D1011740

Religion and Politics
in the Contemporary
United States

Edited by R. Marie Griffith and Melani McAlister

The Johns Hopkins University Press, Baltimore

The Johns Hopkins University Press
2715 North Charles Street
Baltimore, Maryland 21218-4363
www.press.jhu.edu

ISBN 10: 0-8018-8868-9
ISBN 13: 978-0-8018-8868-7

Library of Congress Control Number: 2007940410

A catalog record for this book is available from the British Library.

Special discounts are available for bulk purchases of this book. For more information, please contact Special Sales at 410-516-6936 or specialsales@press.jhu.edu.

The Johns Hopkins University Press uses environmentally friendly book materials, including recycled text paper that is composed of at least 30 percent post-consumer waste, whenever possible. All of our book papers are acid-free, and our jackets and covers are printed on paper with recycled content.

Cover design by Bill Longhauser.

Front cover: Soldiers pray before heading out on a convoy. U.S. Air Force photo by Maj. Tom Crosson. Air Force link, www.af.mil/photos/media_search.asp?q=prayer&page=2.

Back cover: Post-Katrina Memorial Day prayer service, Lower 9th Ward, New Orleans. Photo by Mario Tama, Getty Images.

Religion and Politics in the Contemporary United States

Contents

Leaders and Activists

Media and Performance

Preface

Whereas it was released in 2004, *The Passion of the Christ* was one of the world's most pirated films. Before its release, the *New York Post* showed a bootleg copy of the film to a panel of five reviewers—a rabbi, a Catholic priest, a Baptist reader of the paper, the *Post*'s film critic, and a professor of religious studies—and published their reactions. With large numbers of pirated DVDs available in the United States, the press and Internet bloggers speculated that Christian churches clandestinely screened *The Passion.* Although the film was banned in China, both Catholics and Protestants there reportedly viewed illegal copies of it. The company in Israel with distribution rights declined to distribute it there, but Palestinian Christians, foreign Christian pilgrims, and Muslims in the West Bank nonetheless watched pirated copies of the film. *Passion* bootlegs also circulated in Saudi Arabia, presumably in part because of the controversy over the film in Israel. And unable or unwilling to pay to watch the film in theaters or on legitimate DVDs, Mexicans in both Mexico and the United States purchased cheaper pirated copies instead. These consumers both highlighted economic inequality between Mexico and the United States (as one Mexico City bootlegger told the *Los Angeles Times,* "the two countries aren't equal") and implicitly challenged director Mel Gibson's ownership of the Christ story.[1]

For his part, Gibson struggled to protect his intellectual property rights. Shortly before *The Passion* was released, he screened it for religious leaders, government officials, and media pundits, including the late president of the powerful Motion Picture Association of America (MPAA), Jack Valenti, who hosted the event in his Washington, D.C., office. By the time of the screening, Valenti had effectively enlisted the U.S. government in a war on media pirates, testifying before the Senate Committee on Homeland Security and Governmental Affairs that bootlegging funds terrorism. After the screening, Valenti reportedly praised the film for the way it made "the tears flow easily," and he deflected charges of anti-Semitism by asserting that "people of all religions will find this truly an impressive (and respectful) piece of art and realism." Several months later, Valenti publicly applauded the LAPD when it arrested a man for attempting to videotape *The Passion* during a theater screening.[2]

This brief history of piracy and *The Passion of the Christ* suggests many of the organizing themes for this special issue of *American Quarterly*, including the intercultural and global dimensions of religious politics; the complex relationships between religion and state power; the sometimes conflicted, sometimes compatible aims of religious elites and multitudes; and the politics of religion and media representation. While the United States has long been viewed as a religious nation, the essays in this volume all suggest the importance of these themes for any critical history of the present. The issue brings together an exciting collection of essays on religion and politics in the contemporary United States that incorporates a range of methods and perspectives across the humanities and the social sciences. As might be expected, given recent history, the topic of the Religious Right is well represented here, but so are plenty of other topics that together foreground the political significance of diverse religious traditions in the United States and their implications for our understandings of nationalism, geopolitics, political economy, gender, sexuality, ethnicity, and race. In all of these ways, this special issue attempts to advance vital conversations between the vibrant fields of American studies and religious studies.

This issue of *American Quarterly* was truly a collective endeavor. Initial planning for it was done by my predecessor, Marita Sturken, and I am also grateful to her for her subsequent advice and guidance. Guest editors R. Marie Griffith and Melani McAlister brought their tireless commitment and intellectual brilliance to the project's realization; it has been a pleasure to work with them. I would also like to thank the members of the *AQ* managing editorial board, who read and extensively commented on various manuscripts, including Ruth Bloch, James Kyung-Jin Lee, John Carlos Rowe, Shelley Streeby, and Daniel Widener. Other members of the managing board also provided important advice and help: Sarah Banet-Weiser, Judith Jackson Fossett, Avery Gordon, Greg Hise, Katherine Kinney, Josh Kun, Lisa Lowe, Fred Moten, Laura Pulido, and Henry Yu. In addition, the issue would not have been possible without the fine work of two managing editors, Michelle Commander and Orlando Serrano, as well as editorial assistant Daniel Herbert and interns Matt Nelson and Megan Wagner. Stacey Lynn copyedited the volume with great thoughtfulness and skill, and Bill Longhauser designed the beautiful cover, based on images researched by Melani McAlister.

We are grateful to the Department of American Studies and Ethnicity, the College of Arts and Science, the Critical Studies Department, and the School of Cinematic Arts at the University of Southern California, whose support enabled us to complete this project.

Curtis Marez
Editor
American Quarterly

Notes

1. "News for *The Passion of the Christ*," the Internet Movie Data Base, online at http://www.imdb.com/title/tt0335345/news (accessed July 1, 2007); "Pirated Copies of 'The Passion' Used to Evangelize," AsiaNews.it, March 31, 2004, online at http://www.asianews.it/index.php?l=en&art=558&dos=16&size=A (accessed June 30, 2007); Mark Willacy, "Palestinian Christians Screen 'Passion of the Christ' Amidst Easter Celebrations," correspondent's report, ABC Radio National, April 11, 2004, transcript online at http://www.abc.net.au/correspondents/content/2004/s1085006.htm (accessed June 30, 2007); Reed Johnson, "Inside Mexico's Bootleg Market," *Los Angeles Times*, May 10, 2006.
2. "News for *The Passion of the Christ*," the Internet Movie Data Base; Statement of Jack Valenti, Senate Committee on Homeland Security and Governmental Affairs, "Privacy & Piracy: The Paradox of Illegal File Sharing on Peer-to-Peer Networks and the Impact of Technology on the Entertainment Industry," September, 30, 2003, online at http://www.senate.gov/~govtaff/index.cfm?Fuseaction=Hearing.Testimony&HearingID=120&WitnessID=415 (accessed July 1, 2007). The testimonial from Valenti is reportedly from a letter to Mel Gibson that has been reproduced on several Christian Web sites promoting the film.

Religion and Politics in the Contemporary United States

Introduction
Is the Public Square Still Naked?

R. Marie Griffith and Melani McAlister

In 1984, the Protestant minister Richard John Neuhaus published a groundbreaking book, *The Naked Public Square*. Articulating a critique that would serve as a profoundly influential touchstone for a generation of religious intellectuals, Neuhaus lamented that the public life of the nation no longer included a significant or sufficient recognition of a common religious foundation. The public sphere was "naked," stripped of its legitimate status as a place of moral discourse. A Lutheran who would soon convert to Catholicism and a former liberal who had now become a conservative, Neuhaus argued that "politics is in large part a function of culture." Beyond that, he proposed, "at the heart of culture is religion," whether or not it is called by that name.[1] Without a shared religious point of reference, no society could debate or resolve conflicts in values. The Moral Majority Coalition, founded just five years earlier, might have too strident a view, he argued, but it had made a crucial point: religion not only has a role in politics; it is at the heart of the enterprise. Readers then and later would see *The Naked Public Square* as a formative, early salvo in what would come to be understood (with only partial accuracy) as the "culture wars" between a liberalizing, secularizing, multicultural America on the one hand and a more traditional, conservative, and religious nation on the other.

Twenty years later, as part of a symposium on the book's legacy published in the journal *First Things*, the legal scholar Mary Anne Glendon looked back in anger at the changes that had taken place since the 1980s. Since Neuhaus wrote, she contended, the secularization of society and the marginalization of religious belief had only intensified. Legal rulings and public policies were tightening the space of religious expression. And "state-sponsored secularism" was eroding the ability of religious institutions to function freely (requiring, for example, that Catholic Charities provide health care to its employees that included prescription drug coverage for contraceptives). Writing three years after September 11, Glendon proffered what was surely intended as a chilling comparison:

If present legal trends continue, it is not fanciful to suppose that the situation of religious believers in secular America will come to resemble dhimmitude—the status of non-Muslims in a number of Islamic countries.

The dhimmi is tolerated so long as his religion is kept private and his public acts do not offend the state religion. Naturally, key positions in society must be reserved to those who adhere to the official creed.[2]

Glendon could assume that many readers would share her sense of persecution: by the early twenty-first century, despite the ubiquitous influence of religious discourse in U.S. public life, it was not uncommon for religious people, Christians in particular, to declare themselves under siege.

Glendon is a profoundly conservative intellectual, and her level of panic about the imminent demise of the rights of believers surely sets her apart from the vast majority of religious people in the United States. But her concerns were not unique. Although conservative Christians have been most vocal about decrying "the war on Christians" (not to mention the related "war on Christmas"), commentators across the political spectrum have expressed increasingly outspoken concerns about the "marginalization" of faith. From Joseph Lieberman to Barack Obama, from liberal evangelicals to mainstream Muslims, politicians and observers have decried the lack of attention to religion, and lack of respect for religious people, in U.S. politics. Not for the first time in U.S. history, there is a profound sense of crisis about the unsettled relationship between religion and politics in our public life.

These concerns, although in some sense perennial ones, conspicuously quickened after September 11, 2001. In the wake of the attacks, which instantly became identified with the shadowy category of "Islamic fundamentalism," Islam was repeatedly vilified; indeed, by 2004, 44 percent of people in the United States said they believed that "Islam was a religion of violence."[3] Policymakers and pundits, aware of the delicacy of this situation and cognizant of the implications with regard to allies in Saudi Arabia and elsewhere, often worked to moderate such disparagements. They did so by distinguishing sharply between "good" religion, which seemed calm, rational, and moderate in its claims on public life; and "dangerous" religion, which is to say any form of Islam that positioned itself or its adherents as "anti-American."[4] The larger "problem," however, as self-styled experts from Samuel Huntington to Sam Harris have explained, is that "Islam" does not recognize a distinction between religious and secular law, that is, between church and state. Its failure to do so, in this logic, is part of what inclines Muslims to fanaticism: they refuse to recognize the limits of religion within a secular state.[5]

Figure 1.
Martin Luther King Jr. and Nun. Martin Luther King Jr. and others in the 1965 march from Selma to Montgomery. King brought a prophetic sense of the power of faith to activate social change. Photograph by Bruce Davidson, courtesy Magnum Photos.

As we discuss below, there are considerable intellectual problems with these distinctions. But there is also a larger irony, since the first years of the twenty-first century involved intensified battles over church-state separation in the United States. Christian conservatives decried a court decision that stopped the public display of the Ten Commandments in an Alabama courthouse, and called for the right to teach religiously based creationism in public schools.[6] The most recent Supreme Court decision pertaining to abortion clearly reflects the conservative Catholic position held by five of the nine justices. There is at the very least a tension between the valorization of secularism, when comparisons to Islam are at hand, and the simultaneous call for more religion in the public sphere, where U.S. politics is concerned. Different interests are at stake in different conflicts, so that what appears to be an infringement of religious rights to one party in a particular case may look like crucial protections from religion to another. Our enduring disagreements, in any case, indicate a more general public confusion about what "separation of church and state" actually *means*—as a constitutional doctrine, a public value, or a protection of minority rights.[7]

The purpose of this special issue is to examine some of the multiple and conflicting ways that religion matters in U.S. politics today. Writing from a

variety of scholarly disciplines and with distinctive topical expertise, the authors featured here explore numerous modes through which religious faith has mobilized political action, be it conservative, liberal, or—as with much of what is chronicled here—not clearly classifiable as either. This issue also explores the meanings of "religion" for people who might contest the term—those who are "spiritual but not religious," for example, or activists who engage symbols of faith and community but who may not necessarily consider themselves members of a specific religion. Several essays also examine the meanings of secular identity, humanist politics, and/or the complex evocations of "civil religion" in American life.

Figure 2.
Madonna Pro Vida. A pro-life activist praying at a demonstration in Washington, D.C., in January 2005, on the 32nd anniversary of *Roe v. Wade.* Photograph by Tim Sloan, courtesy AFP/Getty Images.

The risk here is that a journal issue on *religion* and *politics* in the contemporary United States will wrongly romanticize any of these categories as unified or ontological, when each is as shifting and as complicated as another, and subject to multiple paradoxes and negotiations. Sometimes, the working of religion in U.S. politics is prophetic, while at other times it is deeply reactionary. As often as it appears to liberate or empower one group of people, it manipulates, displaces, and exploits another. The very need to trade in normative evaluations about religion and politics, as witnessed by media treatments of Islam and evangelicalism no less than by scholarly assessments, perhaps bespeaks an enduring hope that "good" religion—progressive, disruptive, and justice-oriented—will prevail, while "bad" religion—reactionary, conformist, and violent—will expire. That hope seems to be peculiarly acute in the post-9/11 context in which we live today, a world in which the antireligious screeds of Sam Harris, Richard Dawkins, and Christopher Hitchens, on the one side, and the nostalgic pinings for Puritan–style religiosity of David Brooks, on the other, pass for thoughtful public reflection about religion rather than being more properly pegged as the ill-informed, ideologically driven rants they are.[8]

In this introduction, we discuss a series of topics—theoretical, methodological, and historical—that undergird our own understanding of the issues at stake in analyzing the vexed nexus of religion and politics in the United States today. First, we lay out the dual genealogies of religious studies and American studies, and the possibilities for shared conversation. We then discuss at length some significant theoretical debates about religion, secularism, and the public sphere, including thinkers whose work provides particularly valuable context for this issue. Third, we analyze several key cultural and political trends in the 1990s that are vital to understanding the current moment, which we follow with an examination of the complexities of the identifications of "Left" and "Right" in religious politics. We conclude with a brief discussion of the essays overall.

Our goal for this issue is not only to provide an entrée into understanding the impact of religion on politics, or politics on religion, but also to present new and sophisticated models for thinking productively about religion within American studies. It should be noted that several contributors to this volume teach in or received a PhD from a department of religion, which makes this issue unique in *American Quarterly*'s long history. With this multidisciplinarity in mind, the specific contributions of this special issue are, we hope, as much methodological as topical, in that the authors draw on history, sociology, cultural studies, and political science to examine religion, not as a rarefied or transcendent object, but as a part of the daily lived experience of people inside and outside the United States. A focus on "lived religion" has, in fact, recently become a standard concern in religious studies, in part because it allows scholars to move beyond a singular focus on the theological debates of the learned elite or the public statements of a few leaders. Many of the essays in this issue share a commitment to this kind of careful engagement with the social experiences and cultural practices of ordinary people. However, this does not and has not precluded engagement with religious and secular thought, attention to religious leaders, or sustained ideological critique of some of the views and values of religious actors. All of these approaches are represented here, and they offer, we believe, a sense of the rich possibilities that can emerge from a sustained conversation between the study of religion and American studies.

Disciplines and Multidisciplinarity: Distinctive Legacies, Collective Conversations

The study of religion, as a broad interdisciplinary field, has historically been a closer cousin to the disciplines of anthropology and sociology than to American studies. It traces its origins back to European intellectuals—notably Durkheim, Weber, Marx, and Freud—with William James considered the earliest and most important U.S. thinker. Mary Douglas and Clifford Geertz have been two of the major influential scholars in more recent times, with Jonathan Z. Smith and Talal Asad standing tall in the field today. Early contributors to the field were particularly concerned with exploring the contours of so-called primitive religions in exotic locations and with developing evolutionary schemas that typically placed modern forms of monotheism (chiefly Protestantism) at the hierarchical apex. In recent years, academic religionists have devoted considerable attention to investigating the history of the discipline, including the multiple forms of racism, nationalism, and presumptions of Western superiority that have suffused modern analytic categories of religion.

Scholars of *American* religion and religious history represent a rather different intellectual formation, although they find themselves today in a similar moment of self-questioning. Most are indebted less to Durkheim et al. than to Perry Miller and other Puritan scholars, as well as to those who were at one time deemed (rightly or wrongly) "church historians," including Philip Schaff, Peter Mode, William Warren Sweet, Sidney Mead, and Sydney Ahlstrom. Originally trained and later housed in departments of history or in liberal Protestant divinity schools, many U.S. religious historians in the latter half of the twentieth century began migrating into university departments of religion, where they were challenged to reconsider the pastoral, theological, and missiological traces of their field. Given this legacy, the question of whether one could be both a practitioner and a scholar of religion has vexed Protestant scholars of religion more acutely—or at least more publicly—than it has their Jewish, Catholic, or Buddhist peers.[9]

What matters most about these dual genealogies in the study of American religion, at least for the purposes of this special issue, is their convergence today with several other intellectual models of critique and reassessment. More specifically, just as it is the case that religionists have been revisiting and in a clear sense apologizing for their historical self-centeredness and blindness to other subjectivities, so too has American studies engaged in its own lengthy project of self-scrutiny and redirection. The puzzle for many of us who have been involved in both fields is why, after all this time, they seem to speak so little to each other—or, put differently, to make so little impact when they do.

We have been intrigued, for instance, to hear recent calls on the part of American studies scholars for more attention to religion at ASA conferences and in our scholarship, as if religion has not somehow been there all along.[10] It may well be the case that in the last twenty years it was possible, indeed quite easy, to get a degree in American studies or its allied fields without learning much beyond the very basics of U.S. religious history. But the argument that religion is somehow terra incognita for recent American studies scholarship ignores many of our impressive intellectual traditions and resources. If those of us working on the twentieth century have paid relatively less attention to religious issues than those who examine Emersonian transcendentalism, nineteenth-century reform movements, or colonial contact, there remains nonetheless a rich scholarship on faith, politics, and culture in this later period—with attention to topics ranging from the Scopes trial of 1920 to the civil rights movement, from the coalescence of occultism, faith, and power in Theosophy and Vedanta to more contemporary mixings in *Buffy the Vampire Slayer*.[11] Perhaps the issue is less that American studies has not examined religion than that we have been seized by a kind of historiographic amnesia. In our view, American studies does have a great deal to learn from religious studies (and the reverse is also true, though perhaps for different reasons—a subject for another conversation). One clear gain for American studies scholars delving into religious studies is increased awareness of that field's long, self-conscious, and productive engagement with the very category of "religion" itself, as a category no less simple or transparent than "race," "nation," and other organizing themes of our work. That body of valuable analytic theorizing ought not to be ignored.[12]

This special issue of the *American Quarterly* maps a fresh cooperative venture between religious studies and American studies and so represents, we believe, a way forward that bypasses the false and moralizing dichotomies between "good" and "bad" religion that we have already noted. In each of the articles featured here, the categories of *religion* and *politics* relate to one another in distinctive ways; often enough, in fact, the very use of these terms changes from one article to the next. We highlight that definitional dissonance here not as a weakness but as a positive contribution achieved by this sort of collaborative, interdisciplinary work. Still, recognizing the theoretical baggage carried by these terms as well as the multiple audiences to whom we hope this special issue will appeal, we offer a brief lexical guide to their current usage here.

A Short Glossary of Terms: Religion, Secularism, and the Public Sphere

Within American studies as well as other fields, scholarship invoking the public sphere inevitably refers back to Habermas, who famously valorized the "bourgeois public sphere" as a site where modern Europeans made "rational use of their rationality." In the cafes and coffee houses of early modern Europe, Habermas argues, men read and talked and debated. There, a particular form of political rationality emerged, suitable for the rise of capitalism and the modern nation-state. Without the stifling intellectual habits of the courts and the dead hand of the aristocracy shaping them, bourgeois men learned to respect, and be convinced by, "the unforced force of the superior argument."[13]

The Habermasian model has been venerated, vilified, and constantly re-worked by a generation of scholars. Critics have pointed out the exclusion of women and people of color from this original framing of the public sphere—an exclusion of which Habermas was certainly aware but considered contingent: for him, the public sphere, like the Enlightenment itself, carried the seeds of its own universalization. Others have productively used the concept of the public sphere but have expanded its base and redefined its character. Habermas had articulated a "rational" public sphere, which he closely associated with the secularizing and individualizing process of the Enlightenment; more recent scholars have attended as well to the work of "irrationality"—affect, pleasure, and longing—in constructing meaning and constituting publics. Examining popular culture as a site of extrarational but meaningful "work," or exploring community organizations, including religious ones, as sites of affective public-ness, scholars have dramatically expanded the notion of the "public sphere" to include everything from the politicized fashions of zoot-suiters to fan sites on the Internet.[14] As a result, in both scholarly writings and the parlance of public intellectuals, "the public sphere" has come to mean less the rational bourgeois public sphere pioneered in Enlightenment Europe, and something more like "a space of intentional, broad-reaching conversation"—a far less rigorous but perhaps more useful definition.

When it comes to religion, debates about the public sphere have generated tremendous fervor among political theorists, public philosophers and theologians, and religious actors themselves. John Rawls and Richard Rorty, for instance, have famously argued that individuals should restrain themselves from injecting religiously based argumentation into public discussions of political and legal policies; and their lengthy defenses of this position—one version being Rawls's early ideal of public reason, another Rorty's dictum that religion is a "conversation-stopper"—have generated deep support for the notion that religion must be privatized.[15] In Rorty's approving words, the "happy, Jeffersonian compromise that the Enlightenment reached with the religious" serves rightly to keep religion out of politics, "making it seem bad taste to bring religion into discussions of public policy."[16] Such arguments have inspired not only admirers and emulators, but also countless critics who propose a range of rationales for bringing religion back into political argumentation within the public sphere.

Jeffrey Stout, a liberal public philosopher and the current president of the American Academy of Religion, has argued forcefully that a religion-free public sphere is neither possible nor desirable. In his 2005 book *Democracy and Tradition*, he writes:

> Secular liberals, sensing the demise of the religious Left, might want to argue that the only way to save our democracy from the religious Right is to inhibit the expression of religious

reasons in the public square. Aside from whatever theoretical errors might lie behind this argument, it is foolhardy to suppose that anything like the Rawlsian program of restraint or what Rorty calls the Jeffersonian compromise will succeed in a country with our religious and political history. So the practical question is not whether religious reasons will be expressed in public settings, but by whom, in what manner, and to what ends.[17]

Stout's model for reimagining the prospects as well as the limits for religion in public speech is, we think, a useful one for those who want to think about the democratic possibilities for religious conversation.

Utilizing a range of thinkers from Ralph Waldo Emerson through Ralph Ellison to Cornel West, Stout argues for a robust form of pluralism, "one that citizens with strong religious commitments can accept and that welcomes their full participation in public life without fudging on its own premises." That is to say, religious persons ought not to be forced to conceal the religious reasons for their views, even if it is sometimes more prudent to avoid sectarian public discourse in order to offer persuasive arguments (regarding a policy issue, for instance) to religiously diverse audiences. At the same time, Stout urges religious persons not simply to intensify their own group commitments while retreating from identification as American citizens; such a course leads only, he argues, to "full-fledged separatism, which involves commitment to a group that is small enough and uniform enough to eliminate ambivalence altogether, at least for a while." It may seem appealing at times to retreat to such communities—particularly in the current context, deeply riven by political disagreements and various so-called culture wars, defined in great part by religious arguments. Still, Stout asks, "why would I want to confine my *discursive* community to the people who already agree with me on all essential matters? Isn't part of the point of trying to hold one another responsible discursively that we do not agree on everything and therefore *need* to talk things through?"[18] Such questions intend to challenge a basic temptation faced by self-styled religious *and* secular citizens in the United States: that of surrounding themselves only with like-minded persons in a world deemed hostile to their commitments.

Still, the questions remain: does religion have, or should it have, a particular status in regard to the public? Is religion only (to quote Stephen L. Carter's term of opprobrium) an "individual metaphysic"—a kind of covert, rather shameful hobby?[19] Or, to turn the tables, why do secular commitments to moral values not receive the same legal protections as religious commitments to those same values? (Rorty makes an apt objection here to the fact that "only *religious* conscientious objectors to military service go unpunished," not those whose antiwar positions derive from merely "secular" premises.[20]) Where should legal and judicial thinkers draw the lines?

One of the points of perennial confusion in these heated debates about religion in the public sphere is how "religion" itself is to be defined against what is usually taken to be its opposite, "secularism." The anthropologist Talal Asad, a distinguished figure in the contemporary study of religion who has been deeply influenced by Foucault, has challenged understanding of the foundational categories of religious and secular. In the essays collected in *Genealogies of Religion*, Asad analyzes the rise of religion in the European Christian West and argues that scholars have inappropriately generalized from that experience to construct "universal" definitions. In a famous critique of Clifford Geertz, Asad challenges Geertz's definition of religion as a set of symbolic meanings that are attached to ideas about the general order of the universe. Religion, for Geertz, was a way of seeing and ordering the world, expressed through ritual and/or doctrine. A scholar, particularly an anthropologist, could locate the presence of "religion" without confusing it with any of its particular cultural expressions. Asad disagrees, arguing that Geertz's view "is in fact a view that has a specific Christian history."

> It is not too unreasonable to maintain that "the basic axiom" underlying what Geertz calls "the religious perspective" is *not* everywhere the same. It is preeminently the Christian church that has occupied itself with identifying, cultivating, and testing belief as a verbalizable inner condition of true religion.[21]

Asad's point about the modern Protestant creation of religion—as, among other things, a matter first and foremost of *belief*—has had a powerful impact on the field of religious studies. Beyond such intellectual circles "religion" often continues to be construed rather carelessly as a definable, universal, and even natural phenomenon.[22]

Calling into question a dominant paradigm for religion is, however, to pose a larger problem, one that Asad's own work does not answer: how, given the Western Protestant legacy of religious categories, can or should we talk about "religion" at all? Scholars of religion are currently engaged in quite impassioned definitional debates about this vexed dilemma (which has bearing, among other things, on the place and function of religion departments in academia), and the political stakes are surely high.[23] But alternative models have been slow to gain ground in this context. Academic commentators, rather, have taken seriously Asad's injunction to avoid assuming that we know in advance what religion comprises and instead to problematize the constitution of this concept in particular places and times. This *American Quarterly* special issue aims to do just that.

Inevitably, Asad's argument about the modern creation of a universal defi-nition of religion includes close attention to questions about the secular and secularism.[24] In his reading, articulated most thoroughly in *Formations of the Secular*, "secularism" as a doctrine pertains, first and foremost, to the construc-tion of a rights-bearing individual whose right to (religious) belief is separate from the state. It has also to do with the historical necessity and the norma-tive value of the "privatization of religion" out of public life, a value retained, he argues, even in the face of the rather obvious failures of the secularization thesis. In the modern West, however, Asad argues, the admission of religion into the public sphere is often based on a more or less explicit set of criteria about *which* religions or beliefs are "useful" or modern: those that promote civil society or contribute to liberal values are seen as acceptable, for instance, while those that undermine such values are rejected.[25] Here, Asad reminds us that the public sphere remains a romanticized fantasy, a place in which those who believe their own voices are adequately heard are often not cognizant of those whose speech is not free. "The point here is that the public sphere is a place *necessarily* (not just contingently) articulated by power. And everyone who enters it must address power's disposition of people and things, the de-pendence of some on the goodwill of others."[26] If Asad's critique takes aim at the notion of the enlightened rights-bearing individuals who equally engage the secular state, still more does it aim to challenge the very premises of liberal pluralistic community such as imagined by Stout. For such a community is both historically contingent—emerging at a certain time out of particular circumstances indebted to modernity—and also dependent on a set of values neither universally held nor freely sustained: values upheld by means of state force and constant enforcement, a public sphere articulated by power.

The relationship between the religious and the secular is, then, far more complicated in Asad's reading than in other work wherein one or the other category has been more or less taken for granted. Those who call today for a more secular politics, Asad insists, are either naive or disingenuous about "the ambition of the secular state itself," failing to recognize or acknowledge its regulatory interventions. A privatized religion under such current circumstances is toothless and ultimately inconsequential, he argues; and, in any case, the categories of "politics" and "religion" are thoroughly imbricated. Asad urges contemporary readers not to take these categories for granted but persistently to inquire "how, when, and by whom" they are defined so as to understand better the varied interests at stake in the clash of visions between a political order perceived as religious and one promoted as secular.[27] This special issue notably includes several essays that discuss the reach of the secular and the power of the state: Kevin Schultz, for example, examines the legal decisions from the 1950s that promoted a "neutral state" regarding religious activity in the public schools. Here, the activism of U.S. Catholics and Jews was essential to limiting the use of school grounds for Protestant proselytizing.

Despite their differences from each other, both Stout's model of a pluralistic discursive community and Asad's interpretation of the contested secularism that saturates this ideal prove useful, we think, to the project of framing this special issue. This is so, incidentally, *not* because we believe that either thinker gets everything right. Each model surely has its own limitations and indeed, as we have already shown, there are substantial disagreements between them. Asad's work essentially refutes the liberal underpinnings for much of Stout's own program, for example; while Stout's model of a generous, democratic community counters the defense of illiberal religion to which Asad's arguments ultimately seem to lead. But both thinkers appeal to us for their intelligent, rigorous, and disciplined engagement with crucial matters of our time pertaining to the intersections of religion and politics in the contemporary United States. And these probing, provocative modes of inquiry stand front and center in the diverse scholarly investigations featured here.

Genealogies of the Contemporary: New Kinds of Diversity

This collection of essays explores both the status of religiously engaged politics in our current moment and the possibilities for interdisciplinary investigations of a set of urgent questions about the nature of U.S. political and cultural life. These questions are not asked or answered ahistorically. There is, of course, a long and multifaceted history of both religious activism and political religiosity in the United States, which has been richly documented by generations of U.S. historians. Just in the last twenty years, scholars have examined topics ranging from the religious beliefs of the "founding fathers" to the international origins of religious pacifism to the socioreligious meanings of the "home birth" movement.[28]

Our goal is not to summarize or reprise that scholarship, but to highlight its importance for this special issue. Any understanding of "religion and politics in contemporary America" requires that we understand the meaning of the *contemporary* in light of the politics of the past. Several of the articles in this issue take up specific historical questions. Barbara Savage's essay on the political vision of African American intellectual and activist Benjamin Mays at midcentury, Laura Levitt's exploration of the history of Jewish secularism, and Neil Young's analysis of the activism of Mormons working against the ERA in the 1970s, among others, offer nuanced accounts of earlier struggles over the politics of belief.

Although debates about the proper role of religion in public life have a long provenance and an impressive intellectual pedigree, we argue that, starting in the 1990s, the issue of "religion and politics" became the topic of an intensified and ultimately tension-filled conversation—among policymakers, activists, and religious organizations. Religious and secular people negotiated a political terrain that had been dramatically reshaped by immigration, invigorated religious movements, globalization, and an ever-expanding commodity culture. Of the many issues that would be relevant to a full explication of the contemporary religio-political landscape, here we briefly examine three: the impact of immigration patterns, the development of a new media landscape, and the increasing focus among religious believers upon transnationalism and diversity.

First is the long-term impact of the Immigration and Nationality Act of 1965, which expanded the number of immigrants from Latin America, Asia, Africa, and the Middle East. This expansion had, and continues to have, major consequences for religious affiliation and participation in the United States. Over the course of forty years, the numbers of Muslim and Buddhist immigrants, in particular, rose noticeably, as each year increased the total number of immigrants from Asia and the Middle East, and these groups began to have children and grandchildren. Despite the fact that a relatively high percentage of the immigrants from Asia are Christian, as are almost all immigrants from Latin America, the long-term result has been a dramatic increase in the religious diversity in the United States.[29] The percentage of Protestant Christians has dropped from 64.3 to 50.4 percent of the population since 1974, while the percentage of Catholics has remained steady at about 25 percent.[30] Among those who identify as Christian, Baptists are the largest Protestant group, at 16 percent of all people in the United States; Mormons total 1.3 percent of the population, and Pentecostals and Charismatics are 2.6 percent. (This last number is misleading, however, since it counts only those who identify with a Pentecostal or Charismatic denomination. Many other Christians, including more that half of Latino Catholics, are Charismatic in practice.)[31]

The total percentage of Jews, Muslims, Buddhists, Hindus, and others is still relatively small, between 5 percent and 8 percent of the population, but that is a substantive increase from 0.5 percent in 1974. After Christians, the second largest "religious identification" in the United States is "no religion" or "unaffiliated." This group has doubled in the last thirty years, from 6.8 to 14.25 percent. For many communities, a consciousness of this diversity has enabled a blending of ethnic and religious activism that has created new kinds of alliances and identifications. In this issue, Prema Kurien, Jane Iwamura, and Luis León all explore the impact of this diversity, which enables various groups—in these cases, South Asians, Japanese Americans, and Chicano activists—to create distinct community identities that articulate, but also complicate, religious practices.

A second significant change in the 1990s involves the new media landscape. Although conservative Christians, in particular, have long been savvy utilizers of radio and television—consider the early broadcast empires of evangelist Aimee Semple McPherson in the 1920s and Catholic archbishop Fulton J. Sheen in the 1950s, not to mention the later television ministries of Pentecostal healers such as Kathryn Kuhlman, Oral Roberts, and many more—the rapid escalation of cable and satellite TV in the 1990s substantially increased the global reach and audiences for religious broadcasting.[32] Equally significant was the striking visibility of loosely religious themes (and the occasional occult fantasy) on broadcast television, from *Touched by an Angel* and *Joan of Arcadia* to *The X Files* to *Battlestar Galactica*. Religious activists have sometimes made savvy use of the familiarity of such images, as when evangelicals developed "Hell Houses" to compete with the secular Halloween haunted house. As Ann Pellegrini explains in this issue, the images that make Hell Houses "work" are frequently drawn from popular culture and horror, even as they have aimed to critique both.

Popular culture has provided one venue for the articulation of what Robert Wuthnow and others have described as the move from "dwelling" to "seeking" in U.S. religious life—a trend away from lifelong commitments to particular religious institutions and toward a more marketplace-oriented and contingent view of faith. The very phrase "spiritual but not religious" captures the sensibility through which people tend to experience their faith as fundamentally *mobile*, significantly emotional, and only loosely articulated. With the rise of new spiritual movements in the 1970s, individuals who self-consciously claimed the right to selectively engage with a variety of spiritual practices had a great deal more to choose from: they could combine, for example, a bit of Buddhism with a flirtation with crystals and loosely Christian beliefs in salvation. Distance from any mainstream religious doctrine was precisely the point. There were important continuities between these postmodern practices and earlier forms of nontraditional spirituality; for example, as Trysh Travis discusses in this

Figure 3.
Hindu Girls. Sisters Dancing by Raina Batra. Working with photographer Wendy Ewald, children who are members of the Hindu Bhavan in Morrisville, N.C., took photographs of their community as part of the Five Faiths Project of the Ackland Museum of Art. Photograph © Wendy Ewald.

issue, the loose supernatural vision of Oprah's Book Club has its origins in a Progressive Era spirituality New Thought, which focuses on the self-healing of the individual. At the turn of the twenty-first century, however, a booming industry of "higher-power"-oriented popular culture has brought the religious marketplace into the living room.[33]

The rise of the Internet has dramatically expanded the terrain of religious expression, communication, and cultural consumption, in large part because its low entry costs and broad reach created significant openings for smaller or more dispersed religious communities.[34] As with popular culture in the past, the impact of the Web's particularities—its new rhetorics, visual cultures, fraught interactivities, and distinctive forms of nonlinearity—are all but impossible to anticipate, and observers of the striking explosion in online religion disagree as to whether the Internet has served to fracture religious identities or to consolidate them. Online, Muslims from around the world debate religious principles with each other and with non-Muslims, Jews can place a prayer at the Western

Figure 4.
Queer Spirit. Members of "Q-Spirit" (Queer Spirit) gathering on September 11, 2002, to remember victims of September 11 with a ceremony of drums, hugging, and healing in the National AIDS Memorial Grove in San Francisco. Photograph by Thomas Hoepker, courtesy Magnum Photos.

Wall, Pagans and Wiccans construct Web sites to introduce their beliefs to the skeptical and educate believers about ceremonial practices, Branch Davidians use e-mail to regroup after Waco, and on and on. If the Web has provided occasions for groups to highlight their religious and political distinctiveness, it has also expanded the possibilities for border-crossing conversations. The broad-ranging, eclectic, and wildly popular site Beliefnet is one example of a space that invites informal discussions that can go well beyond more formal attempts at ecumenical dialogue.[35]

A third contemporary development we wish to highlight is the growing engagement of U.S. believers with the rest of the world. By the 1990s, the diverse set of changes that we have come to call "globalization" made it increasingly difficult to think of religious identities, or any others, as solely contained by national borders. Cross-national religious communities are not a new phenomenon, and several contributors in this volume trace instances in which global politics played a key role for religious self-consciousness: Clarence Hardy examines the ways in which African American Pentecostal preaching women in the interwar years worked to craft postnationalist and postracialized visions of religious community, Jodi Eichler-Levine and Rosemary Hicks examine the recent mobilizations on Darfur as examples of engaged internationalism that draw in a range of believers; and Prema Kurien explores the links between politics in India and religious identifications among Indian immigrants in the United States.

But after September 11, transnationalism took on a new currency for believers, although in very different ways for different groups. Muslims in the United States, for example, were immediately faced with the "clash of civilizations" rhetoric that positioned them as inherently transnational, as framed by the threat of "global Islamic radicalism." As Edward Curtis argues in this issue, the carryover effects of Middle East politics already had a significant impact on African American Muslim communities in the 1950s and 1960s. After 9/11, Evelyn Alsultany contends in her contribution here, Muslims could be (partially) extricated only if they proclaimed an America-first identity. For some, displays of nationalism likely came easily; for others, the expectations surely carried the strong taint of coercion. In addition, the U.S. Muslim community is itself quite diverse, not only politically, but culturally and linguistically as well. Two-thirds of the U.S. Muslim population is composed of immigrants, and these come from sixty-eight different countries. Of all U.S. Muslims, approximately one-third are born in the United States (more than half of those are African American); 33 percent were born in the Arab region or Iran, and almost 20 percent in South Asia.[36]

At the same time, Christians in the United States have become acutely conscious of the emergence of what Philip Jenkins calls "next Christendom"—the numerical growth and political power of the churches of the global south. In the last thirty years, millions of people in Latin America, Africa, and Asia have converted to some form of Christianity; today approximately 60 percent of all Christians live outside the United States and Europe, and the trend is increasing.[37] This recognition of Christians outside the West is not new, of course; Catholics have a deeply held sense of a global church of which they are only a part, and Protestant and Catholic missionaries have embodied a commitment to a global faith. But for U.S. Christians, the self-conscious recognition and embrace of their own impending minority status has had a profound effect. On the one hand, it has been extraordinarily liberalizing, leading to an increased interest in global issues of all sorts, from genocide in the Sudan to the HIV-AIDS epidemic. On the other hand, it has played a major role in strengthening both Pentecostals and theological conservatives, who have found ready allies among Christians in the global south.

These developments, in demographics, media utilization, and global consciousness, have set the stage for the contemporary scene that this special issue explicitly aims to scrutinize. In the last fifteen years, and especially since the 2000 election, people in the United States have become acutely conscious of the politics of religion—and particularly the visibility and power of what is most often called the Religious Right or the Christian Right, or, more recently, "theocratic politics."[38] The greatest spur to new academic and journalistic interest in religion today remains this phenomenon. Composed of specific constituencies of conservative evangelical Protestants and conservative Catholics, the Religious Right has reaped widespread attention and analysis—indeed, it is worth noting that our call for papers regarding this special issue on religion and politics garnered far more submissions on white evangelicals than on most other topics combined—and has rapidly spawned numerous countermovements of varying strength and size. The Religious Right hovers conspicuously over this issue, then, as a site of power, a source of intellectual interest, and an impetus for religious and political opposition. But the Right does not exist in a vacuum; left-leaning religious activists, and many whose political identities are a mix of both the Right and the Left, are also making themselves a social force to be taken seriously.

Political Identities and Institutions: Religious Right, Left, and In-Between

Religious conservatives' political activism certainly did not begin in the 1980s. It can be traced back at least to the nineteenth century: fiercely contested issues such as slavery and woman's suffrage, for example, included religious campaigners on both sides, in both North and South. So did public debates over science, public education, immigration, and many other questions at various historical moments. By the post–World War II period, conservative Christians were reacting intently both to changing dynamics of religion and sexuality (the Kinsey Report, the Beats) and to the civil rights movement; and by the Goldwater campaign of 1964, right-wing religious organizations were organized, energized, and increasingly active.[39]

But Christian conservatives achieved new self-confidence and ambition with a series of events that converged in the late 1970s and 1980s, making that period a uniquely significant and formative one. These include the 1979 founding of the Moral Majority, the election of Ronald Reagan in 1980 (who spoke to the Christian Right more effectively than Jimmy Carter did, despite the latter's open evangelical faith), the fundamentalist takeover in the 1980s of the Southern Baptist Convention (the once theologically diverse denomination that bred Carter, Bill Clinton, and Al Gore), and the founding of the Christian Coalition in 1989. As the electoral power of conservative Christians grew too great to ignore, scholars and journalists began to attend, sometimes obsessively, to this new Religious Right. Leaders such as Jerry Falwell and Pat Robertson, both of whom had made their names in large part through their media empires, garnered early publicity and rallied supporters with their vocal opposition to civil rights and feminism, as well as their enthusiastic support for Israel and commitment to the cold war. In rallying against abortion, evangelicals made significant alliances with Catholics; while, regarding Israel, they often connected with particular groups of Jewish activists. As these examples begin to indicate, the Religious Right is perhaps best described in that early period as a shifting coalition, in which evangelicals were quite powerful but were also finding ways to work more ecumenically on issues they deemed important to their overall project of "saving America."[40]

In the late 1990s, nationally organized evangelicalism began to evolve into a more politically, racially, and theologically diverse movement, with leaders such as T.D. Jakes, Joyce Meyer, Rick Warren, Creflo Dollar, and Joel Osteen rising to compete against the old fire-and-brimstone bugbears like Robertson and Falwell. Today, although most U.S. evangelicals still identify themselves as political and theological conservatives, the newer generations are more culturally savvy, practical minded, and oriented toward popular culture. Evangelicals' energetic commitment to social activism has not diminished, but it now encompasses a far broader range of issues. Today, added to the older but ongoing concerns about sexuality, evolution, public prayer, and patriotism, are environmentalism (grounded theologically in the ideal of stewardship for God's creation, e.g., "What Would Jesus Drive?"), global poverty, the perceived threat of so-called Islamic fundamentalism, and opposition to the persecution of Christians internationally. In some of these broad concerns, particularly on U.S. foreign policy toward the Muslim world, opposition to global sexual trafficking, and environmentalism, evangelicals have again made significant interreligious alliances with Jewish and Catholic conservatives. They have also made strategic links with both secular and religious liberals on issues such as global warming and enforced prostitution. Illustrations of such dynamics appear in this special issue: Michael Lindsay explores the complicated political identities of evangelical policymaking elites, while Brian McCammack examines evangelical environmentalism as a new kind of common ground for liberal and conservative evangelicals. More globally engaged and more comfortable with their own worldliness, the new evangelicals see themselves as worlds apart from the self-involved Americanism of the televangelist generation.[41]

The "Religious Left" has also begun in recent years to make itself known as an intellectual and political force. One of the most important figures in the group is Michael Lerner, who founded *Tikkun* magazine in 1986. *Tikkun* began as a call for renewal of the Jewish Left, supporting a broadly progressive politics, feminism and gay rights, and a "loving criticism" of Israeli policies toward the Palestinians. Lerner himself has recently focused on constructing an ecumenical spiritual Left, and his latest book, *The Left Hand of God*, became a best seller.[42] The Religious Left also includes groups such as the Religious Coalition for Reproductive Choice, which calls itself "pro-faith, pro-family, pro-choice"; the Interfaith Alliance, a nonpartisan advocacy organization that was founded to "challenge the radical religious right" and that broadcasts on Air America Radio; the Baptist Joint Committee for Religious Liberty, composed of progressive Baptists who uphold their tradition's strong support of religious liberty and church-state separation; and the Institute for Welcoming Resources, which represents churches that welcome gays and lesbians. Religious progressives also include evangelicals such as Tony Campolo, Brian McLaren, and Jim Wallis of Sojourners, all of whom made their names chiefly through writing and activism: they don't pastor megachurches or head media empires. The evangelical Left is not always as progressive on gender and sexuality issues as on other issues; leaders such as Wallis are pro-life rather than pro-choice, while homosexuality and women's ordination present difficulties among some leftist religious groups. Their focus is chiefly on poverty, racial injustice, and global inequality, as well as spiritual renewal. This vision is increasingly influential, especially among younger evangelicals. The Religious Left overall was profoundly influenced by the post–9/11 militarization of U.S. policy. Nowhere has it been more active in recent years than in opposition to the politicized events engineered in the name of the "war on terror." In magazines, at rallies, and on the Web, religious people have spoken from their faith to protest the Iraq war, the treatment of prisoners at Guantánamo and Abu Ghraib, and the accelerating diminution of civil rights in the United States.

The Religious Left, no less than the Religious Right, is interested in forwarding the visibility and power of religious speech, although its constituents hold a range of views as to the propriety and limits of religion's role in the public sphere. Like their conservative counterparts, liberal religious leaders have found it useful to cooperate across religious lines with other people of faith on issues of common concern (this cooperation often includes Christians, Jews, and Muslims, but less frequently Sikhs, Hindus, or Pagans). Religious leftists also share with Religious Right leaders a deep-seated ambivalence toward secular culture, often seen as dangerously complicit with global consumerism and the deep injustices and inequalities resulting from North American habits of consumption. Among Christians in particular, the Religious Left seems to differ most sharply overall from the Religious Right in the distinct notions of sin held by each constituency: Christian liberals today, like their predecessors, tend to focus on sin in the social and political sphere, whereas their conservative counterparts remain concerned foremost with individual sins of the spirit (unbelief) or the body (sexuality), with somewhat less attention paid to social, political, and economic inequities. This is changing for a number Christian conservatives, some of whom have become quite active in advocating for debt relief for Africa or more funding for global HIV-AIDS programs. In this, they have worked with more liberal Christians and secular people as well. The concern with "sins of the body" remains, however: conservative evangelicals, for example, have been key to ensuring that one-third of all U.S. money for HIV-AIDS prevention is tied to promoting sexual abstinence.[43]

It may be precisely in these areas of global social concern that the investments—indeed, the definitions—of religious politics, particularly Christian

Figure 5.
Lerner and Neuhaus. In 2006, Rabbi Michael Lerner and Rev. Richard John Neuhaus debated the role of religion in politics on *Meet the Press*. Photograph by Alex Wong, courtesy Getty Images for *Meet the Press*.

conservatism, are most clearly shifting. Since the late 1990s, for example, there has been a dramatic upsurge in activism to end modern slavery and sexual trafficking. It is hard to describe opposition to modern slavery as either a uniquely "liberal" or "conservative" position, and the movement has included not only evangelicals from across the spectrum (including liberals such as Sojourners as well as political moderates, such as those at the International Justice Mission or the global development organization World Vision) but also, not surprisingly, a group founded by a Quaker professor of sociology, Free the Slaves,[44] as well as the largely secular American Anti-Slavery Group.[45] Popular culture played no small role in the larger antislavery mobilization: in spring 2007, the movie *Amazing Grace*, directed by Michael Apted, was released to great acclaim, particularly among religious activists. The film recounted the story of William Wilberforce, the nineteenth-century British MP who led the campaign for the abolition of the slave trade. The film itself was financed by Philip Anschutz, a billionaire social conservative who has been a major backer of the Christian Right, supporting groups who oppose everything from gay rights to abortion to the teaching of evolution.[46] But modern antislavery activists, who include many high school students, have made their own meanings, as a wide range of groups embraced the film as a chance to identify themselves with Wilberforce's righteous campaign for social justice.

Among many religious groups in the United States, then, the Left/Right dichotomies are muddy, even if they remain politically powerful. U.S. Muslims, for example, tend to be very liberal on issues such as the war in Iraq, opposition to the Patriot Act, and, to some degree, social spending. But they also, though not uniformly, tend to be social conservatives.[47] In this they track closer to the politics of African American Protestants and many Catholics, who frequently hold both liberal and conservative positions. (African American Christians still lean heavily Democratic, while Latinos, largely Democratic, are considered potential swing voters in some areas—or were, until the most recent battle over immigration legislation.) And, as John McGreevy analyzes in this issue, the history of the Catholic relationship to the Democratic Party is enormously complicated, to a significant degree because of the politics of race and the charged, ever divisive issue of abortion.[48]

The contest over the shape of religious politics has occurred at the level of policy ideas no less than doctrine and values. Starting in the 1980s and mushrooming in the 1990s, a newly confident and well-connected generation of religious intellectuals worked to raise awareness, legitimize religious concerns in policy-making, and increase funding for faith-based organizations in general. These intellectual leaders—many but not all of them Christian, who crossed political and denomination lines—were fully aware of the political force that evangelicals in particular had begun to wield in the 1980s. Several were deeply influenced by Reinhold Niebuhr, whose status as one of the twentieth century's great public intellectuals exemplified the kind of respectability and intellectual power that the think-tank generation would like to see as their own.[49] (Niebuhr's life and work are reexamined in this issue by Michael Thompson, who argues that Niebuhr's model of religious realism can provide a model for an engaged social consciousness today.) These religious intellectuals did not always constitute a coherent or even congenial group; they spanned the political and theological spectrum, from the deeply conservative to left-liberal. They included Christians and Jews as well as people of other faiths. But what they had in common was a desire to be taken seriously *as* intellectuals and as policy shapers, not only as activists. They wanted, as Richard Neuhaus had put it in *The Naked Public Square*, "a seat at the table"—not a place on the streets.

Intellectual respectability has perhaps been particularly important for evangelicals, who have long been rendered in popular films as country bumpkins duped by ministerial con artists and who are still stereotyped as less educated and less intellectually engaged than the rest of the population. Indeed, one of the major players in the Religious Right today, the Southern Baptist Richard Land, is proud to advertise himself as a graduate of Princeton University; that Ivy League undergraduate degree has given him tremendous caché in evangelical and political circles. Elsewhere in academia, there has been an important rise in evangelical scholars teaching in prestigious departments across the university; in particular, evangelical historians such as Mark Noll and George Marsden, both now residing at the University of Notre Dame, have made it both respectable and desirable to be in (and "take back") the universities from the secularists, who, in the view of some, turned campuses into seething cauldrons of antireligious hostility and decadence.[50]

The think tank revolution emerged from this combination of intellectual engagement, search for respectability, and a revitalized sense that religious people could and should place themselves more visibly in policy-making centers. Neuhaus himself was central to the founding of one of the earliest, most influential, and ultimately most conservative of the think tanks, the Institute for Religion and Democracy. Founded in 1981, the IRD quickly became a bastion of conservative thinking on foreign policy; in the 1980s, it backed a strong anti-Soviet posture and advocated U.S. support for the contras in Nicaragua. It also published vociferous critiques of liberation theology. More recently, it has become a leading voice in support of the Iraq war and opposition to gay marriage. But, as Diane Winston discusses in this issue, the IRD's main goals were primarily focused on the mainline U.S. Protestant churches, which it argued had become too liberal, theologically and politically. From the mid-1980s, the IRD developed a "call to renewal," and an action plan aimed at challenging—more accurately, undermining—Methodist, Presbyterian, and Episcopal church structures, as well as the ecumenical National Council of Churches.[51] The IRD has gone on to play a significant role in supporting the conservative faction of the U.S. Episcopal church in the conflicts that have deeply divided the global Anglican community over issues of homosexuality, women's roles, and biblical literalism.[52]

Several other important think tanks are Christian based but self-conscious about expanding their ecumenical footprint. The Institute for Global Engagement and the International Center for Religion and Diplomacy offer moderate conservative and liberal visions, respectively, of the importance of bringing religion into the apparatus of foreign policy.[53] The Ethics and Public Policy Center, which addresses both domestic and foreign policy, has a capacious intellectual reach and a commitment to creating a new kind of ecumenical conservatism. Its research programs—one each for evangelicals, Jews, Islam, and Catholics—produce sophisticated policy studies on issues ranging from economics to the media to immigration.[54] The Institute for Jewish and Community Research, in San Francisco, is less oriented toward national policy but equally interested in crossing lines between academic research and community advocacy. There are many other, similar organizations.[55]

When the Bush administration came into office, one of its signature programs was the Office of Faith-Based and Community Initiatives. Launched in early 2001, the program was designed to increase the funding available to faith-based social service organizations. Religious organizations had long received public funding for their social service work, and groups such as Catholic Charities, Habitat for Humanity, and Hadassah International Medical Relief had for years run programs that did not include proselytizing. But the faith-based initiative took that issue further; now, even groups committed to proselytizing as part of their programs would be eligible for government support.[56]

The most significant impact was probably internationally; by 2006, the Bush administration had almost doubled the percentage of foreign aid money going to religious groups. This rise in government funding almost certainly reflects the reality that Americans of a variety of faiths are doing a great deal more *work* internationally. But according to a major investigative report by the *Boston Globe*, the funding decisions are also explicitly political, as religious conservatives close to the administration have targeted USAID for its "liberal" bias, and have successfully pressed for steering money away from secular organizations and toward religious groups.[57] In support of establishing an environment more friendly to religious NGOs, the Bush administration has brought in Andrew Natsios to head AID. Natsios, a former Massachusetts state legislator, is also the former vice president of World Vision, a rapidly expanding evangelical development organization that by 2005 had already become the second-largest recipient of USAID grants.[58]

For FBOs operating within the United States, too, the faith-based initiatives of the Bush administration have been as much about politics as they have been about faith or social service. In a remarkable memoir of his time in the Office of Faith-Based and Community Initiatives, former White House staffer David Kuo argues that the biggest irony of the program was its very paucity: despite overblown rhetoric and the implied promise that local groups would receive infusions of cash, very little *new* money actually went to community-based groups in the United States, either religious or secular. But money was redistributed, with religious groups getting a larger share of the pie, and Kuo

Figure 6.
Bush and FBOs. President Bush addressing one of the White House conferences on faith-based initiatives in March 2006. Photograph by Doug Mills, for the *New York Times*, courtesy Redux.

recounts how funding decisions consistently benefited Christian, and particularly evangelical, organizations over others. For example, when a new ratings program was put into effect to evaluate proposals to be supported by the Capital Compassion Fund, the administration stacked an "independent review board" with "well-meaning" Christians. Kuo was not on the committee, but he later had dinner with a woman who was. The group had instructions to score organizations objectively, according to a particular list of requirements. "But," Kuo quotes the woman acknowledging, "when I saw one of those non-Christian groups in the set I was reviewing, I just stopped looking at them and gave them a zero." In this issue, Tanya Erzen discusses the "redemptive" narratives of Chuck Colson's Prison Fellowship, which received significant government funding to offer prison rehabilitation programs that depended on Christian conversion.

The major beneficiary of the faith-based initiative, however, seemed to be the Bush administration itself, which soon realized that it could reap political benefits by holding massive conferences aimed at "training" churches and other groups how to access federal funds. Attendees came away highly enthusiastic about an administration they thought was listening to their concerns and which they assumed, wrongly, was all but promising them funding. During the 2004 election season, the administration scheduled a dozen such conferences in key battleground states.[59] (This series of meetings was challenged as unconstitutional, but the court rejected the suit by a 5–4 Supreme Court decision in June 2007.[60])

All of these developments together illuminate new and potent ways that religion and politics intersect in the contemporary United States. Plainly, religious actors are engaged in a variety of activities that can (and, we think, should) be construed as political: they lay claims on particular public spaces as necessarily religious; make movies and write books to forward their views; deal directly with the power of the state to define and delimit religion; and work outside the state to enact religious ideals on a global scale. These and more are sites of social performance and social struggle, where persons learn what it means to be "religious" and where they in turn practice working with and against those meanings.

Organization and Content of this Special Issue

While it may well be impossible to set clear parameters around the categories of religion and politics, the process of coediting this issue has introduced us to the wealth of exciting research now being pursued in this field. The nineteen essays featured here are organized into four thematic sections that highlight the overlapping categories of state power, global imaginaries, religious and political leadership, and media and performance. Of course, the divisions through which we have grouped this diverse body of work are meant to be suggestive and by no means typologically prescriptive. Nor do they mark disciplinary boundaries: in each section, historians are mixed with sociologists, political scientists with humanists, and of course religious studies scholars mingle with those whose primary scholarly home is American studies.

Five essays are grouped under the heading of "Engaging State Power." Each of these effectively treats distinct conflicts between religious actors and political, legal, or judicial authorities. The first piece, Kevin Schultz's "Favoritism Cannot Be Tolerated," is a case study of the debate over the Gideons' attempt to distribute Bibles to public school children during the 1950s; among other things, the study works to show the surprisingly recent provenance of the legal norm pertaining to "religiously neutral" schools. Next, Evelyn Alsultany analyzes a series of post-9/11 public service announcements that attempted, in various ways, to "Americanize" U.S. Muslims. Neil J. Young's article offers a new window on Mormon political activism by exploring Mormon women's work against the proposed equal rights amendment, while Brian McCammack's "Hot Damned America" unpacks recent developments in evangelical activism on both sides of the global warming debate. Rounding out this section is John McGreevy's article on the complex relationships between U.S. Catholics and the Democratic Party in recent decades. Though markedly divergent in subject matter, these pieces share an explicit interest in religious groups' dealings with state power in the contemporary United States.

Our second set of essays comes under the rubric "Politics of the Global," as these four pieces deal concretely with religious groups that intentionally look beyond national borders to find legitimacy in a transnational context. Edward Curtis examines the layered religious and political alignments made by African American Muslims during the Arab cold war. In "'As Americans' Against 'Genocide,'" a firsthand look at current activism surrounding Darfur, Jodi Eichler-Levine and Rosemary Hicks explore interreligious as well as international cooperation and conflict, as US activists simultaneously confronted the crisis in Darfur and the politics of the war on terrorism. Clarence Hardy analyzes the investments in diaspora and transnationalism in early Black Pentecostal circles, long before such terms had acquired the currency they hold today, while Prema Kurien analyzes the global politics surrounding "Hindu" and "South Asian" identities in the United States. Once again, these articles necessarily focus on the conflictual relationships, as well as the sometimes unexpected convergences, that develop when religion and politics intersect on a global stage.

Our third category, "Leaders and Activists," shifts quite intentionally away from broader social and cultural contexts in order to highlight a number of important thinkers and activists whose intellectual, political, and spiritual leadership has made a crucial difference in both historical and contemporary contexts. Barbara Savage's analysis of Benjamin Mays recuperates the influence of this towering intellectual upon the theological visions and social role of African American churches. Next, Laura Levitt rereads the work of several writers in the journal *Judaism*, published by the American Jewish Congress starting in the 1950s, for what they may tell us about the possibilities for Jewish secularism in the contemporary United States. Michael Thompson takes us back to Reinhold Niebuhr's erstwhile programs for prophetic Christianity —controversial then, and still a source of profound disagreement today—as a means of rethinking religion's role in U.S. foreign policy." Luis León analyzes the example of Cesar Chavez for insight into Latin American Catholic modes of melding religious with political ideals. Finally, Michael Lindsay surveys the worldviews and political activism of the new evangelical elites who in recent years have accrued extraordinary power in a variety of political and cultural arenas. Together, these essays offer innovative paradigms for thinking about leadership and activism over the long term.

No collection of pieces on religion and politics in our current moment would be complete without paying close attention to popular culture, entertainment, and the news. In the fourth section on "Media and Performance," then, several scholars examine the complex ways that believers have engaged,

Figure 7.
Women at Prayer Vigil. Iraqi doctor Rashad Zaydan from Baghdad prays alongside others in a vigil for peace in Iraq in 2006. The gathering included people from several faiths, including Jews, Muslims, and Christians. Photograph by Jason Reed, courtesy Reuters.

claimed, and performed "belief" in public culture. Ann Pellegrini's exploration of Christian "Hell Houses"—the alternatives to "haunted houses" that have flowered in recent years—introduces us to the successful performative modes by which evangelicals have exploited Halloween for witnessing to the fiery horrors of hell and the sweet blessings of heaven. In a different vein, Jane Iwamura examines the Manzanar Annual Pilgrimage, a combined festival, political forum, and religious experience that unites Japanese Americans across religious groups, forging what she terms a "new civil religion." Diane Winston investigates how media have missed the story of religion and politics in the United States, and highlights the limited understandings that journalists bring when they do report on religion. Tanya Erzen's "Testimonial Politics" offers a comparative look at evangelical ex-gay narratives and Christian stories of prison conversions, focusing on the ideological assumptions and persuasive power of their shared narratives of personal redemption. Trysh Travis ends the volume with an analysis of the combination of loose spiritual longings and self-help that undergirds the broad popular allure of Oprah Winfrey's Book Club.

Any one of these four themes could easily work as the subject for a much larger anthology of essays on religion and politics in contemporary America, but we believe readers are well served by seeing these all together under one cover. Unlike many recent scholarly books on religion and politics that focus almost obsessively on white Protestants (with occasional Catholics or Jews thrown in for good measure), this issue highlights a range of diverse religious, ethnic, and racial groupings; and we have been delighted to learn that so many scholars at different points in their careers are pursuing work in such areas. But if we have learned of work-in-progress among current scholars of American studies and religious studies, the process of editing this issue has also made it all the more clear how much we need more of this kind of work, and how much room there is for new modes of analysis and arenas of study. Greater attention to new religious movements and to interreligious encounters, including political alliances across religious lines, is sorely needed, as is more work on parachurch institutions and organizations that play an increasingly significant role in current politics. Debates over contentious issues such as gender and sexuality, tradition and innovation, continue to beg for deeper analysis both within studies of contemporary Christianity and beyond, perhaps especially in more recent religious and interreligious movements in the United States. There is, in short, much to admire in current scholarship, and yet much work still to be done. If a few readers are inspired by this issue to venture out into new territory on religion and politics, the task will have been more than worthwhile.

Notes

We thank Laura Cook Kenna, Ruth Feldstein, Leigh Schmidt, and an anonymous reviewer for their feedback on the introduction, Julie Passanante Elman for research assistance, Maureen Kentoff for help in procuring image permissions, Stacey Lynn for her helpful copyediting, and Curtis Marez for his patient, engaged, and insightful work on every aspect of this special issue.

1. Richard John Neuhaus, *The Naked Public Square: Religion and Democracy in America* (Grand Rapids: Eerdman's, 1984), 27.
2. Mary Ann Glendon, "The Naked Public Square Now: A Symposium," *First Things* (November 2004), 12–14, quote on 13.
3. Pew Forum on Religion and Public Life, "Views of Islam Remain Sharply Divided," September 9, 2004, at *http://pewforum.org/docs/index.php?DocID=54*. A 2003 poll showed similar results: "Growing Number of Americans Say Islam Encourages Violence among Followers," at *http://pewforum.org/press/index.php?ReleaseID=20*. (These and following Web addresses accessed June 29, 2007).
4. See, for example, the organization Freedom House, which waves the banner of "religious freedom" as a cover for an agenda that paints Islam as the primary threat and Christians the primary victims. Freedom House's Web page is *http://www.freedomhouse.org/template.cfm?page=1*. In 2005, the Center for Religious Freedom moved to the Hudson Institute. On Freedom House, see Diana Barahona, "The Freedom House Files," *Monthly Review*, March 3, 2007, at *http://mrzine.monthlyreview.org/barahona030107.html#_edn5*. See also Nina Shea, *In the Lion's Den* (Nashville, Tenn.: Broadman and Holeman, 1997).

On the cultural work done by the image of Muslims as a threat, see Mahmood Mamdani, *Good Muslim, Bad Muslim: America, the Cold War, and the Roots of Terror* (New York: Pantheon, 2004). On the facetiousness of the category "Islamic fundamentalism," see Olivier Roy, *Globalized Islam: The Search for a New Ummah*, rev. ed. (New York: Columbia University Press, 2006).

5. Samuel Huntington, *The Clash of Civilizations and the Remaking of World Order* (New York: Free Press, 2002); and Sam Harris, *The End of Faith: Religion, Terror, and the Future of Reason* (New York: Norton, 2005), and *Letter to a Christian Nation* (New York: Knopf, 2006). More recently, Harris has written, "It is time we recognized—and obliged the Muslim world to recognize—that 'Muslim extremism' is not extreme among Muslims. Mainstream Islam itself represents an extremist rejection of intellectual honesty, gender equality, secular politics and genuine pluralism. The truth about Islam is as politically incorrect as it is terrifying: Islam is all fringe and no center. In Islam, we confront a civilization with an arrested history. It is as though a portal in time has opened, and the Christians of the 14th century are pouring into our world" (*http://www.truthdig.com/report/item/20060207_reality_islam/*).

6. An excellent analysis is found in Ira C. Lupu et al.'s "Religious Displays and the Courts," Report by the Pew Forum on Religion and Public Life, June 2007, at *http://pewforum.org/assets/files/religious-displays.pdf*. Legal scholar Susanna Dokupil focuses on the Ten Commandments case in "Thou Shalt Not Bear False Witness: 'Sham' Secular Purposes in Ten Commandments Displays," *Harvard Journal of Law and Public Policy* 28.2 (Spring 2005): 609–50.

7. The scholarly treatment of these paradoxical questions is, of course, immense. For a recent, very clear, and useful account, see Christopher L. Eisgruber and Lawrence G. Sager, *Religious Freedom and the Constitution* (Cambridge, Mass.: Harvard University Press, 2007).

8. Richard Dawkins, *The God Delusion* (New York: Houghton Mifflin, 2006); Christopher Hitchens, *God Is Not Great: How Religion Poisons Everything* (New York: Twelve Books/Hachette Book Group, 2007); David Brooks, *On Paradise Drive: How We Live Now (and Always Have) in the Future Tense* (New York: Simon & Schuster, 2005).

9. The most valuable recent account of the American religious history subfield's own history is John F. Wilson, *Religion and the American Nation: Historiography and History* (Athens: University of Georgia Press, 2003).

10. See, for example, the long conversation on the H-AmStdy list in May 2007 (discussion thread titled American Studies and Religion). In a related field, see the recent essay by Andrew Preston, "Bridging the Gap Between the Sacred and Secular in the History of American Foreign Relations," *Diplomatic History* 30.5 (November 2006): 783–812.

11. Michael Kazin, *A Godly Hero: The Life of William Jennings Bryan* (New York: Knopf, 2006); Leigh Eric Schmidt, *Hearing Things: Religion, Illusion, and American Enlightenment* (Cambridge, Mass.: Harvard University Press, 2002); Jana Riess, *What Would Buffy Do: The Vampire Slayer as Spiritual Guide* (New York: Jossey-Bass, 2004). Obviously, these are just a few examples.

12. In addition to works we discuss briefly in this introduction, other useful texts that appraise and scrutinize basic theories of religion include Daniel L. Pals, *Eight Theories of Religion*, 2nd ed. (New York: Oxford University Press, 2005); Mark C. Taylor, ed., *Critical Terms for Religious Studies* (Chicago: University of Chicago Press, 1998); Jonathan Z. Smith, *Relating Religion: Essays in the Study of Religion* (Chicago: University of Chicago Press, 2004); Tomoko Masuzawa, *In Search of Dreamtime: The Quest for the Origin of Religion* (Chicago: University of Chicago Press, 1993); David Chidester, *Savage Systems: Colonialism and Comparative Religion in Southern Africa* (Charlottesville: University of Virginia Press, 1996); Daniel Dubuisson, *The Western Construction of Religion: Myths, Knowledge, and Ideology*, trans. William Sayers (Baltimore: Johns Hopkins University Press, 2003); and Robert A. Orsi, *Between Heaven and Earth: The Religious Worlds People Make and the Scholars Who Study Them* (Princeton, N.J.: Princeton University Press, 2005).

13. Jürgen Habermas, *The Structural Transformation of the Public Sphere* (New York: Polity, 1992), and *The Philosophical Discourse of Modernity* (Cambridge, Mass.: MIT Press, 1990), 107.

14. See Craig Calhoun, ed., *Habermas and the Public Sphere* (Cambridge, Mass.: MIT Press, 1993), especially contributions by Nancy Fraser and Michael Schudson. See also the Black Public Sphere Collective's *The Black Public Sphere* (Chicago: University of Chicago Press, 1995).

15. John Rawls, *Political Liberalism* (New York: Columbia University Press, 1993); Richard Rorty, "Religion As Conversation-stopper," in *Philosophy and Social Hope* (London: Penguin Books, 1999), 168–74. For a clear discussion of these positions, as well as a rationale for an alternative view, see Jeffrey Stout, *Democracy and Tradition* (Princeton, N.J.: Princeton University Press, 2004), chap. 3.

16. Rorty, "Religion As Conversation-stopper," 169.

17. Stout, *Democracy and Tradition*, 299.

18. Ibid., 296–97, 299.

19. Stephen L. Carter, *The Culture of Disbelief: How American Law and Politics Trivialize Religious Devotion* (New York: Basic Books, 1993), 17. Aiming to define his terms, Carter writes, "When I refer to religion, I will have in mind a tradition of group worship (as against individual metaphysic) that presupposes the existence of a sentience beyond the human and capable of acting outside of the observed principles and limits of natural science, and, further, a tradition that makes demands of some kind on its adherents." Rorty cites Carter's distinction in "Religion As Conversation-stopper," 169.

20. Ibid., 169.

21. Talal Asad, *Genealogies of Religion: Discipline and Reasons of Power in Christianity and Islam* (Baltimore: Johns Hopkins University Press, 1993), 42, 48. Geertz's famous definition of religion appears in the widely read essay "Religion as a Cultural System," originally published in 1966 and reprinted in Geertz, *The Interpretation of Cultures* (New York: Basic Books, 1973).

22. Asad's contribution to the study of ritual and its relation to belief (or "faith") is also relevant here. In his words: "Ritual in the sense of a sacred performance cannot be the place where religious faith is attained, but the manner in which it is (literally) played out. If we are to understand how this happens, we must examine not only the sacred performance itself but also the entire range of available disciplinary activities, of institutional forms of knowledge and practice, within which dispositions are formed and sustained and through which the possibilities of attaining the truth are marked out—as Augustine clearly saw." Asad, *Genealogies of Religion*, 50.

23. The literature here is voluminous, but see especially Russell T. McCutcheon, *Critics Not Caretakers: Redescribing the Public Study of Religion* (Albany: State University of New York Press, 2001); and Tomoko Masuzawa, *The Invention of World Religions: Or, How European Universalism Was Preserved in the Language of Pluralism* (Chicago: University of Chicago Press, 2005).

24. A very useful history of secularism (one that raises different sorts of issues from Asad's) is Susan Jacoby, *Freethinkers: A History of American Secularism* (New York: Henry Holt, 2004).

25. See, in particular, Asad's engagement with José Casanova in his essay "Secularism, Nation-State, Religion," in *Formations of the Secular: Christianity, Islam, Modernity* (Stanford, Calif.: Stanford University Press, 2003), 181–201.

26. Asad, *Formations of the Secular*, 184.

27. Ibid., 199, 200, 201.

28. See, for instance, Jon Meacham, *American Gospel: God, the Founding Fathers, and the Making of a Nation* (New York: Random House, 2006); Joseph Kip Kosek, "Richard Gregg, Mohandas Gandhi, and the Strategy of Nonviolence," *Journal of American History* 91.4 (March 2005): 1318–48; Pamela Klassen, *Blessed Events: Religion and Home Birth in America* (Princeton, N.J.: Princeton University Press, 2001). These are just a few examples among countless others.

29. Barry A. Kosmin, Egon Mayer, and Ariela Keysar, "American Religious Identification Survey," note that the proportion of the Asian American population who are Christian decreased between 1990 and 2001 from 63 percent to 43 percent, "while those professing Asian religions (Buddhism, Hinduism, Islam, etc.) has risen from 15% to 28%." See discussion at http://www.gc.cuny.edu/faculty/research_briefs/aris/religion_ethnicity.htm. See also Diana L. Eck, *A New Religious America: How a "Christian Country" Has Become the World's Most Religiously Diverse Nation* (San Francisco: HarperSanFrancisco, 2001); and Robert Wuthnow, *America and the Challenges of Religious Diversity* (Princeton, N.J.: Princeton University Press, 2005).

30. The sources for the numbers here and in the rest of the paragraph come from the 2001 American Religious Identification Survey (ARIS), carried out by CUNY. Other sources, including the General Statistical Survey, carried out by the U.S. Census Bureau and other organizations; the Pew Forum for Religion and Public Life; and the World Christian Database have all gathered statistics that *generally* align with each other. The percentage of Christians (all denominations) is about 80 percent (between 77 percent and 82 percent). In all cases, the second largest identification among Americans was "no religion" or "unaffiliated," with percentages between 9.4 percent (World Christian Database) and 14.2 percent (ARIS and GSS). The percentage of non-Christian believers varies noticeably, as some questions are differently phrased and difficult to parse. ARIS, for example, shows the lowest number of Jewish, Muslim, Hindu, and Unitarian identification, with 3.7 percent of the total for all non-Christian

groups. However, the authors note that this survey may underestimate the presence of some religious groups, because the survey was conducted only among English speakers and over the phone. All surveys estimate Jewish identification as less than 2 percent (this is religious and not ethnic identification), and Muslims vary from 0.5 percent (ARIS) to 1.6 percent (World Christian Database). Sources: Barry Kosmin and Egon Mayer, American Religious Identification Survey, Graduate Center of the City University of New York, 2001, at http://www.gc.cuny.edu/faculty/research_studies/aris.pdf; the Pew Forum on Religion and Public Life summarizes several surveys at http://pewforum.org/world-affairs/countries/?CountryID=222#3; the World Christian Database numbers are available at the Association for Religious Databases, http://thearda.com/internationalData/countries/Country_234_2.asp.

31. One-third of all U.S. Catholics are Latino, and 54 percent of those identify as Charismatic. Within the Latino population overall, 70 percent are Catholic and just under 20 percent are Protestant. Among all Latino Christians, 39 percent identify as born again or evangelical; this includes 28 percent of Catholics. "Changing Faiths: Latinos and the Transformation of American Religion," a Joint Project of the Pew Forum on Religion and Public Life and the Pew Hispanic Center, released April 2007, available at http://pewforum.org/surveys/hispanic/.

32. Today, Robertson's Christian Broadcast Network has been joined by Trinity Broadcasting Network (which is the largest Christian broadcasting network in the world), Datstar, Family Net, and a host of others.

33. There are several very fine studies of "seekers" and the spiritual marketplace, including Robert Bellah, *Habits of the Heart: Individualism and Commitment in American Life* (Berkeley: University of California Press, 1996); Robert Wuthnow, *After Heaven: Spirituality in America Since the 1950s* (Berkeley: University of California Press, 2000); Robert C. Fuller, *Spiritual, but Not Religious: Understanding Unchurched America* (New York: Oxford University Press, 2001); Wade Clark Roof, *Spiritual Marketplace: Baby Boomers and the Remaking of American Religion* (Princeton, N.J.: Princeton University Press, 2001). See also Leigh Eric Schmidt, *Restless Souls: The Making of American Spirituality* (New York: HarperCollins, 2005); and Lynn Schofield Clark, *From Angels to Aliens: Teenagers, the Media, and the Supernatural* (New York: Oxford University Press, 2005). Additionally, on New Thought, see Beryl Satter, *Each Mind a Kingdom: American Women, Sexual Purity, and the New Thought Movement, 1875–1920* (Berkeley: University of California Press, 1999); Marie Griffith, *Born Again Bodies: Flesh and Spirit in American Christianity* (Berkeley: University of California Press, 2004).

34. Brenda E. Brasher, *Give Me That Online Religion* (New Brunswick, N.J.: Rutgers University Press, 2004); Lorne L. Dawson and Douglas E. Cowan, *Religion Online* (New York: Routledge, 2004).

35. Much has been written about the ways in which Islamic activists use the Internet to solidify a sense of global Muslim identity, although a great deal of it is marked by hyperbole and panic. Useful scholarly approaches are found in Dale Eickelman and Jon W. Anderson, *New Media in the Muslim World: The Emerging Public Sphere* (Bloomington: Indiana University Press, 2003); and Lina Khatib, "Communicating Islamic Fundamentalism as Global Citizenship," in *Reformatting Politics*, ed. Jon Anderson, Jodi Dean, and Geert Lovink (New York: Routledge, 2006). On the Branch Davidians and online networking, see Mark McWilliams, "Digital Waco: Branch Davidian Communities after the Waco Tragedy," in *Religion and Cyberspace*, ed. Morten Hojsgaard (New York: Routledge, 2005), 180–98.

36. These statistics are from the most comprehensive poll of Muslims to date, by the Pew Forum on Religion and Public Life, "Muslim Americans: Middle Class and Mostly Mainstream," May 22, 2007, at http://pewresearch.org/assets/pdf/muslim-americans.pdf. Other polls offer different numbers. The Mosque Study Project, sponsored by the Hartford Theological Seminary and several other organizations, is often cited. The project, which looks at the "ethnic origin" of all U.S. Muslims, not just first-generation immigrants, estimates the South Asian population at 30 percent; Arab and Iranian at 26 percent; and African American at 30 percent. However, this is from a survey of regular mosque participants, not all people who identify as Muslim. The report is at http://www.cair-net.org/mosquereport/Masjid_Study_Project_2000_Report.pdf.

37. Philip Jenkins, *The Next Christendom: The Coming of Global Christianity*, rev. ed. (New York: Oxford University Press, 2007); Andrew Walls, *The Cross Cultural Process in Christian History: Studies in the Transmission and Appropriation of Faith* (Maryknoll, N.Y.: Orbis Books, 2002); and Lamin Sanneh, *Whose Religion Is Christianity? The Gospel Beyond the West* (Grand Rapids: Eerdmans, 2003). Also see Pew Forum on Religion and Public Life, Event Transcript, "The Coming Religious Wars? Demographics and Conflict in Islam and Christianity," at http://pewforum.org/events/?EventID=82, and the

information collected at the Center for the Study of Global Christianity, part of the Gordon-Conwell Theological Seminary, at http://www.gordonconwell.edu/ockenga/globalchristianity/gd.php.

38. Kevin Phillips, *American Theocracy: The Peril and Politics of Radical Religion, Oil, and Borrowed Money in the Twenty-First Century* (New York: Penguin, 2007).

39. The literature on conservative religious mobilization is too extensive to cite fully here, but see especially Leo P. Ribuffo, *The Old Christian Right: The Protestant Far Right from the Great Depression to the Cold War* (Philadelphia: Temple University Press, 1983); Robert C. Liebman and Robert Wuthnow, eds., *The New Christian Right: Mobilization and Legitimation* (New York: Aldine, 1983); and, more recently, Lisa McGirr, *Suburban Warriors: The Origins of the New American Right* (Princeton, N.J.: Princeton University Press, 2001); and Kenneth J. Heineman, *God Is a Conservative: Religion, Politics, and Morality in Contemporary America* (1998; New York: New York University Press, 2005).

40. On Falwell, see Susan Friend Harding, *The Book of Jerry Falwell: Fundamentalist Language and Politics* (Princeton, N.J.: Princeton University Press, 2000). On Robertson, see the somewhat out of date but still useful book by David Edwin Harrell Jr., *Pat Robertson: A Personal, Political and Religious Portrait* (San Francisco: Harper & Row, 1987). Again, the literature on the Religious Right is too voluminous to cite fully here. For critiques of the mobilization of the Religious Right and its usurpation of other strands within evangelicalism, see Randall Balmer, *Thy Kingdom Come: How the Religious Right Distorts the Faith and Threatens America* (New York: Basic Books, 2006); and Michelle Goldberg, *Kingdom Coming: The Rise of Christian Nationalism* (New York: W. W. Norton, 2006).

41. On the "emergent church," see Brian McLaren, *Everything Must Change: Jesus, Global Crises, and a Revolution of Hope* (Nashville, Tenn.: Thomas Nelson, 2007); Dan Kimball, *They Like Jesus But Not the Church: Insights from Emerging Generations* (Grand Rapids, Mich.: Zondervan, 2007); Doug Pagitt and Toby Jones, eds., *An Emergent Manifesto of Hope* (Idlewood, Mass.: Baker Books, 2007).

42. Michael Lerner, *The Left Hand of God: Taking Back Our Country from the Religious Right* (San Francisco: HarperSanFrancisco, 2006). See also Michael Lerner, "Tikkun's 15th anniversary," *Tikkun*, Sept./Oct. 2001, 9ff.

43. Michael Kranish, "Religious Right Wields Clout: Secular Groups Losing Funding Amid Pressure," *Boston Globe*, October 9, 2006, at http://www.boston.com/news/nation/articles/2006/10/09/religious_right_wields_clout/?page=1; General Accounting Office, "Global Health: Spending Requirement Presents Challenges for Allocating Prevention Funding under the President's Emergency Plan for AIDS Relief," April 4, 2006, Report number GAO-06-395, at http://frwebgate.access.gpo.gov/cgi-bin/useftp.cgi?IPaddress=162.140.64.21&filename=d06395.pdf&directory=/diskb/wais/data/gao

44. See Deann Alford, "Free at Last: How Christians Worldwide Are Sabotaging the Modern Slave Trade," *Christianity Today*, March 2007, at http://www.christianitytoday.com/ct/2007/march/13.30.html. International Justice Mission was founded by Gary Haugen, author of the influential *The Good News about Injustice: The Witness of Courage in a Hurting World* (Downers Grove, Ill.: Intervarsity Press, 1999). In 2006, IJM received a $5 million grant from the Bill and Melinda Gates Foundation to support its work against human trafficking. Announcement at http://www.gatesfoundation.org/GlobalHealth/Pri_Diseases/HIVAIDS/Announcements/Announce-060314.htm. The organization Free the Slaves has produced documentaries on slavery and sex trafficking, three of which are being screened worldwide under the auspices of the U.S. State Department. Eric Green, "State Department Offers Film Program on Trafficking in Persons," US INFO, June 8, 2007, at http://usinfo.state.gov/xarchives/display.html?p=washfile-english&y=2007&m=June&x=20070608130830X1eneerg0.3753168.

45. AASG was founded by Charles Jacobs, a Jewish social liberal who has worked closely with synagogues, African American Christian churches, and nonreligious groups. His stances on Islam and the Middle East, however, can be fairly described as reactionary, and, not incidentally, the organization focuses largely on Sudan, where an Islamist government is in power. The AASG Web activism page is http://www.iabolish.com/index.html. Jacobs himself is also founder of the "David Project," which provides speakers and workshops on the Middle East conflict: "The essence of the Middle East conflict," according to Jacobs, "is about Jewish existence and political self-determination in the Middle East in the face of a hostile Arab world and radical Islamists." See the speakers bureau list for the Israel on Campus Coalition, at http://israeloncampuscoalition.org/speakers/cjacobs.htm. The David Project has also recently and quite controversially opposed the building of a mosque in a Boston suburb and was also centrally involved in the controversy over the Middle East studies program at Columbia

University. Judy Rakowsky, "Lawsuits Dropped, But Battles Over Boston Mosque Continue," *Jewish Daily Forward*, June 27, 2007, at http://www.forward.com/articles/11052/. Douglas Feiden, "Hate 101: Climate of Hate Rocks Columbia University," *New York Daily News*, November 21, 2004, at http://www.nydailynews.com/front/story/254925p–218295c.html.

46. Adam Hochschild, "English Abolition: The Movie," *New York Review of Books* 54.10 (June 14, 2007), at http://www.nybooks.com/articles/20278. Anschutz, the oil magnate, financier, and media mogul who in a three-year period was named "the greediest executive in America" by *Fortune* and one of the country's 50 Most Generous Philanthropists by *Business Week*, is the owner of Walden Media and the Regal Entertainment group. Walden produced the film *The Lion, the Witch, and the Wardrobe*, based on the book by the Christian theologian C. S. Lewis, as well as a range of other movies billed as "family-friendly." Jack Shafer, "The Billionaire Newsboy: Making Sense of Philip Anschutz's *Examiners*," *Slate*, March 24, 2005, at *http://www.slate.com/id/2115253/*; Bill Berkowitz, "The Movie, the Media, and the Conservative Politics of Philip Anschutz," Media Transparency, December 2, 2005, at *http://www.mediatransparency.org/story.php?storyID=97*.

47. Muslims overall voted for Bush in 2000 and Kerry in 2004, although African American Muslims voted largely Democratic in both elections. See Zogby International Press Release, "American Muslims Overwhelmingly Backing Kerry; Major Shift from 2000 Election," September 22, 2004, at http://www.zogby.com/News/ReadNews.dbm?ID=869.

48. Raymond Hernandez, "Hispanic Voters Gain New Clout with Democrats," *New York Times*, June 10, 2007, at http://www.nytimes.com/2007/06/10/us/politics/10hispanics.html?ex=1183176000&en=0 2f7de67d242cc74&ei=5070; "Fact Sheet: Latinos and the 2006 Mid-Term Elections," Pew Hispanic Center, November 27, 2006, at http://pewhispanic.org/files/factsheets/26.pdf.

49. Hauerwas discusses the impact of Niebuhr in "The Naked Public Square Now: A Symposium."

50. Mark A. Noll has consistently been credited with helping to inspire higher standards in evangelical scholarship with his influential book *The Scandal of the Evangelical Mind* (Grand Rapids, Mich.: Eerdmans, 1994). For conservative Christian critiques of the modern university, see George M. Marsden, *The Soul of the American University: From Protestant Establishment to Established Nonbelief* (New York: Oxford University Press, 1994), and *The Outrageous Idea of Christian Scholarship* (New York: Oxford University Press, 1997); and D. G. Hart, *The University Gets Religion: Religious Studies in American Higher Education* (Baltimore: Johns Hopkins University Press, 1999); and, for a highly polemical view of religious studies in the modern university directed at college students, see D. G. Hart, *A Student's Guide to Religious Studies* (Wilmington, Del.: Intercollegiate Studies Institute, 2005).

51. Arthur Farnsley, "People Power," *Christian Century*, October 5, 2004, 34–39.

52. Event Transcript: "Global Schism: Is the Anglican Communion Rift the First Stage in a Wider Christian Split?" Pew Forum on Religion and Public Life, May 14, 2007 at http://pewforum.org/events/?EventID=145.

53. The Institute for Global Engagement publishes *The Review of Faith and International Affairs*, which impressively combines scholarship and advocacy. Douglas Johnston, founder of IRD coedited with Cynthia Sampson, *Religion, the Missing Dimension of Statecraft* (New York: Oxford University Press, 1994). See also the fascinating collection by Elizabeth Bucar and Barbara Barnett, *Does Human Rights Need God?* (Grand Rapids, Mich.: Eerdmans, 2005).

54. For example, the vice president of EPPC, who is a frequent commentator on evangelicals and politics, has edited ten books, among them, Michael Cromartie, ed., *A Public Faith: Evangelicals and Civic Engagement* (Lanham, Md.: Rowman and Littlefield, 2003.

55. The Pew Research Center for Religion and Public Life, surely the country's largest and most important think tank on religious and public policy issues, cannot be counted among these activist think tanks, in that it does not have an agenda to promote any particular set of beliefs or to support religious activity. It produces extraordinary research, however, and in some sense the very availability and timeliness of that research has supported the sense of "people of faith" as important political actors.

56. A Pew poll in 2001 showed that most people in the United States supported faith-based funding, despite their church-state concerns. Pew Research Center for the People and the Press, "Faith-Based Funding Backed, But Church-State Doubts Abound," April 2001, at http://people-press.org/reports/display.php3?ReportID=15.

57. Executive Order 13279, Equal Protection of the Laws for Faith-Based and Community Organizations, December 12, 2002, text at http://www.presidency.ucsb.edu/ws/index.php?pid=61375. Farah

Stockman et al., "Bush Brings Faith to Foreign Aid," *Boston Globe*, October 8, 2006, at http://www. boston.com/news/nation/articles/2006/10/08/bush_brings_faith_to_foreign_aid.

58. By far the largest religious organizations receiving USAID funds are Catholic Relief Services and World Vision. See also the *Boston Globe's* chart at http://www.boston.com/news/special/faith_based/ faith_based_organizations.htm. On the remarkable growth of World Vision, see Susan Mary McDonic, "Witnessing, Work, and Worship: World Vision and the Negotiation of Faith, Development, and Culture" (PhD diss., Duke University, 2004).

59. David Kuo, *Tempting Faith: An Inside Story of Political Seduction* (New York: Free Press, 2006), 212.

60. In *Hein v. Freedom from Religion Foundation*, the Court ruled that the plantiffs did not have standing to sue. In general, U.S. citizens do not have the right to sue over federal spending, but claims that spending violates the establishment clause are exempt. In this case, however, the majority ruled that the exemption applies only to spending set by Congress, not by the president. Since the Office of Faith-Based and Community Initiatives was established by Executive Order, it is exempt. Linda Greenhouse, "Justices Reject Suit on Federal Money for Faith-Based Office," *New York Times*, June 26, 2007, at http://www.nytimes.com/2007/06/26/washington/26faith.html?_r=1&oref=slogin

"Favoritism Cannot Be Tolerated": Challenging Protestantism in America's Public Schools and Promoting the Neutral State

Kevin M. Schultz

In 1951, the Gideons of Passaic and Bergen counties approached the Board of Education of Rutherford, New Jersey, with an offer. The Gideons proposed "to furnish, free of charge, a volume containing the book of Psalms, Proverbs and the New Testament to each of the children in the schools of Rutherford from the fifth grade up to the eighth grade, and High School." Besides Protestant proselytizing, which the Gideons did not deny, the letter also claimed that giving out the so-called Gideon Bible would be socially useful: "If God's word is heard and heeded, if it is read and believed, we believe that this is the answer to the problem of juvenile delinquency." The letter also offered to help work out the thorny details of distributing the Bibles to the Rutherford schoolchildren. Having seen several attempts to infuse religion into the public arena stumble because of poor distribution plans, the Gideons did not want to take the chance that their mission would be foiled by a faulty method of delivery.[1]

On November 5, 1951, the Rutherford school board held a public meeting to consider the Gideons' proposal. The hearing started peacefully enough, but quickly a Catholic priest and a Jewish rabbi protested. Both men argued that the Gideon Bible was an overtly sectarian book forbidden under the laws of their respective religions. Then, as now, the Gideon Bible consists of all the New Testament, all the Book of Psalms (from the Old Testament), and all the Book of Proverbs (also from the Old Testament). Each followed the style and manner of the 1611 King James, or Protestant, version. And, despite the direct importation of several parts of the Old Testament, the Gideons excluded any reference to the Old Testament in their Bible. For obvious reasons, then, the Gideon Bible was offensive to Jews, who denied the validity of much of the New Testament, and to Catholics, who used a different version of the Bible, called the Douay Bible.

In addition to the claim of devotional incompatibility, the rabbi and the priest also argued that the unsystematic content of the Gideon Bible could not be considered a legitimate part of the grand tradition of greater Christendom and therefore could not be accepted by the school board based on a claim that the Gideon Bible was an important part of the Western tradition, which might have made it applicable for educational purposes. The Gideons' only motive, they argued, was proselytizing the Protestant faith to New Jersey's schoolchildren, and this, in postwar America, when Catholics and Jews were making considerable headway toward crafting a truly pluralistic society, was unacceptable.[2]

Despite these pleas, the Rutherford Board of Education voted with only one dissenter to allow the Gideons onto public school grounds to distribute their Bible. Nervously, the school board crafted a complex distribution plan that was supposed to minimize any publicity the affair might generate. The board stipulated that the Gideons would be allowed to distribute their Bibles only to students whose parents had signed request forms several weeks prior to the Gideons' arrival. At the urging of legal counsel, the board added that the Gideons could use only the names of pupils whose parents had signed for the Bibles in any announcement of the event and that any announcement about distribution of the Bibles was not allowed to refer to the event's purpose. Finally, the board added that distribution would happen after school, when no other children would be around to witness the event and potentially feel excluded. The board's clear intent was to remove the possibility that it was advocating one religion at the expense of any other.[3]

The numerous precautions did not slow criticism. Under the banner of defending their faith and their nation, Catholic and Jewish civic and religious organizations mounted complaints. They were joined by a collection of liberal civil rights organizations, including the American Civil Liberties Union (ACLU), and several of the civic unity groups that had emerged during the Second World War. In early 1952, just prior to the scheduled distribution of the Gideons' Bibles, a Catholic parent named Ralph Lecoque and a Jewish parent named Bernard Tudor filed a joint injunction against the Rutherford Board of Education, hoping to get the school board to stop the affair until the matter could be sorted out by the courts. After the initial filing, the near-immediate presence of the American Jewish Committee and several Catholic diocesan authorities made it obvious that Lecoque and Tudor were mere figureheads for the national religious groups that had a stake in the case—an accusation made more than once by the defendants' attorneys, who, at one point, called the plaintiff a "dummy" being used to institute the suit on behalf of "the real moving party." To the defendants, this was a case of two aggressive religious upstarts challenging Protestant hegemony.[4]

The fact that neither plaintiff showed up during the early rounds of the trial buttressed the defendants' claim of absenteeism, but that charge turned out to be moot because the plaintiff's accusation was substantial. As reported in court records, the plaintiffs' chief argument was that the Gideon Bible was "a sectarian work of peculiar religious value and significance to the Protestant faith," and each complainant claimed that its distribution violated "the teachings, tenets and principles" of their religions. Therefore, its presence, with direct sanctioning from the state in the form of the school board, constituted not only a breach in the wall of separation between church and state, but an offense to religious minorities. In pluralist postwar America, this could not stand.[5]

Or could it? By early twenty-first-century standards, the Gideons' campaign sounds well beyond the realm of what is legal. Like now, however, such matters were under heavy debate during the midcentury years. Indeed, between 1947 and 1963, five major cases concerning the exact parameters of the wall of separation worked their way through the U.S. court system, each of them eventually ending up in front of the Supreme Court. The decisions of these five cases (known mostly, but not always, by the names of the plaintiffs: *Everton, McCollum, Zorach, Engel,* and *Schempp*) demonstrate the United States Supreme Court's definitive entrance into the debate about religion in the public sphere and its subsequent conclusion that there should exist a firm line between religious advocacy and U.S. public schools. Although religion was a significant component of good Americanism, the Court claimed that it was better for both religion and the state if the two realms remained relatively separate. The last of these cases (*Schempp*) was decided in 1963, meaning that when the Gideons approached the Rutherford Board of Education in late 1951, the question of whether proselytes could be allowed on public school grounds was still open. What would the courts decide? What would be their rationale? What would be that decision's legacy?[6]

★★★★★

The purpose of this essay is to use the relatively obscure case of the Gideons to show that postwar Catholics and Jews were instrumental in the creation of what Michael J. Sandel has labeled a "procedural republic." In 1996, Sandel, a professor of government at Harvard University, published *Democracy's*

Discontent: America in Search of a Public Philosophy. The book contrasted two public philosophies that had competed for hegemony in American life since the nation's founding. The first was civic republicanism, a public philosophy based on an awareness of one's membership within a larger society, and a commitment to consider the duties and responsibilities inherent to belonging to that society. According to Sandel, civic republicanism and its emphasis on duties and responsibilities dominated American life throughout the eighteenth and nineteenth centuries. In the middle of the twentieth century, however, civic republicanism was eclipsed by a second tradition, commonly known as rights-based liberalism. This second philosophy, which also has a long history, embraces individual rights and a neutral state whose main responsibility is to protect these rights.

Sandel is not the only author to cite the middle of the twentieth century as the time when rights-based liberalism rose to prominence in the United States (others include Alan Brinkley, William E. Nelson, and John D. Skrentny), but Sandel is the strongest in arguing that there is no civic commitment in this second public philosophy, only the disparate sense that what it means to be an American is purely ideological, boiling down to the passionate possession of a few individual rights. Being a communitarian interested in creating (he would say *re-creating*) a national sense of belonging, Sandel denigrates the good that has come from rights-based liberalism (since, as he says, liberalism "offered no way to reinvigorate civic life, no hope for reconstituting the political economy of citizenship"), and, indeed, in the Whig history that makes up the second half of Sandel's book, he ignores the very causes that led to liberal individualism's triumph, opting to emphasize the expansion of wage labor (which "conceded as unavoidable the broader condition of dependence") and the decline of community life (which led to "dislocation" as "men and women groped for bearings"), while failing to give credit to the numerous minorities who forthrightly advocated the neutrality needed for fair play and equal treatment. The civil rights movement, for example, makes no substantial appearance. Sensing that the "disuniting of America" reached its culmination with the rise of ethnic and especially racial particularism in the 1960s and 1970s, Sandel views the procedural republic as a dangerous concept, breeding divisiveness and discontent, creating a rights-demanding society that has prevented the United States from creating some much needed solidarity.[7]

Democracy's Discontent is one of many critiques of the "procedural republic" and the general stress on liberal individualism that has arisen since World War II. For instance, Christopher Shannon's *A World Made Safe for Differences: Cold*

War Intellectuals and the Politics of Identity (2001) argues that "the internaliza-tion of authority" at the individual level has incited the creation of numerous "alien norms" that have dismantled the possibility of a unified communal order. In other words, the primacy of liberal individualism during and after World War II has led to the self-deluding triumph of the notion that each man is his own master, which by definition prevents the creation of solidar-ity. Wilfred McClay gave this theme a name in his book *The Masterless: Self and Society in Modern America* (1994), which argued that U.S. intellectuals, always pondering the tension between lionizing the individual and yearning for national solidarity, have conflated the two ideals since the Second World War, thus justifying the triumph of liberal rights–based individualism as a community-making ideal. From a purely philosophical perspective, Alasdair MacIntyre and Charles Taylor have persistently cautioned against too strong a commitment to individualism, with MacIntyre going so far as to dismiss liberal individualism as a "social order" removed from the stabilizing forces of tradition, which thus denies the ability of liberalism to create unity based on a "common good."[8]

There are many merits to Sandel and others' calls for increased national solidarity. For instance, it is hard to deny that the expansion of the industrial state and the growth of the federal government have led to the decline of com-munity and the rise of the sense that people cannot control the events that surround them. And it is also true that a stronger commitment to the duties inherent to being a part of a national community could do much good toward making the United States a kinder, more egalitarian nation. In fact, there is recent evidence that many U.S. citizens would embrace such commitments, if only they had a systematic way to do so. When events prompted the federal government and other institutions to facilitate hard work in the name of the national community (such as after 9/11 and Hurricane Katrina), Americans overwhelmingly responded. The trouble has been with sustaining this sense of solidarity.

My intention here is to provide a bit of context to the history of the triumph of American liberal individualism. At root, I take for granted that rights-based liberalism has actually wrought much good, bringing about things like female suffrage and African American political equality, as well as restrictions on anti-Semitism, anti-Catholicism, and other forms of overt nativism. More specifically, however, this essay demonstrates that the procedural republic did not emerge out of the dislocation brought on by increasing industrialization, but that it was shaped by post–World War II civil rights liberals seeking to delineate and create a pluralistic nation. Foremost in this collection of civil rights liberals were everyday Catholics and Jews working to establish a society that enabled them to be true to their unique characteristics while still granting them the latitude to be labeled Americans.

That religious minorities were vital to the creation of the procedural republic is often forgotten; those derisive of liberal individualism usually cite the divisions of black power and the cultural politics that followed it as principal provocateurs. In the thinking of these critics, the identities that shaped "identity politics" were racial, sexual, or gendered. But it should not be too much of a surprise to find that religious minorities were some of the key groups in deciphering the acceptable boundaries of postwar pluralism. After all, the twentieth century's five signal court cases concerning the separation between church and state occurred immediately after the Second World War but just before the widespread embrace of the civil rights movement, in 1963. Catholics and Jews had different notions of what pluralism would look like, and this often placed them on competing sides of political debates in the 1940s and '50s. This essay, however, examines one case in which Catholics and Jews came together to deny a persistent notion of civic republicanism grounded in a singular founding quality, Protestantism. In the case of the Gideons, Catholics and Jews united to demonstrate that pluralism demands a neutral state and an ideological (not racial, religious, or ethnic) definition of what it means to be an American. This case also suggests that the procedural republic emerged as much from demands by American minority groups searching for equal rights and fair treatment as from anywhere else. And in postwar America, when liberal individualism began its rapid ascent, no groups were more important to this pursuit than religious ones.

*****

The immediate context of the Gideon case was the emerging cold war, when calls for increased religious education and inculcation were on the rise. After a century of struggle that began during the initial expansion of public education in the 1830s, by the 1920s and '30s, most public schools ceased to take direction from a culturally Protestant hegemonic presence, favoring instead rationalization and the scientific method as primary sources of knowledge. In the years between the First and Second World Wars, Bibles were not often distributed to students and prayers were rarely said in public schools. The teaching of evolution went on trial during the Scopes case of 1925, the overall result being that Christian fundamentalists largely retreated from public activism and that textbooks removed both God and Darwin from their content. Nevertheless, some atavistic laws still existed, and in the early 1940s, thirteen states required that school be opened with Bible reading and/or prayer, and thirty-seven states allowed some form of religious observance on public school grounds. But for the most part, U.S. public schools found the light through John Dewey rather than Jesus Christ.[9]

With the rise of the cold war, many in the United States sought to increase the religious content of public education. "Today," said Will Herberg after describing the growth of "progressive" education in public schools, "the climate of opinion is again changing . . . There is a mounting demand that religion be given some sort of place in the program of public education. This sentiment is nation-wide." Polls bear out the assessment. According to a Gallup poll from the early 1960s, 79 percent of people in the United States approved of having religious observances in school. Reciting the Twenty-third Psalm or the Lord's Prayer became relatively commonplace. Mangers began appearing on school lawns. Proposals advocating placing plaques bearing the Ten Commandments on public school campuses rose throughout the decade. For many, reasserting the United States' Christian foundation was the best antidote to communism.[10]

How much religion was actually being taught in U.S. public schools during the postwar period? Quite a bit, in fact. In 1949, the National Education Association (NEA) sent a questionnaire to more than 5,000 superintendents of schools in all regions of the country, asking just this question. More than 2,600 responses came back, revealing that nearly half the school systems in America's large cities (having more than 100,000 residents) had a formal program of religious education, usually taught by a religious leader from one or more faith community. Smaller cities had fewer programs, although one can surmise from circumstantial evidence that schools in smaller communities provided a more implicit form of religious education. Of the more than 700 school systems with formal programs in religious instruction, 15 percent held classes on school grounds during regular school hours despite this being prohibited by federal law. Around 5 percent allowed public school buildings to be used after school. Nearly 500 school districts had created some sort of released-time arrangement, whereby students were free to leave school during school hours to obtain religious training. A remaining 4 percent of school systems occasionally released pupils for an entire day, presumably so they could obtain religious training outside school. The final 10 percent of districts that admitted to having a formal plan of religious education could not be classified under any of these categories. The bottom line was that in 1949 there was a lot of religion being taught in America's schools. In addition, the numbers presented by the NEA survey are probably low because the survey occurred within a year of the Supreme Court's momentous *McCollum v. Board of Education* decision, which outlawed religious education on school grounds during regular hours. (The *McCollum* decision was specifically mentioned by more than 300 superintendents, each of whom said they had dropped formal religious programs from their schools in the twelve months between *McCollum* and the survey.)[11]

In addition to this large amount of religious instruction and inculcation (it is difficult to tell the difference between the two based on the NEA's questionnaire), many Americans felt the need to increase the amount of religion in public schools. But the question was, of course, if, as Supreme Court Justice William O. Douglas said in 1952, "we are a religious people whose institutions presuppose a Supreme Being," how could that idea be institutionalized without the public sanctioning of any particular faith? As a letter from the general assembly of the National Council of Churches of Christ in the U.S.A. put it, "in some constitutional way, provision should be made for the inculcation of the principles of religion, whether within or outside the precincts of the school, but always within the regular schedule of a pupil's working day." How to do this legally was the paramount question.[12]

Protestants most often sought a bland form of Protestantism, such as the Lord's Prayer or the Twenty-third Psalm, which, they hoped, was ecumenical enough not to stir debate. Many times this hope was misplaced, as a Catholic, Jew, or secularist often opposed it. In early 1947, for example, New York City councilman Hugh Quinn introduced a resolution to the New York City Council permitting the reading of the Lord's Prayer at general assemblies in the New York City Public School District. The proposal provoked strong debate, and more than a hundred attendees showed up at the public hearing. Those who were for allowing the Lord's Prayer into public schools suggested that the action would "pave the way to create a better religious atmosphere in public schools and build up the morale of the city's youth." Those against it said the resolution would inject a dose of sectarianism into the school system, the Lord's Prayer being, in their opinion, a Christian prayer. Many clergymen opposed the resolution, as did the ACLU, the Congress of Industrial Organizations (CIO), and several Jewish groups, including the powerful New York Board of Rabbis. Sectarian matters had made the issue divisive. The city council deferred action on the motion, hoping it would go away.[13]

It didn't. In November 1951, the New York State Board of Regents recommended that each school day open with a prayer. Leery of the sectarian issues that would undoubtedly arise, perhaps not more than 300 of the 3,000 school districts in the state adopted the regents' suggestion. The New York City School Board recognized at once the explosive character of the issue, and attempted to craft a compromise in January 1953 whereby New York City schools would sing the fourth stanza of "America," the patriotic hymn, in lieu of any prayer more commonly associated with a particular creed. The compromise placated Protestants, and the Catholic weekly *America* echoed general Catholic approval. Jews, however, were less persuaded, and the New York Board of Rabbis once again objected, this time arguing that the fourth stanza, taken alone, constituted a Protestant prayer. Sectarian divisions again killed the proposal. (The fourth stanza reads: "Our fathers' God to thee/Author of Liberty/To Thee we sing./Long may our land be bright/With Freedom's holy light/protect us by thy might/Great God, our King.")[14]

Indeed, sectarianism was a contentious issue throughout postwar America, and schools were often the battlegrounds. The challenges of Catholics and Jews forced Protestants to search, often in vain, for a plausible religious middle ground. The frustrated *Time* magnate Henry R. Luce, son of Protestant missionaries, suggested to the Church Federation of Greater Chicago, "It is certainly time that Protestants, if they don't do anything else, should unite on a program to bring the knowledge of God to our boys and girls at school." But he offered no solution beyond this plea. At the same time, bills authorizing Bible reading were defeated after hotly contested debates in California in January 1953 and in Illinois in June 1953. Sectarianism was a crucial battleground of postwar pluralism. In struggling to determine how American society could create a nation respectful of minorities while still being reverent toward its dominant character, the courts were left to debate and decide the correct height of the wall of separation between church and state.

This sectarianism, and the subsequent fight for pluralism by Catholic and Jewish minorities, is the necessary context of all of the major United States Supreme Court cases of the postwar years. As *Life* put it in 1955, the "wall of separation" was in reality "an uneasy four-way truce among Catholics, Protestants, Jews and secularists." Will Herberg commented on this in his 1952 essay on "The Sectarian Conflict Over Church and State." In the early 1950s, the wall of separation was not entirely about keeping politics and religion apart for the sanctity of both (as the rhetoric of the debate had been) or about maintaining Protestant hegemony (as the reality of the debate had been), but about making pluralism.[15]

This represented a dramatic and largely unrecognized shift in the rhetoric and justification of the separation of church and state. As historian Philip Hamburger has shown, despite the fact that the First Amendment often comes up in debates about church and state, the principle of separation has very little constitutional foundation and, furthermore, arguments that have suggested that the principle of separation was developed in order to prevent the intrusion of the state into church matters simply masks an uglier history. Rather, the doctrine of separation emerged shortly after the nation's founding as a result of growing fears of churches, especially the Catholic Church. The doctrine first clearly entered public debate in 1800 as a way for Jeffersonian Republicans to criticize and intimidate Federalist clergymen (Jefferson's famous coining of the phrase "wall of separation between Church and State" came in 1802, not during the period when the founders drafted the Constitution). Then, in the middle of the nineteenth century, nativists and, more broadly, American Protestants adopted the principle of separation as a way to keep newly arrived Irish Catholics from obtaining the same social and political rights that Americans with a longer North American pedigree possessed. Protestants argued that a unified and powerful Catholic bloc might attempt to overturn republican government in favor of one controlled by the pope. Thus, to prevent Catholics from capturing free government, Protestants felt they had to deny Catholics equal civil and political rights.

The anti-Catholic tenor of separation discourse lasted until the 1950s, when a secular argument for separation emerged (although the anti-Catholic strain continued to exist at least until after John F. Kennedy's election to the presidency in 1960). This secular defense of separation, which Hamburger does not describe, emerged primarily as a defense of religious pluralism. In midcentury America, Catholics and Jews were clamoring to find a peaceable solution to the problem of pluralism, where minorities with diverse conceptions of the good sought first-class status and social and cultural authority without having to give up all that made them unique. One method they embraced—especially Jews but also, upon occasion, Catholics too—was the principle of separation.[16]

This, of course, led to a conflict between the cold war desire to add religion to the public sphere and the quest to create a nation that could maintain ideological unity while honoring religious diversity. The contentious cases made headlines. Most often, however, short religious devotionals were quietly added to the daily routine of public school children, leaving Catholics and Jews to wonder which cases were worth fighting. Christmas and Easter were celebrated lavishly. The holiday carols chosen for presentation were usually religious. Bibles began to appear more regularly on public school grounds. Despite occasional Catholic approval, the Protestant cast of this type of education was not missed by many. In July 1995, Howard Squadron, whose parents were part of the turn-of-the-century Jewish Diaspora, described at a House of Representatives hearing what it was like growing up in the 1950s:

> Let me recall to you what the public schools I attended were like. They had an overtly Protestant cast. Prayers and bible passages were recited daily. Prayer is not a generic form of expression and bible passages (and translations) were not, are not, and should not be, theologically neutral. The public school religion I encountered had in every case specific theological roots and forms. The prayers said in the public school I attended were distinctly Protestant in content.

Squadron also commented on what he saw as the cultural content of this religiosity. As he saw it:

> The use of Protestant religion was a part of a deliberate effort by the public schools to suggest to the American children of Jewish immigrants that these Protestant rituals represented true Americanism, that the rituals and rhythms of our parents' houses were alien and foreign, worse, to children who desperately wished to be accepted, even "un-American." This use of religion as a means of acculturating aliens caused many painful gaps between parent and child.

A leading historian of religion and education in the United States concluded that Squadron "captured more clearly than most the ways in which many schools operated in the United States."[17]

Catholics and Jews were torn by the increasing religiosity demanded in cold war America. Both groups were fighting for religious pluralism, but they were doing so from different perspectives. In general, Catholics felt religion was a vital component of a child's development, and the leading Catholic organizations wanted sanctioned religion in public schools. However, they did not want that religion to have a Protestant cast. In 1952, the Catholic Bishops of America adopted a resolution warning that the nation faced a grave danger from the "irreligious decay" of its most important institutions, pointedly criticizing public schools for ignoring the importance of religion in the lives of children. But they also worried about the reemphasis of Protestantism in the public schools—the very issue that prompted the formation of Catholic parochial schools in the first place, during the nineteenth century. These fears led to a reaffirmation of parochial schools. Reporting that Catholic schools were "growing at a rapid rate," a front-page report in the *New York Times* claimed in 1952 that Catholic schools had grown by 35 percent between 1942 and 1952, making the total enrollment 4 million, and leading the National Catholic Welfare Conference to organize a quarter-billion-dollar expansion of the Catholic school system. Furthermore, "the increase is expected to continue," wrote the *Times.* Reflecting their rising socioeconomic status, postwar Catholics also began developing a network of private academies in which elite Catholics could enroll their children. Of course, the growth of parochial education led to increased claims of Catholic separatism, so their pluralistic position came at a cost.[18]

Jews were also divided. For the most part, they were suspicious about any religion in the public schools, although the leading Jewish organizations were split over how far Jews should go to fight its presence. The American Jewish Committee and the Anti-Defamation League of B'nai B'rith—two of the more moderate Jewish civic organizations—generally sought a reconciliation of Jewish observances with Christian ones and were less aggressive about the addition of ecumenical prayers in the school day. These organizations, for instance, advocated the celebration of Hanukkah services alongside Christmas ones in public schools. In 1946, they helped Cleveland become a pioneer in crafting joint Hanukkah-Christmas celebrations. A similar situation was crafted at the Dundee Elementary School in Omaha, Nebraska, a public school active in the intergroup relations movement. Historian Edward S. Shapiro has discussed the "elevation of the erstwhile minor holiday of Hanukkah into one of the most widely observed celebrations on the Jewish calendar" during these years, describing the ironic process by which a nationalistic Jewish holiday was transformed into an ecumenical celebration of religious pluralism. Hanukkah's main appeal, concludes Shapiro, is that it comes in December, so Hanukkah's timing coincided with Christmas. Plus, because it focused on children receiving gifts, Hanukkah accorded with the material nature of Christmas celebrations. Hanukkah was also family oriented, did not place barriers between Christians and Jews, and did not require special accommodations that marked Jews as culturally different from their Christian peers. Hanukkah's transformation in these years represented part of what Shapiro has called "the Protestantization of American Judaism."[19]

The American Jewish Congress, on the other hand, was more adamantly against any incursion of religion in the public sphere and, during the midcentury years, it was the most vocal Jewish organization in America. "Separation of Church and State is indispensable if we are to immunize our schools from sectarian divisiveness and strife," the Jewish Congress wrote in a forcefully worded pamphlet. "The principal of separation of Church and State, particularly in the field of public education, is not something abstract and theoretical; it is a necessary and practical guardian and protector of the welfare of American children, and particularly children adhering to minority faiths." Thus, the fight for a high wall of separation between church and state had everything to do with the rights of minorities. "Experience has shown," the pamphlet continued, "that whenever religion intrudes into the public school, sooner or later Jewish children will be hurt."[20]

When the Catholic and Jewish ideals of pluralism clashed, fireworks erupted. Regarding the question of how best to celebrate religious holidays in public schools, one (Catholic) diocesan newspaper declared, "We believe that the time has come for Christians in the public school system and everywhere else to declare in outright fashion that *the United States by culture, tradition, and full right is a Christian country* and must not be allowed to change. For that reason, Christmas in schools must be kept a distinctly Christian feast with a Christian purpose." The paper added: "Non-Christian religious groups [read: Jews], prompted by the presence of many of their children in public schools, are seeking to dilute or to eliminate Christ from Christmas. They are aided and abetted by the secularizing tendency in American life. If both pressures are not resisted, Christmas will lose its whole and wholly Christian meaning." This quotation supports the claim of recent scholarship that one way Catholics proved their credentials as good Americans was by trumpeting the anticommunist, Christian core of the meaning of America. If America was noncommunist and Christian, then Catholics were undoubtedly American.[21]

Similarly contentious debates occurred in New Hyde Park, New York, and Newark, New Jersey, concerning the posting of a plaque of the Ten Commandments. In Ossining, New York, tensions erupted over the placement of a manger at one public school. Examples of other conflicts are numerous. Both Catholics and Jews were fighting for pluralism; they were just using different, self-interested tactics to do so. Most Jews said that successful pluralism depended on a religiously neutral state; being a small minority, this made sense. Catholics, meanwhile, were more comfortable with a form of pluralism that was respectful and even supportive of various groups' religious expressions, even if those expressions occasionally made them look like separatists. This likewise made sense, considering first, that they, like the Protestant majority, were Christians, and second, that because roughly 25 percent of all U.S. citizens considered themselves Catholic, there seemed little chance that Catholics could be easily homogenized.[22] However, their pluralism was often narrower than that of the Jews, and, unlike even the more accommodationist Jews who favored multiple religious celebrations, many midcentury Catholics probably would not have supported celebrating Jewish holidays in schools. They were mostly interested in asserting the Christian foundations of the United States, which would, of course, make them full-fledged members. These differences led Catholics and Jews to oppose one another on numerous issues regarding public schools, including federal funding debates, released-time programs, and the observance of religious holidays. Understanding their struggle for pluralism as a root cause of their contentiousness adds some much-needed context to the public school battles of this era, which have usually been interpreted as a simple quest to keep the state free from religion, and religion free from the state. The battles were instead a struggle about the exact dynamic of pluralism that would create civic peace in a multicultural America.

★★★★★

In this atmosphere, the Gideons were obviously something of nuisance. With the heightened awareness of America's religious pluralism, any religious organization that aggressively sought converts was bound to become contentious. And, in light of the child-focused nature of the postwar suburbs, any attempt to proselytize to children was doubly suspect. The Gideons offended on both accounts. Their unsubtle mission declared an intent to "win men and women for the Lord Jesus Christ" by distributing a Gideon Bible to every person in the nation—a calling they took seriously. And in the immediate aftermath of the Second World War, the Gideons embarked on an ambitious "national campaign . . . to furnish the Word of God free to young people." The idea was to present their bound gift to students at every high school and every middle school in the country.[23]

They were, of course, fought. By 1952, the Gideons were denied access to schools in Rutland, Vermont; Akron, Ohio; York, Pennsylvania; and Oakland, California. Protestant proselytes had no place in America's public schools, these school boards declared, often at the collective urging of Catholic and Jewish parents joining forces to keep the Protestant hegemony from reasserting itself. But the Gideons continued to pursue their mission, and their implacability inevitably landed them in court. Catholic and Jewish litigants came together to fight the Gideons' hardheaded intrusion and the first test case emerged from Rutherford, New Jersey. *Ralph Lecoque and Bernard Tudor v. Board of Education and the Gideons International* was the case, and the key question was whether or not honoring pluralism meant allowing religious advocacy into America's public schools at all. The case worked its way to the United States Supreme Court and has stood as the final word on proselytizing on public school grounds since the Court handed down the decision in 1952.[24]

When the Catholic and Jewish parents sued the Rutherford Board of Education for accepting the Gideons' proposal, the state court upheld the injunction. There was much to discuss before the Gideons could be allowed to proceed. In an order dated February 29, 1952, the Gideons were formally restrained from distributing their Bibles until the case was thrashed out in court. The Gideons had a right to the nation's sidewalks, its parks, and even its hospitals and its military, but as to the public schools, the answer was less clear.[25]

In early 1953, the case finally went to court. The Gideons signed on as codefendants with the Rutherford Board of Education, and, by that time, the child of Ralph Lecoque had transferred to a parochial school. Lecoque's departure affirmed the plaintiffs' argument that reinforcing Protestantism was necessarily divisive, but it was also a blow to the plaintiffs, who had sought to frame the case as two respectful minorities fighting for dignity and respect. Efforts to replace Lecoque with another Catholic parent (a Mrs. Walter Natyniak) were rejected as coming too late. The case, therefore, became simply *Tudor v. Board of Education of Rutherford and the Gideons International.*[26]

In March 1953, New Jersey trial judge J. Wallis Leyden heard testimony. Suggesting the depth of companionship that Catholics and Jews felt regarding the case, the American Jewish Congress and the diocesan authority of the Roman Catholic Church joined forces to prosecute on behalf of Bernard Tudor. They retained Leo Pfeffer to prosecute the case, which was an unsurprising choice considering Pfeffer's long-standing ties to the American Jewish Congress, but it was a bold move nonetheless. Pfeffer was a polemical author and attorney who, in the late 1940s and early 1950s, had become a well-known figure in defending a high wall of separation between church and state. Indeed, Pfeffer sometimes came off as an unbending defender of an implacable wall of separation, but as the author of several leading books on the subject, there was little doubt about his expertise. Pfeffer's presence meant the case was sure to become an important testing ground for the extent to which advocated Protestantism could be brought anywhere near public school classrooms.[27]

The testimony Pfeffer brought forward consisted of a host of religious experts who described the exact points of conflict that Catholics and Jews had with the Gideon Bible. For Jews, the argument was simple. "[The New Testament] presupposes the concept of Jesus of Nazareth as a divinity, a concept which we do not accept," testified Rabbi Joachim Prinz. Several other rabbis testified similarly. Meanwhile, although not of strict legal importance because the Catholic plaintiff had been removed from the case, the prosecutors nevertheless quoted the canon law of the Roman Catholic Church, which holds that "editions of the original text of the sacred scriptures published by non-Catholics are forbidden *ipso jure*." According to canon law of the Catholic Church, reading an alternative form of the Bible is proscribed as a sin.[28]

All this was irrelevant if Pfeffer could not paint the board of education's decision as an "effort to uphold Protestant Christianity through the public school system." If the distribution of Bibles was done carefully enough so as not to antagonize a Catholic or a Jew, what did it matter if the minorities found the Gideon Bible offensive? Completely ignoring the numerous stipulations the board had drafted regarding distribution of the Bibles, Pfeffer said the board's decision to allow the Gideons onto campus was in "direct contradiction" to "democratic education," which, he said, was an educational system based on the notion that, in the words of one witness, "the school people must treat each group with full respect for personality, and where they have differences, [school officials] must respect those differences." This type of "democratic education" was being lionized in the aftermath of World War II as the training ground for young, ideologically sound Americans. Pfeffer conveniently skipped over the fact that many in the United States considered publicly proclaiming faith in God an ideologically sound component of good Americanism too. He nevertheless asserted that the sanctioning of Protestantism was nothing but divisive, and that the board's actions had created an "unconstitutional preference . . . to the Protestant denomination," which was an obvious "infringement of the religious liberty of Catholic and Jewish public school children." Giving state sanction to the Gideons was a dangerous throwback to the early nineteenth-century days of Protestant hegemony, said Pfeffer, and much had changed since then.[29]

The brief submitted upon appeal said as much, and it reads like a "greatest hits" of religious intolerance in the United States. Citing Charles Beard, Ray Billington, and Gustuvus Myers as prominent historians of American bigotry, Pfeffer argued that "in the past, Catholic children in the public schools have been subjected to severe persecution for adhering to this dogma of the Church and refusing to commit sin by participating in the reading of the King James Bible." He referred to an instance when more than one hundred Catholic children were expelled from Boston public schools for refusing to read the King James Bible. He cited another case where a priest's challenge to a legislative mandate requiring Bible reading led the "infuriated Protestant community" to tar and feather the priest and run him out of town. Pfeffer paralleled the Rutherford Board of Education's decision regarding the Gideons to actions during the period of the "anti-Catholic nativism and 'know-nothingness' which disgraced American history in the nineteenth century."[30]

In the case, Pfeffer was at a tactical advantage because the school board had in fact approved access only to the Gideons. It did not matter that no other group had applied. The board's stipulation, as Pfeffer hastened to point out, "is clearly and expressly limited to the Gideons and authorizes only the distribution of their Bible to the public school children." He showed that even the defendant's own witnesses had conceded this point when the superintendent of schools admitted that the "resolution was not authority for me to distribute the Douay Version of the Bible."[31]

Pfeffer concluded his argument by bringing forward several child psychologists who painted a vivid picture of the millions of "minority" children who might have adverse psychological effects because the Gideons had come to their campus to proselytize, sanctioned, as they were, by the school, and therefore, by the state. These "minority" children would be identified as different and would encounter pressures to conform to the majority. Speaking specifically of Jewish children, the prominent New York University psychologist Isador Chein said that "when the New Testament is given to [children] by sources which they consider to be respectable, and . . . from whom they are expected to learn, I think that there can be little question but that a great many Jewish children will be thrown into a state of conflict, perplexity, confusion, and to some extent guilty feeling." Another expert suggested that the school board decision would "leave the left handed implication that the school thought this was preferential in terms of what is the divine word, and that backing of the State would inevitably be interpreted as being behind it." How demoralizing, concluded Pfeffer. What was a child to do when the two chief authorities in his or her life—parent and teacher—conflicted, all because the Rutherford School Board had allowed the Gideons to distribute Bibles on public school grounds![32]

It is worth noting Pfeffer's use of the term *minority* here, obviously referring to Catholic and Jewish schoolchildren. His ultimate claim was that Catholics and Jews were doing their part to accommodate to the ideological demands of mainstream society. They were not demanding separate schools or unique divisions within the schools; they simply wanted the state to remain religiously neutral. Shouldn't mainstream society do its part to accommodate their access to the mainstream? How many more children would be driven to attend parochial schools because of divisive Protestant biases? Wasn't the United States beyond the bigotry and favoritism of yesteryear?

The defense team thought these arguments were inflated—which they were. But the defense could not mount much of a defense. They perpetually cited the case of *Doremus v. Hawthorne,* a case in which the New Jersey Supreme Court upheld the reading of the Lord's Prayer in public schools. *Doremus* was an important precedent, the defense argued, because it demonstrated the Supreme Court's willingness to allow the New Testament onto campus. Pfeffer quickly dispatched the claim on two grounds: first, it was clear that the New Testament consists of much more than simply the Lord's Prayer; and second, *Doremus* did not deal with diversity, which, he said, was the most important issue in the *Tudor* case. "That was a suit brought by some atheists, some individual trouble makers, and so on," Pfeffer said. In the Gideon case, sectarianism was "the basic issue," and, he implied, when good religious Americans disagreed, diversity had to be honored. Mainstream society was what had to bend.[33]

But the central argument put forward by the defense was that the New Testament was not sectarian but a universal book of the Western world, especially important in understanding the creation of American democracy. Claiming that their responsibility was to the parent, not to any religious denomination, the school superintendent, Dr. Guy L. Hilleboe, claimed that "when we have an opportunity to give those parents that kind of literature which is basic in the whole development of our democracy, from its beginnings—even before that; from the founding, from Plymouth Rock to the present time . . . I feel that there is nothing contrary, either morally or legally, in the provision of such materials." And "if any group presents to the schools material which will aid the child to better understand, not only himself, but those around him . . . our obligation is to the parent."[34]

Showing some quick thinking, Pfeffer countered this claim by pointing out that *Das Kapital* was also part of the Western tradition. Would Hilleboe distribute it too? Hilleboe stumbled in his answer. Pfeffer then made his sentiment plain, asking that, since Hilleboe had lent "the facilities of the public school to The Gideon International," would he "not do the same for the Communist International?" Hilleboe meekly said no. This allowed Pfeffer to make the point that the school did in fact have discretion as to which groups would be allowed on campus, and, in the case of the Gideons, it had adjudicated favorably. Allowing just Protestants access could not, according to Pfeffer, be approved. Catholics and Jews, as minorities on the frontline of the diversity debate, deserved protection. At risk, he added, were America's children.[35]

By the end of formal argument, Judge Leyden was clearly sympathetic to Pfeffer's case. Unfortunately for Pfeffer, Leyden also found it beside the point. On March 14, 1953, Leyden ruled that the action of the Rutherford School Board might be "bad policy," but it was constitutional. "I can see no illegal or unconstitutional interference by what is proposed by the Board of Education, with the religious liberty or freedom of the plaintiff or his child, nor can I see any particular preference granted to the Protestant faith."[36] The board was right to allow the Gideons onto school property, said Leyden, because Catholics and Jews and any other religious minority had a right to do so as well. If Americans really were "a religious people whose institutions presuppose[d] a Supreme Being," keeping God off of school grounds did not make much sense. To Leyden, it was the various groups who brought Him there that deserved protection.

As would be pointed out on appeal, Leyden's decision may well have been on solid constitutional grounds, but it was somewhat ignorant of reality. Although the picture Pfeffer painted was overdrawn—with vulnerable students incurring irreparable damage because of their potential but unlikely exposure to a member of the Gideon Society walking across campus after school—Protestants did have the overwhelming numerical advantage in most American school districts (and on most American school boards). Therefore, sanctioning distribution of the Gideons' Bible did seem to be playing favorites. More telling, however, was the fact that the decision arrived at roughly the same time as numerous Protestant complaints about Catholic intrusion onto public school grounds—a claim that, more than anything else, stirred the pot of anti-Catholic animosity in postwar America. In Wisconsin, for example, fourteen school districts had battled over what to do with several public schools that sat in predominantly Catholic neighborhoods. The state chose to cut aid to the schools on the grounds that teachers were given a religious test before they could teach there, that Catholic instruction was included in the curriculum, and that the schools were not operated beyond the eighth grade. Although this is an extreme comparison, was there a difference if the majority population was Catholic or Protestant? Could Protestants have advocates on campus while Catholics could not?[37]

A similar case emerged from New Mexico in 1951. In *Zellers v. Huff*, Lydia C. Zellers sued the state of New Mexico for allowing several of the state's public schools to become effectively parochial schools. Importantly, she was joined by an upstart group called Protestants and Other Americans United for the Separation of Church and State (POAU), which funded and directed Zellers's legal campaign. Upon uncovering that as many as 25 of the public schools in Santa Fe were simultaneously listed as public schools *and* parochial schools, that all of the teachers at these schools were nuns of the same order, that they all taught while wearing traditional habits and insignia, that the nuns were chosen by their religious superiors rather than a secular school board, and that students attended Mass several mornings each week. The court enjoined the 139 nuns from teaching, denied the schools access to public funds, and shut down public schools that sat on church property. The Protestant plaintiffs carried the day. Again, although the case was extreme, Leyden's decision did not fit well with these realities. Why hadn't the court protected the rights of Catholics to bring their religion onto campus? Where was the line that demarcated the differences between these cases of proselytes?[38]

Meanwhile, the Gideon case was creating strange bedfellows—a fact that testified to the widespread appeal of the neutral state in a multicultural America. For example, the Catholic organizations protesting Leyden's decision were joined by two famously aggressive anti-Catholics, Paul Blanshard and POAU. Blanshard was an intellectual and attorney who, in 1949, released a collection of essays called *American Freedom and Catholic Power*, a book that probed the question of how Catholics, under ecclesiastical control, could possess the capacity for the kind of free thinking required in a democracy. His main argument was that lay Catholics could accomplish this only by ignoring the dictates of their church. The book became a runaway best seller, and it defined the terms of American anti-Catholicism for the next decade. Of course, not everyone was happy with the book. The Jesuit theologian John Courtney Murray, S. J., American Catholicism's ablest defender, described Blanshard as the figurehead of the "New Nativism." Will Herberg referred to the increasing anti-Catholicism in postwar America simply as "Blanshardism." But the book still won important converts: John Dewey, for example, led the liberal embrace of Blanshard's ideas by praising the book's "exemplary scholarship, good judgment, and tact."[39]

The second anti-Catholic presence to side with the Catholics in the Gideon case was a group of politicized Protestant leaders who strongly advocated the separation of church and state. Founded in 1949, Protestants and Other Americans United for the Separation of Church and State emerged out of fears that U.S. Catholic institutions were becoming strong enough to challenge the moral authority of the Protestant mainstream, and, as Philip Hamburger has shown, the principle of separation has long been a weapon used to keep upstart religious minorities in check by denying them the capacity to make national claims.[40] In short, POAU sought to counter Catholic unity by creating a unified Protestant opponent and reasserting its power. In an editorial in the *Christian Century*, editor Charles Clayton Morrison, a charter member of POAU, wrote, "Catholicism, with its parochial schools in which not only knowledge about their religion is imparted, but religious devotion is inculcated, is in a position to take advantage of the vacuum in the general culture, and it is acting accordingly. Until Protestantism awakens to the fact that its position is vulnerable to Catholicism on the one hand, and to secularism on the other, its hope of winning America is a blind illusion." "That men do not move over graciously," Thomas F. O'Dea warned elsewhere, "is one of the few undeniable generalizations from history," and thus emerged POAU.[41] That Paul Blanshard and POAU received such widespread support signified the importance of religion in the debates about American pluralism in the 1950s. That they could find common cause with American Catholics in this period indicates the power of the argument for separation.

★★★★★

In the context of the wide-open debates about church and state in the 1940s and '50s, one cannot help but wonder if Leyden wanted his decision appealed. There was at that point considerable wiggle room in the Supreme Court's interpretation of the amount and manner of religious education in public schools, but allowing the Gideons onto public school grounds was something different. And Leyden had to have known that these religious minorities would fight what they saw as a sectarian attempt to insert Protestantism into public education. Perhaps Leyden's decision was deliberately meant to be provocative? Considering, however, that few judges like to have their decisions overturned, it is likely that Leyden's decision was one of conscience.

As everyone expected, the American Jewish Congress and its plaintiff, Bernard Tudor, immediately appealed Leyden's decision. The Gideons agreed to continue the injunction until the matter was finally settled. By now, the case had become something of a testing ground for the Gideons, who were interested in having it play out in the courts so they could know their exact boundaries.[42]

Play out it did. On its own initiative, on October 2, 1953, the New Jersey Supreme Court withdrew the case from the Appellate Division of the Superior Court and placed it on its own calendar, to be argued just three days later. There was no time for the attorneys to do anything but recapitulate the original arguments, meaning that the arguments heard by the New Jersey Supreme Court were the same ones weighed by Leyden. *Amici curiae* from the Synagogue Council of America and the (Jewish) National Community Relations Advisory Council were rushed in, and the New Jersey Supreme Court came down with its decision in early December.[43]

In the end, the New Jersey Supreme Court was considerably more sympathetic to Pfeffer's arguments than Leyden had been. Ruling unanimously, the Supreme Court claimed the board of education had indeed shown preference to one religion over another. By inviting the Gideons on school grounds, "the board of education has placed its stamp of approval upon" Protestant proselytes. The court sympathetically quoted one of the professional witnesses in the case, Dr. William Heard Kilpatrick, who said that non-Protestant students were "not quite as free as the statement on that slip says; in other words, that he will be something of an outcast and a pariah if he does not go along with this procedure." Chief Justice Arthur T. Vanderbilt, who wrote the opinion, powerfully concluded: "Such favoritism cannot be tolerated and must be disapproved as a clear violation of the Bill of Rights." Vanderbilt openly acknowledged that Leyden's decision "ignores the realities of life," and, concluding that the Gideon Bible was undoubtedly a Protestant document, Vanderbilt declared that any attempt to employ "the public school system as a medium of distribution" of the Bibles was ignoring the pluralism that had come to inhabit the meaning of separation of church and state in the early 1950s.[44]

Vanderbilt recognized that the key question in the case was how best to honor pluralism. "The full force of the violation," Vanderbilt wrote, "is revealed when we perceive what might happen if a single school board were besieged by three separate applications for the distribution of Bibles—one from Protestants as here, another from Catholics for the distribution of the Douay Bible, and a third from Jews for the same privilege for their Bible." The question was left unanswered, leaving readers to infer that the obvious reaction would have been against any attempt to have children hear from Jewish or Catholic proselytes. The use of the word "besieged," however, also implies that if the doors of distribution were open, who knows how many sects would come to push their view? And what about communists and atheists, as Pfeffer had suggested? This, presumably, would be worse. The court's point was that schools should not become battlegrounds for ideological groups, and the allowance of the distribution of Bibles, even by the majority, opened the door to controversy. In a pluralistic nation, the state would have to remain neutral.[45]

In the end, the court believed that Pfeffer was on the right track when he pointed out that the United States was finally overcoming its history of religious bigotry. Vanderbilt devoted more than two-thirds of the decision to recapping religious bigotry from AD 313 (when Constantine and Licinius proclaimed the Edict of Milan) to modern America. Vanderbilt's claim was that mid-twentieth-century Americans had finally begun to achieve the goal of tolerance in the name of pluralism. "It took us over 14 centuries and an incalculable amount of persecution to gain the religious tolerance and freedom expounded in 313 A.D. by the rulers of the Roman world," said Vanderbilt, adding that to allow the Gideons to distribute their Bibles on public school grounds "would be to cast aside all the progress made in the United States . . . in the field of religious toleration and freedom. We would be renewing the ancient struggles among the various religious faiths to the detriment of all. This we must decline to do."[46]

The decision was a strong one, well argued, and broad in scope. In 1954, the Gideons appealed the decision to the United States Supreme Court, but, in October of that year, the court chose not to hear the case (*certiorari denied*) which, by law, upheld the New Jersey decision. In the case of religious advocacy in America's public schools, Jews and Catholics could not be sidelined in favor of Protestants, even if that meant limiting the access anyone had to public schools. If diversity could not be adequately recognized, access would have to suffer. The separation between church and state had to be a solid one because to do otherwise would be to allow majority rule, and in the new, more tolerant United States, this was not acceptable.

The Gideon case, in turn, served as an ideological predecessor to the more famous cases that arose in the late 1950s and early 1960s, when the courts made the wall of separation between church and state increasingly high—all in the name of pluralism (the *Tudor* case, for example, was repeatedly cited in the United States Supreme Court's decision in *Schempp*, which outlawed school-sponsored Bible reading). In answering the question of who would have to bend to honor diversity, more and more throughout the 1950s the courts were rejecting the assimilationist ideal, saying mainstream society would have to bend to accommodate its minorities.[47]

On the surface, then, the issue the Gideons seemed to provoke was about shaving the line between church and state just a tiny bit more. What the case underscores, however, is that each of the midcentury challenges to putting religion in the public schools had deep sectarian roots. "One particularly reassuring aspect of the case," wrote the American Jewish Congress after the decision was handed down, "was the cooperation of the local diocesan authorities of the Roman Catholic Church throughout the litigation." Despite the different means by which Catholics and Jews struggled to make pluralism, they came together to fight any reassertion of Protestant hegemony. The American Jewish Congress added: "We believe that this decision will stand as a landmark in the history of religious liberty in this country," and it reprinted the decision in its entirety as an easily distributed pamphlet.[48]

The Gideon case reminds us that sectarian issues were the fundamental context of the numerous United States Supreme Court cases that rose to prominence in the postwar years. It also reminds us that, during the years between the Second World War and the rise of the civil rights movement in the early 1960s, religious divisions—especially those between Protestants, Catholics, and Jews—were the acceptable grounds for hashing out the limits of diversity and for the affirmation that a neutral state that protects the rights of minorities is the most acceptable form of government in a multicultural nation—even if the result is what its opponents have labeled as a heartless "procedural republic." In light of the new kinds of religious pluralism that have emerged since the alteration of America's immigration laws in 1965, the difficulties of accommodation rather than neutrality seem only more relevant.[49] Furthermore, because most of the recent debates about pluralism have focused on—and become entangled with—racial, sexual, or gendered divisions, the "identity" of today's "identity politics" is usually viewed as racial, and sometimes gendered and sometimes sexual. It is, however, often forgotten that the calls for individual dignity that ground identity politics were hashed out earlier, and when this was done in the middle of the twentieth century, no groups were more important to the process than religious ones. This is worth remembering today more than ever, especially as the battle lines of the current culture war reignite debates about the proper contours of religious pluralism, both in the United States and abroad.

Notes

1. The letter is Exhibit P-1 in the "Appendix to Appellant's Brief," *Ralph Lecoque and Bernard Tudor v. Board of Education of the Borough of Rutherford and the Gideons International*, 14 N.J. 31, 100 A.2d 857 (1953), found in State of New Jersey, *Supreme Court of New Jersey*, vol. 305 (Newark, N.J.: Adams Press, 1954), 99a–100a.
2. Ibid., "Brief for Plaintiff-Appellant," 4.
3. Ibid., "Appendix to Appellant's Brief," 9a, 100a, 71a–73a, 101a.
4. Ibid., 24a.
5. Ibid., 3a.
6. The five cases are *Everson v. Board of Education of Ewing Township*, 330 U.S. 1 (1947); Illinois ex rel. *McCollum v. Board of Education* 330 U.S. 203 (1948); *Zorach v. Clauson* 343 U.S. 306 (1952); *Engel v. Vitale*, 370 U.S. 421 (1962); and *Abington School District v. Schempp*, 374 U.S. 203 (1963).

7. Michael J. Sandel, *Democracy's Discontent: America in Search of a Public Philosophy* (Cambridge, Mass.: Harvard University Press, 1996), quotations on 315, 200, and 205. For minorities as part of the problem, see 279–80 and 294–97. Regarding the case's relative obscurity, the only secondary source I know of is four paragraphs in Naomi W. Cohen, *Jews in Christian America: The Pursuit of Religious Equality* (New York, 1992), 191–92. Regarding the rise of rights-based liberalism in the middle of the twentieth century, see Alan Brinkley, *The End of Reform: New Deal Liberalism in Recession and War* (New York: Knopf, 1995), and William Edward Nelson, *The Legalist Reformation: Law, Politics, and Ideology in New York, 1920–1980* (Chapel Hill: University of North Carolina Press, 2001); for its fulfillment from 1965–1975, see John D. Skrentny, *The Minority Rights Revolution* (Cambridge, Mass.: Harvard University Press, 2002).

8. Christopher Shannon, *A World Made Safe for Differences: Cold War Intellectuals and the Politics of Identity* (Lanham, Md.: Rowman & Littlefield, 2001), xvii; Wilfred M. McClay, *The Masterless: Self and Society in Modern America* (Chapel Hill: University of North Carolina Press, 1994); Alasdair C. MacIntyre, *Whose Justice? Which Rationality?* (Notre Dame, Ind.: University of Notre Dame Press, 1988), quotation on 347; Alasdair C. MacIntyre, *Three Rival Versions of Moral Enquiry: Encyclopaedia, Genealogy, and Tradition* (Notre Dame, Ind.: University of Notre Dame Press, 1990); and Charles Taylor, *Sources of the Self: The Making of Modern Identity* (Cambridge, Mass.: Harvard University Press, 1989), esp. 495–521.

9. James W. Fraser, *Between Church and State: Religion and Public Education in a Multicultural America* (New York: St. Martin's Press, 1999), 131–44; R. Laurence Moore, "Bible Reading and Nonsectarian Schooling: The Failure of Religious Instruction in Nineteenth-Century Public Education," *Journal of American History* 86 (March 2000): 1581–99; and David Tyack and Elisabeth Hansot, *Managers of Virtue: Public School Leadership in America, 1820–1980* (New York: Basic Books, 1982).

10. Will Herberg, "Summary Statement on 'the American Tradition on Church and State,'" Articles Unpublished File, RG 14.2, Will Herberg Papers, Will Herberg Collection, Drew University (Madison, N.J.); George Gallup et al., *The Gallup Poll: Public Opinion*, vol. 3 (Wilmington, Del.: Scholarly Resources, 1972), 1779. The most famous crèche, legally speaking, was that in Ossining, New York, which first appeared in 1956; on Ten Commandment plaques, see Leo Pfeffer, "Memo of Law in Opposition," May 15, 1957, "CLSA Materials Jan.-June 1957" (New York: American Jewish Congress). Thanks to Marc Stern for granting me access to these files.

11. The NEA data is reprinted in the *American Jewish Year Book, 1951* (New York: American Jewish Committee, 1951), 48–49.

12. Douglas's famous quotation comes from his opinion in *Zorach v. Clauson*. For the National Council of Churches of Christ quotation, see the *American Jewish Year Book, 1954* (New York: American Jewish Committee, 1954), 50.

13. *New York Times*, March 1, 1947, 16. For the argument of the New York Board of Rabbis, see Harold H. Gordon, "Letter to the editor," *New York Times*, March 5, 1947, 24.

14. The story is recounted in the *American Jewish Year Book, 1954*, 52–53, and *America*, January 31, 1953, 471.

15. Luce is quoted in the *American Jewish Year Book, 1947–1948* (New York: American Jewish Committee, 1948), 25; the 1953 Bible reading bills are discussed in the *American Jewish Year Book, 1954*, 52; *Life*, December 26, 1955, 56; and Will Herberg, "The Sectarian Conflict Over Church and State," *Commentary* 14 (November 1952): 450–64.

16. Philip Hamburger, *Separation of Church and State* (Cambridge, Mass.: Harvard University Press, 2002). See also Gregg Ivers, *To Build a Wall: American Jews and the Separation of Church and State* (Charlottesville: University of Virginia Press, 1995).

17. Fraser, *Between Church and State*, 144–45.

18. For the Catholic Bishops of America quotation, see the *American Jewish Year Book, 1954*, 49; Benjamin Fine, "Catholic Schools Raise Enrollment to 4,000,000 Peak," *New York Times*, May 30, 1952, 1; and for the development of elite Catholic schools, see Milton M. Gordon, *Assimilation in American Life: The Role of Race, Religion, and National Origins* (New York: Oxford University Press, 1964), 210–12.

19. The Cleveland case and the Dundee Elementary School are discussed in the *American Jewish Year Book, 1951*, 50–51. Regarding "the Protestantization of American Judaism," Shapiro also emphasizes the changing nature of Jewish worship and the timing of sermons. Edward S. Shapiro, *A Time for Healing: American Jewry since World War II* (Baltimore: Johns Hopkins University Press, 1992), 166–68.

20. Leo Pfeffer and Phil Blum, "Public School Sectarianism and the Jewish Child," May 1957, 2, in "CLSA Materials Jan.–June 1957."

21. Quoted from Pfeffer and Blum, "Public School Sectarianism," 11. For Catholics' credentials as good Americans, see John T. McGreevy, *Catholicism and American Freedom: A History* (New York: Norton, 2003), 211–12.
22. For these numbers and for an elaboration of these arguments, see Kevin M. Schultz, "Religion as Identity in Postwar America: The Story of the Last Serious Attempt to Put a Question on Religion in the United States Census," *Journal of American History* 93 (September 2006): 359–84.
23. The quotation comes from the Constitution and By-Laws of the Gideons International, included as Exhibit P–7 in "Appendix to Appellant's Brief," *Tudor v. Board*, 105a.
24. In addition to the various school districts listed here, the Gideons were protested in Boston, Sandwich, and Bourne, Massachusetts, and in the Connecticut State Board of Education. See "Brief for Plaintiff-Appellant," *Tudor v. Board*, 13. For the case's place as the final word, see Marc D. Stern, *Religion and the Public Schools: A Summary of the Law* (New York: American Jewish Congress, 1993), 20.
25. J. Wallace Leyden, "Order for Stay Pending Determination," February 29, 1952, reprinted in "Appendix to Appellant's Brief," *Tudor v. Board*, 7a.
26. "Appendix to Appellant's Brief," *Tudor v. Board*, 24a–25a.
27. On Catholics and Jews joining forces, *New York Times*, October 4, 1953, 65; Will Maslow and Shad Polier, two prominent attorneys from Jewish organizations, joined Pfeffer when the *Tudor* case was appealed to the U.S. Supreme Court.
28. "Appendix to Appellant's Brief," *Tudor v. Board*, 28a–29a.
29. On "democratic education," see ibid., 58a–59a; on the "unconstitutional preference," see "Brief for Plaintiff-Appellant," *Tudor v. Board*, 6.
30. "Brief for Plaintiff-Appellant," *Tudor v. Board*, 11–13.
31. Ibid., 8–9.
32. For Chein's quotation, see "Appendix to Appellant's Brief," *Tudor v. Board*, 42a–43a; for the second expert, ibid., 56a.
33. *Doremus et al. v. Board of Education of the Borough of Hawthorne et al.*, 342 U.S. 429 (1952); for its use in the *Tudor* case, see "Appendix to Appellant's Brief," *Tudor v. Board*, 65a–66a.
34. "Appendix to Appellant's Brief," *Tudor v. Board*, 75a–76a.
35. Ibid., 81a–91a.
36. Ibid., 96a.
37. The public reaction to the schools in Wisconsin is noteworthy: the response was the formation of the Protestant Bill of Rights Committee, which sought to have the state disown these public schools. The story is retold in the *American Jewish Year Book, 1953* (New York: American Jewish Committee, 1953), 46.
38. *Zellers v. Huff*, 55 N.M. 501 (1951). For POAU's involvement in the case, see Sarah Barringer Gordon, "The Almighty and the Dollar: Catholics, Protestants, and School Funding at Mid-Century," working paper, quoted with permission of the author, 29–31.
39. Paul Blanshard, *American Freedom and Catholic Power* (Boston: Beacon Press, 1949). For the book's place in midcentury intellectual life, see John T. McGreevy, "Thinking on One's Own: Catholicism in the American Intellectual Imagination, 1928–1960," *Journal of American History* 84 (June 1997): 97–131. See also John Courtney Murray, "Paul Blanshard and the New Nativism," *The Month* (April 1951): 214–25, quotation on 216; and Herberg, "The Sectarian Conflict Over Church and State," 456. The Dewey quotation is found in McGreevy, "Thinking on One's Own," 97.
40. Hamburger, *Separation of Church and State*, esp. 479–83.
41. *The Christian Century*, April 17, 1946, 493; Thomas F. Odea, "The Missing Dialogue," in *Facing Protestant-Catholic Tensions*, ed. Wayne Cowan (New York: Associated Press, 1960), 57–58. In POAU, Morrison was joined by John Mackay, president of the Princeton Theological Seminary; Edwin McNeill Poteat, president of the Colgate-Rochester Divinity School; and the Methodist bishop G. Bromley Oxnam. This was respectable company, consisting of powerful interests in American intellectual life. See "Protestant v. Catholics," *Time*, April 8, 1946, 68–69, and "Unbrotherly Division," *Time*, November 5, 1945, 61.
42. *New York Times*, October 4, 1953, 65.
43. Ibid.
44. *Bernard Tudor v. Board of Education of the Borough of Rutherford and the Gideons International* 14 N.J. 31 (1953).

45. Ibid.
46. Ibid.
47. In 1962, the U.S. Supreme Court outlawed "innocuous" prayer in the case of *Engel v. Vitale*. In 1963, it removed school-sponsored Bible reading in the case of *Abington v. Schempp*.
48. American Jewish Congress, "In Defense of Religious Liberty," Church + State Misc. File, Box 37, RG I–77, Papers of the American Jewish Congress, American Jewish Historical Society, New York.
49. For a vivid account of America's post–1965 religious diversity, see Diana L. Eck, *A New Religious America: How a "Christian Country" Has Become the World's Most Religiously Diverse Nation* (San Francisco: HarperSanFrancisco, 2001).

Selling American Diversity and Muslim American Identity through Nonprofit Advertising Post-9/11

Evelyn Alsultany

In the weeks after 9/11, patriotic advertising campaigns flooded highway billboards, radio, magazines, newspapers, and television. Some corporations used the tragedy directly or indirectly to market and sell their product. General Motors launched a campaign, "Keep America Rolling," offering zero percent financing deals on new cars and trucks. The New York Sports Club encouraged New Yorkers to "Keep America Strong" by joining the gym on September 25.[1] Some corporations, such as AOL/Time Warner, MSNBC, Ralph Lauren, Sears, and Morgan Stanley advertised that they would not be advertising, instead buying advertising space on billboards, magazines, and television to express their condolences, solidarity, and an inspirational message.[2] Recovery from tragedy came with a corporate sponsor and was endorsed by President Bush and Mayor Giuliani, who encouraged citizens to fight terror through shopping, to practice citizenship through consumerism.

Corporations were not alone in producing post-9/11-specific advertisements: nonprofit organizations (e.g., the Ad Council), civil rights groups (e.g., the American Civil Liberties Union, the Council on American-Islamic Relations, etc.), and the U.S. government have also been involved in post-9/11 advertising. For example, the Ad Council, which produces public service announcements (PSAs), created an extensive advertising campaign that was aired on mainstream network television. Some ads directed persons who had lost family members in the attacks to sources of financial assistance, some alerted the public to challenges they might face in raising their children in the aftermath of tragedy, some told the public how they could get involved and be of assistance, and others aimed to unify the United States across racial lines and inspire patriotism.[3] More than an educational or emotional response to tragedy, post-9/11 nonprofit advertising sought to "sell" ideas about an imagined American community and redefine American identity and citizenship.[4] Notions of who "counted" as an American shifted after 9/11. The government's antiterror campaign involved interviewing nearly 200,000 Arabs and Muslims; detaining and deporting thousands of Arabs, Muslims, and South Asians; instituting special registration requirements for Arabs and Muslims; and shutting down Muslim charities and other organizations. Congressional passage of the USA Patriot Act enabled increased surveillance that included wiretapping, monitoring of bank transfers, and extra searches at airports. The government's practice of detaining, deporting, and profiling those who appear to be Arab, Middle Eastern, or Muslim marked these identities as suspect and therefore un-American.[5]

In addition to government practices that defined Americans and Arabs/Muslims as binary opposites, government and media discourses relied on old Orientalist tropes that positioned American national identity as democratic, modern, and free and the Middle East as primitive, barbaric, and oppressive.[6] For example, President Bush's speeches were replete with references to the United States as a democratic nation saving others—Afghanistan and Iraq—from oppression and tyranny and bestowing on them democracy and freedom. His infamous statements, "They hate us for our freedom" and "You are either with us or you are with the terrorists," established a dominant binary paradigm for understanding the post-9/11 climate: American versus Arab/Muslim. Furthermore, President Bush's speeches positioned Christianity and Islam in opposition to each other by stating that the war against terrorism would be a *crusade* against evil-doers.[7] At the same time, however, Bush made statements that seemed to unravel this binary framework by distinguishing the religion of Islam from the actions of the terrorists, such as "the terrorists practice a fringe form of Islamic extremism . . . that perverts the peaceful teachings of Islam" and "the enemy of America is not our many Muslim friends."[8] While such distinctions outraged some of Bush's allies, for others in the United States these statements operated to create the illusion of a sensitive administration. For instance, when the USA Patriot Act was passed, many who expressed alarm at the disproportionate impact it would have on Arabs and Muslims were often met with a reminder of Bush's statements about Islam being a religion of peace, which was used as evidence that the government would not treat Arabs and Muslims badly. Despite such statements, the dominant discourse of the War on Terror and subsequent government actions confirmed the binary framework of good and evil, Americans and Arabs/Muslims.

One way that this framework materially manifested was through individual vigilante acts: hate crimes. Hundreds of Arabs, Muslims, and those mistaken for Arab or Muslim were attacked or harassed, their businesses burned, and some murdered by individuals who perceived themselves as patriots. Reports indicate that perpetrators of hate crimes said such things as "go back to your country" or "I am an American" or some kind of racial slur during the act of violence.[9] After 9/11, as Leti Volpp has argued, the category of the American citizen went through a process of resignification, defined over and against the category of the terrorist.[10] The conception of the American citizen became suddenly and momentarily centered on multicultural diversity in opposition to Arabs and Muslims (and those who are mistaken for Arab or Muslim, such as South Asians and Iranians) who came to be marked as noncitizen terrorists.

A 2004 nationwide survey conducted by Cornell University found that 44 percent of people in the United States favored some kind of restriction on Arab and Muslim American civil liberties—which included registering one's place of residence with the government and racial profiling. The poll also found that 74 percent characterized Islamic countries as oppressive to women; 50 percent perceived Muslims as violent, dangerous, and fanatical; and one-third indicated that a majority of Muslims are hostile to the United States. In addition, it reports that only 27 percent agreed that Muslim and Christian values are similar, and 47 percent indicated that the "Islamic religion is more likely than others to encourage violence among its believers." These figures indicate that at least half of U.S. citizens see Islam as dangerous and as having values fundamentally different from Western/Christian ones.[11] These figures also demonstrate the convergence and culmination of government practices, government and media discourses, and individual acts and perceptions that criminalized and racialized Arabs and Muslims.[12] This is not to say that Arabs, Muslims, and South Asians were unproblematically included within an imagined American community before 9/11 or that racism toward other racialized groups in the United States ended on 9/11. Notions of American national identity are fraught with contradictions and are continually in the process of being formed and re-formed. After 9/11, however, there emerged an ideological moment that, supported by a range of individual and institutional discourses and practices, defined U.S. citizens as diverse and united in the "War on Terror," over and against Arabs and Muslims, who were represented as un-American, terrorists, enemies.

This essay examines how nonprofit advertising participated in refiguring an imagined American community after 9/11. In what follows, I compare three advertising campaigns: the Ad Council's "I am an American," the Council on American-Islamic Relations' "I am an American Muslim," and the U.S. Department of State's "Shared Values Initiative." I argue that, in an effort to deconstruct the binary opposition between American citizen and Arab Muslim terrorist, these PSAs reproduced restrictive representations of diversity. How was diversity used to resist this binary racial configuration? How were American or Muslim identities packaged, marketed, and sold through nonprofit advertising and how did these campaigns differ when directed at domestic or international audiences? What role did Muslims play in this process? An examination of these discourses on diversity reveals the content and limits to American cultural citizenship at this particular historical juncture.[13]

"I Am an American"

The Ad Council has been producing public service advertisements on behalf of the government and nonprofit organizations since 1942 to raise public awareness on a variety of social issues ranging from the prevention of child abuse, domestic violence, drug use, and drunk driving, to education on seat-belt use, racism, and discrimination. The Ad Council's public service announcement "I am an American" was created in direct response to the hundreds of hate crimes against Arabs, Muslims, and Sikhs and began airing on television ten days after 9/11. The advertisement features a diverse group of people, one by one stating: "I am an American." The range of diversity includes Latinos, Caucasians, African Americans, Caribbean Americans, South Asian Americans, Native Americans, Asian Americans, young and old people, as well as urban and suburban men and women, a fireman, and a woman who appears to be a nun. The advertisement ends with the written words "E Pluribus Unum—Out of Many, One," followed by a young girl of about three or four years of age, who appears possibly to be Latina, silently waving an American flag and smiling (see fig. 1). The soundtrack to the PSA, composed mainly of violins, sounds like an anthem in its solemn disposition.[14]

"I am an American" aims to discourage further attacks on Arabs, Muslims, and Sikhs by promoting unity through the marker "American," which is signified as a diverse designation. The ad seeks to appeal to viewers to be tolerant and accepting of people who look or sound different from themselves and to encourage "Americans" not to discriminate against each other. Some of the "Americans" featured in the PSA have accented English, signaling that English is their second language and thus that they are first-generation immigrants. Nonetheless, the ad does not present a range of languages, only English with various accents. As the Ad Council Web site explained: "Diversity is what defines America. In the wake of this national tragedy, it is time to embrace our differences and celebrate that diversity, rather than let it divide us. Our

Figure 1.
Still from the Ad Council's PSA "I am an American." Created pro bono by GSD&M for the Ad Council. Reproduced with the permission of the Ad Council.

nation's motto sends a message that has never been more appropriate—E Pluribus Unum, or Out of Many, One. We are all Americans and our differences create the very foundation and spirit that define this nation."[15] Difference is identified as defining the nation; American identity is defined as diverse. But what kind of diversity is acceptable? How is diversity defined?

Despite seeking to deconstruct the binary between the citizen and the terrorist, Arabs, Muslims, and Sikhs are not specifically included in this diverse display. There are no visible markers of anything Arab, Muslim, or Sikh in the ads—no veil, no mosque, no turban, no beard; no distinctive Arab, Muslim, or Sikh clothing; and no Arab accent. There is an African American man wearing a suit and bow tie in the advertisement, who could possibly be part of the Nation of Islam, but this is ambiguous. There is one young woman who appears to be South Asian American and a young man who might be South Asian American or could possibly be Arab American, but there is no clear indication of their identities. The young man who might possibly be South

Asian or Arab American has a difficult time articulating that he is an American because he is overcome with emotion. While all of the individuals clearly state, "I am an American," the ambiguously Arab man, as the only one who has difficulty articulating his American identity, is distinguished in the advertisement as someone for whom it is especially meaningful to be an American. The fact that Arabs were blamed for 9/11 but South Asians were also subject to attacks, harassment, deportation, and surveillance demonstrates that these identities are conflated by the general U.S. public. The Ad Council continues this conflation through the ambiguous representation of this Arab/South Asian man as an American. Nonetheless, those that were most targeted after 9/11 were persons who wore religious symbols, such as veils and turbans, and the conspicuous absence of any religious identification from the "ambiguously" marked Arabs or South Asians raises serious questions: why is Islam (and a Sikh identity that was often mistaken as Muslim) ignored in this ad? Are these groups unrepresentable in a mainstream campaign that promotes a vision of a proudly diverse American citizenry?

The ad responds to national crisis through diversity-patriotism, whereby racialized groups are temporarily incorporated into the imagined community of "Americans." Amid legislation to deport Arabs, Muslims, and South Asians and end affirmative action, the idea/ideal of diversity is mobilized urgently and expediently, motivated in response to trauma, and it serves to comfort and heal the nation. Although diversity takes ideological precedence in the post-9/11 period, it is unlikely to take precedence indefinitely. As Omi and Winant have stated, one of the consequences of centuries of American racial dictatorship is that "American" identity has been defined as white.[16] Despite the fact that U.S. citizenship has been historically defined as white and repeatedly redefined as such through immigration policies, attacks on affirmative action, and other legal and governmental mechanisms, hegemonic whiteness is temporarily suspended in the national imaginary and replaced by diversity as the paradigm of American citizenship—with exceptions. Latinos, Asian Americans, and African Americans are refigured as "American" alongside whites. The ad promotes what appears to be an inclusive and diverse United States, but this is done through ambiguously including Arabs and South Asians while excluding unambiguous markers of Muslim or Sikh identity. The ambiguous assimilative diversity-patriotism that is mobilized by the Ad Council affirms the binary between "the citizen" and "the terrorist."

The defining of a diverse U.S. citizenry in opposition to Arabs and Muslims did not begin on 9/11. Melani McAlister argues that after 1945, "there was a move away from the distinctly modern concern with the construction of a unified (white, masculine) national and racial identity toward a construction of the national subject as disjointed and diverse, gendered both masculine and feminine, and ultimately multiracial" and that the Middle East was central to the development of this form of nationalism.[17] Both McAlister and Wahneema Lubiano have written about the centrality of narrating African American soldiers as heroes of the Gulf War to redefining a diverse U.S. citizenry.[18] McAlister notes that "the images of diversity and strength of U.S. armed forces simply did not include Arab Americans."[19] Multiculturalism was defined in opposition to the Arab/Muslim enemy. The post-911 discourse continues the Gulf War representation of multicultural U.S. citizens vis-à-vis the Arab/Muslim enemy.[20] "I am an American" functions to create an imaginary multiracial and equal America, yet it does not solve the dangerous configuration of Americans versus Arabs/Muslims, but rather functions to mobilize ambiguous assimilative diversity to unite Americans in supporting the government's "War on Terror" against Arabs and Muslims.

"I am an American Muslim"

While the Ad Council does not directly address the relationship between Arab and Muslim Americans and American citizenship, the Council on American-Islamic Relations (CAIR), the largest Muslim civil liberties and advocacy organization in North America, does. CAIR's mission is "to enhance understanding of Islam, encourage dialogue, protect civil liberties, empower American Muslims, and build coalitions that promote justice and mutual understanding."[21] Since its establishment in 1994, CAIR has sought to promote a positive image of Islam and Muslims in the United States, through media relations, lobbying, education, and advocacy. Among their many post-9/11 initiatives are their "National and Worldwide Condemnation of Terrorism" and "Not in the Name of Islam" campaigns—both of which denounce terrorism as part of an effort to correct public assumptions that Muslims support terrorism. CAIR was among 120 Muslim groups to support a fatwa (Islamic religion ruling) against terrorism and extremism.

Despite the group's work in condemning terrorism and educating the public about Islam, CAIR has been attacked by conservatives, who have accused the group of being a front for terrorism, specifically for Hezbollah and Hamas. CAIR officials have stated that such accusations stem from the group's differing perspectives on particular issues. For example, while they are critical of Hamas and Hezbollah, they refuse to join in the U.S. government's blanket condemnation of these groups. In addition, they have urged the U.S. government to stop shipments of weapons to Israel and have opposed the pro-Israel lobby in Washington. Such stances have sometimes made it difficult for CAIR to work with government officials. Senator Barbara Boxer of California, for example, revoked a certificate of appreciation that she had issued to the group, in order not to be perceived as supporting terrorism.[22]

One of CAIR's post-9/11 initiatives was an advertising campaign, "Islam in America," to foster understanding of Islam in the United States and to counter anti-Muslim rhetoric. The campaign includes one television public service announcement and six print advertisements.[23] The first print ad of the series appeared in the Sunday, February 16, 2003, edition of the *New York Times*. Each of the six ads is designed to address one aspect of Islam and to educate the public about it. Seeking to move away from the Hollywood Arab Muslim villain and government framing of a clash of civilizations between the West and the East, the ads attempt to redefine Islam and its relationship to America. Through the slogan "I'm an American Muslim," CAIR tries to break down the constructed opposition between American and Muslim, to include Muslims in the imagining of America, and to draw a parallel between the diversity of America and the diversity within Islam. In other words, compatibility between Americans and Muslims and the possibility of patriotic American Muslim identity is established through the language of diversity, presenting another version of diversity-patriotism. The advertisements assert that "American" and "Muslim" are compatible by articulating a number of discourses, including a Muslim legacy of military service to the U.S. nation, to replace the notion that Muslims are violent fanatics who hate the United States.

The television PSA takes place in a studio. The background is blank and the synthesizer music creates a hopeful atmosphere. The featured Muslim speakers appear to be in their twenties, thirties, and forties.

Narrator: America is the land of diversity and service.
African American man: I am an African American. My forefathers overcame the trials of slavery.
Native American woman: I am Native American. I'm a journalist, wife, and mother.
White man: I am of European heritage. One of my ancestors was a member of the Continental Congress.
Latina (in a hijab): I'm Hispanic American. I've been a girl scout since I was six years old and now I'm a troop leader.
African American man: I served in our nation's armed forces, as have many of my relatives.

Native American woman: My father served two terms of duty in Vietnam.
White man: Another fought for freedom at Gettysburg.
Latina: Two of my uncles fought for our country in the Korean War.
African American man: And I am an American Muslim.
Native American woman: And I am an American Muslim.
White man: And I am an American Muslim.
Latina: I am an American Muslim.
Narrator: Muslims are part of the fabric of this great country and are working to build a better America.

This advertisement operates to relay three interrelated messages. First, it seeks to delink Islam from Arabs. By not representing any Arabs in its multiethnic display of "American Muslims," it serves to correct the common conflation that all Arabs are Muslim and all Muslims Arab. Second, through invoking slavery, representing a Native American, and speaking of ancestors, the notion that Muslims are "foreign" or "new" immigrants and therefore un-American is challenged. Instead, a narrative of a Muslim legacy in the United States is established. Third, Muslims are represented as productive citizen-patriots who serve their country by being a girl scout, by fighting for the nation, and by having ancestors who also fought for the nation. Thus this advertisement claims that Muslims are American by virtue of their legacy of patriotic service to the nation, and patriotism is defined by one's willingness to go to war and fight/die for the United States.

The discourses that are mobilized to include Muslims within American cultural citizenship are centered upon notions of the United States as a melting pot nation and upon service to the nation, and are expressed in a variety of ways for men and women and for U.S.-born and foreign-born citizens. Diversity is expressed through representing Latinos, African Americans, Native Americans, and European Americans as Muslim Americans (or rather, as "American Muslims"). Service to the nation is articulated for men through military service as the quintessential enactment of patriotism, and for women through being a girl scout or participating in volunteer or relief work. Foreign-born citizens are included in American citizenship through establishing a length of time living in the United States and service to the government/nation.

While speech is the means through which to declare and establish one's American identity in the Ad Council's PSA, in the case of CAIR, speech is not enough but requires action (e.g., military service) and even oath taking. One print ad features Arab Muslim American girls taking their Girl Scout oath, pledging to serve their country as well as God (see fig. 2).

WE'RE AMERICANS AND WE'RE MUSLIMS

**On my honor, I will try:
To serve God and my country.
And to help people at all times.**

The members of Santa Clara Muslim Girl Scout Troop #856 have made a pledge to serve their community, their country and God. The American values that we all cherish—like service, charity and tolerance—are the same values that Muslims are taught to uphold in daily life.

Muslim life and worship are structured around the Five Pillars of Islam—faith, prayer, helping the needy, fasting, and pilgrimage. The third pillar teaches that all things belong to God and are only held in trust by humans, so as Muslims we are expected to share a percentage of our wealth every year to help the poor.

Devotion to God and the teachings of Islam strengthen our commitment to community and country. Like Americans of all faiths, we use the principles of our religion to guide us in an ever-changing world, and we teach our children to respect the values that make our country a secure place for all Americans.

WE'RE AMERICAN MUSLIMS

COUNCIL ON AMERICAN ISLAMIC RELATIONS

Number two of fifty-two in the *Islam in America* series
To learn more about the series, visit www.americanmuslims.info

"We're Americans and we're Muslims."

"On my honor, I will try: To serve God and my country. And to help people at all times."

The members of Santa Clara Muslim Girl Scout Troop #856 have made a pledge to serve their community, their country, and God. The American values that all cherish—like service, charity, and tolerance—are the same values that Muslims are taught to uphold in daily life.

Muslim life and worship are structured around the Five Pillars of Islam—faith, prayer, helping the needy, fasting, and pilgrimage. The third pillar teaches that all things belong to God and are only held in trust by humans, so as Muslims we are expected to share a percentage of our wealth every year to help the poor.

Devotion to God and the teachings of Islam strengthen our commitment to community and country. Like Americans of all faiths, we use the principles of our religion to guide us in an ever-changing world, and we teach our children to respect the values that make our country a secure place for all Americans.

"We're American Muslims."[24]

Figure 2.
Islam in America series, 2 of 52.
Photograph courtesy of the Council
on American-Islamic Relations.

The advertisements produced by the Council on American-Islamic Relations, as well as by the Ad Council, take the form of a performative speech act. Defining the self becomes a means for inclusion in the imagined diverse American nation. Through "oath taking," and testifying to one's identity, the speakers not only illustrate that they are "good Muslims," but also display to other Muslims how to be a "credit to one's race." In the case of CAIR, the emphasis is not only on speaking, declaring, or taking an oath, but also on articulating enactments of service to the nation. American values are defined as "service, charity, and tolerance" and these are situated as identical to Muslim values. American and Muslim values, unbeknownst to most Americans, are in fact the same, according to CAIR's PSA. In addition, Islam actually teaches Muslims to be patriotic, creating charitable, tolerant citizens who serve their community and country. Muslim interest in the security of the American nation is expressed as Muslims take an oath from a young age to serve their country and God.[25]

As serving the nation takes precedence in the articulation of American Muslim identity, other ways to serve the nation besides military and Girl Scout service are also identified, such as working for the U.S. government or being active in the PTA (Parent-Teacher's Association). One ad features a photo of a family—husband, wife wearing a headscarf, and two children who are probably four and six years old. They look South Asian, but it turns out the woman is Puerto Rican (see fig. 3):

WE'RE AMERICAN AND WE'RE MUSLIMS

MY NAME IS AMINAH KAPADIA, and I'm a wife, a mom and a student. I'm studying for a Masters degree in education, and I volunteer at our children's school, where I'm also active in the PTA. I was born in Philadelphia, to Puerto Rican parents, and have lived in the United States my entire life. My husband, Zubin, is from India, but has called America home for more than thirty years. He's an attorney and former economic officer for the U.S. Department of State. Now he spends his time running a consulting firm and coaching our sons' T-ball and soccer teams.

Like many Americans, my husband and I face the challenge of raising our children in an unpredictable world. That's why the basic principles of our religion, like tolerance, justice and devotion to family, are a central part of our lives. As the Prophet Muhammad told us, "The best of you is he who is best to his family. None of you will have faith until he wants for his brother what he wishes for himself."

We believe the security of our nation is dependent upon the strength of our families, and Islam teaches us the values that provide that strength.

WE'RE AMERICAN MUSLIMS

Number five of fifty-two in the *Islam in America* series.
To learn more about the series, visit www.americanmuslims.info

My name is Aminah Kapadia, and I'm a wife, a mom, and a student. I'm studying for a Master's degree in education, and I volunteer at our children's school, where I'm also active in the PTA. I was born in Philadelphia, to Puerto Rican parents, and have lived in the United States my entire life. My husband, Zubin, is from India, but has called America home for more than thirty years. He's an attorney and former economic officer for the U.S. Department of State. Now he spends his time running a consulting firm and coaching our son's T-ball and soccer teams.

Like many Americans, my husband and I face the challenges of raising our children in an unpredictable world. That's why the basic principles of our religion, like tolerance, justice, and devotion to family, are a central part of our lives. As the Prophet Muhammad told us, "The best of you is he who is best to his family. None of you will have faith until he wants for his brother what he wishes for himself."

We believe the security of our nation is dependent upon the strength of our families, and Islam teaches us the values that provide that strength.

"We're American Muslims."[26]

Figure 3.
Islam in America series, 5 of 52. Photograph courtesy of the Council on American-Islamic Relations.

This advertisement demonstrates the convergence of a variety of discourses: diversity, service to the nation, Muslim and American shared values, the interconnection between Islam and national security, and the significance of heterosexual family values. This is a multicultural Muslim American family: they are Puerto Rican and Indian. The advertisement states that the Puerto Rican woman was born in the United States while her Indian husband was not. Nonetheless, his legitimacy as an American is claimed by virtue of the length of time he has been in the country (thirty years) and his patriotic service (he has worked for the U.S. government). Furthermore, he is a successful, middle-class, family man and thus a productive and desirable citizen-patriot. He participates in "American" activities such as coaching his son's T-ball and soccer teams.

Though a distinction is made between those born here and those born abroad, a legitimate claim to American identity is established through length of time in the United States, diversity, and service to the government. Meanwhile, the woman was born in the United States, and to complicate her identity and challenge even further what the general public purports to "know" about Islam and Muslim women, she is of Puerto Rican descent. Thus, Muslims can be of any background and Muslim women are not necessarily oppressed and confined to the private sphere. Although she is married and a mom and has many home and family responsibilities, she still pursues a master's degree while being involved in her children's lives—volunteering at their school and as a member of the PTA. Finally, by affirming that "the security of our nation is dependent upon the strength of our families, and Islam teaches us the values that provide that strength," the ads link Islam, heterosexual family values, and national security.

The 9/11 tragedies became an opportunity not only to reformulate who is a citizen, but also what constitutes American values. According to polls, the primary reason Bush's supporters voted for him had to do with "moral values." Freedom of speech and freedom of religion are not the values citizens affirmed in voting for Bush. Rather, the "moral values" that are currently central to conservatives are the heterosexual family, belief in God, and opposition to abortion.[27] According to the CAIR PSAs, Muslim family values are not that different from how President Bush might define American values. This is particularly significant given the domestic controversy over gay marriage. Though CAIR does not make an explicit statement against homosexuality, it does clearly accentuate its support for the heterosexual family as the foundation for a secure nation. Not only is the organization seeking to connect with other Americans through the rubric of tolerance and diversity, but also by linking heterosexuality with religion. These advertisements target other religious Americans, presumably the majority of Americans and, in doing so, seek to place Islam on the same level as other faiths, particularly Christianity and Judaism.

While some of CAIR's advertisements seek to stress similarities between Islam and "America," others seek to correct misperceptions of Islam. Since dominant narratives in the West about Islam often revolve around the oppressed, veiled Muslim woman, CAIR seeks to correct these misperceptions by featuring hijab-wearing Muslim women as active in the public sphere. One ad consists of a photo of an Arab Muslim American woman wearing a headscarf and text that reads:

> My name is Manal Omar. I've earned a Master's degree from Georgetown University, and I've won several national public speaking awards. I'm a development researcher for an international corporation. I vote. I'm active in politics, and I belong to several civic organizations.
>
> I am an American Muslim woman and I wear hijab.
>
> I choose to wear hijab—a headscarf and modest attire—because the practice is integral to my religious beliefs, and because I am proud to be a Muslim woman. In Islam, both women and men are encouraged to dress modestly, thereby allowing a person to be judged on the content of his or her character, and not on physical appearance.
>
> To me, hijab is a symbol of my confidence and self-respect.
>
> "I'm an American Muslim."[28]

This Arab Muslim American woman is a model citizen: educated, professional, and involved in politics. Challenging the image of the oppressed veiled Muslim woman, she is not hidden away at home but actively participates in the public sphere and has even won national public speaking awards. The hijab is explained: it is asserted as her choice and as an expression of her beliefs. Her statement that dressing modestly allows one to be judged by character as opposed to appearance resonates with Martin Luther King's speech in which he dreams of a day when people will be judged by the content of their character and not by the color of their skin. Evocative of the civil rights movement, the statement invites other Americans to practice tolerance and diversity.

The main message these ads seek to convey is that Muslim values are compatible with American values. Thus a variety of dominant discourses are mobilized to make this possible: diversity, legacy, patriotism and national service, belief in God, and the significance of the heterosexual family unit. Just as the United States is a diverse, multiethnic nation, so too is Islam a diverse and multiethnic religion, according to the PSAs. Muslims are not foreign invaders but have a long history in the United States. They have served and contributed to the nation for more than a hundred years. In addition to having a rich legacy, Muslim Americans today are concerned about national security and are patriotic, like other Americans. Also like other Americans, Muslims believe that faith in God and maintaining the heterosexual family are fundamental components of a successful nation. Ultimately, Muslim Americans, like other Americans during this time of diversity-patriotism, are American first and Muslim second: "We're American Muslims." "American" is the privileged identity here and "Muslim" is packaged, marketed, and sold in ways that emphasize its likeness to, not difference from, American values.

These specifications effectively lead to other exclusions. What about those who do not actively serve the nation through military service, who do not work for the government, are not heterosexual, or not religious? Are they not equally American? In contesting the exclusion of Arabs and Muslims from the American national imaginary, other exclusionary mainstream narratives are utilized. As Akhil Gupta and James Ferguson have written, strategies of resistance can be complicit with strategies of power: "Practices that are resistant to a particular strategy of power are never innocent of or outside power, for they are always capable of being tactically appropriated and redeployed within another strategy of power, always at risk of slipping from resistance against one strategy of power into complicity with another."[29] While the Ad Council and the Council on American-Islamic Relations were clearly aiming to produce a more inclusive framework for American citizenship, these public service announcements participate in the formation of a particular exclusionary version of diversity that requires individuals to approximate a patriotic sameness in order to gain access to cultural citizenship. Such efforts at inclusion, in other words, erase cultural differences and exclude noncitizens.

CAIR's ad campaign falls within the "good Muslim/bad Muslim" paradigm. Mahmood Mamdani claims that the public debate post-9/11 has been most influenced by Samuel Huntington and Bernard Lewis, who both believe that the world is divided between the East and the West.[30] While Huntington positions all Muslims as a threat, Lewis distinguishes between good, secular Westernized Muslims and bad, religious fanatical Muslims. Mamdani critiques this perspective and also President Bush's speeches on Islam as a religion of peace, stating that what makes a Muslim "good" or "bad" within this framework is not his relationship to Islam, but rather, his relationship to the United States and argues that all Muslims are positioned as bad until they prove their allegiance to the nation. The CAIR ads clearly position Muslims as on the side of America within the binary framework of "with us or with the terrorists."

After September 11, 2001, Arab and Muslim Americans are in a position of having to display their ability and willingness to assimilate in order to have a chance at becoming American cultural citizens. CAIR, for example, seeks to prove that American Muslims are "good Muslims" in order to gain entry into the post-9/11 American imagined community and attempt to secure their safety in the United States. The practice of diversity during the "War on Terror" reveals the essence of diversity in the United States, requiring assimilation and displays of patriotism. Thus, PSAs that actively participate in shaping and articulating a diverse America post-9/11 either avoid symbols of cultural/religious difference, or if such symbols are shown, their compatibility with American values is emphasized.

Advertising the Nation Abroad

Using advertising for the purpose of nation building and patriotism is certainly not unique to the United States. Communist countries are known for their noncorporate advertising. The streets of Havana are marked by billboards of Cuban flags and statements such as "Hasta La Victoria Siempre" ("Always until victory") and "Viva La Revolucion" ("Long live the revolution"), that seek to promote patriotism and nationalism, inspire hope for and commitment to revolution, and promote pride in being a Cuban. Similarly, England's "Cool Britannia" campaign, pursued by Tony Blair after the labor party won the 1997 election and launched through a Ben and Jerry's ice-cream flavor of the same name, was used to change and sell Britain's national image.[31] The objective of the campaign was to modernize England's image from one of imperialism, monarchy, and old, white, stuffy traditions to "a young, stylish, post-imperial nation with leading edge creative cultural industries" and to change their national slogan from "Rule Britannia" to "Cool Britannia." It included promotional videos of "New Britain" and a pop version of "God Save the Queen," as a way to refashion and sell Britain's new image as a multicultural modern nation, both internally and externally.[32] Cool Britannia was criticized for seeking to create a multicultural image without addressing the legacy and remaining reality of racism. It was also disparaged for seeking to define a national culture that is broad and complex. In early 2002, the British Tourism Authority restrategized its public relations campaign and began using "UK OK," invoking Britain's monarchic past and present and seeking to keep open a range of possible meanings.[33]

The examples of Cuba's patriotic billboards and the UK's Cool Britannia campaign demonstrate that it is not uncommon for nations to market themselves like a product for internal and/or external consumption. Governments use public relations campaigns to perform the ideological work of (re)defining a national image and ideas associated with that nation. As Mark Leonard has written: "Today all modern nations manage their identities. They use logos, advertising campaigns, festivals and trade fairs to promote a national brand."[34]

In the case of the United States, "public diplomacy" emerged as an important form of "political warfare" during the cold war, and such efforts have been revived since the start of the "War on Terror."[35] The U.S. government after 9/11 sought to manage its identity abroad by establishing the "Office of Strategic Influence" to market America's "War on Terror" outside the United States. In February 2002, the office closed after a media scandal in which classified information was leaked to and published in the *New York Times*, alleging that the Office of Strategic Influence would be manufacturing support for U.S. policies through the dissemination of misinformation to foreign governments and media sources.[36] In early 2003, the White House created the "Office of Global Communications" after President Bush issued an executive order establishing the need for strategic communications overseas to promote the interests of the United States abroad.[37] An "Advisory Group on Public Diplomacy for the Arab and Muslim World" was established to advise the government on how best to conduct *strategic influence* in the Middle East. The advisory group, in its report, outlines a strategic plan to initiate a public relations arm to U.S. policies. The plan encourages greater funding of public diplomacy efforts; an increase in staff training in the Arabic language and recruitment of Arab and

Muslim American government employees; the establishment of "American corners," "American Knowledge Libraries," and American studies centers in the Middle East; strengthening American universities in the Middle East; a publication initiative in which American books are translated from English into Arabic; technology initiatives; educational fellowships and exchanges; and the establishment of a think tank, among other initiatives.[38]

This extensive campaign makes clear that winning the "War on Terror" requires not only military and financial strength, but also ideological hegemony through the various means outlined above. In other words, there are various levels of warfare, including ideological warfare. As Tucker Eskew, director of the White House's Office of Global Communications, has stated, "we're fighting a war of ideas as much as a war on terror,"[39] explicitly referring to the ideological and repressive state apparatuses that are central to the U.S. imperial project.[40] The report makes the importance of ideological hegemony clear and thus argues for increased funding for public diplomacy initiatives abroad:

> The United States today lacks the capabilities in public diplomacy to meet the national security threat emanating from political instability, economic deprivation, and extremism, especially in the Arab and Muslim world. Public diplomacy is the promotion of the national interest by informing, engaging, and influencing people around the world. Public diplomacy helped win the Cold War, and it has the potential to help win the war on terror.[41]

As Liam Kennedy and Scott Lucas have written, "in the promoting of 'freedom' to foreign audiences, public diplomacy is inextricably connected with the development and implementation of U.S. foreign policy, charged with the awkward task of reconciling interests and ideas" (325). In other words, winning the "War on Terror" and ending the presumed crisis in national security depends on ideological hegemony, influencing people around the world through promoting American national interests, particularly through popular culture and advertising campaigns. Public diplomacy has "politicized the international spread of American popular culture."[42]

A popular culture campaign is currently being operated by the U.S. government in the Middle East. Radio Sawa (Radio Together), located in Dubai, broadcasts pop music in English and Arabic (from Britney Spears to Amr Diab) and news from an "American" perspective in several Arab nations, including Jordan, Iraq, Morocco, Sudan, Yemen, and Qatar.[43] The Broadcasting Board of Governors decided to focus on music with sporadic news interludes after research indicated that music would be the most effective way to garner listeners. Al-Hurra Television (The Free One), broadcast out of Virginia to counteract the negative light cast on the United States by Al-Jazeera, features a mix of news and popular culture, including magazine shows with segments on exercise, fashion, technology, and movies, twenty-four hours a day.[44] *Hi Magazine*, launched in 2003 and suspended at the end of 2005, was an Arabic language monthly magazine sold in Lebanon, Jordan, the West Bank and Gaza, Israel, Algeria, Egypt, Cyprus, and several Gulf nations.[45] The articles were written by Arab Americans and strove to highlight similarities between youth in the United States and in the Middle East. These initiatives sought to produce and package a particular version of American national identity for Arabs and Muslims in the Middle East and South East Asia to consume. Its stated objective was to influence the "hearts and minds" of the opposition and to reduce hatred toward the United States. As President Bush stated regarding Al Hurra television, it will "cut through the hateful propaganda that fills the airwaves in the Muslim world."[46] The combined annual budget for these three public relations campaigns was $100 million in 2003.

In addition to the aforementioned initiatives, the U.S. government through the Department of State and CAMU, the Council of American Muslims Understanding (created after 9/11 and funded by the State Department), spent $15 million on the "Shared Values Initiative."[47] Charlotte Beers, a corporate advertising executive who created the Uncle Ben's campaign, was hired by the U.S. government to market and sell the nation like a product abroad. The campaign, "meant, in part, to correct a mistaken image of American hostility to Islam that research showed was prevalent in the Arab and Muslim world," included videos, newspaper ads, and radio spots seeking to "establish a recognition that Americans and Muslims share many values and beliefs [and] demonstrate that America is not at war with Islam."[48]

The U.S. media dubbed the advertisements the "Muslim-as-Apple-Pie" campaign. They consist of several Muslims in their daily lives discussing the good life they live in the United States. The ads were aired between October 28 and December 10, 2002, during the Muslim holy month of Ramadan in Pakistan, Malaysia, Kuwait, Saudi Arabia, United Arab Emirates, Bahrain, Oman, Qatar, and Indonesia. They were refused by Egypt, Lebanon, and Jordan because they were perceived as contradictory: portraying Muslims "testifying" to the freedom and respect they experience living in the United States while not acknowledging the detentions, deportation, and racial profiling Muslims have been subjected to since 9/11.

These ads seek to demonstrate to Muslims abroad that Muslims in the United States live prosperous lives free of harassment, and therefore there is no need to hate the United States. Five ads were produced, each featuring the story of one U.S. Muslim. Devianti Faridz, a female Indonesian graduate student of broadcast journalism at the University of Missouri, testifies that "the values that I was taught as a child in Bandung are the values they teach here in America." Another ad featured Farooq Muhammad, a paramedic with the New York Fire Department, who states: "We are all brothers and sisters. Here I am one human being taking care of another." Dr. Elias Zerhouni, the director of the National Institutes of Health, is featured in another ad, saying: "I am basically an immigrant here, and the tolerance and support I have received myself is remarkable." Abdul-Raouf Hammuda, a bakery owner in Toledo, Ohio, states: "Religious freedom here is something very important. Muslims are free to practice their faith in totality" (fig. 4). The text that accompanies his advertisement reads as follows:

> I was born and raised in Tripoli, Libya. I came to America to go to school. After I graduated, I really saw the opportunity this country would have for me as a businessman.
>
> I went through four or five businesses that failed before I succeeded with the Tiger Lebanese Bakery. We make the greatest pita bread in the nation. I added some dishes from the African nations of Libya, Morocco, and Tunisia, we put a deli in, and it was received very well. My wife is my right-hand person, and I have been very fortunate to have my children help me part time at the bakery.
>
> My customers are probably 75% non-Muslims, 25% Muslims. Since 9/11, we've had an overwhelming sense of support from our customers. I believe Americans in general respect the Islamic faith. Religious freedom here is something very important, and no one has ever bothered us.
>
> I was also one of the co-founders of the Toledo Islamic Academy, the first school of its kind in the state of Ohio. We started with about 50 students, and now we are from pre-K through high school and bursting at the seams.
>
> America is a land of opportunity, of equality. My children converse in Arabic, they can read Koran, they know the Sunnah, we're free to worship in mosques. We are happy to live here as Muslims and preserve our faith.

Hammouda's narrative affirms several U.S. nationalist tropes, particularly the United States as a "land of opportunity" and a "land of (religious) freedom and equality." Stating that he came to this country to go to school and stayed to open a now successful business implies that the United States provides educational and financial opportunities for all peoples regardless of religion, race, or culture. His narrative stresses that non-Muslims are supportive of his business, signifying that anti-Muslim discrimination is not a problem in his

Figure 4.
Open Dialogue—Hammuda, Council of American Muslims for Understanding. Produced in collaboration with the U.S. government in 2002.

adopted country. He furthermore states that he is not only able to practice his religion, but he is also actively involved in creating and maintaining a Muslim community and future generations of Muslims. The advertisement also includes an image of him praying in public at an amusement park, presumably with three of his sons. While Muslims praying in public is a far from ordinary occurrence in the United States, it is pictured as if commonplace, symbolizing public acceptance of Islam. Hammouda's narrative revives U.S. nationalist tropes of opportunity, freedom, and equality in the service of denying discrimination or hatred against Muslims.

Another ad, that of Rawia Ismail (see fig. 5), a teacher in Toledo, Ohio, also stresses religious freedom and the ease with which she is able to practice her religion and be accepted by non-Muslims. In addition, she stresses that Muslims and Americans have similar values. Her text reads:

> I'm a schoolteacher in a public school in Toledo, Ohio, in the United States of America. I also teach my own children in Saturday school, Islamic school.
>
> I was born in Beirut, Lebanon, and came to the United States in 1984. I have four beautiful children. I decided to become a teacher because I enjoy working with children more than anything.
>
> At the Islamic Center I teach the kids about an hour of religion, an hour of Arabic, they have some lunch in between, and then we all do prayers together. This is something I have found to be the only way of life for me and my family. Being a Muslim means everything to me.
>
> In my neighborhood, I see that all the non-Muslims care a lot about educating their children and family values, just as much as I do. I didn't see any prejudice anywhere in my neighborhood after September 11. My neighbors have always been supportive, truly.
>
> I wear a hijab in the public school classroom where I teach. Children ask me a lot of questions. I have never had any child that thought it was weird or anything like that. And they like the fact, both them and their parents, that they're introduced to a different culture.
>
> I work a lot at getting the kids to understand that the most important thing is that we should work on our similarities rather than our differences.

Ismail is a teacher in two schools: a public school and an Islamic school. Her involvement in an Islamic school signifies that she is involved in creating future generations of Muslims. Her involvement in the public school illustrates that her life in the United States is not restricted to a Muslim enclave, but rather, that she is part of the American public, where her difference/diversity is valued. Scenes of her teaching at the public school provide visual evidence to support her narrative. She also states that non-Muslims in

Figure 5.
Open Dialogue—Ismail, Council of American Muslims for Understanding. Produced in collaboration with the U.S. government in 2002.

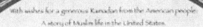

America care about family values, responding to the presumption that Muslims perceive Americans as lacking in values, particularly family values, and she insists that her neighbors have always been friendly and supportive of her as a Muslim. Her final statement about the importance of similarities over differences is a message to Arabs and Muslims not to hate the United States for differences, but to embrace similarities in values and in humanity.

These ads collectively seek to prove that Muslims live prosperous lives, are not marginalized, and are included as part of the core of U.S. society—in leading government positions (e.g., director of the National Institutes of Health), as paramedics, students, teachers, and business owners with predominantly non-Muslim clients (who want to eat Arabic food, or consume Arab culture). Muslims in the United States raise their children speaking Arabic and as Muslims, and are involved in the Islamic school. These ads draw on discourses of the United States as a land of opportunity, freedom, equality, and diversity as truth claims. The message of these advertisements is that people of all religions get along in the United States and Islam is respected; Muslims can be themselves there without barriers. The campaign seeks to remake "America" into a nation that is not against Islam, despite waging war against Arabs and Muslims at home and abroad. The intended audience is Muslims in the Middle East and Southeast Asia, who presumably assume that Muslims face discrimination and hate in the United States. Unlike the CAIR ads that seek to demonstrate that Islam shares values with America, these ads from the Shared Values Initiative seek to prove that American values do not conflict with Muslim values. With a different target audience from the CAIR ads, Muslims abroad as opposed to non-Muslims in the United States, these ads assert that American values, defined as freedom, equality, and respect for diversity, provide Muslims with opportunities for a prosperous life in the United States; they are values that not only benefit Muslims, but also values from which they can learn.

The U.S. Shared Values campaign emphasizes that Muslims are recent immigrants and are treated fairly in a country in which they are foreigners, while the CAIR ads emphasize that Muslims are not recent immigrants and therefore are part of the American nation. The messages are similar in some ways, but the differences in target audiences mean that the messages negate each other. If Muslims were truly part of the U.S. national community in the way that the government claims in their Shared Values campaign, then there would have been no need for CAIR to produce their "I am an American Muslim" ads, with their message to fellow Americans that Muslims are Americans too. This is not to say that some Muslims do not live prosperous lives free of harassment in the United States, but rather that not all Muslims do. Mosques have been attacked and burned, and these attacks are not restricted to the months after 9/11, but continue today.[49]

Many critics responded to the U.S. government's public relations campaign with questions as to how it could believe that a media campaign would solve problems rooted in foreign policy: if the government wants to change opinions about the United States in Muslim countries, then the way to do so would be through changing foreign policies. The fact that the media is being used to address or cover a policy problem garners greater suspicion and animosity toward the United States for presuming an ignorant audience. As one journalist wrote,

> Middle Eastern papers were nearly unanimous in arguing that American support of Israel and its occupation of Iraq are the issues that fuel anti-American sentiment—and Al Hurra can do little to disguise this. The Jordan *Times* put it in terms even an American could understand: "No amount of sweet words and pretty pictures will change the reality of an Israeli occupation, soon in its 37th year, or the chaos in Iraq, both of which can be directly attributed to American policy. No one here is going to be convinced of America's benign intentions as long as these issues remain unresolved. It all seems so obvious, at least to most of the people of this region, that, to borrow the phrase of an American cultural icon, "doh!"[50]

The U.S. message of freedom was met with suspicion and seen as propaganda by many. "Freedom," as Kennedy and Lucas assert, became a signifier of American imperialism—"the empire for liberty" (325).

Even the Advisory Group on Public Diplomacy for the Arab and Muslim World concedes that the problem is actually rooted in U.S. foreign policy:

> We fully acknowledge that public diplomacy is only part of the picture. Surveys indicate that much of the resentment toward America stems from real conflicts and displeasure with policies, including those involving the Palestinian-Israeli conflict and Iraq. But our mandate is clearly limited to issues of public diplomacy, where we believe a significant new effort is required.[51]

Nonetheless, policy resolutions have yet to be issued. Instead, initiatives have been passed to secure military, economic, and ideological hegemony. As the U.S. government uses elements of popular culture (advertising, pop music, etc.) to sell ideology or brand national identity like a commodity, such an approach raises questions about the use of popular culture to cover policy issues and influence public opinion abroad. It also raises important issues about the reception of such initiatives, especially since this particular campaign was not as successful as anticipated, as reflected in the resignation of Charlotte Beers in 2005, the suspended production of *Hi Magazine*, and the removal of the Shared Values campaign from the internet.[52] Viewers in the Middle East and elsewhere had made clear that they were not likely to confuse the rhetoric of U.S. respect for Islam with the realities of U.S. foreign policy.

It is not unusual for the rhetoric of diversity to be mobilized during times in which the United States is least multicultural, or rather most discriminatory, in order to cover actual racist policies and practices. The "War on Terror," because it is so explicitly anti-Arab and anti-Muslim, with its attacks on Arabs, Muslims, and those mistaken for Arab/Muslim "at home" and abroad, requires the rhetorical production of diversity. Some civil rights groups and nonprofit organizations were responding to material realities (i.e., hate crimes) through ideological products with the intention of altering the material reality through "selling" the ideology of diversity and producing racial harmony in the public. The U.S. government, by contrast, "sells" the ideology of diversity to conceal the blatant discriminatory practices it enacts daily. All of these efforts seek to brand national identity and sell an ideological product. The impact of the message, however, depends on circulation and the relationship between the viewer/consumer and the message.

Circulation is bound up in questions of access to resources and access to mainstream media outlets. While the Ad Council broadcasted its PSA repeatedly for months after 9/11 and for weeks after the first and second anniversary of 9/11 on network television, CAIR, facing financial constraints, had each of its PSAs printed in the *New York Times* once, totaling six times. CAIR's television PSA made it onto the FOX network once, only when the TV drama *24* depicted Arab terrorists seeking to destroy the United States, and CAIR lobbied for fair representation. The producers of Fox and *24* agreed to air the PSA at some point during the same day as the program (not during the duration of the program). The chance of the American public viewing CAIR's PSA is minute compared to the probability of people viewing the Ad Council's PSA on numerous occasions. The Ad Council's message of ambiguous multiethnic American national identity was circulated and consumed by the U.S. public exponentially more often than CAIR's campaign was. It is likely that hundreds of millions of U.S. viewers saw the Ad Council's "I am an American" PSA repeatedly after 9/11, as it was broadcast for months on mainstream channels and during prime-time programming after 9/11. In contrast, CAIR estimates that 1 million people might have seen its ads in the *New York Times* and that approximately 6 million have seen their other campaigns on CAIR's Web site or in local newspapers, demonstrating how limited resources also leads to limited circulation.

While economic strength and access to mainstream media institutions guarantee a more visible and frequent circulation of a particular message, they do not guarantee the interpellation of that message by viewers/consumers.[53] As Stuart Hall has written, "ideas only become effective if they do, in the end, *connect* with a particular constellation of social forces."[54] The failure of the U.S. government's public diplomacy campaign, despite hundreds of millions of dollars spent and access to global media outlets, demonstrates that even if a particular message reaches millions, interpellation is not guaranteed. However, if the message is not widely circulated, it is difficult to evaluate its potential effectiveness (e.g., CAIR). The Ad Council's PSA was presumably effective, as it reached millions of viewers. While it did not stop hate crimes against Arabs, Muslims, and South Asians, and while some viewers likely rolled their eyes at the hypocrisy of the message, it did potentially contribute to a diverse imagined American community.

These PSAs do not necessarily respond to views held by the majority of the U.S. public (polls indicated that approximately half of people in the United States perceive Arabs and Muslims as violent and dangerous, indicating that the rest presumably do not), but rather, they react to and make visible the discourses that hold ideological hegemony. CAIR challenges the notion that Muslims are violent and have values incompatible with U.S. values. The Ad Council challenges the notion that only whites are American. The Shared Values initiative challenges the notion that the United States is at war with Islam. Ultimately, these campaigns reveal that ideological meanings, particularly around American national identity, are not fixed and are constantly being reworked. However, from the perspective of post-9/11 ideological formations, the terms within which Muslim American citizenship can be articulated are restricted to discourses on the "War on Terror," in which Muslims are positioned as a threat to the U.S. nation. Thus while CAIR responds that Muslims are not a threat to the nation, the Ad Council leaves this question ambiguous by excluding Muslim and Sikh religious symbols from its PSA. In contrast, the U.S. government's message to Muslims abroad is that Muslims are safe in the United States and that the country is not a threat to Muslims worldwide. Despite these various ideological campaigns, U.S. Muslims after 9/11 must prove their loyalty to the nation for a chance at being imagined as part of the diverse national community.

Notes

I thank members of the *AQ* board for their helpful comments on an earlier version of this article. Special thanks to Melani McAlister for her in-depth feedback on several earlier drafts and for her encouragement and engagement with my work.

1. For example, see the *New York Times*, September 21–24, 2001, specifically September 22, 2001, A26, and September 23, 2001, A47.
2. Life insurance and pharmaceutical companies had a field day advertising in the face of tragedy. LIFE (an insurance company) advertised: "Life Insurance Isn't For the People Who Die, It's For the People Who Live," capitalizing on the loss of human life and resulting financial burden faced by many families. Meanwhile, Pfizer, a pharmaceutical company, advertised: "At Pfizer we discover and develop medicines. We wish we could make a medicine that would take away the heartache." For example, see *Newsweek*, October 8, 2001.
3. For more on post-9/11 patriotism, see Ella Shohat and Robert Stam, *Flagging Patriotism: Crises of Narcissism and Anti-Americanism* (New York: Routledge, 2007).
4. My use of the term *imagined community* comes from Benedict Anderson, *Imagined Communities: Reflections on the Origin and Spread of Nationalism* (New York: Verso, 1991).
5. For reports on the government's practice of detaining and deporting Arabs and Muslims after 9/11, see, for example, "ADC Fact Sheet: The Condition of Arab Americans Post-9/11," March 27, 2002, *http://www.adc.org/index.php?id=282* (accessed March 7, 2007); "Equal Employment Opportunity Commission (EEOC) Fact Sheet," January 13, 2003, *http://www.adc.org/index.php?id=1682* (accessed March 7, 2007); and "America's Disappeared: Seeking International Justice for Immigrants Detained after September 11," January, 26, 2004, *http://www.aclu.org/FilesPDFs/un%20report.pdf* (accessed March 7, 2007). For the impact of 9/11 on Arab and Muslim communities, see Nadine Naber, "The Rules of Forced Engagement: Race, Gender, and the Culture of Fear among Arab Immigrants in San Francisco Post-9/11," *Cultural Dynamics* 18.3 (2006): 235–67.
6. Edward W. Said, *Orientalism* (New York: Vintage Books, 1979).
7. "Remarks by the President Upon Arrival, the South Lawn" Office of the Press Secretary, September 16, 2001, *http://www.whitehouse.gov/news/releases/2001/09/20010916-2.html* (accessed May 14, 2007).
8. "Address to a Joint Session of Congress and the American People," Washington, D.C., Office of the Press Secretary, September 20, 2001, *http://www.whitehouse.gov/news/releases/2001/09/20010920-8.html* (accessed May 14, 2007).
9. For example, see Human Rights Watch, "'We Are Not the Enemy': Hate Crimes Against Arabs, Muslims, and Those Perceived to Be Arab or Muslim, after September 11," vol. 14, no. 6 (G), November 2002, http://www.hrw.org/reports/2002/usahate/index.htm#TopOfPage (accessed March 7, 2007); The Sikh Coalition, "One Year After Brutal Attack, Sikh Hate Crime Victim Files Civil Suit Against Attackers," July 12, 2005, http://www.sikhcoalition.org/ca_rhill.asp (accessed, March 7, 2007); and Jim Forman, "Store Owner Fights Back After Attack," KING5 News, Seattle, Washington, February 22, 2007, http://www.king5.com/topstories/stories/NW_022107WABclerkattackKC.22f8ce0b.html (accessed March 7, 2007).
10. Leti Volpp, "The Citizen and the Terrorist," in *September 11 in History: A Watershed Moment?* ed. Mary L. Dudziak (Durham, N.C.: Duke University Press, 2003), 147–62.
11. The Media and Society Group, "MSRG Special Report: Restrictions on Civil Liberties, Views of Islam, and Muslim Americans," and "MSRG Special Report: U.S. War on Terror, U.S. Foreign Policy, and Anti-Americanism," Cornell University, Ithaca, N.Y., December 2004, *http://www.comm.cornell.edu/msrg/report1a.pdf* and *http://www.comm.cornell.edu/msrg/report1b.pdf* (both accessed March 7, 2007).
12. For a discussion of the increased racialization of Arab Americans post-9/11, see Nadine Naber and Amaney Jamal, eds. *Arab American Identities Before and After September 11th: From Invisible Citizens to Visible Subjects* (Syracuse, N.Y.: Syracuse University Press, 2007).
13. My use of the term *cultural citizenship* comes from Renato Rosaldo, "Cultural Citizenship, Inequality, and Multiculturalism," in Race, Identity, and Citizenship, ed. Rodolfo D. Torres, Louis F. Mirón, and Jonathan Xavier Inda (Oxford: Blackwell, 1999): 253–61. For more on the media's role in shaping multiculturalism, see Ella Shohat and Robert Stam, *Unthinking Eurocentrism: Multiculturalism and the Media* (New York: Routledge, 1994).
14. The "I am an American" public service announcement can be viewed at the Ad Council's Web site. See *http://www.adcouncil.org/default.aspx?id=141* (accessed March 7, 2007).

15. "I am an American" (2001–present), the Ad Council, *http://adcouncil.org/default.aspx?id=141* (accessed May 14, 2007).

16. Michael Omi and Howard Winant, *Racial Formation in the United States: From the 1960s to the 1990s* (New York: Routledge, 1994), 66.

17. Melani McAlister, *Epic Encounters: Culture, Media, and U.S. Interests in the Middle East, 1945–2000* (Berkeley: University of California Press, 2001): 270.

18. Wahneema Lubiano, "Talking about the State and Imagining Alliances," *Talking Visions: Multicultural Feminism in a Transnational Age*, ed. Ella Shohat (New York and Cambridge: The New Museum/MIT Press, 1998), 441–50.

19. McAlister, *Epic Encounters*, 259.

20. For more on representation of the Gulf War, see Ella Shohat, "The Media's War," *Social Text* 28 (Spring 1991): 135–41.

21. The Council on American-Islamic Relations (CAIR), *www.cair-net.org* (accessed March 7, 2007).

22. Neil MacFarquhar and David Johnston, "Scrutiny Increases for a Group Advocating for Muslims in U.S.," *New York Times*, March 14, 2007, A1.

23. CAIR planned to produce fifty-two print PSAs as part of their "Islam in America" campaign, but ended up producing only six for financial reasons.

24. The ads can be viewed at *http://www.americanmuslims.info/archive.asp* (accessed March 7, 2007).

25. See the Girl Scouts' Web page at *http://www.girlscouts.org/who_we_are/facts/* (accessed March 7, 2007).

26. Found at *http://www.americanmuslims.info/archive.asp* (accessed March 7, 2007).

27. See poll results at *http://www.cnn.com/ELECTION/2004/pages/results/states/US/P/00/epolls.0.html* (accessed March 7, 2007).

28. See CAIR print ads at *http://www.americanmuslims.info/archive.asp* (accessed March 7, 2007).

29. Akhil Gupta and James Ferguson, "Culture, Power, Place: Ethnography at the End of an Era," in *Culture, Power, Place: Explorations in Critical Anthropology*, ed. Akhil Gupta and James Ferguson (Durham, N.C.: Duke University Press, 1997), 18–19.

30. Mahmood Mamdani, *Good Muslim, Bad Muslim: America, the Cold War and the Roots of Terror* (New York: Pantheon, 2004).

31. Eugene McLaughlin, "Rebranding Britain: The Life and Times of 'Cool Britannia,'" *BBC and the Open University*, *http://www.open2.net/newbrit/pages/features/features_mclaughlin.htm* (accessed March 7, 2007).

32. Ibid.

33. Ibid.

34. Mark Leonard, "Cool Britannia," *The New Statesman*, *http://markleonard.net/journalism/coolbritannia/* (accessed March 7, 2007).

35. Liam Kennedy and Scott Lucas, "Enduring Freedom: Public Diplomacy and U.S. Foreign Policy," *American Quarterly* 57.2 (June 2005): 309–33. For more on U.S. public diplomacy, see Penny M. Von Eschen, "Enduring Public Diplomacy," and Ron Robin, "Requiem for Public Diplomacy?" *American Quarterly* 57.2 (June 2005): 335–43 and 345–53, respectively. Also see Penny Von Eschen, *Satchmo Blows Up the World: Jazz Ambassadors Play the Cold War* (Cambridge, Mass.: Harvard University Press, 2004).

36. James Dao and Eric Schmitt, "A Nation Challenged: Hearts and Minds; Pentagon Readies Efforts to Sway Sentiments Abroad," *New York Times*, February 19, 2002, A1, 6. Also see CNN, "Pentagon Closes Down Controversial Office," February 26, 2002, *http://archives.cnn.com/2002/US/02/26/defense.office* (accessed March 7, 2007).

37. Office of the Press Secretary, "Executive Order: Establishing the Office of Global Communications," January 21, 2003, *http://www.whitehouse.gov/news/releases/2003/01/20030121-3.html* (accessed March 7, 2007).

38. Report of the Advisory Group on Public Diplomacy for the Arab and Muslim World, "Changing Minds, Winning Peace: A New Strategic Direction for U.S. Public Diplomacy in the Arab and Muslim World," Edward P. Djerejian (chairman), submitted to the Committee on Appropriations, U.S. House of Representatives, October 1, 2003, http://bakerinstitute.org/Pubs/Miscellaneous/Peace.pdf (accessed March 7, 2007).

39. Andrew Buncombe, "Bush Launches Magazine to Teach Young Arabs to Love America," *Independent News and Media* (UK), July 18, 2003, *http://news.independent.co.uk/world/americas/article96619.ece* (accessed March 7, 2007).

40. Louis Althusser, "Ideology and Ideological State Apparatuses," *Lenin and Philosophy, and Other Essays* (New York: Monthly Review Press, 2001).

41. Advisory Group, "Changing Minds," 13.

42. Kennedy and Lucas, "Enduring Freedom," 315.

43. See *http://www.radiosawa.com/* (accessed March 7, 2007).

44. See *http://www.alhurra.com/* (accessed March 7, 2007).

45. Found at *http://www.himag.com/* (Web site no longer available).

46. President George W. Bush, "State of the Union, 2004," January 20, 2004, *http://www.whitehouse. gov/news/releases/2004/01/20040120-7.html* (accessed March 7, 2007).

47. Found at http://*www.opendialogue.com* (Web site no longer available).

48. Advisory Group, "Changing Minds," 72.

49. See, for example, "FBI Investigating Mich. Mosque Attacks," *USA Today*, February 16, 2006, *http:// www.usatoday.com/news/nation/2006-02-16-michigan-mosque_x.htm* (accessed March 7, 2007), and "Frederick Mosque Possible Target of Hate Crime: Windows Broken at Building 3 Times," *NBC4. com*, Maryland, February 28, 2007, http://www.nbc4.com/news/11138569/detail.html (accessed March 7, 2007).

50. Ed Finn, "Unhip, Unhip Al Hurra: The Middle East Hates Its New TV station," *Slate.com*, February 20, 2004, *http://slate.msn.com/id/2095806* (accessed March 7, 2007).

51. Advisory Group, "Changing Minds," 9.

52. The site http://*www.opendialogue.com* (which is no longer available) included a section for visitors to post comments.

53. My use of interpellation is based on Louis Althusser, "Ideology and Ideological State Apparatuses," in *Lenin and Philosophy and Other Essays* (New York: Monthly Review Press, 2001), 85–126.

54. Stuart Hall, "The Problem of Ideology: Marxism without Guarantees," *Journal of Communication Inquiry* 10 (1986): 28–44, quote on 42.

"The ERA Is a Moral Issue": The Mormon Church, LDS Women, and the Defeat of the Equal Rights Amendment

Neil J. Young

For two days in June 1977, fourteen thousand women packed Salt Lake City's convention center for Utah's International Women's Year conference. Across the country, each state convened an IWY conference to discuss various issues affecting women, most notably the equal rights amendment. Utah's IWY conference ranked as the nation's largest state conference, by far eclipsing the second biggest, of six thousand participants in California, a state twenty times more populous than Utah. In Utah, the organizational skills of the Church of Jesus Christ of Latter-day Saints ensured the conference's record crowds. The Mormon Church wanted to counteract the perceived liberal slant of participants in other state conferences by flooding the Utah meetings with faithful church members.

From the church's highest leadership ranks, word went out that every church ward was to recruit at least ten women to attend the Utah IWY conference. A church memorandum directed ward bishops and Relief Society presidents to tell selected women they had been "called" to attend and that they should defeat every conference proposal. When more than thirteen thousand Mormon women arrived at the Salt Palace, they overwhelmed conference organizers, who had expected two thousand attendees. These thirteen thousand women steered the conference in keeping with church directives by harassing various speakers, voting on platforms before discussion and soundly defeating every proposal. The Utah IWY conference had been a masterful performance on behalf of the Mormon Church in repudiating liberal agendas of the 1970s, particularly the equal rights amendment.[1]

The historiography of the Equal Rights Amendment has largely ignored the Mormon Church's role in the political battle. Jane J. Mansbridge's study *Why We Lost the ERA* references the church in just one sentence when she locates anti-ERA opposition in "the fundamentalist South . . . and in the Mormon states of Utah and Nevada, where the Mormon church actively fought the ERA." Mary Frances Berry notes the church president's official opposition to the amendment, but fails to examine any organized role the church played in the ERA's defeat.[2] Mormon-centered studies, however, have offered notable supplements to the ERA's historiography. These works have attributed the church's part in preventing the amendment's ratification to its hierarchal nature and Mormons' solid deference to that hierarchy.[3] As one work's representative argument puts it, Mormons defeated the ERA "by *merely* flexing their considerable organizational muscle."[4]

While this essay acknowledges that the church's organizational structure provided the means by which LDS members could act in opposition to the proposed constitutional amendment, it finds the structure-based argument particularly lacking in its capacity to answer adequately *why* members of the church would believe they must act in keeping with the church's counsel regarding a political matter. To say that the Mormon Church is a hierarchical institution fails to provide sufficiently for why members followed its pronouncements regarding the ERA. For Mormons, particularly the women who constituted the bulk of Mormon grassroots anti-ERA efforts, opposing the ERA allowed them to demonstrate to each other their right standing with the church through their obedience to its directives, both religious and political, and to signal to themselves and to others their "exalted" destiny in the afterlife.

Across the nation, Mormon women stepped forward to carry out their church's fight against the equal rights amendment. Most remembered having never heard of the ERA until learning about it at church. Ruth Peterson Knight was raising three small children in Virginia when she received an anti-ERA pamphlet in church one Sunday. She quickly decided that if the church was against the ERA, she would oppose it too, and became active in a letter-writing campaign that deluged the Virginia legislature with thousands of anti-ERA epistles.[5] Others, such as Arda Harman in Las Vegas and Eleanor Ricks Colton in Washington, D.C., learned of the ERA for the first time when the church called them to fight against the amendment. At first overwhelmed by the prospect of waging a political battle they did not know was raging across the country until their church told them of it, these women threw themselves into the task of becoming experts on why the Mormon Church opposed the ERA and of working to ensure the amendment's defeat. "I pledged that I would do everything I could to understand the reasons for the Church's opposition to the ERA," Eleanor Colton remembered, "and try to explain them through my own firm testimony of the gospel of Jesus Christ."[6] The Mormon

Church activated thousands of women like these across the country, almost all political neophytes, and asked them to step to the frontline of their fight against the ERA.

Sociologist Rebecca Klatch has argued that the unique characteristic of the New Right, the network of people and organizations that began to coalesce in the 1970s, was the "visible presence of women" in this conservative movement.[7] The thousands of Mormon women who worked to defeat the ERA were a critical component of the New Right's ascendancy. But aside from assisting the conservative resurgence building in the 1970s, these women had personal motivations for battling against the ERA's ratification. In fighting against women's rights in the 1970s, Mormon women outwardly revealed to each other their internal acceptance of the church's teachings about proper gender roles, male-female relations, and the submission of women. Like Puritans eager to show each other that they belonged in the community of the elect, Mormon women battled the ERA to prove to their church, their co-religionists, and themselves that they embodied Mormonism's most fundamental beliefs. As Mormon theology heightened its emphasis on women's subordinate status and domestic place, the ERA fight provided women with an opportunity to resist some of those limitations by becoming public political actors for the church. In a decade marked by increasing conservatism within theological Mormonism regarding the role of women and by a decreasing prominence for women within institutional Mormonism itself, Mormon women asserted themselves by utilizing the network of their weakened Relief Society organization to carry the weight of the Mormon Church's biggest political effort ever.[8] I argue that the Mormon Church helped defeat the equal rights amendment because Mormon women seized the opportunity of a political engagement to serve their church, to secure their eternal fate, and to expand their own power within Mormonism by working to defeat the movement for equality for all women in the United States.

This essay also maintains that the history of religion and the history of U.S. politics need to be examined together. To observe merely that evangelicals or Catholics or Mormons have voted for a particular candidate or issue barely scratches the surface of historical analysis. Blending U.S. religious and political history allows us to better see the motivations, the machinations, and the mass mobilizations that compel people of particular religious faiths to support certain political objectives. Historians necessarily treat religious faith not as an unchanging, eternal truth, as the devout do, but as a historical object, ripe for analysis. In examining shifts and changes in the theological emphases of a particular faith at a certain historical moment, we can begin to understand how religious teachings are often tied to current conditions. Also, through comparing the political actions of a religious body to the contemporaneous doctrinal teachings of that group, we can begin to understand better how religiously devout citizens understand their political action as an outgrowth of their deepest spiritual convictions. More important, we can see how religious institutions utilize certain teachings and beliefs to bring about a desired political objective.

The Proposed Amendment

Both houses of Congress passed the equal rights amendment, which proposed equality of rights under the law regardless of sex, in the spring of 1972. By December 1974, thirty-three states had passed the amendment, just five less than the number required for ratification.[9] Pro-ERA supporters sensed imminent victory, and five years remained to secure the ERA's ratification. Yet the momentum quickly abated. When the ratification period ended, the ERA fell just three states shy of becoming a constitutional amendment.

Initially, the Mormon Church issued no statement regarding the equal rights amendment. Meanwhile, Mormon legislators, both in Congress and in the legislatures of Hawai'i, Idaho, Colorado, and California helped ratify the ERA in their states.[10] During the summer of 1972, a majority of candidates to the Utah legislature, regardless of party affiliation, expressed support for the amendment in a survey conducted by the *Deseret News*, the church's daily newspaper.[11] Two years later, the *Deseret News* surveyed church members in Utah and found that 63.1 percent of them favored ratification.[12] As the state legislature's 1975 session opened, thirty-four of the seventy-five members, 70 percent of whom where church members, indicated their intent to vote for the amendment.[13] With just a few more votes, Utah could be the thirty-fifth state to ratify the amendment. Yet only a month later, the Utah legislature, with solid public approval, voted the amendment down fifty-four to twenty-one on February 18, 1975.[14] What had happened in such a short time to overturn the supportive numbers for the ERA in Utah's general population and its state legislature? The Mormon Church had at last entered the fray and issued its position against the amendment. As the *Herald Journal* of Logan, Utah, foretold: "Church Stand Apparently Dooms ERA Amendment."[15]

The day before the Utah legislature's opening session in 1975, the Mormon Church killed the ERA's chances in Utah by publishing an anti-amendment editorial in the "Church News" section of its *Deseret News.* Citing "the fact that men and women are different, made so by a Divine Creator," the editorial characterized the ERA as "not only imperfect but dangerous" and "so broad that it is inadequate, inflexible and vague" and that it "would work to the disadvantage of both men and women."[16] For Mormons, editorials in the *Deseret News*'s "Church News" section are more than journalistic opinion. Reading the anti-ERA editorial in 1975, church members would have believed that the First Presidency (the Church's ruling trinity of the president and his two counselors) had issued a divinely authorized prophetic proclamation. (A church officer officially confirmed what Mormons already generally believed when he went on record as saying in 1979 that "Church News" editorials "represent the viewpoint of the First Presidency of the church.")[17] With one editorial, the Mormon Church ensured the ERA's defeat in the Utah legislature, but preventing the amendment's ratification elsewhere would take more work.

"We Have a Living Prophet"

Why did the Mormon Church wait nearly three years to enter the political battle over the equal rights amendment? In the initial exuberance of multistate ratification, anti-ERA forces, particularly Phyllis Schlafly's STOP ERA organization, made a delayed, but eventually successful, entry into the fray.[18] The historian D. Michael Quinn attributes the church's belated anti-ERA stand not to national political trends but to changes in the church's leadership. Quinn argues that Harold B. Lee, church president when Congress passed the ERA, believed that the burgeoning women's movement presented the greatest test to the church's authority, but he wanted the church to remain out of the ERA debate because he feared confronting an issue he felt some Mormon women supported. A more committed conservative than some of his predecessors, Spencer W. Kimball, Lee's successor upon his death in December 1973, shared no such fear and moved the church into its critical position among the chief players in the anti-ERA coalition.[19] But even if President Lee had been unwilling to mount an official challenge to the ERA, critical church pronouncements about the president as "Prophet" during his administration and that of his predecessor, Joseph Fielding Smith, provided a firm foundation upon which President Kimball could launch a successful campaign against the ERA.

Mormons have not always seen their president as a prophet. Before 1955, D. Michael Quinn notes that every mention of the church's leader in *Deseret News* articles referred to him as "President." The honorific "Prophet" was reserved only for Joseph Smith, the church's founder, and prophets from the Bible and the *Book of Mormon*. Yet during David O. McKay's popular presidency from 1951 to 1970, church publications began occasionally referring to him as "Prophet." By the late 1960s, "President" had become interchangeable, if not synonymous, with "Prophet," thanks to routine references to the latter in church publications and at General Conferences, the semiannual church convention held each April and October.[20]

Emphasis on the prophet and prophecy proliferated in the early 1970s. In three years, three different men—Harold Lee, Joseph Fielding Smith, and Spencer Kimball—assumed the church's presidency.[21] A *Deseret News* editorial commented: "In many organizations such rapid turnover at the top could readily bring on confusing shifts of direction and with them a feeling of hesitancy and uncertainty. By contrast, the feeling within the church during this historic period has been one of stability and clear purpose, of constancy amidst change."[22] More than that, the successive deaths allowed the church to strengthen the image of church presidents as prophets through General Conference talks in which speakers praised the prophecy of the deceased president and heralded the ascending president's divine prophetic authority.[23] By Kimball's presidency, it was as likely that he be referred to as "Prophet" as that he be spoken of as "President."

The political consequences of such a transformation cannot be overstated. By strengthening the president's role as God's mouthpiece on earth, rather than simply the administrative head of His church, the church's leadership strengthened its influence over all matters, including political issues, in the lives of Mormons. In earlier years, various church presidents had tried unsuccessfully to use their position to achieve political ends. Most notably, from 1932 to 1944, almost 70 percent of Mormons backed Roosevelt and the New Deal, despite President Heber J. Grant's repeated denunciations of FDR and the frequent anti-Roosevelt *Deseret News* editorials.[24] Lacking prophetic status, church presidents saw Mormons regard their political statements as ignorable opinions rather than divine proclamations that had to be obeyed.

By the 1970s, however, the transformation of the Mormon Church president into prophet was complete. During the Reagan era, Mormons fell in line with church proclamations on issues including abortion, gay rights, Sunday closing laws, and gambling.[25] This political authority was secured first in the equal rights amendment battle as church leaders tested their ability to mobilize members toward a political objective.

But why did the church decide to use the equal rights amendment as a testing ground for a national political presence? Perhaps the church's leadership felt that the amendment ratification process lent itself to the type of participation the church could most successfully produce. With just 2.7 million U.S. members by 1980, the Mormon Church could have little influence in a presidential election. But the localized process of ratification carried out in fifty state legislatures meant the that the church was able to focus on states where it could be most effective: in Utah, where Mormons controlled the legislature; in Nevada and Idaho, with significant Mormon populations in both the citizenry and legislature; and even in Virginia, where a small, but politically active Mormon population could disproportionately affect the legislative process. Since 1.3 million, or nearly half, of the church's U.S. membership resided in Utah, Nevada, and Idaho, the church could offer itself to the anti-ERA movement as the best source for preventing ratification in the intermountain West. Also, though only twenty-six thousand Mormons lived in Virginia, the fact that half were concentrated in the politically active D.C. suburb counties of Arlington and Fairfax likely led the church to believe it could guarantee the ERA's defeat there.[26] Anti-ERA success, and indeed the success of much of New Right politics, depended upon the effective strategies of coalition politics. In its foray into New Right politics, the Mormon Church could use the ERA battle to show its political allies the significant contribution it could make to a national conservative coalition.

But for more than just procedural reasons, the ERA battle appealed to Mormon leaders because of the issue itself. Indeed, the church continually justified involvement in the amendment battle by arguing that the "ERA is a moral issue."[27] A bid for a constitutionally protected equality of the sexes struck at the very core of Mormonism's deepest beliefs about the gender-specific roles for men and women in life. Because the question of the amendment concerned key Mormon beliefs about life's most fundamental aspects in a way that other political issues, such as taxation and national defense, did not, the church's hierarchy understood that this political battle would resonate with its membership like no other political issue could. And by first using a perceived "moral issue" to broach the subject of active political participation, the church could later expand its influence to include a variety of political issues. The Mormon Church entered the fight over the equal rights amendment because it recognized the particular way its institutional structure could influence the ratification process, but also because the substance of the amendment challenged the church's most important teachings about the proper role of women.

"The Lord's Plan": Salvation and the Place of Women

Women have had an unusual history in the Mormon Church. In some ways, the course of their social status flows counter to that of most women in the United States. In Mormonism's early days, women shared with men in highly public roles. After Utah's settlement in 1847, Mormon women enjoyed rights far earlier than other U.S. women: the rights to own property, to conduct business, and to file for divorce because of incompatibility. In 1870, Utah became the first state to enfranchise women, although the Wyoming territory already had done so. A Mormon became the first woman in the nation elected to a state senate spot, defeating her own husband in 1896.[28]

Life's difficulties in Utah's early days meant that all residents had to contribute their abilities to the public community. Yet the economic and political stability of the church in the twentieth century spelled the end of Mormon women's public prominence. Beginning in the 1920s, church women watched their autonomy and standing erode as General Authorities emphasized Victorian notions of domesticity while minimizing the legacy of female autonomy. By the 1970s, Mormon women regularly heard and read the instruction to, as the title of one *Ensign* article stated, "Maintain Your Place As a Woman." In doing this, Mormon women were to reject the worldly lures of career, self-fulfillment, and independence in favor of the "eternal" womanly responsibilities of marriage, motherhood, and submissiveness. Most pointedly, church teachings in the 1970s continuously warned Mormon women to spurn the popular calls to liberation that feminism and its projects, such as the ERA, advocated. Liberation was a guise, Mormon leaders contended, that promised fulfillment but would destroy the timeless and divinely created distinctions between man and woman that ordered life.[29]

As the church increased its emphasis on motherly obligation and female subordination, it also restructured itself to reflect the male-female hierarchy it championed. In 1970, the church's First Presidency revoked the independent financial status of the Relief Society, the auxiliary organization to which all Mormon women belong. No longer an autonomous unit, the Relief Society and its leadership would henceforth be monitored and guided by a completely male leadership that was simultaneously increasing its institutional power while also directing the church in a national battle against the expansion of women's rights. Relief Society president Barbara B. Smith would later liken the church's new organizational setup to the proper relationship between husband and wife. "The priesthood presides," she explained in an interview in *Ensign*. "This isn't my plan. It's the Lord's plan, and leaders who apply it and husbands and wives who abide by it know not only that it works, but also that it gives each party his or her greatest joy."[30]

The church's new organizational structure not only resembled the ideal Mormon marriage, but also mimicked the unique Mormon notion of salvation. It should first be noted that Mormons do not worry about salvation so much as they do about exaltation. In Mormon doctrine, unlike most Christian theology, the realm of hell is small, containing only the world's most evil people. Unlike mainstream Christianity, which splits eternity into just heaven and hell, Mormon theology minimizes hell and expands heaven into tiers. Mormons believe, then, that all humans will live in glory. The question for Mormons is which realm of glory they will deserve based on their life on earth. The highest realm of heaven is the celestial kingdom, where families dwell together forever and continue to procreate, expanding their own universe infinitely. The next two tiers, the terrestrial and telestial kingdoms, have decreasing degrees of glory. In effect, Mormons do not so much seek salvation, that is, pardon from damnation, for they essentially have assurance of that. Rather, Mormons strive for exaltation in the celestial kingdom, the highest of the heavenly realms, with the greatest glories and closest proximity to God.

Exaltation, however, cannot be reached alone. While individuals can earn salvation, only temple-married couples will be exalted in the celestial kingdom. Marriages are not merely earthbound unions in Mormonism, but eternal pairings in which partners are "sealed" to each other in a temple ceremony. Thus, in Mormonism, exaltation cannot be received by grace, nor earned through individual works if one of those works is not entering into a sealed marriage. As the *Encyclopedia of Mormonism* explains, exaltation to the celestial kingdom "is available to . . . a man and wife."[31] Just as the Relief Society lost its organizational autonomy to the church's male authorities in 1970, Mormon women reach exaltation only by submitting themselves in marriage to a priesthood-holding Mormon man.[32] And unlike the equal rights amendment's bid to apply laws regardless of sex, Mormon theology places sexual difference and male-female interdependency at the heart of its conception of exaltation. Told that the ERA would eradicate the basic distinctions between the sexes and loosen men and women from the gender-based obligations of marriage, Mormon men and women opposed the ERA because it contradicted their most fundamental beliefs about the nature of both life and the afterlife.

They also opposed it in order to increase their exaltation within the celestial kingdom. Like the church's administrative structure and like the arrangement of its realms of the afterlife, the celestial kingdom too is tiered. Those at the very highest sphere of the celestial kingdom will live in more glory than those below them. Thus, in Mormonism, while there may be some assurance of an eternity in the celestial kingdom for a devout, married member, that same member believes that his or her family's eternal positioning might be further improved by additional earthly activity.[33] This ethos of perpetual striving for a greater heavenly reward played a role in influencing thousands of Mormons to engage in political activity to defeat the equal rights amendment, for they believed they were increasing their celestial exaltation and demonstrating their eternal destiny to each other.[34]

Landslide in the Salt Palace: Utah's IWY Conference

Originally, the Mormon Church made no plans to involve itself in Utah's International Women's Year conference, scheduled for June 24–25, 1977. The United Nations had proclaimed 1975 as the "International Women's Year." In response, President Ford created the National Commission for the Observance of IWY, which allocated money for fifty state conferences and a national conference to be held in Houston in November 1977. The commission formulated sixteen resolutions for each state to vote on, covering various issues including the equal rights amendment. Each state conference would also elect delegates for the national conference. Despite the diverse issues considered, most people perceived the state IWY conferences as a referendum on the equal rights amendment. And as each state held its IWY conference, the delegations enthusiastically voted in support of resolutions backing the proposed amendment. Because of this, church leaders in Utah initially thought it best to steer Mormon women away from the state's IWY conference, fearful that their participation might be interpreted as a support of feminism, in general, and the ERA, in particular.[35]

But plans changed when someone in the church's leadership realized that a carefully orchestrated mass influx of Mormon attendees at the conference could tip the scales against a pro-feminist, pro-ERA agenda. For five days in June 1977, Relief Society president Barbara B. Smith met with a four-person team to develop a strategy for turning the Utah IWY conference into a church-controlled affair.[36] The group assisting President Smith included Moana Ballif Bennett, a Relief Society board member and frequent speechwriter for Smith; Oscar McConkie Jr., a senior partner in the church's law firm; Wendel Ashton, the church's director of the Public Communications Department; and Georgia

Bodell Peterson, president of "Let's Govern Ourselves," a conservative, anti-ERA organization in Utah. These five, three of whom were women, crafted a plan for the IWY conference, and Ashton acted as a liaison between their group and the Special Affairs Committee, the church's policy-making board for social issues.[37] Certainly President Smith must have viewed this as a propitious opportunity to show church leadership that the Relief Society and its thousands of Mormon women, even if weakened by the 1970 reorganization, could play a major role in carrying forward the Mormon Church's emergence onto the national political scene.

Meanwhile, Ezra Taft Benson's office called all of the church's regional representatives in Utah, informing them of the IWY conference and of the church's plan that each ward send at least ten women to the conference.[38] After the phone call, Benson's office distributed a letter on Relief Society letterhead further elaborating the steps each ward should take to ensure high Mormon participation in the conference. "This is a follow-up on the phone call you received from President Ezra Taft Benson's office, and here is what should be done," the letter began. Stake Relief Society presidents were instructed to remind their women to read all *Deseret News* articles regarding the IWY convention and to make sure that "at least ten women and hopefully many more from each ward" attended the conference. "We hope Mormons everywhere will participate in the meetings and become part of the decision making process," the letter concluded.[39]

How each ward selected its ten designates varied. In some wards, the Relief Society president asked women to accompany her to the meetings. In other wards, the bishop (equivalent to a male pastor) "called" women to represent the ward at the conference. These different types of selection would have carried vastly different meaning for the women.

Aside from the very highest echelons of the church's leadership, the Mormon Church is an entirely lay ministry operation run by volunteers who retain their secular occupations. As part of a hierarchical organization, all men, from local ward bishop to regional representative, are "called" to their positions by the man directly above them. At the ward level, the bishop calls men and women from his congregation to fill the various positions, such as Relief Society president, primary teacher, organist, and door greeter. Mormons believe that a calling is a revealed, divine appointment, not a human-made decision. A ward bishop, for example, presents his selection for a calling to God and seeks confirmation of his choice through prayer. Thus, as the *Encyclopedia of Mormonism* explains, "when leaders select members to fulfill callings . . . members understand that callings have divine approval."[40] Given this divine sanction, few Mormons decline their calling, believing also that blessings, both on earth and in the afterlife, come to those who graciously accept their callings. In accepting and fulfilling their callings, Mormons add to their work toward exaltation in the celestial kingdom.[41]

So, when ward bishops in the summer of 1977 selected women from their wards to attend Utah's IWY conference, most women, whether specifically told so or not, believed that this was not a voluntary invitation, but a calling from God. Even in wards where Relief Society presidents *asked* the women to go to the IWY conference, as opposed to *called* them, since only male bishops can issue callings, the Relief Society presidents often did this by reading letters of instruction from the highest ranks of the church's leadership, thus apparently passing on a calling to these women from higher authorities.

It also appears, based on accounts, that the specificity of instructions given to these women regarding what to do at the IWY conference varied from ward to ward. Many Mormon women attended antifeminist, anti-ERA workshops organized by the Conservative Caucus of Utah, an organization led by Dennis R. Ker, a Mormon bishop. Though not an official church organization, the Conservative Caucus utilized the church's highly organized Relief Society network via its comprehensive telephone tree to spread the invitation to Mormon women to attend any of the caucus's fourteen workshops that would prepare them for participating in the state convention.[42] At these workshops, leaders instructed the women to vote no on all resolutions, no matter how good they might seem, because some of them "had been deceitfully written and baited with hidden hooks," as one woman remembered them being described.[43] While the Mormon Church had no official connections with the Conservative Caucus of Utah's workshops, it would have been hard for the average Mormon woman to know this. Made aware of the workshops through her Relief Society network, a Mormon woman likely would have thought she was attending the preconference workshop, surrounded by other women from her own ward no less, at the behest of the same church that had also called her to attend the state convention later that month. In this light, while the church could publicly claim to a skeptical national media that it had no role in directing its women in how to vote at the state convention, it could also rest assured that its women would perceive these meetings as church organized and directed and that the instructions given in the workshops were church approved and inspired.[44]

Of course, not every Mormon woman who attended the Utah IWY conference participated in the Conservative Caucus's workshops. Also, many Mormon women remember hearing no specific instructions from their leaders about what to do at the IWY conference. However, even without instruction, most of the women still understood what was expected of them. Dixie Snow Huefner, a Utah IWY conference participant, remembered that the calls made through the church's telephone tree relayed not so much a nonpartisan encouragement for women to participate in a community event, but rather an urgent warning that Mormon women were needed to offset the anticipated feminist nature of the conference and, as her Relief Society president told her, to reflect "church standards" at the meeting. Huefner's Relief Society president then sent her a copy of the conference preregistration form marked up to highlight the workshops that Mormon women ought to attend, including the session on the ERA. "It seems obvious that members did not need to be told explicitly how to vote," Huefner recalled. "Their attitudes about the conference had already been shaped."[45]

Of the nearly fourteen thousand women who packed the Salt Palace convention hall for the Utah IWY conference, thirteen thousand belonged to the Mormon Church. These women commandeered the convention's proceedings and defeated every proposed resolution, even one motion to curb pornography.[46] But the attendees had really come to the Salt Palace because of the equal rights amendment. When the votes were tallied, the resolution "The Equal Rights Amendment should be ratified," lost in a landslide: 8,956 votes to 666. The Salt Palace erupted in cheers upon hearing the resolution's lopsided defeat.[47]

Finally, the attendees selected Utah's fourteen delegates and five alternates for the national IWY conference in Houston later that year. Of the nineteen elected, eighteen were Mormon, five of whom were Relief Society leaders. All nineteen had expressed opposition to the ERA as their primary motivation for serving as a delegate to the national convention.[48] The Utah IWY conference concluded as a resounding rebuke to the national pro-ERA movement and as a testament to the Mormon Church's ability to activate its women through the Relief Society network to accomplish its political goals. Successful first in Utah, the Mormon Church repeated this strategy of utilizing the Relief Society network to flood the state IWY conferences with Mormon women in states as diverse as Hawai'i, Florida, New York, Mississippi, Washington, Alabama, Montana, and Kansas.[49] And Mormon women seized the opportunity to serve their church, accepting a political mission wrapped in a discourse of religious calling.

The Battle in Sin City: Stopping the ERA in Nevada

The Mormon Church identified Nevada as a state where it could prevent the ERA's ratification. Though constituting just 10 percent of the population, Mormons in Nevada, repeatedly instructed by the church that they should "pray to the Lord for guidance, and go to the polls and vote," often represented more than 30 percent of Nevadan voters in any given election.[50] From 1975 to 1978, Nevadan Mormons applied enough pressure on state legislators to make sure the state senate never passed the ERA.

Having watched the amendment be repeatedly defeated in the senate, ERA backers in Nevada hoped that a 1978 ballot referendum on the amendment might change its fate. Most candidates in the 1978 campaign demurred on voicing their position on the ERA, saying instead they would support the results of the referendum, so pro-ERA forces hoped that an apparent amendment-supporting majority of Nevadans could ensure at last the ERA's ratification in the state. Shortly before the election, a poll showed a slight majority of Nevadans intended to vote for the ERA's ratification. Inspired by this challenge, the Mormon Church's leadership in Nevada mounted a last-ditch effort against the amendment.[51]

The weekend before the election, Mormon leaders held a meeting for approximately two thousand Las Vegas–area Saints. Because more than 50 percent of Nevada's population lived in greater Las Vegas, church leaders targeted their anti-ERA campaign to the metropolitan area.[52] The two thousand Mormons gathered at the Saturday evening meeting witnessed a spirited presentation on how they could help defeat the ERA by enlisting as many members from their wards as they could for a full-out final assault. The next evening, Sunday, November 5, wards and stakes all over Las Vegas organized special assemblies so that all area Mormons could learn about what the church expected of them in the remaining days before the election.[53] Deb Turner's experience that evening was common. Her North Las Vegas stake held a meeting, which all married couples had been asked to attend. At the meeting, Turner listened in horror as church leaders described the new world that passage of the ERA would create, with women dragged to the frontlines in war and unisex bathrooms providing havens for rapists to attack women. "But wait! There was a way we could stop this," Turner recalled,

> They just happened to have a bunch of literature . . . and had broken the community up
> into geographical areas for us to canvas (which just coincidentally corresponded to the wards
> and stakes) and we could go door-to-door handing out literature and telling people why they

should vote against passage of the ERA. Only the women were to canvas the neighborhoods
. . . so people could see that women were opposed to the ERA. . . . They had already broken
down our ward into the streets and blocks they wanted each one of us to canvas. . . . I took
what had been assigned to me and did the street I was assigned.[54]

Throughout greater Las Vegas, nine thousand Mormon women like Turner
spread out over the city in similar fashion. The church later boasted that every
Mormon in Las Vegas was contacted and reminded to vote and that anti-ERA
pamphlets were placed on almost every doorstep in the metropolitan area. The
day of the election, 95 percent of all eligible Mormons in Nevada showed up to
vote. Having rallied its members and widely disseminated through its women
its anti-ERA message, the Mormon Church brought about a rousing two-to-
one defeat for the referendum on the equal rights amendment in Nevada. The
church guaranteed that one more state would not ratify the amendment.

Sonia Johnson, Mormons for ERA, and the Threat of Excommunication

In January 1978, Sonia Johnson and three other Mormon women in northern
Virginia organized Mormons for ERA (MERA). Johnson, the ward organist
and a former Relief Society teacher and president, knew nothing, like many
Mormon women, about the ERA until she learned of it at church. "And everything I heard about it was bad," she remembered. In April 1977, the stake
president for northern Virginia visited Johnson's ward to deliver a sermon on
why the church was opposing the ERA, a message that primarily consisted of
him reading a First Presidency statement against the amendment. Following
this, Mormon leaders in northern Virginia organized the Virginia LDS Women's
Coalition (VLDSCC), an anti-ERA organization all Mormon women were
encouraged to join. Those who did were then "set apart," signifying a church
calling had been extended and accepted. The VLDSCC quickly ballooned
to sixteen thousand members, and it joined with other Virginia anti-ERA
groups in lobbying state legislators, circulating anti-ERA literature, holding demonstrations, and collecting signatures for anti-ERA petitions, many
gathered before and after church services. Though accounting for less than 1
percent of Virginia's population, Mormons wrote approximately 85 percent
of the anti-ERA letters Virginia state legislators received.[55]

Incensed by the church's role in the ERA battle, Johnson and three other
women organized Mormons for ERA to oppose the church's work against the
amendment. Johnson, who held a PhD in education from Rutgers University
but remained a homemaker, had recently become interested in feminism,

devouring books such as *The Female Eunuch* and *The Feminine Mystique*.[56] Initially, MERA remained small and local, but it counted a thousand members nationwide by 1981.[57] Many more supporters sent money to MERA but refrained from joining, or even signing their letters, for fear of reprisals from the church. These secret donors understood what Johnson would learn: the Mormon Church would not ignore a woman challenging its authority.[58]

While the Mormons for ERA group seemed minuscule in light of the thousands the church had activated to oppose the amendment, the church still wanted to quiet the voices of protest raging from the group. No one represented a bigger public threat to the church's power over its members than Johnson herself. Johnson's testimony supporting the ERA before a Senate Subcommittee on Constitutional Rights in 1978 had thrust her into the national spotlight, and she traveled throughout the country speaking out on the role the Mormon Church was playing in defeating the ERA.

Johnson most enraged the church leadership when she announced that President Kimball had received no divine revelation guiding the church's opposition to the ERA, but that God instead had revealed to her that the church should support the amendment.[59] Johnson's flouting of established church doctrine regarding the president's prophetic status helped strengthen the conviction in most Mormons that her work, and that of Mormons for ERA, was outside of the church's will and the first step toward apostasy. Indeed, faithful Mormons questioned whether those who supported the amendment could even call themselves Mormons, and church leaders helped support that doubt. Hartman Rector Jr., a General Authority of the church, sent Teddie Wood, one of the Mormons for ERA's founders, a letter voicing such an accusation. "The Lord has spoken through his Prophet Spencer W. Kimball," Rector wrote to Wood. "If you are really serious about being a Mormon, you will sustain the Prophet. . . . So far as I am concerned—you are not a 'Mormon' and should'nt [*sic*] make pretenses that you are—certainly you don't represent the rank and file membership of the Church." Sonia Johnson frequently answered her phone to the voice of an enraged member yelling at her that she was not a Mormon.[60]

While Mormons for ERA's leaders weathered challenges to their spiritual authenticity, other pro-ERA Mormons experienced various forms of discipline from their leaders. Wanda Scott of Utah County was released from her calling as Relief Society teacher after she voiced support for the amendment. The bishop of Sonia Johnson's mother in Logan, Utah, warned her of the precarious status of her church membership after she signed a pro-ERA letter and threatened to revoke her temple recommend if she continued to support the amendment. Many other stake presidents issued no such warning and instead denied temple recommends to those women who were unaligned with the prophet's admonition.[61]

The revocation of a temple recommend was one of the harshest ways a bishop could discipline a member. In Mormon temples, worthy Saints perform sacred rituals that relate to salvation and exaltation. Unlike Mormon wards, temples are closed to the public. Indeed, not even all Mormons may enter a temple. Temple admission, instead, extends only to faithful Mormons whose bishops judge them worthy to hold a temple recommend card. In yearly interviews, ward bishops assess the worthiness of a member with questions that include, "Do you sustain the [Church] President . . . as a Prophet, Seer, and Revelator, recognizing no other person on earth as authorized to exercise all priesthood keys?" and "Do you earnestly strive to live in accordance with the accepted rules and doctrines of the Church?" and "Will you earnestly strive to do your duty in the Church . . . and to obey the rules, laws, and commandments of the Church?"[62] A temple recommend tangibly signifies one's right standing with the church, and thus with God. Only those who regularly retain their temple recommends can hope to spend eternity in the celestial kingdom. And those with temple recommends frequently engage in temple work in order to further exalt themselves in the afterlife through earthly activity. Thus, revoking one's temple recommend has frightening eternal consequences.[63] By refusing temple recommends to various Mormons who supported the equal rights amendment, the church sent a strident message of the timeless importance for each member in following the prophet's will.

Fearful of the growing prominence of Sonia Johnson and Mormons for ERA and their mutinous potential, the church excommunicated Johnson by letter in December 1979. The letter reminded Johnson that she had never been dissuaded "from seeking the ratification of the equal rights amendment." The church was excommunicating Johnson not because of her political views, the letter maintained, but because she was "not in harmony with church doctrine concerning the nature of God in the manner in which He directs His church on earth."[64]

Johnson's excommunication achieved a double success for the church. First, it effectively minimized Mormon support for the ERA by instilling the fears of a similar fate for those who worked against the church's political objectives. Mormons for ERA's membership flatlined at a thousand in 1981, a paltry number in light of the church's approximately 3 million American members in 1980.[65] Conversely, thirteen thousand Mormon women in Utah had turned the IWY conference into an anti-ERA protest; nine thousand Saints had canvassed Las Vegas on behalf of the church's anti-ERA mission; sixteen thousand church members in northern Virginia had joined the church's anti-ERA organization there. Across the country, Mormons by the thousands, mostly women, worked locally to defeat the equal rights amendment that their church so vigorously opposed. That Mormons for ERA could amass no more than a thousand members nationwide, many of whom considered themselves to be Mormon only out of tradition rather than active participation, demonstrates the difficulty, indeed the near impossibility, for church members to organize a movement that challenged the church's official position. Mormons for ERA, then, was little more than the tiniest drop of dissent in a very large bucket of Mormon loyalists.

Second, and perhaps more important to the church's own long-term objectives, the excommunications of Sonia Johnson and other ERA supporters strengthened the ability of the church's hierarchy to command complete obedience from its members—no matter the issue, ecclesiastical or political. The 1970s not only had witnessed the church's organized attack on the equal rights amendment, but had also revealed an equally well orchestrated movement by the church to solidify in members the belief that they were led by a prophet whose voice was animated by God and that they could gain salvation and exaltation only through active, faithful membership in the Mormon Church. At the same time, Mormon women watched the church undercut the Relief Society's independence while it increased emphasis on women's dependence on and subservience to their husbands. Faithful Mormon women, fearful of earthly judgments and their heavenly consequences, fell in line to support the church's actions against Johnson, to demonstrate their submission to the prophet's absolute authority over all matters, and to question the true Mormon identity of any dissenting members. Shirley Sealey, of Highland, Utah, expressed typical feelings about pro-ERA Mormon women: "In my opinion . . . [they] aren't aware of the gospel and . . . aren't living it." "Usually active women aren't for the ERA," she continued.

> I think there might be a few . . . If they are really living the gospel of Jesus Christ, they don't have these kinds of feelings. Now the way I think, if we believe in a prophet . . . that's why we belong . . . If we don't want to follow that prophet, what are we in the church for? We'd better get out. Because even when you join a club . . . you follow the rules or else you leave. And so a lot of people that are speaking out . . . [about] the ERA—well, our prophet is against it and tells us we shouldn't fight for the ERA because the principles of it are against our Gospel principles. But our prophet and the church are certainly for women being upheld and honored. In fact, women are cherished in the church.[66]

As N. Eldon Tanner, the church's second highest ranking official, stated in the opening pages of the August 1979 issue of *Ensign*: "When the prophet speaks the debate is over." Acknowledging the swirling controversies of the day, not least the equal rights amendment, Tanner reminded his readers that "True Latter-day Saints" faced no dilemma choosing between following the prophet or the ways of the world. True Mormons, Tanner instructed, "who heed [the prophet's] counsel will be partakers of the promised blessings which will not be enjoyed by those who fail to accept his messages."[67] Against this backdrop of strident orthodoxy and authoritarianism, the Mormon Church launched its first national political effort with the committed work of its faithful members.

But Mormons who opposed the ERA were not merely sheep following a controlling master. Certainly, the Mormon Church emphasized its authoritarian and exclusivist theology as it prodded Mormons to political action. But this emphasis, while important, cannot completely explain Mormons' willingness to engage in a political battle on their church's behalf. Mormons worked to defeat the ERA not simply because they believed they had to, but also because they wanted to. Fighting the ERA gave Mormons the opportunity to add to their strivings for exaltation in the celestial kingdom by opposing what the church depicted as one of the greatest evils of their day: feminism. Also, the public nature of so much of the anti-ERA work—the marches, conferences, workshops, and rallies—allowed Mormons to perform for one another their alignment with the church and its teachings.

For Mormon women, the chance to fight the ERA allowed them to work within restricted roles while subtly challenging them. As they assisted the church's political objectives, they resisted some of its most constricting expectations for them as women. Instructed to spurn public life for domestic responsibilities, Mormon women seized the opportunity to take the leading role in the Mormon Church's emergence onto the national political stage. Under the auspices of religious calling and societal preservation, LDS women used their weakened but still impressive Relief Society network to show the church that they were useful not only as housewives but also as effective political actors. In doing so, Mormon women did not seek to topple Mormonism's strict gender hierarchy as much as loosen some of its tightest constraints. In opposing equality for American women, Mormon women grabbed a little more power and opportunity for themselves.

Notes

1. "Women at Utah Meeting Oppose Rights Proposal," *New York Times*, June 26, 1977; John M. Crewdson, "Mormon Turnout Overwhelms Women's Conference in Utah," *New York Times*, July 25, 1977; Martha Sontagg Bradley, "The Mormon Relief Society and the International Women's Year," *Journal of Mormon History* 21.1 (Winter 1995): 105–67; Dixie Snow Huefner, "Church and Politics at the Utah IWY Conference," *Dialogue: A Journal of Mormon Thought* 11.1 (Winter 1978): 58–75.

2. Jane J. Mansbridge, *Why We Lost the ERA* (Chicago: University of Chicago Press, 1986), 3; Mary Frances Berry, *Why ERA Failed: Politics, Women's Rights, and the Amending Process of the Constitution* (Bloomington: University of Indiana Press, 1986), 76.

3. See D. Michael Quinn, "The LDS Church's Campaign Against the Equal Rights Amendment," *Journal of Mormon History* 20.2 (Fall 1994): 85–155, and *The Mormon Hierarchy: Extensions of Power* (Salt Lake City: Signature Books, 1997), 373–406; O. Kendall White Jr., "Overt and Covert Policies: The Mormon Church's Anti-ERA Campaign in Virginia," *Virginia Social Science Journal* 19 (Winter 1984): 14–16, and "Mormonism and the Equal Rights Amendment," *Journal of Church and State* 31.2 (Spring 1989): 249–67; Marilyn Warenski, *Patriarchs and Politics: The Plight of the Mormon Woman* (New York: McGraw-Hill, 1978), 181–224; James Coates, *In Mormon Circles: Gentiles, Jack Mormons, and Latter-day Saints* (Reading, Mass.: Addison-Wesley, 1991), 127–34; and, Robert Gottlieb and Peter Wiley, *America's Saints: The Rise of Mormon Power* (New York: G. P. Putnam's Sons, 1984), 201–13.

4. Gottlieb and Wiley, *America's Saints*, 21; italics added.

5. Ruth Peterson Knight Oral History, interviewed by Matthew K. Heiss, 1990, 26–27, James Moyle Oral History Program, archives, Family and Church History Department of The Church of Jesus Christ of Latter-day Saints, Salt Lake City, Utah.

6. Eleanor Ricks Colton, "My Personal Rubicon," *Dialogue: A Journal of Mormon Thought* 14.4 (Winter 1981): 102; Arda Harman, "The Equal Rights Amendment Defeated in Nevada, a Report by Arda Harman, July 1984," photocopy of typescript, archives, Family and Church History Department of The Church of Jesus Christ of Latter-day Saints, Salt Lake City, Utah.

7. Rebecca Klatch, "Coalition and Conflict Among Women of the New Right," *Signs: Journal of Women in Culture and Society* 13.4 (Summer 1988): 672. For other works on the role of women in the New Right's battles against women's rights, especially the ERA, see Theodore S. Arrington and Patricia A. Kyle, "Equal Rights Amendment Activists in North Carolina," *Signs: Journal of Women in Culture and Society* 3.3 (Spring 1978): 666–80; David W. Brady and Kent L. Tedin, "Ladies in Pink: Religion and Political Ideology in the Anti-ERA Movement," *Social Science Quarterly* 56.4 (March 1976): 564–75; Iva E. Deutchman and Sandra Prince-Embury, "Political Ideology and Pro- and Anti-ERA Women," in *The Equal Rights Amendment: The Politics and Process of Ratification of the 27th Amendment to the Constitution*, ed. Sarah Slavin (New York: Haworth Press, 1982), 39–55; Rebecca Klatch, *Women of the New Right* (Philadelphia: Temple University Press, 1987); Kristin Luker, *Abortion and the Politics of Motherhood* (Berkeley: University of California Press, 1984); and Susan E. Marshall, "Ladies Against Women: Mobilization Dilemmas of Antifeminist Movements," *Social Problems* 32.4 (April 1985): 348–62.

8. On Mormonism's increasing conservatism in the 1970s regarding the role of women, see Laurence R. Iannaccone and Carrie A. Miles, "Dealing with Social Change: The Mormon Church's Response to Change in Women's Roles," *Social Forces* 68.4 (June 1990): 1231–50.

9. Berry, *Why ERA Failed*, 63–67.

10. Quinn, *The Mormon Hierarchy*, 375.

11. Margaret I. Miller and Helene Linker, "Equal Rights Amendment Campaigns in California and Utah," *Society* 11.4 (May/June 1974): 42.

12. "Most Favor Full Rights for Women," *Deseret News*, November 15, 1974.

13. Warenski, *Patriarchs and Politics*, 208; Gottlieb and Wiley, *America's Saints*, 203.

14. Quinn, *The Mormon Hierarchy*, 377.

15. "Church Stand Apparently Dooms ERA Amendment," *Logan Herald Journal*, January 19, 1975, quoted in Quinn, *The Mormon Hierarchy*, 377.

16. "Equal Rights Amendment," *Deseret News*, January 11, 1975; Warenski, *Patriarchs and Politics*, 205.

17. Peter Gillins, "'Circle of Gold' Pyramid Plan Headed for Utah Court Ruling," *The Provo Herald*, February 27, 1979.

18. Berry, *Why ERA Failed*, 65–68.

19. Quinn, *The Mormon Hierarchy*, 376.
20. *Ibid.*, 363.
21. *Ibid.*, 863–64.
22. "Editorial," *Deseret News*, July 8, 1972, quoted in Spencer W. Kimball, "We Thank Thee, O God, for a Prophet," *Ensign*, January 1973, 33.
23. In the 1970s, Mormons heard or read nearly thirty General Conference talks and *Ensign* articles on the subject of the prophet and/or prophecy.
24. Gottlieb and Wiley, *America's Saints*, 69–70; Quinn, *The Mormon Hierarchy*, 358.
25. Richard N. Ostling and Joan K. Ostling, *Mormon America: The Power and the Promise* (San Francisco: HarperSanFrancisco, 1999), 111–12.
26. Bernard Quinn et al., *Churches and Church Membership in the United States 1980: An Enumeration by Region, State and County Based on Data Reported by 111 Church Bodies* (Atlanta: Glenmary Research Center, 1982), 1, 14, 19, 25.
27. "First Presidency Reaffirms Opposition to ERA," *Ensign*, October 1978, 63.
28. Ostling and Ostling, *Mormon America*, 77; Quinn, *The Mormon Hierarchy*, 44, 373; Warenski, *Patriarchs and Politics*, 1–13.
29. Harold B. Lee, "Maintain Your Place As a Woman," *Ensign*, February 1972, 48–56.
30. "Editorial," *Ensign*, January 1971, 97; "Women and the Church: A Conversation with Sister Barbara B. Smith, Relief Society General President," *Ensign*, March 1976, 11; Gottlieb and Wiley, *America's Saints*, 197–98; Quinn, *The Mormon Hierarchy*, 374.
31. Margaret McConkie Pope, "Exaltation," in *Encyclopedia of Mormonism: The History, Scripture, Doctrine, and Procedures of the Church of Jesus Christ of Latter-day Saints*, ed. Daniel H. Ludlow, 5 vols. (New York: Macmillan, 1992), 2: 479; Alma P. Burton, "Salvation," in *Encyclopedia of Mormonism*, 3: 1256–57; Douglas J. Davies, *The Mormon Culture of Salvation: Force, Grace and Glory* (Aldershot, U.K.: Ashgate, 2000), 154–55; Ostling and Ostling, *Mormon America*, 164–65; Warenski, *Patriarchs and Politics*, 226–29.
32. Since Mormonism has no professional clergy, all "faithful and worthy" Mormon men are ordained to the priesthood, authorizing their leadership both in the church and the family. Mormon women cannot hold the priesthood. Richard C. Elsworth and Melvin J. Luthy, "Priesthood," in *Encyclopedia of Mormonism*, 3: 1137.
33. Burton, "Salvation," 1256–57; Pope, "Exaltation," 479; Bruce R. McConkie, *Mormon Doctrine* (Salt Lake City: Bookcraft, 1958), 109–10, 238–40, 390, 602–3; Davies, *The Mormon Culture of Salvation*, 66–67; Ostling and Ostling, *Mormon America*, 332.
34. While the connection between Mormonism's theology of salvation and anti-ERA activism needs more attention, my argument here draws on the works of sociologists who have argued about the complicated and multiple connections between motivation and theology for different people engaged in the same acts, especially, Ziad Munson, "When a Funeral Isn't Just a Funeral: The Layered Meaning of Everyday Action," in *Everyday Religion: Observing Modern Religious Lives*, ed. Nancy Ammerman (Oxford: Oxford University Press, 2007), 121–35; and Rhys Williams and Jeffrey Blackburn, "Many Are Called but Few Obey: Ideological Commitment and Activism in Operation Rescue," in *Disruptive Religion: The Force of Faith in Social Movement Activism*, ed. Christian Smith (New York: Routledge, 1996), 167–85.
35. Bradley, "The Mormon Relief Society," 108–12; Quinn, *The Mormon Hierarchy*, 378.
36. Smith was president of the Relief Society for the entire Mormon Church. Like the church itself, the Relief Society is organized in a federated structure with authority that extends from the church's headquarters down through every level of the hierarchy to each ward—or congregation—itself.
37. Bradley, "The Mormon Relief Society," 132–33; Quinn, *The Mormon Hierarchy*, 378–79.
38. Benson was then president of the Quorum of the Twelve, the group of a dozen men directly below the First Presidency in the church's leadership hierarchy.
39. Letter to "All Regional Representatives in Utah," June 3, 1977, quoted in Bradley, "The Mormon Relief Society," 127–28; Quinn, *The Mormon Hierarchy*, 379. A stake is the Mormon equivalent of a Catholic parish and contains many wards (Mormon congregations) within it.
40. Brian L. Pitcher, "Callings," in *Encyclopedia of Mormonism*, 1: 250.
41. *Ibid.*, 248–50; Davies, *The Mormon Culture of Salvation*, 177–78.
42. Bradley, "The Mormon Relief Society," 134; Quinn, *The Mormon Hierarchy*, 379.
43. Bradley, "The Mormon Relief Society," 135.

44. Through Don LeFevre, a church spokesman, the Mormon Church acknowledged to the *New York Times* that it had encouraged its women to take part in the IWY Conference but claimed its influence over the women in how to act at the conference had extended only so far as to encourage the women to "vote for correct principles." LeFevre did concede that the women had been provided with information materials that outlined both how to register at the conference and the church's positions on various issues, including the E.R.A., "in case they had any questions." LeFevre quoted in Crewdson, "Mormon Turnout Overwhelms Women's Conference."

45. Huefner, "Church and Politics at the Utah IWY Conference," 58, 67.

46. Crewdson, "Mormon Turnout Overwhelms Women's Conference"; "Women at Utah Meeting Oppose Rights Proposal"; Gottlieb and Wiley, *America's Saints*, 202; Ann Terry, Marilyn Slaght-Griffin, and Elizabeth Terry, eds., *Mormons and Women* (Santa Barbara, Calif.: Butterfly Publishing, 1980), 111.

47. Bradley, "The Mormon Relief Society," 145, 160; Huefner, "Church and Politics at the Utah IWY Conference," 62; Crewdson, "Mormon Turnout Overwhelms Women's Conference"; and "Women at Utah Meeting Oppose Rights Proposal."

48. Bradley, "The Mormon Relief Society," 148; Huefner, "Church and Politics at the Utah IWY Conference," 61.

49. "At Women's Parley Conservative Bloc Exceeds Liberals," *Honolulu Star-Bulletin*, July 9, 1977.

50. Spencer W. Kimball, "God Will Not Be Mocked," *Ensign*, November 1974, 4.

51. James T. Richardson, "The 'Old Right' in Action: Mormon and Catholic Involvement in an Equal Rights Amendment Referendum," in *New Christian Politics*, ed. David G. Bromley and Anson Shupe (Macon, Ga.: Mercer University Press, 1984), 215, 222.

52. Janet Brigham, "Beyond the Glitter," *Ensign*, February 1979, 38.

53. Richardson, "The 'Old Right' in Action," 222.

54. Deb Turner, e-mail message to author, January 26, 2003. Deb Turner is a pseudonym.

55. Sonia Johnson, *From Housewife to Heretic* (Garden City, N.J.: Doubleday, 1981), 101, 102–105, 359; O. Kendall White Jr., "A Feminist Challenge: 'Mormons for ERA' as an Internal Social Movement," *Journal of Ethnic Studies* 13.1 (Spring 1985): 34–35; Quinn, *The Mormon Hierarchy*, 390, 395.

56. Johnson, *From Housewife to Heretic*, 46, 90–99; Heather Kellogg, "Shades of Gray: Sonia Johnson's Life Through Letters and Autobiography," *Dialogue: A Journal of Mormon Thought* 29.2 (Summer 1996): 84.

57. Though the ratification period for the ERA was to end in 1979, Congress controversially extended the window three years until June 30, 1982. Berry, *Why ERA Failed*, 70.

58. Johnson, *From Housewife to Heretic*, 153.

59. Terry, *Mormons and Women*, 76, 44.

60. Hartman Rector Jr., letter to Mrs. Teddie Wood, August 29, 1978, in White, "A Feminist Challenge," 44; Karen DeWitt, "The Pain of Being a Mormon Feminist," *New York Times*, November 27, 1979.

61. Amy L. Bentley, "Comforting the Motherless Children: The Alice Louise Reynolds Women's Forum," *Dialogue: A Journal of Mormon Thought* 23.3 (Fall 1990): 40; Johnson, *From Housewife to Heretic*, 202–3; White, "A Feminist Challenge," 37.

62. From *Temple Recommend Form Book*, Instructions to Interviewing Authorities, Church of Jesus Christ of Latter-day Saints, Salt Lake City, Utah, 1979, quoted in Terry, *Mormons and Women*, 62–63.

63. Robert A. Tucker, "Temple Recommend," in *Encyclopedia of Mormonism*, 4: 1446–47; McConkie, *Mormon Doctrine*, 557, 703–6; Davies, *The Mormon Culture of Salvation*, 39–40, 72–76.

64. Ben A. Franklin, "Mormon Church Excommunicates a Supporter of Rights Amendment," *New York Times*, December 6, 1979; "Mormons Eject E.R.A. Activist," *New York Times*, December 9, 1979.

65. Kenneth A. Briggs, "Mormon Church at 150: Thriving on Traditionalism," *New York Times*, March 30, 1980.

66. Terry, *Mormons and Women*, 89.

67. N. Eldon Tanner, "First Presidency Message: 'The Debate Is Over,'" *Ensign*, August 1979, 3, 2.

Hot Damned America: Evangelicalism and the Climate Change Policy Debate

Brian McCammack

> If evangelicals were to take climate change, the environmental issues, seriously, do it from a biblical standpoint—not a secular ideology here but from a biblical standpoint, developing their own voice—there's no question Washington would pay heed.
> —Reverend Richard Cizik, National Association of Evangelicals[1]

Glaciers are melting and threatening the survival of polar bears, weather seems to be more extreme and erratic, and the global mean temperature appears to be steadily rising—all consequences, scientists argue, of global climate change. One could learn this much—and also that the United States is lagging far behind other industrial nations, particularly in the European Union, in addressing climate change—from Al Gore's documentary *An Inconvenient Truth* or any number of news reports. But Gore and the news media have largely failed to acknowledge that a brewing sea change in the traditional political engagement among an unlikely group—evangelical Christians—perhaps represents America's greatest hope for instituting climate change legislation. No longer focusing their political engagement almost exclusively on issues such as abortion and gay marriage, a segment of evangelical Christian leaders has broken rank with the politically conservative leadership and begun to address climate change in ways that suggest real possibility for change, both politically and in terms of faith. Yet this group continues to encounter strong resistance from such popular evangelical leaders as James Dobson and Charles Colson, who refuse to believe that climate change is an issue evangelicals are morally obligated to address and fear that it may become a wedge within evangelicalism, irreparably dividing what has been a fairly cohesive political force over the past quarter century.

An analysis of evangelical Christians' role in climate change policy proves both urgent and fruitful for two main reasons. First, evangelicals have risen to a point of prominence wherein they seem to possess great influence in American politics, making their impact on future climate change policy potentially quite significant. Considered simply as a voting bloc, evangelical Christians are a force to be reckoned with, making up roughly 30 percent of the American population.[2] Second, and perhaps more important, the response to climate change within the evangelical community has been quite discordant, thereby offering valuable insight into the complex and oft-misunderstood group labeled "evangelical." It is important to realize, whether from the perspective of policymakers, environmentalists, or evangelicals, that, as a group wielding significant political capital, evangelicals are currently deeply divided on the issue of climate change policy. Like secular politicians and activists, evangelicals disagree on two main facets of decision making regarding climate change—economics and science. Unlike their secular counterparts, evangelicals address a unique third area that, for them, is the basis for all decision making: the scriptures. In large part because the Bible is open to interpretation when it comes to environmental issues, evangelicals are neither a monolithic mass nor inflexible in their environmental beliefs. While it is no doubt cliché to frame the issue in such a way, the fact remains that there are rhetorical, theological, and ideological battles to be won. Evangelicals are in the midst of not only deciding upon an appropriate response to climate change, but also whether or not that response is worth pursuing at the expense of or in addition to such steadfast evangelical political issues as abortion and gay rights.[3]

Despite sharing many common values, not all evangelicals map their spiritual beliefs onto political and social action in the same way; in fact, while all evangelicals are *theologically* conservative, they are not necessarily all *politically* conservative.[4] Evangelicals interpret the scriptures diversely, sometimes emphasizing different chapters and verses in support of their worldview. Some place importance on personal responsibility and morality; these believers, typically cast as political conservatives, have dominated evangelical political agendas and media representations in recent history. Others tend to believe that social justice issues are more critical to following biblical teachings; these evangelicals are typically cast as politically liberal and marginal to the evangelical political leadership. While "conservative" and "liberal" are loaded terms politically, I nonetheless employ them throughout this essay as useful shorthand when speaking about evangelicals and their approaches to environmental stewardship. Here the terms simultaneously imply a distinct polarity on climate change policy while also affording the flexibility of a continuum that includes more moderate environmental views.

While there is certainly room for unique, more complex evangelical approaches to environmentalism, evangelical leadership has eschewed any sort of productive dialectical discourse, instead tending to exhibit two distinct and irreconcilable positions.[5] One group, which I will call liberal evangelical environmentalists, generally accepts the scientific claim that climate change is occurring in part due to anthropogenic effects and interprets biblical mandates to mean that action should be taken to reduce manmade carbon emissions and mitigate environmental impacts. Liberal evangelical environmentalists are represented by the Evangelical Environmental Network (EEN) and, most recently, the Evangelical Climate Initiative (ECI). Among the group's foremost supporters are Rick Warren, best-selling author of *The Purpose-Driven Life*; Richard Cizik, NAE vice president of government affairs; Jim Ball, executive director of EEN; and Leith Anderson, president of the National Association of Evangelicals. The other group, which I will call conservative evangelical environmentalists, often remains skeptical of scientific evidence supporting the anthropogenic climate change theory and interprets biblical mandates to mean that no action should be taken to reduce emissions, even if climate change is occurring. Rather than attempt to mitigate environmental impacts—a prohibitively costly proposition, they argue—conservative evangelical environmentalists believe the more sensible approach is to promote economic development aiding adaptation to environmental changes.[6] Conservative evangelical environmentalists are represented by the Interfaith Council for Environmental Stewardship (ICES) and, more recently, the Interfaith Stewardship Alliance (ISA).[7] The most prominent ISA supporters are conservative evangelical heavy hitters such as Charles Colson, founder of Prison Fellowship Ministries, and James Dobson, Focus on the Family founder. But the most vocal conservative evangelical environmentalist is E. Calvin Beisner, ISA spokesman and associate professor of historical theology and social ethics at Knox Theological Seminary, who almost exclusively outlines the conservative side's environmental theological underpinnings—a subject of paramount importance in evangelicalism, a faith whose bedrock is the Bible.[8]

Theory and Practice: Biblical Interpretations and Practical Applications

Evangelicals' biblical interpretation is crucial to their role in the climate change debate—and, more broadly, environmental stewardship—precisely because the Bible plays so central a role in evangelical faith. While liberal Protestants may tend to invoke more secular ethical or moral arguments for environmentalism, evangelical environmentalists—both liberal and conservative—return to the

Bible as their guiding text.[9] Somewhat less clear is exactly how the Bible should be interpreted. Conflicting theological interpretations focus mainly on two different biblical principles—stewardship and concern for the poor.

The debate over biblical environmentalism has historically focused on how to reconcile the ideas of dominion and stewardship.[10] In Genesis 1:28, humankind is given dominion over the environment: "God blessed them and said to them, 'Be fruitful and increase in number; fill the earth and subdue it. Rule over the fish of the sea and the birds of the air and over every living creature that moves on the ground.'" And in Genesis 2:15, man is commanded to be a steward to the garden: "The LORD God took the man and put him in the Garden of Eden to work it and take care of it."[11] The conservative perspective on these verses and others is articulated chiefly by E. Calvin Beisner, who argues that "linking these two commissions together—cultivate and guard the Garden, and fill, subdue and rule the Earth—implies that God intended, and still intends, mankind to transform the Earth from wilderness into garden."[12] Beisner envisions an active role for humankind in its relationship to the environment and makes no apologies for what many would agree are the negative effects of environmental exploitation. The cultivation of wilderness might have seemingly little to do with twenty-first-century environmental stewardship, let alone climate change policy, but Beisner argues that "this Biblical principle also applies to debates over global warming. Rising atmospheric carbon dioxide concentrations might result in some increase in global average temperature. However, increasing CO_2 levels also result in enhanced plant growth and reduce desertification. This fact is firmly established and must not be ignored" and he goes on to espouse the benefits of global warming in reducing species extinction.[13] In this sense, then, conservative evangelical environmentalists see carbon dioxide emissions as actually fulfilling both the subdue-and-rule and be-fruitful-and-multiply commands of dominion, turning wilderness into the garden and transforming previously unfarmable areas into regions hospitable to plant growth.[14] In other words, good stewards are necessarily those who exercise active dominion over the earth's resources. Even though Beisner argues for the beneficial effects of increased CO_2 levels on the earth's biological systems, he seems aware that this claim could be easily disputed by those who argue that the costs of increased CO_2 levels far outweigh the benefits. Citing Psalm 19:1–6, Beisner's answer to this argument is that God is too wise and his creation too adaptable to be much negatively affected by mankind's activities.[15] Such a construction, along with Beisner's argument that CO_2 emissions are actually beneficial for the environment, could easily be taken as a blank check for environmental exploitation. By contrast, liberal evangelical environmentalists have historically interpreted the same passages from Genesis in such a way as to explicitly limit this type of anthropocentrism.

A typical liberal evangelical environmentalist interpretation of stewardship is that of Ron Sider, president of Evangelicals for Social Action, who writes that "the Bible teaches . . . that the non-human creation has worth and significance, quite apart from its usefulness to humanity . . . Anyone who thinks God created the non-human world merely for the benefit of persons has not read the Bible carefully."[16] While liberal evangelical environmentalists see Jesus's version of dominion (read as a type of servanthood in Matthew 20) as the template for man's dominion over the earth, Beisner argues that to interpret "Christ's suffering servanthood [as] . . . the real model of human dominion over the earth" is a mistake because "while indeed all of man's tilling of the earth should be service to God, it is inaccurate to say that it is service to the earth itself. Rather, man's cultivating the earth is designed . . . to cause the earth to serve man."[17] In making this distinction, Beisner alludes to a very real risk liberal evangelical environmentalists run when they advocate a more biocentric view of stewardship, a risk that threatens the roots of evangelical belief. Because of Christianity's reverence of God as Creator, any attempt to worship anything other than God—in this case, the earth—is antithetical to scriptural teachings. Occasionally, liberal evangelical environmentalists' rhetoric does open itself to accusations of nature worship, despite their best efforts to the contrary. For example, *Redeeming Creation*, a book offering a liberal evangelical environmentalist approach to stewardship, argues that evangelical Christians should heed the "call to accept our rightful place in creation as its servant and protector . . . By Christ's example we are instructed to put the welfare of the nonhuman world above our own, to seek its good first, to rule as servants."[18] The direct emphasis on an inversion of the man-nature hierarchy is enough to make many evangelicals uncomfortable. The Cornwall Declaration, adopted by the conservative evangelical Interfaith Council for Environmental Stewardship (the predecessor of the newly formed Interfaith Stewardship Alliance) and released in the spring of 2000, reflects this angst:

> Many people believe that "nature knows best," or that the earth—untouched by human hands—is the ideal. Such romanticism leads some to deify nature or oppose human dominion over creation. Our position, informed by revelation and confirmed by reason and experience, views human stewardship that unlocks the potential in creation for all the earth's inhabitants as good.[19]

One sees reiterated here the desire to turn the earth into the garden by "unlock[ing] the potential in creation" (natural resources) paired with a dismissal of nature reverence. Perhaps sensing the tenuous position of defending a more biocentric version of environmental stewardship on a biblical basis, liberal evangelical environmentalists have recently begun downplaying this approach in favor of one based on treatment of the poor in society, an area that has long been the province of conservative evangelical environmentalists.[20]

Although poverty has lately become the primary focus of liberal evangelical environmentalists, an acknowledgment of the relationship between poverty and environmental issues has always been evident in the movement. EEN's 1994 Declaration on the Care of Creation, for instance, states: "We recognize that human poverty is both a cause and a consequence of environmental degradation."[21] Yet this earlier approach buries these considerations below an emphasis on stewardship and does not deal with climate change directly, mostly because a decade ago liberal evangelical environmentalists began by focusing on the Endangered Species Act—an issue that did not lend itself favorably to highlighting the interplay of poverty and environmentalism.[22] More recently, as the movement has matured, the focus has gradually shifted to put climate change at the forefront of the evangelical environmentalist agenda. In fact, it seems apparent that a change in focus on environmental issues actually facilitated a shift in theological focus. While endangered species are not particularly conducive to utilizing more anthropocentric New Testament theology, climate change's potential affects on humankind—including rising sea levels and more intense heat waves, droughts, floods, and hurricanes—are direct, thus affording evangelicals an opportunity to engage a theology more familiar, and perhaps less offensive, to the laity.[23] The 2002 Oxford Declaration on Global Warming takes this approach as well, but the most publicized campaign prior to ECI was the 2002 EEN "What Would Jesus Drive?" ad campaign (WWJDrive for short), which riffed on the popular "What Would Jesus Do?" slogan and implored drivers to think about whether or not Jesus would drive an SUV, or a similar vehicle, that gets excessively poor gas mileage. The implication of the ad campaign was that since SUVs contribute disproportionately to climate change through their excessive greenhouse gas emissions, Jesus would do the ecologically conscientious thing and not drive such vehicles. Though the impetus for the campaign was rooted in stewardship, a letter from campaign leaders addressed to U.S. auto executives reveals a more anthropocentric agenda, stating that pollution due to automobiles is "warming the planet, contributing to causes of war and increasing the burden on the poor."[24]

Following the 2002 WWJDrive campaign, the Sandy Cove Covenant and Invitation adopted by the National Association of Evangelicals (NAE) on June 30, 2004, at the Creation Care Conference was the most notable evangelical statement on climate change prior to ECI's 2006 *Call to Action*. The covenant "invite[s] our brothers and sisters in Christ to engage with us the most pressing environmental questions of our day, such as . . . the important current debate about human-induced climate change,"[25] an important step because the NAE represents a much broader base of evangelicals than the EEN, to which much of the movement had been previously confined. In the wake of the covenant, the NAE has been no stranger to the argument that evangelical Christians should push for action on climate change policy based on a biblical need to care for the poor. John Houghton, evangelical Christian and former chairman of the scientific working group of the Intergovernmental Panel on Climate Change (IPCC), stated in a March 2005 presentation to the NAE that "there is already a strong tendency in the world for the rich to get even richer while the poor get poorer.[26] The impacts of human induced climate change will tend to further bolster that trend."[27] In effect, environmentalism has been turned into something more closely resembling humanitarianism.

With the 2006 Evangelical Climate Initiative, liberal evangelical environmentalists continue to simultaneously work at broadening their base while driving home the poverty issue. Backed by a media blitz that included a press conference and print ads in both the *New York Times* and *Christianity Today*, the ECI recruited more than eighty signatories, many of whom represented an extension beyond typical liberal evangelical environmentalist boundaries. As Jim Ball noted, "It's a very centrist evangelical list, and that was intentional. When people look at the names, they're going to say, this is a real solid group here. These leaders are not flighty, going after the latest cause."[28] The signers to ECI's *Climate Change: An Evangelical Call to Action* advocate social justice that is both biblically based and urgent, arguing that "millions of people could die in this century because of climate change, most of them our poorest global neighbors."[29] To achieve their desired ends, liberal evangelical environmentalists may have found that it pays to craft a message more universally palatable to evangelicals. While creation care represented what at least seemed like a new—and potentially hazardous—theological approach to man's relationship with the environment, arguing climate change from the angle of its impact on the poor strikes a more familiar chord with evangelicals. With this shift, movement leaders may be addressing what could be termed a triage mentality on the part of evangelicals: the idea that with limited resources (financial and otherwise), only a finite number of issues warrant attention. By folding environmental issues into the context of addressing poverty, movement leaders avoid adding another issue to an already crowded plate full of such hot-button issues as abortion and gay rights. If there was any doubt at all about why liberal evangelical environmentalists believe climate change is worthy of their attention, Richard Cizik puts that doubt to rest, definitively stating: "Environmentalists say the Earth is in jeopardy. The Earth will go on. I believe human beings are in jeopardy. Those who say, 'Well, you're caring about plants and animals more than people.' Au contraire, this is about people."[30]

Of course, in a sense, liberal evangelical environmentalism's newfound anthropocentric humanitarianism merely mimics an already established conservative evangelical environmentalist approach. The spring 2000 Cornwall Declaration, considered by some to be "the first major statement politically conservative evangelicals have made on the environment,"[31] takes aim directly at global warming, stating that "some unfounded or undue [environmental] concerns include fears of destructive manmade global warming, overpopulation, and rampant species loss." The Declaration goes on to say that these problems "tend to be speculative," are "of concern mainly to environmentalists in wealthy nations," are "of very low and largely hypothetical risk," and that solutions "are unjustifiably costly and of dubious benefit." The reference to cost applies most directly, it argues, to the poor: "Public policies to combat exaggerated risks can dangerously delay or reverse the economic development necessary to improve not only human life but also human stewardship of the environment. The poor, who are most often citizens of developing nations . . . are often the most injured by such misguided, though well-intended, policies."[32] Similarly, the Interfaith Stewardship Alliance, in a 2006 press release responding to ECI's *Call to Action*, directly states that "effort[s] to cut greenhouse gases hurt the poor. By making energy less affordable and accessible, mandatory emissions reductions would drive up the costs of consumer products, stifle economic growth, cost jobs, and impose especially harmful effects on the Earth's poorest people."[33] So while liberal evangelical environmentalists view climate change from the perspective of how the *environmental consequences* of climate change will affect the poor, their conservative counterparts focus on the potential *economic impacts*. Both sides cast themselves as defenders of the poor, but disagree on the scientific basis and economic impacts of climate change. Consequently, the challenge for liberal evangelical environmentalists now is less about proving and defending their theological foundations and more about arguing the scientific legitimacy of reports that anthropogenic emissions are contributing to a potentially catastrophic warming of the earth. This shift opens up entirely new problems for those seeking to mobilize evangelicals on environmental issues since so many remain deeply suspicious of science.

Politics and Climate Change Science

Fueled in part by the creation-evolution debate, many evangelicals detest what they see as the nearly religious significance science has taken on in contemporary culture. In an August 2005 *Christianity Today* editorial, Andy Crouch makes a direct connection between creationist thinking and skepticism regarding climate change science. Crouch writes, "If evangelicals mistrust scientists when they make pronouncements about the future, it may be because of the history of antagonism between biblical faith and evolution," and he goes on to say that "perhaps no result of the creation-evolution stalemate is as potentially disastrous as the way it has stymied courageous action on climate change."[34] To combat this mistrust, liberal evangelical environmentalists have turned to evangelical scientists to bridge the credibility gap, taking pains to point out evangelical scientists who argue for the validity of data suggesting global mean temperatures are rising. An early example of this tactic is Howard A. Snyder's suggestion in a 1995 *Christianity Today* article titled "Why We Love the Earth" that Christians "become informed on environmental issues. A number of books and other publications by Christian writers and scientists are now available," implicitly arguing that Christians should turn first and foremost to Christian writers when looking for the truth on scientific matters.[35] If, as Andy Crouch notes in his *Christianity Today* editorial, "all science is ultimately a matter of trust," evangelicals seem to trust fellow evangelical scientists more than their secular counterparts. More recently, the most notable instances of an evangelical partiality to Christian scientists are the repeated references of liberal evangelical environmentalists to Sir John Houghton, former chairman of the scientific working group of the IPCC. Andy Crouch suggests the IPCC's conclusions should be taken seriously because the international scientific body was "chaired for many years by the evangelical Christian Sir John Houghton."[36] Intended to speak to an evangelical audience, this article and other EEN and ISA documents strive to show that Houghton is a fellow believer, a man worthy of trust. Houghton himself often invokes his faith when speaking about climate change science. In an interview with the EEN-published *Creation Care Magazine*, he says that "the discipline of science is a marvelous area to operate in. Why? Because it's God's science and we're looking for truth . . . I was also conscious that I had God's help in [Chairing the IPCC's Scientific Assessment]."[37] Houghton's strategy, adopted by the liberal evangelical environmentalist movement, is perhaps all the more effective given evangelicals' emphasis on personal testimony; in a sense, he evangelizes his audience with the word of climate change science, much like evangelicals seek to spread the word of God.[38]

A typical conservative evangelical environmentalist response to climate change science is similar to the conservative Republican response: to highlight both its scientific uncertainty and theoretical nature. Roy Spencer, a research scientist at the University of Alabama, Huntsville, argues in an ISA document that

> manmade global warming is a *theory*, and not a scientific observation. How much of the current or predicted warming a scientist (or anyone else) believes is due to mankind ultimately comes down to how much faith that person has in our present understanding of what drives climate fluctuations, the computer climate models that contain that understanding, and ultimately, in how fragile or resilient is the Earth.[39]

Again, one sees tied up in this discussion of uncertainty two elements that speak directly to evangelicals: the resilience of the earth (recall Beisner's reference to Psalms) and a reference to having faith in science. Subtract blatant biblical references, and the current conservative evangelical environmentalist stance on climate change science begins to look strikingly similar to George W. Bush's first-term position on the issue. While the vast majority of the scientific community insists that global warming is indeed occurring and is at least in part due to anthropogenic greenhouse gas emissions, Bush administration officials continued to advocate more scientific study rather than immediate action. In remarks made on June 11, 2001, Bush emphasized the uncertainty involved with climate change science, and repeatedly referred to what scientists "do not know." He noted:

> We do not know how much effect natural fluctuations in climate may have had on warming. We do not know how much our climate could or will change in the future. We do not know how fast change will occur, or even how some of our actions could impact it . . . And, finally, no one can say with any certainty what constitutes a dangerous level of warming, and therefore what level must be avoided.[40]

The Bush administration's stance on climate change has evolved over the course of his administration, however. A June 2005 news release titled "Fact Sheet: President Bush Is Addressing Climate Change" mutes the uncertainties emphasized in his policy four years prior, simply admitting that "we know that the surface of the Earth is warmer, and that an increase in greenhouse gases caused by humans is contributing to the problem"[41] and promoting economic development to deal with climate change. Rather than emphasizing uncertainty about the very existence of anthropogenic climate change, Bush has now begun emphasizing the uncertainty inherent in predicting the precise effects of such change, lending slightly more credence to climate change science. Late in 2006, the Department of the Interior went even further by proposing to list the polar bear as a threatened species, an animal whose polar habitat is literally thought to be melting as a direct result of climate change.[42] Although it is difficult if not impossible to label the Bush administration as proactive on climate change legislation, and it remains unclear to what extent Bush's evangelical faith informs his climate change policy, his administration's stance may be very slowly coming to more closely resemble liberal evangelical environmentalism than it once did.

Compared to the Bush administration's wariness, the stance of James Inhofe, evangelical Christian and former chairman of the Senate Committee on Environment and Public Works, can be characterized as outright hostility. Inhofe goes far beyond merely questioning the certainty of global warming (though he does that often, as well), consistently calling climate change "the greatest hoax ever perpetrated on the American people."[43] Whereas movement toward acceptance can be seen, if not in practice then at least in rhetoric, on the part of the Bush administration, Inhofe shows no willingness to budge on his position that climate change is a hoax. And the connections between his stance and his personal evangelical Christian beliefs seem much clearer. The closing comments of a 2003 Inhofe speech read like an evangelical sermon as he exhorts his listeners to uphold all that is good and decent about the United States:

> With all the hysteria, all the fear, all the phony science, could it be that manmade global warming is the greatest hoax ever perpetrated on the American people? I believe it is. And if we allow these detractors of everything that has made America great, those ranging from the liberal Hollywood elitists to those who are in it for the money, if we allow them to destroy the foundation, the greatness of the most highly industrialized nation in the history of the world, then we don't deserve to live in this one nation under God.[44]

Inhofe's rhetoric seems reflective of historian James Davison Hunter's assertion that "the evangelical heritage has long identified itself with the hopes and promises of America. Evangelicals view themselves as having helped to create and sustain all that is good in America: its traditions of moral virtue; its ethic of work, commitment, and achievement; and its political and economic institutions."[45] Taken in conjunction with Inhofe's own evangelical Presbyterian faith, it seems clear that Inhofe is consciously appealing to his conservative evangelical constituents. He plays to their distrust of science by calling much of it "phony," condemns Hollywood elitists whom many evangelicals see as morally bankrupt, and ties it all to a threat upon America's religious and economic traditions. Inhofe has brought up climate change several times in a religious context. In a January 2005 speech, he said that "put simply, man-induced global warming is an article of religious faith to the radical far left alarmists,"[46] and during an April 2005 speech he stated that "for the alarmists, global warming has nothing to do with science or scientific inquiry. Science is not about the inquiry to discover truth, but a mask to achieve an ideological agenda. For some, this issue has become a secular religion, pure and simple."[47] When one recalls the evangelical angst over science becoming a faith within the secular community, it becomes apparent that Inhofe is likely both reflecting his own personal religious concern while also appealing to his evangelical constituency. While Inhofe's hostility toward climate change science could be chalked up purely to a conservative Republican agenda, loyalty to campaign contributors in the oil and gas industries, or loyalty to his oil-rich Oklahoman constituency, it is hard to ignore the religious rhetoric when Inhofe himself is an evangelical and his rhetoric so closely matches that of the conservative evangelical environmentalists.[48]

Politics and Climate Change Economics

It is clear, then, that the evangelical stance on climate change science directly affects whether or not evangelicals believe emissions reductions policies should be instituted. Yet these policy positions also rely on biblical applications to economics that extend beyond New Testament social justice commands to care for the poor. While liberal evangelical environmentalists advocate emissions restrictions and immediate action to address climate change based upon the idea of biblical prudence (roughly equivalent to the secular idea called the precautionary principle), their conservative counterparts use biblical prudence to advocate more research before instituting such policies. For example, E. Calvin Beisner invokes prudence as it is represented in Proverbs 22:3 (which reads: "A prudent man sees danger and takes refuge, but the simple keep going and suffer for it")[49] to argue in the conclusion, titled "Applying Biblical Prudence to Global Warming," of a 2006 Interfaith Stewardship Alliance document that a prudent person foresees danger and hides himself . . . Given all the uncertainties of global warming, . . . it is crucial that we adopt a decision process that can guide us through the labyrinth of errors to a sound outcome—one that, in particular, does not impose greater risks and harms on the most impoverished and powerless people among us.[50]

The main tenets of conservative evangelical environmentalist ideology—adherence to the Bible, suspicion of climate change science, and concern for the poor—come together to inspire prudent action. Prudence, in this case, dictates more research before any action is taken, implicitly prioritizing protecting the economy rather than the environment, a position that is evident in much conservative evangelical environmental discourse. The spring 2000 Cornwall Declaration comes very close to making economic considerations more important than environmental ones, stating that "a clean environment is a costly good; consequently, growing affluence, technological innovation, and the application of human and material capital are integral to environmental improvement. The tendency among some to oppose economic progress in the name of environmental stewardship is often sadly self-defeating."[51] The environment is cast as just another commodity in a market economy ("a costly good"), perhaps no less or more valuable than an SUV rolling off the production line. The declaration also implies that those who do not rely solely on the market to solve these problems are necessarily opposed to economic progress, a claim that is not clearly supportable. Such a construction threatens to negate the biblical mandate to be good stewards of an earth that God created, instead subsuming the "clean environment" into man's market economy; any ethical or spiritual arguments carry no weight unless they assume a dollar value. The declaration takes the prototypical conservative economic approach to environmental problems: affluence and innovation are the solutions to environmental problems and the rest will take care of itself. In fact, much of the Cornwall Declaration is focused on a conservative economic approach to environmental stewardship, so much so that the biblical foundation of stewardship seems nearly lost.[52] The conservative evangelical environmentalist approach to economics and the environment is strikingly similar to the Bush administration position, articulated in part by the statement that "President Bush is dedicated to climate change policies that grow economies, aid development, and improve the environment."[53] The goals of climate change policy are phrased such that economic prosperity is the main goal, and addressing environmental issues becomes secondary or even tertiary. This affinity for business goes beyond conservative evangelical environmentalists and politicians; even liberal evangelical environmentalists have, to an extent, prioritized the protection of business interests.

A 2006 Evangelical Climate Initiative document quotes CEOs of corporations such as BP, DuPont, and General Electric that confirm the threat of climate change and call for action, offering inspiration while also perhaps soothing the concerns of evangelicals who might worry that emissions restrictions would hurt big business.[54] Former NAE president Ted Haggard, a vocal believer in the validity and urgency of global warming, has said that evangelicals "want to be pro-business environmentalists," making it unclear whether protecting business interests or the environment is the top priority.[55] Despite this lingering concern for the effects on big business, liberal evangelical environmentalists in general advocate immediate action on climate change—interpreting biblical prudence in terms of potential impacts on the environment, not on the economy. John Houghton, for example, argues:

> When it comes to future climate change, it would not be prudent to rule out the possibility of surprises . . . [though] much stronger in the argument for precautionary action is the realisation that significant anthropogenic climate change is not an unlikely possibility but a near certainty; it is no change of climate that is unlikely . . . to "wait and see" would be an inadequate and irresponsible response to what we know.[56]

To address the potential threat and respond prudently, liberal evangelical environmentalists argue that action must be taken now, because the costs of ignoring climate change are much greater than the costs of addressing it, in spite of scientific uncertainty. Similarly, Andy Crouch, in a *Christianity Today* editorial, applies the precautionary principle to the environment and likens it to Pascal's wager, translating the "better safe than sorry" idea into terms that might resonate with evangelicals. He writes,

> believe in God though he does not exist, Pascal argued, and you lose nothing in the end. Fail to believe when he does in fact exist, and you lose everything. Likewise, we have little to lose, and much technological progress, energy security, and economic efficiency to gain if we act on climate change now—even if the worst predictions fail to come to pass.[57]

Crouch sees only positives resulting from instituting climate change policy—technological progress, energy security, and economic efficiency. It is a vision that conservative evangelical environmentalists believe is a case of having one's cake and eating it too; for them, economic prosperity and emissions reductions are mutually exclusive. Crouch's editorial prompted a direct response from the Interfaith Stewardship Alliance, whose E. Calvin Beisner writes that "Crouch turns a blind eye to both the costs of CO_2 emission reduction and the benefits of increasing CO_2. His wager is a false analogy to Pascal's. In Pascal's, there was nothing to lose if the believer in God turned out wrong but everything to gain if he turned out right; in Crouch's wager, there are many costs and benefits of varied kinds to be identified, measured, and compared."[58] Beisner argues that benefits from economic growth are proven while benefits from emissions reductions are unproven and points to benefits of increased CO_2 concentrations, suggesting that these possible benefits of inaction far outweigh the economic costs of action.[59] For Beisner and the ISA, even if climate change is occurring, facilitating adaptation through economic development is a more prudent solution than pursuing costly mitigation strategies. But do any of these arguments resonate with evangelical voters, or are the debates among the leadership taking place in a sort of rhetorical vacuum? A turn to empirical data, however spotty, may shed some light on this issue.

Environmental Attitudes of the Evangelical Masses and a Look to the Future

Several polls and sociological studies have attempted to gauge evangelical environmental attitudes; although the results of these studies are varied, in general they have found that no aspect of Christian religious belief other than a fundamentalist biblical literalism is an accurate predictor of negative environmental attitudes.[60] A 1995 study also found that "among clergy, evangelicals are least environmental" when compared to Catholics and mainline Protestants, which indicates that awareness and engagement with evangelical environmentalism is not widespread and perhaps prevalent among only very high level elites.[61] Yet these studies generally use data more than a decade old, when climate change had not yet galvanized evangelical leadership. It seems unlikely that most evangelical leaders even broached environmental issues with their congregants a decade ago; it is a likelihood that continues to grow, however, as prominent evangelical leaders and organizations become increasingly engaged in the issue and garner media coverage.[62] For that reason, newer data from national polls may offer more insight into the evangelical laity's views on climate change.

A 2004 poll conducted for PBS's *Religion and Ethics Newsweekly* found that, when asked how important they thought "combating global warming and other environmental threats" was, only 45 percent of evangelicals answered that they believed it was extremely or very important, as compared to 53 percent of the general population.[63] Clearly an 8 percent gap represents a fairly significant difference in relation to the general population, but with 45 percent of evangelicals admitting climate change is an important problem, the skepticism among that group does not appear either overwhelming or monolithic in nature.

A 2006 poll conducted by ABC News, *Time*, and Stanford University obtained similar results, but cast them in a much different light, finding

> little resonance for [the 2006 ECI *Call to Action*] among evangelical white Protestants. They're less likely than others to think about their personal impact on the environment, to see global warming as a threat to the global environment, or to say the government should address it. Evangelicals also are no more likely than others to think scientists agree on the issue—and they're 12 points less likely than other Americans to trust environmental scientists in the first place.[64]

Perhaps these findings are unsurprising, but they contradict ECI's own polling, which suggests that evangelicals may be more receptive to scientific claims regarding climate changes. The ECI study found that "overall, three out of four evangelicals tend to support environmental issues and causes such as reducing global warming or protecting wilderness areas from development, including one out of four who tend to support these issues strongly."[65] Though these results are intended to show evangelical support for addressing global warming in particular, they seem to be just vague enough to preclude any definitive claims about evangelicals' true attitudes toward the particulars of climate change policy. The same study also found that "a majority of evangelicals (54%) also believe that a person's Christian faith should generally encourage them to support environmental issues."[66] In comparison to the three out of four evangelicals who support environmental issues, this number seems curiously low, particularly given that *both* liberal and conservative evangelical environmentalists push a biblical basis for Christian environmentalism. Yet perhaps the most striking finding of the entire study was that "half [of evangelicals] went so far as to say steps need to be taken to reduce global warming, even if there is a high economic cost to the U.S. Even among evangelicals who are political conservatives, over four out of ten believe global warming must be reduced even if there's a high economic cost, and half feel we must begin addressing the issue immediately."[67] Ten percent, while a significant difference between evangelicals as a whole and politically conservative evangelicals, is not as much as one might have expected, particularly on a question that deals with taking action regardless of economic cost. If this poll is any indication, then there may be hope for liberal evangelical environmentalists who advocate taking action on climate change and are less concerned about the economic cost than their conservative counterparts are.

The future of evangelical engagement with environmental issues is anything but clear. On the one hand, there are several reasons to believe that liberal evangelical environmentalists are growing in strength—their biblical message is becoming more focused and viable, they appear to be broadening and better publicizing the movement, and climate change science appears to be on their side. On the other hand, there seem to be just as many reasons to believe that conservative evangelical environmentalists will continue to find success—their biblical interpretations have withstood disagreement, they have support from deeply entrenched evangelical power structures, and their adaptation and economic development solution is much more consistent with the current U.S. political approach to climate change. While the liberal evangelical environmentalist movement appears to be growing in strength, it suffers not only from resistance from conservative evangelicals, but internally as well. Liberal evangelical environmentalists struggle with themselves over what moral issue should take priority—is it worth advocating action on climate change if it means sacrificing political influence on issues such as abortion and gay marriage and perhaps being cast as liberals? Evangelicals are unlikely, after all, to see confirmations to the Supreme Court of justices as conservative as Samuel Alito and John Roberts if Congress remains under the control of the Democratic Party.

If nothing else, liberal evangelical environmentalists exhibit an awareness of these challenges. NAE's Richard Cizik admits that "it is hard to oppose [Bush] when he has the moral authority of the president and a record of standing with us on moral issues like abortion."[68] EEN's "Global Warming Briefing for Evangelical Leaders" takes an ambivalent approach to the Bush administration, stating that "while currently insufficient to meet the challenge of climate change, the Bush Administration's efforts to address global warming have helped to set the stage for more significant action."[69] Clearly most liberal evangelical environmentalists are hesitant to condemn the president outright for his environmental policy, yet some go a step further. A March 2004 *Sojourners Magazine* article called for readers to "get rid of the president" in the 2004 election cycle, and *Creation Care Magazine* articles have lent vocal support to the 2004 McCain-Lieberman Stewardship Act and the 2005 Bingaman resolution, both of which go further than the Bush administration in addressing climate change.[70] These steps may indicate that evangelicals are becoming more willing to broaden the core set of issues upon which they base their voting choices; despite solidarity with Bush on abortion and gay marriage, evangelicals were willing to let environmental issues assume a more central role. A Democratic-controlled Congress that seems more ready than previous Congresses to take on climate change will begin to put these allegiances to the test, though it may not be until the 2008 presidential election that one can get an accurate sense of how much traction environmental issues has truly gained with evangelicals.

Perhaps one of the more effective strategies liberal evangelical environmentalists have recently employed is to directly link climate change with traditionally conservative issues. A 2006 ECI print advertisement run in *Christianity Today* states in part that

> with the same love of God and neighbor that compels us to preach salvation through Jesus Christ, protect unborn life, preserve the family and the sanctity of marriage, defend religious freedom and human dignity, and take the whole Gospel to a hurting world, we the undersigned evangelical leaders resolve to come together with others of like mind to pray and to work to stop global warming.[71]

Clearly anticipating the key issues of importance to its evangelical readership, the ad places climate change among them, thereby seeking to alleviate concerns that becoming involved in the issue somehow necessarily makes one politically "liberal" across the board. ECI directly addresses this concern in its "Frequently Asked Questions" document, which first articulates the biblical basis for stewardship, then argues that "climate change is not a liberal issue. It is a profound problem for people Jesus loves, people Jesus died to save."[72] No matter how savvy and far-reaching ECI may be, however, the fact still remains that ISA represents a coherent and powerful opposition.

The ISA's opposition is powerful enough, in fact, to deter two prominent NAE officials, Richard Cizik and then-president Ted Haggard, from signing the ECI *Call to Action.*[73] This development was clearly frustrating for Calvin DeWitt, who said that "a year ago, it looked as though evangelicals would become a strong, collective voice for what we call 'Creation care' and others may call environmentalism . . . [Haggard's and Cizik's lack of action] will have negative consequences for the ability of evangelicals to influence the White House, unfortunately and sadly."[74] The discord among the evangelical leadership surely affects not only their political power but their influence among the evangelical laity as well; the lack of a coherent message seems likely to confuse the masses. At this point, though the liberal evangelical movement appears to be gaining momentum, the liberals still do not hold the same sway that conservative evangelicals do on this issue. The next few years will be critical in determining which group succeeds in articulating a coherent stance on climate change. Although the issue of global warming remains in question at least for some, its inherent uncertainties are attenuated with each passing year (the most recent IPCC report, released early in 2007, assessed the likelihood of anthropogenic climate change at 90 percent or more), forcing the real battle between conservative and liberal evangelical environmentalists to occur on the economics of the issue. For liberal evangelical environmentalists, the challenge is in convincing fellow evangelicals that emissions reduction policies (1) will not hurt them economically (or will be worth the hurt) and, more important, that (2) such policies are the best way to address the effects of climate change and fulfill the biblical obligation to the poor of the world.

Climate change, along with other social humanitarian issues such as genocide, human rights, and the AIDS epidemic may yet prove to be a catalyst for evangelical political realignment encompassing more traditionally "liberal" issues. Of course, the promise of a less politically conservative evangelicalism has come before, only to be squashed by the ascendance of the Christian Right. Robert Wuthnow argues that in the 1960s and 1970s, "it appeared that the gap between religious liberals and conservatives might be bridged by a significant segment of the evangelical community," but that these voices were drowned out by evangelicals mobilizing around the *Roe v. Wade* Supreme Court decision and elections of the early 1980s.[75] If climate change proves to inspire a sustained iteration of the change that glimmered and then faded some forty years ago, the current internal evangelical fight over the issue raises two distinct possibilities: on the one hand, a liberalizing, centrist evangelical consensus about climate change that succeeds in broadening the evangelical agenda to include environmental and social justice issues; on the other hand, discord within evangelicalism, splintering the faith into new centrists with a broad social agenda and old traditionalists with a narrower moral agenda. Key to the ultimate success of either liberal or conservative evangelical environmentalists, however, may be the observable (and nearly impossible to ignore) impacts of climate change—irregular weather patterns, severe storms like Hurricane Katrina, melting ice caps, and the like—which are wholly out of their control. These natural events have already proven critically important in driving the urgency of religious and political responses to environmental questions. For evidence of this, one only has to look to conservative evangelical Pat Robertson, who reversed course and admitted that 2006's summer heat wave convinced him of global warming's legitimacy.[76] In a sense, then, only nature itself holds the answers to how hot and how damned the United States will become.

Notes

Many thanks are due to Susan Curtis, Leigh Raymond, and especially P. Ryan Schneider for their insightful suggestions and criticisms at various points in the development of this essay, which unquestionably made the finished product a better one.

1. Religion and Ethics NewsWeekly, "Evangelicals and the Environment," http://www.pbs.org/wnet/religionandethics/week920/cover.html (accessed June 5, 2007).
2. Estimates vary widely in part because researchers and scholars have found it difficult to agree upon what exactly the term *evangelical* means, but 30 percent appears to be a reasonable figure.
3. While this essay necessarily deals with theological and scientific issues, I do not pretend to be either a theologian or a scientist; I do not attempt to interpret biblical passages or hard scientific evidence on my own. Instead, I endeavor to analyze the state of the theological and scientific debates centering on environmental stewardship and climate change policy.
4. Although "evangelical Christian" is a term that has been used by the news media interchangeably with terms such as "Christian conservative," "Christian Right," "Christian fundamentalist," and so on, these do not accurately describe a significant number of self-described evangelical Christians. I contend that the definition offered by Mark Noll, an evangelical and a scholar, is appropriate, in a sense bridging the gap between scholarly and self-applied definitions. Following British historian David Bebbington, Noll sees "the key ingredients of evangelicalism as conversionism (an emphasis on the 'new birth' as a life-changing religious experience), Biblicism (a reliance on the Bible as ultimate religious authority), activism (a concern for sharing the faith), and crucicentrism (a focus on Christ's redeeming work on the cross)," all of which are characteristics that not only differentiate evangelicals from mainline Protestants, but also shape the ways in which they respond to climate change. See Mark A. Noll, *The Scandal of the Evangelical Mind* (Grand Rapids, Mich.: William B. Eerdmans, 1994), 8. Noll's book is a plea for evangelicals to embrace intellectual life. He is a professor of Christian thought at Wheaton College, an evangelical school in Illinois.
5. It is because these two groups—both liberal and conservative evangelical environmentalists—line up closely with so-called liberal and conservative political approaches to climate change policy that I refer to them as such. Again, this denotation does not refer to their theological orientation or even their broader political orientation; it instead refers solely to their stance on climate change.
6. The most recent Intergovernmental Panel on Climate Change (IPCC) assessment advocates a combination of mitigation and adaptation strategies. See IPCC Working Group II, *Climate Change 2007: Climate Change Impacts, Adaptation and Vulnerability: Summary for Policymakers*, at *http://www.ipcc.ch/SPM13apr07.pdf* (accessed June 5, 2007).
7. While the ISA is indeed "interfaith," it is largely evangelical, as evidenced not only by its leadership, but also by its direct engagement with the NAE and its oppositional evangelical group, the Evangelical Climate Initiative. Although the ISA was founded in November 2005, yet another group, created in May 2007 and calling itself the Cornwall Alliance for the Stewardship of Creation, has already supplanted ISA as the primary conservative evangelical environmentalist group working from the principles of the Cornwall Declaration. The Cornwall Alliance appears to have become a more unapologetically exclusive evangelical organization, dropping "Interfaith" from its title and trumpeting its formation as something announced (solely) by evangelical leaders (see http://www.cornwallalliance.org/docs/Announcement.pdf [accessed June 5, 2007]). That said, the succession from ICES to ISA to the new Cornwall Alliance should be seen as changes in name only rather than radical departures from previous groups. Indeed, the people and organizational documents carry over nearly seamlessly from one group to the next; E. Calvin Beisner, for example, remains the organizational spokesman for the Cornwall Alliance (see *www.cornwallalliance.org* for more information). For these reasons and because of the Cornwall Alliance's organizational infancy, in this essay I continue to refer to the ISA and not the Cornwall Alliance as the primary conservative evangelical environmentalist organization.
8. Before the analysis of biblical interpretations can proceed, I must address the distinction between beliefs and practices of the evangelical leadership and the laity. While the laity surely has its own diversity of biblical interpretation, the theological conclusions I analyze are by and large limited to the evangelical leadership. There are inevitably pitfalls to this type of analysis, but the assumption is that evangelical leadership anticipates and influences, if not represents, the attitudes of the masses.
9. For a conservative perspective, see E. Calvin Beisner, *Where Garden Meets Wilderness: Evangelical Entry into the Environmental Debate* (Grand Rapids, Mich.: Acton Institute for the Study of Religion and

Liberty, 1997), 43. The liberal perspective is embodied by Evangelical Environmental Network, "On the Care of Creation," *http://www.creationcare.org/resources/declaration.php* (accessed June 5, 2007).

10. This essay mainly seeks to examine evangelical environmentalism as it has engaged climate change. For a more historical perspective on the movement, see David Kenneth Larsen, "God's Gardeners: American Protestant Evangelicals Confront Environmentalism, 1967–2000" (PhD diss., University of Chicago, 2001).

11. *Holy Bible: New International Version* (Colorado Springs, Colo.: International Bible Society, 1984).

12. E. Calvin Beisner, "Biblical Principles for Environmental Stewardship," in Interfaith Stewardship Alliance, "An Examination of the Scientific, Ethical and Theological Implications of Climate Change Policy," *http://www.interfaithstewardship.org/pdf/ISA_Climate_Change.pdf* (accessed June 5, 2007), 14.

13. Beisner, "Biblical Principles for Environmental Stewardship," 15.

14. For a balanced and readable account of the science underlying climate change theory, see John Houghton, *Global Warming: The Complete Briefing*, 3rd ed. (Cambridge: Cambridge University Press, 2004). For a good reference on the areas of agreement as well as areas of uncertainty in climate change science, see Donald A. Brown, *American Heat* (Lanham, Md.: Rowman & Littlefield, 2002), 103–17.

15. See Beisner, "Biblical Principles for Environmental Stewardship," 13.

16. Ron Sider, "Message from an Evangelical: The Place of Humans in the Garden of God," *The Amicus Journal* 17 (Spring 1995): 13.

17. Beisner, "Where Garden Meets Wilderness," 15.

18. Fred Van Dyke et al., *Redeeming Creation: The Biblical Basis for Environmental Stewardship* (Downers Grove, Ill.: InterVarsity Press, 1996), 97.

19. Interfaith Council for Environmental Stewardship, "The Cornwall Declaration on Environmental Stewardship," http://www.stewards.net/CornwallDeclaration.htm (accessed June 7, 2007).

20. For a secular take on climate change's potential impacts on the poor, see Brown, *American Heat*, 92–94, who culls most of his information from the Intergovernmental Panel on Climate Change (IPCC) 2001 assessment.

21. Evangelical Environmental Network, "An Evangelical Declaration on the Care of Creation," http://www.creationcare.org/resources/declaration.php (accessed June 5, 2007).

22. An early attempt to apply New Testament theology to Creation Care failed to significantly alter the movement's rhetoric. See Calvin B. DeWitt, ed., *The Environment and the Christian : What Does the New Testament Say about the Environment?* (Grand Rapids, Mich.: Baker Book House, 1991).

23. Liberal evangelical environmentalists tend to rely heavily on verses from the book of Matthew in arguing a biblically based concern for the poor.

24. John Porretto, "Religious leaders ask automakers to build more fuel-efficient products," The Associated Press State & Local Wire, November 21, 2002.

25. National Association of Evangelicals, "The Sandy Cove Covenant and Invitation," http://www.nae.net/index.cfm?FUSEACTION=editor.page&pageID=121&IDCategory=9 (accessed June 5, 2007).

26. The IPCC is the foremost international organization researching climate change. It released comprehensive assessment reports in 1990, 1995, 2001, and 2007.

27. John Houghton, "Climate Change—a Christian Challenge and Opportunity," *http://www.creationcare.org/resources/climate/houghton.php* (accessed June 5, 2007).

28. Laurie Goodstein, "Evangelical Leaders Join Global Warming Initiative," *New York Times*, February 8, 2006.

29. Evangelical Climate Initiative, *Climate Change: An Evangelical Call to Action*, http://www.evangelicalclimateinitiative.org/statement (accessed June 5, 2007).

30. Quoted in Bill Moyers's PBS program *Moyers on America: "Is God Green?"* at http://www.pbs.org/moyers/moyersonamerica/print/isgodgreen_transcript_print.html (accessed June 5, 2007).

31. "Evangelicals attack environmentalists," *Christian Century*, May 3, 2000, 497.

32. Interfaith Council, "The Cornwall Declaration."

33. Interfaith Stewardship Alliance, "Vast Majority of Evangelicals Not Represented by 'Evangelical Climate Initiative'," *http://biz.yahoo.com/prnews/060208/dcw045.html* (accessed March 8, 2006).

34. Andy Crouch, "Environmental Wager: Why Evangelicals Are—But Shouldn't Be—Cool toward Global Warming," *Christianity Today*, August 2005, 66.

35. Howard A. Snyder, "Why We Love the Earth," *Christianity Today*, May 15, 1995, 15.

36. Andy Crouch, "Environmental Wager," 66. Crouch's invocation of Houghton is far from an isolated incident; an EEN global warming fact sheet makes sure to note that the IPCC's "first three scientific assessments, in 1990, 1995, and 2001, were chaired by Sir John Houghton, an evangelical Christian," and the 2006 *Climate Change* further emphasizes Houghton's strong evangelical faith by stating that "from 1988–2002 the IPCC's assessment of the climate science was Chaired by Sir John Houghton, a devout evangelical Christian." See Evangelical Environmental Network, "EEN's Global Warming Briefing for Evangelical Leaders," http://www.creationcare.org/files/global_warming_briefing.pdf (accessed June 5, 2007), 2, and Evangelical Climate Initiative's *Climate Change.*

37. "Interview with Sir John Houghton on the Mall in Washington, D.C." *Creation Care Magazine,* Summer 2005, *http://www.creationcare.org/magazine/summer05.php* (accessed June 5, 2007).

38. In fact, that is precisely what John Houghton did when he "converted" Richard Cizik to realizing the "truth" of climate change science in 2002. See Moyers, *Moyers on America,* and Terry Gross, "Green Evangelist Richard Cizik," radio interview, *Fresh Air,* from WHYY and National Public Radio, http://www.npr.org/templates/story/story.php?storyId=6646568 (accessed June 5, 2007).

39. Roy W. Spencer, "Global Warming: How Much of a Threat?" in Interfaith Stewardship Alliance, "An Examination of the Scientific, Ethical and Theological Implications of Climate Change Policy," *http://www.interfaithstewardship.org/pdf/ ISA_Climate_Change.pdf* (accessed June 5, 2007): 5.

40. "Bush Administration Position: Remarks by the President on Global Warming," *Congressional Digest,* January 2004, 8.

41. White House News Release, "Fact Sheet: President Bush Is Addressing Climate Change," June 30, 2005, http://www.whitehouse.gov/news/releases/2005/06/20050630-16.html (accessed June 5, 2007).

42. U.S. Department of the Interior, "Interior Secretary Kempthorne Announces Proposal to List Polar Bears as Threatened Under Endangered Species Act," *http://www.fws.gov/home/feature/2006/12-27-06polarbearnews.pdf* (accessed June 5, 2007).

43. "Global Warming Debate," *Congressional Record,* January 4, 2005, S18.

44. "Science of Climate Change," *Congressional Record,* July 28, 2003, S10022.

45. James Davison Hunter, "The Shaping of American Foreign Policy," in *Evangelicals and Foreign Policy,* ed. Michael Cromartie (Washington, D.C.: Ethics and Public Policy Center, 1989), 72.

46. "Global Warming Debate," S18.

47. "Four Pillars of Climate Alarmism," *Congressional Record,* April 7, 2005, S3348.

48. Neither conservative nor liberal evangelical environmentalists have formally acknowledged or endorsed views forwarded by Bush or Inhofe, yet their approaches to climate change science bear so much resemblance to one another that it is worth pointing out. Additionally, although neither Bush nor Inhofe has explicitly aligned himself with either evangelical group, Inhofe in particular has been quite critical of the ECI. See Moyers, *Moyers on America.*

49. *Holy Bible: New International Version,* Proverbs 22:3.

50. Beisner, "Biblical Principles for Environmental Stewardship," 17.

51. Interfaith Council, "The Cornwall Declaration."

52. See, in particular, the "aspirations" of the signers of the Cornwall Declaration, found in the Interfaith Council's "Cornwall Declaration."

53. White House News Release, "Bush Is Addressing Climate Change." Also see White House News Release, "Climate Change Fact Sheet," May 18, 2005, http://www.whitehouse.gov/news/releases/2005/05/20050518-4.html (accessed June 5, 2007). See Spencer Abraham in *Science* 305 (July 30, 2004) for the outline of Bush's plan, and Paul Higgins in *Science* 306 (December 17, 2004) for a scientific reply.

54. See Evangelical Climate Initiative, "Scientific and Business Perspectives on Climate Change," http://www.evangelicalclimateinitiative.org/pub/scientific_business_perspectives_fact.pdf (accessed June 5, 2007). Similar concerns are evident in EEN publications. See, in particular, Evangelical Environmental Network and Creation Care Magazine, "EEN's Global Warming Briefing for Evangelical Leaders," http://www.creationcare.org/files/global_warming_briefing.pdf (accessed June 5, 2007).

55. Laurie Goodstein, "Evangelical Leaders Swing Influence Behind Effort to Combat Global Warming," *New York Times,* March 10, 2005.

56. John Houghton, *Global Warming,* 229–30. For similar arguments from the movement, see also Evangelical Environmental Network, "Hurricanes, Climate Change, and the Poor," *http://www.creationcare.org/files/hurricane_briefing.pdf* (accessed June 5, 2007); "Heat Stroke: The Climate for

Addressing Global Warming Is Improving," *Christianity Today*, October 2004, *http://www.christiani-tytoday.com/ct/2004/010/10.26.html* (accessed June 5, 2007); Evangelical Environmental Network, "A Call to Action: On Global Warming," *Creation Care Magazine*, Spring 2004, *http://www.creationcare.org/magazine/spring04.php* (accessed June 5, 2007).

57. Andy Crouch, "Environmental Wager," 66.

58. E. Calvin Beisner, "No Sure Bet: Two Replies to Andy Crouch's 'Environmental Wager,'" *http://www.interfaithstewardship.org/content/printarticle.php?id=150* (accessed June 5, 2007). For a similar response, see also Kenneth W. Chilton's piece in the same article.

59. Predictions of economic costs of instituting climate change policy (more specifically, the Kyoto Protocol) vary widely. For a good overview of "predicted climate impacts from global warming," derived mainly from the IPCC reports, see Brown, *American Heat*, 87–92.

60. See James L. Guth et al., "Theological Perspectives and Environmentalism among Religious Activists," *Journal for the Scientific Study of Religion* 32.4 (1993): 373–82; Heather Hartwig Boyd, "Christianity and the Environment in the American Public," *Journal for the Scientific Study of Religion* 38.1 (1999): 36–44; Douglas Lee Eckberg and Jean T. Blocker, "Varieties of Religious Involvement and Environmental Concerns: Testing the Lynn White Thesis," *Journal for the Scientific Study of Religion* 28.4 (1989): 509–17; and Andrew Greeley, "Religion and Attitudes Toward the Environment," *Journal for the Scientific Study of Religion* 32.1 (1993): 19–28.

61. James L. Guth et al., "Faith and the Environment: Religious Beliefs and Attitudes on Environmental Policy," *American Journal of Political Science* 39.2 (1995): 373.

62. Add to that varying definitions of "evangelical" and "literalism," not to mention a wide variety of methodologies across studies and polls, and it becomes virtually impossible to draw any hard and fast conclusions, particularly from older data.

63. Greenberg Quinlan Rosner Research Inc., "Religion and Ethics Newsweekly Frequency Questionnaire," April 5, 2004, http://www.pbs.org/wnet/religionandethics/week733/questionnaire.pdf (accessed June 5, 2007), 7. White evangelicals are somewhat less likely to see global warming as an extremely or very important threat, at 40 percent of respondents. The racial divide evident in evangelical environmental views is an important area for further research, particularly as Hispanic evangelicalism continues to grow.

64. ABC News/ *Time*/Stanford University, "Intensity Spikes Concern on Warming; Many See a Change in Weather Patterns," March 25, 2006, *http://abcnews.go.com/images/Politics/ 1009a1GlobalWarming.pdf* (accessed March 27, 2006). See also ABC News/ *Washington Post*, "Most Think Global Warming Has Begun But Differ with Scientists on Urgency," June 6, 2005, http://abcnews.go.com/images/Politics/983a3GlobalWarming.pdf (accessed June 5, 2007).

65. Ellison Research, "Nationwide Study Shows Concerns of Evangelical Christians over Global Warming," February 2, 2006, *www.evangelicalclimateinitiative.org/pub/ polling_report.pdf* (accessed June 5, 2007).

66. Ibid.

67. Ibid.

68. Blaine Harden, "The Greening of Evangelicals: Christian Right Turns, Sometimes Warily, to Environmentalism," *Washington Post*, February 6, 2005.

69. Evangelical Environmental Network, "Global Warming Briefing."

70. See Bill McKibben, "Sins of Emission," *Sojourners Magazine* 33.3 (March 2004): 8–12; Evangelical Environmental Network, "A Call to Action"; Jim Ball, "Progress in Senate on Addressing Global Warming," *Creation Care Magazine*, Summer 2005, *http://www.creationcare.org/ magazine/summer05.php* (accessed June 5, 2007).

71. Evangelical Climate Initiative, "Our Commitment to Jesus Christ Compels Us to Solve the Global Warming Crisis," www.evangelicalclimateinitiative.org/pub/ct_ad.pdf (accessed June 5, 2007).

72. Evangelical Climate Initiative, "Frequently Asked Questions (FAQs)," *http://www.evangelicalclimateinitiative.org/faq* (accessed March 8, 2006).

73. Cizik's name actually appeared as a signer on the *Christianity Today* print ad, but was removed on all subsequent ECI documents.

74. Alan Cooperman, "Evangelicals Will Not Take Stand on Global Warming," *Washington Post*, February 2, 2006. Haggard had previously signed the Sandy Cove Covenant; Cizik had signed both the covenant and the Oxford Declaration.

75. Robert Wuthnow, *The Struggle for America's Soul: Evangelicals, Liberals, and Secularism* (Grand Rapids, Mich.: W.B. Eerdmans, 1989), 35. See also Robert Wuthnow, *The Restructuring of American Religion: Society and Faith since World War II* (Princeton, N.J.: Princeton University Press, 1988), 374.

76. "Heat Convinces Robertson of Global Warming," *Reuters*, August 3, 2006, *http://www.msnbc.msn.com/id/14171691/* (accessed August 7, 2006).

Catholics, Democrats, and the GOP in Contemporary America

John T. McGreevy

True story: It is the day before Pope John Paul II's funeral, in April 2005. Assembling in Rome are the members of the official delegation of the United States government, including President and Mrs. Bush and a number of Catholic senators and representatives. Two of those Catholic senators are Democrats Dick Durbin of Illinois and John Kerry of Massachusetts.

As the two of them walk across St. Peter's Square, bystanders stop Kerry every few steps to bemoan his defeat in the presidential election just a few months before. Some of these admirers—including a few Italian priests—drape themselves over Kerry's lanky frame for group snapshots.

Then a single priest stops Kerry and Durbin. He warns Kerry that he will have to answer, perhaps in hell, for his position on abortion.

That priest is from Minnesota.

*****

Unraveling this vignette requires attention to three interlocking narratives. The first is the story of the once-happy but now troubled marriage between Catholics and the Democratic Party. The second is the history of the fight over public access, not to abortion, but to birth control. The third is the emergence of a new generation of bishops, priests, and lay intellectuals, suspicious of both theological and political liberalism, and eager to take a more adversarial posture toward modern society.

The first story of Catholics and Democrats is the most familiar. Most Catholics, clustered along the East Coast and in the Great Lakes region, voted Democratic in presidential elections for most of the twentieth century, an alliance jump-started by Al Smith's failed 1928 presidential campaign and cemented by Franklin Roosevelt's charisma, the early programs of his New Deal, and his sympathy for U.S. workers. (Roosevelt thrilled Catholic activists by quoting from Pius XI's 1931 encyclical on the economy, *Quadragesimo anno*, at a massive rally in Detroit during the final days of the 1932 campaign.)[1] Many Catholic voters drifted toward the popular Dwight Eisenhower in the 1950s, but a remarkable 78 percent voted for Catholic war hero John Kennedy in 1960. As late as 1968, two of the three Democratic candidates for president, Eugene McCarthy and Robert Kennedy, were serious Catholics on the liberal wing of the Democratic Party, and support from white Catholics in the North almost pushed the eventual Democratic nominee, Hubert Humphrey, past Richard Nixon. As Howard Dean recently put it, "the Democratic Party was built on four pillars—the Roosevelt intellectuals, the Catholic Church, labor unions, and African Americans."[2] (Dean ignores white southerners, the most reliable members of the pre–civil rights era Democratic Party, but the observation is accurate for the party in the North.)

George McGovern proved incapable of sustaining this Catholic backing in 1972, in part because the Democratic Party in the heady years between 1968 and 1972 became associated with a cultural liberalism that some Catholic voters, especially working-class whites, found unsettling. (Humphrey, during the bitter days of the 1972 Democratic primaries, inaccurately but effectively tarred McGovern as favoring "abortion, acid, and amnesty [for Vietnam-era draft evaders].")

Much of this uneasiness with the national Democratic Party in the late 1960s and early 1970s revolved around black-white racial tension, with working-class white Catholics in the North appalled by Democratic support for forced busing programs to alleviate racial imbalance in the public schools, and suspicious of efforts to integrate lily-white (and heavily Catholic) construction and trade unions. The sympathy for African American civil rights displayed by many priests and nuns in the late 1960s evoked among some white Catholics a raw sense of betrayal. One segregationist priest in Chicago, defying his archbishop and the head of his religious order, became an alderman as an advocate for the "forgotten minority" of white home owners.[3] J. Anthony Lukas's study of the busing crisis in Boston, *Common Ground*, pivoted on the role of the church, attempting to mediate between Catholic politicians and judges eager to end racial segregation (but often themselves living in suburban enclaves), and working-class white Catholics often incapable of welcoming African Americans, even African American Catholics, into their midst.[4] Neither Democratic Party nor church leaders devoted much attention to Latino Catholics in the late 1960s. However United Farm Workers' organizing campaigns led by Cesar Chavez and supported by Robert Kennedy in California's Central Valley, and subsequent cries of betrayal from Catholic landowners in the region, revealed a parallel set of political and religious divides.

As the various racial tensions of the 1960s and 1970s ebbed, abortion took center stage. But not right away. Until the early 1970s, most Democrats seemed more conservative than Republicans on abortion. Republican governors, including Nelson Rockefeller in New York and William Milliken in Michigan, signed or advocated laws loosening state restrictions on abortion. By contrast, Senator Edward Kennedy assured his constituents as late as 1971 that "abortion on demand is not in accordance with the value which our civilization places on human life." George McGovern's first choice for running mate in 1972, Senator Thomas Eagleton of Missouri, held pro-life views, as did McGovern's eventual running mate, Kennedy in-law and Peace Corps founder Sargent Shriver.[5]

Roe v. Wade made everything more partisan. In the last major statewide referendum on abortion before *Roe v. Wade*, Michigan's Catholics persuaded the state's voters to reject a measure eliminating state restrictions on abortion. (Working-class Catholic voters, often union members, proved decisive in the outcome.) Giddy with victory, staffers at the Michigan Catholic Conference began to lobby for increased welfare benefits to poor parents, as part of a "planned, integrated attack on those socio-economic inequities which prompted thousands of women (and men) to consider abortion preferable to protecting the lives of their unborn babies."[6]

Two months later the U.S. Supreme Court in *Roe v. Wade* eliminated almost all state restrictions on abortion. The number of abortions rose dramatically, to 1.5 million a year by 1980. This jump-started a grassroots anti-abortion movement, perhaps the largest social movement of the immediate post–civil rights era, led, funded, and supported in its first years by Catholics. At the same time, abortion rights became central to the modern women's movement in the United States (more so than in most of Europe), and these activists called the Democratic Party their home. Now no politician could dodge the issue (as Robert Kennedy had in 1968), and a generation of Catholic Democrats, some principled, some pragmatic, adopted a pro-choice stance.

They did not pay an electoral price. Catholic voters during this period were only modestly less pro-choice than the general population—a point worth emphasizing—and tended not to make abortion a voting issue. The number of pro-life Catholic Democrats holding high office dwindled, a decline marked by the 1984 Democratic Party platform, which described reproductive freedom as a "fundamental human right." (The same year, New York's Cardinal John O'Connor chastised Geraldine Ferraro, Walter Mondale's vice presidential running mate, for her pro-choice views, and New York's Governor Mario Cuomo defended his pro-choice position in a widely publicized speech at Notre Dame.)

In 1992, leading Democrats notoriously prevented Pennsylvania's Governor Robert Casey, the country's most prominent pro-life Catholic Democrat, from speaking at the party's national convention.

The Republican Party moved in the other direction. Its most prominent congressional voice became an Illinois Catholic, Congressman Henry Hyde, who endeared himself to Catholic conservatives by attacking the use of Medicaid funds for abortions. ("I stand before you," Hyde would tell Catholic audiences in the 1970s, "a 652-month-old fetus.") More important, for the first time prominent evangelical theologians such as Francis Schaeffer and ministers such as Jerry Falwell threw themselves into the anti-abortion campaign, and their enthusiasm helped propel a pro-life candidate, Ronald Reagan, into the White House.[7]

Bill Clinton stemmed this Catholic drift into the Republican Party during the 1990s, and the relationship of Catholic politicians to their bishops faded from the headlines. (A new cluster of pro-choice Catholic Republicans in states where pro-life politicians have little hope for election to statewide public office, including Arnold Schwarzenegger in California and George Pataki and Rudy Giuliani in New York, also complicated the picture.) But in 2004 Democrats nominated John Kerry, a pro-choice Catholic, for president. A few bishops battered the Kerry campaign with prohibitions, or threatened prohibitions, on his receiving Communion. Kerry himself, when asked about abortion in the second presidential debate, offered a windy soliloquy "about life and about responsibility" that begged the hard questions.

In the aftermath of Kerry's defeat, Democrats began to pick up the pieces. As part of this effort, Democratic pollster Stanley Greenberg—famous for his analysis of Reagan Democrats in Macomb County, Michigan—and an associate, Matt Hogan, polled white Catholics.[8] Greenberg and Hogan paid special attention to Democratic defectors, the small but crucial group of white Catholic Democrats, especially in Ohio and other battleground midwestern states, who voted for Clinton in 1996 but supported George W. Bush in 2004. (Clinton carried white Catholics by seven points in 1996, Gore lost them by seven points in 2000, and Kerry lost white Catholics by fourteen points in 2004.) In an election in which notions about morality played an important role, these Catholic Democrats named abortion as their "single greatest moral concern." Indeed, Galston, a onetime Clinton aide, recently argued that vetoing the partial-birth abortion ban was the "single worst political mistake that Bill Clinton made in his eight years. . . . If there was ever an issue to take off the table, that was it."

The Supreme Court nominations of John Roberts and Samuel Alito also testified to the durability of the abortion debate. A Catholic Kabuki theater marked Roberts's confirmation hearings, especially, with the liberal Catholic lions on the Senate Judiciary Committee, including Kennedy from Massachusetts, Durbin from Illinois, and Patrick Leahy from Vermont, probing the Catholic Roberts on his views on privacy and individual rights, while Catholic conservatives tied to the Bush administration muttered about anti-Catholic litmus tests. (Roberts's wife, Jane Sullivan Roberts, a College of the Holy Cross graduate, has also donated her legal talents to Feminists for Life.) Tim Russert on *Meet the Press* asked Durbin to explain how as a congressman he had once called for *Roe v. Wade* to be overturned, but now, as a senator, termed opposition to *Roe v. Wade* "out of the mainstream." Durbin, in turn, recalled that he came to Washington holding pro-life views but discovered that many opponents of abortion were unwilling to make exceptions for victims of rape or incest. Even more troubling, so many "opponents of abortion were also opponents of family planning. This didn't make any sense to me."[9]

*****

Durbin's last point is intriguing, if inevitably self-interested. Understanding the contemporary American abortion debate requires a return to the dimly recalled history of the public debate about contraception. In 1930, Pius XI, the same pope who just three months later in *Quadragesimo anno* would condemn "individualist economic teaching," chose, in *Casti connubii*, to define all contraceptive use as immoral.

By then, as Margaret Sanger and other birth-control advocates delighted in pointing out, Catholics remained the only sizable lobby opposed to liberalization of laws regarding birth control. The issue began to flare up: Should the Army issue condoms to Catholic soldiers? Should Community Chest fund-raising drives contribute to Planned Parenthood chapters? The most heated debates took place in Massachusetts and Connecticut, where nineteenth-century laws (written by Protestants, not Catholics) that prohibited even married couples from purchasing contraceptives remained on the books. (Doctors evaded the law by prescribing contraceptives for "health" reasons.)

Catholics in Massachusetts defeated a first push to change the state's laws in 1940. In 1948, reformers tried again and Massachusetts voters again pushed them back, urged on by an archdiocesan-funded effort, with a billboard and radio campaign, emphasizing that "Birth Control Is Still against God's Law."

Sermon outlines distributed to all priests in the Boston Archdiocese explained that "the prohibition of birth control is not a law peculiar to the church any more than are the laws against murder, theft, perjury, or treason."

The Archdiocese of Boston won this battle only to lose the war. Leslie Tentler's *Catholics and Contraception*, now required reading for any bishop, priest, or layperson opining on this subject, details how confidence in church teaching on birth control collapsed over the next two decades.[10] The causes included the increasing frustration of married couples, especially married women, wed in their early twenties after World War II and bearing six, seven, eight, or more children; the conviction of priests, especially priests listening to their most idealistic and loyal parishioners in the confessional, becoming convinced that obeying church teaching and the sexual abstinence it required damaged as many marriages as it helped; and the unease among theologians about a natural-law teaching presumably accessible to reason that only Catholics found reasonable. By the mid-1960s many bishops hoped for a change in church teaching, and priests knew that their parishioners, some after agonized soul-searching, had abandoned it.

In 1965, a young Massachusetts Democrat named Michael Dukakis introduced a measure in the state legislature to legalize contraceptive use for married couples. Advised behind the scenes by Jesuit John Courtney Murray, Boston's archbishop, Richard Cushing, declined to oppose the measure. Then laboring over the *Declaration of Religious Freedom* at the Second Vatican Council, Murray composed a statement for Cushing insisting that it is not "the function of civil law to prescribe everything that is morally right and to forbid everything that is morally wrong." Given that contraceptive devices had "received official sanction by many religious groups within the community," Cushing, channeling Murray, urged Catholics to respect the religious freedom of their fellow citizens.[11] Two years later, just before his death in 1967, Murray regretted that church teaching on contraception "went too far," reaching for "too much certainty too soon."

★★★★★

From a pro-life perspective, this debate over birth control, and the widespread rejection of the 1968 papal encyclical rejecting "artificial" birth control, *Humanae vitae*, could not have been more ill timed.[12] As early as 1965, theologians such as Richard McCormick, S.J., were privately alerting their colleagues that "there is going to be a strong play for widening acceptable indications for abortion" and asking for assistance in distinguishing, in both the public and the Catholic mind, between contraception and abortion. A few Catholic conservatives, such as William F. Buckley Jr., even (briefly) advocated a liberalization of abortion laws for the same reason, respect of conscience, articulated by Murray in regard to contraception.

The alienation of Catholic women from church teaching on contraception also provided pro-choice organizations with an opportunity. Groups such as the National Abortion Rights Action League (NARAL) self-consciously promoted Catholic women as spokespersons in the state battles over abortion in the late 1960s and early 1970s, exploiting the reputation of a church perceived as incapable of acknowledging women's experiences. Even the bishops' point man on the abortion issue, Bishop James McHugh, privately conceded that the credibility of the Vatican on sexual and gender issues, in large part because of the debate over contraception, was such that official statements on abortion risked aggravating "the problems of *Humanae vitae*."

There matters stood until the election of Karol Wojtyla as Pope John Paul II in 1978. Over a generation, John Paul II's passionate pro-life stance shaped the U.S. abortion debate, as did his opposition to capital punishment. Most Americans still support legal abortion in some circumstances, but since the early 1990s, remarkably, support for the position that abortion should be legal in all circumstances has declined, while support for making abortion illegal in all circumstances has increased. That George W. Bush, in his tribute to John Paul II on the pope's death, sounded more like a Catholic bishop than a non-Catholic president, with references to his support for a "culture of life," reflected the late pope's influence as much as Karl Rove's ongoing effort to sway Catholic voters.[13]

In retrospect, John Paul II's conservative views on abortion and sexual ethics mirrored a wider withdrawal from 1960s-style liberalism in U.S. intellectual life, certainly in its Catholic variant. At the level of ideas, philosophers such as Alasdair MacIntyre attacked the "Enlightenment project" and a liberalism predicated on a false sense of moral neutrality. At the level of policy, Daniel Patrick Moynihan, Mary Ann Glendon, and James Q. Wilson cast jaundiced eyes on some liberal social-welfare policies and no-fault divorce. In the narrow world of Catholic polemics, neoconservatives such as Michael Novak, Richard John Neuhaus, and George Weigel pushed Catholic liberals to acknowledge the achievements of market capitalism, the importance of the two-parent family, and the unstable foundations of liberal church-state jurisprudence.

The moment passed. Trolling much of the Catholic press now means drowning in screeds. Sermons on the "crisis of fatherhood," the "decay of family life," and the need to check the "deceptive charm" of a culture unwilling to cultivate the virtue of "obedience" substitute for empirical analysis. We "slouch toward Gomorrah" in Robert Bork's heated phrasing. In retrospect, the 1996 imbroglio at Neuhaus's *First Things* over the "judicial usurpation of politics" marked a sectarian warning shot. (The magazine's editors warned that recent Supreme Court decisions on abortion, especially, meant that matters "have reached or are reaching the point where conscientious citizens can no longer give moral assent to the existing regime.")[14] More recent attacks by the neocons on the Jesuits, on those Catholics (including some bishops) who upheld traditional end-of-life teaching during the Terri Schiavo melodrama, and on the new archbishop of San Francisco as overly sympathetic to gays are only the most recent volleys.

Part of this rhetorical overkill stems from disappointment. John Paul II, despite his extraordinary charisma, did not stem the drift away from official church teaching on most of the hot-button sex and gender issues. More Catholic couples now use birth control than at the beginning of John Paul II's papacy, and the Greenberg/Hogan polling data highlight the sympathy of Catholic voters, even practicing Catholic voters supporting President Bush, for same-sex civil unions.

Within the church, John Paul II's frequent condemnations of contraception, his fiat against discussion of women's ordination, his refusal to appoint as bishop any priest not willing to defend *Humanae vitae*, and his characterization of the modern United States as a "culture of death," fostered a more sectarian mood. In August 2006, Bishop Thomas Doran of Rockford, Illinois, solemnly (and offensively) listed the "sacraments" of the Democratic Party as "abortion, buggery, contraception, divorce, euthanasia, feminism of the radical type, and genetic experimentation and mutilation." These Democratic positions, Doran cheerfully informed Rockford Catholics, "place us squarely on the road to suicide as a people."[15]

More politely, Denver archbishop Charles Chaput described Catholics as "timid" in a "culture that grows more estranged from the gospel with every year." Or, as Chaput explained two years ago to the *New Yorker's* Peter Boyer: "We're at a time for the church in our country when some Catholics—too many—are discovering that they've gradually become non-Catholics who happen to go to Mass. That's sad and difficult, and a judgment on a generation of Catholic leadership. But it may be exactly the moment of truth the church needs."[16]

To Chaput and other like-minded Catholics, the primary obstacle to a new evangelization is a "liberal culture" entrenched in the media, the universities, and, crucially, within the church itself. In an eerie echo of the 1960s, these spokespersons urge their coreligionists to reject not just the mainstream media but the Catholic mainstream as well. Protect your children at Steubenville, a countercultural Catholic college in Ohio, instead of lobbing them to the wolves at Boston College or Notre Dame. Former Pennsylvania senator Rick Santorum even blamed Boston liberalism—instead of, say, Cardinal Bernard Law—for that archdiocese's implosion during the sexual-abuse crisis, a dubious claim given what the Philadelphia district attorney has recently told us about sexual abuse in that archdiocese.

This more apocalyptic ecclesiastical mood blended with the waning of the Catholic subculture over the past thirty years and the felt need of a significant minority of young Catholics for more familiarity with the faith they professed. Much like mainline Protestants and Jews, Catholic leaders of the 1970s and 1980s never solved the larger puzzle of what serious catechetical education might entail in a more mobile, fragmented society. Sociologist Christian Smith's recent surveys suggest that Catholic young people are notably uninformed about their own religious heritage.[17] At Notre Dame, where I teach, more than half of the students did not attend Catholic high schools, one marker of the attenuation of the institutional subculture. A colleague claims that some of her juniors and seniors, almost all Catholic, cannot identify Pontius Pilate.

The more committed Catholic young people lurch between service to the church and society through volunteer programs and a defensive circling of the wagons. One local conservative student newspaper recently carried the following headline: "Can Women Be Priests? A Full Defense of the Authoritative Church Position, and Why It Cannot and Will Not Change."

★★★★★

Given these three contexts: the relationship of Catholics to the Democratic Party, the partisan cast of the abortion debate since *Roe v. Wade,* and the more sectarian tone in recent Catholic life, perhaps the real surprise is that the priest from Minnesota didn't insist on escorting John Kerry to hell himself.

Still, a new political moment and a new papacy do contain hints of change. Emily's List, the pro-choice fund-raising operation, remains the most important source of independent funds in the Democratic Party. But Robert Casey Jr., a pro-life Catholic Democrat, received the enthusiastic backing of chastened party leaders in his successful 2006 Pennsylvania senatorial race against Rick Santorum, and a number of pro-life Catholic Democrats won high-profile races across the country. (Casey's background as the Catholic-school-attending scion of a Democratic family from Scranton, and Santorum's vocal participation in the culture wars, his decision to homeschool his children, and his association with "JPII"-style Catholics, made this U.S. Senate race the most expensive in U.S. history, a clash in Catholic styles as well.)

Democrats for Life now claims thirty-two Democratic congressional representatives as pro-life, many of whom have endorsed the organization's 95–10 initiative, aimed at reducing the number of abortions in the United States by 95 percent in ten years. Cardinal Theodore McCarrick, chair of the bishops' task force on Bishops and Catholic Politicians, recently cautioned against importing the "intense polarization and bitter battles of partisan politics" into the church, and commended off-the-record discussions with and information sessions for Catholic politicians. McCarrick's successor as archbishop of Washington, Donald Wuerl, infuriated neoconservatives by refusing to comment on pro-choice speaker of the House Nancy Pelosi's installation, complete with a Catholic Mass celebrated at her alma mater, Trinity University. New York's Cardinal Edward Egan recently described Hillary Clinton and pro-choice Catholic Republicans George Pataki and Rudy Giuliani as "friends of mine."[18]

Pope Benedict XVI's view about the relationship between religion and politics will become more clear over time. His record suggests skepticism about Catholic politicians recording 100 percent NARAL voting records. Still, the first years of his papacy also suggest a willingness to engage rather than merely admonish fellow Catholics about contested issues. The recent plea of the former San Francisco archbishop William Levada, now prefect of the Congregation of the Doctrine of the Faith, for more discussion of the problem of Catholic politicians, abortion, and Communion also reminds us that the abortion question is not simply a problem in the United States. (In the fall of 2006, the Italian press buzzed with discussion of meetings between center-left Christian Democrat Rosy Bindy and top Vatican officials, including Benedict XVI, on matters of sexual ethics. On his recent trip to Brazil, Benedict XVI generated a wave of commentary when questioned on the plane about the passage of less restrictive abortion laws in Mexico.) Instead, it is a case study for the universal church of how Catholics vote and work within societies that do not embody the norms of Catholic social thought.

None of this denies the hypocrisy of many Catholic Democrats (and some Catholic Republicans) on the abortion issue. It simply recognizes that the hot-house ecclesiastical climate created in the last decade of John Paul II's papacy, which endures in the bishops he appointed and some of the young people he inspired, nurtured a kind of romantic purity, a prophetic denunciation of a U.S. society for which Catholics are, after all, in large part responsible.

That these tensions between Catholic social thought and U.S. politics will continue to roil political waters seems clear. In the short term, pro-choice Catholic Republicans such as Rudy Giuliani and pro-life Catholic Democrats such as Robert Casey, Jr., make the abortion issue more controversial within both parties, as well as between them. Recent ballot measures on stem cell research in Missouri (which the local archbishop compared to slavery), abortion in South Dakota (which rejected a law that banned abortions without any exception for rape and incest), and gay marriage both mobilize (and polarize) voters. The affinity of some Catholics for the neoconservative movement within the Republican party also seems enduring, and of course the ideas of Catholics Anthony Kennedy, Clarence Thomas, John Roberts, Antonin Scalia, and Samuel Alito—the majority in *Gonzalez v. Carhart* (2007), the recent Supreme Court decision upholding state bans on partial-birth abortion—will continue to shape American jurisprudence.

The long-term forecast is hazier. The dispirited character of contemporary U.S. Catholicism, with Mass attendance falling, a sharp decrease in the number of Catholic couples choosing marriage within the church, low rates of vocations to the religious life, and the massive trauma of the sexual abuse crisis, suggests a diminished role. The history of the mainline Protestant denominations—central to American identity and public life in 1950, invisible now—is not reassuring for Catholic leaders.

Still, Catholics remain the nation's single largest church, claiming the allegiance of roughly one-quarter of the population. One unexpected lever for change may come from the Vatican, where the focus on the global South, especially the flourishing church in Africa, looks to be a major theme of Benedict XVI's papacy. More predictable pressures will come from the waves of Latino Catholic immigrants and their descendants exercising the franchise not just in California, Arizona, and Texas, but in Georgia and Illinois. With the notable exception of Florida's Cuban Catholics, these Latino Catholics, primarily Mexican American, have historic ties to the Democratic Party in some of the same ways as Poles and Irish once did. But evangelical Protestant Latinos proved significantly more likely in 2004 to support George W. Bush than John Kerry, and their number is growing at a steady pace in both Latin America and the United States as nominal Catholics switch to more fervent and intimate Pentecostal and evangelical congregations. At the same time, constant immigration and relatively high birth rates replenish the Latino Catholic population in the United States, with an inevitable effect on church life. The relationship of Cardinal Roger Mahony of Los Angeles with Latino Catholics in his own archdiocese has been controversial, but it is significant that Latino organizers of the largest parade for immigrants' rights in U.S. history, 500,000 estimated in Los Angeles in April 2006, asked him to march at its head. (Mahony's fluent Spanish and work as a young priest in California's Central Valley in support of the United Farm Workers' organizing campaigns make him an unusual link between the late 1960s and contemporary concerns.) Catholic bishops across the country have also been active in support of such organizing campaigns as Justice for Janitors.

The Italian priests standing with John Kerry in St. Peter's Square did not, one imagines, admire Kerry's inarticulate position on abortion. Instead, they opposed the American invasion of Iraq, and the mores of a society that permits record economic inequality. This European Catholic vision overlaps but is not identical with that of John Kerry, Nancy Pelosi, Rudy Giuliani, Rick Santorum and Benedict XVI. But they are all Catholic. And how these swirling crosscurrents, caged within the world's biggest and most global institution, are translated into an American idiom will mark the next chapter in the relationship between Catholicism and politics in the United States.

Notes

An earlier version of this article appeared as "Shifting Allegiances: Catholics, Democrats, and the GOP" in *Commonweal*, September 22, 2006 (133.16), 14–19.

1. John T. McGreevy, *Catholicism and American Freedom: A History* (New York: Norton, 2003), 151ff.
2. See Jeffrey Goldberg, "Central Casting," *The New Yorker*, May 29, 2006 (82.15), 62–71.
3. John T. McGreevy, *Parish Boundaries: The Catholic Encounter with Race in the Twentieth-Century Urban North* (Chicago: University of Chicago Press, 1996), 231–34.
4. J. Anthony Lukas, *Common Ground: A Turbulent Decade in the Lives of Three American Families* (New York: Knopf, 1985).
5. McGreevy, *Catholicism and American Freedom*, 279–80.
6. Ibid., 277.
7. The rise of the Religious Right has been recounted by numerous scholars as well as journalists; one useful account is William Martin, *With God on Our Side: The Rise of the Religious Right in America* (New York: Broadway Books, 1996). Hyde quoted at http://www.georgiabulletin.org/local/1979/01/25/a (accessed July 2, 2007).
8. The results are available at http://www.democracycorps.com. A more comprehensive analysis of the Democrats' prospects that draws on the Greenberg/Hogan analysis is "The Politics of Polarization," by William A. Galston and Elaine C. Kamarck, available at third-way.com.

9. "NBC News' Meet the Press," transcript for July 24, 2005, available at *http://www.msnbc.msn.com/id/8658626/* (accessed July 2, 2007).

10. Leslie Woodcock Tentler, *Catholics and Contraception: An American History* (Ithaca, N.Y.: Cornell University Press, 2004).

11. McGreevy, *Catholicism and American Freedom*, 237–38.

12. Tentler, *Catholics and Contraception*; Peter Steinfels, *A People Adrift: The Crisis of the Roman Catholic Church in America* (New York: Simon & Schuster, 2003), 253–75.

13. "President's Statement on the Death of Pope John Paul II," April 2, 2005, *http://www.whitehouse.gov/news/releases/2005/04/20050402-4.html* (July 2, 2007).

14. "The End of Democracy? The Judicial Usurpation of Politics," *First Things* 67.1 (November 1996): 18.

15. Bishop Thomas G. Doran, "Reaping the Whirlwind of Abortion," *Observer*, August 11, 2006; posted online at *http://www.rockforddiocese.org/observer/observer.asp?a=5#bishop* (accessed July 2, 20007).

16. Peter Boyer, "A Hard Faith," *The New Yorker*, May 16, 2005 (81.13), 65.

17. Christian Smith, *Soul Searching: The Religious and Spiritual Lives of American Teenagers* (New York: Oxford University Press, 2005).

18. McCarrick quote at *http://www.beliefnet.com/story/193/story_19383_1.html*; Egan interview with New York WNBC reporter David Ushery at http://whispersintheloggia.blogspot.com/2007/01/egan-john-carroll-got-it-right.html (accessed July 2, 2007).

Islamism and Its African American Muslim Critics: Black Muslims in the Era of the Arab Cold War

Edward E. Curtis IV

Rather than treating African American Muslims as marginal Muslims, a species of Muslim largely separate from immigrant Muslims, this essay adopts black Muslim perspectives on the history of Islamism, the twentieth-century transnational ideology that sees Islam as both a political system and a religion. I argue that the contours of Islamic identity and practice among African Americans after the Second World War developed partly in response to nascent Islamist missionary efforts led by ideological participants in the so-called Arab cold war. During this era, Islamic missionary activity became a well-funded and well-organized component of Saudi Arabia's foreign policy. Several international organizations, local Islamic centers, and tract societies targeted U.S. blacks as potential allies in the struggle to construct Islamic religion as a response to Arab socialism and nationalism. As foreign and immigrant Muslim missionaries reached out to African American Muslims in the 1960s, they claimed the authority to interpret what constituted legitimate Islamic practice, encouraged African American Muslims to join their missionary organizations, and in some cases, challenged the Islamic authenticity of indigenous African American Muslim groups and leaders.

This contact and competition with the missionaries had far-reaching implications and important repercussions for African American Muslim religious practice and political identity. In one sense, African American Muslim reactions to the Islamist call reflected the ideological and cultural diversity of the thousands of African Americans who called themselves "Muslim." It is no surprise—given that there were more than a dozen different African American Muslim networks and groups by 1960—that African American Muslim responses would differ. In addition to creating the famous Nation of Islam and well-known Moorish Science Temple, African American Muslims by this date had either established or come to dominate the leadership of many Ahmadi Muslim mosques, the Islamic Brotherhood (or the State Street Mosque of

Brooklyn), the Addeynu Allahe Universal Arabic Association, the Fahamme Temple of Islam and Culture, and the First Mosque of Pittsburgh, which reportedly had subcharters in Kirkwood and St. Louis, Missouri; Philadelphia, Pennsylvania; Cleveland, Ohio; and Jacksonville, Florida.[1] Rather than attempting to describe all of these groups' reactions to the new missionary activity, however, I will limit my discussion to three strains of African American Muslim hermeneutics, exemplified respectively by Malcolm X, the Nation of Islam, and Shaikh Daoud Ahmed Faisal, the founder of the State Street Mosque. I show how Shaikh Daoud Ahmed Faisal aligned his community of believers with Islamist ideology; how Malcolm X became the student and ally of these new foreign and immigrant missionaries, though he resisted their politicized interpretation of Islam; and finally, how members of Elijah Muhammad's Nation of Islam rejected the missionaries' claims to ultimate religious authority and instead defended Elijah Muhammad's prophetic voice. These differing reactions are important, if for no other reason than they disprove the notion, at least implied in the arguments of many Islamophobes, that foreign Islamist missionaries have been pied pipers leading all indigenous U.S. Muslims toward the deadly ideology of violent jihad.

While restoring the historical agency of indigenous Muslims who responded in complex ways to foreign and immigrant Muslim groups and ideologies, this account also argues for some shared repercussions among African American Muslims. As a result of the increased immigrant and foreign Muslim presence in the United States, many more African American Muslims began to use canonical Islamic texts, including the Qur'an and in some cases, the *hadith* (the sayings and deeds of the Prophet Muhammad and his companions) to articulate ethical, theological, political, and socioeconomic visions for themselves and other U.S. blacks. This adoption of sacred texts altered not only the aesthetics of African American Muslim religious practices, but also the communal identity of persons who now thrust themselves into an age-old, transnational conversation about the meaning of these texts. Increasing African American Muslim identification with the rest of the Muslim world also became manifest in African American Muslim visual art and poetry. Many African American Muslims literally drew and rhymed themselves closer to the imagined worldwide community of Muslim believers. Finally, I discuss how this shift in African American Muslim consciousness had significant but diverse political implications, as African American Muslims came to hold differing interpretations of their obligations to the worldwide community of Muslims and the heritage of Islam.

Twentieth-Century African American Islam in Transnational Context

After the Second World War, religious and cultural exchange between indigenous African American Muslims and foreign Muslims, especially from the Middle East, expanded dramatically. In one sense, this expansion of ties was an acceleration of trends that began decades before, during the flowering of Islam as a twentieth-century African American religious tradition.[2] As the modern anticolonial struggle among persons of African descent became an international black freedom discourse, more and more African Americans and English-speaking people of color began to link the self-determination of African-descended people to the fate of Muslim persons and Muslim-majority lands. The nineteenth-century pioneer in this regard was Edward Wilmot Blyden, the African American Liberian professor and politician, whose English-language works, read in Britain, the Americas, and West Africa, praised Islam, the Qur'an, and West African Muslim society as effective vehicles of modern black manhood and nationalism.[3] Blyden's linkage of Islam and black nationalism was perpetuated in the English-speaking black world by the Universal Negro Improvement Association (UNIA). Arnold Ford, the musical director of the UNIA, included allusions to Allah in some of his movement songs, and the UNIA's *Negro World* supported pan-Islamic attempts to resist European imperialism. Marcus Garvey, the UNIA's founder, even compared himself to the Prophet Muhammad, though he was careful to contrast what he deemed his political aspirations with the religious goals of the Prophet.[4] Another African American leader, Timothy Drew, went further, proclaimed himself a Muslim prophet, and established the Moorish Science Temple in 1920s Chicago. Noble Drew Ali insisted that black Americans were Muslim in religion, Asiatic in race, and Moorish in nationality, and called on "Moors" to return to their original religion of Islam and their true national identity.[5] Foreign Muslim missionaries also promoted the link between black peoplehood and Islam in the 1920s, and South Asian missionaries from the Ahmadiyya community of Muslims successfully recruited hundreds, if not thousands, of African Americans to Islam in this era.[6] Established in 1889 in the Punjab by Ghulam Ahmad (d. 1908), the Ahmadiyya movement was a modern messianic group that sought the revival of Islam. Many of Ahmad's followers believed him to be a *mujaddid*, or a renewer of religion; the Islamic *mahdi*, an important figure in Islamic eschatology; and the Christian messiah. Though the group would face claims of heresy from other Muslims, Ahmadis were among the most successful Muslim missionaries in the first half of the 1900s.[7] In 1920,

South Asian Ahmadi missionary Muhammad Sadiq arrived in the United States, and as an astute observer of America's racialist society, quickly focused his evangelizing on African Americans. He promised black converts that they would experience true brotherhood and equality in Islam, claiming that "there is no question of color" in the East.[8] He also offered Islam as the cultural and religious heritage of African Americans, stolen from them when the "Christian profiteers brought you out of your native lands of Africa and in Christianizing you made you forget the religion and language of your forefathers—which were Islam and Arabic."[9] The Ahmadi newspaper, the *Moslem Sunrise*, featured the stories of great black ancestors in Islam, persons such as Bilal ibn Rabah, the first prayer caller, and included pictures of black American Ahmadi leaders such as P. Nathaniel Johnson, or Sheik Ahmad Din.[10] The Ahmadiyya also influenced many of the early independent African American mosques. The First Mosque of Pittsburgh, for example, supported an Ahmadi teacher for a time, and the First Cleveland Mosque was established by a former Ahmadi, African American Wali Akram, in the 1930s.[11] It is also possible that W. D. Fard, the mysterious Detroit salesman who established the Nation of Islam in 1930, was influenced by Ahmadi interpretations of Islam.[12] But whether or not Fard was touched by the Ahmadi missionaries, it is clear that Elijah Muhammad was. Muhammad and his cadre of intellectuals regularly quoted, verbatim, from Ahmadi literature, including Ahmadi translations of the Qur'an.[13]

In sum, from the time of its origins as a topic in international black English-language discourse, Islam was associated if not with an explicit black political nationalism then at least with ideas of black self-determination and shared historical destiny. African American Islam was also an international discourse shaped in part by contact and exchange with persons from Muslim-majority lands. But after the Second World War, during the era of decolonization and the "rising tide of color," African American interests in the link between black nationalism and Islam became even more prominent.[14] More and more persons in the African American diaspora identified Islam and Muslims as potential allies in the struggle against European neocolonialism and white supremacy, often framing the domestic struggle for civil rights as part of a global struggle for the self-determination of all persons of color. Malcolm X, for example, famously spoke of the 1955 Afro-Asian Conference of nonaligned countries in Bandung, Indonesia, as a turning point in the affairs of the world, as people of color everywhere vowed not only to reject the yoke of neocolonial political control, but also to eschew a colonized consciousness. After the 1956 Suez Crisis, Egyptian president Gamal Abdel Nasser emerged as a powerful symbol of victory in this third-world struggle against imperialism and inspired admiration among many African Americans, especially those associated with Elijah Muhammad and the Nation of Islam. When Nasser hosted the Afro-Asian conference in 1958, Elijah Muhammad telegrammed the Egyptian president to assure him that "freedom, justice and equality for all Africans and Asians is of far-reaching importance, not only to you of the East, but also to over 17,000,000 of your long-lost brothers of African-Asian descent here in the West." Some members of the Nation of Islam hung Nasser's picture in their homes. Nasser was received enthusiastically by Muslims and non-Muslims alike when he visited Harlem in 1960.[15]

Black American interests in Islam and the Muslim Orient went beyond the explicitly political, but even cultural and aesthetic identification with various things Islamic was often viewed as a form of political protest against the racial status quo. Several well-known African American jazzmen became converts in the 1940s and 1950s, largely under the missionary umbrella of the Ahmadiyya movement. Many of them played for Dizzy Gillespie. Antiguan Alfonso Nelson Rainey became Talib Dawud. Tenor saxophonist Bill Evans became Yusef Lateef. Lyn Hope converted and changed his name to Hajj Rashid. According to Gillespie, they converted in order to fight Jim Crow and the stigma of "being colored." In 1953, *Ebony* covered this trend by publishing an article titled "Moslem Musicians Take Firm Stand against Racism."[16] During this period, the Nation of Islam also embraced jazz artist converts, and jazz groups played at temple and mosque events.[17]

The broader African American interest in things Islamic and Muslim and the heightened profile of black Muslims such as Elijah Muhammad and Malcolm X also attracted the gaze of Muslims overseas. Nasser, for example, responded to Elijah Muhammad's 1958 telegram, extending his "best wishes to our brothers of Africa and Asia living in the West." Elijah Muhammad visited Egypt in 1959, and one of his sons, Akbar Muhammad, studied there during the 1960s.[18] These contacts between Egypt and the NOI begin to indicate the extent to which African American Muslims became potential foreign policy allies and symbols of political struggle, not only in the grand struggle for the freedom of all formerly colonized peoples, but also in the more local and regional struggles waged by differing interest groups in the Middle East. To understand foreign and immigrant Muslim engagement, especially Arab Muslim engagement with African American Muslims, it is necessary to explore more deeply how the financial, diplomatic, and cultural outreach of Arab Muslims was often colored by these local and regional interests. In the postwar era, the neocolonial elites and newly empowered military juntas who had seized authority within political boundaries initially drawn to serve European and U.S. interests were forced to negotiate the interference of superpowers, the pull of regional desires for pan-Arab unity, and the challenge of the Palestinian-Israeli conflict.[19] Part of their struggle was ideological, and although various national elites may have celebrated the solidarity of all formerly colonized peoples and touted both pan-Arabism and pan-Islamic unity, such rhetoric was often deployed to buoy their own national legitimacy and manage popular opinion.[20]

One seldom mentioned but pivotal crucible of African American Muslim and foreign Muslim interaction was what Malcolm Kerr famously referred to as the "Arab Cold War." The Arab cold war was a conflict waged primarily between the Kingdom of Saudi Arabia and Nasser's Egypt, which were locked in both ideological and military struggles from 1958 through the 1960s. The battle of ideas commenced shortly after Nasser successfully entered into a political union with Syria in the winter of 1958. The United Arab Republic (UAR), as the two states became known, signaled the growth of both revolutionary socialism and pan-Arabism, the movement to unite all Arab peoples into one political entity expressing their shared historical and linguistic roots. A few months later, when revolution overturned the Iraqi monarchy and an uprising occurred against President Sham'un in Lebanon, monarchs throughout the Middle East feared that Nasserism might actually succeed. The Arab cold war continued into the 1960s, perhaps reaching its apex in 1962, when Egypt sent troops to support the leftist revolution in Yemen. Saudi Arabia threw its financial and political clout behind the Yemeni monarchy.[21]

But Saudi Arabia and its allies also forged a secondary front in this war, an ideological effort designed to bolster its legitimacy in the West and among Muslim states and persons. This was a battle for hearts and minds, and it was joined through Saudi Arabia's generous support and careful organization of global missionary activities. Up to this point, missionary societies such as the Muslim Brothers in Egypt and the Society of the Call and Guidance in South Asia aspired mostly to change Islamic practices within historically Islamic lands.[22] By the 1960s, however, Saudi Arabia's aid allowed these groups' ideas to be broadcast, printed, and distributed around the world. In 1961, Saudi Arabia established a new university in Medina committed to the training of Muslim missionaries. The following year, as tension over Yemen escalated, the government also supported the founding of the Muslim World League, whose statement of purpose included a commitment to global missionary work. Not surprisingly, the conference was strongly anti-Nasser, promoting a vision of pan-Islam that hoped to counter the powerful Arab populist.[23] An impressive array of Muslim personages attended the organization's inaugural meeting, including Mawlana Mawdudi of Pakistan and Said Ramadan of Egypt. One of the most influential intellectuals of Islamic reform and revival in the twentieth century, Pakistani ideologue and Jama 'at-i Islami (Islamic party) founder Mawdudi argued that the *shari'a*, or Islamic law and ethics, provides God's blueprint for all human societies, which should be organized into an Islamic state.[24] Egyptian representative Said Ramadan was the son-in-law of Hasan al-Banna, the founder of the Muslim Brothers, an Islamist organization that Nasser came to oppose as he consolidated power in postrevolutionary Egypt. Seeking refuge from Nasser's repression in 1958, Said Ramadan immigrated to Switzerland, where he established, with Saudi assistance, the Centre Islamique des Eaux-Vives, an institution that became one of the nodes in a transnational Islamist intellectual network.[25] Like other Muslim Brothers, Ramadan insisted that Islam was a total way of life, applicable as much to public affairs as to private morality.[26]

Students, visitors, and refugees from the Middle East brought these Islamist ideas with them to the United States during the late 1950s and early 1960s. Confronting what they considered to be overly assimilated American Muslims, some Arab students immediately challenged the "liberal" and "Westernized" practices of various Muslim persons and organizations.[27] At the Islamic Center of New England, which had been built partly with a 1962 donation from King Saud, students made available various pieces of Islamic literature not previously translated into English.[28] In 1963, students from a variety of Muslim-majority countries gathered at the University of Illinois, Urbana-Champaign, to establish the Muslim Students Association (MSA). Among the founding members were three Muslim Brothers from Egypt. Using their positions on college campuses, these activists helped to make the MSA one of the most successful immigrant-led organizations in propagating Islamist ideas throughout North America.[29] In some cases, student advocates met African American Muslims who were already proponents of Islamist ideologies; in other cases, they confronted African American Muslims who had never heard the Islamist message.

African American Islamism in the Era of the Arab Cold War

One African American pioneer who had already articulated Islamist ideas in print by 1950 was Caribbean immigrant Shaikh Daoud Ahmed Faisal (d. 1980), reportedly the son of a Moroccan father and a Jamaican mother. Echoing the

Islamist call that all societies must be governed by the Islamic *shari'a*, his book, *Islam the True Faith: The Religion of Humanity*, proclaimed that human beings should submit their societies to the authority of God, the Prophet, and the *shari'a*.[30] Shaikh Daoud was a pioneer who successfully converted hundreds, if not thousands, of African Americans to a Sunni interpretation of Islam at his Brooklyn-based State Street mosque. His adventuresome spirit led him to establish a short-lived Muslim village in rural New York State, but he achieved his greatest success as leader of the mosque in Brooklyn. In 1939, he leased a brownstone at 143 State Street in Brooklyn Heights, just a block away from the heart of the Arab American community on Atlantic Avenue. He called his congregation the Islamic Mission of America in New York.[31] Shaikh Daoud welcomed both indigenous and immigrant Muslims to his mosque, where he warned them not to let the allure of the material world take them away from their Islamic practice.[32]

Before most Muslim missionaries had arrived from Afro-Eurasia, Shaikh Daoud's intellectual life bore the influence of Islamic reform and renewal movements. His publications, which often borrowed from other Muslim missionary tracts, sought to inform the American public on the basics of Islamic religion. They described the holy cities of Mecca and Medina, reproduced large excerpts from the Qur'an, taught believers how to make the *salat*, or daily prayers, and detailed and praised contemporary Muslim heads of state. As a New Yorker, Shaikh Daoud came to know Muslims who traveled to the city from various countries, especially diplomats who worked at the United Nations.[33] In the 1950 edition of *Islam the True Path*, he acknowledged the assistance not only of his wife, Khadijah, but also M. A. Faridi of Iran, Bashir Ahmed Khan of Pakistan, and others from Afro-Eurasia.[34] The sheikh was also pictured in this volume wearing light-colored Arab robes, sitting cross-legged on a prayer rug, or oriental carpet. In his hands he held the Qur'an, deeply contemplating its contents in the manner of an Old World Islamic scholar.

His mission was devoted to converting everyone in the United States to what he considered to be the only true religion of humankind. The profession of Islamic faith, he said, was a prerequisite to peace and security, as was Islam's implementation as a form of government and law based on the Qur'an. The holy book, he argued, "contains the complete Revelations of 'Allah,' the 'Almighty God,' the Lord of the worlds with the complete Laws for the government and guidance of humanity and as a protection for us from evil. The Criterion of all Laws is enclosed in the Holy Quran."[35] Shaikh Daoud's old-time missionary techniques, evangelical in tone, were harshly critical of Jews and Christians who ignored the truth that would set them free. He practically begged them to convert to Islam, warning that no one would be saved, no one would have "true religion," unless and until they became Muslims. Attacking the growing ecumenism among some American monotheists after the Second World War, Shaikh Daoud explicitly rejected the idea that all Abrahamic faiths were equally valid paths to salvation.[36] His criticism of Jews and Christians was grounded both in an Islamic critique of Jewish and Christian religious claims and in his experience as an African American New Yorker who had faced discrimination at the hands of some Jews and Christians. "The Jews of America are the proudest of all the people," he claimed. "If by chance a man of colour would move into their neighborhood they would raise such a rumpus which would give one cause to believe that that one person had committed murder."[37] He also criticized Christianity as a form of white supremacy. "Christianity," he claimed, is but a "social order, a philosophy, based on certain principles of White Supremacy, that White people are superior to their human brethren who are not White." Like other twentieth-century African American converts to Islam, he viewed Christianity as "an instrument of conquest."[38]

On the one hand, Shaikh Daoud's comments about Jews and Christians sound similar to other Islamic traditions of anti-Jewish and anti-Christian polemic grounded in a sense of religious superiority and particularity—a rhetorical mode hardly unique to Islam.[39] On the other hand, Faisal's critique also reflects a reading of history shaped by the racist contexts in which he was living—in 1950 and after, white Jews and Christians, from this black man's point of view, did indeed seem like godless creatures when they discriminated against people of color in their own neighborhoods and in foreign lands.[40] In asserting that Islam was the solution to such problems, Shaikh Daoud was participating in multiple discourses international and local in scope. He did not resort to violence to achieve his end; instead, he relied on quintessentially American missionary techniques: he wrote missionary tracts, preached of divine justice and the chance of salvation, and established a successful congregation devoted to his teachings.[41] According to one scholar, he assiduously avoided any politically subversive activities and instructed his followers to follow all U.S. laws.[42]

In fact, some of his followers left the Islamic Mission precisely because they believed Shaikh Daoud to be overly supportive of the political status quo.[43] Many of them found their fellow congregants at the State Street mosque to be morally lax and insufficiently pious. In the 1960s, some of Faisal's followers broke away to form the Ya-Sin (pronounced yah-seen) mosque, which sought to separate from mainstream society so that believers could adhere as strictly as possible to *shari'a*. They were influenced in part by Hafis Mahbub, a Pakistani member of the Tablighi Jama'at, a Muslim reform group known mainly for its emphasis on spiritual purification and world renunciation over political entanglements. In 1960, Faisal reportedly hired Mahbub as a religious teacher. African American followers Rijab Mahmud and Yahya Abdul-Karim adopted Mahbub's call for "personal transformation" by living a life in strict adherence with the ethical example of the Prophet Muhammad of Arabia.[44] Women at Ya-Sin often covered themselves with both a head scarf and a face veil. Some men practiced polygamy.[45] Their movement would become known as Darul Islam, or the abode of Islam. By the 1970s, leader Yahya Abdul-Karim would declare that Muslims should avoid participation in U.S. politics and eschew friendships with all Americans, non-Muslim and Muslim, alike, if they did not practice the "correct" form of Islam. Eventually, the movement spawned other African American Muslim groups, including the network of twenty mosques led by Jamil al-Amin, the former H. Rap Brown, who became known for his urban revitalization work in Atlanta.[46] All of these African American Islamist groups dreamed of a morally revived Islamic society, but they sought to realize that goal largely by personal example and the organization of utopian communities, not through violent *jihad*. Though many of these African American Muslims shared the same basic Islamist ideas, they were fractured into different groups with different leaders, and they often translated Islamism into an American idiom.

Malcolm X in the Missionary Maelstrom

Despite the growing power of Islamist ideas, many African American Muslims in the age of the Arab cold war rejected the arguments and authority of the Muslim missionaries and the ideology of Islamism. This was especially true in Elijah Muhammad's Nation of Islam (NOI), which was harshly criticized by Sunni Muslims of all stripes for its black separatist version of Islam. The rise of the NOI's profile as the most popular African American Muslim movement in the United States coincided with the increased presence and impact of foreign and immigrant Muslim missionaries. Most Americans, including immigrant Muslims, knew little about the NOI until the late 1950s. Then, in 1959, New York's WNTA-TV aired a five-part series about the movement, hosted by Mike Wallace, titled "The Hate That Hate Produced."[47] Following that program, stories about the NOI appeared in national magazines such as *Time* and *U.S.*

News and World Report. This coverage was generally negative, criticizing the movement as an anti-American or black supremacist organization. African American civil rights leaders, including Roy Wilkins of the National Association for the Advancement of Colored People (NAACP), denounced the NOI as a hate group.[48]

As negative portrayals in the mainstream press and criticism from black leaders increased, more and more Muslims in the United States joined to condemn, dispute, and reject the teachings of Elijah Muhammad and the NOI. Their criticism of the NOI was a public performance of Muslim identity that expressed the growing cultural power of foreign and immigrant Muslims. By making such public pronouncements, whether they had been formally trained in the Islamic religious sciences or not, these self-appointed spokesmen for Islam attempted to define the doctrinal boundaries of Islamic religion. As Malcolm X, the chief spokesperson for Elijah Muhammad, made his way around the college lecture circuit, he was constantly hounded by Muslim students and others who considered themselves the guardians of "true" Islam. He mustered Qur'anic verses and his best exegetical rhetoric to defend Elijah Muhammad's unique Islamic mythos, but to little avail among his critics. Malcolm's inability to bring them over to his side seemed to bother him or at least to intrigue the famous debater. In 1962, for example, one Muslim student at Dartmouth, Ahmed Osman, traveled to NOI Mosque No. 7 to question Malcolm about Islam. After grilling Malcolm in the question-and-answer section of his talk, Osman came away "unsatisfied." When Osman began to send Malcolm literature from the Centre Islamique des Eaux-Vives in Geneva, Malcolm read it and asked for more. In another incident, Arab students from UCLA surrounded Malcolm after a March 1963 appearance on the Ben Hunter Show in Los Angeles. After hearing the students argue that his belief in white devils was un-Islamic, Malcolm became quite disturbed, according to journalist Louis Lomax, who was accompanying Malcolm at the time.[49]

These students and the larger trend of which they were part had a profound influence on Malcolm's religious life.[50] Perhaps their criticism of Elijah Muhammad's Islamic legitimacy was one contributing factor in Malcolm's defection from the NOI in 1964. But even if Malcolm left for other reasons—such as Elijah Muhammad's moral failings and the NOI's lack of direct political action[51]—his subsequent profession of Islam certainly adopted the ideas and symbols of the new Muslim missionaries. After Malcolm X broke away, he turned to Dr. Mahmoud Youssef Shawarbi, a University of Cairo professor and Fulbright Fellow in the United States who was teaching at

Fordham University.[52] Malcolm knew of Shawarbi through the numerous immigrant Muslims, especially students, who had been confronting him after his various lectures and appearances. "Those orthodox Muslims whom I had met, one after another, had urged me to meet and talk with a Dr. Mahmoud Youssef Shawarbi," he said in his *Autobiography*.[53] Shawarbi encouraged Malcolm to make the *hajj*, the annual pilgrimage to Mecca, and instructed him in the fundamental elements of Sunni Islam.[54] After training Malcolm in the rudiments of Sunni Islamic thought and practice, Shawarbi gave Malcolm a letter of recommendation, a copy of *The Eternal Message of Muhammad* by the renowned pan-Islamist Abd al-Rahman Azzam, and the phone number of Azzam's son, who happened to be married to the daughter of Saudi Prince Faysal.[55] The elder Azzam was one of pan-Islam's most important figures. A father of Arab nationalism and a distinguished Egyptian diplomat, Azzam was a chief architect of the Arab League and served as its first secretary general from 1945 to 1952. But like so many others, he lost favor after Nasser came to power, finding refuge in Saudi Arabia, where he became a leading polemicist and author.[56] His *Eternal Message of Muhammad*, available in a 1993 edition, was a prime example of a popular modern Islamic polemic that both defended Islam against Western critics and advocated a vision of the ideal Islamic nation-state. Islam, Azzam said, was a "faith, a law, a way of life, a nation, and state." Contrary to Western assumptions, Azzam implied, Islam was a highly modern religious tradition that promoted tolerance, removed superstition, and encouraged mercy, charity, industriousness, fairness, and brotherhood in the hearts and minds of its adherents.[57]

Malcolm read the book while flying over the Atlantic Ocean on his way to Mecca, and then met Azzam himself during the pilgrimage. On April 13, 1964, Malcolm departed JFK International Airport with a one-way plane ticket to Jidda, Saudi Arabia.[58] When Malcolm arrived on the Arabian Peninsula, Saudi authorities detained him for special interrogation. After fretting for some time, Malcolm telephoned Azzam's son, Dr. Omar Azzam. The Azzams immediately interceded with the proper authorities, vouching for Malcolm when he faced an examination by the *hajj* court, the legal entity that decides whether one is a legitimate Muslim able to participate in the pilgrimage. In addition, the elder Azzam insisted that Malcolm stay in his suite at the Jedda Palace Hotel. Later, the Saudi government officially extended its welcome when the deputy chief of protocol, Muhammad Abdul Azziz Maged, gave Malcolm a private car for his travels around the kingdom.[59]

Because of the Saudis' hospitality, and because of what he witnessed during the pilgrimage rites, Malcolm issued a strong endorsement of Sunni Islam.

He argued, famously, that Islam was a religion of racial equality and brother-hood—which is what his Saudi hosts hoped to hear. After Malcolm completed the pilgrimage, Prince Faysal invited him for an audience. The prince quizzed Malcolm about the Nation of Islam, carefully suggesting that if what he had read in Egyptian papers were true, they did not practice the real Islam. Further, the prince reminded Malcolm that due to the abundance of English literature on Islam "there was no excuse for ignorance, and no reason for sincere people to allow themselves to be misled."[60] Prince Faysal, constructing himself as an authority on proper Islamic practice, apparently wanted to make sure that Malcolm understood the meaning of his royal hospitality.

Malcolm sustained these relationships with various Saudi-financed mission-ary groups until his untimely death. During September 1964, Malcolm left for another pilgrimage to Mecca.[61] During this *umra*, or "lesser" pilgrimage, Malcolm underwent training as an evangelist by the Muslim World League, the organization that had been established in 1962 to propagate an Islamist interpretation of Islam around the world. Shaykh Muhammad Sarur al-Sab-ban, secretary general of the organization and a descendant of black slaves, supervised his education. The University of Medina granted Malcolm several scholarships for U.S. students who wanted to study there. According to Rich-ard W. Murphy, then second secretary at the U.S. embassy in Jidda, Malcolm granted an interview to a Jiddan newspaper, *al-Bilad,* in which he "took pains . . . to deprecate his reputation as a political activist and dwelt mainly on his interest in bringing sounder appreciation of Islam to American Negroes."[62]

Though these missionaries had a profound effect on Malcolm, he had a serious disagreement with some of them about the question of black political liberation in the United States. One of Malcolm X's last press interviews was given to *Al-Muslimoon*, a journal published by Said Ramadan's Centre Islamique des Eaux-Vives in Geneva. Malcolm had visited the Islamic center's director, Said Ramadan, in 1964. As mentioned above, Ramadan, son-in-law of Muslim Brothers' founder Hasan al-Banna, was one of several persons who helped to establish the league with the support of Saudi Arabia. Like Dr. Omar Azzam, Ramadan strongly asserted the view that Islam was both a religion and a state, the solution to all of humanity's economic, cultural, and political problems, including the oppression of black persons in the United States. In his written questionnaire, Ramadan challenged Malcolm about his continued focus on racial identity and the need for black liberation, asserting that the conversion of Americans to Islam would solve such problems. Malcolm X completed his answers to Ramadan's questions on February 20, 1965, one day before his assassination. Malcolm disagreed with Ramadan's view and insisted that while he would always be a devout Muslim, his first duty in life was to work for the political liberation of all black persons around the globe.[63] While Malcolm was no less committed to Islam as a religious and spiritual path, he rejected the view that Islam could offer a specific solution to every political problem. "My fight is two-fold, my burden is double, my responsibilities multiple . . . material as well as spiritual, political as well as religious, racial as well as non-racial," he told a crowd in Cairo. "I will never hesitate to let the entire world know the hell my people suffer from America's deceit and her hypocrisy, as well as her oppression."[64] Malcolm remained as committed as ever to a program of political liberation that remained outside the purview of his commitments as a Sunni Muslim. Though he had received Arab Muslims' financial support, their religious imprimatur, and their friendship, Malcolm resisted the Islamist view of his allies and sponsors.

Instead, Malcolm's break with the Nation of Islam freed him to articulate a powerful pan-Africanist politics.[65] By the time he had declared his independence from Elijah Muhammad in 1964, Malcolm had already cultivated ties to other black nationalists in New York and had met several leaders of the nonaligned movement, including President Sukarno of Indonesia, President Castro of Cuba, and President Nasser of Egypt.[66] He furthered such connections throughout his travels in 1964, much of which he spent in Africa. During his May visit to Nigeria, he proudly acquired a new title, "Omowale," or the son who had come home. That year, Malcolm also met with Kwame Nkrumah, president of Ghana; Milton Obote, president of Uganda; and Jomo Kenyatta, president of Kenya; and he attended two Africa Summit Conferences, where he represented his own Organization of Afro-American Unity, a group he had modeled on the Organization of African Unity.[67] Until his death in February 1965, Malcolm also sharply criticized U.S. foreign policy toward Africa, especially U.S. support for Moise Tshombe's regime in the Congo. He stated, correctly it turns out, that the United States had supported the overthrow of Patrice Lumumba, who had helped to expel Belgian forces, and he wondered aloud whether he should recruit African American freedom fighters to fight Tshombe's regime.[68] In a similar way, his domestic politics focused on finding black solutions to black problems, and his rearticulations of black nationalist themes included calls for racial solidarity in the face of white supremacy. His politics may have been radical, but they were not Islamist. Malcolm X did not believe Islamism was the solution to the problems of black people. Only black people, reaching across continents and across confessional lines, could solve black problems.

Transnational Reverberations in the Nation of Islam

The rejection of the Islamists' authority was even more profound in the NOI, which would not permit other Muslims to define what it meant to be an authentic Muslim, as Elijah Muhammad himself made clear: "Neither Jeddah or Mecca have sent me! I am sent from Allah and not from the Secretary General of the Muslim League," he said, referring to the Muslim World League, created in 1962.[69] The NOI had its own system of rituals and code of ethics, which relied more on the prophecies of Elijah Muhammad than on the *shari'a*. But intellectuals in the NOI were not indifferent to the criticisms of other Muslims. Elijah Muhammad and his lieutenants were extremely sensitive to public opinion and vulnerable to attacks from other Muslims, as outlined in the examination of Malcolm X's efforts to defend Elijah Muhammad above. Like Malcolm X, they were also influenced by the new ideas, texts, pamphlets, translations, stories, and symbols circulated by the Muslim missionaries in the United States. The NOI's reactions show just how important the missionaries and their ideas were to the development of African American Islam and American Islam as a whole.

For example, *Muhammad Speaks*, the NOI's newspaper of record from 1961 until the middle 1970s, frequently published endorsements of Elijah Muhammad and the NOI by mainstream Asian Muslim leaders. Like other so-called new religious movements, the NOI used appeals to traditional religious authorities in an effort to legitimate their movement.[70] In addition to citing foreign authorities to counter charges of illegitimacy, a whole cadre of intellectuals inside the organization, including NOI ministers and newspaper columnists, responded to Muslim criticisms of Elijah Muhammad's Islamic bona fides by constructing him as a qur'anically sanctioned prophet. For example, the prominent Nation of Islam cartoonist Eugene XXX, or Eugene Majied, frequently incorporated images and passages from the Qur'an into his drawings of Elijah Muhammad, who was depicted variously as a doctor healing the "deaf and dumb Negro," as a Daniel fighting off critics, or as a Moses plaguing Pharaoh Lyndon Johnson.[71] Others, including Minister Abdul Salaam and columnist Tynnetta Deanar, fiercely defended their prophet by citing the Qur'an.[72] A few NOI intellectuals sought ideological rapprochement with the critics by reinterpreting the mission of Elijah Muhammad in terms more suitable to Sunni orthodoxy or asking the critics to adopt a more sympathetic, theologically pluralistic view of Elijah Muhammad's claims.[73]

This engagement with Elijah Muhammad's critics represented a remarkable moment of contact and confrontation. As a result, NOI intellectuals increasingly read Islamic texts, especially the Qur'an. In some cases, this deeper engagement with Islamic texts and traditions led to dissension and outright rebellion among NOI intellectuals, as was the case with Elijah Muhammad's son, Wallace D. Muhammad.[74] However they answered the question of Elijah Muhammad's legitimacy, all of these intellectuals, card-carrying members of the NOI and defectors alike, had something in common. They had become part of an old Islamic tradition—a transnational conversation about the meaning of the Holy Qur'an.[75]

This moment of contact and confrontation also led to a shift in the mental geography of many African American Muslims in the NOI, as artists and poets incorporated new Islamic names, places, dates, figures, and ideas in their historical imaginings of black identity. This deployment of Islamic signs was part of a larger trend in black American culture that represented a re-Orientation of African American politics and religion toward the Middle East more generally, as Melani McAlister has argued.[76] But for African American Muslim members of the NOI, this was a collective reorientation not only toward the Middle East, but also toward other places and times in which blacks/Muslims had lived. African American Muslims in the NOI located the story of black/Muslim people in many epochs and locales, including ancient Egypt, Muslim West Africa, Asia, a mythical Arabia, and the classical period of Islam during and immediately after the time of Prophet Muhammad of Arabia. These black Muslims "moved across" time and space, constructing their contemporary identities by imagining who they had been in the past.[77]

Such re-Orientation is expressed perfectly in a 1967 poem by William E. X published in *Muhammad Speaks*:

From the Land of the Hot Sun
The Tigris and the Nile
From the Sun Baked Valleys of Egypt
To the Faraway Himalayas
Down Again into Tibet
And China
And then Pygmy Country
Where Tiny Black People Grow Very Tall
In their Smallness
Of Stature
Black Man!
Turkey, Iran, Iraq and Persia
Lands of Splendor
And the Prayer is to Allah
And the Tongue is Arabic

Sometimes Different
But the Melodic Beauty
Is One and Same
Black Man!
Black Man
Giant of Giants.[78]

In this poem, titled "Black Man," black/Muslim geography includes Asia, which had been constructed as a racial home by African American Muslims at least since the 1927 publication of Noble Drew Ali's *Holy Koran of the Moorish Science Temple*. Brother William's poem recognizes the diverse linguistic, phenotypical, and geographic roots of blacks/Muslims, but insists that on the whole blacks are still one and the same. In his poetic romp around Asia and Africa, Brother William sees the Muslim "black man" as possessing a common god, language, and character—all of which are viewed as Islamic. Whether the black man lives in the Middle East, China, or even Tibet, he is, at heart, a Muslim. There are countless other examples of this re-siting of black Muslim identity, including several cartoons by NOI artist Eugene Majied that drew on elements of classical Islamic history to create and celebrate black Muslim time and space.

In one such cartoon, Majied retold the story of Khawlah bint Azdar, a heroine of the campaign to conquer Damascus in 634–35 CE. The likely source for Majied's narrative was Syed Sulaiman Nadwi's *Heroic Deeds of Muslim Women*, a book offered for sale in *Muhammad Speaks* by Books and Things, a Muslim bookstore on Lenox Avenue in New York City.[79] Majied's transliterations of Arabic names and his recounting of the story parallel the Nadwi version in precise fashion. This reliance on Nadwi's text helps to illustrate the flow of ideas from the missionaries to African American Muslims inside the NOI, since Nadwi was a prominent Sunni Muslim scholar from India.[80]

In Majied's cartoon, a male teacher at the University of Islam, the primary and secondary school of the NOI, addresses veiled female students in a history class. He proclaims that "no woman of the Caucasian West can compare in bravery, valor, or martyrdom with our Muslim sister[s] of that time!"[81] Women, according to the teacher, followed men into war and tended to horses, weapons, and the wounded. They buried the dead and fed the living. But in the siege of Damascus, the teacher explained, women were forced into a more aggressive role. "The people," the teacher said, "were under the heels of the Romans, and were being fed Christianity (much like the American so-called Negro today)."[82]

Abu Bakr, the first caliph of Islam, "directed Khalid Bin Walid [a general] to lay siege on Damascus—and remove the death-grip of Christianity."

Such parallels, drawn between the Muslims of Arabia and the black Muslims of the United States, were a frequent feature of NOI discourse during the 1960s, as NOI members reached into the history of Islam to understand their own history and the trials of their prophet in America. The comparison of Muslims in the golden age of Islam and Muslims in North America also shows how the introduction of Islamic ideas from abroad does not necessarily lead to widespread agreement on their meaning. The signs, once present, can be appropriated in any number of ways.

As Majied's tale continues, we learn that Muslim forces had effectively sealed the ancient city of Damascus, when another "Roman" army of ninety thousand marched on Muslim forces in a place south of Damascus called Ajnadayn. The Muslims, only twenty-four thousand strong, were outnumbered. In response, Khalid ibn al-Walid ended the siege on Damascus and turned his forces toward Ajnadayn. The Damascenes, however, saw a chance for revenge and attacked the contingent's rearguard, the section in which Muslim women were traveling. One particularly brave woman, Khawlah bint Azdar, swore in the name of God to fight the "infidels" unto death. Under attack, Khawlah grabbed a tent pole and subdued one of the assailants, crying "Allah is the Greatest!"[83] Soon her comrades followed suit. By the time they had finished, thirty Damascenes were dead and the honor of the Muslim women was saved. "Thus," the teacher announced, "the names of those brave women of Islam—Khaula . . . Afira . . . Afara . . . Salmah—will live in history." He added that "by following Messenger Elijah Muhammad, today's black woman will make history!"[84]

Whether it was through cartoons or poems, this kind of re-Orienting of African American mental geography toward the Muslim world had important implications for NOI members' sense of religious community. Though some of their symbols, texts, and narratives had been adopted from foreign and immigrant missionaries, members of the NOI reappropriated such raw materials in their own understandings of what it meant to be a Muslim. Black Muslims in the NOI looked beyond the black Atlantic world to form their communal identities and created narratives that linked the history of black people to this history of Islam. They felt allegiance not only to the black nation but also to a community of Muslims who might be members of several different nations. Elijah Muhammad and many of his followers did not define the collective identity of blacks *exclusively* in terms of a desire for a separate nation or polity. Many in the NOI constructed black identity in terms of a shared history that was defined by its Islamic character. Of course, members offered differing understandings of their shared black/Islamic heritage, and they sited Islam in multiple times and places. Refusing to locate the history of blacks in one country or even on one continent, these stories adopted a transnational perspective toward black identity that rested upon its common Islamic roots. The radical implications of such identity making would become clear in the 1970s and beyond, when some black intellectuals, especially Chancellor Williams, Molefi Asante, and later, Henry Louis Gates Jr., came to depict Islam as an enemy to or at least a foreign element within African cultures and civilizations.[85] Such reactions, dubbed "black orientalism" by Sherman Jackson, are difficult to imagine in the absence of a culturally influential and institutionally successful African American Islam. At the least, it is clear that Islam, however constituted, had become a potent signifier of black identity for some African Americans and that other African Americans resisted this remaking of black identity in Islamic terms.

Conclusion: Political Refractions of Transnational Encounters

But the political implications of African American re-Orientations toward Islam were not as clear. Several scholars of the NOI have insisted, for decades now, that the insular, "cultic" qualities of Elijah Muhammad's NOI, in addition to the organization's millennialism and Victorian gender relations, as well as its Puritanism and embrace of the Protestant work ethic, rendered the group an unwitting, decidedly conservative agent of the political status quo.[86] Such approaches seem to reflect the view, stated famously by Sacvan Bercovitch, that groups like the Nation of Islam, though appearing at first to look like manifestations of dissent, have actually functioned in U.S. history as vehicles of social control, since their teachings have not attacked the root causes of oppression.[87] This argument, that the absence of a direct and organized assault on the political economy and patriarchy of the United States effectively sustains the status quo, reflects only a partial view of political action and resistance. Rebellion, as Robin D. G. Kelley argues, also includes cultural acts of resistance that reject the values and expectations of the powerful.[88] In this sense, the NOI's activities, and the growth of Islam more generally among black Americans, were extremely rebellious in the 1960s. During the 1950s, as Penny Von Eschen has pointed out, "the Nation of Islam permitted a space—for the most part unthinkable in the Cold War era—for an anti-American critique of the Cold War."[89] During the Vietnam era, in the middle of a civil rights movement that was an important component of U.S. foreign policy, many in the Nation of Islam and other African American Muslims rejected American nationalism, refused to serve in Vietnam, criticized the civil rights movement as hollow, and challenged the legitimacy of the nonofficial state religion, Christianity. The way these Muslims dressed and talked—in addition to the pictures they drew and the poems they wrote—questioned the cultural foundations of the state and its legitimacy to rule. The fact that U.S. government officials associated members of the NOI with violent revolution, despite the lack of any organized effort in the movement to confront authorities with violence, indicates the extent of the ideological challenge.[90] According to one observer, the NOI was among the most watched organizations in the government's Counter-Intelligence Program (COINTELPRO).[91] Surely, this evidence indicates that the message of the Nation of Islam and its members was politically dangerous in some way.

The political implications of this Islamist flowering were also multivalent. The radical call for God's sovereignty over all the earth and the establishment of the United States as an Islamic nation was reflected and refracted in an array of community programs and political platforms. Shaikh Daoud, as we have seen, preached the necessity of establishing God's rule over all the earth, but relied on nonviolent missionary work as his means to accomplish this end. The younger critics of Daoud's supposed passivity cried even more loudly about the moral bankruptcy of the West and its evil ways, but in most cases, they sought separation from mainstream society, not violent revolution. For example, Sheik Tawfiq (d. 1988), an African American from Florida, founded the Mosque of the Islamic Brotherhood in Harlem, New York. Stressing the call of Islamic universalism, the idea that Islam crossed all racial barriers, African Americans, Hispanics, and others prayed together, established housing and education programs, and ran small businesses in the heart of the United States' largest city. In 1971, Yusuf Muzaffaruddin Hamid, who was a student of Pakistan's Jamaʿat-i Islami, established the Islamic Party of North America, which advocated the creation of an Islamic state in North America through a mass religious revival.[92] These African American Sunni Muslim leaders mingled regularly with foreign and immigrant *imams*, who were now entering the United States in larger numbers, due to 1965 reforms in immigration policy and financial support from Saudi Arabia and other Gulf countries. After the 1973 and 1974 OPEC oil embargo, the price of oil skyrocketed, and at least some of those petrodollars were used to support the missionary efforts created during the Arab cold war. By the early 1980s, according to one scholar, twenty-six communities "were receiving the services of leaders provided by the Muslim World League."[93] While infused with a powerful jeremiad and the call for an Islamic revolution, however, their rhetoric led mainly to a moral revival, not violent *jihad*. Even when African American Muslims engaged in violent *jihad* during this era, it was directed toward other African American Muslim groups, not the government or larger society.[94] There is simply no hard evidence indicating that their radical rhetoric led to organized terrorism or violent revolution on a mass scale.

As in the case of the Nation of Islam, it might be tempting to conclude that the political impact of these utopian groups was conservative, but such arguments would once again ignore the ideological and cultural resistance that the groups offered. Some African American Islamists became effective spokespersons in the United States for foreign Muslim causes, including those in Palestine, Afghanistan, Bosnia, and Chechnya, and while some funds were raised for these causes, American Muslim support was mainly moral in nature, as supporters gave fiery speeches from the pulpit on Fridays and discussed the issues in conferences and study groups.[95] Some American Muslims, including African American Muslims, would eventually become entangled in violent jihadist networks, and a few African American Muslims have even been convicted of aiding al-Qa'ida or other terrorist groups, but these are rare, if dramatic cases.[96]

In some ways, the culture of African American Islam from the 1970s until today has borne the imprint of the contact and confrontation with foreign and immigrant Muslims during the 1960s. In the 1970s, W. D. Muhammad, the son of Elijah Muhammad, would change the name of the Nation of Islam to the World Community of al-Islam in the West and ask his followers to observe the ethical, theological, and ritual directives of Sunni Islam.[97] He also reached out to foreign Muslims, accepted Egyptian president Anwar Sadat's offer of scholarships to attend Egyptian universities, and placed a Sudanese shaykh educated at the University of Medina as the prayer leader of the Chicago temple.[98] But despite these ties, he would tailor Sunni Islamic teachings to the African American experience, advocating a platform of political, economic, and social reforms that were transnational in style but local/national in their content.[99] In a sense, he had truly internalized the reformist attitudes of the Muslim missionaries by focusing so intently on the scriptures of Islam; but his close readings did not always agree with theirs. The same was true for other African Americans who sought to apply the texts of Islam to their own circumstances. By the 1990s, some of these efforts produced progressive political positions on a variety of issues, especially on gender. Islamic studies professor Amina Wadud issued an academic manifesto called *Qur'an and Woman*.[100] Eventually, she would challenge the taboo of a woman leading a mixed gender prayer.[101] Similarly, African American women at the grass roots interpreted the Qur'an and *hadith* as documents of womanist liberation.[102] More and more African American Muslims would travel abroad to study the classical Islamic sciences in the aftermath of the Arab cold war, but when they came back from foreign *madrasas* and Muslim universities, their interpretations of Islam were still infused with an African American sensibility focused on the problems facing Muslims in the United States.[103]

The interaction of African American Muslims with ideological players in the Arab cold war may have changed the contours of African American Islamic culture, but it did not undermine African American Muslim religious or political agency. On the contrary, African American Muslims often appropriated the cultural and intellectual resources of the missionaries into an Islam that reflected their own interests. Greater transnational ties between African American Muslims and Muslims abroad have led to an ever larger variety of Islamic religious expression in black America. Some African American Muslims have joined both new and traditional Sufi orders, the mystical groups of Islam, including the West African–based Tijaniyya and the Philadelphia-based fellowship of Shaykh M. R. Bawa Muhaiyaddeen.[104] There is an important, if small, number of black Shi'a Muslims as well—the result of Shi'i outreach from the 1970s until today.[105] Minister Louis Farrakhan, who reconstituted the Nation of Islam in 1978, has incorporated more and more Sunni Islamic texts and traditions into his religious practice and sought strong ties to foreign Muslim leaders, but he has also continued to claim a special place for black inter/nationalism and his own interpretations of Elijah Muhammad's teachings within the Nation of Islam.[106] All of these groups, and their differing religious and political outlooks, reflect the vitality of an African American Islam both transnational and local.

Notes

1. See Aminah Beverly McCloud, *African American Islam* (New York: Routledge, 1995), 9–40.
2. See Michael A. Gomez, *Black Crescent: The Experience and Legacy of African Muslims in the Americas* (Cambridge: Cambridge University Press, 2005), 274; Sylviane A. Diouf, *Servants of Allah: African Muslims Enslaved in the Americas* (New York: New York University Press, 1998), and Allan D. Austin, *African Muslims in Antebellum America: Transatlantic Stories and Spiritual Struggles* (New York: Routledge, 1997).

3. See Edward Wilmot Blyden, *Christianity, Islam, and the Negro Race* (1887; Edinburgh: Edinburgh University Press, 1967); Hollis Lynch, *Edward Wilmot Blyden: Pan-Negro Patriot, 1832–1912* (London: Oxford University Press, 1967); Hollis Lynch, ed., *Selected Letters of Edward Wilmot Blyden* (Millwood, N.Y.: KTO Press, 1978); and Richard Brent Turner, *Islam in the African-American Experience*, 2nd ed. (Bloomington: Indiana University Press, 2003), 47–59.
4. Randall K. Burkett, *Garveyism as a Religious Movement* (Metuchen, N.J.: Scarecrow Press, 1978), 178–81. Garvey's pan-Africanism was influenced partly by Dusé Mohammed Ali, publisher of the *African Times and Orient Review*.
5. See Susan Nance, "Respectability and Representation: The Moorish Science Temple, Morocco, and Black Public Culture in 1920s Chicago," *American Quarterly* 54.4 (December 2002): 623–59, and "Mystery of the Moorish Science Temple: Southern Blacks and American Alternative Spirituality in 1920s Chicago," *Religion and American Culture* 12.2 (Summer 2002): 123–66; Arthur Huff Fauset, *Black Gods of the Metropolis: Negro Religious Cults of the Urban North* (1944; Philadelphia: University of Pennsylvania Press, 2002), 41–51; Peter Lamborn Wilson, *Sacred Drift: Essays on the Margins of Islam* (San Francisco: City Light Books, 1993); Yvonne Y. Haddad and Jane I. Smith, *Mission to America: Five Islamic Sectarian Communities in North America* (Gainesville: University Press of Florida, 1993), 79–104; Ernest Allen Jr., "Identity and Destiny: The Formative Views of the Moorish Science Temple and the Nation of Islam," in *Muslims on the Americanization Path?* ed. Yvonne Y. Haddad and John L. Esposito (New York: Oxford University Press, 2000), 163–214; Turner, *Islam in the African-American Experience*, 71–108; Edward E. Curtis IV, *Islam in Black America: Identity, Liberation, and Difference in African-American Islamic Thought* (Albany: State University of New York Press, 2002), 45–62; and Gomez, *Black Crescent*, 203–75.
6. See Turner, *Islam in the African-American Experience*, 109–46; Haddad and Smith, *Mission to America*, 49–78; and cf. Robert Dannin, *Black Pilgrimage to Islam* (New York: Oxford University Press, 2002), 34–40, 99–103.
7. See further Yohanan Friedman, *Prophecy Continuous: Aspects of Ahmadi Religious Thought and Its Medieval Background* (Berkeley: University of California Press, 1989).
8. *Moslem Sunrise*, October 1921, 41.
9. *Moslem Sunrise*, April and May 1923, 184.
10. See *Moslem Sunrise*, October 1932/January 1933, 31–33, and July 1922, 119.
11. See, respectively, McCloud, *African American Islam*, 24–27, and Dannin, *Black Pilgrimage to Islam*, 96–108.
12. See Elijah Muhammad, *Message to the Blackman in America* (1965; Newport News, Va.: United Brothers Communication System, 1992), 164.
13. Compare "The Holy Qur-an," *Muhammad Speaks*, February 12, 1965, 8, with Ahmadi Qur'an scholar Muhammad Ali, *The Holy Qur'an*, 2nd ed. (Columbus, Ohio, and Lahore: Ahmadiyyah Anjuman Isha'at Islam, 1951), and *Muhammad Speaks*, September 9, 1963, 9, with Maulana Muhammad Ali, chap. 19, "Jihad (Hadith)," in *A Manual of Hadith* (Lahore: Ahmadiyyah Movement for the Propagation of Islam, n.d.), 256n3.
14. See "The Middle East in African American Cultural Politics, 1955–1972," in Melani McAlister, *Epic Encounters: Culture, Media, and U.S. Interests in the Middle East since 1945*, updated ed. (Berkeley: University of California Press, 2005).
15. See Brenda Gayle Plummer, *Rising Wind: Black Americans and U.S. Foreign Policy, 1935–1960* (Chapel Hill: University of North Carolina Press, 1996), 257–66, 285, and C. Eric Lincoln, *The Black Muslims in America*, 3rd ed. (Grand Rapids, Mich.: William B. Eerdmans, 1994), 225.
16. See McCloud, *African American Islam*, 20; Dannin, *Pilgrimage to Islam*, 58–59; Dizzy Gillespie and Al Frazer, *To Be or Not to Bop* (New York: DaCapo, 1979), 293; Turner, *Islam in the African-American Experience*, 139; Mustafa Bayoumi, "East of the Sun (West of the Moon): Islam, the Ahmadis, and African America," *Journal of African American Studies* (October 2001): 259; and "Moslem Musicians Take Firm Stand against Racism," *Ebony* (April 1953): 111.
17. Robin D. G. Kelley, "House Negroes on the Loose: Malcolm X and the Black Bourgeoisie," *Callaloo* 21.2 (1998): 425; Louis Lomax, *When the Word Is Given* (Cleveland: World Publishing, 1963), 191; and Edward E. Curtis IV, *Black Muslim Religion in the Nation of Islam, 1960–1975* (Chapel Hill: University of North Carolina Press, 2006), 170–173.

18. Lincoln, *Black Muslims*, 226, 227; and Claude Andrew Clegg III, *An Original Man: The Life and Times of Elijah Muhammad* (New York: St. Martin's Press, 1997), 135–136, 189.

19. See further Fawaz A. Gerges, *The Superpowers and the Middle East: Regional and International Politics, 1955–1967* (Boulder, Colo.: Westview, 1984).

20. See Malik Mufti, *Sovereign Creations: Pan-Arabism and Political Order in Syria and Iraq* (Ithaca, N.Y.: Cornell University Press: 1996).

21. Malcolm H. Kerr, *The Arab Cold War, 1958–1964: A Study of Ideology in Politics*, 2nd ed. (London: Oxford University Press, 1965), 21–22, 53; and see also Michael C. Hudson, *Arab Politics: The Search for Legitimacy* (New Haven, Ct.: Yale University Press, 1977).

22. Reinhard Schulze, "Institutionalization [of *da'wa*]" in *Oxford Encyclopedia of the Modern Islamic World*, ed. John L. Esposito (New York: Oxford University Press), 1:346–50; and James P. Piscatori, *Islam in a World of Nation-States* (Cambridge: Cambridge University Press, 1986).

23. Reinhard Schulze, "Muslim World League," in *Oxford Encyclopedia of the Modern Islamic World* 3:208–10.

24. See Charles J. Adams, "The Ideology of Mawlana Mawdudi," in *South Asian Politics and Religion*, ed. Donald E. Smith (Princeton, N.J.: Princeton University Press, 1966), 371–97; Hamid Enayat, *Modern Islamic Political Thought* (Austin: University of Texas Press, 1988), 101–10; John L. Esposito, *The Islamic Threat: Myth or Reality*, 3rd ed. (New York: Oxford University Press), 129–35.

25. Hans Mahnig, "Islam in Switzerland: Fragmented Accommodation in a Federal Country," in *Muslims in the West: From Sojourner to Citizens*, ed. Yvonne Y. Haddad (New York: Oxford University Press, 2001), 75–76. And for a contrast, see Said Ramadan's son, Tariq Ramadan, *Western Muslims and the Future of Islam* (New York: Oxford University Press, 2005).

26. See Geneive Abdo, *No God but God: Egypt and the Triumph of Islam* (New York: Oxford University Press, 2000); Nazih N. Ayubi, *Political Islam: Religion and Politics in the Arab World* (London: Routledge, 1991); and Gilles Kepel, *Muslim Extremism in Egypt: The Prophet and the Pharaoh* (Berkeley: University of California Press, 1985).

27. Yvonne Y. Haddad and Jane I. Smith, eds., *Muslim Communities in North America* (Albany: State University of New York Press, 1994), xxi.

28. Mary Lahaj, "The Islamic Center of New England," in *Muslim Communities*, ed. Haddad and Smith, 299–300.

29. Larry Poston, *Islamic Da'wah in the West* (New York: Oxford University Press, 1992), 79.

30. See further Shaikh Daoud Ahmed Faisal, *Islam the True Faith: The Religion of Humanity* (Brooklyn, N.Y.: Islamic Mission of America, 1965), n.p.

31. Marc Ferris, "To 'Achieve the Pleasure of Allah': Immigrant Muslims in New York City, 1893–1991," in *Muslim Communities*, ed. Haddad and Smith, 212.

32. See McCloud, *African American Islam*, 21–24; and Dannin, *Black Pilgrimage to Islam*, 63–67.

33. Ferris, "To 'Achieve the Pleasure of Allah,'" 214.

34. "Author's Note," in Shaikh Daoud Ahmed Faisal, *Al-Islam: The Religion of Humanity* (Brooklyn, N.Y.: Islamic Mission of America, 1950), 7–8.

35. Ibid., 51.

36. Ibid., 15–16. Compare Will Herberg, *Protestant, Catholic, and Jew: An Essay in American Religious Sociology* (Garden City, N.Y.: Doubleday, 1955).

37. Ibid., 49–50.

38. Ibid., 60.

39. See, for example, Regina M. Schwartz, *The Curse of Cain: The Violent Legacy of Monotheism* (Chicago: University of Chicago Press, 1997).

40. For accounts of the relationships between blacks and Jews in the United States, see V. P. Franklin et al., eds., *African Americans and Jews in the Twentieth Century: Studies in Convergence and Conflict* (Columbia: University of Missouri Press, 1998); Cheryl Lynn Greenberg, *Troubling the Waters: Black-Jewish Relations in the American Century* (Princeton, N.J.: Princeton University Press, 2006); and Eric J. Sundquist, *Strangers in the Land: Blacks, Jews, Post-Holocaust America* (Cambridge, Mass.: Harvard University Press, 2005).

41. For classic accounts of these "American" missionary strategies, see, for example, William R. Hutchison, *Errand to the World: American Protestant Thought and Foreign Missions* (Chicago: University of Chicago Press, 1987); William G. McLoughlin Jr., *Revivals, Awakenings, and Reform* (Chicago: University of

Chicago Press, 1978); and Edith Blumhofer and Randall Balmer, eds., *Modern Christian Revivals* (Urbana: University of Illinois Press, 1993).

42. Dannin, *Black Pilgrimage to Islam*, 64.
43. R. M. Mukhtar Curtis, "The Formation of the Dar ul-Islam Movement," in *Muslim Communities in North America*, 54.
44. Dannin, *Black Pilgrimage to Islam*, 66–68.
45. McCloud, *African American Islam*, 71.
46. See Sherman A. Jackson, *Islam and the Blackamerican: Looking Toward the Third Resurrection* (New York: Oxford University Press, 2005), 48–49.
47. Louis E. Lomax et al., "The Hate That Hate Produced," on "Newsbeat," WNTA-TV, July 23, 1959, a transcript of which is available in a declassified FBI report. See SAC, New York, office memorandum to director, FBI, July 16, 1959, available through *http://wonderwheel.net/work/foia/1959/071659hthp-transcript.pdf* (accessed May 1, 2007).
48. E. U. Essien-Udom, *Black Nationalism: A Search for an Identity in America* (Chicago: University of Chicago Press, 1962), 73–74.
49. Louis A. DeCaro Jr., *On the Side of My People: A Religious Life of Malcolm X* (New York: New York University Press, 1996), 159–60, 201–2.
50. See DeCaro, *On the Side of My People*, especially 159–293. And compare Turner, *Islam in the African-American Experience*, 174–237, and Curtis, *Islam in Black America*, 85–105.
51. See Malcolm X and Alex Haley, *The Autobiography of Malcolm X* (New York: Ballantine, 1965), 266–317.
52. Ferris, "To 'Achieve the Pleasure of Allah,'" 215.
53. Malcolm X and Haley, *Autobiography of Malcolm X*, 318.
54. Bruce Perry, *Malcolm: The Life of a Man Who Changed Black America* (Barrytown, N.Y.: Station Hill, 1991), 261–64; and DeCaro, *On the Side of My People*, 202–3.
55. Malcolm X and Haley, *Autobiography of Malcolm X*, 320.
56. Yaacov Shimoni, *Political Dictionary of the Arab World* (New York: Macmillan, 1987), 105–6.
57. Abd al-Rahman 'Azzam, *The Eternal Message of Muhammad*, trans. Caesar E. Farah (Cambridge: Islamic Texts Society, 1993).
58. DeCaro, *On the Side of My People*, 206.
59. Malcolm X and Haley, *Autobiography of Malcolm X*, 331–33.
60. Ibid., 348.
61. Perry, *Malcolm*, 322.
62. DeCaro, *On the Side of My People*, 336.
63. The interview is reproduced in *February 1965: The Final Speeches*, ed. Steve Clark (New York: Pathfinder, 1992), 252–55, and on the Web at Malcolm-X.Org: http://www.malcolm-x.org/docs/int_almus.htm (accessed August 28, 2006).
64. DeCaro, *On the Side of My People*, 233, 238–39.
65. See "Notes on the Invention of Malcolm X" and "Malcolm X and the Failure of Afrocentrism" in Gerald Early, *The Culture of Bruising* (Hopewell, N.J.: Ecco Press, 1994), 233–58.
66. See George M. Fredrickson, *Black Liberation: A Comparative History of Black Ideologies in the United States and South Africa* (New York: Oxford University Press, 1995), 277–97; and Gomez, *Black Crescent*, 348–55.
67. Malcolm X and Haley, *Autobiography of Malcolm X*, 323–72; Gomez, *Black Crescent*, 372; Curtis, *Islam in Black America*, 96–99.
68. See Malcolm X, *February 1965: The Final Speeches*, ed. Clark, 20–21; and Clayborne Carson, *Malcolm X: The FBI File* (New York: Carroll and Graf, 1991), 79–80.
69. "Mr. Muhammad Answers Critics: Authority from Allah, None Other," *Muhammad Speaks*, August 2, 1962, 3.
70. James R. Lewis, *Legitimating New Religions* (New Brunswick, N.J.: Rutgers University Press, 2003), 13–14. For an NOI example, Sylvester Leaks, "the Messenger of Allah as Seen by an Islamic Leader from Pakistan," *Muhammad Speaks*, May 8, 1964, 3.
71. See "Our Great Physician," *Muhammad Speaks*, June 1962, 14; "As It Was in the Days of Daniel, So It Is Today," *Muhammad Speaks*, June 19, 1964, 9; and "As It Was with Pharaoh So It Is Today," *Muhammad Speaks*, July 17, 1964, 9.

72. See "First Printing of Holy Qur'an in U.S.," *Muhammad Speaks*, August 17, 1973, 23, and "Women in Islam: Is the Honorable Elijah Muhammad the Last Messenger of Allah?" *Muhammad Speaks*, September 16, 1965, 19.
73. See "Allah and His Messenger," *Muhammad Speaks*, January 1, 1965, 1; and "Where Others Fail, Our Messenger Succeeds," *Muhammad Speaks*, May 14, 1965, 3.
74. See Zafar Ishaq Ansari, "W. D. Muhammad: The Making of a 'Black Muslim' Leader (1933–1961)," *American Journal of Islamic Social Sciences* 2.2 (1985): 248–62.
75. See further Curtis, *Black Muslim Religion*, 65.
76. McAlister, *Epic Encounters*, 86.
77. See Thomas A. Tweed, *Crossing and Dwelling: A Theory of Religion* (Cambridge, Mass.: Harvard University Press, 2006); and Jonathan Z. Smith, *Map Is Not Territory: Studies in the History of Religions* (Chicago: University of Chicago Press, 1978).
78. *Muhammad Speaks*, July 7, 1967, 22.
79. See *Muhammad Speaks*, February 14, 1969, 26.
80. According to Robert Coolidge, Nadwi was the rector of Darul Uloom Nadwatal Ulama in Lucknow, India; personal correspondence with the author, December 22, 2004.
81. *Muhammad Speaks*, December 17, 1965, 27.
82. "Muhammad's Message," *Muhammad Speaks*, December 24, 1995, 27. See also "Dimashk," in *Encyclopaedia of Islam*, 2:277.
83. *Muhammad Speaks*, January 28, 1966, 27.
84. *Muhammad Speaks*, February 4, 1966, 27.
85. Jackson, *Islam and the Blackamerican*, 99–129.
86. One argument for the movement's gender conservatism can be found in E. Frances White, *Dark Continent of Our Bodies: Black Feminism and the Politics of Respectability* (Philadelphia, Pa.: Temple University Press, 2001), 43. For counterarguments and qualifications, see Cynthia S'thembile West, "Nation Builders: Female Activism in the Nation of Islam, 1960–1970" (PhD diss., Temple University, 1994); and Curtis, *Black Muslim Religion*, 95–130. For critiques of the NOI on other scores, see Essien-Udom, *Black Nationalism*, 286–87, 339; and Hans A. Baer and Merrill Singer, *African-American Religion in the Twentieth Century: Varieties of Protest and Accommodation* (Knoxville: University of Tennessee Press, 1992), 143.
87. See further Sacvan Bercovitch, *The American Jeremiad* (Madison.: University of Wisconsin Press, 1978).
88. Ibid.
89. Penny M. Von Eschen, *Race against Empire: Black Americans and Anticolonialism, 1937–1957* (Ithaca, N.Y.: Cornell University Press, 1997), 174.
90. See "Nation of Islam: Cult of the Black Muslims," May 1965, available through the FBI's Web site at http://foia.fbi.gov/nation_of_islam/nation_of_islam_part02.pdf (accessed May 1, 2007).
91. In 1967, the FBI included "black nationalist hate groups" in COINTELPRO. See Frank T. Donner, *The Age of Surveillance: The Aims and Methods of America's Political Intelligence System* (New York: Knopf, 1980), 178, 212–13.
92. See McCloud, *African-American Islam*, 64–72; and Dannin, *Black Pilgrimage to Islam*, 66–71.
93. Poston, *Islamic Da'wah in the West*, 39.
94. See Dannin, *Black Pilgrimage to Islam*.
95. See Jackson, *Islam and the Blackamerican*, 73.
96. See, for example, United States District Court, Western District of Washington at Seattle, *United States of America v. Earnest James Ujaama*, at http://fl1.findlaw.com/news.findlaw.com/hdocs/docs/terrorism/usujaama82802ind.pdf (accessed May 1, 2007).
97. For background, see Clifton E. Marsh, *The Lost-Found Nation of Islam in America* (Lanham, Md.: Scarecrow Press, 2000), 67–78, 101–28.
98. Curtis, *Islam in Black America*, 115, 120–21.
99. See, for example, W. Deen Mohammed, *Focus on Al-Islam* (Chicago: Zakat Publications, 1988).
100. Amina Wadud, *Qur'an and Woman* (New York: Oxford University Press, 1999).
101. See Amina Wadud, *Inside the Gender Jihad: Women's Reform in Islam* (New York: Oxford University Press, 2006).

102. See Carolyn Rouse, *Engaged Surrender: African American Women and Islam* (Berkeley: University of California Press, 2004).

103. See Jackson, *Islam and the Blackamerican*, and Imam Zaid Shakir, *Scattered Pictures: Reflections of an American Muslim* (Haywood, Calif.: Zaytuna Institute, 2005).

104. See McCloud, *African American Islam*, 88–94, 248; Dannin, *Black Pilgrimage to Islam*, 248, 255–56; and Jackson, *Islam and the Blackamerican*, 50–51, 191–98. For one example of the influence of the Bawa Muhaiyaddeen Fellowship on an African American Muslim, see Gwendolyn Zoharah Simmons, "Are We Up to the Challenge? The Need for a Radical Re-ordering of the Islamic Discourse on Women," in *Progressive Muslims: On Justice, Gender, and Pluralism*, ed. Omid Safi (Oxford: Oneworld, 2003), esp. 235–39.

105. Poston, *Islamic Da'wah in the West*, 108–9.

106. See further Mattias Gardell, *In the Name of Elijah Muhammad: Louis Farrakhan and the Nation of Islam* (Durham, N.C.: Duke University Press, 1996).

"As Americans Against Genocide": The Crisis in Darfur and Interreligious Political Activism

Jodi Eichler-Levine and Rosemary R. Hicks

On April 30, 2006, thousands of people gathered on the Mall in Washington, D.C., to join celebrities, politicians, and the leaders of the interreligious Save Darfur Coalition in demanding U.S. intervention in Sudan. Early that morning, we and about fifty other community members boarded a bus in our northern Manhattan neighborhood and departed for the capitol. On arriving, we were met by a flood of banners and T-shirt slogans as attendees from a multitude of states, synagogues, colleges, churches, high schools, and humanitarian groups paraded onto the Mall. With their declarations, these activists demonstrated that the coalitional focus on human rights abroad was deeply intertwined with domestic issues of representation and interaction, as well as with collective narratives of national identity. We focus here on how this Washington, D.C., rally and a similar one the following September in New York City served as theaters in which participants enacted their own religious and ethnic identities while positing commonality and difference with others. In addition, we chart the dynamics that unfolded in these spaces as attendees identified with genocide victims, African and otherwise, while simultaneously declaring the ability to save them.[1]

The stories narrated at these events relied on multiple factors: the growth of U.S. military power, rising international debates over genocide, and changing political alliances built partly around investments in the Middle East and Africa. In this article, we consider the messages participants conveyed regarding their views on religion, pluralism, and power in the United States and abroad. We examine how these ideas depended on the many individual and community histories that attendees brought with them to the events and reconstructed in the process of evoking their power as Americans to "save." We also discuss what some of the interactions that occurred before and during the April rally and at the September follow-up demonstrate about the kinds of coalitions built around such salvific efforts, and explore the deployment of a comparatively new narrative: American interreligious humanitarian activism.

Here we go beyond abstract narratives of pluralism to the concrete dynamics of how different people employed the concept of genocide in defining American ethnic and religious identities. Further, we examine how the story of the U.S. citizenry's ability to stop genocide resonated among various marginalized groups and how they demonstrated their Americanness by assuming the identities of powerful saviors. In other words, we examine how particular groups underlined their Americanness and their relationships to each other by claiming the power to control a very specific kind of crisis in Sudan.

"Save Darfur": A Collaborative Experiment in American Interreligious Activism

The conflict in Darfur, a major province in the west of Sudan, emerged in 2003 just as the twenty-one-year civil war in southern Sudan was ending. International entities (including evangelical Christian groups and the Bush administration) had intervened to help broker peace deals for the conflict in the south, which contributed to both halting the violence between Muslims and Christians there and opening the country's abundant oil reserves to U.S. corporations. Inhabitants of the Darfur region subsequently rebelled, citing the government's lack of attention to their economic crises and Darfurian exclusion from oil revenues. The rebel Sudanese Liberation Army's 2003 manifesto invited Arab and African Darfurians to oppose the discriminatory policies of the government in Khartoum. This, in turn, led to reprisals from government-sponsored troops and militias, with many in the United States—including the Save Darfur Coalition—describing the conflict as one of Arab militias attacking black African villagers.[2]

According to witnesses, militias have committed grave human rights violations in the Darfur region as fighting between rebel groups and government troops has escalated. More than 2 million people have since been displaced, and both observers and journalists have detailed widespread torture and murder. In most recent estimates, more than 200,000 people have died and millions more in the region are in need of humanitarian aid.[3]

Mahmood Mamdani, in his recent comparison of U.S. and U.N. involvement in Iraq and Darfur, notes that although the U.N. Commission on Darfur was created "in response to American pressure," it nevertheless concluded in 2005 that the Sudanese government did not in any way "pursue a policy of genocide." Mamdani has elsewhere chronicled the British origins of the rhe-torical divide between a supposedly Arab North Africa and an African South, and discusses contemporary uses of this distinction. In his work, Hishaam Aidi charts the recent deployment of racial and religious dichotomies in descriptions of the Sudanese conflict. He contends, quoting Alex de Waal, that

> the Arab-African dichotomy is historically and anthropologically bogus. But that doesn't make the distinction unreal, as long as the perpetrators subscribe to it . . . Darfurian Arabs, too, are indigenous, black and African. In fact, there are no discernible racial or discernible religious differences between the two: all have lived there for centuries; all are Muslims.[4]

De Waal, one of the few firsthand observers of the political process in Sudan, questions the efficacy of U.S. involvement. He points to mistakes U.S. officials have made in identifying figures powerful enough to effect changes and the inability of U.N. peacekeepers to stop the killing.[5] Despite these problems, the Save Darfur Coalition has marshaled millions of Americans with their emotionally resonant calls for military involvement in Darfur and pressure on the United Nations.

As Aidi notes, in 2004 the American Jewish World Service and other or-ganizations helped form the coalition, who described themselves then as "an alliance of over 100 faith-based, humanitarian and human rights organizations [whose] mission is to raise public awareness and to mobilize an effective uni-fied response to the atrocities that threaten the lives of two million people in the Darfur region."[6]

In 2005, the Save Darfur Coalition prompted Congress to designate July 15–17 "a national weekend of prayer and reflection for Darfur" and launched a Web site and other public relations efforts, including a "Million Voices for Darfur" postcard campaign.[7] This effort to inundate President Bush with notes about the situation was featured prominently at the April 2006 rally and cul-minated in June 2006, when Democratic Senator Hillary Clinton and Senate majority leader, Republican Bill Frist, jointly signed the millionth card. In January of 2007 the coalition successfully pressured Bush to mention Darfur in his State of the Union address, and subsequently e-mailed activists in key states to call their senators on the Armed Services Committee so as to request specific military maneuvers.[8] The following month, the coalition utilized funds from anonymous donors to engage in a media blitz involving, among other things, advertisements in many of the most highly trafficked subway stations in New York City, full-page ads in prominent national newspapers, and televi-sion and magazine spots featuring well-known celebrities. Controversy quickly ensued over the use of coalition funds for publicity instead of aid to refugees, as well as over the coalition's military plan (which aid workers in Sudan argued could both harm relief efforts and expose workers to physical danger). As a result of pursuing these strategies, executive director and founding coalition member David Rubenstein was fired in June of 2007—just days after Bush announced the enactment of economic sanctions that Rubenstein and other coalition members had long lobbied. For his part, Rubenstein described the contested sanctions as "too little and too late."[9]

As of 2007, the coalition's members include more than 150 national and regional nonprofit groups, encompassing some organized primarily on the basis of race (such as the National Association for the Advancement of Colored People, or NAACP), others organized primarily on the basis of political or human rights (Amnesty International), and still others delimited in terms of religion (the Union for Reform Judaism).[10] These three categories—race, politics, and religion—are the focus of our study, as all three overlap in complicated ways and connect American issues to international ones. Thus, in this article we speak not of religious identities or ethnic identities, but ethno-religious ones, particularly as they are formed through these contested narratives of political activism.

Prevailing ideas about "ethnicity," "race," and "religion" developed out of eighteenth- and nineteenth-century European understandings of Christianity and scientific inquiry and have influenced each other greatly. Though these modern categories are often simplified and separated for many reasons, including political expediency, we use the term "ethno-religious" here to highlight the complex interplay between them that occurs in everyday life.[11] As we discuss below, the Save Darfur Coalition's highly promoted Jewish–African American Alliance belies any simple narrative of religious identity and reveals the multivalent nature of inter-"religious" political activism. While Rabbi David Saperstein (director of the Union for Reform Judaism's Religious Action Center and NAACP board member) represented one half of this alliance, Reverend Gloria White-Hammond (co-pastor of the Bethel AME Church in Boston and chairwoman of the "Million Voices" campaign), represented its completion.[12] Further, we must note here that ethnic, economic, and religious complexities contribute to specific kinds of relations *inside* ethno-religious groups, and not only among them.[13]

In addition to foregrounding the complexity of religious identity, stories told at the rallies highlighted the changing histories that members of various ethno-religious traditions have in relation to contested terms of Americanness.

Different understandings of slavery, pan-Africanism, civil rights struggles, the Iranian hostage crisis, and September 11 complicate the terms by which some have gained acceptance in the United States and the extent to which they identify with it. Rally participants referenced many such historical realities in their speeches, plotting them into sometimes clashing narratives of religious identity and interreligious activism. As we discuss, the contestations among various representatives regarding *which* ethno-religious Americans could be included in the endeavor to "save" Darfur reveal their different notions about models of diversity and activism in the United States.

Evangelical Christians were active in Sudan prior to the Darfur crisis. During the 1990s, they lobbied for American intervention after reports that Christians in southern Sudan faced attacks from roving Arabs. The Arab Muslim foe was a familiar adversary to these advocates, and many depicted the Darfur crisis in similar terms as a clash between Arabs and black Africans. The conflict was also sometimes described in contrasting religious terms, despite the fact that almost all involved are Muslim. Likewise, organizers of the Save Darfur Coalition portrayed the Sudanese government as a specifically Muslim aggressor in this 2005 *Washington Times* op-ed piece co-written by the National Association of Evangelicals' vice president of governmental affairs, Richard Cizik, and Rabbi Saperstein:

> While the Sudan government has heeded President Bush's call to cooperate in the war on terror and with the January 2005 Comprehensive Peace Agreement that ended the two-decade-long Sudan civil war between *the Muslim government* in the north and Christian and Animist population in the south, it has failed to disarm and disperse the Janjaweed militias responsible for the daily slaughter of civilians.[14]

At the time this piece was printed, importantly, the Sudanese government had included Christian members for almost six months.

Some speakers and attendees likewise tapped into the theme of Muslim Arabs as a menace to a Jewish-Christian alliance and to Jewish, black African, and Jewish-African interests. These conflations did not go unchallenged. In the following sections, we examine the dynamics of this interreligious coalition, the roots of the emotionally evocative narratives on which suggested alliances hinged, and how these elements changed between the rallies of April and September 2006.

"I Have a Nightmare": Jewish Americans, African Americans, and Narratives of Redemption

In a country where Jews are slightly less than 2 percent of the population, Jewish organizations constituted nearly one-third of the rally sponsors.[15] Four of the eleven institutional members of the group's executive committee were Jewish, as were 34 of the 117 national supporting groups listed.[16] Although no official demographic breakdown of rally attendance exists, a disproportionate number of participants also identified as Jewish (according to their T-shirts and banners). Meanwhile, African American leaders appeared alongside Jewish leaders on the rally speakers' list, thus marking the event as politically significant for both groups. Contemporary appeals to Jewish–African American cooperation pivoted around the stories these groups told about their shared histories of activism, their own memories of persecution, and their own vested interests in the history and politics of the Middle East. We consider here the power of group narration and explore how ethno-religious identities were formed in relation to each other and to a particular concept of "America" as enforcer of international human rights.

The racial identities of Jews and African Americans have changed continually throughout the twentieth century; in fact, each group's identity is often figured in terms of the other's. For example, the whiteness of American Jews is a relatively recent construction. Eastern European Jews arriving in the late nineteenth century were initially categorized as unwhite, "Hebraic," or provisionally white, but not *white enough*. For these Jews, whiteness came accompanied by—perhaps even caused by—upward mobility in the years following World War II.[17]

Relationships between blacks and Jews did not commence in the 1960s, nor was this iconic decade simply a halcyon era of cooperation, despite famous images like that of Jewish theologian Abraham Joshua Heschel marching arm-in-arm with Dr. Martin Luther King Jr.[18] Jewish-black interaction always involved a push and pull of identity. Many Americans have since portrayed Jewish–African American connections in terms of a "decline and fall," citing racial tensions in the 1960s and 1990s in Brownsville and Crown Heights, Brooklyn, as well as Jewish outrage at the anti-Jewish comments of Nation of Islam leader Louis Farakhan.[19] Other scholars have discussed divisions the 1967 war caused between Jewish nationalists and African nationalists, the latter of which increasingly supported pan-Africanism and viewed Israeli military power as neocolonial.[20]

One task of the Save Darfur event appeared to be mending the rifts between African and Jewish Americans by uniting them in a common cause of international intervention. The unmentioned organizational issue in this endeavor, as in previous ones, was *which* African Americans, and which first-generation Africans in America, to include. At the April rally, "African American" was almost always a metonymic reference for Christian. Additionally, African Muslims *in* America—specifically, Darfurians—were originally not included as participants. Organizers thus attempted to renew a particular Judeo-Christian alliance by collectively narrating themselves as powerful American protectors of voiceless victims—this time, of black bodies in Darfur.

Numerous rally presenters drew from the idealized social capital of the 1960s, while simultaneously pointing toward the future of joint activism.[21] Rabbi David Saperstein, for example, inverted Martin Luther King Jr.'s most famous address when he proclaimed his "nightmare" for today's world.

> We stand here on the Nation's Mall, hearing still the echoes of Dr. King's dream. But we, the Jews of America, we whose people have been the quintessential victims of ethnic cleansing and genocide, join with a rainbow of Americans of conscience to speak not of remembered dreams but of ongoing nightmares.
>
> For I have a nightmare today that because of the world's apathy and indifference hundreds of thousands more Darfurians will die. Will you let that happen?
>
> I have a nightmare that despite the committed efforts of our President, Congress, and ourselves, we will commit the most tragic political sin good people can make—we will be too late. Will you let that happen?[22]

By evoking King, Saperstein wielded a powerful common narrative, a site of *in-between-ness* designed to bring together those assembled. Simultaneously, Saperstein claimed *uniqueness* for Jews, speaking of "we, the Jews of America, we whose people have been the quintessential victims of ethnic cleansing and genocide." He was not alone in figuring Jewish action in terms of remembrance and the Holocaust, thus moving between universality and particularism. The United States Holocaust Museum issued the 2004 "Genocide Alert" for Darfur, and the Holocaust hovered over much of the language in the "Jewish" Million Postcards material, which read: "Instead of mourning a genocide, what if we could STOP one? As Jews, we have a particular moral responsibility to speak out and take action against genocide."[23] According to the coalition, Jews not only have a special sense of empathy for genocide as victims par excellence; they also have a special responsibility and, as Jewish *Americans*, a special *power* to stop genocide. In Saperstein's words, Jews do not only remember the Holocaust; they are the "quintessential" genocide victims. The question of Holocaust uniqueness has long been debated; some academics and activists argue that the Holocaust is an exceptional event in history, while others contend that insisting on Holocaust uniqueness turns Holocaust defenders into genocide deniers by hiding other tragedies.[24] For Saperstein, being part of this "quintessential" community allowed him to identify other instances of genocide, such as Rwanda and, now, Darfur.

By including non-Jewish victims in the category of genocide, Saperstein and those at the Holocaust Museum opened the possibility for others to join them in their status as responsible survivors. Identifying "genocide" necessitates action from countries that are party to the U.N. Convention Against Genocide.[25] Likewise, identifying oneself as a victim of genocide necessitates activism. Memories of genocide and mourning for victims were thus funneled into an active, *salvific* mode of protest, transforming commingled Jewish and African American narratives of suffering into an American tale of redemption: Judeo-Christians saving Darfur from invading Arab Muslims. Several narratives were interwoven in utilizing genocide to unite Jewish and African American groups that are in many ways dissimilar—including over the issue of supporting Israel. While criticism of Israel is a hotly contested topic for Americans across the political and religious spectrum, condemning an ostensibly Arab aggressor in Sudan seemed to serve as a powerful and emotionally resonant rallying point for many, though certainly not all, attendees.[26] Likewise, identifying "genocide" was here a measure of building a pan-African identity based on ethnicity instead of religion (Rwanda, Southern Sudan, and now Darfur) that separated "Arab" African Muslims from "black" African Muslims and reincorporated the latter into a new alliance.

Not only were racial and religious identities folded into one another during the April rally, but time and space were condensed, as well. "I Have a Dream" was translated from a recollection of past American religious activism into a model for future interreligious action and future interethnic coalitions. During tremendous upheavals, communal traumas are commonly remembered in terms of one another, and the complicated process of remembering involves overlapping cycles of narrative borrowing.[27] Such situations call for a conceptualization of religious (and activist) cultures that foster in-between spaces of speech. In Homi Bhabha's terms, culture, including social narratives, occurs in translation between groups.[28] In this case, narratives of suffering were simultaneously plotted as narratives of *redemption*. Indeed, they were the very grounds on which redemptive enactments were based, as previous victims rose up to speak for the now "silent." This new narrative was performed on one of the most multivalent sites in America's civic landscape: the National Mall. The Reverend Al Sharpton drew upon its history as he included African Americans in the category of those powerful enough to identify genocide because of identification *with* genocide. Sharpton also connected Americanness to the ability to *stop* genocide, then lay claim to that power for the assembled crowd:

> This has been a long struggle, but now, when we see you here today, on the same ground that Martin Luther King came, on the same grounds that civil rights and civil liberties came, we know when America comes together, we can stop anything in the world. History will write that we came together in the first decade of the twenty-first century and stopped genocide in Sudan.[29]

"History *will* write" of the rally, argued Sharpton. Like Saperstein, he took the long view *forward* by looking *backward*: King *once* stood here and was inscribed into "history," and those standing here today *will* be. As Francesca Polletta argues, protest narratives afford a special vantage point on time: "narratives not only make sense of the past and present but, since the story's chronological end is also its end in the sense of moral, purpose or telos, they project a future. This is the basis for self-identity and action."[30] At the Save Darfur rallies, moral condemnations of genocide included only certain tragedies, thus incorporating only certain actors in this victim-turned-vindicator teleology.

"Never Again, Again": Narratives of Genocide

Many at the rally described the horrors of Darfur in terms of the Holocaust, figuring catastrophes that both preceded and followed it on its terms. Numerous attendees carried signs proclaiming "Never Again, Again," making this phrase stand in metonymically for the very concept of genocide. The phrase was not just an imperative, but a history: "Never Again, *Again*" narrated the multiple failures to stop genocide in Armenia, Germany, Cambodia, Rwanda, Bosnia, and now Darfur, making genocide no longer solely a Jewish purview. The United Nations proclaimed the first *International* Holocaust Remembrance Day in January of 2006, also broadening the "never again" dictum into a schema in which Holocaust imagery becomes a universal mandate for intervention. U.N. Secretary General Ban Ki-moon hinted as much on the Remembrance Day's second annual observance when he declared that "the International Day in memory of the victims of the Holocaust is thus a day on which we must reassert our commitment to human rights."[31]

Inaugural speaker Elie Wiesel elaborated on this theme at the April rally.

> Remember, silence aids the killer, never his victims. We are here today because if we do nothing, Al Qaeda and the world's number one holocaust denier, the infamous ruler of Iran, Ahmadinejad will send terrorists there. We are here to voice our compassion for the victims and our anger at leaders who are timorous, complacent, and unwilling to take risks . . . Darfur today is the world's capital of human suffering. Not to offer our help, not to urge our governments to intervene in every manner possible is to condemn us on grounds of inhumanity. Darfur deserves to live. We are the only hope . . . Let the appeal go out from here, strong and loud, for the sake of our humanity, Save Darfur.[32]

Wiesel moved rapidly from the story of Holocaust to the contemporary "war on terror" and to Darfur. He conflated a variety of eras and issues in a brief rhetorical span, contrasting the rally's location in the center of human freedom with Darfurians at the center of "human suffering" and drawing both together in their respective "capitals" under the menace of similar foes. Wiesel juxtaposed humanity and holocaust, or, humanity and inhumanity, and used this commentary to bridge multiple concerns. In the process, he consolidated both the identities of victims *and* the identities of victimizers, thus portraying them as historically fixed and mutually exclusive. Not all attendees agreed with Wiesel, however; many were distressed to hear human rights rhetoric used to evoke and justify the "war on terror" and contemporary U.S. wars in Afghanistan and Iraq—thus demonstrating how narratives can congregate *and* segregate diverse coalitions.[33]

U.S. action during the Holocaust was iterated even in performances that were not explicitly Jewish. Consider the speech of Brian Steidle, a former U.S. Marine captain and advisor to African Union forces, who had traveled the United States to display his photographs from Darfur.[34] "We have the power, here, in America," he informed the crowd, "the people have the power to stand up, and say 'genocide—never again!'"[35] Steidle spoke in the language of Holocaust remembrance while embodying military intervention. Like other figures that day, he promoted the chant of "Never Again" as a universalized interdiscourse, crafting this story to fit "between" the narratives of assembled groups. For some Jewish rally participants, connection with the Holocaust was one of the more moving aspects of the rally. Others, however, were disturbed by the continuing trend of building Jewish identity on its legacy.[36] Meanwhile, certain coalition members publicly decried being excluded from both the rally and the narrative regroupings altogether.

One attendee later expressed her ambivalence, questioning the event's success in building a genuine multiracial and interfaith coalition, while simultaneously voicing the rally's importance to her as a Jew:

At the rally there were thousands of Jews. While I enjoyed seeing many friends and familiar faces, I wondered what kind of coalition had really been achieved, whose voices we were really hearing, and whether we had gathered together truly to help affect [sic] change in Darfur, or to let ourselves, as Jews, off the hook—as if to say "we stood up and shouted 'Never Again,' now we are absolved of our responsibility."

But what troubled me even more so was the under current of racism that I couldn't help but feel. Israeli flags being flown. A young boy, sitting on his father's shoulders, carrying a sign that read "Arabs in Khartoum, just because we don't believe in Mohammad doesn't mean you can kill us!" So much racism embedded in our community, so much propaganda and misinformation. Standing there in Washington after hours and hours of work I felt so torn—as an individual I feel so powerless to affect [sic] change, and so I do the only thing I can do and shout. But when I shout among thousands I can't help but wonder if it is the voices decrying genocide the world hears, or the voices of racism and fear.[37]

The attendee raises questions about many of the dynamics we observed at the rally, including the interrelated issues of voice and power that we address in our final section. Ultimately, her online observations reveal the complications involved in shaping this interreligious activism. She was there for one kind of coalition; the family with the anti-Arab sign was there for another one.

This blogger also connected some attendees' support of Israel with racism against Arabs and criticized the conflation of Arabs and Muslims with victimizers: "Arabs in Khartoum, just because we don't believe in Mohammad doesn't mean you can kill us!" read the boy's sign. Who is "*we*"? Darfurian Muslim victims? Jews? Both, in the form of Jews standing in for (religiously ambiguous) Darfurians? The Holocaust and African crises were not the only genocides mentioned that day. Bosnia, a conflict in which European Muslims were killed, was also cited. Muslims were thus included as victims of genocide—in Europe and in Africa—but were identified under ethnic categories around which ostensibly similar ethnic communities in the United States could mobilize. Meanwhile, attention to Arab Muslim victims was conspicuously absent.

At the actual rally, most representatives were careful not to cast Arabs as Nazis—despite the fact that this allusion was prevalent in the promotional video, in packets circulated among religious communities before the event, and in the press packet available that day. In fact, the Save Darfur Coalition had only recently refrained from identifying the perpetrators as "a government-backed *Arab* militia known as Janjaweed."[38] In contrast, the evangelical representative at the April rally continued to interpret the conflict in racial terms while omitting the common Muslim identity of all involved:

Let me say it bluntly, the regime in Khartoum does not consider African Darfurians to be human beings. It is very clear that those in power in Khartoum intend to "empty" Darfur of its large non-Arab African population.[39]

In the "Background" provided for their interfaith educational materials, the Save Darfur Coalition identified the perpetrators only as "government-backed militias, known collectively as the Janjaweed," and omitted the word "Arab" from their April 30 "Darfur Backgrounder and Policy Talking Points" press packet insert. However, they still included a *New York Times* editorial piece (dated April 29) identifying the antagonists as "Arab militias that *call themselves* the janjaweed and are backed by Sudan's government" who, "not satisfied with the numbers of murders and rapes of men, women, and children—a vast majority of them Muslim—in their ethnic cleansing campaign . . . are attempting to eliminate entire African tribes from the countryside" (emphasis added). Samantha Power, one of the first journalists to report on the crisis and a speaker at both rallies, also described the militias bent on "ethnic-cleansing" as "janjaweed" . . . after arguing elsewhere that no one in Darfur uses the term "janjaweed" self-referentially.[40]

As demonstrated here, coalition attempts to rejuvenate an alliance between African and Jewish Americans involved complex dynamics—including contestations over ethno-religious categories and defining Americanness in terms of military intervention against genocide. These debates hinted at otherwise unspoken issues on many attendees' minds: Israel's relationship with various Arab neighbors and relationships between Arab and black Muslims in both Africa and the United States.

Melani McAlister has examined how racial politics have impacted U.S. understandings of the Middle East, and the contours of the "dominant discourses that have represented the region as a resource for American nationalism and a site for the expansion of U.S. power." Black, Christian, and Jewish nationalists in the United States have historically worked independently and cooperatively, as Aidi concurs, "to claim certain cultures, spaces and eras of the Arab world as theirs for their own purposes." Though African Americans have historically been ambivalent about Zionism, Aidi adds, all groups "have long imbued the 'Orient' with redemptive significance."[41] The story of Darfur-as-contemporary-Holocaust often reiterated such older themes and was used to (re)build alliances between African American (Christians) and American Jews. Many Muslims—including African Americans, Arab Americans, and Darfurian refugees—contested their exclusion from this alliance. We now turn to how these contestations revealed intra-Muslim tensions over the nature of authentic Islam, as well as intra-ethnic tensions between African American Muslims and Christians over authentic African identity. As far as Americanness, all Muslim coalition members oppose genocide. Importantly, though, they enacted American identity in terms of this specific moral claim rather than in terms of military power.

Muslims, Arabs, Africans, and Americans: How/Do We Hyphenate?

Many speakers urged Jewish and African American participants to unite under the common moral status of survivors and mourners of genocide and to blend their claims to the lands of Africa and the Middle East. They then endeavored to collaborate with white evangelicals, who had long been active in these regions, in order to utilize American power to "save" black bodies from invading Arabs. As Yvonne Haddad, Jane Smith, and John Esposito note, contested appeals to the ostensible "Judeo-Christian" heritage of the American nation are increasingly cited as a basis for building future American identities: "[After 1965,] a definition of America as Protestant, Catholic, and Jewish was promoted as an alternative to the melting-pot metaphor. Immigrant Muslims, for the most part latecomers to the American scene, have actively sought recognition, some even calling for a definition of America as Judeo-Christian-Muslim."[42] Speakers' related, but disparate, appeals to American moral authority recalled the difficulties *some* Christians and Jews have had in gaining access to Americanness and nuanced contemporary accounts of American egalitarian "Judeo-Christian" identity. Meanwhile, the near-exclusion of Muslim participants from the rally troubled the coalition's own narratives of religious diversity and pluralistic equality.

The Save Darfur Coalition includes several important Muslim organizations, such as the American Society for Muslim Advancement (ASMA), the Council on American Islamic Relations (CAIR), the Islamic Society of North America (ISNA), the Islamic Circle of North America (ICNA), the American Islamic Forum for Democracy, the Muslim Public Affairs Council, and the Muslim American Society Freedom Foundation.[43] Nevertheless, Muslim rally presenters were included only at the last minute. In response, CAIR (self-described as "America's largest Muslim civil liberties group") organized its own interreligious rally at one of the nation's largest Islamic centers in Cincinnati, where attendees likewise signed Save Darfur postcards. CAIR also issued a press statement the day after the April event indicating the ongoing tensions within American Muslim communities over who has authority to authentically represent American Islam: "It is unfortunate that the Save Darfur Coalition chose not to list any mainstream American Muslim groups in the rally program . . . This disturbing omission calls into question the coalition's true agenda at the rally."[44] According to CAIR, the few Muslims included in Washington, D.C., were not sufficiently "mainstream." As this statement shows, the question of *whether* to represent Islam at this rally was beset by another, larger dilemma: *how?* This is not simply an *intra*religious debate; it is also an *inter*ethnic one.

Conflations of "Muslim" with "Arab" in the United States have only worsened since 2001, as many rhetoricians attempt to separate "Islam" from "the West." In addition to masking the existence of Arab Christians and Arab Jews, this conflation denies recognition to the many diverse Muslim communities in America, including one of the largest groups: African Americans. Sherman Jackson has recently discussed how current tensions between "immigrant" and "indigenous" American Muslims revolve around claims to authentic Africanness, authentic Americanness, and authentic Islam. These struggles are contingent upon both groups' "mutually conflicting relationship to American whiteness," he contends. Upwardly mobile and generally well-educated Arab and South Asian immigrants of the 1960s were not confined to the fixed pole of "blackness," but distanced themselves from this designation by climbing the economic and social ladder. Further, as Islam grew more prevalent in black communities, he argues, African American Christians began to defensively reiterate American anti-Arab bias in the hopes of preventing their constituents from converting. The result: "Black Orientalist" tales of Arab invaders destroying indigenous African civilization.[45] Aidi largely agrees with this assessment, noting that conflicts in Sudan are often portrayed in these suspect terms. Particularly after 2001, Aidi argues, various communities invested in the Middle East and Africa renewed their historical coalitions around a poignantly familiar trope: violent Arab conquests.[46]

The equality of Muslims—especially Arab Muslims—remained ambiguous in the months leading up to the April Save Darfur rally and at the actual event. This was particularly evident in the pre-rally promotional materials, in the controversy over Muslim speakers, and in the statements of official representatives. In these venues, Islam was generally either excluded or portrayed as a specifically Arab religion while Arabs were identified as perpetrators of genocide. Prior to the April rally, for example, religious leaders could access an array of resources for mobilizing their congregations on the Save Darfur Web site. Among these were several "Action Packets" ("Christian Faith," "Jewish," "Interfaith," and "General Faith"), though none for Islam—despite the fact that the sole insert designed to mobilize Muslim Americans identified all 400,000 fatalities in Darfur as Muslim deaths.[47]

Religious leaders could also utilize the coalition's educational film, which included narrative commentary from military envoy Brian Steidle. Steidle described the conflict as one between "Arabs from the Middle East who had migrated in" and "the African world," and argued that the "government who is predominantly Arab chose their Arab allies" over black Africans. Steidle also modeled American military intervention in one segment. Against a soundtrack of rotating chopper blades he described with technical precision how it felt to capture the "Arab janjaweed" under the camera's red scope instead of under a gun. "When you shoot from a helicopter you get a lot of vibration and it's nice to get clear shots. And sometimes you wish, maybe . . . you did have a rifle."[48]

During his public appearance at the April rally, Steidle spoke only of his identification with the Darfurians, encouraging participants to do likewise. "Ana Sudani!" (I am Sudanese!) he proclaimed, making his affiliation with particular Sudanese clear. What was unclear to most participants was that the language in which he made the statement was Arabic—a language commonly used to bridge regional Sudanese dialects. As in Steidle's comments, "Sudani" was almost always presented as a black and religiously ambiguous African identity at the April rally—and generally one that needed saving from Muslim Arabs.

Despite the historical tensions between black Muslims and immigrant Muslims from Arabia and South Asia, American Muslims from all backgrounds were cautious of the politicized stereotypes running through various characterizations of the Darfur crisis. Imam A. Rashied Omar, a black South African Muslim leader living in Indiana, highlighted this concern as far back as 2004, arguing that "it would be simplistic to attribute the carnage in Darfur purely to motives of racism as has been implied in much of the media reporting of Arabs against Africans," and urging Americans to "purify and heal our souls and rid our communities from the scourge of racism through a vigorous education campaign."[49]

Similarly, Reverend Sharpton attempted to decry discrimination, while simultaneously claiming the capacity to save. "Now is the time to speak for children who cannot speak for themselves. We are not anti-Muslim, we are anti-murder. We are not anti-Arab, we are anti-annihilation," he chanted, though in the process positioning the "we" of which he is a part as specifically *not* Muslim and *not* Arab, and alluding to the victimizers in such terms.

As we have discussed, most representatives at the Save Darfur rally demonstrated complex relations to Muslims—relations that were highly dependent on the ethnicity of the Muslims in question. Some evangelicals, white and black, evinced antagonism toward Arab Muslims but paternalism toward "African" (i.e., black African) Muslims. Meanwhile, the broadened "Never Again" mandate did not serve as an open-ended framework encompassing *all* genocides in an archetypical narrative, but only genocides perpetrated by particular actors and not others against particular victims and not others. Specifically, in the narrative voiced by Wiesel and renarrated by Steidle and evangelical Christians, the genocide that should not be repeated is that which Arabs/Muslims ostensibly do, not that from which they historically or currently suffer.

"THIS TIME WE CAN"—Religious Pluralism and American Agency

As organizers urged attendees to adopt the refrain "we have the power to stop [genocide]," they deliberated over the ethno-religious contours of American moral agency as well as collaborated in building a common enemy.[50] In the process, most speakers also continually described Darfurians as voiceless victims in need of American intervention. Days before the rally, Alan Cooperman of the *Washington Post* reported that

> organizers rushed this week to invite two Darfurians to address the rally after Sudanese immigrants objected that the original list of speakers included eight Western Christians, seven Jews, four politicians, and assorted celebrities—but no Muslims and no one from Darfur.[51]

The continual iterations that American Christians, Jews, and (possibly) Muslims have the power to *save* black Africans were sometimes reminiscent of American Protestant appeals to act on behalf of voiceless nonwhites in other eras. In this section we examine how various speakers used these calls for intercession to replot past salvation narratives with different actors, thus moving previously marginalized groups into positions of power by insisting on the powerlessness of others.

Christian members of the coalition most explicitly shouldered this mantle of salvation. Only the "Christian" packet Sample Prayer asked God to forgive their failure to believe that "*you* have *empowered us* to protect our brothers and sisters" (emphasis added). Further, "AS CHRIST GAVE SIGHT TO THE BLIND," the Christian insert proclaimed, "we can give voice to the voiceless" (emphasis in original). At the rally, Geoff Tunnicliffe, international director of the World Evangelical Alliance, called upon "the 100's of million[s of] evangelical Christians in the world to join with others across the globe in responding to the Biblical exhortation of Proverbs 31:8–9: *Speak up for those who cannot speak for themselves, for the rights of all who are destitute. Speak up and judge fairly; defend the rights of the poor and needy.*"[52]

"We can either speak out and become agents of justice, or remain silent and be rendered irrelevant," argued African American evangelical leader and Coalition Executive Committee member White-Hammond in her explicit appeals to act on behalf of rape victims. She also connected voice with agency, but did not always depict Darfurians as voiceless. Rather, they were leaders of the call to justice—albeit ones who needed others to join "their chorus." White-Hammond declared that "the voices of women . . . are crying out from the deserts of Darfur. They blend with those echoing from the mountainous terrain of Bosnia and the hill country of Rwanda."[53] She disrupted the tale of voiceless victims at times by echoing their spoken mandate for help. Though there is not sufficient space to explore this theme here, narratives of Darfurian helplessness persist most noticeably in the emphasis then and since on victimized womanhood. Appeals to masculinity were also used as an index of authentic Americanness and a measure of unity, as is hinted at by the overwhelmingly male representation of clergy, politicians, and members of the military, and their continual evocation of the racialized specter of rape.[54]

Darfurians were much more sensitive about the efforts of their ostensible saviors than organizers imagined or admitted. In fact, as Cooperman noted,

> keeping the peace within the diverse Save Darfur Coalition has not been easy. Tensions have arisen, in particular, between evangelical Christians and immigrants from Darfur, whose population is almost entirely Muslim and deeply suspicious of missionary activity.[55]

At the April rally, one Sudanese man, though not a Darfurian, did figure prominently. Simon Deng had endured years of slavery during the country's earlier southern conflict. This African-turned-American citizen confirmed Americans' roles as voices of the voiceless, plotting himself first as a silent *Sudanese victim* approving the salvific American mandate and then as an authoritative *American* empowered to enact it. As with Jewish and African American narratives, the space between these two poles was the space in which he found his voice—first as a victim on behalf of others like himself, and then as an American on behalf of other silent sufferers. Throughout the process, the important distinctions for Deng were not ones of race or religion, but nationality and victimhood. To be an American is to *not* be a victim; rather, it is to overcome victim status by intervening elsewhere:

> I stand here *as a victim* of the atrocities that are happening in Sudan . . . Today, I am standing here *as the voice of those who have no voice, my fellow victims* who are living . . . in the hell that has become Sudan.

> . . . And today, especially you the young ones, we are making history by speaking loudly that genocide must end now . . . young people are using their voices to *speak up for those who can't speak for themselves.*
>
> The violence in Sudan is *not* a question of black versus Arab or Islam versus Christianity; it is a question of humanity.
>
> *My fellow Americans,* particularly leaders of the African American community, we must become strong, vocal advocates for the people of Sudan during *their* time of need.[56]

Two important Darfurian representatives did appear at the rally in the same five-minute slot allotted to Deng. Lawyer and human rights activist Salih Mahmoud Osman and Tragi Mustafa, "The Darfur refugee [who] founded Save Women–Sudan," were silenced by time constraints.[57] In contrast, much time was devoted to buttressing Sharpton's call for protecting voiceless Darfurian children. Two children from Darfur were led on to the stage to address the assembled audience of thousands. They were almost completely silent, speaking reluctantly only after being prodded to offer a few words.

After much criticism of the April rally, the speakers list at the September event included several representatives from Darfurian organizations as well as more Arab and Muslim Americans. However, the DVD featuring Steidle and describing the conflict in religious terms was also available there, demonstrating that ethno-religious debates continue over African American identity, Muslim American identity, and how Islam fits into pluralistic models of religious activism and moral authority. In this case, these debates are integrally tied to descriptions of genocide and calls for U.S. military intervention.

During the course of the rally, genocide was depicted as something some Americans have suffered and something Americans actively prevent but certainly *not* something in which they participate. By inviting particular representatives and not others to lead the call for *saving* "voiceless" black bodies, organizers tapped into contested narratives of agency regarding *which* ethno-religious Americans have the power to protect, as well as *who* they should protect, *from* whom, and where. American Muslims endeavored to insert themselves into this narrative as ethno-religious Americans against genocide and to claim the moral authority this stance provides, meanwhile contesting varied attempts to conflate genocide with Arabs and/or Muslims.[58] Further, they pursued this American identity partly by silencing some of their own concerns about what they have experienced as U.S.-supported and U.S.-directed oppression at home and abroad.

Postscript: Human Rights and Military Might

On September 17, 2006, protestors convened in the sunny East Meadow of Central Park for the "Global Day for Darfur," a gathering timed to coincide with United Nations General Assembly meetings in New York. At the April rally, focused on instigating American political involvement, participants had stood in, and spoken *for*, Sudanese victims. One of the stated goals of the September rally, in contrast, was to involve the United Nations. Some participants arrived in Central Park wearing blue hats to signify a United Nations peacekeeping force, with many of high school and college age sporting bright blue berets. Amnesty International volunteers provided pale blue bandanas to those who did not come "equipped." At this rally attendees sprawled on the grass throughout the meadow and—between musical acts and speakers—were urged to text the president from their mobile phones.

The physical space of protest had shifted from Washington, D.C., the *national* capital, to New York City, home of the United Nations. Simultaneously, protestors moved from *embodying the victims* to primarily *embodying their rescuers*. Somewhat struck by the prevalence of beret- and camouflage-clad youth around us, we mused over these bodies dressed as peacekeeping soldiers at a time when other young Americans are *literally* suited up for war.[59] The protestors' dress that day combined the stated human rights goals of the rally with a collective overlay of militarism. Former U.S. Secretary of State Madeleine Albright carefully countered concerns over American imperialism when she argued that "the protection of the innocent is a universal responsibility . . . this issue is not about trying to promote one religion over another because all the sides in Darfur are Muslim . . . this is not about politics; it is about people."[60]

As mentioned, Alex de Waal (director for the Social Science Research Council program on AIDS and social transformation, fellow of the Harvard Global Equity Initiative, and director of the London-based Justice Africa) argues that U.S. and U.N. military intervention in Sudan may be counterproductive to ending the Darfur conflict. De Waal was one of the only mediators involved in brokering the May 2006 Darfur Peace Agreement in Sudan. In addition to asserting that the U.S. State Department has incorrectly assessed, and thus negatively affected, the situation in Darfur, he argued in a November 2006 article that

> military intervention won't stop the killing. Those who are clamouring for troops to fight their way into Darfur are suffering from a salvation delusion. It's a simple reality that U.N.

troops can't stop an ongoing war, and their record at protecting civilians is far from perfect . . . The crisis in Darfur is political. It's a civil war, and like all wars it needs a political settlement . . . fix the politics first and the peacekeeping will follow. It's not a distant hope: the political differences are small.[61]

Like Albright, de Waal cites politics instead of religion. Rather than downplay U.S. interests by evoking genocide, however, he insists on attending to economic and political issues underlying the Sudanese conflicts. The "Global Day for Darfur" events often concealed the complexities of geopolitical realities while revealing the emotional stakes and ambivalences involved in marshaling U.S. power against Arab invaders. We have noted the emotional resonance of many narratives utilized by rally attendees and speakers as they enacted their transformations from victims of genocide to powerful American protectors. Simon Deng, though not Darfurian, spoke to his "fellow Americans" as one empowered to intervene on behalf of silent/silenced others. Like members of African American and Jewish groups, he claimed Americanness by assuming the power to stop genocide. White evangelicals did likewise. Also marginalized from the American mainstream in the mid-twentieth century, their success in securing American political intervention in southern Sudan was a similar kind of claim to American moral authority and power. At one point in the day, a white evangelical speaker specifically grounded late-twentieth-century evangelical political prominence within a broader and older American narrative. Referencing the liberation of Nazi camps, he claimed: "America has been the world's conscience and halted . . . genocide when it raised its evil head in Europe. We have a moral obligation to do the same in Africa."[62]

Historically, however, the United States has been reticent to label atrocities "genocide" while they are occurring, did not become party to the Convention on Genocide until the 1980s (with reservations), and did not intervene in any post–World War II instances of genocide until Kosovo in 1999.[63] The Save Darfur Coalitions call for American action under a "Never Again" mandate can thus be seen not only as claims to American power, but emotionally evocative mobilizations of American *will*, in short, as attempts to reshape American identity into that of citizens who don't just witness the unfolding of ostensibly ethno-religious crises, but militarily intervene. When U.S. ratification of the Convention on Genocide was disputed, convention advocate Senator William Proxmire of Wisconsin noted that emotional resonance is essential in moving Americans to act against atrocities: "The overwhelming majority of Americans agree with the treaty's supporters but they aren't excited about it. They are not moved emotionally. They rarely listen."[64]

At the Save Darfur rallies, emotional narratives of embattled identity transformed into agential power were poignant in varying ways. For Jewish communities witnessing the death of the last generation of Holocaust survivors, the need to act feels paramount, particularly in light of Iranian president Ahmadinejad's denials of the Holocaust and anti-Israel rhetoric. For many African American communities, histories of slavery, continual civil rights struggles, twentieth-century religious divisions, apartheid, and ongoing conflicts in Africa combine into a frightening mélange that effectively recalls the danger of powerlessness. These multiple concerns were often explicitly mapped onto contemporary apprehensions about U.S. security via a common trope (Arab invasion) that tapped into a more tangible climate of fear. In the meantime, Muslim and Arab American participants endeavored to insert themselves into contemporary narratives of Americanness and American moral authority by silencing their own fears of genocide elsewhere.

We are not suggesting that any participants at these events politically manipulated the crisis in Darfur intentionally, nor do we doubt their sincerity, their experiences of trauma, or their earnest desires to stop horrendous violence and loss of life. We, too, attended the April rally out of such concerns. Since then and in this article, we have sought to understand why particular alliances around this issue and calls for questionable military action continue to garner support when these well-intentioned maneuvers may prolong the terrible conflict *and* while other devastating crises (including similar and greater levels of rape, murder, and displacement in Uganda and the Congo) go unmentioned.

We have emphasized here that understanding interreligious endeavors in the United States—particularly interreligious political activism—requires situating participants in the context of changing historical realities and historical understandings, both national and international. Each interaction involves multiple shifting narratives of religious identity that depend not only on interrelated experiences of gender, ethnicity, and economic standing, but also on collective histories *as* Americans in an increasingly globalized world. These continually contested narrations converge dynamically in each interaction according to the various interpretations brought to and renarrated *through* the event and—in this case—on the very space in which it occurs. In the process, new narratives of American religious pluralism are created and contested, as each opportunity provides fodder for the next round.

Notes

Many thanks to the editorial board of *American Quarterly* for their suggestions, as well as to special editors Melani McAlister and R. Marie Griffith for their invaluable comments and assistance. All provided significant guidance in the production of this article, but are certainly not to blame for any shortcomings or errors contained herein.

We take the language of our title from the Save Darfur Coalition's own framing in its promotional materials. "As Americans . . . we must do something to help those who suffer, and THIS TIME WE CAN." Save Darfur Coalition, "Background on the Crisis in Darfur," *http://millionvoicesfordarfur.com/pdf/Darfur%20Christian%20Faith%20Action%20Packet%202006.doc* (accessed May 2, 2006).

1. We refer to performance here in the sense of Judith Butler's work on performance and power, including *Gender Trouble: Feminism and the Subversion of Identity* (New York: Routledge, 1990), and *Excitable Speech: A Politics of the Performative* (New York: Routledge, 1997).

2. Quoted in Samantha Power's history of the conflict, "Dying in Darfur," *The New Yorker*, August 30, 2004, *www.newyorker.com/printables/fact/040830fa_fact1* (accessed January 21, 2007).

3. "Third Periodic Report of the United Nations High Commissioner for Human Rights on the human rights situation in the Sudan," *http://www.ohchr.org/english/index.htm* (accessed August 7, 2006). See also UNHCR, "Human Rights Resolution 2005/82," edited by United Nations Office of the High Commissioner for Human Rights: U.N., 2005. While the Save Darfur Coalition cites 400,000 deaths, most agencies cite the United Nation's statistics from Ernest Harsch's "Darfur Facing Even Greater Horror" in the U.N.-sponsored *Africa Renewal 20.3 (October 2006): 3.*

4. Mahmood Mamdani, "The Politics of Naming: Genocide, Civil War, Insurgency," in *London Review of Books* 29.5 (March 8, 2007), and *When Victims Become Killers: Colonialism, Nativism, and the Genocide in Rwanda* (Princeton, N.J.: Princeton University Press, 2001). Aidi, "Slavery, Genocide and the Politics of Outrage: Understanding the New 'Racial Olympics,'" *Middle East Report* 234 (Spring 2005), *http://www.merip.org/mer/mer234/aidi.html* (accessed February 15, 2007); Alex de Waal, "Tragedy in Darfur," *Boston Review* (October–November 2004).

5. Alex de Waal, "I Will Not Sign," *London Review of Books* 28.23 (November 30, 2006).

6. Found at *http://www.savedarfur.org/about/coalition* (accessed May 10, 2006.)

7. Save Darfur Coalition, "Darfur: A 21st Century Genocide" (Washington, D.C.: New Media Mill, 2005), a video created and distributed by the coalition.

8. See Senate Resolution 172 (2005). George W. Bush, "State of the Union Address," http://www.whitehouse.gov/stateoftheunion/2007/index.html (accessed February 3, 2007). David Rubenstein, Save Darfur Coalition, "Urgent—Call Your Senator," February 5, 2007, electronic communication.

9. Stephanie Strom and Lydia Polgreen, "Darfur Advocacy Group Undergoes a Shake-Up," *New York Times*, June 2, 2007; Rubenstein quoted in the May 29, 2007, Coalition press release, "Save Darfur Coalition Responds to President Bush's Sanctions Announcement," *http://www.savedarfur.org/newsroom/releases/save_darfur_coalition_responds_to_president_bushs_sanctions_announcement/* (accessed 2 June, 2007).

10. See *http://www.savedarfur.org/about/signatories* (accessed August 13, 2006). The members of the "Executive Committee," however, are primarily religious: the American Jewish World Service, the American Society for Muslim Advancement, the Jewish Council for Public Affairs, the National Association of Evangelicals, the National Council of Churches of Christ in the USA, the Union for Reform Judaism, and the United States Conference of Catholic Bishops all have religious ties. The remaining members are Amnesty International USA, Citizens for Global Solutions, Darfur Peace and Development, the International Crisis Group, the NAACP, and United States Holocaust Memorial Museum.

11. For an overview of this scholarship, see Henry Goldschmidt, "Introduction," in Henry Goldschmidt and Liza McAlister, eds., *Race, Nation, and Religion in America* (New York: Oxford University Press, 2004), 1–31.

12. See *http://www.naacp.org/about/leadership/natboard/* (accessed August 13, 2006).

13. Whereas assimilation into the "melting pot" was once valued, debates over what came to be called "multiculturalism" exploded in the 1980s and 1990s, involving postcolonial theorists and scholars in ethnic studies. Attention to "religious pluralism"—inflected by ideas of multiculturalism—followed. As Linda Hutcheon contends, though, in her "Crypto-Ethnicity" portion of "Four Views on Ethnicity" (*PMLA* 113 [January 1998]), multiculturalism has often failed to live up to its ideal of celebrating

(to say nothing of providing equality for) different ethnic cultures in the United States. David Hollinger argues likewise and urges moving toward a "postethnic America" in which embracing hybridity over rigid identity politics becomes the modus operandi for public life (*Postethnic America: Beyond Multiculturalism* [New York: Basic Books: 2006]).

14. Richard Cizik and David Saperstein, "Human Rights Opportunity for Bush," *Washington Times*, November 14, 2005 (emphasis added).

15. Lawrence Kotler-Berkowitz, "An Introduction to the National Jewish Population Survey 2000–01," *Sociology of Religion* 67.4 (2006): 387–90.

16. See *http://www.savedarfur.org/about/signatories* (accessed July 30, 2006).

17. Karen Brodkin, *How Jews Became White Folks, and What That Says about Race in America* (New Brunswick, N.J.: Rutgers University Press, 1998), 1–24, 138–75. Eric Goldstein complicates and deepens this picture by examining the ambivalence of Jewish race assignment in terms of shifting Protestant notions of the black-white divide and Jews' own changing self-designations. Goldstein, *The Price of Whiteness: Jews, Race, and American Identity* (Princeton, N.J.: Princeton University Press, 2006), 202–30.

18. Hasia Diner, *In the Almost Promised Land* (Baltimore: Johns Hopkins University Press, 1995).

19. Jack Salzman and Cornel West, *Struggles in the Promised Land: Towards a History of Black-Jewish Relations in the United States* (New York: Oxford, 1997), 1–21.

20. Michael Lerner and Cornel West, *Jews and Blacks: Let the Healing Begin* (New York: Putnam, 1995). Melani McAlister also examines how representations of Arabs and the Middle East have long been important for African American identity formation in *Epic Encounters: Culture, Media, and U.S. Interests in the Middle East since 1945* (2001; Berkeley: University of California Press, 2005).

21. On social capital, see James M. Jasper and Francesca Polletta, "Collective Identity and Social Movements," *Annual Review of Sociology* 27 (2001).

22. Found at *http://rac.org/Articles/index.cfm?id=1576&pge_prg_id=4575* (accessed July 25, 2006).

23. "Jewish Insert," *http://www.savedarfur.org/faith* (accessed May 2, 2006).

24. Gavriel D. Rosenfeld, "The Politics of Uniqueness: Reflections on the Recent Polemical Turn in Holocaust and Genocide Scholarship," *Holocaust and Genocide Studies* 13.1 (Spring 1999): 28–61.

25. United Nations General Assembly Resolution 260 (III)A, "Convention on the Prevention and Punishment of the Crime of Genocide," adopted December 9, 1948. http://www.hrweb.org/legal/genocide.html (accessed February 7, 2007). Article 1 states that genocide is "a crime under international law," which contracting parties "undertake to prevent and punish"; Article 5 requires that the parties "provide effective penalties of persons guilty of genocide."

26. McAlister examines the emotional valence of these particular narratives in *Epic Encounters*.

27. James Young, *Writing and Re-Writing the Holocaust: Narrative and the Consequences of Interpretation.* (Bloomington: Indiana University Press, 1988).

28. Homi Bhabha, *The Location of Culture* (New York: Routledge, 2004), 83.

29. Al Sharpton, "Speech," Washington, D.C., April 30, 2006.

30. Francesca Polletta, "'It Was Like a Fever': Narrative and Identity in Social Protest," *Social Problems* 45.2 (1998): 139.

31. Found at *http://www.un.org/holocaustremembrance/* (accessed February 3, 2007).

32. Elie Wiesel, "Speech," Washington, D.C., April 30, 2006.

33. For some varying political views from attendees, see, for example, "Live the Questions," *http://livethequestions.blogspot.com/2006/05/rallies-rule-and-rally-rules-i-spent.html*, *http://photosfollowingmyfootsteps.blogspot.com/2006/07/saving-darfur-43006-washington-dc.html* (both accessed August 22, 2006), and Michael Reynolds, "Love Beams Won't Do It," *http://donklephant.com/2006/05/01/love-beams-wont-do-it/* (accessed August 28, 2006.)

34. "Confirmed Speakers" list, "Save Darfur Now" press packet, April 30, 2006.

35. Brian Steidle, "Speech," April 30, 2006, Washington, D.C.

36. On reactions, see: *http://orthodoxparadox.blogspot.com/2006/05/save-darfur-rally.html* (accessed August 10, 2006); and *http://drewkaplans.blogspot.com/2006/05/yesterdays-darfur-rally-holocaust.html* (accessed August 16, 2006). The Associated Press, "Celebrities, Activists Rally for Darfur," published on CNN.com (accessed May 1, 2006).

37. Found at *http://volleyrav.blogspot.com/2006/05/reflections-on-april-30th-save-darfur.html* (accessed August 22, 2006).

38. Quote from the Coalition's "Unity Statement," 2004.
39. Geoff Tunnicliffe, international director of the World Evangelical Alliance, recited verbatim this prepared statement, which was provided to reporters via the press packet.
40. Power, "Dying in Darfur."
41. McAlister, *Epic Encounters*, 11; Aidi, "Slavery, Genocide, and the Politics of Outrage."
42. "Introduction: Becoming American—Religion, Identity, and Institution Building in the American Mosaic," in *Religion and Immigration: Christian, Jewish, and Muslim Experiences in the United States*, ed. Jane Smith, Yvonne Yazbeck Haddad, and John Esposito (Walnut Creek, Calif.: Alta Mira Press, 2003), 2.
43. U.S foreign policy is a primary factor in whether immigrant Muslims even *want* to be American and *how*, argues current ISNA president Ingrid Mattson in "How Muslims Use Islamic Paradigms to Define America," in *Religion and Immigration*, 119–26. Mattson contends these identifications depend on how various Muslims classify the American nation under Islamic law—something that is determined not only by U.S. actions in and toward Muslim nations, but also by the various Islamic narratives through which Muslims can interpret them.
44. CAIR press release, "CAIR Asks Why No Muslim Groups to Speak at Darfur Rally," April 30, 2006. See also "CAIR-Cincinnati: Muslim Community Sponsors Darfur Prayer," CAIR "News Releases," May 2, 2006, *http://www.cair.com/default.asp?Page=articleView&id=2131&theType=NR* (accessed February 12, 2007).
45. Sherman Jackson, *Islam and the Blackamerican* (New York: Oxford, 2005). Many scholars of U.S. Islam have devoted specific attention to aspects of these tensions and the histories, both separate and shared, of immigrant and indigenous Muslims in the United States. See, for example, Aminah Mc-Cloud, *African American Islam* (New York: Routledge, 1995); E. E. Curtis, *Islam in Black America: Identity, Liberation, and Difference in African-American Islamic Thought* (Albany: State University of New York Press, 2002); and Richard Brent Turner, *Islam in the African American Experience* (Bloomington: Indiana University Press, 1997). Like Jewish–African American relations, South Asian Muslim and Arab Muslim relations with African Americans began long before the 1960s, but were inflected differently after the civil rights movement (see Jane I. Smith, *Islam in America* [New York: Columbia University Press, 1999]).
46. Aidi adds, quoting de Waal, that these have become reflexive narratives for Africans as "[Darfurian leaders] too learned to characterize their plight in the simplified terms that had proved so effective in winning foreign sympathy for the south: they were the 'African' victims of an 'Arab' regime." ("Slavery, Genocide, and the Politics of Outrage.")
47. "400,000 MUSLIMS HAVE BEEN KILLED IN DARFUR," read the headline of the "Muslim Insert," *http://millionvoicesfordarfur.com/pdf/Darfur%20Muslim%20Insert.pdf* (accessed May 2, 2006). The same statistics ("400,000 dead; 2.5 million displaced; 3.5 million at risk of starvation") and photo of African children emblazon all inserts, but this piece is the only one to detail the religious identity of the victims. Importantly, after the April 30 rally and in preparation for the September rally in New York, a "Muslim Faith Action Packet" was added. The original action packets were found at *http://millionvoicesfordarfur.com/pdf/Darfur%20Christian%20Faith%20Action%20Packet%202006.doc*, *http://millionvoicesfordarfur.com/pdf/Darfur%20Jewish%20Faith%20Action%20Packet%202006.doc*, *http://millionvoicesfordarfur.com/pdf/Darfur%20Interfaith%20Faith%20Action%20Packet%202006.doc*, and *http://millionvoicesfordarfur.com/pdf/Darfur%20General%20Faith%20Action%20Packet%202006.doc* (all accessed May 2, 2006, but since removed and revised).
48. Brian Steidle, quoted in the coalition's video, "Darfur: A 21st Century Genocide."
49. Omar, imam of the Islamic Society of Michiana (Indiana) drew from his "A belated Muslim response to the humanitarian crisis in Darfur" (South Bend, Indiana, July 23, 2004), which was the second component of the "Sample Sermon, Homily, Dvar Torah, Jumu'ah Khutbah" portion of the "Interfaith Action Packet." Though Omar describes his response as "belated," Imam Feisal Abdul Rauf, founder of ASMA, member of the Save Darfur Coalition Executive Committee, and one of the original signatories of the "Unity Statement" in 2004, contends that "we and other organizations horrified by the human rights violations have been urging specific actions since the crisis began" (quoted in "Faith-Based Coalition to Hold 'Week of Prayer and Action for Darfur,'" press release).
50. Save Darfur Coalition, "Responsive Reading: For the People of Darfur," 2006, press packet.
51. "Groups Plan Rally on Mall to Protest Darfur Violence: Bush Administration Is Urged to Intervene," *Washington Post*, April 27, 2006.
52. As noted, Tunnicliffe's statement was provided in the press packet.

53. Quoted in Save Darfur Coalition, "Faith-Based Coalition to Hold 'Week of Prayer and Action for Darfur' to Generate 1 Million Postcards Urging President Bush to End Genocide," March 21, 2006, press packet. Gloria White-Hammond, "Keeping Our Sisters Safe: Women Unite to Stop Rape of Sudanese," *Boston Herald*, February 20, 2005 (also provided in the press packet).

54. Rosemary R. Hicks, "Religion, Race, Rape, and Rights: Building Interreligious Coalitions around Female Sexuality and Military Humanitarianism," paper presented at "After Pluralism: Reimagining Models of Interreligious Engagement," Columbia University, New York, October 11–13, 2007.

55. Cooperman also pointed to the dual nature of the word *save* when iterated by evangelicals, and the problems this had caused the Coalition: "Some Darfur activists also have complained about the involvement in the rally of Kansas-based evangelical group, Sudan Sunrise. Last week . . . Sudan Sunrise changed its web site to eliminate references to efforts to convert the people of Darfur. Previously, it said it was engaged in 'one on one, lifestyle evangelism to Darfurian Muslims living in refugee camps . . .' and appealed for money to 'bring the kingdom of God to an area of Sudan where the light of Jesus rarely shines.'"

56. "Simon Deng's Remarks/Former slave in southern Sudan/(New York City)/'SAVE DARFUR: Rally to Stop Genocide'/National Mall, Washington, DC—30 April 2006" (emphasis added), from "Save Darfur Now" press packet.

57. "Confirmed Speakers," press packet.

58. Imam Omar urged Muslims to "*to add our voices* to those insisting that the Sudanese government disarm and disband the Janjawid and that it provide full access for humanitarian workers and international human rights monitors." He went on to describe the upcoming fact-finding mission sponsored by ISNA and led by African American Muslim leader (and former Nation of Islam leader) Imam W. D. Muhammad—thus alluding to the collaborative alliances formed between African American and immigrant Muslims in recent years.

59. Thanks to Professor Elizabeth Castelli, who noted the prevalence of popularized militarism at evangelical youth rallies in a discussion at the Columbia Institute for Research on Women and Gender, September 15, 2006.

60. Madeleine Albright, "Speech," New York, September 17, 2006.

61. De Waal, "I Will Not Sign."

62. Richard Cizik of the National Association of Evangelicals, "1 Year After Bush Administration Declared Darfur Violence a 'Genocide,' Progress Is Minimal, Evangelical Official Says," *http://releases.usnewswire.com/GetRelease.asp?id=52965* (accessed May 2, 2006). This September 9, 2005, article was also posted on the NAE's Web site *http://www.nae.net/* (accessed May 2, 2006).

63. Samantha Power, *A Problem from Hell: America in the Age of Genocide* (New York: Basic Books, 2002), xi–xxi, 161–69, 443–74.

64. Quoted in Power, *A Problem from Hell*, 156. Mamdani argues that Power argues for the need to expiate American guilt over inaction in Rwanda, though—as in Darfur—American action could not solve the underlying political crisis ("The Politics of Naming").

From Exodus to Exile:
Black Pentecostals, Migrating Pilgrims, and Imagined Internationalism

Clarence E. Hardy III

The American Negro no longer conceives of his destiny as bounded by the limits of the United States. He is seeking alliances and creating loyalties that transcend the boundaries of our American commonwealth. The Negro, in his racial relationship at least, is internationalist. He is becoming a citizen of the world.

—Robert Park, 1923

New World Africans are deeply modern in the sense of being exiles, banished from their native lands and forced to live lives as perennial "outsiders," finding a "home" only in a dynamic language and mobile music—never in a secure land, safe territory or welcome nation. The fundamental theme of New World African modernity is neither integration nor separation but rather migration and emigration.

—Cornel West, 1993

Beyond Exodus: Blackness, Religion and Collective Identity

When popular evangelist and preacher Ida Robinson heard in 1924 rumors that the United Holy Church, the same Pentecostal denomination that had ordained her, would soon stop ordaining women (at least publicly), she received a divine vision after a ten-day fast that instructed her to "come out on Mount Sinai" and "loose the women." Robinson's vision motivated her to establish a new regional "confederation of churches," later called the Mount Sinai Holy Church of America, based in her new home of Philadelphia to provide, at least in part, institutional space for women to exercise clerical leadership. Her extension to women of the exodus metaphor so prevalent in black Protestantism emerged as she reckoned with the reality of an increasingly scattered black religious community. In an earlier vision that set the stage for her career as an evangelist and preacher, Robinson, a migrant who was born in Hazelhurst, Georgia, in 1891 and reared in Pensacola, Florida, saw the new possibilities for religious leaders that the mass migration of black people to cities promised. In her vision she saw "a great church being born in the city, with people coming from the North, South, East and West."[1]

Reckoning with how evolving conceptions of community and collective identity generated both the language and the institutional context for black Pentecostal growth during the modern period invites scholars to develop a more textured sense of the role religion has played in black life in the United States. This article will examine how, in the early decades of the twentieth century, black religious leaders—especially women Pentecostal preachers—sought a new basis for (religious) community beyond old "man-made" (and white-made) divisions of region, race, and nations. They drew on black Holiness traditions, which began in the 1880s and '90s and were remade in the context of the Pentecostal revivals in the early years of the new century, to embrace the broader world. The most noted of these revivals was one a band of black Holiness worshippers sparked in 1906 at the Azusa Street Mission in Los Angeles. The Azusa revival was a broad religious awakening that bridged various groups, encompassing local whites, Mexicans, and Russians. Lasting several years, it became the mythical point of origin for worldwide Pentecostalism, as it served as one context wherein black Holiness leaders began to see themselves on a global stage. By forging an exilic rhetoric that extended beyond the exodus narrative, which had so gripped black Protestantism in the decades just before and after the Civil War, black Holiness leaders, often inspired by Azusa, helped their followers of migrating pilgrims adapt as their institutions began to span regional and racial divides.

Years before the terms *diaspora* and *transnationalism* entered into the scholarly analyses of the possibilities for black global culture, Pentecostals understood that the communal fragmentation cities helped create also produced the possibilities for human connection beyond the boundaries of regions and even nation-states.[2] Women Pentecostal leaders such as Robinson, whose religious networks extended from the South into northern cities during the interwar period, understood that difference—the separation of members from one another—generated a new basis for unity and collective identity. Decades after its founding, Mount Sinai would extend its reach even to Cuba, Guyana, and South America.[3] Long before scholars would declare Pentecostalism a global option that rivaled Catholicism and Islam's worldwide reach in our contemporary world,[4] Robinson's visions made real in Mount Sinai were "articulations of diaspora," to borrow a phrase from Stuart Hall, in which cultural practices and communities across regions and even oceans were "related as much through differences as through their similarities." The moments of dispersal and unity

Robinson imagined and preached about were like joints in the body—points of separation that were also points of linkage and connection—that provided the possible basis for collective coordination and movement.[5]

To focus on the construction of racial and collective identities within religious discourse is to situate religion as one cultural arena among many where black people defined themselves and their relationship to the larger (white) society. Racial formation in the United States, in fact, was deeply intermeshed with blacks' adoption of Christianity; the enslaved became black as they became Christian in the years just before the Civil War.[6] And when the Civil War confirmed for many the reality of a Christian god who emancipated Africans as he had the early Israelites, this understanding helped generate the mass conversions that secured Christianity's majority status within African America for the first time and ratified how blacks would frame Christianity after the guns of war fell silent.[7] The newly emancipated established their separate institutions around the story of Exodus in the wake of what many black people saw as the war's divine judgment on the South. "Most prominent in southern blacks' appropriation of Christianity," historian Katherine Dvorak has argued, "was their sense of community as liberating and liberation as communal."[8]

As large numbers moved to northern cities in the opening decades of the twentieth century, black migrants from the South and elsewhere created new conceptions of blackness and community during the interwar period. Translating the political and social aspects of the New Negro movement into cultural terms, Alain Locke, in an essay that carried the same title as the singular collection it introduced, celebrated how racial identity had developed in a "new and enlarged way." In Harlem, Locke found "the pulse" of the black world, where the "Negro mind" could extend beyond the "cramped horizons" that American prejudices allowed. Locke's *The New Negro* was one example among many of how black intellectuals and artists engaged in the "practice of diaspora" during the interwar years as they linked themselves to "the growing group consciousness of the dark-peoples."[9]

Cheryl Sanders, a scholar of black Holiness and Pentecostal traditions, inspired by Cornel West's focus on migration as the central metaphor for black modernity, has argued in recent years that the notion of exile enables a sharper focus on "intragroup identity" and better characterizes the expressive individuality of black culture and black Pentecostals in the modern era.[10] At the margins of a fading Victorianism of the 1880s and '90s, and while exodus piety still predominated, an exilic discourse began to emerge from reformers within black Protestantism who struggled with the cultural conformity of the time only to flower as migrants carried these perspectives to the urban North. As Paul Gilroy reminds us, "travelling cultures" can foster not only "transcultural" exchange but also "outernational" perspectives for a black people never entirely at home in U.S. society.[11] As southern black Holiness traditions transmuted into the mobile Pentecostal cultures that hopeful migrants discovered and carried across boundaries of territory and of gender, Christians reconceptualized racial identity and religious community. Like the writers and intellectuals Robert Park described in 1923 who were newly enchanted with Pan-Africanism, black Pentecostals did not see their "destiny as bounded by the limits of the United States" but rather forged identities within a more globally inflected Christian faith.

Migrants, whatever their religious identity, did not find the Promised Land they had hoped for in the North (or West). What they found instead was a broader space to further interrogate old conceptions of racial identity they had already begun to question as Reconstruction's promise faded. Whether they found themselves in the ranks of emerging black Holiness groups hoping finally to escape sin and stultifying conformity or among emigrationists seeking to remake Africa for Christ and civilization, the children of slaves began to embrace the global stage as the principal context for constructing notions of (black) communal identity and the divine. They moved beyond the exodus narrative and toward stories of exile, diaspora, and Babylon as they set the stage for a new architecture in their language of religious community and their descriptions of God.

"On the Plains of Dura": Pentecostals in Babylon

The quest for holiness that shaped the increasingly internationalist posture of many in the 1920s and '30s emerged just after the Civil War. In the decades after the war, black separatism, which animated the rise of Baptist and Methodist national organizations, more deeply embraced the cramped horizon of American expectations than the possibilities for kinship and life beyond the Atlantic. Frantz Fanon's exploration of the "fact of blackness" in his *Black Skin, White Masks* provides a point of departure for assessing the forging of a black identity that took place as black Baptists built a broad association on a national scale. The Baptist struggle for recognition and social power forms the crucial backdrop for the emergence of black Holiness leadership and culture in the closing decades of the nineteenth century.[12] "For not only must the black man be black," Fanon writes, "he must be black in relation to the white man."[13]

Black people's adoption of Christianity not only marked the emergence of racial identity, but it also established rhetorical and institutional connections with a larger, predominantly Christian society. Needing the resources to build local churches at home and abroad and sharing their aspirations to civilize Africans on both continents, black religious leaders necessarily cooperated with white northern religious organizations as they built their own separate national institutions to garner respect while surviving Jim Crow and the constant threat of violence from widespread lynching and the Klan.[14] Whether in the "unlikely sisterhood" between black Baptist women in the Women's Convention of the National Baptist Convention and northern-based white women's mission societies or black Baptist Lott Carey's alliance for missionary work in Liberia with the American Colonization Society (however dubious its motives), black religious leaders could not—even if they had wanted to—escape "the presence of white people or the effects of their power."[15] As historian David Wills has persuasively argued, although the exodus narrative helped define black Protestants as they struggled to establish Methodist and Baptist organizations that were truly national in scope, these were not venues "to escape religious interaction with whites," but rather collective arrangements for "restructuring" their relationship with those who ruled their society.[16]

When most of the descendents of slaves decided not to leave the United States for Africa after the war and remained in the South, they knew they would have to share the same land with people who vacillated between "paternalism and violence."[17] The majority responded as the black North Carolina Baptist State Convention did when attendees pledged to "use every exertion . . . to harmonize the white and colored races, so that they may be in peace in the same country."[18] In the North, sharing territory with whites in perpetuity framed the tragic ambiguity that animated black political life even before slavery's bloody demise in the South.[19] As Henry Highland Garnett observed in his 1843 speech before the Black National Convention in Buffalo: "It is impossible, like the children of Israel, to make a grand exodus from the land of bondage. The Pharaohs are on both sides of the blood-red waters."[20] Religion scholar Eddie Glaude argues that the debate surrounding Garnett's rejection of the exodus story and its political passivity for the more revolutionary options of slave insurrection disclosed the ambiguity at the heart of black "exodus politics" in the United States. Two ideals sat uneasily together. When participants in the convention rejected, by the slimmest of margins, Garnett's call for a slave insurrection, participants embraced however uneasily a "nation language that simultaneously accents the idea of racial solidarity and identifies with America" and they illuminated how, caught between two commitments, the tragic became a constitutive element of black political culture.[21]

Inspired by theorists Nancy Fraser and Jürgen Habermas, historian Evelyn Brooks Higginbotham demonstrates in her influential study *Righteous Discontent* how a language of respectability, especially among black Baptist women, became a "bridge discourse that mediated relations between black and white reformers" as African Americans built religious societies with a national presence.[22] In effect, the language of decorum, deportment, and restraint exemplified in the political and religious activity of black Baptist clubwomen tied together race and respectability—developing the language of respectability into the intimate face of the contested collective identity black people forged after the Civil War. "Respectability," Higginbotham writes, "demanded that every individual in the black community assume responsibility for behavioral self-regulation and self-improvement along moral, educational, and economic lines."[23] This tension between black self-determination and U.S. nationalism shaped black collective identity and defined a politics of respectability for a people navigating a Jim Crow country that would prefigure the emphasis on surveillance that animates the regulating procedures of the modern nation-state.[24] Invoking Sartre's famous description of Jews as "overdetermined from the inside," Fanon described black identity in colonial contexts. "I am overdetermined from without," Fanon wrote. "I am the slave . . . of my own appearance."[25] Black Baptist leaders labored under the burdensome gaze of their white counterparts as they worked to knit their new organizations before an audience that haunted and shaped their institutional aspirations. As one prominent spokesman of an early black Baptist convention warned his colleagues in 1869: "Brethren, we are watched. We are not accepted as a body or denomination qualified to manage our own missionary and educational work, and many of those who most discredit our capacity . . . have set themselves up as our benefactors."[26]

While the politics of respectability pivoted on bodily awareness before unsympathetic "benefactors," participants in black Holiness culture practiced ritualized denials of self-awareness that differentiated them from established Baptist and Methodist churches as they developed new and different conceptions of religious community. Holiness leaders sought to remake for a new age the conversion-brokered religion of their enslaved ancestors that celebrated a lack of self-consciousness in ritual practice. "When the spirit strikes me," one former slave reported to interviewers at Fisk University in the 1930s, "I lose all sense of the world."[27] Before the Civil War, this escape from the world was most vividly expressed in the "invisible" church outside the gaze of their white overlords. While interracialism characterized many of the prewar worship settings, the former slave Emily Dixon of Mississippi preferred being "in the woods" without white overseers: "Us could go to de white folks' church but us wanted ter go whar we could sing all de way through an' hum 'long an' shout, o' all know, jist turn loose lak."[28] Another former slave—Cordelia Jackson from South Carolina—demonstrated how ecstatic religious practice marked not only the possibility for escape from the physical world but also escape from the expectations of whites and the larger community—even if only for a moment. White people told stories about religion because they were afraid of it, Jackson told her interviewer from the Works Progress Administration, but "I stays independent of what white folks tells me when I shouts."[29]

But as the nineteenth century came to a close, what black Holiness leaders offered was not simply a return to the old ways. The initial innovators of the black Holiness tradition in 1880s and '90s inaugurated a language steeped in biblical themes and cadences that embraced a focus on interiority in speaking about God and the religious life, even as it provided space to question the nature and basis of black solidarity, if not the larger project of racial uplift. Remembering how central the religious experience of sanctification was to his ministry, one of the preeminent early Holiness leaders, Charles Price Jones, recaptured a focus on interiority over the communal identity of exodus piety:

> When I first gave myself to the Lord to be sanctified, (this was in 1894 at Selma) I had no idea at all of taking up holiness as a fad, or an ism, or a creed, or the slogan of a "cult". I just wanted to be personally holy. I just wished to make my own calling election sure to my own heart by walking with God in the Spirit. As a Baptist I had doctrinal assurance; I wanted spiritual assurance, heart peace, rest of soul, the joy of salvation in the understanding of a new heart, a new mind, a new spirit, constantly renewed and comforted by the Holy Ghost.[30]

During an increasingly tumultuous period for black people after Reconstruction, Holiness leaders asserted that no human institutions, including churches, could provide ultimate security. Upon starting his ministry, Jones was asked whether he would join a lodge (i.e., a local branch of a fraternal organization), as most prominent black leaders did, but he was said to ask "how could he, being a preacher, teach the *people* to trust God when *he himself* was not trusting God but trusting the lodge?"[31]

Taking their cues from Alexander Campbell earlier in the century, William Christian in the 1880s, followed by other Holiness leaders such as Jones and Charles Harrison Mason in the Mississippi Delta during the 1890s, felt that the emerging institutional arrangements among black Baptists stifled the vitality of old slave religious practices they saw as the simplest expressions of the earliest church.[32] Even as black Baptists struggled to forge a national association after the war, these leaders believed that the growing denominational structures put too much focus on "man-made" doctrines instead of Christ and fostered corruption and consumerism rather than the racial uplift that leaders promised.[33] "Like the Christians (sometimes known as Campbellites)," Holiness leader Charles Price Jones argued, "we beleive [*sic*] that we ought to HONOR THE NAME of Christ as it is honored in the New Testament and not put human nicknames on Christ's bride, since there is only one name by which we may be saved."[34] As black Holiness leaders moved away from the Baptist (and Methodist) communions they started in, the nomenclature they adopted for their associations (e.g., Christian's Church of the Living God founded in Wrightsville, Arkansas, in 1888, or the Church of God in Christ [COGIC], cofounded by Jones with Mason in 1897) came directly from New Testament phrases that individual religious visions and prophesies inspired and confirmed.

Beginning with Christian, Holiness leaders rejected Baptist and Methodist leaders' increasing emphasis on a public piety that was outwardly respectable. They rejected all practices they could not find a defense for within scripture. The only acceptable public prayer in William Christian's Church of the Living God, for decades after its founding, was the Lord's Prayer as recorded in the New Testament.[35] "Damnation is threatened on long prayers," Christian wrote. "I want you to understand, Christ never told us to pray what we please. Christ Jesus quietly told his disciples what to pray."[36] In his early writings, the most prolific of the pioneering Holiness leaders, C. P. Jones, praised the Bible's Joseph for having "none of the men-pleasing, crowdfearing spirit" he believed characterized his own age wherein "everybody is joining a combination, brotherhood, a social or religious trust, a mutual help and mutual admiration society." Consequently, Jones bemoaned: "Every man is closing his eyes and lips to the faults of his particular brotherhood, denominational, Masonic or otherwise."[37] Christian's rejection of denominationalism anticipates Jones's rejection of the politics of respectability and the concern for the outer display of public piety as the intimate face of the broader ongoing institutional struggle for collective identity. In the poem "Memory and Conscience," composed in 1899, Jones chides the cult of respectability's politics:

Go on, go on, indulge your grieving lust,
All men are sinners, none are true and just,
Just hide yourself, don't let the people know,

Keep under cover all the sin you do:
Keep a bold face, respectability
Is the great thing; what means hypocrisy?"
Thus by one sin we lose the love of truth.[38]

When Jones and his colleague Charles Harrison Mason established their Holiness body, the Church of God in Christ (COGIC), in 1897 after their expulsion from the state Baptist association, they, like Christian, worked to forge their followers into a biblical people. But where William Christian would largely reject the folk practices of slave religion, Mason worked especially hard to identify the most suspect of slave religious practices like the shout and religious dance as biblically defensible.[39] After Mason visited a revival in 1906 at Azusa Street in Los Angeles, generally considered the birthplace of Pentecostalism, he came back to his Memphis headquarters convinced that COGIC should embrace the glossolalia practiced so fervently in California. When he and Jones split over the issue, Mason took the name of the group and reestablished COGIC as a Pentecostal group in November of 1907. Mason's group would become the largest Pentecostal body (white or black) in the United States, with an aggressively (and occasionally stridently) biblical culture. Several years after the church's founding, one Baptist minister in southeastern Texas warned his Baptist colleagues about Mason's Church of God in Christ: "You fellows better be careful if you go down there. Them damned niggers got the Bible cold, on everything they say. They're going exactly by it."[40]

With the beginning of the mass migration of black people to the industrialized North, Mason adopted a conscious "strategy of sending evangelists to accompany the northerly migration of African Americans" to spur his biblically oriented group into new urban environments. COGIC's urban growth was so phenomenal that one observer has noted that a denomination birthed in a simple country church in Mississippi had become in a few decades "a predominantly urban church" with "fewer rural churches than the Baptists and Methodists." Their membership increases, primarily in the cities, enabled the group to grow from 50,000 to more than 400,000 adherents in just four to five decades of existence.[41] Other Pentecostal groups experienced similar growth in the midsized and larger cities of both the North and South. And women were the primary engines of growth as both members and evangelists during those years when Holiness language would evolve into the even more globally oriented Pentecostalism. Women evangelists and preachers, called "church mothers," acted within male-led denominations such as COGIC or acted as overseers and bishops in their own right, leading and managing their own regional and multiregional church bodies.

But even before the mass migration of blacks began in earnest with the First World War, Holiness leaders anticipated the shift from exodus to Babylon that Pentecostal groups would more fully develop after the war. Remembering the motto "denominationalism is slavery" that sparked the Holiness movement, which would lay the groundwork for Pentecostalism, Jones, Mason's original cofounder of COGIC, wrote:

> We stood [instead] for the communion of the Holy Ghost. We served in the denomina-
> tions if allowed, but we served Christ in the life of His people instead of a denominational
> "image in the plains of Dura." But alas! the sectarian spirit is hard to conquer. We are soon
> contending for our crown, our doctrine, our way, our sect instead of the Lord.[42]

For Jones and his Holiness compatriots, denominations including his own emerged like the glorious man-made statue Nebuchadnezzar built demanding obeisance from the Jewish faithful while they were in Babylonian exile on the "plains of Dura." Holiness leaders asserted that denominations were like Nebuchadnezzar's idol, that is, opportunities for public display over "man-made" creations instead of opportunities for true worship of God. And although Jones confessed that the "sectarian spirit" was "hard to conquer," in confessing his hope for "the communion of the Holy Ghost" instead of the denominationalism of his own followers, he anticipated black people's shift from the exodus narrative to that of Babylon as they sought new bases for community beyond the collective and institutional identities black people had forged after Reconstruction. Women Pentecostal leaders in particular gave rhetorical and institutional substance to these hopes for a "communion of the Holy Ghost" that bridged regions, race, and nation as both migrating pilgrims and heathens began to imagine their identities as black and religious from a broader perspective that was not as tied to white Americans or even to their own status as Americans.

"Of United Universal Ones": Toward a Horizon beyond Nations

Shortly after Emancipation, black Baptist observers from the North believed that the power some black women exercised within rural religious communi-ties in the South was an unfortunate heritage from the days of bondage and undoubtedly among the "vices and irregularities inseparably attendant upon the state of slavery." Though these "church mothers" or "gospel mothers" were, according to one missionary, Charles Satchel, in the late 1860s, "outside of the New Testament arrangement," the women nevertheless claimed "to be under the special influence of the Spirit" and began to "exercise an authority, greater in many cases, than that of ministers."[43] Whether this less formal expression of leadership actually had a more ancient pedigree that stretched beyond slavery to Africa is unclear, but after many black women found their influence waning in congregational settings after emancipation, black Holiness (and later Pentecostal) networks allowed many to experience a resurgence in their power and influence over new congregations.[44]

This new power would take shape as women led Pentecostal bands into northern cities under the jurisdiction of male-led denominations such as C. H. Mason's COGIC or established themselves as bishops and central overseers over entire regional and multiregional church bodies they founded, led, and controlled. Within COGIC, church mothers "dug out," that is, planted and nurtured, new churches as they established a parallel structure to male clergy. They exercised separate spiritual authority over the women in the congregation, and they had profound influence over the entire congregation, often constraining the power of male pastors. Church mothers in the Women's Department of COGIC established in 1911 "defined the content of their own roles" without interference from men and male pastors who wanted to make significant changes in an individual congregation's worship practice had to reckon with a church mother's informal power over the entire parish.[45]

Women such as Lucy Smith of Chicago, Rosa Horn of Harlem, Ida Robinson of Philadelphia, and Mary Magdalena Tate of Tennessee were frequently addressed as "Mother" as they built regional religious empires, often with themselves at the center, through active radio ministries. But even though they were addressed in a similar fashion as church mothers in the COGIC, they exercised far greater authority. Where church mothers within COGIC wielded informal power within individual congregations, these women served as clerical leaders over multiregional networks of churches. In the early decades of the twentieth century, Mary Magdalena Tate, the first woman in the United States to head a predominantly black denomination as chief overseer and bishop, faced the near constant possibilities of schism that the mass migration of her members to the North, combined with male unease over women's leadership, helped produce.[46] Tate founded a new denomination in 1903, and in 1908 the General Assembly of the Church of the Living God, Pillar and Ground of the Truth formally named her head and overseer. Although her religious network was concentrated mostly in the mid-South, Georgia, and Florida, Tate's denomination overlapped with much of Robinson's Mt. Sinai confederation in northern cities. The Church of the Living God spanned more than twenty states, including the nation's capital, with churches spreading as far north as Connecticut and Pennsylvania by the time of her death in 1930.[47]

Given how similar the names were for the church bodies they led and the distinctive doctrinal positions they held in common, Tate and William Christian might have shared some association when she began her ministry in the mid-South and Midwest, leading a loose confederation of church bands called the "Do Rights" from 1895 to 1902.[48] Whatever connection they might have shared, Mother Tate—the name her followers most commonly called her—appealed to a strategy Christian initiated among black Holiness groups in the 1880s and '90s that sought to recapture a time before denominations in an effort to forge followers into a biblical people that perfectly revived the spirit of the earliest church. Like Christian, Tate saw denominational divisions as unscriptural and understood these divisions as a sign not only of idolatrous behavior but also of an impending divine judgment that would come with the world's end. Tate in one early scriptural tract written around 1915 described the "beast" in Revelation as the "wicked" "first man" who ignores God and offers his mark and image to "wicked men and women, who like the first man, continue to 'frame up' false church names and to organize people." She condemns those who want to build "beastly kingdoms" or "sect denominations." In the years just before national prohibition was declared Tate had hopes that God would call her church members "out of wine drinking and all of the other sins of Babylon" as they navigated tumultuous times. "There is damnation in wearing the wrong church name" Tate wrote, "[but] salvation in wearing the right church name according to the Word of God and His Holy Spirit."[49]

While the revival at Azusa Street has come to symbolize how radically Pentecostals embraced the importance of crossing the boundaries set between nations and peoples in a single miraculous event in Los Angeles, Tate demonstrates how in an age of migration and industrialization, Holiness language evolved initially from believers' doubts about human institutions and developed into Pentecostal language that bridged boundaries of race and nation. Holiness rhetoric had been baptized in the fire of Pentecostal revivals in Los Angeles and then spread as male and female Pentecostal ministers and evangelists expanded this new faith into the Northeast and Midwest from the South over boundaries of territory and gender. Evangelism, of course, had provided an initial drive for much of this evolution, and women Pentecostal leaders in particular adopted an evangelical tone as they envisioned a broader mission field that extended far beyond their local congregations. Mother Rosa Horn of Harlem and Lucy Smith of Chicago found that radio evangelism not only made them more recognizable than Tate, but it had also buttressed a larger sense of religious community unmoored from institutional demands and responsibilities. Horn, a South Carolina–born dressmaker turned preacher, founded the Mount Calvary Assembly Hall of the Pentecostal Faith Church for All Nations in 1926. The windows circling her original building in Harlem with the message "Jesus Saves" in English, French, and Spanish demonstrates how transnationalism began to flow from evangelism and stamped the Holiness ranks with a more internationalist orientation.[50] Though an "instrument of the devil," radio allowed Horn to knit together a religious community beyond the categories of denominations and church bodies. As she told one newspaper reporter:

> It is impossible to state accurately how many infidels have been converted and brought back to the church; how many healings have been wrought; how many estranged families have been reunited, and generally how much sunshine and cheer have been brought into the lives of many people. Even other ministers have told me that their lost members have returned to their churches.[51]

Tate, absent from the radio waves and its opportunities for evangelism, rooted the indivisibility of the church in the same biblical language William Christian did. She framed her religious community as a simple expression of New Testament piety and the earliest church. But for Tate exile had truly come to define the Church of the Living God from its inception. "It shall always be remembered and told from one generation of the Church to another," she wrote, "that the Church of the Living God . . . was once a stranger and the founders thereof were pilgrims and sojourners in a land which they knew not." Although the upheaval of World War I and the subsequent mass migration of her parishioners troubled Tate, she was convinced that this "exodus of the Ethiopian [i.e., black] people" was divinely initiated. Tate assured her followers that it was God himself who had caused the "destructive battle" of war that had "scattered [her church] abroad to every place like a great fire" and reached "nearly every state of the union from 1914 to 1924."[52] Although she might have exaggerated its impact, mass migration and not evangelism per se had established and fundamentally shaped the kind of religious community she led in the early decades of the twentieth century.

Knowing that her parishioners were less tied to their former homes in the South, Tate reconfigured the language of Holiness and an indivisible biblical church to knit together a religious community that bridged sharp regional divisions. The migration forced Tate and Tate's church to consider their ties to one another instead of their connections, formal and otherwise, to the possible outside observers before whom they would need to be respectable. Tate urged her followers never to allow any regional division within her church family. In an evocative section titled, "Of United Universal Ones" that nearly concludes her central governing document, the *General Decree Book*, she wrote:

> There shall never be a Mason-Dixon Line, nor a middle wall of petition, nor any division or separation or difference of any description between the Saints and Churches herein named. North, South, East and West, home or foreign in the United States of America or in the Isles thereof or in any and all other lands and countries and Isles thereof . . . There shall never be anticipated, or indulged or otherwise practiced or in any way at all acts of state or sectional prejudices and differences among any of the members.

"Satan shall never seduce the true Saints into such confusions," Tate argued, because they would not allow "various manners of educations and of languages used" or the "dispositions of some sections and people's [*sic*] . . . to stop the love and unity and ones [i.e., oneness] of the true people and Saints of God."[53]

Even though her missionary activity beyond the United States was relatively minor, Tate's mention of languages, peoples, foreign lands and islands rather than just the mainland demonstrates how an awareness of the world beyond U.S. borders bubbles up from conceptualizing cultural and political work in ways that span regional dimensions. Tate's refusal to accept what her (white) countrymen had divided established not only unity within her communion, but also allowed these migrating pilgrims to view themselves from man-made national borders and allow that outside reality to define both peoples and individuals. Cultural and literary historian Michelle Stephens has reminded us how Fanon saw nationalism and transnationalism as coupled and emerging together as colonized peoples searched out the very possibilities of a national consciousness. As Fanon concluded his speech to the 1959 Second Congress of Black Artists and Writers in Rome: "It is at the heart of national consciousness that international consciousness lives and grows. And this two-fold emerging is ultimately only the source of all culture."[54] Tate's spiritual empire mirrors that imagined by figures such as Marcus Garvey who have generally been described simply as black nationalists and seem quite different from Pentecostals like Tate who often prided themselves on their ability to cross the racial boundaries. But what makes them notably connected with their Pentecostal counterparts is that they framed their collective identity as actors in global terms beyond U.S. identity and aspirations. As Stephens explains, "Marcus Garvey held up an alternative model for the representation of a diasporic black political community, the notion of a worldwide black empire that would shadow the travels of the Western imperial powers." Garvey and other Caribbean colonials such as Claude McKay and C. L. R. James "reimagined political identity, black specifically, in non-national and non-ethnocentric terms."[55]

Pentecostals' imagined internationalism emerged from different cultural networks and a different historical legacy than the transnationalism of Garvey or that of emergent Islamic alternatives. Pentecostal transnationalism was generated more securely from within U.S. possibilities and was more imagined than real prior to the vigorous missionary activity black Pentecostal denominations would undertake after World War II. Caribbean migration to northern cities deepened United Negro Improvement Association's (UNIA) dominant presence in Harlem and other northern neighborhoods and helped insure that Garvey and the developing proto-Islamic movements emerged more sharply from without. From Masonic underpinnings the Moorish Science Temple and Nation of Islam (NOI) imagined an Asiatic Black Nation connecting all non-Europeans to a primordial past when ancient Egyptians reigned and black civilization was believed to emerge in Asia. In seeing people of African descent primarily as "Moorish" or as "Asiatic Black Men," these religionists argued implicitly that foreign lands were ultimately more significant in defining who black people were and to whom they belonged than the United States was.[56] This message offered escape from the clutches of a land organized against black interests. As one early observer of the Moors argued: "Complete emancipation through a change of status from 'Negro' to 'Asiatic' promised an easy way to salvation."[57]

By the early years of U.S. entry into the First World War many (black) Pentecostals had developed an ambiguous relationship with the American state, partially because of their embrace of a biblical citizenship beyond country that prompted them to support pacifism. C. H. Mason and other Pentecostals had advised young men to resist the draft upon the U.S. entry into the World War I, and Federal officials, wondering whether these acts of resistance represented a broader threat, established a measure of government surveillance over Mason and the Church of God in Christ during its early years. Through his support of Liberty Bonds and his willingness to denounce strongly the Kaiser, Mason ultimately demonstrated his allegiance to the U.S. government and its war effort, while never quite renouncing his pacifist stance.[58]

Adherents of Noble Drew Ali and his Moorish Science Temple struck a similarly uncertain tone. This group, a precursor to the later Nation of Islam, issued "Nationality and Identification" cards, emblazoned with iconography from Islam and Morocco, with a statement placing its bearer under the laws of

Allah and promising him or her the "birthrights" of Moorish Americans that would ultimately promote inclusion in U.S. society as full citizens. With the cards in hand, many Chicago members thought that carrying them would "restrain" white people from "disturbing or harming [their] holder[s]" reportedly prompting many members to "accost white people of the streets . . . showing their membership cards" and "sing[ing] the praises of their prophet [Noble Drew Ali]." In a flyer given to temple governors and sheiks in the late 1920s to read before each meeting, Ali instructed his leadership to "inform all members that [they] must end all radical agitating speeches while at work, in their homes or on the streets" and to "stop flashing your [ID] cards at Europeans, it causes confusion." In the end, Ali urged his followers to remember their card was for spiritual salvation and not political protest that could be read as seditious behavior. In Ali's words: "We did not come to cause confusion; our work is to uplift the [American] nation. [59]

What Mother Tate (along with other Pentecostals) and the Moors (followed later by the Nation of Islam) represented were two, often competing, attempts to define themselves and their followers beyond their apparent links to the larger (white) society in the United States. Ali, when he discussed what made what he called the "Moorish Divine National Movement" significant and powerful, explained that when followers were "incorporated in this government" of the Moors they could now become "recognized by all other nations of the world."[60] In their quest to escape (white) man-made divisions black religionists reached for the world beyond the nation's borders and as they did, new conceptions of the divine emerged that would convey the materiality of the divine. In the wake of the mass migrations after World War I, black activists and religionists reconceived the separatism that had animated the rise of black independent denominations in the decades immediately after slavery. Black organizational networks, religious and otherwise, spanned the old regional divisions shaping how black people would define community to meet the demands of a new world. While black Holiness and Pentecostal leaders (of both sexes) asserted independence from (white) outsiders, onlookers, and benefactors, the Baptist churches and religious societies from which these religious leaders had emerged were immersed in the very muck of the American terrain and a necessary embrace of their white counterparts.

Historian Beryl Satter, in noting the stiff competition between Marcus Garvey and Father Divine, questioned how the followers of a Marcus Garvey in the UNIA, which focused on "race consciousness and race purity," could later be drawn in large numbers to Father Divine, who proclaimed his own status as God incarnate and his Peace Mission movement with its stance of "race neutrality." Satter speculated that the charismatic Father Divine was attractive because he shared UNIA's focus on economic empowerment and its embrace of New Thought language and beliefs that suggested "one's thoughts could literally create one's material reality."[61] But after the First World War, new (religious) groups emerged. These, such as Marcus Garvey and his followers, all reconfigured their emphasis on racial uplift and respectability by placing less emphasis on the interests of whites and more on the possibilities beyond U.S. society. This common perspective might have also attracted members of the UNIA to the Peace Mission. But while Garvey and his religious and intellectual heirs represented a different approach to race and nation from the uneasy interracialism black Pentecostals developed, they both depended on new ways to conceptualize collective identities that would transcend the racial dynamics that existed after the failed promise of Reconstruction. In the process of imagining themselves on the global stage, they both sought to escape from the human boundaries drawn between peoples in regions and nation-states.

Father Divine was the apotheosis of the nonracialist promise only ephemerally realized in the idealized memories of Azusa Street among the earliest Pentecostals. Divine's followers often practiced the glossolalia that usually distinguished Pentecostals from the rest of Christendom, and Father Divine himself, when still called George Baker, attended the 1906 revival at Azusa Street—the place Pentecostals would recognize as the birthplace of Pentecostalism—where he reportedly spoke in tongues as well.[62] Despite his stronger links to Charles Fillmore, Unity, and the New Thought movement of the prior century, Father Divine incarnated as well Jones's early search for a new basis for religious community beyond racial identity. In worship, members of the Peace Mission imagined a day even in the South when race consciousness and segregation would not define black reality. As members of the Peace Mission movement sang in the 1940s: "Away down in Texas, and in the farthest parts of the south, we shall eat and drink together, racism shall be wiped out."[63] With a stance that went far beyond "race neutrality" toward a perspective of determined nonracialism, Divine's ministry, which reached its height in Harlem during the 1930s and then continued in Philadelphia in the '40s, represented a radicalization of the sentiments for unity found in Tate's attempts to hold her church fellowship together. Nothing captured Divine's sentiments more than his simple refusal to describe people as white or black in an age obsessed with notions of racial purity. (He described people instead as "dark-complected" and "light complected.")[64] His rejection of race paralleled his rejection of national identity. "I am none of your nationalities," Father Divine once said in reference to his divine identity and his ultimate allegiance to nation states. "You don't have to think I AM an American. . . . I AM none of them."[65]

On the horizon of their vision as an imagined nation, black religious people, like their secular counterparts, hoped for a perspective unmoored from their U.S. identity and reality. Like the horizon, this perspective could be seen but never truly reached. It could be imagined and could inspire even if it did not truly exist. Black Pentecostals, like most born in the United States, were inseparably of the nation even as they reached beyond its borders in their imaginations, their writings, and in their religious practices. As they pressed toward the cultural and physical boundaries of both the nation they imagined and of the one for which they held a sharply circumscribed citizenship, they shaped anew their sense of who they were and where they might finally belong.

Notes

I am grateful to the Louisville Institute for the financial resources that supported much of the research for this paper. My fellow Coolidge Fellows with Cross Currents in the summer of 2006 provided the first audience to the paper that would form the basis of this article. My colleagues in the Religion Department of Dartmouth College, after hearing a version of this article, provided me with additional context for sharpening the presentation of my ideas. Melani McAlister, Marie Griffith, David Daniels, and Sylvester Johnson all read earlier versions of this article and provided helpful comments for revision. All the remaining mistakes and limitations are, of course, mine.

Sources for the opening quotations are Robert E. Park, "Negro Race Consciousness as Reflected in Race Literature," *American Review* 1.5 (September–October 1923): 515, and Cornel West, *Keeping Faith: Philosophy and Race in America* (New York: Routledge, 1993), xiii.

1. For an account of Ida Robinson's visions, see Harold Dean Trulear, "Reshaping Black Pastoral Theology: The Vision of Bishop Ida B. Robinson," *Journal of Religious Thought* 46.1 (Summer–Fall 1989): 21. For additional biographical information about her life, music, and sermons, see Harold Dean Trulear, "Ida B. Robinson: The Mother as Symbolic Presence," in *Portraits of a Generation: Early Pentecostal Leaders*, ed. James R. Goff Jr. and Grant Wacker (Fayetteville: University of Arkansas Press, 2002), 309–24, and Bettye Collier-Thomas, *Daughters of Thunder: Black Women Preachers and Their Sermons, 1850–1979* (San Francisco: Jossey-Bass, 1998), 194–210.
2. For a genealogy of the term *diaspora*, its relation to Jewish intellectual history, and its entrance into scholarly and activists' analyses of black internationalism in the postwar period, see Brent Hayes Edwards, "The Uses of *Diaspora*," *Social Text* 66 (Spring 2001): 45–73.
3. Collier-Thomas, *Daughters of Thunder*, 194.
4. David Martin, *Pentecostalism: The World Their Parish* (Malden, Mass.: Blackwell, 2002).
5. I have adopted both the reading of Stuart Hall's ideas and the metaphor of joints from Brent Edwards. See Edwards's "The Uses of *Diaspora*," 64–66. For Stuart Hall's central article on articulation, see his "Race, Articulation, and Societies Structured in Dominance," in *Black British Cultural Studies: A Reader*, ed. Houston Baker, Manthia Diawara, and Ruth H. Lindeborg (Chicago: University of Chicago Press, 1996), 16–60.
6. Michael A. Gomez, *Exchanging Our Country Marks: The Transformation of African Identities in the Colonial and Antebellum South* (Chapel Hill: University of North Carolina Press, 1998), 15–16.
7. Dan Fountain, "Christ Unchained: African American Conversions During the Civil War Era," *Ohio Valley History* 3.2 (Summer 2003): 31–48.
8. Katharine L. Dvorak, "After the Apocalypse, Moses," in *Masters and Slaves in the House of the Lord: Race and Religion in the American South, 1740–1870*, ed. John B. Boles (Lexington: University Press of Kentucky, 1988), 173.

9. Alain Locke, "The New Negro," in *The New Negro* (1925; New York: Atheneum, 1989), 14. For the development of the political and social movement of the New Negro in the opening decades of the twentieth century into a more culturally oriented Harlem Renaissance, see Ernest Allen Jr., "The New Negro: Explorations in Identity and Social Consciousness, 1910–1922," in *1915: The Cultural Moment,* ed. Adele Heller and Lois Rudnick (New Brunswick, N.J.: Rutgers University Press, 1991), 48–68. The phrase "practice of diaspora" comes from Brent Hayes Edwards's brilliant examination of black transnational print culture in New York and Paris. See his *The Practice of Diaspora: Literature, Translation, and the Rise of Black Internationalism* (Cambridge, Mass: Harvard University Press, 2003).

10. Cheryl J. Sanders, *Saints in Exile: The Holiness-Pentecostal Experience in African American Religion and Culture* (New York: Oxford University Press, 1996), viii–ix, 143–44.

11. Paul Gilroy adopts the term "travelling cultures" from James T. Clifford's "Travelling Cultures," in *Cultural Studies,* ed. Lawrence Grossberg et al. (New York: Routledge, 1992). See his *The Black Atlantic: Modernity and Double Consciousness* (Cambridge: Harvard University Press, 1993), 17.

12. This notion that African Americans constructed a national Baptist denomination in an effort to achieve visibility and social power comes from James Melvin Washington's *Frustrated Fellowship: The Black Baptist Quest for Social Power* (Macon, Ga.: Mercer University Press, 1986).

13. Frantz Fanon, *Black Skin, White Masks,* trans. Charles Lam Markmann (New York: Grove Press, 1967), 110.

14. For an example of this cooperation on the local church level, see Thomas Armstrong, "The Building of a Black Church: Community in Post Civil War Liberty County, Georgia," *Georgia Historical Quarterly* 66.3 (Fall 1982): 346–67.

15. Evelyn Brooks Higginbotham, *Righteous Discontent: The Women's Movement in the Black Baptist Church, 1880–1920* (Cambridge, Mass.: Harvard University Press, 1993), 88–119; Sandy D. Martin, *Black Baptists and African Missions: The Origins of a Movement, 1880–1915* (Macon, Ga.: Mercer University Press, 1989), 12–19, 219–20; David W. Wills, "Exodus Piety: African American Religion in an Age of Immigration," in *Minority Faiths and the American Protestant Mainstream,* ed. Jonathan D. Sarna (Urbana: University of Illinois Press, 1998), 164.

16. Wills, "Exodus Piety," 164.

17. Paul Harvey, *Redeeming the South: Religious Cultures and Racial Identities among Southern Baptists, 1865–1925* (Chapel Hill: University of North Carolina Press, 1997), 52.

18. Quoted in Harvey, *Redeeming the South,* 52.

19. Inspired by Sidney Hook's *Pragmatism and the Tragic Sense of Life* (New York: Basic Books, 1974), Eddie Glaude frames black political life around this notion of the tragic. See Eddie Glaude, *Exodus! Religion, Race, and Nation in Early Nineteenth-Century Black America* (Chicago: University of Chicago Press, 2000), 166–67.

20. Quoted in Glaude, *Exodus!* 156.

21. Glaude, *Exodus!* 167.

22. Higginbotham, *Righteous Discontent,* 197; Nancy Fraser, *Unruly Practices: Power, Discourse, and Gender in Contemporary Social Theory* (Minneapolis: University of Minnesota Press, 1989), 174.

23. Higginbotham, *Righteous Discontent,* 196.

24. Linking together surveillance with state mechanisms of control, Michel Foucault argues: "The exercise of discipline presupposes a mechanism that coerces by means of observation." See his *Discipline and Punish: The Birth of the Prison,* trans. Alex Sheridan (New York: Vintage Books, 1977), 170.

25. Fanon, *Black Skin, White Masks,* 116.

26. Quoted in Harvey, *Redeeming the South,* 63.

27. Clifton H. Johnson, *God Struck Me Dead: Voices of Ex-Slaves* (Cleveland: Pilgrim Press, 1969), 92.

28. George Rawick, ed., *The American Slave: A Composite Autobiography* (Westport, Conn.: Greenwood, 1972–), Supplement series 1, Mississippi, vol. 6, part 1, 623.

29. Rawick, *The American Slave,* Supplement series 1, South Carolina, vol. 3, part 3, 5.

30. Otho B. Cobbins, ed., *History of Church of the Christ (Holiness) USA, 1895–1965* (New York: Vantage Press, 1966), 23–24.

31. J. H. Green, introduction to Charles Price Jones, *An Appeal to the Sons of Africa: A Number of Poems, Readings, Orations and Lectures, Designed Especially to Inspire Youth of African Blood with Sentiments of Hope and True Nobility as well as to Entertain and Instruct All Classes of Readers and Lovers of Redeemed Humanity* (n.p.: Truth Publishing, 1902), xv.

32. I am thankful to David Daniels for suggesting to me Campbell's influence on William Christian. For the suggested associations between Mason and Christian, see David D. Daniels, "Charles Harrison Mason: The Interracial Impulse of Early Pentecostalism," in *Portraits of a Generation*, ed. Goff and Wacker, 259. For a discussion on the Holiness challenge to the struggle over religious institutionalization in the closing decades of the nineteenth century, see David Douglas Daniels, "The Cultural Renewal of Slave Religion: Charles Price Jones and the Emergence of the Holiness Movement in Mississippi" (PhD diss., Union Theological Seminary, 1992), 59–95.

33. John Giggie, "God's Long Journey: African-Americans, Religion, and History in the Mississippi Delta, 1875–1915" (PhD diss., Princeton University, 1997), 196–204.

34. Charles Price Jones, *The Gift of the Holy Ghost in the Book of Acts* (Los Angeles: National Publishing Board of the Church of Christ [Holiness], 1996), 40, quoted in Dale T. Irvin, "Charles Price Jones," in *Portraits of a Generation*, ed. Goff & Wacker, 41.

35. Alvin M. Harrell, *The First One Hundred Years: The History of the Church of the Living God*, (Rialto, Calif.: Harrell, 1993), 20–25.

36. William Christian, *Poor Pilgrim's Work in the Name of the Father, Son and Holy Ghost* (Texarkana: Joe Erlich Print, 1896), 24.

37. Jones, *An Appeal to the Sons of Africa*, 29.

38. Ibid., 42.

39. For more on Mason's distinctive role, see Daniels, "The Cultural Renewal of Slave Religion," 88, 186–88.

40. Charley C. White, as told to Ada Morehead Holland, *No Quittin' Sense* (Austin: University of Texas Press, 1969), 120.

41. C. Eric Lincoln and Lawrence H. Mamiya, *The Black Church in the African American Experience* (Durham, N.C.: Duke University Press, 1990), 82.

42. Cobbins, *History of the Church of Christ*, 27.

43. *American Baptist*, June 26, 1868, as quoted in Washington, *Frustrated Fellowship*, 109.

44. For the African legacy evident in female leadership roles, see Cheryl Townsend Gilkes, "The Politics of 'Silence': Dual-Sex Political Systems and Women's Traditions of Conflict in African-American Religion," in *African American Christianity: Essays in History*, ed. Paul E. Johnson (Berkeley: University of California Press, 1997). For an example of women's waning influence in congregational life during the later half of the nineteenth century, see Brown, "Negotiating and Transforming the Public Sphere: African-American Political Life in the Transition from Slavery to Freedom," in Black Public Sphere Collective, ed., *The Black Public Sphere: A Public Culture Book* (Chicago: University of Chicago Press, 1995).

45. Cheryl Townsend Gilkes, "'Together and in Harness': Women's Traditions in the Sanctified Church," in *African American Religious Thought*, 636; see also Anthea D. Butler, "Church Mothers and Migration in the Church of God in Christ," in *Religion in the American South: Protestants and Others in History and Culture* (Chapel Hill: University of North Carolina Press, 2004).

46. Kelly Willis Mendiola, "The Hand of a Woman: Four Holiness-Pentecostal Evangelists and American Culture, 1840–1930" (PhD diss., University of Texas, Austin, 2002), 291–92.

47. Helen M. Lewis and Meharry H. Lewis, *Seventy-fifth Anniversary Yearbook of the Church of the Living God, Pillar and Ground of the Truth, 1903–1978* (Nashville, Tenn.: New and Living Way, 1978), 9–10.

48. One distinctive practice, for example, that Christian's group and Tate's group share is using water instead of wine or grape juice for the Communion rite. They have similar explanations and defenses for the practice as well. See Harrell, *The First One Hundred Years*, 106–14; Christian, *Poor Pilgrim's Work*, 11–12; Mary Magdalena Tate, *The Constitution Government and General Decree Book of the Church of the Living God, Pillar and Ground of the Truth* (Chattanooga, Tenn.: New and Living Way, 1924), 65.

49. Mary Magdalena Tate, "The Name of the Lord Is a Strong Tower; the Righteous Runneth into It, and Is Safe," in *Mary Lena Lewis Tate: Collected Letters and Manuscripts*, ed. Meharry H. Lewis (Nashville: New and Living Way Publishing, 2003), 22.

50. For a brief, biographical essay on Horn, along with a small selection of her sermons, see Collier-Thomas, *Daughters of Thunder*, 173–93. For Horn's place in the Harlem community and religious life, including descriptions of her church building, see Cheryl Lynn Greenberg, *"Or Does It Explode?" Black Harlem in the Great Depression* (New York: Oxford University Press, 1991), 59, and James Campbell, *Talking at the Gates: A Life of James Baldwin* (New York: Viking, 1991), 36.

51. "Church of All Faiths Now Favorite of Air Waves," *Amsterdam News*, October 31, 1936, Sherry Sherrod DuPree African-American Pentecostal and Holiness collection, 1876–1989, Box 10, Folder 17, Schomburg Center for Research in Black Culture, New York Public Library, New York.
52. Tate, *General Decree Book*, 59.
53. Ibid., 58–59.
54. Michelle A. Stephens, "Black Transnationalism and the Politics of National Identity: West Indian Intellectuals in Harlem in the Age of War and Revolution," *American Quarterly* 50.3 (September 1998): 592; Frantz Fanon, *The Wretched of the Earth*, trans. Constance Farrington (New York: Grove Press, 1963), 247–48.
55. Michelle Stephens, "Re-imagining the Shape and Borders of Black Political Space," *Radical History Review* 87 (Spring 1997): 173. See also Michelle Stephens, *Black Empire: The Masculine Global Imaginary of Caribbean Intellectuals in the United States, 1914–1962* (Durham, N.C.: Duke University Press, 2005), esp. chap. 3.
56. Nathaniel Deutsch, "'The Asiatic Black Man': An African American Orientalism?" *Journal of Asian American Studies* 4.3 (September 2001): 196–98.
57. Arthur Huff Fauset, *Black Gods of the Metropolis: Negro Religious Cults of the Urban North* (Philadelphia: University of Pennsylvania Press, 1944), 42.
58. Theodore Kornweibel Jr., "Bishop C. H. Mason and the Church of God in Christ during World War I: The Perils of Conscientious Objection," *Southern Studies* 26 (Fall 1987); Grant Wacker, *Heaven Below: Early Pentecostals and American Culture* (Cambridge, Mass.: Harvard University Press, 2001), 248–49.
59. [Flyer], Box 1, Folder 3, Moorish Science Temple of America collection, 1926–1967, Schomburg Research Library for Black Culture, New York Public Library, New York.
60. Noble Drew Ali, *Moorish Literature* (n.p.: n.p., 1928), 6. Box 1, Folder 2, Moorish Science Temple of America collection, 1926–1967.
61. Beryl Satter, "Marcus Garvey, Father Divine, and the Gender Politics of Race Difference and Race Neutrality," *American Quarterly* 48.1 (January 1996): 44.
62. Jill Watts, *God, Harlem U.S.A.: The Father Divine Story* (Berkeley: University of California Press, 1992), 25. For more on Azusa Street's role as the mythical origin of the Pentecostal movement, see Joe Creech, "Visions of Glory: The Place of the Azusa Street Revival in Pentecostal History," *Church History* 65 (September 1996): 405–24.
63. Charles Samuel Braden, *These Also Believe: A Study of Modern American Cults and Minority Religious Movements* (New York: Macmillan, 1949), 19.
64. See Robert Weisbrot, *Father Divine: The Utopian Evangelist of the Depression Era Who Became an American Legend* (Boston: Beacon Press, 1983), 100–102. See also Braden, *These Also Believe*, 25–26.
65. Quoted in Jill Watts, *God, Harlem U.S.A.*, 88.

Who Speaks for Indian Americans?
Religion, Ethnicity, and Political Formation

Prema Kurien

In this era of "multicultural citizenship," the politics of immigrant groups can have powerful impacts, affecting their countries of residence and ancestry.[1] This is particularly the case when these groups develop organized means such as ethnic lobbies to represent their interests. There is a large body of literature addressing the role of domestic ethnic lobbies in shaping U.S. foreign policy, but most of this literature focuses on lobbies representing well-established U.S. ethnic groups such as Jews, African Americans, Armenians, Irish, and Cubans. Virtually no attention has been paid to ethnic lobby groups of immigrants who have entered the country since the passage of the 1965 Immigration Act. While it often takes a generation or two for new immigrant groups to enter into the political mainstream of their new homelands, some newer groups have reached this point and are now beginning their foray into national politics. [2]

Several analysts have noted that the Asian Indian American community is emerging as a powerful political influence in U.S. politics.[3] This article provides a brief overview of the patterns of civic activism of a variety of Indian American groups in the United States and examines the role that religion and transnational interests play in the formation of Indian American ethnic constituencies. Specifically, I focus on the development and activities of two types of organizations: those mobilizing under a Hindu umbrella and secular or multireligious Indian American groups, which often adopt the label "South Asian." Hindu organizations represent political Hindu interests, and South Asian organizations represent pluralist subcontinental groups that are explicitly against the political Hindu movement. Thus, these two types of organizations often have conflicting goals and strategies. I examine the objectives of the Hindu and the South Asian groups and some of the specific issues on which these two types of organizations have opposed each other. In the final section, I focus on the United States India Political Action Committee (USINPAC), formed in 2002 to represent "the Indian American community" on Capitol Hill and raise the issue of how this national-origin-based organization will arbitrate between the two types of supranational lobby groups.

My analysis draws on a ten-year study of the emergence and development of political Hinduism in the United States, the strategies of Indian Muslim and secular groups to challenge this mobilization, and a book on the new forms, practices, and interpretations of Hinduism in the United States.[4] Besides participating in the activities and programs of twelve Hindu American organizations in Southern California and New Jersey, I conducted detailed interviews with leaders and many of the members (more than 120 first- and second-generation Hindu Americans in all). I have also studied a Muslim Indian organization, an Indian Christian church, and a secular coalition of Indian American activists in Southern California. In addition to this primary research, I have been following the activities of Indian Americans around the country by reading Indian American newspapers (*India Abroad, India West, India Post, India Journal*) and the international magazine *Hinduism Today*, published from Hawai'i. However, the primary source of data for this article comes from an analysis of publications and Web sites of groups belonging to the two types of organizations, in addition to interviews I conducted with some leaders and members of three South Asian organizations.

The larger issue that I am interested in understanding is how certain types of groups come to be recognized as the authentic voices of a community by U.S. policymakers. What types of voices are included in this process and what types are excluded? How do local and national policymakers adjudicate between different types of groups, each claiming to represent the community? While this article does not provide the answers, it demonstrates the complexity of identity formation and mobilization by immigrant groups and shows why these questions are important.

Contemporary Ethnic Interest Groups

The large-scale immigration from countries in Asia, Latin America, and the Caribbean is transforming the contours of the U.S. economy, society, and culture.[5] Contemporary immigrants have affected U.S. politics through their voting behavior and their participation in local administration, and so far this has been the focus of the research on the political behavior of post-1965 immigrants.[6] However the involvement of contemporary immigrants in ethnic interest groups or lobbies at the national level is likely to be more consequential, since the context within which such groups operate has changed in significant ways over the past few decades. First, ethnic interest groups today operate in a context in which globalization and transnationalism challenge definitions of assimilation, patriotism, and citizenship.[7] Second, new forms of technology such as the Internet significantly affect the capacity of groups to disseminate information, to formulate and articulate interests, and to mobilize in support of these interests. For both these reasons, the ethnic advocacy organizations of contemporary immigrants are likely to adopt different agendas and strategies when compared to those of the earlier waves of immigrants.

An intense debate has raged among political scientists about the effect of the contemporary context on the functioning of ethnic interest groups. Some scholars believe that globalization and multiculturalism legitimize the pursuit of parochial concerns by ethnic lobbies and will thus further the balkanization of the foreign policy process.[8] Others argue that ethnic advocacy organizations representing the interests of new groups, aided by new forms of technology, will further democratic participation by a more diverse group of U.S. citizens and will also result in the spread of American values around the world.[9] However, only careful case studies of newer ethnic lobbies can address the question of which of these two scenarios is more likely. This article is a step in that direction.

The literature dealing with ethnic lobbies implies that one of the keys to success is the use of a nation-state organization to articulate common goals that transcend any internal divisions. But what happens when internal cleavages are so fundamental as to possibly prevent the development of a unified platform? Heather Gregg argues that the development of competing Armenian lobbies in the United States did not hurt or undermine the Armenian cause but on the contrary actually helped to promote the success of Armenian lobby efforts. She points out that this was because "although the two lobbies have different approaches to influencing Washington, they mostly agree on policy objectives."[10] Studies of the Jewish lobbies in the United States discuss the lack of unity within the community and the opposition Zionists initially had to face from anti-Zionist Jewish groups. But in the long term, the opposition dissipated and pro-Zionism emerged as the official U.S. Jewish position.[11] However, it is not clear if either type of solution is likely in the Indian American case. First, political Hindu groups and South Asian groups often disagree on policy objectives; and second, the opposition to the platform of political Hindu groups is quite strong among sections of the Indian American community and is unlikely to diminish over time.

While not dealing with ethnic lobbies, another body of literature examines the tendency of many newer immigrant groups to mobilize on the basis of "new" supranational identities in the contemporary period. There are two major bodies of work in this regard: one focused on alliances formed due to common religious affiliation, and the other looking at panethnic coalitions based on region of origin. [12] What are the similarities and differences between the two types of mobilizations, and how does each affect the ethnic community and the wider society? This issue has been relatively neglected, mainly because the two bodies of literature have been produced by different groups of scholars. While religious and panethnic groups may have overlapping agendas, their goals may also be in conflict. [13] Particularly in the latter case, it is important to determine which type of group is more successful in shaping policy. It is also important to understand whether lobbies representing religious groups and panethnic groups experience different outcomes from nation-state lobbies. Since Indian Americans have all three types of lobby groups, they make a good test case to examine such questions.

Indian Americans and Civic Activism

In a 2002 article, James M. Lindsay, vice president of the Council on Foreign Relations, identified Indian Americans as most "likely to emerge as a political powerhouse in the U.S." over the next few years. [14] Indian Americans form the wealthiest and fastest growing ethnic group in the United States and, at 2.3 million in 2005, are now the second-largest Asian community in the country. [15] Despite this increase, Indian Americans are still a relatively small group in terms of numbers, so their influence on U.S. politics is largely due to their position as a "donor machine" rather than a "voter machine." [16] While James Lindsay estimated that Indian Americans contributed around $8 million to federal election campaigns in the three elections prior to 2004, [17] an Indian American leader states that the community contributed "at least $7 million" in the 2000 presidential campaign alone. [18] Another analyst at the Council on Foreign Relations indicates that Indian Americans raised $5 million for the Democratic Party and $1.5 million for the Republican Party in 2004. [19] Indian Americans have also been able to develop the largest ethnic caucus on the Hill: the Congressional Caucus on India and Indian Americans, founded in 1994, has 176 members, and the India caucus in the Senate has 37 members. The geopolitical significance of the Indian subcontinent as a result of the nuclearization of India and Pakistan and the events of 9/11 have meant that the U.S. government is now well aware of the need to carefully balance the competing interests of these two countries. The rise of India as a key economic player in what Thomas Friedman describes as a "flat world" is a further reason that Indian American lobby groups and their influence on policy is an important issue to study.[20]

In the past decade, Indian Americans mainly have been entering the public sphere in the United States in two distinct ways: around a pan-Hindu identity, and on the basis of a secular Indian subcontinental, or "South Asian," identity (which despite the label is composed overwhelmingly of Indian Americans). Many of the pan-Hindu organizations are supporters of political Hinduism: some are involved with U.S. branches of Hindu nationalist groups existing in India; others are independent Hindu American organizations that share some of the ideological assumptions of the Hindu nationalist groups. The South Asian groups usually comprise a coalition of secular Hindus, leftist South Asian academics, *Dalits* (mobilized members of lower caste groups, which were formerly classified as "Untouchable"), and Indian Muslim and Christian groups all banding together on an anti-Hindutva platform. Relationships between Hindu and South Asian groups are often characterized by tension and hostility. At the heart of the difference between Hindu and South Asian organizations lie two different conceptions of "Indianness"—a Hinducentric one that defines India as a Hindu country under attack from Muslims, Christians, and secularists within and without the country, and a secular, multireligious, and multicultural conception that emphasizes the importance of developing harmonious relationships between groups and countries in the Indian subcontinent. There are also several political education groups and professional groups that identify and mobilize as "Indian Americans" or "Asian Americans," but many share the ideology of either the Hindu or the South Asian organizations mentioned and are also involved with these organizations in some capacity.[21] All of these organizations use the Internet as an important recruitment and mobilization tool.

Multiculturalism and Ethnic Formation

The ideology and practice of contemporary multiculturalism plays an important role in creating and explaining the patterns of mobilization of Indian American groups. Multiculturalism permits, even demands, the construction of a public ethnic identity, as opposed to a purely private one. Multiculturalism leads to the institutionalization of ethnicity and to ethnic formation among immigrant groups as individuals face pressure (both from the wider society and from within the ethnic community) to organize into groups on the basis of cultural similarity and to have ethnic representatives "speak for the community" and its concerns. Since official "recognition" can secure social, economic, and political resources in a multicultural society, the "struggle for recognition" is now becoming the central form of political conflict in multicultural societies, spurring ethnic mobilization among a range of groups.[22]

In another publication I have argued that multiculturalist policies, despite their intended goal of facilitating the integration of immigrants and winning their loyalty, seem to often do the reverse, strengthening immigrant attachment to the ancestral homeland and giving rise to diasporic nationalism.[23] There are several reasons for this, but briefly, multiculturalism allows immigrant groups to gain membership in the United States as "ethnic" Americans. Thus, paradoxically, immigrants become American by becoming ethnic. Becoming ethnic involves a process of group unification and mobilization around allegiance and loyalty to the ancestral homeland (or region, or religion), so not surprisingly, ethnic leaders try to whip up ethno-nationalism among immigrants.

Despite the fact that ethnic categorization is generally by virtue of national origin, mobilizing on the basis of an allegiance to the ancestral homeland is viewed as politically threatening, since it calls into question the patriotism of the groups to their current homelands. This means that immigrants mobilizing as ethnics have to be careful to emphasize and demonstrate their loyalty to their country of residence, particularly when they emerge in the public sphere. For this reason, religion has long been recognized as an acceptable and nonthreatening basis for community formation and expression, particularly in the United States. As sociologist Stephen Warner points out, immigrants were able to hold on to their religious identity and practices even in the assimilationist era of U.S. history.[24] Since religion and religious institutions often play a central role in the process of ethnic formation, they become more important in the immigrant context in the United States than in the home country, increasing the power of such organizations to construct and impose authoritative versions of ethnicity. Having to be the repository of ethnicity also transforms immigrant religion.[25] As de facto ethnic institutions, most immigrant religious organizations also develop regional and national associations to unify the group, define their identity, and represent their interests. Consequently, different religious groups tend to develop definitions of nationality from their own perspective, resulting in variations in the construction of homeland culture and identity along religious lines, sometimes exacerbating tensions between them.

In the United States, the historical legacy of religion being the most legitimate form of ethnic expression, the political success of Jewish groups, the mobilization of Christian evangelicals, and the establishment of faith-based initiatives have all reinforced the tendency of other groups to mobilize around religion. In the Hindu American case, a conjunction of additional factors— Hindus being a majority in the homeland, but a racial and religious minority in the United States, anti-Islamic sentiment in the United States, the history of Hindu nationalism as a reaction to Western colonialism and racism, its recent resurgence in India, and the encouragement of diasporic Hindu nationalism by the *Bharatiya Janata Party* (BJP, the Indian People's Party) government that was in power between 1998 and 2004—contributed toward the mobilizing of Hindu Americans.

The Formation of Hindu American Political Organizations

It is likely that Hindu Indian Americans are a smaller proportion of the Indian American population than they are in India (where they are more than 80 percent), since Indians from Sikh and Christian backgrounds seem to be overrepresented in the United States.[26] Since the U.S. census does not collect data on religion, there are no official figures on how many Indian immigrants in the United States are from a Hindu background. However, national surveys conducted in the late 1990s estimated Hindus to be a little more than 1 million, most believed to be immigrants from India and their children.[27] Since 1.7 million of the U.S. population identified themselves racially as "Asian Indians" in the 2000 census, Hindus probably constitute around 60 percent of the total Indian American population.[28] As mentioned, the number of Indians in the United States grew to 2.3 million in 2005. However, we do not know if the proportion of Hindus changed during that period.

Unlike most other established religions, Hinduism does not have a founder, an ecclesiastical structure of authority, or a single canonical text or commentary. Consequently, Hinduism in India consists of an extraordinary array of practices, deities, texts, and schools of thought. Hindu umbrella organizations, whose goal in India has been to unite, educate, and mobilize Hindu Indians of different backgrounds in support of Hindu interests, were well positioned to take on this role in the United States as well. Most of these umbrella organizations are organizationally or ideologically linked to Hindutva (Hindu nationalist) organizations in India.

Hindu nationalism first emerged as a reaction to British colonialism and was explicitly codified in the 1920s. The first major Hindu nationalist organization, the *Rashtriya Swayamsevak Sangh* (RSS, the National Indian Volunteer Corps), was established in 1925 to serve the cause of Hindu unity and defense. In the contemporary period, Hindu nationalism achieved a resurgence from the late 1980s with the Ram temple movement calling for the building of a temple to Lord Ram in a town in North India, on the site of a sixteenth-century mosque. Hindutva supporters claim that the Babri mosque had been over a temple commemorating the exact place of Lord Ram's birth. The Ram movement was spearheaded by the *Vishwa Hindu Parishad* (VHP, World Hindu Council), founded in 1964 as a transnational organization to promote Hinduism and Hindu unity among Hindus in India and abroad. The *Bajrang Dal*, a militant youth activist organization of the VHP, was founded in the 1980s during the Ram movement. The BJP, established in 1980, was able to achieve a meteoric rise by adopting Hindu nationalism as its central plank in the late 1980s. The watershed event that first propelled the BJP onto the national stage was the demolition of the Babri mosque on December 6, 1992, by a mob of Hindu nationalists, despite the attempts of the central government to prevent it. The BJP came to power in India at the head of a coalition government in 1998 and remained in control until the summer of 2004, when it was defeated in national elections. The different, interlinked organizations that are at the core of the Hindu nationalist movement are collectively referred to as the *Sangh Parivar* (the family of [Hindu] organizations).

The rise of the contemporary Hindutva mobilization in India has been marked by violence against Muslims, and also against Christian missionaries and recent converts (mostly lower caste or tribal) to Christianity. Two of the most serious incidents took place in December 1992, when the Babri mosque was demolished, and in 2002, when the state of Gujarat witnessed what several groups of independent investigators have characterized as an organized, state-sponsored pogrom against Muslims, ostensibly in retaliation against a Muslim mob attack on a train carrying Hindu activists and their families.[29] After the violence had been brought under control, Muslims in Gujarat were warned by members of the VHP that if they wanted to return to their villages, they should "do so as a subject, not an equal" and that they should learn to "live like a minority."[30] As we will see, these two incidents played an important part in mobilizing both Hindutva and anti-Hindutva groups in the United States.

The VHP of America (VHPA), a branch of the VHP in India, was the earliest Hindu American umbrella organization and was founded in 1970 on the East Coast by four members of the RSS and was formally incorporated in 1974.[31] It now has chapters in most of the fifty states. Although the VHP in India is militantly nationalistic, perhaps partly because it is registered in the United States as a nonprofit, tax-exempt religious organization, which is therefore forbidden to pursue political activities, the VHPA has officially remained devoted to promoting Hinduism and pursuing cultural and social activities. However, unofficially, VHP members and activists are networked with a range of Hindu organizations and groups around the country and in India, including those that are more overtly political. The HSS (*Hindu Swayamsevak Sangh*), the overseas branch of the RSS organization in India, was established in New Jersey in 1977. Despite the establishment of these groups in the 1970s, the Hindutva movement in the United States gained support only in the late 1990s due to a combination of four factors: the ethnicization of Hinduism, the coming to power of the BJP in India, the use of the Internet as an instrument of mobilization, and the perceived need by Hindus for political action to obtain recognition and resources in the United States.

An important development in the institutionalization of Hinduism in the United States was the development of an ecumenical, pan-Indian Hinduism and a concomitant gradual solidification of the India = Hindu equation. For instance, John Fenton discusses the way in which the "India Center" in Atlanta, meant to be a facility for all religious groups to use, was taken over by a group of Hindus who constructed an ecumenical temple in the mid-1980s, thus alienating some Indian religious minorities.[32] Again, Sandhya Shukla argues that the Cultural Festival of India organized in 1991 in New Jersey by the Swaminarayan group of Hindus projected a Hinducentric vision of India.[33] Raymond Williams points out that the ecumenicalism that in the early period was forged out of necessity due to the diversity and small numbers of Hindu immigrants in a region had by the mid-1980s "become a conscious strategy to develop a new form of Hinduism among immigrants."[34] As he indicates, the VHPA was a key player in this development. By the mid-1980s, the organization had chapters in twenty-eight states and about seventy-five cities and was also networked informally with Hindu groups, temples, and religious leaders at the national and local levels.[35] Although the VHP in India also emphasized ecumenicalism and nationalism, their message fit in better in the United States, where the ecumenicalism was occasioned by the diversity within the Hindu American community, the huge expense involved in constructing new temples and centers, and the need to develop a coherent ethnic identity. The India = Hindu equation also conformed well to the American tradition of ethnicizing religion. Recognizing this, the VHPA exhorted Indians in the United States to be an example to those in India in the development of ecumenicalism and nationalistic pride. In a resolution passed at the tenth Hindu Conference in

New York in 1984, the VHPA urged "all the Hindus of the world—back home and abroad—to act in a broad and nationalistic manner rising above their personal beliefs and creeds, parochial languages, and provincial and sectarian considerations."[36] Ecumenicalism and nationalistic pride became the central planks of the American Hinduism that began to be increasingly publicized by spokespersons of Hindu American organizations in this period.

Despite the development of Hindu nationalism within a section of the Hindu American community during the mid- to late 1980s, the Hindutva voice was overpowered by secularists.[37] For instance, the emphasis on Hindu solidarity used in the first press statement of the Hindu Federation of America (HFA), an organization founded in 1985 by a small group of Hindus in the San Francisco Bay Area, was denounced by several organizations, including the VHPA. Dr. Mahesh Mehta, general secretary of the VHPA, expressed concern about the very concept of Hindu solidarity, arguing that "when we speak of Hindu Solidarity, we are speaking of taking a stand, even antagonizing, if necessary, powerful forces such as Christianity."[38]

Hindu groups from around the country participated in the Ram movement and contributed money and sanctified bricks to build the temple at Ayodhya, and by the early 1990s Hindu nationalism was on the ascendancy in the United States.[39] The demolition of the Babri mosque on December 6, 1992, energized American Hindu nationalist groups to come out more publicly. The VHPA started to openly emphasize the need for Hindu unity and also became more militant and more overtly political.[40] The Internet became a major site for Hindu nationalist propaganda and mobilization from the early 1990s. The Hindu nationalist message also began to be carried by several Indian American newspapers. The coming to power in 1998 of the BJP, the party that supported Hindu nationalism, gave the Hindutva cause more legitimacy within Hindu circles both in India and in the United States, and Hindu umbrella organizations in the United States began to use some elements of the Hindutva platform to unify and politically mobilize Hindu Americans. *Sangh Parivar* organizations and affiliates in the United States registered a "phenomenal growth" from the late 1990s.[41]

Not surprisingly, the Hindu nationalist message, with its emphasis on the need for Hindu pride and assertiveness, is particularly attractive to Hindus in the United States who experience becoming a racial, religious, and cultural minority upon immigration and must deal with the largely negative perceptions of Hinduism in the wider society.[42] In the United States, religion has become an important magnet for Indians from a Hindu background to coalesce around in their effort to obtain recognition and resources as American ethnics.[43] One strategy that Hindu community leaders have been following for a long time is to emulate the model of Jewish Americans. As a highly successful group that is integrated into mainstream American society while maintaining its religious and cultural distinctiveness, close community ties, and connections with the home country, U.S. Jews are viewed as a group that has been able to "fit in" while remaining different. This is the route to success that Hindu Americans also want to adopt in their quest to stake a position in American society. Many Hindu organizations have also formed alliances with Jewish groups.

The control that Hindu groups have been able to gain over Indian American politics can be seen by the comment of Narayan D. Keshavan, a special assistant to Congressman Gary L. Ackerman (one of the former cochairs of the Congressional Caucus on India and Indian Americans), who told *India Post* journalist Prashanth Lakhihal that "there are scores of congressmen and dozens of senators who clearly equate the growing Indian American political influence to the 'Hindu Lobby'—very much akin to the famed 'Jewish Lobby.'"[44] Hindu umbrella groups and leaders in the United States, as in India, demonstrate considerable hostility toward Muslims, and to Christians to some extent. They have also strongly opposed the attempts by academics and secularists to develop a South Asian American identity.

While a variety of Hindu American groups seek to influence policy, a Hindu American Foundation (HAF) was formed in the summer of 2004 ostensibly to consolidate these demands and to "provide a voice for the . . . Hindu American community." In the short period since its formation, the HAF has become a well-known and influential organization. Its Web site indicates that the organization "interacts with and educates government, media, think tanks, academia and public fora about Hinduism and issues of concern to Hindus locally and globally."[45] The group also describes itself as "promoting the Hindu and American ideals of understanding, tolerance and pluralism." Although spokespeople indicate that the organization is not affiliated with any religious or political organizations or entities, its president, Mihir Meghani, has been an active member of the VHPA and the HSS and is the author of the central essay on the BJP philosophy, titled "Hindutva: The Great Nationalist Ideology," on the BJP Web site.[46] This political slant can be seen in many of the activities of the organization. In 2004–2005, the organization held events to educate legislators about "issues of concern to Hindu Americans," such as the abuses to Hindus in Muslim majority areas such as Kashmir, Bangladesh, and Pakistan. They also allied with Jewish organizations on an anti-Muslim platform. For instance, in the meeting with the American Jewish Committee in San Francisco held in October 2004, Mihir Meghani noted the "declining number of Hindus in India owing to growth rate and dubious methods of conversion to other faiths" and compared it to the demographic decline faced by Jews in Israel. He also spoke about "the shared risks they face from neighbors with long histories of terrorism."[47]

Since the Hindutva movement is based on a definition of Indian identity and culture that marginalizes or excludes secularists, Muslims, Christians, and Dalits, these groups have formed organizations that individually and in coalition attempt to oppose political Hinduism. Some, like the South Asian organizations, are explicitly secular, and even antireligious. However, all of the other groups mobilized against political Hinduism through the use of religion and religious organizations. In fact, groups such as Indian Christians united to develop a national organization only in response to the Hindutva threat. The Internet played an important role in these mobilizations as well.

The Formation of Anti-Hindutva Organizations

South Asian American Groups. The politics of multicultural recognition, combined with the reality of racism, also means that groups that "look alike" are frequently lumped together and treated as though they are the same. Over time, as various groups that are lumped together have interacted in the United States, they have become aware of common problems and goals. Thus, the tendency for racial categorization and the recognition of commonalities by those so categorized has often given rise to panethnicity, particularly among members of the second and later generations. Groups that are lumped together, such as "blacks," "Asians," "Native Americans," and "Latinos," have developed ethnic solidarity by adopting the ascribed category and reinterpreting the history of the individual groups to create a common heritage.[48] Like religious groups, panethnic coalitions are also able to mobilize politically without being seen as unpatriotic. This is the logic that explains the formation of South Asian American groups.

Like the Asian American movement of the late 1960s, the South Asian American movement began on college campuses in the late 1980s.[49] As South Asians encountered each other, they discovered how much they had in common—from their historical, social, and cultural heritage to their experiences of racialization in the United States.[50] They thus came together to challenge the exclusion of South Asian voices within Asian American umbrella organizations and to mobilize as a progressive coalition against the religious bigotry that seemed to be sweeping through their communities.[51] This background explains the concern of South Asian groups for social justice issues, their emphasis on inclusivity, and their secular orientation.

When I first began my study of South Asian organizations, I was interested in finding out why politically oriented Indian Americans chose to mobilize under a South Asian, rather than an Indian, identity. I was told by Nirav Desai, a leader at the Subcontinental Institute, an educational organization based in Washington, D.C., that sought to develop a South Asian American political identity, that besides the need to be inclusive and to address the common concerns of the community in the United States, there were two additional reasons that motivated the founders (all of Indian origin) to make the institute a South Asian organization. First, they realized that policymakers often "wanted to talk about issues in terms of South Asia;" and second, they wanted to show that their loyalties were not split with another government.[52] Similarly, journalist Sarah Wildman suggests that the desire to be perceived as a patriotic American partly motivates politically active Indian Americans to adopt a South Asian identity. In an article on South Asianness she quotes Kris Kolluri, an Indian immigrant and senior policy adviser to the then House minority leader, Dick Gephardt, as saying, "What you're seeing is not only a movement to stand up for our civil rights but also a movement to ensure that the larger society knows that we are Americans."[53]

There are several local South Asian American groups, but a national South Asian American organization that is policy oriented and constituted primarily of Indian Americans is the South Asian American Leaders of Tomorrow (SAALT). They describe their mission as developing leadership and fostering civic engagement by South Asians in all sectors of U.S. society.[54] The organization focuses on domestic issues of concern to the South Asian community, such as immigration, discrimination, hate crimes, and civil rights, and its goal is to develop a unified voice to address these concerns. Its leaders claim that their target audience is the younger generation and that one of their central goals is to provide guidance and support for this group. They say that they are not interested in getting involved in the geopolitics of South Asia and, therefore, as a rule, do not address issues related to the subcontinent.

Other South Asian organizations, however, try to address both foreign and domestic issues. One such organization is Friends of South Asia (FOSA), which was founded in the Silicon Valley area at the turn of 2001/2002 when tensions between India and Pakistan were particularly high and threatened to break out into a nuclear conflagration. The organization claims that its basic mission is "to achieve a peaceful, prosperous, and hate-free South Asia," one in which "the rights of all minorities are respected and protected; regardless of religious, ethnic, sexual or other differences."[55] Its activities include sponsoring talks and organizing protests, rallies, and campaigns around issues affecting the South Asian community. There are also many issue-based coalitions, such as the Coalition against Communalism (CAC), formed in the San Francisco Bay Area in December 1992 in the wake of the demolition of the Babri mosque.[56] Some of these types of coalitions are discussed further in the next section.

Indian Muslim American Organizations. There are various Indian Muslim American organizations. One of the best known is the American Federation of Muslims from India (AFMI), formed in 1989 as a social service organization dedicated to the uplift of Muslims in India who, for a variety of reasons, remain well behind the Hindu community in terms of education, income, and employment. The activists are mainly established professional men, several of whom are medical doctors. Their programs focus particularly on improving the educational status of Indian Muslims. However, subsequent to the demolition of the Babri mosque, the opposition to Hindutva and the promotion of secularism, and communal harmony in India became an important goal. Since 1994, AFMI formed a coalition with Dalit groups to support the advancement of all underprivileged groups in India. AFMI also works with other organizations, such as the Indian Muslim Relief Council (IMRC), and national Muslim organizations such as the Muslim Public Affairs Council (MPAC), and the Council on American Islamic Relations (CAIR) to politically mobilize American Muslims and stay in regular contact with legislators.

Another Indian American Muslim group, the Indian Muslim Council (IMC), was formed in 2002 after the Gujarat riots. On its Web site, the organization indicates that it was formed at that time because Indian Muslims in the United States realized "it was time to act. Gujarat 2002 was clearly only the more visible tip of a dangerous iceberg [and] the poison of Hindutva-fascism had not only reached alarming proportions in India, but had also insidiously infiltrated many institutions and individuals in the USA, particularly those related to India."[57]

Indian Christian American Organizations. While national organizations to represent particular Indian Christian denominations have existed for decades, a national organization to represent all Indian Christian Americans was forged only in the year 2000. The impetus was an official visit to the United States in September 2000 by the Indian prime minister, Atal Bihari Vajpayee, the head of the BJP-led government. A coalition of Indian Christian organizations held a demonstration on Capitol Hill on September 14 to protest the violence against Christian churches in India under the BJP government, and a Federation of Indian American Christian Organizations of North America (FIACONA) was subsequently formed on October 28, 2000, in Washington, D.C. According to the press release announcing the formation of the FIACONA, the organization was formed to "counter the activities of [the] BJP-RSS-VHP-Bajrang Dal nexus . . . We are fully aware that this neo-Nazi group has infiltrated many mainstream think tanks and political groups in the U.S. particularly in Washington and in New York under the cover of cultural organizations or political educational forums. Members of these organizations often disassociate themselves with RSS-VHP-Bajrang Dal nexus openly, while maintaining very close ties with them informally . . . We are particularly concerned about their increasing assault on the Christian Churches and members of the defenseless Christian communities in India."[58] The FIACONA has forged alliances with American Christian, Indian Muslim, and Dalit groups to form an anti-Hindutva front that publicizes and protests the actions of the Sangh Parivar against minorities.

American Dalit Organizations. The visit of the Indian prime minister to the United States in 2000 also mobilized Dalit groups in this country. On September 8, 2000, when Mr. Vajpayee was speaking at the United Nations, a Dalit coalition group, the Federation of Ambedkarites, Buddhists, and Ravidasi Organizations of North America (FABRONA), organized a protest in New York against the "atrocities and genocides of Dalits [Untouchables] of India" under the BJP government. The press release argued that the "BJP Alliance Government has been responsible for promoting Hindu Fundamentalism . . . thus making living hell for Dalits, Christians, Muslims, Sikhs, Tribals and other minorities."[59] Religion has played an important role in organizing and galvanizing Dalit American groups as well. A variety of Dalit groups have formed in the United States and Canada to publicize Dalit oppression, and according to Gail Omvedt, an academic focusing on Dalit issues, this was due to "integration and motivation" provided by the Guru Ravidass religious institutions patronized by Dalits in these two countries.[60]

Hindu and South Asian Groups in Opposition

In an earlier work, I examined some of the organizations that fell under the Hindu and South Asian umbrella, paying particular attention to the response of the two types of groups to the events of September 11, 2001, since 9/11 was a watershed for both types of organizations, propelling them into activism and into the American public sphere in very different ways. In the post-9/11 period, Hindu groups who had been overlooked in the interfaith events that were organized in the wake of 9/11 mobilized to bring Hinduism to the attention of the administration and policymakers. They challenged the post-9/11 attempt to enlarge the "Judeo-Christian" tradition into an "Abrahamic" one (by including Muslims), since they feared that this would further marginalize Hindus within the country. Finally, they also mobilized to draw attention to the difference between Hinduism and Islam, to criticize Islam and Muslim countries, and to press their point that India had nothing in common with Islamic countries like Pakistan and Bangladesh and should therefore not be lumped together with them under the South Asian rubric. South Asian groups on the other hand, mobilized to present a united front against hate groups and to challenge immigration policies such as the special registration required of immigrants from predominantly Muslim countries, the racial profiling and arrests of South Asians, and the hate crimes experienced by the community.[61]

After 9/11, Hindu leaders strengthened their efforts to forge alliances with Israeli groups on an anti-Islamic platform, increased their attacks on Pakistan and Bangladesh, particularly with respect to their treatment of Hindu minorities, and launched attacks against "Abrahamic" religions, especially Christianity and Islam, arguing that such monotheistic and history-centered religions are inherently intolerant and violent.[62] South Asian groups continued to mobilize on an anti-Hindutva platform. In November 2002, leftist Indian American academics and activists mobilizing under a Campaign to Stop Funding Hate (CSFH) platform released a report demonstrating that a prominent Indian American charity organization, the India Development Relief Fund (IDRF), which claimed to be nonpolitical and nonsectarian, actually had close ties with Hindu nationalist groups in India and had been diverting some of the millions of dollars earmarked for nonreligious humanitarian causes toward supporting such groups.[63] The authors of the report were successful in getting software corporations such as Cisco and Oracle to stop their matching contributions to IDRF and in obtaining the endorsement of more than three hundred academics in the United States for their campaign. The attack against the IDRF galvanized several Hindu groups in the United States to come out strongly in defense of the organization, and the criticism actually increased the contributions to the charity.[64] In the spring of 2005, a Coalition Against Genocide (CAG) composed of thirty-five different South Asian, secularist, Indian Muslim, and Indian Christian groups successfully lobbied to have the U.S. administration deny a visa to Narendra Modi, the chief minister of Gujarat held responsible for the anti-Muslim violence in that state. Modi had been invited to the country by the Asian American Hotel Owners' Association (an organization dominated by Indian Americans) as the chief guest for the 2005 annual convention.[65]

Most recently, Hindu and South Asian organizations have clashed over a very different issue: the depictions of India and of Hinduism in U.S. school textbooks. Indian American parents have long been concerned about the inaccurate and negative depiction of India in U.S. textbooks. Indian American Internet groups feature frequent discussions about insensitive, ignorant, Eurocentric teachers and classmates and the pain they cause Indian American students. The portrayal of Hinduism in these textbooks has been a particular concern of Hindu American parents. Hindu American mobilization began in the fall of 2004, when the school district in Fairfax, Virginia, put forward a new set of world history textbooks for public review. Hindu American parents, with the support of a Hindu organization, the Vedic Friends Association, mobilized and were relatively successful in making some changes in the way Indian history was taught in their district. One textbook was rejected and eight others were revised.[66] Based on this success, Hindu American groups decided to organize and turn their attention to school textbooks in other regions of the country.

In the summer of 2005, the California State Board of Education opened up its process of textbook review for sixth-grade social studies texts to the public. Two Hindu American groups, the Vedic Foundation (VF) based in Austin, Texas, and the Hindu Education Foundation (HEF), a group composed of members from around the country and from India participated in the textbook review process. The efforts of the VF and the HEF were backed by the Hindu American Foundation (HAF). The VF-HEF combine proposed more than 117 edits to the content on India and Hinduism covered by the textbooks. While some of the edits corrected blatant errors or gratuitous insults, the changes that would become controversial fell into one of three categories. First, material referring to the plurality of deities and beliefs and forms of worship in Hinduism was redacted, and the texts were revised to portray Hinduism as a monotheistic religion based on Vedic texts. Second, the caste system was dissociated from Hinduism, its hereditary nature was not mentioned, and passages describing its oppressive nature were modified. Finally, references to patriarchy or the unequal treatment of women were erased. Ninety-one of these edits were originally accepted by the Curriculum Commission, and these edits were to be presented and ratified at a meeting on November 9, 2005. However, Michael Witzel, professor of Sanskrit and Indian studies at Harvard University was informed about the efforts of the Hindu groups in early November, and on November 8, he sent a letter to the California Board of Education with signatures from forty-six other prominent academics specializing in Indian studies. The letter urged the board to reject the controversial edits proposed by the Hindu groups on the basis that they were "not of a scholarly but of a religious-political nature . . . primarily promoted by Hindutva supporters." Witzel also argued that the same revisions that the Hindu groups were trying to make in California textbooks had been temporarily inserted in textbooks in India when the Indian central government was led by the BJP and had since been removed when that government was voted out of power.

Through a spate of articles on Internet Web sites, discussion groups, newspapers, and magazines both sides—those opposed to the efforts of the VF-HEF-HAF combine and those supportive of these groups—tried to get their views heard by a wider public. Groups that mobilized to oppose the edits of the Hindu groups included South Asian studies scholars, South Asian groups such as FOSA, secular Indian American groups such as the Coalition against Communalism (CAC) and the Campaign to Stop Funding Hate (CSFH), and Dalit groups such as the Ambedkar Center for Justice and Peace and the Guru Ravidass Gurdwaras of California. Articles by members of this side meticulously traced and publicized the links between the Vedic Foundation, Hindu Education Foundation, Hindu American Foundation, and Hindutva groups in the United States and India, and criticized the changes as trying to promulgate an upper caste, male, North Indian, sanitized view of Indian history and deny oppression.[67] Groups supportive of the VF, HEF, and HAF on the other hand, denounced the scholars, secular Indian American and Dalit groups, as "anti-Hindu." They argued that the treatment of Hinduism in the California textbooks did not comply with the standards set by the California State Board of Education and that Hindus were merely demanding that Hinduism be treated with the same consideration and respect as other groups.[68] Several of the pro-Hindu writers pointed out that Jewish, Muslim, and Christian traditions were presented respectfully (and even erroneously), from the point of view of the practitioners of the religion. In contrast, they argued that the treatment of Hinduism in the textbooks was so biased and focused on the negative that it was causing grievous psychological harm to Hindu American children.[69] Members of the California State Board of Education found themselves caught in the cross fire and were placed in the difficult position of having to adjudicate between the two sides, each claiming to represent the Indian American community. After a series of public and private meetings, the California State Board members finally voted to overturn most of the contentious changes proposed by the VF-HEF.

In response, the Hindu American Foundation and an association of Hindu parents in California filed a legal case against the California State Board of Education. In early September 2006, the judge overseeing the case ruled that the challenged texts comply with the applicable legal standards for materials on religious and historical subject matter. However, he also ruled that the California Board had not complied with the regulations governing the textbook approval process and that it needed to prepare more detailed regulations for future textbook adoptions. On the basis of this ruling both sides claimed a victory. South Asian groups opposed to the edits pointed to the fact that the judge had discussed and rejected each of the Hindu groups' substantive challenges to the current texts, while the Hindu American Foundation contended that the court had recognized procedural irregularities in the way the edits proposed by the Hindu groups had been challenged by the South Asian academics.

An Attempt to Forge Unity: The USINPAC

Recognizing that the internal divisions within the community were preventing it from gaining political clout in the United States, a United States–India Political Action Committee (USINPAC), modeled on the highly successful American Israel Public Affairs Committee (AIPAC), was formed in late 2002 to create a "political brand" to represent Indian Americans in Washington. The organization claims that its mission is "to impact policy on issues of concern to the Indian American community." It is particularly interested in targeting members of the India Caucus on the Hill. Besides strengthening U.S.-India relations in defense, trade, and business, the goals of the organization include increasing the numbers of Indian Americans in the government, ensuring that the community is protected from hate crimes and civil discrimination, and advocating for Indian American business and professional groups. The USINPAC seems to be emerging as the key organization representing the Indian American community on Capitol Hill and the White House. But how does it "represent" the Indian American community? How does it balance the often competing demands of Hindu versus pluralist Indian groups and define "issues of concern" to the community?

The organization has been attempting to project itself as moderate and pragmatic and has come under attack from both Hindu and South Asian organizations. For instance, Hindu groups have criticized the organization's support for the candidacy of Bobby Jindal, the first Indian American elected to Congress in the contemporary period, since he converted from Hinduism to Christianity in his teens. They have also attacked the USINPAC for not presenting the Hindu perspective on the 2002 Hindu-Muslim riots in the state of Gujarat and on other sensitive communal issues and for not speaking out against South Asian studies scholars who, they claimed, undermine "brand India" by focusing on the negative aspects. Leftist South Asian groups on the other hand criticized the USINPAC for allying with "Zionist" groups like the AIPAC on an anti-Muslim platform, for not speaking out against the Patriot Act but only asking for Indians to be exempted from the special registration, and for supporting the International Higher Education act of 2003, which they argued is an attempt to create a monitoring committee to control the work of university professors focusing on world affairs, which would negatively impact South Asian studies scholars.[70]

While the organization came under some criticism from Hindu and South Asian groups in the early period of its formation, more recently it seems to be gaining the respect and admiration of the community. It has also received a lot of praise from independent political analysts for its role in successfully lobbying members of Congress to support the historic civilian nuclear deal between India and the United States.[71] The question is whether the community unity apparently forged on the nuclear deal is likely to last, particularly on matters on which the subgroups are deeply divided. On such issues, will one side come to project itself as the voice of the Indian American community, as in the Jewish case, or will the subgroups be able to work out a middle ground from which they can address issues of concern to the community? If the former, which group will this be, and if the latter, what will this middle ground look like?

Conclusion

Most multicultural policies are based on the assumption that there is an "authentic" community voice. As we have seen, however, this can be problematic.

Hindu, South Asian, and national-origin groups such as USINPAC all form under the auspices of multiculturalism, but they each have different agendas. So, which is the authentic voice of Indian Americans? Looking at the way policymakers seem to have responded so far, it does seem as though the arguments of the pluralist coalition often have triumphed over those of the Hindu organizations. This is probably because the Hindu organizations, particularly those that are seen as being allied with extremist anti-Christian groups, have a harder case to make, especially in the contemporary context in which Christian evangelical groups have a lot of political clout. However, in the long run, Hindu groups could start making inroads into the U.S. political system since they are better organized than South Asian groups and have more resources.

We have seen that Hindutva groups as well as many of the anti-Hindutva groups are entering American politics using religion as the basis of solidarity and organizational support. As this article shows, the ethnicization and politicization of religion can lead to a variety of sobering consequences. In the Indian American case it has polarized the community into Hindu versus non-Hindu groups, and Hindu versus secular groups, as well as reinforced tensions between South Asians of different religious backgrounds. Tensions created within the Indian American community due to the efforts of Hindutva and anti-Hindutva groups could spill over to the wider society, as both sides in the conflict are forging alliances with other U.S. groups (such as Jews, larger Muslim and Christian coalitions, and progressive organizations), leading to the development of competing ethnic lobbies and the possible exacerbation of religious tensions within this country.

Both Hindutva and anti-Hindutva groups also use transnational resources and the Internet to mobilize their constituencies. Are their efforts leading to the balkanization of policy as feared by some political scientists, or are they furthering democratic participation as predicted by others? As we have seen in the California textbook case, Indian American groups are pressing for changes in the organization and functioning of U.S. institutions and are therefore raising new problems for policymakers. In the long run, however, it is likely that these challenges will lead to the widening of multiculturalism and democratic participation in the country.

Immigrant diasporic politics will have a decisive impact in shaping the political contours of the United States in the twenty-first century. Such politics challenge conventional understandings of nationhood and citizenship and create dilemmas for multicultural societies trying to institutionalize pluralism. The rise of religion as an important political force further complicates the situation. Indian Americans are a rising political force in this country and a group wherein there is a deep cleavage based on religious identity. This case study of their mobilization patterns provides some hints regarding how religion and panethnicity might interact, when and how supranational and nation-state forms collide, and finally, how globalization, multiculturalism, and new forms of technology shape the goals and methods of contemporary ethnic lobbies.

Notes

1. Tony Smith, *Foreign Attachments: The Power of Ethnic Groups in the Making of American Foreign Policy* (Cambridge, Mass.: Harvard University Press, 2000).
2. Charles M. Mathias Jr., "Ethnic Groups and Foreign Policy," *Foreign Affairs* 59 (Summer 1981): 979.
3. Walter Andersen, "The Indian-American Community Comes into Its Political Own," *India Abroad*, September 1, 2006, A12–13; Michael Forsythe and Veena Trehan, "India's Clout in U.S. Congress Assisted by GE, Boeing, JP Morgan," *Bloomberg*, July 17, 2006; James Lindsay, "Getting Uncle Sam's Ear," *Brookings Review* 20.1 (Winter 2002): 37–40; Mike McIntire, "Indian-Americans Test Their Clout on Atom Pact," *New York Times*, June 5, 2006.
4. Prema A. Kurien, *A Place at the Multicultural Table: The Development of an American Hinduism* (New Brunswick, N.J.: Rutgers University Press, 2007).
5. See Frank D. Bean and Gillian Stevens, *America's Newcomers and the Dynamics of Diversity* (New York: Russell Sage Foundation, 2003); George J. Borjas, *Friends or Strangers: The Impact of Immigrants on the U.S. Economy* (New York: Basic Books, 1990); Diana Eck, *A New Religious America: How a "Christian Country" Has Become the World's Most Religiously Diverse Nation* (New York: HarperCollins, 2001); Charles Hirschman, Josh Dewind, and Philip Kasinitz, eds. *The Handbook of International Migration: The American Experience* (New York: Russell Sage Foundation, 1999); Julian L. Simon, *The Economic Consequences of Immigration* (Cambridge: Blackwell, 1989); Roland Schmidt Sr., *Language Policy and Identity Politics in the United States* (Philadelphia: Temple University Press, 2000); Neil J. Smelser, William Julius Wilson, and Faith Mitchell, eds. *America Becoming: Racial Trends and Their Consequences* (Washington, D.C.: National Academy Press, 2001).
6. Louis DeSipio, *Counting on the Latino Vote: Latinos as a New Electorate* (Charlottesville: University of Virginia Press, 1996); María C. García, *Havana, USA: Cuban Exiles and Cuban Americans in South Florida, 1959–1994* (Berkeley: University of California Press, 1996); Eduardo Guarnizo, "On the Political Participation of Transnational Migrants: Old Practices and New Trends," in *E Pluribus Unum? Contemporary and Historical Perspectives on Immigrant Political Incorporation*, ed. Gary Gerstle and John Mollenkopf (New York: Russell Sage Foundation, 2001), 213–66; Michael Jones-Correa, *Between Two Nations: The Political Predicament of Latinos in New York City* (Ithaca, N.Y.: Cornell University Press, 1998); Karthick S. Ramakrishnan, *Democracy in Immigrant America: Changing Demographics and Political Participation* (Stanford, Calif.: Stanford University Press, 2005); Alex Stepick, Guillermo Grenier, Max Castro, and Marvin Dunn, *This Land Is Our Land: Immigrants and Power in Miami* (Berkeley: University of California Press, 2003).
7. Arjun Appadurai, *Modernity at Large: Cultural Dimensions of Globalization* (Minneapolis: University of Minnesota Press, 1996); Rainer Bauböck, *Transnational Citizenship: Membership and Rights in International Migration* (Aldershot, U.K.: Edward Elgar, 1994); William R. Brubaker, ed., *Immigration and the Politics of Citizenship in Europe and North America* (Lanham, Md.: University Press of America, 1989); Michel S. Laguerre, *Diasporic Citizenship: Haitian Americans in Transnational America* (London: Macmillan, 1998); Yasmin N. Soysal, *The Limits of Citizenship: Migrants and Postnational Membership in Europe* (Chicago: University of Chicago Press, 1994); Steven Vertovec, "Transnational

Challenges to the 'New' Multiculturalism," ESRC Transnational Communities Programme Working Paper, WPTC-01–06, *http://www.transcomm.ox.ac.uk (accessed February 3, 2006).*

8. Samuel Huntington, "The Erosion of American National Interests," *Foreign Affairs* 76.5 (September/October 1997): 28–49; Arthur Schlesinger Jr., *The Disuniting of America* (New York: W. W. Norton, 1992); Smith, *Foreign Attachments,* makes the same argument in a more nuanced way.

9. Michael Clough, "Grass-Roots Policymaking: Say Good-Bye to the 'Wise Men,'" *Foreign Affairs* 73. 1 (January/February 1994): 2–7; Yossi Shain, *Marketing the American Creed Abroad: Diasporas in the U.S. and their Homelands* (Cambridge: Cambridge University Press, 1999).

10. Heather S. Gregg, "Divided They Conquer: The Success of Armenian Ethnic Lobbies in the U.S.," Rosemary Rogers Working Paper Series, No. 13 (Cambridge, Mass.: Massachusetts Institute of Technology, 2002), 10.

11. Daniel J. Elazar, *Decision Making in the American Jewish Community* (Philadelphia: Jewish Studies Group, 1972); David H. Goldberg, *Foreign Policy and Ethnic Interest Groups: American and Canadian Jews Lobby for Israel* (Westport, Conn: Greenwood Press, 1990); I. L. Kenan, *Israel's Defense Line: Her Friends and Foes in Washington* (Buffalo, N.Y.: Prometheus Books, 1981).

12. In regard to alliances formed to common religious affiliation, see José Casanova, *Public Religions in the Modern World* (Chicago: University of Chicago Press, 1994); Yvonne Y. Haddad, ed., *The Muslims of America* (New York: Oxford University Press, 1991); Jane Smith, *Islam in America* (New York: Columbia University Press, 1999); Gerald Sorin, *Tradition Transformed: The Jewish Experience in America* (Baltimore: Johns Hopkins University Press, 1997). For examples of work that focuses on panethnic coalitions based on region of origin, see Yen Le Espiritu, *Asian American Panethnicity: Bridging Institutions and Identities* (Philadelphia: Temple University Press, 1992); Felix M. Padilla, *Latino Ethnic Consciousness: The Case of Mexican Americans and Puerto Ricans in Chicago* (Notre Dame, Ind.: Notre Dame University Press, 1985); Mary C. Waters, *Black Identities: West Indian Immigrant Dreams and American Realities* (New York/Cambridge: Russell Sage Foundation/Harvard University Press, 1999).

13. See Pierrette Hondagneu-Sotelo and Kara Lemma, "Clergy Advocacy for Immigrants: A Comparison of the Sanctuary Movement and Clergy and Laity United for Economic Justice" (paper presented at the American Sociological Association annual meeting, Anaheim, Calif., August 18–21, 2001), who discuss Protestant and Catholic church leaders in Southern California becoming involved in social activism for immigrant rights due to their large Mexican and Central American constituencies, a platform that overlaps with that of Latino coalitions in that region. On the other hand, Arun Kundnani, "An Unholy Alliance? Racism, Religion, and Communalism," *Race and Class* 44.2 (2002): 71–80, writes about Hindu groups in Britain that were mobilizing on the basis of an anti-Islamic platform, which was weakening the Asian coalition in that country.

14. Lindsay, "Getting Uncle Sam's Ear."

15. In 2000, the median household income of foreign-born Indians was $68,500, compared to $53,400 for native-born whites (U.S. census figures). The Indian community registered a growth rate of 105.87 percent between 1990 and 2000 and 38 percent between 2000 and 2005. According to the 2005 American Community Survey of the U.S. Census Bureau, the Indian American population in the United States was 2,319,222.

16. Michael Lind, "The Israeli Lobby," *Prospect,* April 1, 2002.

17. Lindsay, "Getting Uncle Sam's Ear."

18. Sumeet Chhibber, "Indian Americans, Speak Now and Be Heard," *Sulekha.com,* March 31, 2003 (accessed March 31, 2003).

19. Manjeet N. Kripalani, "A New Kind of Indian Power," January 20, 2007, *Los Angeles Times,* archived at the Web site of the Council on Foreign Relations, www.cfr.org/publication/12467/ (accessed March 8, 2007).

20. Thomas Friedman, *The World Is Flat: A Brief History of the Twenty-first Century* (New York: Farrar, Straus and Giroux, 2005).

21. For instance, the Indian American Forum for Political Education (IAFPE) and the Indian American Center for Political Awareness (IACPE) are political education groups. Examples of professional groups are the American Association of Physicians of Indian Origin (AAPI) and Asian American Hotel Owners Association (AAHOA).

22. Nancy Fraser, *Justice Interruptus: Critical Reflections on the "Post Socialist" Condition* (London: Routledge, 1998), 11.

23. See Prema Kurien, "Multiculturalism and Ethnic Nationalism: The Development of an American Hinduism," *Social Problems* 51.3 (2004): 362–85.
24. Stephen R. Warner, "Work in Progress: Toward a New Paradigm for the Sociological Study of Religion in the United States," *American Journal of Sociology* 98 (1993): 1058.
25. See Fenggang Yang and Helen Rose Ebaugh, "Transformations in New Immigrant Religions and their Global Implications," *American Sociological Review* 66 (2001): 269–88.
26. The figure for Hindus in India is based on census reports that count Dalit groups as Hindu. However, many Dalits object to their being included within Hinduism. For more information on the Indian American religious affiliation, see Raymond Williams, *Religions of Immigrants from India and Pakistan: New Threads in the American Tapestry* (Cambridge: Cambridge University Press, 1988), 37; Pyong Gap Min, "Immigrants, Religion and Ethnicity: A Comparison of Korean Christian and Indian Hindu Immigrants," in *Revealing the Sacred in Asian and Pacific America*, ed. Jane Naomi Iwamura and Paul Spickard (New York: Routledge, 2003), 125–43.
27. Tim W. Smith, "Religious Diversity in America: The Emergence of Muslims, Buddhists, Hindus, and Others," *Journal for the Scientific Study of Religion* 41.3 (2002): 581–82.
28. The Harvard Pluralism Project provides two estimates for 2000: 1,285,000 from the 2000 *World Almanac*, and 1,032,000, from the 2000 *Britannica Book of the Year*, www.pluralism.org/resources/statistics/tradition.php (accessed June 30, 2007).
29. There is now some question about whether the Godhra train incident was due to an accident or a mob attack. Some of the independent commissions also seemed to think that the pogrom had been planned earlier.
30. Amy Waldman, "A Secular India or Not? At Strife Scene, Vote Is Test," *New York Times*, December 12, 2002, A18.
31. Prashanth Lakhihal, "Sudershan to Salute Hinduism's Growth," *India Post*, 2001, 59.
32. John Fenton, *Transplanting Religious Traditions: Asian Indians in America* (New York: Praeger, 1988).
33. Sandhya Shukla, "Building Diaspora and Nation: The 1991 'Cultural Festival of India,'" *Cultural Studies* 11.2 (1997): 296–315.
34. Raymond Williams, *Religions of Immigrants from India and Pakistan*, 52.
35. Ibid., 53.
36. Cited in Williams, *Religions of Immigrants from India and Pakistan*, 53.
37. Jean Bacon, *Life Lines: Community, Family, and Assimilation among Asian Indian Immigrants* (New York: Oxford University Press, 1996), 32.
38. "Hindu Federation Launches Bold Effort for Unity," *Hinduism Today*, November 1985, 1, archived at *www.hinduismtoday.com* (accessed November 10, 2005).
39. Arvind Rajagopal, "Hindu Nationalism in the United States: Changing Configurations of Political Practice," *Ethnic and Racial Studies* 23.3 (2000): 474.
40. Arvind Rajagopal, *Politics After Television: Hindu Nationalism and the Reshaping of the Public in India* (Cambridge: Cambridge University Press, 2001), 238–39.
41. Lakhihal, "Sudershan to Salute Hinduism's Growth," 59.
42. Ramesh Rao et al., "A Factual Response to the Hate Attack on the Indian Development and Relief Fund (IDRF)," 2003, *http://www.letindiadevelop.org/thereport/synopsis.html (accessed February 4, 2004)*.
43. See Kurien, *A Place at the Multicultural Table*.
44. Lakhihal, "Sudershan to Salute Hinduism's Growth."
45. Found at http://*www.hinduamericanfoundation.org* (accessed March 3, 2006).
46. For information on Meghani's involvement with the VHPA and HSS, see Rao et al., "A Factual Response," 2. His essay can be found at http://*www.bjp.org/history/htvintro-mm.html* (accessed September 4, 2001).
47. Press release, October 20, 2004, archived at http://*www.hinduamericanfoundation.org (accessed March 25, 2006)*.
48. Espiritu, *Asian American Pan-ethnicity*.
49. Vijay Prashad, "Crafting Solidarities," in *A Part, Yet Apart: South Asians in Asian America*, ed. Lavina Dhingra Shankar and Rajini Srikanth (Philadelphia: Temple University Press, 1998), 107.

50. Nazli Kibria, "The Racial Gap: South Asian American Racial Identity and the Asian American Movement," in *A Part, Yet Apart: South Asians in Asian America*, ed. Lavina Dhingra Shankar and Rajini Srikanth (Philadelphia: Temple University Press, 1998), 69–78; Prashad, "Crafting Solidarities," 114.
51. Prashad, "Crafting Solidarities," 112.
52. Nirav Desai, telephone interview with the author, February 25, 2003.
53. Sarah Wildman, "All for One," *The New Republic*, December 24, 2001, *www.thenewrepublic.com122401/diarist122401.html* (accessed February 18, 2002).
54. See their Web site at http://*www.saalt.org.*
55. See http://www.friendsofsouthasia.org/about (accessed September 2, 2006).
56. "Communalism" is a term used in South Asia to refer to forces that create tensions and conflicts between religious groups. See http://*www.cac.ektaonline.org/about/* (accessed September 2, 2006).
57. See http://*www.imc-usa.org/cgi-bin/cfm/whoweare.cfm* (accessed September 2, 2006).
58. See http://*www.fiacona.org/Press%20Releases/010920 PR_discuss_forming_FIACONA.htm* (accessed September 2, 2006).
59. See http://*www.ambedkar.org/News/hl/PROTESTBY.htm* (accessed September 2, 2006).
60. Gail Omvedt, "Dalits Mobilising," *The Hindu*, May 27, 2003, archived at http://*www.countercurrents.org/dalit-omvedt270503.htm (accessed September 2, 2006).*
61. Prema Kurien, "To Be or Not to Be South Asian: Contemporary Indian American Politics," *Journal of Asian American Studies* (October 2003): 261–88.
62. See, for instance, the article by Rajiv Malhotra, "Problematizing God's Interventions in History," Sulekha.com, March 19, 2003, now posted at *http://rajivmalhotra.sulekha.com/blog/post/2003/03/problematizing-god-s-interventions-in-history.htm*, and the presentation by Swami Dayananda Saraswati at the Global Dharma Conference in Edison, New Jersey, June 2003.
63. See Sabrang Communications, "The Foreign Exchange of Hate: IDRF and the American Funding of Hindutva," http://www.proxsa.org/newsflash/index.html, 2002 (accessed May 12, 2003). An independent study conducted in the United Kingdom came to much the same conclusion about Hindu organizations in that country. (See the report by Jonathan Miller of channel 4 in Britain, http://www.channel4.com/news/homez/stories/20021212/guj/html [accessed December 12, 2002]).
64. Anil Padmanabhan and Ishara Bhasi, "Fund Fracas," *India Today*, March 24, 2003.
65. See *http://www.coalitionagainstgenocide.org/* (accessed April 4, 2006).
66. Maria Glod, "Wiping Stereotypes of India Off the Books," *Washington Post*, April 17, 2005, C17.
67. Indian American Public Education Advisory Council, "Section VI: Timeline of the Hindutva California Textbook Campaign and the Academic/Indian American Community's Response," http://indiantruth.com (accessed February 21, 2006); Sunaina Maira and Raja Swamy, "History Hangama: The California Textbook Debate," *Siliconeer* 7.2 (February 2006), http://siliconeer.com/past_issues/2006/february2006.html (accessed March 2, 2006).
68. Rajiv Malhotra and Vidhi Jhunjhunwala, "Academic Hinduphobia," Outlookindia.com, http://www.outlookindia.com (accessed February 10, 2006).
69. Vishal Agarwal, "California Textbooks Controversy: Politicization of an Academic Issue by Hindu-Haters," India-Forum, http://www.india-forum.com, January 23, 2006; Kalavai Venkat, Kalavai, "The California Textbook Trial," Sulekha.com blogs, December 6, 2005, http://www.sulekha.com/blogs.blogdisplay.aspx?cid=40019 (accessed December 8, 2005).
70. For the Hindu perspective, see comments following the article by Sumeet Chhibber, "Indian Americans, Speak Now and Be Heard," March 31, 2003, w*ww.sulekha.com/expressions/column.asp?cid=305794* (accessed March 31, 2003), and the article by Beloo Mehra, "Political Coming-of-Age for Indian-Americans," June 17, 2003, *www.sulekha.com/column.asp?cid=305830* (accessed June 18, 2003). For the South Asian point of view, see the articles by Zeeshan Farees, "USINPAC: Buying Zionist Influence, Selling Indian Interests," and the editorial by Ra Ravishankar and Shefali Chandra, "Brahminizing the Diaspora," both in *Ghadar*, June 2004, *www.ghadar.insaf.net/June2004 (accessed May 28, 2005).*
71. Andersen, "The Indian-American Community"; Forsythe and Trehan, "India's Clout in U.S. Congress"; McIntire, "Indian-Americans Test Their Clout."

Benjamin Mays, Global Ecumenism, and Local Religious Segregation

Barbara Dianne Savage

In his 1971 memoir, *Born to Rebel*, the religious scholar and educator Benjamin Mays wrote that it would be "a sad commentary on our life and times if a historian writing in the year 2000 can still truthfully say that the most segregated institution in the United States is the 'Church of the Living God.'"[1] A southern black man born in the late nineteenth century, Mays's life spanned the eras of Jim Crow, World Wars I and II, civil rights, and black power. But he did not live to see the millennium or the failure of his own prophecy.

Born in South Carolina in 1894 to tenant farmer parents, Mays made the improbable rise to a distinguished career spent at the administrative helm of two black educational institutions, first, the School of Religion at Howard University during the 1930s, and then, from 1940 to 1967, at Morehouse College. From both positions, Mays became one of the most prominent and influential black theologians, educators, and public intellectuals of the twentieth century.

His own road to a formal education was long and winding, delayed by his family's financial hardship and the racial inequities in southern public education. Eventually, and quite remarkably, at age twenty-six, he graduated with honors from Bates College in 1920, and later, at age forty-one, earned a doctorate in religion from the University of Chicago in 1935, making him one among a small cohort of academically trained black theologians. His was an unusually rich background that included the southern black rural religious world in which he was raised, the Baptist church in which he was ordained, the northern (mostly white) liberal theological institutions in which he thrived as a scholarship student, and the Jim Crow South to which he returned and where he worked for all of his life.

Memories of Mays's stature have been eclipsed by the outpouring of attention to his Morehouse student Martin Luther King Jr., who claimed him as his mentor and whom Mays would later eulogize in 1968. In his own time, Mays was called one of the most powerful black men in America and widely recognized as one of the most important public theologians of the twentieth century.[2] Because Mays, unlike King, was blessed with a long life, his books and articles, his speeches, his sermons, and his political columns span a half century of American history, starting in the 1930s.[3]

Mays's early and eager engagement with global religious organizations provided him with opportunities to travel the world. In this way, Mays's life is more emblematic than it is unusual. Many other prominent politically engaged African American religious intellectuals in the pre–civil rights era came to a concept of global politics in just this way, through travels to and participation in ecumenical world gatherings. For that reason, our understandings of African Americans and international politics also must make way for religious universalism as one route to a compelling critique of colonialism and of the oppression of people of color around the globe.[4]

Earlier in the twentieth century, W. E. B. Du Bois had warned of the weariness of black double consciousness, of seeking to reconcile being both black and American. Would that it were that simple. For Mays, the challenge was far more complicated because he was a southern black religious liberal, an identity described by terms normally held in juxtaposition and rarely joined. In fact he was all of that, as were many other men and women of his region and his race and his faith and his politics.

Perhaps the advantage of a multiple consciousness is a learned aptitude for abiding with irreconcilable contradictions. Mays advocated a church universal, albeit distinctly Christian, that could build a worldwide movement for social justice; at the same time, he understood the innately local nature of religious and racial policy and practice. He argued that Christianity ought to be color blind and desegregated, while at the same time he adhered to a belief in the political necessity of black controlled institutions, especially churches and colleges. Still, Mays did not believe only in the power of the sacred or of private institutions; he coupled that with a faith in an interventionist egalitarian state believing that both church and state were essential to achieving racial equality.

Toward the end of his life, Mays came to understand better that local churches, black and white, served not only as religious sanctuaries but as racial and political ones as well. As a whole, neither blacks nor whites wanted to sacrifice institutions with distinctive cultural, theological, and political natures; born and bred in segregation, each group's churches had grown its own separate way and neither group wanted them to be subsumed in a quest for liberal universalism or color-blind Christianity.

Mays clung to his faith in the possibilities of global religious enterprises, but he repeatedly confronted the difficulty of convincing local religious organizations to embrace the lofty tenets of a church universal and of global ecumenism. Putting those worldviews into local practice proved extremely difficult and often impossible. Indeed, a full half century after the civil rights movement and a decade into the twenty-first century, racially separate Christian churches still dominate today's religious landscape. The reasons for that rest in the complicated history of race, religion, and politics present even before the founding of the Republic, but here presented through the narrative of a politically and religiously engaged black twentieth century life.

*****

Mays's thinking about the hypocrisy of American Christianity was deeply influenced by his travels outside the United States. His tenure as dean of Howard's school of religion from 1934 to 1940 provided him with the opportunity to participate in several international ecumenical conferences where world race relations was a central topic of discussion. He attended the World Conference of the YMCA in Mysore, India, and the Oxford Conference on the Church, Community and State, both held in 1937; he also traveled to Amsterdam for a 1939 conference of 1,500 young Christians from around the world.

What struck Mays as most remarkable about these gatherings was that "members of different races and nations met on a plane of absolute equality" where they could take communion together as Christians and where they imagined themselves to be part of a "universal church that transcends all national, racial or class barriers and cuts across all theological presuppositions." He also repeatedly witnessed vigorous debates on resolutions urging Christian churches to end segregation on the basis of race or color in worship and in more informal fellowship activities. Although the resolutions passed with majority support, they did so only after white delegates from South Africa resolutely offered a spirited theological defense of segregation in both church and state.[5]

Traveling broadened Mays's exposure to issues of color, class, and religion beyond the American example. On his 1937 trip to India, his first of three, he met with Gandhi, whose nonviolent work he had long admired, as did many other black Americans in the late 1920s and 1930s. Leaders and intellectuals as diverse as Du Bois, Marcus Garvey, and A. Philip Randolph embraced Gandhi's anticolonialist and, later, his anticaste positions. African American newspapers and journals across the political spectrum were full of coverage of

Gandhi's life and campaigns in both South Africa and India. The journeys of African Americans to India and the visits from Indians to African American communities also were closely covered.[6]

African American Christians such as Mays were especially drawn to the example of Gandhi's spiritual and political commitments, finding in a Hindu, and apparently without hesitation, a twentieth-century embodiment of the teachings of Jesus. Mays saw Gandhi putting into practice an ethos of love, a commitment to help the most disadvantaged, and a willingness to confront repressive regimes. Mays recast Gandhi and his teachings into Christian terms while accepting and remaining uncritical of his Hinduism. Although he eagerly embraced lessons learned from other faith traditions, Mays's universalist visions were nonetheless firmly framed and ultimately limited by his Christian beliefs.

Mays was but one in a long line of black theologians and religious leaders who made the journey to India. In a ninety-minute meeting with Gandhi, Mays came to better understand that nonviolence was not simply passive resistance but rather was "an active force" and something to "be practiced in absolute love and without hate." In a series of articles that he published upon his return to the United States, Mays argued that African American Christianity was especially compatible with the principles and strategies endorsed by Gandhi.[7]

In his travels through the Middle East on that same trip, Arab Muslims challenged Mays to defend his belief in Christianity in the face of white American Christian hypocrisy and the practices of racial segregation. Mays vividly recounted a conversation on a train from Jerusalem to Cairo with an Arab who criticized American racism and American Christianity's role in it. "When I kept telling him that we were all Christians," Mays explained, "he was bewildered. Finally he said, 'In my religion when once one embraces the faith of Islam, race makes no difference. That is why I cannot understand how you Christians behave as you do towards each other.'" In the end, Mays reported, the man "expressed little faith in our Christianity and little in our democracy" and challenged him to rethink his commitments to both.[8]

Although these early opportunities for international travel were formative factors in Mays's own intellectual, political, and spiritual growth, he also recognized how little authority the world conferences to which he traveled exerted over local beliefs and practices in the United States and elsewhere. The Oxford Conference passed strongly worded resolutions against racial segregation, but Mays knew that churches in South Africa or the United States would not heed that sentiment. That conference also produced an outline for the future establishment of a World Council of Churches in which Mays would later participate.

Despite these developments, Mays felt it was futile to expect that such efforts would advance the cause of justice, peace, and racial equality:

> Nothing we said at Oxford will have any influence on the governments of the world with respect to their armament plans. . . . Nothing we did at Oxford will change Hitler and Germany in their ruthless warfare against the Jews and nothing we did there will destroy Italy's ambition to reestablish the Roman Empire. The communists and fascists in Spain will continue to fight despite what we said at Oxford. Segregation in God's church will continue in America and in South Africa after Oxford.[9]

Mays also connected the issue of racial injustice in the United States with political persecution around the world and called on Christian churches to combat both. "This being true," he wrote, "the persecution of the Jews in Germany and Poland, the complete subjugation and exploitation of the Bantu in South Africa, the disfranchisement and economic prescriptions of Negroes in the United States, the treatment of Aborigines in Australia, the Anglo-Indian problem in India, and the struggle of suppressed peoples everywhere—all these must be the immediate concern of God's Church."[10]

In the end, what did give Mays some hope was his feeling at these ecumenical gatherings that there was "such a thing as a *Universal Church*" that could stretch across national, racial, class, and theological divisions. And, again, he got that feeling from the sheer power of the experience of sharing worship and communion with groups of people from all around the world. This fed his belief in "interracial fellowship" as both a symbol and a practice of a Christian church engaged in common work for the greater good.[11]

★★★★★

The desire and the prospect for interracial fellowship were weak among both blacks and whites in the United States. Mays recognized this even as he put the idea to good rhetorical use in attacks against segregation more generally. While he chastised white churches for closing their doors to black worshippers or explicitly restricting membership to whites, he defended all-black churches and denominations by explaining that they developed only as a necessary response to the exclusionary practices of white Christians. This is a historical vision of the founding of independent black denominations that veers sharply from the more traditional and the more nationalist claims about this development as an act of political defiance.

Mays acknowledged that the proliferation of segregated black churches also was driven by a "growing racial consciousness" and by "the desire of the Negro to manage and direct his own religious activities." He cautioned that even though black churches would never turn away white worshippers, "Negroes themselves would question the motives of white people if they sought in large numbers to join Negro churches." What he called the "dual religious system" was actually a more complicated issue to resolve. This was especially true once one ventured beyond his call for all Christian churches to open their doors to everyone regardless of race, about as limited a version of interracial fellowship as one could imagine.[12]

Despite his own persistence on this issue, Mays was not particularly optimistic about the prospects for interracial fellowship or for a more progressive, politically engaged and unified American Christian community. Two formidable ideas stood in opposition even to the ideal of an interracial fellowship. The first, already touched upon, was the apprehension among both blacks and whites that such a change would eventually eradicate churches predominated by their own race. The second was a stated fear among whites that it would lead inevitably to interracial sex and marriage.[13] When he was asked in 1939 to predict the state of American Christianity in a decade, Mays's most optimistic prediction was that "by 1950 Negroes and white people who want to exercise Christian fellowship will not have to sneak and hide as much as they do now," an unfortunate choice of words for those already afraid that church integration would bring on interracial marriage and sex.[14]

Indeed, even the most "liberal" white Protestants were unwilling to confront the question of interracial marriage at that time. Mays and several other African Americans served as members of committees convened by the Federal Council of Churches in the mid-1940s on race and religion. One of those, the Commission on the Church and Minority Peoples, convened in 1943 with a charge to gather facts about the relations between blacks and whites, between Jews and Gentiles, and between recent immigrants and other Americans. When the commission held a series of regional conferences on race relations, the fear of intermarriage, especially between black men and white women, emerged as the biggest source of tensions and resistance to any change in race relations. This was true for every region and not just the South.[15] The most optimistic conclusion from the commission's meetings was that "it is not necessary to want a man for a brother-in-law before treating him as a brother." For whites, that distinction affirmed a notion of equality while still strictly maintaining marriage and sex prohibitions as if the incest taboo applied to fraternal relations between the races. So it was that the commission urged churches to declare intermarriage "not a sin, but perhaps unwise."[16]

Mays and others proposed report language to strengthen what they perceived as a weak position on the legality of interracial marriage. "In a democratic and Christian society such as we dream of in America," they wrote, "there can be no legal limitation, based on race, creed, or national origin alone, upon free relationships among people." When the council adopted its final commission report on the conferences on race and religion in 1946, it included no mention of the intermarriage issue. All references to it had been marked out by hand in the penultimate draft with the simple notation "eliminate." The final statement merely condemned segregation as "a violation of the gospel of love and human brotherhood" and proposed more study to "work on an unsegregated Church and an unsegregated society."[17]

*****

As part of its midcentury commemorations, the *Pittsburgh Courier* asked Mays in 1950 to assess the progress of black churches over the previous half century and to predict their status at the turn of the next.[18] Sharing in the sense of optimism of the immediate post–World War II period, Mays forecast the next fifty years as "decades of integration." He actually predicted an end to black churches, quite surprisingly something he represented as a sign of progress and a good thing:

> There will be no Negro church in the year 2000 and there will be no white church. There will exist only Christian churches in the year 2000. . . . In the year 2000 the names of all denominations with Negro or colored designations will have been changed. The words "Negro Baptists" will not appear in the Federal Census of Religious Bodies in the year 2006. Nor will the designations CME, AME, and AMEZ. If we become Christian enough, avoid war and survive, racial designation in matters of religion will be history in the year of our Lord 2000.[19]

This 1950 prediction was more than a mere exercise in millennial prophecy, for Mays continued to call for a fully integrated church throughout that decade. In a lecture on the Christian's duty in race relations given at Yale's divinity school in 1952, he broadened the political nature of his appeal and urged all Christian churches to integrate, to support the NAACP, and to instruct its members to disobey unjust laws related to segregation. Although he did not retract his prediction of the inevitability of an integrated church, he did seek to mollify and reassure those who were uneasy with some of the practical consequences of such an outcome. He predicted that "there would be little change in the membership of congregations if racial restrictions were completely removed" but still that "over a relatively long period the racially designated church would disappear, and Christians would cease to think in terms of race or culture."[20]

Mays acknowledged here the reality of the complications that a move toward integrating churches would bring. Although he believed that black congregations on the whole would be more willing to welcome white members than white churches would be accepting of black members, he also knew that many black people also would oppose the full integration of the churches. "Many fear that their leadership would be threatened," he explained, "if the racial church were abolished." But Mays had little patience for that view, concluding that "the Negro church may be just as un-Christian at this point as the white church."[21] Mays seemed most interested in seeing black and white churches united as a way of modeling interracial unity and desegregation, even at the risk of weakening or destroying black churches as independent black institutions.

The notion of a church universal remained a driving force not only in Mays's advocacy of a desegregated American church but also in his early embrace of the movement toward a world council of churches that had evolved out of the 1939 World Conference in Oxford that had made such a profound impression on him. When the First Assembly of the World Council was held in 1948 in Amsterdam, Mays was elected to a five-year term on its Central Committee. When the council convened in the United States in fall 1954 in Evanston, Illinois, Mays was given the honor of delivering an address to counter one given by a representative of the Dutch Reformed Church of South Africa who defended segregation and apartheid as practical necessities defensible within Christian doctrine.[22]

In his rebuttal speech, titled "The Church Amidst Ethnic and Racial Tension," Mays made a case against racial discrimination and segregation within Christian institutions based on a reading of early church history, the Bible, and the findings of modern science. In many ways, this speech expanded upon ideas that Mays had been preaching for decades but which now drew more attention because of his and the council's growing prestige, symbolized by the spectacular pageantry surrounding the event itself. Mays laid out a complex series of connected arguments from the report the council's own working group on race had prepared. He based part of his argument on the fixed nature of the physical characteristics of color and race itself. "Segregation on the basis of color or race is a wicked thing," he said, "because it penalizes a person for being what God had made him and for conditions over which he has no control." But at the same time as Mays relied on notions of immutability, he also argued that modern science had proved that physical markers used to categorize according to "race" did not rest on any deeper biological or human difference. "At long last science has caught up with religion," he teased, "for it was Paul who declared on Mars Hill nineteen centuries ago that God made of one blood all nations of men."[23]

Advancing a line of historical reasoning that presaged theories of race as a construction, Mays told his audience that the racial bar in the church was not something innate to Christianity's early history but was of modern origin. "It was when modern western imperialism began to explore and exploit the colored peoples of Africa, Asia and America," he said, "that the beginning of segregation and discrimination based on color and race was initiated." It was only then, he reported, that color became associated with "inferiority" and whiteness with "superiority." Having said all that, Mays then asked, if no basis existed in the Bible, in church history, and theology, "how can segregation and discrimination in the Church be justified?'" For him, segregation was the great scandal in the church, especially in South Africa and the United States.[24]

The speech moved his World Council audience to interrupt Mays with applause ten times and to give him an extended standing ovation. The talk was reported and reprinted widely, including in pamphlet form; excerpts were broadcast or quoted on local and national radio. Coming as it did only months after the *Brown* decision, his remarks generated considerable attention in this country and abroad. That also meant that some listeners heard or read the speech as yet another radical attempt to move the country too rapidly into a postsegregation world. This surprised Mays because every world assembly since 1928 had condemned segregation and racism through speeches and resolutions. Indeed, the very repetition of that protest, without meaningful change, had led even him to write about the futility of such work.[25]

The fact that this world assembly was held on American soil also made a difference in the reach and reception of its message on race. Some white American listeners objected not just to that message but especially to the race of the messenger. Mays would later recount that he received "more vilifying letters" on account of that speech than from any other in fifty years of public life. One listener took up Mays's immutability argument and twisted it to ask him, "Why can't a Nigger just go on bein' a Nigger like God dun made em, and be happy?"[26] Despite that, Mays judged the meeting to have been a great success, but he resigned himself to the fact that, just as with all the other world assemblies, "the character of the local churches was hardly changed by any of the activities of the conference." Here again the global and the local had collided.

★★★★★

The end to the legal sanction to segregated public education in the *Brown* decision added fire to Mays's arguments against what he called the "voluntary" segregation in religion that he contrasted with secular practices. He argued that it was even more scandalous for Christian churches to maintain their racially exclusive policies, since as completely private institutions they had the freedom both to impose and to lift them.[27] Mays urged churches to open their doors to all as a way of supporting the morality of the Court's edict even though the law did not apply to them.[28] In an article in the liberal Protestant magazine *Christianity and Crisis*, Mays countered scriptural and historical justifications for segregated churches and implored Christian churches to assume a leadership role in the pursuit of racial justice. "If the Churches needed a *legal* basis for doing what the *Gospel has ordered* for nineteen centuries," he wrote, "they have it in the recent decision of the Supreme Court."[29]

The distinction Mays made between the law that governs the state and the law that governs moral relations also points to the difficulty of calling on churches to act as if they were public or political institutions, rather than private and religious ones. Public institutions were subject to legal edict, even if only reluctantly so, but the churches were not. The wall separating the public sphere of law and policy-making and the private sphere of worship and freedom of religious choice was not a porous one, as it stood in part to protect and divide two worlds that were sometimes in conflict, or even when, as in the case of racial segregation, they had been in harmony.

In the decade following the *Brown* decision, Mays defended the continuing existence of private black colleges such as Morehouse College, where he presided. In 1943, Mays had been among the presidents of similar institutions who had formed the United Negro College Fund (UNCF), which dedicated itself to raising the necessary funds to preserve those schools. Like Morehouse, most of the affiliated colleges were in the South and had been founded with religious support.

In 1958, Mays began a three-year term as the president of the UNCF. By then, the really important practical question was why white philanthropists and others should continue to support private black colleges and universities in the face of legal decisions that opened the way, in principle, for black students to seek enrollment in white institutions. Mays and his colleagues in the UNCF had begun even before *Brown* to argue that the best way to protect black colleges from extinction was to make them as good as comparable white institutions, enabling them to compete equally for students.[30] Mays tried to reassure black institutions that they would not perish but would flourish in an integrated society. But he was prescient in his concern that integrating blacks into white higher education would rob historically black colleges of some of their best students and thus deprive those institutions of needed resources.[31] That is the argument that Mays and other supporters of black educational institutions made not only immediately after the *Brown* decision but in the 1960s and 1970s as well.

His predictions about the effect of integration in higher education proved far more accurate than his many prophecies on integrating churches. He reiterated that idea in 1962 as part of a fund drive appeal on behalf of the UNCF. "In fact," he said then, "the prestige colleges and universities in America are not interested in providing a program that would take the most disadvantaged Negro students and prepare them for graduate and professional training. This is our task and if the UNCF colleges do not wrestle with it, nobody else will." Mays warned that "without these colleges thousands of Negro students would never be trained" and the race and the nation also would lose large numbers of "qualified leaders."[32]

Mays made essentially the same argument in 1965. "The white institutions in this country are not greatly concerned about improving the quality of education for all Negroes," he explained. Using a term that Du Bois had coined for other purposes, Mays argued, apparently without irony, that white institutions "are concerned only about the talented tenth."[33] The possibility of ceding the training of the race's leadership class to white institutions disturbed Mays greatly. So too did his growing realization of the practical consequences that any significant move toward interracial churches might bring for black ministers. Mays continued to be concerned about the relatively limited numbers of educated and seminary-trained black clergy, a subject about which he had written and spoken since the 1930s.

Mays now used the specter of church integration to add fire to his arguments for the urgency of increasing the black educated clerical class at the same time that his protégé King emerged as a national figure as a result of the Montgomery bus boycott. In a 1955 column titled "Who Will Preach to Negroes in 1980," Mays combined his concern about the declining numbers of educated black clergy with the fear that as a consequence, educated black Christians might turn to white churches or white ministerial leadership of black churches. Saying that he was not opposed to either on principle, which was consistent with his other public stances, he explained that he would still "like to see Negroes have their share of the ministerial leadership in the desegregated tomorrow." Mays ended with a call for black churches to rid themselves of "an illiterate ministry" and for black religious and educational leaders to unite around a common goal of preparing educated preachers.[34]

In 1959, Mays argued that a demand for highly educated black ministers would "speed up the process of desegregation" by discouraging unenlightened, uneducated black preachers from founding more small or storefront churches. His wish for an educated ministry was often coupled with his continued discomfort with small, mostly holiness and Pentecostal churches. He still harbored his early belief that the leadership and proliferation of those churches were somehow implicated in holding the race back.[35]

To believe, as Mays did, that black churches were essential to black political advancement required a reconciliation with the fact that those local institutions were male led but female dominated in numbers and in financial support. For him, it seems, the gender problem in black churches was not the overwhelming presence of women, but the relative absence of men in the pews and the unpreparedness of the men who assumed the pulpit. Mays longed for an educated black male clerical class that could double as local political leadership and partner with the work of those already dedicated black church women.[36]

In his view, it was not the case that men led and women did not, but rather that leadership was one of the defining characteristics of black masculinity. That sentiment also remains central to Morehouse College's mission. Before, during, and after the era when King, Morehouse's most famous graduate, was providing a heroic example of an educated young black southern religious political leader, Mays was lobbying hard for black men to take up the mantle of leadership. In his mind, well-educated black ministers were needed especially then to preserve and further the gains being made through litigation and changes in the laws of segregation.

Mays's vision of creating a trained black ministry culminated after fifteen years of groundwork with the founding of the Interdenominational Theological Center ("ITC") at Morehouse in 1958. The center brought together under one administrative umbrella four black seminaries affiliated with Methodist, AME, CME, and Baptist denominations, and later added two others linked to the Presbyterian and Church of God in Christ. Here, Mays was able to model his ideas of institutional consolidation and ecumenical cooperation, at least among African Americans. ITC also welcomed both men and women who sought clerical training, subject to denominational practices.[37]

★★★★★

Despite Mays's own growing concerns about the potential consequences of an integrated Christianity on the black ministry itself, he continued to promote interracial and ecumenical alliances throughout this period as he had done over the previous three decades. He felt especially honored to be asked to chair the Conference on Religion and Race held in Chicago in January 1963. A gathering of more than seven hundred religious leaders, the conference marked the first time that Protestant, Catholic, and Jewish religious bodies had gathered for the express purpose of attacking racism in the United States at all levels of society, including within the religious bodies themselves. Writing at the time, Mays hoped then that the consolidation of religious forces could at the very least encourage local communities to accept changes in the law and to "work against racial bias at the local level," including in individual congregations.[38]

There were those at the meeting, however, who were fearful of the broader political consequences of sacrificing black churches at the altar of interracial Christianity or integrated fellowship. Just that complaint was raised by Anna Arnold Hedgeman, a savvy African American political activist with a long record of experience in a variety of religious, women's, labor, and government positions. At the meeting, Hedgeman observed Catholic, Jewish, and Protestant religious leaders speaking about their faiths and moral responsibilities for helping to solve the racial crisis. But she was disturbed that there had been "no presentation of the Negro church," of its achievements and strengths.

Mays spoke at the conference, as did King, who gave the closing address. While Hedgeman praised their oratory, she wanted them to say more. Since Mays was a co-convener of the meeting, it was his speech that most disappointed Hedgeman:

> Dr. Mays could easily have indicated that there would be need for much conversation between Negro and white church leaders, for the only real power the Negro leader has ever had was within his own church. Would the Negro be willing to play a secondary role if churches merge? Could he have confidence in the leadership of the white churches? These questions were not discussed.[39]

Although she had worked for decades in ecumenical work among blacks and whites, including among white women's religious groups, Hedgeman feared that African American churches would be imperiled if they were silently subsumed under the broad political umbrella of "Protestantism." For her the conference was "really the same old story." She issued a press statement to that effect, saying that "again we were the porters of the conference and not really having our great religious experience properly related to the whole thing." Ironically, Hedgeman was soon to be approached by the National Council of Churches, for whom she successfully organized the outpouring of 40,000 white Protestants at the March on Washington.[40]

Mays experienced the year 1963 and the remainder of the decade as many did: a roller-coaster ride of promise, achievement, and trauma. In the months following the meeting on race and religion, Medgar Evers was assassinated in his driveway in Mississippi, the March on Washington was celebrated as a triumph, four little girls died in a church bombing in Birmingham, and John Kennedy met a sniper's bullet in Dallas. At that point, Mays wrote a letter to his former student King in which his grief for Kennedy and his fears for King were palpable: "President Kennedy's death was almost more than I could take. If they hated him, you know they love you less. I hope that you will take every precaution as you move around."[41]

By 1964, Mays had tempered his earlier optimism that American churches might lead in the fight for social justice, as he resigned himself to the notion that there had been a failure of leadership by white American churches in the decade since *Brown*. If local white churches had acted in a moral and religious way, he argued in the *Christian Century*, years of "turmoil and bitterness" would have been avoided: "We might not have had Little Rock, Oxford, New Orleans. Even the sit-ins might have been unnecessary." He saw white churches now doomed to follow rather than to lead in the moves already under way toward desegregation in public arenas. His vision of an integrated church had not faded entirely, however, as he continued to imagine a world of black and white co-pastors and a day when "Negro and white Christians will worship together, sing together, pray together, share each other's joys and sorrows." But he continued throughout this period to chide white churches for their silence on the race question even though "the false god segregation is dead." He began to see churches primarily as private racial sanctuaries held immune from any legal claims from a desegregated secular order. Mays feared as a consequence that "the haven of exclusion will be in God's house."[42]

The end of the 1960s brought little good news or much of anything good that would stir any sense of hope for Mays. This pattern of joy and despair continued in the years that followed with the passage of civil rights legislation, the killing of Malcolm X, and then with the assassinations of first King and then Robert Kennedy in 1968. Mays delivered a eulogy for King at Morehouse, admitting that losing him was like losing a son for the childless Mays. Violent outbreaks in the nation's urban areas marked the summer that followed, including in protests in the streets of Chicago during the Democratic convention. This was also a period of other personal transitions for Mays. After over a quarter century at the helm, Mays retired, in his early seventies, from the presidency at Morehouse in 1967. In 1969, his wife, Sadie, became ill and died after more than four decades of marriage, robbing the couple of the more leisurely pace expected together in his retirement.

The emergence of black power in this period challenged the notions of interracialism that were so much a part of Mays's political and moral philosophy and marked the generational change and the growing chasm that separated Mays from younger, vocal advocates of black nationalism, those on black college campuses like Morehouse, and increasingly, on white college campuses too.[43] Just as King had done, Mays became a vocal opponent of the war and predicted that no military victory was possible there. "But we must get a victory," he explained, "that will wipe out poverty, disease, and ignorance here in the U.S. in urban areas and in the rural areas. If we can spend enough to kill one enemy, we can spend enough to build a society where none will be hungry, none will suffer from malnutrition, and none will be poorly housed." Mays also began in this period to add a strong critique of poverty to his traditional emphasis on racial inequalities.[44]

★★★★★

Mays's views on integration also began to shift in the 1970s as he grew both more skeptical that it would be achieved at all and more concerned about its impact on black communities and black leadership. He began to warn black audiences not to be "swept off their feet by the glamour of an integrated society" and against integrating themselves out of existence. The problem, as he saw it, was that integration means that "you move from black to white and never from white to black" with grave consequences for black institutions, especially educational ones.[45]

His long-standing commitment to education drew Mays back into public life when in 1969 he was elected to the Atlanta school board, and later assumed its presidency.[46] This experience gave Mays a firsthand view of the difficulty of integrating the public schools, even under the duress of court orders directed at state-financed public institutions. He also saw many experienced black teachers, principals, and administrators lose their jobs or be demoted as a consequence of integrating that school system. In an article titled, "Integration Not All Gain," Mays observed that "I have not heard of a single white teacher losing his or her job because of integration."[47] This prompted Mays to ask "did black leadership sleep" in not anticipating the discrimination that would ensure in the process of desegregation itself.[48]

At the same time that he was wrestling with the challenges of the Atlanta school system, Mays became increasingly alarmed by the poverty and despair then facing many black urban communities, as proven through statistical accounts and exposes of black-on-black violence, drug use, joblessness, inadequate health care, and poor housing conditions. "I have a great fear for the future of black people," Mays said at a black ecumenical conference in 1971. "We cry 'Black is Beautiful,' we sloganize 'Black Power,' we go around calling each other 'sister' and 'brother,'" he observed, but warned that "until black people stop killing themselves and stop fighting themselves, the salutations 'sisters' and 'brothers' are sounding brass or tinkling cymbals."[49]

Mays's most pressing concern, however, was black poverty, both in cities and in rural areas. That is what moved him to reassess some of his earlier positions concerning the place of black churches and their role in black communities. He continued to lose faith in white churches, writing in 1971 that "the white church belongs to the powerful ruling majority and it serves for the most part the privileged in our society."[50] More than ever, Mays embraced a service model for black churches in which he called on "affluent black churches" to minister to the needs of the black poor. "If the black church does not wrestle incessantly with, and minister daily to the needs of black people," he wrote, "no other church group will." He called those institutions the "church of the living God" that had to serve first as the "bridge to connect the middle class blacks and the poor blacks" and perhaps also as a "bridge" to affluent white churches that might want to offer assistance. But most emphatically, Mays called on the black middle-class church to "cast its lot more and more with the black poor, the semi-illiterate, the under-employed, the unemployed, those who live on the brink of poverty, the boys and girls who have no father."[51]

This is a move away from his earlier emphasis on a prophetic messianic vision of black churches as savior of American Christianity or as a balm for American political wrongs. Here, Mays endorsed a vision of black churches dedicated to a social services model that in the 1930s he had believed them to be incapable of supporting financially. Now, he directed black churches to help poor black children by adopting schools, setting up dropout programs, and establishing mentoring programs. He had lost faith in the state's commitment to help or to help enough. "If the black church does not do it," he warned, "it will hardly be done."[52]

But even in the post–civil rights period, Mays had not abandoned entirely his vision of a broad role for religious leadership, black and white. "The Negro church is still the most segregated or separate institution Negroes own," Mays wrote in 1968. He then asked but did not answer this question: "Should it remain that way?"[53] He still preached a gospel of racial reconciliation in which Christian churches would take the lead in stabilizing communities where attempts to integrate schools and neighborhoods were met by white flight to the suburbs.

Increasingly, however, Mays saw the need for black religious leadership to try to unite what he saw as deep divisions among black people, both economic and political. He still believed that only the churches could do what most needed to be done: "If the church, Black and White, cannot bring Black and White, the rich and the poor, the educated and the ignorant together as brothers in order to establish a just society for all," he warned, "we are not the church but a series of social clubs."[54] In this way, Mays saw the civil rights movement as a triumph of black church leadership, but evidence of continued white resistance led him to conclude that ultimately it also bore witness to a failure of white religious leadership. "For the most part," he concluded, "the churches were conspicuous by their absence in speech or action."[55]

The central problem, which Mays had acknowledged after his attendance at World Council meetings, was that religious institutions are among the most local of organizations. If they were to act as moral and political agents, then that had to happen locally at the congregational level, where community intervention was most needed and most effective. Even as national religious organizations had endorsed an end to segregation, without local follow-up and commitment, that sentiment rang hollow. "It is at the local level," Mays observed in 1974, "where implementation of the Gospel of Christ is most difficult." By then, he was urging all local churches to join an even broader fight against war, poverty, and racism.[56] Evidence of local resistance was not hard to come by. His friend and fellow Georgian Jimmy Carter had worked since 1955 to get his own church to delete a color bar to membership from its policies; in 1976, as president-elect of the United States, Carter led the fight again, and this time prevailed, with his congregation voting to abandon the exclusion of anyone from worship or membership based on race, but not without considerable dissent in a vote of 120 to 66. Mays praised Carter but concluded by observing that "the churches in the United States are still the most segregated spot on Sunday at 11 o'clock in the morning."[57]

★★★★★

A few years before his death in 1983, Mays published an article revisiting his experiences at the international conferences he had written about so eloquently four decades earlier. In his search for evidence of progress in uniting black and white churches during the intervening years, Mays claimed that, unlike in 1939, no white church would then refuse entry to a black worshipper. But he also admitted that "so far as integrating the churches by merging them, I see no chance of that taking place in the twentieth century." This was an acknowledgment of the failure of his earlier predictions; he blamed institutional resistance from both black and white church bodies for the continued existence of segregated churches.[58]

At the same time that Mays bemoaned the lack of progress in integrating the churches, he lavished praise on black colleges and universities, stressing their importance in training black leaders and strengthening black communities. Mays ended his article with the hope that by the middle of the twenty-first century the country would have moved "further along the road to a truly democratic America."[59] But he made no new prediction about the integration of black or white churches or about their potential for uniting in the arena of race relations.

The keenest irony, of course, is that the end of legalized segregation had the least immediate effect on the racially segregated sector of society that Mays cared about the most: churches. Other institutions, including black newspapers, black colleges, black schools, black small businesses, were disadvantaged or destroyed by the forces surrounding the drive toward desegregation. In some cases, state intervention played a key role, as with the schools, and in others, as with the press and businesses, market forces caused major losses. Because they are voluntary, private, nonprofits, churches were immune to market forces and legal edict. By their very natures, as culturally and politically specific entities and the most local of community-based institutions, they lend themselves to independent, idiosyncratic self-perpetuation from generation to generation.

In the post–civil rights era, the growth of a new, larger, and more stable black middle and professional class did bring new financial resources to many urban churches. That growth and financial stability have enabled some of those churches today to better meet the social service needs of black communities. Black megachurches, whose origins Mays traced back to the black urbanization of the great migration, have proliferated and now include those in cities and in suburbs and those that embrace a prosperity gospel rather than the social gospel. Regardless of their size or theological orientation, however, their ever increasing numbers is at odds with Mays's predictions of the disappearance of black churches into an integrated Christianity by the year 2000. One consistency, however, is the dearth of other black institutions, preserving local churches as unrivaled community and political resources now as in the 1930s.

Mays lived out the complexities of being a southern black liberal Protestant who believed that black and white churches should function as progressive political agents, resting on the moral foundation of global Christian universalism and an enduring faith in the institution of American democracy. His repeated use of the prophetic form was more than a rhetorical device. It reflected a broadly "American" faith in progress, the specific hope for progress in race relations, and a messianic way of seeing human history that was rooted in his Christian faith. In his vision, claiming a central, crucial role for black institutions, black religious leaders, and black religious discourse, he addressed these linked issues in politically and philosophically astute ways. Yet in his lifetime and in ours, the continued existence of the "race church," whether black or white, remains a fact of American life. As well, the search for a progressive politics of religious globalism remains as elusive today as during his long life.

Notes

1. Benjamin Mays, *Born to Rebel: An Autobiography* (Athens: University of Georgia Press, 1971), 264.
2. *Walking Integrity: Benjamin Elijah Mays, Mentor to Martin Luther King Jr.*, ed. Lawrence Edward Carter Sr. (Macon, Ga.: Mercer University Press, 1998), 5, 19. On Mays's intellectual influences, see, Randal M. Jelks, "Mays's Academic Formation, 1917–1936," in *Walking Integrity*, 111–29.
3. Mays' embrace of both social science methodology and liberal theology was reflected in two seminal books in black religious studies, the first a 1933 national social scientific study of black churches, which he coauthored, and the second, his 1934 dissertation-based study of black religious thought based on a large body of black literature, sermons, and songs. Benjamin E. Mays and Joseph Nicholson, *The Negro's Church* (New York: Institute of Social and Religious Research, 1933; reprint, Ayer Company, 1988); Benjamin Mays, *The Negro's God as Reflected in His Literature* (New York: Atheneum, 1938; reprint, Greenwood Press, 1969). In addition to those and his autobiography, Mays also wrote *Seeking to Be Christian in Race Relations* (New York: Friendship Press, 1957), and *Lord, the People Have Driven Me On* (New York: Vantage Press, 1981), and edited *A Gospel for the Social Awakening: Selections from the Writings of Walter Rauschenbusch* (New York: Association Press, 1950). His published writings also include newspaper columns and magazine articles, including nearly 1,600 weekly columns for the national edition of the *Pittsburgh Courier* between 1946 and 1981. His records at Howard University's

Moorland Spingarn Research Center (referred to hereafter as "Mays Papers") also include more than eight hundred unpublished addresses, lectures, and sermons, as well as an extensive correspondence collection spanning his long public life. Carter, *Walking Integrity*, 425.

4. Religion is a paradoxical but particularly promising and understudied route for examining global orientations among African Americans, including conceptions and constructions of diaspora. See, for examples, R. Marie Griffith and Barbara Dianne Savage, eds., *Women and Religion in the African Diaspora: Knowledge, Power, and Performance* (Baltimore: Johns Hopkins University Press, 2006), and James T. Campbell, *Songs of Zion: The African Methodist Episcopal Church in the United States and South* (New York: Oxford University Press, 1995). Scholars have given considerable attention to the global outlook of African American intellectuals and activists in the twentieth century, especially in its embrace of Africa and anticolonialism. See, for example, Robin D. G. Kelley, "'But a Local Phase of a World Problem': Black History's Global Vision, 1883–1950," *Journal of American History* 86 (December 1999): 1045–77, Brenda Gayle Plummer, *Rising Wind: Black Americans and U. S. Foreign Affairs, 1935–1960* (Chapel Hill: University of North Carolina Press, 1996); James H. Merriweather, *Proudly We Can Be Africans: Black Americans and Africa, 1935–1965* (Chapel Hill: University of North Carolina Press, 2002); Melani McAlister, *Epic Encounters: Culture, Media, and United States' Interests in the Middle East, 1945–2000* (Berkeley: University of California Press, 2001); Carol Anderson, *Eyes Off the Prize: The United Nations and the African American Struggle for Human Rights, 1944–1955* (New York: Cambridge University Press, 2003).

5. Benjamin Mays: *Born to Rebel*, 157–62, 165–67; "The Church Surveys World Problems," *The Crisis* 44.10 (October 1937): 299, 317; and "World Churchmen Score Prejudice," *The Crisis* 44.11 (November 1937): 341.

6. Mays, "The Color Line Around the World," *Journal of Negro Education* 6.2 (April 1937): 134–43. Sudarshan Kapur, *Raising Up a Prophet: The African-American Encounter with Gandhi* (Boston: Beacon Press, 1992), 3–8, 13, 26–27. On the theological and political significance of traveling to India for African American religious intellectuals, see Dennis Dickerson, "African American Religious Intellectuals and the Theological Foundations of the Civil Rights Movement, 1930–55," *Church History* 74.2 (June 2005): 217–35.

7. Kapur, "Raising Up a Prophet," 81–82, 87–93, 95–97; Mays, *Born to Rebel*, 155–56.

8. Mays, "The Eyes of the World Are Upon America," *Missions* 35.2 (February 1944): 74–79.

9. Mays, "The Church Surveys World Problems," 299, 316, 317; and "World Churchmen Score Prejudice," 341.

10. Benjamin Mays, "Amsterdam on the Church and Race Relations," *Religion in Life: A Christian Quarterly* 9.1 (Winter 1940): 102.

11. Mays, "The Church Surveys World Problems," 316.

12. Benjamin Mays, "The American Negro and the Christian Religion," *Journal of Negro Education* 8.3 (July 1939): 532, 533.

13. Benjamin Mays: "Christian Youth and Race," *The Crisis* 46.12 (December 1939): 365, 370; and "The American Negro," 537.

14. Mays, "The American Negro," 537–38.

15. See Minutes, The Commission on the Church and Minority Peoples, September 16, 1943. Accounts of individual meetings include: Consultations on the Church and Minority Peoples, St. Paul, Minnesota, March 10, 1944; Conference on the Church and Minority Peoples, Seattle, Washington, March 14, 1944; Consultations on the Church and Minority Peoples, Los Angeles, California, March 20, 1944; Minutes, The Commission on the Church and Minority Peoples, April 21, 1944, and May 8–10, 1945, National Council of Churches Records, Presbyterian Historical Society, Philadelphia.

16. The two quotations are from Minutes, Commission on the Church and Minority Peoples, September 16, 1943, and Consultations on the Church and Minority Peoples, Los Angeles, March 20, 1944, respectively, National Council of Churches Records, Presbyterian Historical Society.

17. Memorandum on Community Tensions: The Church and Race, Special Meeting, Federal Council of Churches of Christ in America, March 5–6–7, 1946, Columbus, Ohio, 6–7; The Church and Race Relations, An Official Statement, approved by the Federal Council of Churches of Christ in America at a Special Meeting, Columbus, Ohio, National Council of Churches Records, Presbyterian Historical Society; George Edmund Haynes, "Along the Interracial Front," "Pull Down Barriers! Vote Three National Bodies," press release, Department of Race Relations, Federal Council of Churches, March 29, 1946, National Council of Churches Records, Presbyterian Historical Society.

18. Benjamin Mays, "Fifty Years of Progress in the Negro Church—Tremendous Gains Since 1900—Full Integration in All Churches Seen in 50 Years," *Pittsburgh Courier*, 1950, Mays Papers.
19. Ibid.
20. Benjamin Mays, "The Christian in Race Relations," Henry B. Wright Lectures, Yale University Divinity School, April 16, 1952, 3.
21. Mays, "The Christian in Race Relations," 4.
22. Letter from W. A. Visser 't Hooft, World Council of Churches, to Mays, December 16, 1953, Mays Papers.
23. Benjamin Mays, "The Church Amidst Ethnic and Racial Tensions," speech to the Second Assembly of the World Council of Churches, August 21, 1954, Mays Papers.
24. Ibid.
25. Mays, *Born to Rebel*, 260–61.
26. Ibid., 261.
27. Benjamin Mays: "The Quicker We Clear Up the Racial Mess in U.S.A., the Better It Will Be for the World," *Pittsburgh Courier*, March 7, 1953; and "In Order to Save Its Own Soul, the Church Must End All Forms of Segregation in Worship," *Pittsburgh Courier*, February 28, 1953.
28. Benjamin Mays: "Challenge to the Churches Issued by U. S. Supreme Court Decision," *Pittsburgh Courier*, July 10, 1954; "Will Churches Meet the Challenge Offered Them by the High Court," *Pittsburgh Courier*, July 24, 1954; and "We Serve Other Gods," *Pittsburgh Courier*, February 26, 1955.
29. Benjamin Mays, "The Church Will Be Challenged at Evanston," *Christianity and Crisis* 14.14, August 9, 1954, 108.
30. Benjamin Mays: "Women's Division of United Negro College Fund," speech, April 11, 1950; and UNCF dinner speech, Philadelphia, May 7, 1952, Mays Papers.
31. Benjamin Mays: "He Doesn't Believe Negro Institutions Will Perish in an Integrated Society," *Pittsburgh Courier*, July 17, 1954; "College for Negroes in a Segregated Society," speech, February 20, 1955; "The Past, Present, and Future of the Thirty-One Colleges That Make Up the United Negro College Fund," speech, April 5, 1956; address delivered before the Inter-Alumni Council, Detroit, June 18, 1957; "Why Support the United Negro College Fund," speech, Buffalo, May 7, 1958; and address to the United Negro College Fund, Cleveland, April 22, 1959, Mays Papers.
32. Benjamin Mays: "Why Do We Come?" UNCF Capital Fund Drive, October 1962; and "The Future Role of the Private Negro College," speech given at Morehouse College, April 28, 1961, Mays Papers.
33. Benjamin Mays, "The Second Hurdle," *Pittsburgh Courier*, April 24, 1965, Mays Papers.
34. Benjamin Mays, "Who Will Preach to Negroes in 1980?" *Pittsburgh Courier*, May 23, 1955.
35. Benjamin Mays, "The Negro in Christian Ministry," speech given in Greenwich, Connecticut, March 6, 1959, 11–12, Mays Papers. Mays was not alone in this view, which was common among African American critics of black churches, including Carter G. Woodson and E. Franklin Frazier, both of whom wrote foundational texts in African American religious studies: Woodson, *The History of the Negro Church* (Washington: Associated Negro Press, 1921), and Frazier, *The Negro Church in America* (New York: Schocken Books, 1964). On Woodson, see Barbara Savage, "Carter G. Woodson and the Struggle for a 'United Black Church,'" *A. M. E. Church Review* (Fall 2000): 13–20.
36. On the role of women in the National Baptist Convention, see Evelyn Higginbotham's pioneering *Righteous Discontent: The Women's Movement in the Black Baptist Church, 1880–1920* (Cambridge, Mass.: Harvard University Press, 1993). On black women and the varieties of their religious activism, see Judith Weisenfeld, *African American Women and Christian Activism, New York's Black YWCA, 1905–1945* (Cambridge, Mass.: Harvard University Press, 1997); Judith Weisenfeld and Richard Newman, eds., *This Far by Faith: Readings in African American Religious Biography* (New York: Routledge, 1996). For astute analyses of gender relations in churches with female preachers, see Wallace Best, "'The Spirit of the Holy Ghost Is a Male Spirit': African American Preaching Women and the Paradoxes of Gender," in *Women and Religion*, ed. Griffith and Savage, 101–27; and Wallace Best, *Passionately Human, No Less Divine: Religion and Culture in Black Chicago, 1915–1952* (Princeton, N.J.: Princeton University Press, 2005).
37. Mays, *Born to Rebel*, 234–40. On religious women as activists, see Cheryl Townsend Gilkes, "Exploring the Religious Connection: Black Women, Community Workers, Religious Agency, and the Force of Faith," in *Women and Religion*, ed. Griffith and Savage, 179–98.

38. Benjamin Mays, "My View: The National Conference on Religion and Race," *Pittsburgh Courier*, February 2, 1963.

39. Anna Arnold Hedgeman, *The Trumpet Sounds: A Memoir of Negro Leadership* (New York: Holt, Rinehart, 1964), 175–77. Mark Chapman, *Christianity on Trial: African American Religious Thought Before and After Black Power* (Maryknoll, N.Y.: Orbis Books, 1996), 139–41. For more on the meeting, see Mathew H. Altmann, *Race: Challenges to Religion, Original Essays and An Appeal to the Conscience* (Chicago: H. Regnery, 1963).

40. "Negro Clergy and Laymen Active in All Phases of Historic Conference on Race and Religion," ANP release, January 23, 1963; Anna Hedgeman interview, 179–81, Black Women's Oral History Project interviews, Schlesinger Library, Radcliffe College, Harvard University; Civil Rights Documentation Project, interview with Anna Arnold Hedgeman, July 25, 1967, and August 28–29, 1968, Moorland Spingarn Research Center, Howard University.

41. Freddie Colson, "Mays as Mentor to King," in *Walking Integrity*, ed. Carter, 209.

42. Benjamin Mays: "Let the Pastors Declare Themselves," *Pittsburgh Courier*, June 1, 1963; "The Church Should Have a Policy," *Pittsburgh Courier*, June 8, 1963; "And God Was Embarrassed," *Pittsburgh Courier*, May 18, 1963; "And They Call It Christian," *Pittsburgh Courier*, November 23, 1963; "Southern Ministers Get Another Chance," *Pittsburgh Courier*, March 7, 1964; "The Churches Will Follow," *Christian Century*, April 22, 1964, 514; "Will the Churches Be the Last," *Pittsburgh Courier*, January 1, 1965; and "Why the Churches Will Be the Last," *Pittsburgh Courier*, September 18, 1965.

43. Benjamin Mays: "Prisoner in Harkness Hall," *Pittsburgh Courier*, May 3, 1969; "Where Are the Answers," *Pittsburgh Courier*, December 14, 1968; "Black Dorms No Solution," *Pittsburgh Courier*, March 22, 1969; "Black Students—Helping? Hurting?" *Pittsburgh Courier*, May 17, 1969; and "Killing Black Colleges," *Pittsburgh Courier*, June 13, 1970, Mays Papers.

44. Benjamin Mays, "White Power vs. Black Power," speech, n.d., Mays Papers.

45. Benjamin Mays, "Let Us Not Ingrate or Segregate Ourselves Out of Existence," speech given at Grambling College, November 13, 1968; and "Integration Not All Gain," *Pittsburgh Courier*, July 5, 1969.

46. Benjamin Mays, "Man in a New Job," *Pittsburgh Courier*, January 24, 1970.

47. Mays, "Integration Not All Gain."

48. Mays, "Are Black Teaching Jobs Lost for Good," *Pittsburgh Courier*, July 8, 1972.

49. Benjamin Mays, "The Black Man's Environment and His Minority Status: A Challenge to the Black Church," speech given to the Black Ecumenical Commission, Boston, July 30, 1971, Mays Papers.

50. Ibid. Du Bois had held this view in the 1930s but extended it to all churches, both black and white. For more on Du Bois's views on churches, see Barbara Savage, "W. E. B. Du Bois and 'the Negro Church,'" *The Annals of the American Academy of Political and Social Science* 568.1 (March 2000): 235–49. On debates about the public role of black churches, see Barbara Savage, "Biblical and Historical Imperatives: Toward a History of Ideas About the Political Role of Black Churches," in *African Americans and the Bible*, ed. Vincent Wimbush (New York: Continuum, 2000).

51. Mays, "The Black Man's Environment and His Minority Status."

52. Benjamin Mays, "The Church and the Development of Black Leadership in America," speech given February 20, 1978, Conference on Blacks and Religion, University of Tennessee, Knoxville, Tennessee, Mays Papers.

53. Mays, "Where Are the Answers."

54. Benjamin Mays, "The Urgent Need of Reconciliation in Today's World: A Challenge to the Church," *Criterion* 11.3 (Spring 1972): 11–12.

55. Benjamin Mays, "The Church: New Challenges for Survival," *Tuesday Magazine* 9.2 (February 1974), 15 (*Tuesday Magazine* was a monthly magazine carried as an insert in major national newspapers, with a combined circulation of 2.3 million), Mays Papers.

56. Mays, "The Church: New Challenges for Survival," 13.

57. Benjamin Mays, "Church Integrated?" *Pittsburgh Courier*, December 4, 1976.

58. Benjamin Mays, "Progress and Prospects in American Race Relations," *Journal of Ecumenical Studies* 16.1 (Winter 1979): 128, 132.

59. Ibid.

Impossible Assimilations, American Liberalism, and Jewish Difference: Revisiting Jewish Secularism

Laura Levitt

To remain marked as other even in the process of becoming citizens, of becoming incorporated into the nation, still haunts contemporary Jewish experience as well as efforts to explain Jewish difference. Although it may be said that the French and American revolutions brought Jews into the dominant cultures of the West, they also set limits on this very promise of inclusion.[1] In this essay I am interested in these limits as they have been enacted and reenacted in the United States, especially after the mass migration of Eastern European Jews to this country at the turn of the last century.[2] I am concerned about the ways tolerance works to both regulate and maintain a deep ambivalence around Jews, Jewishness, and Judaism in U.S. society, even in the present.

Writing about Jewish difference and the legacy of Jewish emancipation in Western Europe, political theorist Wendy Brown explains that

> to be brought into the nation, Jews had to be made to fit, and for that they needed to be transformed, cleaned-up, and normalized, even as they were still marked as Jews. These triple forces of recognition, remaking and marking—of emancipation, assimilation, and subjection; of decorporatization as Jews, incorporation as nation-state citizens, and identification as different—are what characterize the relation of the state to Jews in nineteenth-century Europe and constitute the tacit regime of tolerance governing Jewish emancipation.[3]

The regime of tolerance Brown describes, with its contradictory appeals and desires, aptly captures the ambivalent position of Jews in the United States. Working against this use of tolerance, I want to think about the ways Jews do not fit into the now long accepted litany of differences—race, class, gender, sexuality—as well as how the presumed "whiteness" of some Jews has served to make invisible the ways Jewish difference continues to make a difference in how Jews figure in U.S. culture. And, coupled with this, I want to call attention to what has been the most acceptable form of Jewish difference,

Jewishness defined as religious difference. This way of marking Jews as the same but different, the notion that they simply go to a different "church" has itself come to mark Jews who oddly enough do not define their Jewishness in these religious terms.

Alongside this problem, I am also interested in how this vision of acceptable Jewish difference as religious difference, a kind of community of faith, also differs from the ways many observant Jews understand themselves as followers of Jewish law who may or may not attend synagogue services. By retracing the legacy of Jewish emancipation in the West alongside a legacy of Jewish enlightenment and modernity as experienced in Eastern Europe and then seeing what happened as these two distinct visions of Jewish modernity came into conflict in the United States in the early twentieth century under the umbrella of the liberal inclusion Brown describes, I want to challenge the vision of tolerance offered in the West. I do this by showing how this vision of inclusion had no place for Eastern European Jewish secularism, the legacy of Yiddish secularism that characterized the Jewishness of so many of these immigrant Jews. I use this case to reconsider the legacy of liberal inclusion for Jews and what it might mean for there to be a place for secular Jews in the United States.

I return to this cultural legacy because it remains the inheritance of the vast majority of U.S. Jews. By retelling the story of Eastern European Jews coming to the United States at the turn of the last century, I want to show a more complicated legacy of impossible assimilation as a clash between different modern configurations of Jewishness. In other words, the legacy of Jewish emancipation and enlightenment in the West—inclusion on the basis of religious pluralism—and the traditions of worldly Eastern European Jewish enlightenment were set in conflict as Eastern European Jews struggled to figure out what it was going to mean for them to become Americans at the turn of the twentieth century.

By returning to the problem of Jewish assimilation in this way I ask, at what cost have Jews been accepted into the dominant culture of America? What has it meant for especially Eastern European Jews to refashion their Jewishness to fit into American middle-class Protestant culture? Part of what I will argue is that in order to be accepted as citizens of liberal nation-states such as the United States, Jews had to conform to the norms of this culture, remaking themselves and their Jewishness into something familiar. They were to become a version of the same with a minor difference. And yet, as Brown argues, this process has within it an inherent contradiction. It both promises acceptance and effaces this same promise.[4] In other words, liberal assimilation produces a subject who is almost but not quite dominant. The harder this subject tries to fit in, ironically, the more s/he differs. Instead of sameness, these efforts produce an excess that always marks this subject as other. In the case of Jewish assimilation, the not quite dominant status of Jews can be seen in the ways so many continue to identify as Jewish but not as religious. As I have argued elsewhere, liberal assimilation is always haunted by its partial production of versions of the same. The harder U.S. Jews try to fit in, the more they end up demonstrating their Jewish difference. Hence, the joke: Jews are just like everybody else only more so. By looking more closely at the impossibility of liberal inclusion, like Brown, I want to imagine other forms of social inclusion that need not rely on merely tolerating difference.

By taking seriously the ongoing effects of and the necessarily incomplete character of the assimilation of Eastern European Jews into American culture at the beginning of the twentieth century alongside the not quite assimilation of an earlier generation of Western European Jews into the dominant culture of Protestant America, I hope to shed new light on the contradictions that continue to haunt contemporary U.S. Jewish life. To this end, in what follows I offer a somewhat schematized account of the differing eastern and western legacies of Jewish enlightenment and modernization that came into conflict in the early part of the twentieth century in the United States. I will then return to the archives to look specifically at the legacy of Yiddish Jewish secularism. By offering a reading of some of the arguments posed by the last of the Yiddish secular thinkers, ironically in the pages of the English language journal *Judaism: A Quarterly of Jewish Life and Thought*, a publication founded in 1952 with the explicit goal of reviving Jewish religious thought, I will challenge the liberal presumption that Jewish identity must be understood as a form of private faith.[5] Using some of the challenges these Yiddish thinkers posed to precisely these liberal American cultural presumptions in the first half of the twentieth century, I ask readers to reconsider what it might mean to claim a more complicated and decidedly less Protestant Jewish position in the present. Because these thinkers explicitly refused to adhere to precisely these Protestant religious norms, even as their movement was coming to an end, their arguments remain relevant.

As they make clear, *religion*, *race*, *class*, and even *ethnicity* have never been able to fully or accurately describe what it means to be a Jew in the United States.[6] The containment of Jewish difference within such narrow categories as required by liberal pluralism is no longer viable. By having to pin down what, in essence, is most salient about Jewish difference, other, often crucial, pieces of Jewishness drop out. Jewishness is cultural and ethnic and religious in many but not all instances. Jewishness exceeds notions of ethnicity because there are multiple Jewish ethnicities and because it can include forms of religious expression beyond privatized faith. Thus, in order to appreciate what it means to claim a Jewish position, a Jewish identity, the common rubrics of liberal pluralist difference—race, class, and gender and/or sexuality—just do not fit, nor does the overarching notion of religion, although that has been the most salient and acceptable form of claiming Jewish difference in the United States.

Social Amelioration, or Religion as the Means to Emancipation

> The Jewish communities, during the stormy struggle for emancipation and enlightenment in the nineteenth century, achieved adjustment to the general social order on the primary basis of religious tolerance. . . . The Synagogue was, accordingly, the primary instrument of adjustment to modern life, and acknowledged as the center of Jewish loyalty and identification.
> —Herbert Parzen, 1959

In 1959 in the pages of *Judaism*, Herbert Parzen, a Conservative rabbi and, at the time, a contributor to numerous Anglo-Jewish periodicals, notes the crucial role of religious tolerance and the centrality of the synagogue to Jewish emancipation in Western Europe.[7] He uses this account to draw a sharp contrast between East and West and in so doing follows closely Jewish historian Paula Hyman's account of what it meant for Western Jews to enter into the dominant cultures of Western liberal nation-states. As she explains,

> The entry of Jews into the general body politic and the transformation of the Jewish community from a self-governing corporate body with police powers to a voluntary religious association challenged the very nature of Jewish self-understanding. Increasingly, Jews were seen, and defined themselves, as adherents of a religious faith rather than as members of a religio-ethnic polity, a people-faith. Their rabbis became religious functionaries—preachers and spiritual counselors—rather than judges and interpreters of the law.[8]

I open this discussion with these accounts of the transformation wrought by Jewish emancipation as a way of making clear the material and social implications of what it meant for Jews to become citizens of Western nation-states. These Jews not only pledged allegiance to these states in order to take on the rights and responsibilities of citizenship, but they also gave up a great deal in this process. Prior to emancipation, Jews were, as Hyman indicates, a "self-governing corporate body." Jewish communal authorities had both police and judicial powers. Emancipation, or more precisely, using the language of the late eighteenth century, "civic amelioration," meant that the political and social integration of the Jews into Western culture came at a price.[9] Not only did Jews lose their communal autonomy; they were also required to re-create themselves as Jews. They made Jewish communal life into a voluntary religious association, something completely at odds with what had been a traditional Jewish self-understanding.[10] What is striking in this regard is even the historian's difficulty in pinpointing this loss. What was it that the Jews had been before emancipation? Hyman herself struggles to find words adequate to explain this Jewish self-understanding. In her text the difficulty is signified by her use of the hyphenated terms "religio-ethnic polity" and "people-faith."

The process of political emancipation in the West in effect re-created Judaism as a religion. It used familiar categories of faith to assure that this people within a people would not be a threat to their new nation-states. Even so, the Jews had to find a way to still be recognized as a communal entity. Religion as a voluntary commitment of faith and communal practice enabled Western European Jews to maintain their commitment to an ongoing Jewish communal life without remaining a separate self-governing corporate body. In other words, what religion offered to Jews in the liberal West was a Protestant version of religious community that they could apply to themselves as Jews. Given this, one of the lasting legacies of political emancipation in the West was the formation of Jewish religious denominations as we now know them. Since affiliation was a matter of choice facilitated by capital (like the term *denomination* itself, from *denominate*, "to issue of, express in terms of a given monetary unity"), these Jewish communities produced a variety of congregational options that allowed for certain differences among Jews while also reinforcing the notion that what links all Jews is a common faith.[11] As Hyman notes:

> This transformation of Judaism and the Jewish community facilitated the emergence of denominations within Judaism, particularly in America, where the voluntary nature of the Jewish community was most fully realized. Any group of Jews who could muster the requisite financial and human resources to establish a synagogue, school, or journal were free to do so and thereby to disseminate their conception of Judaism.[12]

Although political emancipation was the product of the age of reason, the end of the rule of religion, for Jews in the West, this version of the rule of reason brought with it, ironically, a reaffirmation of religion, and specifically of religion as a kind of faith. For Jews to become enlightened as Jews was to remake Jewishness into a matter of individual faith. As I have already suggested, the problem was that Jewishness never fit easily into Western notions of religion as simply a matter of individual faith.

This lack of fit was not simply because the presumed category of religion was Christian, but also because it was an enlightenment construct. As Robert J. Baird and others have argued, "religion" as a category was produced by the enlightenment. It was built on a Protestant model, with an emphasis on individual, private, and voluntary confessions of faith.[13] To become citizens of liberal nation-states such as the United States, enlightened Jews needed to redefine themselves as adherents to a Jewish religious faith and voluntary community.[14]

As I have argued elsewhere, this was never an easy process. In many instances Jews were the other within the "more civilized" dominant cultures of the West, atavistic throwbacks, members of a more primitive people, the people of the Old Testament that had to be superseded. In many cases Jewish loyalty to the nation as opposed to the Jewish community remained an issue. Thus, even as Judaism was religiously privatized, the liberal state maintained an interest in supervising Jewish communities. This can be seen in state efforts to control even the most "private" of matters, such as marriage and sexuality.[15] Here public and private enactments were intertwined. Liberal states used the control of sexuality under the auspices of liberal marriage and proper or middle-class morality as a way of judging Jewish fidelity to the state. So, although rabbis were free to perform weddings and divorces in France, the first state to emancipate their Jews, even in these matters rabbinic authority was granted only by the nation-state. In performing presumably religious rites, rabbis in effect became agents of the state, acting by virtue of the power vested in them, not by their denominations, or by God, but rather by the power of the state.[16] In these ways, again, Jewishness, although a matter of private faith, was very much about state-sanctioned collectivity. And, in the United States, Jews took their cues in these matters from the dominant culture and its Protestant majority.

In the nineteenth century, as various denominations of U.S. Protestantism were becoming increasingly privatized and feminized, Jews followed suit.[17] As U.S. Jewish historian Karla Goldman has demonstrated, in the United States public worship among Protestants was marked by its decidedly feminine character.[18] The image of church pews filled with devoted women had a particular impact on the transformation of Jewish worship. In contrast to the bourgeois norms of Western Europe, in the United States middle-class

Jewish women were expected to show their devotion in public by attending synagogue worship services. They more than met these cultural expectations and, as Goldman shows, their growing presence in synagogue services had material effects. In the United States the architectural structure of synagogues changed to meet this new expectation. Synagogues were literally restructured: women's sections were first expanded, and later, mixed pews become a part of Jewish worship in many liberal Jewish congregations. Despite such dramatic changes, as Goldman's work indicates, these reforms were not without conflict. Although the women came to synagogue, their presence at services did not mean that they were granted communal authority, even in the most liberal of these institutions.[19] Nevertheless, changing gender norms were only one example of how powerfully Jewish political emancipation came to transform Jewish self-understanding.

In the early part of the twentieth century, this liberal Protestant version of Jewishness came into direct conflict with a very different understanding of Jewish enlightenment, the modern vision of Eastern European Jews. As millions of Jews immigrated to the United States, these religious practices were very much at odds with the forms of Jewish life they were accustomed to in Eastern Europe. Not only did many of these newly arrived Jews not recognize the liberal religious practices as Jewish; they did not have any simple way of explaining their own very different forms of enlightened Jewish expression.

Jewish Enlightenment in the East

> Jewish Secularism originated in Eastern Europe, and was imported to this country as part of the social baggage of Eastern European immigrants.
> —Herbert Parzen, 1959

Although it is often assumed in popular imagination that culturally backward Eastern European Jews were enlightened only as they made their way west, as the above passage suggests, this was not the case.[20] The other, and perhaps even more important, story of Jewish enlightenment for U.S. Jews took place in Eastern Europe.[21] Although Eastern European Jews were never granted political emancipation, they were very much affected by the legacy of the Haskalah or Jewish enlightenment well before they reached the shores of the United States. It is this inheritance that interests me as it has come to shape contemporary expressions of Jewishness.[22]

The notion of "modernity" or cultural enlightenment as enacted in Eastern Europe is not a simple matter. Recent scholarship has increasingly challenged any unitary reading of these processes.[23] Although much of the scholarship on Jewish enlightenment has privileged the experience of Central and Western European Jews, Eastern European Jews complicate the ways rationality, secular education, and the study of science, philosophy, and literature became a part of Jewish self-understanding in Eastern Europe. Here "secular," in English, became the term for what was understood as a series of worldly knowledges and practices. It did not necessarily bring with it the privatization of Jewish religious observance. In some instances, there was a wholesale rejection of religious practice; in others, there was an embrace of any variety of worldly political and cultural enactments. To be clear, in the East, modernity and enlightenment rarely led to political emancipation as they did in the liberal nation-states of the West. Instead they offered new modes of sometimes uniquely Jewish cultural and political expression (modern Hebrew and Yiddish literatures and various forms of Jewish nationalism), as well as more universal expressions of culture and politics to which Eastern European Jews adhered.

In other words, for the Jews of Eastern Europe, enlightenment values were not necessarily linked to remaking Jewishness into a matter of faith or, for that matter, denominations. Enlightenment was enacted in other venues and on other terms.[24] Here modernization was not a matter of becoming bourgeois; in fact, for many Eastern European Jews, poverty and political disenfranchisement led to more radical forms of enlightened politics. These Jews became involved in socialism and communism as Jews. They accentuated their Jewish particularism even as they participated in these larger political movements. In Eastern Europe, Jews used the languages of socialism, communism, and nationalism to envision their own transformed versions of modern Jewish communal life.

For some, this meant seeing the Jewish people as their own nation. This nation was conceptualized as either a separate entity within the boundaries of Eastern Europe or as a nation with their own independent state and their own forms of modern Jewish cultural expression. In all of these ways, Eastern European Jews used the expansive public dimensions of traditional Jewish life, those aspects of rabbinic Judaism as an autonomous political and social entity that Western Jews gave up in order to become citizens of liberal nation-states, to construct their own enlightened Jewish positions. In the East and, eventually, in the Yiddish speaking world of U.S. Jews, these autonomous forms of Jewish communal life were greatly expanded. And, in the early part of the twentieth century, it was these enlightened secular Jews who took on leadership roles in the immigrant community.[25] They used culture as well as politics to solidify their own enlightened notions of Jewish community.

By focusing on the distinctiveness of Jewish culture, they took pride in the creation of new Jewish literatures in both Hebrew, their ancient sacred tongue, and Yiddish, their modern Jewish vernacular. Eastern European Jews created modern Hebrew as a living language, even as they transformed Yiddish into modern poems, stories, novels, and plays.[26] It should also be noted that still other groups of Eastern European Jews wrote Jewish poetry, novels, and short stories in both Polish and Russian.[27] In all of these instances, Eastern European Jews used Western enlightened cultural forms to fashion themselves as modern Jews. Instead of reconstituting their Jewishness as a form of bourgeois religion, they both mimicked and transformed enlightened cultural expressions and politics to make sense of their own lives. They staged performances as well. Making powerful use of the Yiddish theater, they literally enacted their discomforts, remaking them into both art and artifice.[28]

Worldly versus Religious Jews

For many Eastern European Jews, modernity meant liberation from the restraints of a more stringent religious way of life. Their new modern Jewish identities were no longer bound by ritual practice; they were worldly, or, as they were to call themselves in the United States, "secular." The Yiddish term for what is often referred to as "secular" Jewishness is *weltlikh*, deriving from the Yiddish word for world or universe. It describes, in the broadest terms, a kind of Jewish cosmopolitanism that included both rational and nontheistic ways of being in the world as Jews.[29]

Given this legacy of enlightenment, the encounter with those Jews already in the United States was somewhat confusing. Although these more acculturated Jews offered a model of how to succeed, there were few Eastern European analogies to this explicitly religious form of enlightened Jewishness.[30] In Eastern Europe, the notion of enlightenment went hand in hand with a sense of worldliness. It was primarily on these terms that Eastern European Jews' deferred hope for political emancipation rested. But, of course, what they found in the United States was something quite different. Here there was little place for their worldly forms of enlightened Jewishness. Instead they found themselves being asked to enter into what Mordecai Kaplan described as the only form of acceptable Jewish difference in their new home.

> In this country, as well as all other countries where the Jews have been emancipated, the synagogue is the principal means of keeping alive the Jewish consciousness. . . . [It] is the only institution which can define our aims to a world that would otherwise be at a loss to understand why we persist in retaining our corporate individuality.[31]

Faced with this very different strategy, the question was, how much of these other forms of enlightened Jewish expression would these new immigrants be able to maintain?

The vast majority of Eastern European Jews who came to this country at the turn of the last century were the least educated, the poorest, and the most desperate. My argument is not that these Jews were particularly enlightened but rather that even these Jews had a very different sense of what it might mean to be modern as they entered the United States. And so it was that Eastern European Jewish immigrants brought with them a mixture of pride, shame, nostalgia, and joy in the Yiddish culture and politics they left behind.[32] Most still spoke and read Yiddish in their new home, learning about the world through the pages of a vibrant U.S. Yiddish press.[33] They learned how to become Americans through these papers. As Riv Ellen Prell and other Jewish historians have argued, the Yiddish press played an active role in assimilating Eastern European immigrants into the middle-class norms of American culture.[34] In other words, these papers not only taught immigrants how to dress, how to speak, and how to decorate their homes, but they also continued to influence their politics.

In addition to reading Yiddish newspapers, these immigrants also kept alive other parts of their Eastern European Jewish culture. They went to the Yiddish theater on the Lower East Side of New York City and sought out traveling Yiddish theatrical productions as they played in smaller venues across the country.[35] They continued to enjoy the diet they had known in Eastern Europe, now increasingly understood as simply Jewish. These immigrants performed these secular rituals that kept them linked to the Jewish culture of Eastern Europe even as they strove to assimilate into U.S. society. Although there were pockets within this community that remained loyal to the radical socialist politics they brought with them to the United States, and still others who remained observant of *Halacha* or Jewish law, most of these immigrants had only vague relations to any of these traditions.[36] For these Jews, coming to the United States was not an all-or-nothing proposition.

What is difficult in the present is trying to characterize the "religious" practices of all Eastern European Jews, not only those who remained religiously observant but also those who had begun to give up their religious commitments in Eastern Europe. There were any number of permutations among and between what was cultural and what was religious or Halachic in terms of diet, foods, and everyday practices. When asked why certain foods were or were not eaten, immigrant Jews offered numerous explanations. In other words, not all who kept some semblance of a kosher diet did so as a religious obligation. For many it was just what their families had done, it was familiar and comforting, and they did not do so out of religious obligation. Such practices had many, even contradictory, meanings for those who performed them.

These Jews should not be confused with what we now think of as "Orthodox" Jews. Here again the terms and categories of "religion" obscure historical and cultural differences. "Modern Orthodoxy," for example, began as a Western European movement. It was a response to religious reform, and its leaders included figures such as Samson Raphael Hirsch, who believed it was possible to be fully modern in the public sphere and fully observant at home. For him, the issue was that the reformers had gone too far.[37] Nevertheless, to speak of "Modern Orthodoxy" in the present in the United States is to recognize strands of this Western European tradition as it merged with some of the practices of only some observant Eastern European Jews. And this is only part of the story. The arrival of Orthodox and Hasidic refugees, especially after 1945, has come to reshape Orthodox Judaism in the United States yet again.[38] These later refugees brought with them the remnants of their traditional communities in order to rebuild them and have been extremely successful in these efforts.[39]

The Demise of Yiddish Secular Culture Revisited: The Move to *Judaism*

Although most scholars agree that the unraveling of Yiddish secular culture in the United States occurred in the late 1950s and early 1960s, there is less agreement about why this culture came to an end as a vernacular communal practice.[40] I want to take a step back and see this problem in a larger historical context, remembering both the end of Jewish immigration in the 1920s on the one hand, and the traumatic destruction of the center of secular Yiddish culture in Eastern Europe with the Holocaust on the other. To do this, I turn to feminist poet and writer Irena Klepfisz, a child survivor of the Holocaust who grew up after the war in some of the last of these secular, Yiddish-speaking communities in the United States. By illustrating the complexity of this historical moment, her account sheds light on the ways that the end of Yiddish as a secular vernacular in the United States was not so much about the ideology of Yiddish secularism as about the larger historical forces that led to the end of these communities. For Klepfisz, both the power of assimilation after the end of the great migration of Eastern European Jews to the United States in the 1920s and the Holocaust made Yiddish secular culture increasingly a less viable way of being Jewish in the United States after the Second World War.

In Klepfisz's account, these losses are palpable. For her, secular Yiddish culture offers contemporary Jews a path not taken. It is a viable alternative to the narrow, religiously construed Jewishness of dominant U.S. Jewish culture. By telling this story in its brokenness, her account also prefigures the kinds of postvernacular Yiddish cultural expression addressed in Jeffery Shandler's remarkable study, *Adventures in Yiddishland: Postvernacular Language and Culture*, on new ways of being Jewish that build on that culture in innovative and surprising ways that speak to younger generations eager to claim other forms of Jewish cultural expression as their own.

In her essay "Secular Jewish Identity: *Yiddishkayt* in America," Klepfisz describes her own encounter with the demise of Yiddish secular culture in the United States. For her, the world of Yiddish in the United States was a new home. It was the space in U.S. culture that defined her Jewishness. And although her own first language was Polish, and along the way she learned to speak Swedish and English, Yiddish was the language of her mother's secular Jewishness and her own. For Klepfisz, being a U.S. Jew meant being a secular Bundist, a Jewish socialist who spoke and read Yiddish.[41] Growing up in the shadows of the Holocaust, she found herself a part of yet another community that was dying, although as she explains in her essay, she did not realize this at the time. It is only much later as an adult that she came to understand that the U.S. Yiddish-speaking world in which she was raised no longer exists.

It is with great sadness that Klepfisz writes about the loss of this *yidishe svive*, this Yiddish-speaking world. The loss is complicated; not all is lost. Klepfisz believes that secular *Yiddishkayt* can be revived in new forms. She believes there is both a need and a desire for this kind of Jewish cultural expression in the present. She believes there is a place for a kind of broken Yiddish culture, a secular Yiddish culture for those who no longer speak the language of their ancestors but who bring other things to this cultural legacy. These other commitments include feminist and queer politics, jazz and art, literature and film.[42]

As Klepfisz explains, these contemporary Jews present not only a "totally new phenomenon, Yiddishists without knowledge of the Yiddish language but deeply committed to the survival of Yiddish culture;" they also include a growing movement of Jews committed to fully reclaiming Yiddish language, literature, music, and theater in the present. In other words, although the vast majority of secular, assimilated, and liberal religious Jews may not speak Yiddish fluently, these Jews nevertheless may present a viable future for Yiddish secular culture in the United States.[43]

Despite these signs of hope, what Klepfisz clearly describes in her essay is a generational loss. As the immigrants who came to the United States between 1880 and 1920 and their children began to die, and without an ongoing influx of new Yiddish speakers coming into this world, it became difficult to sustain these communities. And, although refugees like Klepfisz and her mother helped bring new life into this Jewish world after the war, the reality was that there were no more secular Yiddish speakers left in Europe after the Holocaust. Although many Eastern European Jews and their children continued to speak Yiddish, by the second and third generations, the number of Yiddish speakers in the United States also dwindled.

What is it about U.S. culture and the specific experiences of these immigrants that made sustaining Yiddish—much less its various secular cultural expressions—so difficult? One partial answer to these questions can be found in the pages of *Judaism*, a journal that was founded in the early 1950s to meet the needs of a new generation of U.S. Jews. As I will demonstrate, here we find Jewish secularists grappling with precisely these issues. I focus on this journal and its first decade of publication because it is a pivotal moment in the consolidation of the kind of religious expressions of Judaism and Jewishness I have argued become hegemonic in the postwar United States. The journal expresses the desire to affirm a profoundly religious notion of Judaism, and in the process it also traces in its pages the last breath of what were explicitly secular and cultural forms of Jewish identification that become increasingly unlivable after the war. In *Judaism* we find the convergence of these quite disparate versions of U.S. Jewish identification and literally see how, in order to survive, Yiddish secularists try to reimagine their movement in increasingly religious terms.

★★★★★

The only enduring type of pluralism which the structure of American life envisages lies in the field of religion. . . . It is within the rubric of religious pluralism, therefore, that the basis for permanent survival of the Jewish group as an indigenous element of American Life is to be sought.

—Robert Gordis, 1952

Judaism marks a Jewish embrace of religious pluralism, and yet in the process of solidifying this vision, the journal also allows the last generation of U.S. Yiddishists to offer traces of a road not taken, their efforts to maintain secular Yiddish positions and communities. And yet, as they become increasingly desperate, they come to find themselves advocating for a reinvention of their explicitly secular movement in religious terms, agreeing with Gordis's assessment of the future of U.S. Jewish life. There is a sad irony to these essays. They show explicitly the generational tensions in defining Jewishness and increasingly make clear that, as Kaplan suggested, in the United States, the future depends on redefining Judaism as ultimately and only in religious terms.

Judaism, a journal of the American Jewish Congress, was first published in 1952. As Robert Gordis, a Conservative rabbi and professor of biblical exegesis at the Jewish Theological Seminary, explained in the opening essay of the very first issue, this new journal was dedicated to a revival of Judaism after Hitler and after the founding of the State of Israel.[44] Gordis inaugurates the journal with a commitment to reassessing the Jewish religious tradition as a basis for the future of the Jewish people.[45] He also suggests that like the journal itself, there is in the American Jewish community more broadly a kind of religious revival, especially among a new generation of U.S. Jews, Jews no longer satisfied by the enlightened answers provided by reason and science.

By highlighting the limitations of the secular discourse of science, Gordis goes on to argue for religion as the basis for ethical judgment and insists on the new journal's commitment to reassessing Judaism as a religious tradition. As he explains: "The Jewish community can boast of a number of valuable periodicals concerned with various aspects of Jewish life, but we regard it as an indefensible lacuna that practically none is primarily concerned with the philosophy, ethics, and religion of Judaism as a factor in the contemporary world."[46] *Judaism* was established in order to meet these needs.

Judaism carries within its pages traces of the various forms of Jewish cultural, political, and intellectual life it was leaving behind, and this included the legacy of secular Yiddish culture. This is why, especially in its early years, it included explicitly secularist essays. Nevertheless, reading through the pages of the first fifteen years of the journal, one notices that the pieces about Yiddish secularism grow increasingly sparse, and by 1960 they are primarily about the demise of this cultural formation and what might be done to transform these legacies for the future. And, by the mid-1960s, the definition of secularism itself shifts. It no longer refers to Jewish worldliness but rather, quite explicitly, to the absence of religion, with virtually all discussions of secularism now focused on Israeli and not U.S. Jewish culture.[47] Reading these early essays shows why Yiddish secularism did not survive and how this form of Jewish cultural identification gave way to religious definitions of American Jews, Jewishness, and Judaism.

I now want to turn more directly to two of these essays, Herbert Parzen's "The Passing of Jewish Secularism" and Saul L. Goodman's "Jewish Secularism in America." What these writers describe, and even Gordis suggests at the end of his inaugural essay, is that, in the United States, it is only through religious pluralism that Jews can survive as Jews. But need this still be the case? Is it possible to imagine a place for other forms of cultural difference, including the various broken versions of secular Jewishness that continue to exist in the United States? These are the issues that animate both essays as another way of understanding the status of U.S. Jews even in the present. Although in both instances the writers are very much concerned about the future of Jewish secularism, they each offer vivid critical descriptions of U.S. culture to make their cases. In what follows I build on these descriptions to challenge these cultural norms in the present.

"The Passing of Jewish Secularism"

Parzen opens his 1959 essay by addressing what he sees as the dual impasse faced by conscientious secularists. As he explains, "in separating themselves from the Synagogue—the basic institution of the historical tradition as the inevitable instrument for the survival of organized Jewish life in America, they are committed to foster a substitute—a secular Jewish culture sufficiently resourceful to reward them with self-fulfillment and to assure group survival."[48] Secularists need to have a central institution, a substitute for the synagogue on the one hand. And, on the other, they need to become contemporary. Although "Jewish secularism was destined to flourish temporarily and artificially in this country," this is no longer the case.[49] It may have made sense to an immigrant generation of Eastern European Jews, but it is no longer viable; its adherents are aging and have little to offer to a new generation of U.S.-born Jews. Parzen continues by saying that Jewish secularism "can no longer serve as an agency for self-fulfillment and survival."[50] He explains that the only form of cultural difference that is recognized and respected in the United States is religious difference.

> American culture is unitary and national, by design and intent. The only exception is religion. And though there is a clear-cut contemporaneous tendency to de-emphasize this tradition, the separation of Church and States is, nevertheless, a regnant rule in American thought

and life; it decisively directs, likewise by design and intent, that religious phases of American civilization shall be diverse, discrete, and necessarily, pluralistic.[51]

This account is offered as what we might now call a reality check, a reminder to the remnant of Jewish secularists that their program no longer makes any sense. He continues, "Thus, religious pluralism is the law of the land." This is in sharp contrast to secularist notions of cultural pluralism that were developed in Eastern Europe. As Parzen explains, in the United States as in Western Europe, Jews "achieved adjustment to the general social order on the primary basis of religious tolerance."[52] It was expected that Jews would conform to the cultural patterns of the state and not maintain separate cultures. Parzen is frustrated that these seemingly simple truths have not been taken up by Jewish secularists, who seem to go on as if they were living elsewhere, insisting that they can maintain their old ways even in the United States.

As it turned out, by and large Parzen was right: secular forms of Jewishness were dying. Before assessing the "perilous position of present-day secularists in the United States," circa 1959, Parzen makes one final point that is worth reiterating. He clarifies that Jewish secularists should not be confused with assimilationists. This is a crucial point, one reaffirmed almost thirty years later by Irena Klepfisz. As Parzen explains, "secularists must be differentiated from assimilationists. The first planned to preserve Jewish peoplehood and its culture, the second sought absorption or 'integration' in the dominant civilization."[53] As Parzen makes clear, secularists were very much committed to Jewish culture and a Jewish future. What is painful is that their strategies did not survive in the United States. By the end of the twentieth century, it had become virtually impossible to recognize the differences. Given this, by 1986 Irena Klepfisz had to fight hard to make the case that it was possible to be a committed secular Jew, a notion that sounds like an oxymoron to most contemporary U.S. Jews.

And yet it is precisely the memory of these secular traditions that helps explain the contradictions that so many contemporary Jews experience around their own Jewish positions in the present. Rereading Parzen helps us recall that these traditions were a part of the "social baggage" that Eastern European Jews brought with them to this country.[54] He also reminds us that the loss of these traditions is part of the price that eastern European Jews paid to become U.S. citizens. They had to give up these forms of Jewish cultural expression to become a part of the dominant culture. To assimilate into the dominant Protestant culture of the United States, Jews were required to identify their Jewishness as a form of religious faith to remain visible as Jews.

Having made these cogent arguments, Parzen concludes his essay by looking at specific Jewish secularist positions and explaining where he thinks they go wrong. He moves from general Zionists, to labor Zionists, to Yiddishists, and finally to a group he calls native Jewish intellectuals. He demonstrates how and in what ways each of these groups failed, but he saves his most vehement critique for this final group who persist "in a sort of no-man's land, on the periphery of Jewish life and on the margins of American culture, discontented, dismayed, disjointed." For Parzen, the message is clear, for all of these Jews there is no future. Appealing to Jewish tradition, he concludes his essay by describing these Jews as *nishmatin artilain*, 'naked souls,' meandering about the world without balance and without consistency! This, it seems to me, is the fate of Jewish secularists in the United States."[55] In this way Parzen ultimately rejects Jewish secularism in order to assure a more stable Jewish future. In the United States, Jews need to position themselves as a religious group to survive as Jews, and none of these groups was willing to do this.

"Jewish Secularism in America"

By way of contrast, Saul L. Goodman attempts to tell a different, but again not uncritical, story about the future of Jewish secularism in his essay "Jewish Secularism in America: Permanence and Change." The subtitle of this essay conveys the tension at its heart. Goodman wants permanence as well as change and is willing, in a sense, to let go of the secular in order to save Jewish secularism.

Goodman wrote this essay while directing New York's Yiddish secular Sholom Aleichem Schools. He wrote from within the Yiddish secular world as both an educator and a scholar. Although like Parzen he is critical of what was happening to Jewish secularism in the United States, he very much wanted there to be a future for this movement. Precisely because he was committed to the future of American Jewish secularism, he was willing to consider change, even radical change. Goodman went so far as to suggest the viability of Jewish secularists self-consciously joining religious Jewish communities to make this possible.

At the heart of Goodman's essay is his struggle to come to terms with religion as a secularist. For him, religion had already come to structure Jewish life in the United States. His question was what are secularists to do with this reality? After providing a brief overview of the origins of Jewish secularism in the nineteenth century and the crises faced at the eve of the Second World

War, including a disillusionment with not only the promises of emancipation gone sour in Western Europe and a lack of faith in the larger promises of progress at the heart of the enlightenment more broadly, he makes his case. As he explains,

> in addition to these altered internal factors within the Jewish community, the general climate of opinion in America was radically different now. Modern man became disillusioned with technical-material progress that did not satisfy his hunger for genuine loftiness, did not give him a *raison d'être*, and left a void in place of the old faith that promised immortality, permanence, and tranquility.[56]

Goodman builds on this disillusionment. Like Parzen, he wants something to take the place of this old faith in reason. He wants a new foundation since he too no longer finds it in reason or science.

In this way, Goodman sets up his quest to reclaim "religion" as a secularist. He uses this broader disillusionment and longing for a lost idyllic past in order to reconsider some of the basic tenants of Jewish secularism. By challenging the opposition between religion and Judaism within some of the earliest U.S. proponents of Jewish secularism, Goodman hopes to make it easier for other secularists to reconsider the merits of religious community for the future. He turns to the writing of Jewish secularist Leibush Lehrer in order to present this secularist position so that he can then take it apart point by point.

As Goodman explains, in the late 1930s Lehrer argued that Judaism was not to be equated with religion. According to Lehrer, religion was in essence an individual psychic experience that could not be confused with Judaism. "Judaism is mainly *a code which regulates the lives of Jews as belonging to a collectivity.*"[57] Lehrer suggested that even the English term *secular* makes no sense when applied to Judaism. Judaism need not be secularized since it was never a religion. Moreover, as Goodman goes on to explain, the Yiddish term *Weltlikh* and the English word *secular* are clearly not one and the same thing. In other words, *secular* is not the opposite of *religion*. In the case of Yiddish secular Jews, not being religious did not mean that they were not committed to Jewish culture and Jewish tradition.

I think it helpful to quote from Goodman's text at some length to fully express the way he builds on this earlier Yiddishist position citing Lehrer explicitly.

> In Judaism the essence is not theological but rather legalistic; not metaphysical sanctions but sociological functions; not whether you have faith in God but whether you observe the sancta (*Mitzvoth*) is what counts. Which is another way of saying that the true substance of

Judaism is expressed in folkways, observances, in culture, in tradition, in Law, (*Halakhah*), and conduct; not in "fear of the Lord", not in piety, nor in creedal dogmas. "Judaism" is primarily a folk idea, a concept of conduct.[58]

Here the distinctions are sharp. Judaism is presented as a unique cultural formation that is anything but a religion. Yet in order to make this case, Lehrer appeals to the kinds of Jewish stereotypes most often deployed by Christians against Jews. Jews are legalistic and clannish as opposed to spiritual and universal. According to Goodman, this is the secularist position at its most extreme and most pernicious in terms of how dominant U.S. culture would see it given its rootedness in Protestant Christianity.

Although there is something to be said for this notion of Judaism as a legal, cultural, and social folk tradition whose sole purpose is the survival of the Jewish people, Goodman believes there is more to it than just this. He suggests that even for secularists, Judaism offers something that is also transcendent, something that could be understood using the language of religion.

In the final portion of his essay, Goodman presents his own constructive argument. Like Parzen and Gordis, Goodman sees the future of the Jewish people in America as contingent upon the redefinition of the Jewish people as a religion. "American Jewish community life, including its secular-cultural elements, should be put into a religious framework." Using the work of Jewish sociologists to make his case, he explains that there can be no Jewish communal future without an accommodation to the dominant norms of U.S. culture. "[I]n order to get the sanction of America to Jewish group survival, we must declare ourselves to be a religious community. Inasmuch as America will not consent officially to a permanent ethnic or linguistic separateness, our descendants will not exert themselves to preserve their Jewishness."[59] This is the crucial point. In order to find a place for secularists among already established explicitly religious Jewish communities, those sanctioned by the dominant culture secularism must become, in a sense, religious.

Goodman concludes his essay by offering one final "American twist to the concept of Jewish secularity" by appealing to John Dewey's distinction between the adjective *religious* and the noun form *religion*.[60] As Goodman explains, "the adjective religious denotes an attitude, a disposition, a commitment." According to Dewey, "any activity pursued in behalf of an ideal and against obstacles and in spite of threats of personal loss because of conviction of its general and enduring values is religious in quality."[61] In other words, Goodman used Dewey to bolster his position for claiming the language of religion. He argues that for Jews to do whatever it takes to secure the survival of the Jewish people,

Jewish values, and Jewish practices, the explicit goals of Jewish secularism, they are, in Dewey's sense, "religious." For Goodman, religious secularism, although seemingly an oxymoron, is, nevertheless, a way of securing a future for secular Jews. As he explains: "The Jewish secular conception is an attempt by all who are seeking to identify themselves with the Jewish group through modern means; it is an attempt to harmonize the prevalent ideas of modern culture with the historic Jewish heritage."[62]

In this way Goodman ends his essay by placing his efforts to renovate Jewish secularism within a broader historical framework and uses Dewey, the quintessential American thinker, to do this. As Goodman reads it, in every generation, Jewish secularists have rethought their Jewish inheritance in the present. They have sought to reconcile modern culture and Judaism. Jewish secularists have attempted time and time again to offer "satisfactory rationale" for what it means to be a modern Jew. In Goodman's case, U.S. culture demanded that he embrace a new form of Jewish religiousness even as a secular Jew.[63] Although this schematization, this rigid adherence to the terms of liberal assimilation made sense for Goodman in 1959, I want to suggest that in 2007 it is time to reconsider this wager and the ongoing effects of this embrace of liberal pluralism. In order to allow for the diversity of Jewish expression both historically and in the present, it would be worthwhile to consider the implications of what it would mean not to define Jewishness in religious terms. Instead U.S. Jews might consider claiming the diversity of Jewish expression outside of the confines of religious pluralism.

Toward the Future

Like Goodman and Parzen, I too end with thoughts about the future of Jewish secularism but at a different historical juncture. There is, of course, no going back to their specific world. The community out of which Goodman wrote no longer exists. In this essay I have returned to Goodman, Parzen, and others to remember that there was a Jewish secularism, that the vast majority of U.S. Jews did not necessarily come to this country at the turn of the twentieth century with the notion that Jews were a religious minority. I have returned to this tradition to better explain the place of Jews in U.S. culture and what it might mean for Jews to more fully accept our own complicated positions as Jews who never quite fit into a religious definition of our Jewishness. What this earlier generation of explicitly Jewish secularists reminds us is that some of our own discomforts are not of our own making. They remind us that U.S.

culture, despite its promise of inclusion, still finds it difficult to embrace cultural differences. Moreover, they remind us that liberal inclusion has always been only partial. In Brown's terms, "the triple forces of recognition, remaking and marking—of emancipation, assimilation and subjection" all remain operative. To be accepted as Jews into U.S. culture we have had to remake our Jewishness into a form of private religious faith containing our Jewish difference to the "church and home." By returning to the archive of *Judaism*, I have tried to show how this model of Jewish inclusion has never quite fit the realities of Jewish existence in the United States, especially after the vast migration of Eastern European Jews to this country in the early twentieth century. Moreover, this problem was not unknown to precisely these same Jews. Secular Yiddishists were quite clear about the limitations of liberal inclusion. Although I am not interested in resurrecting their particular solutions, I appreciate their early articulation of the problem. By seeing these issues spelled out by an earlier generation of Jews, I believe we can more fully appreciate the need to resist this legacy in the present. This is very much the vision of many contemporary U.S. Jews involved in creative new forms of Jewish communal expression.[64] These new Jews are increasingly interested in not only revisiting Eastern European Jewish secularism, but also in exploring various other nonreligious forms of Jewish academic, cultural, and political expression.[65]

Liberal assimilation is never complete. As a process it is necessarily ongoing and partial, even as it holds out the promise of completion. We need to let go of this mechanism. For the vast majority of U.S. Jews, the descendants of Eastern European immigrants, this process of assimilation was a repetition with a difference. Like their predecessors, Jews who came from Central and Western Europe, these Jews tried to redefine themselves as religious to fit into U.S. culture, but the definition was not quite accurate. Although all of these Jews were compelled to assimilate into liberal religious norms, their efforts remained fraught; their Jewishness did not fit easily into this model of acceptable social difference. As I have argued, some overtly resisted this imperative. This was especially so in the case of secular Jews who refused to define themselves as religious. Given this, contemporary American Jews have been left a series of contradictions. American Jews are both too religious and not religious enough, too American and not nearly American enough.[66] The question of what it means to be an American Jew remains contradictory. Given that Jews are, as Yiddish literary critic Samuel Niger put it, "a historic ethico-cultural, and socio-politico-economico-psychological phenomenon," there remains no easy or simple way of containing Jewish difference.[67] Instead of changing, I believe we need to reconsider these norms for acceptance and their ongoing effects. I have returned to the writings of Jewish secularists because these Jewish thinkers worked hard to resist adhering to the category of religion in defining themselves as American Jews.

By reclaiming the complexity of Jewish modernization and enlightenment offered to Jews at the beginning of the twentieth century, we remember that there are other ways to be Jews in the United States. We need not continue to adhere to the failed promises of liberal inclusion. The example of Eastern European Jewish secularists suggests the impossibility of this model as well as what it might mean to challenge the notion of religious pluralism as a means to Jewish social acceptance. They make clear that for this to happen it is not Jews who must change but, rather, U.S. culture and its notions of cultural inclusion. By letting go of liberalism as this defining discourse, it might be possible to imagine other ways of describing and inhabiting positions Jewish or otherwise eccentric to the dominant culture of the United States in the present and in the future.

Notes

This essay was inspired by the work of Janet Jakobsen and Ann Pellegrini, especially the special issue of *Social Text* they edited, "World Secularisms at the Millennium," *Social Text* 64, 18.3 (Fall 2000), and their coauthored book *Love the Sin: Sexual Regulation and the Limits of Religious Tolerance* (Boston: Beacon Press, 2004). A version of this essay was originally written for their collection *Secularisms* (Durham, N.C.: Duke University Press, forthcoming [2008]). That essay is titled "Other Moderns, Other Jews: Revisiting Jewish Secularism in America." I am indebted to Janet and Ann for critical editorial suggestions and advice on that essay.

1. For more on this problem, see Wendy Brown, *Regulating Aversion: Tolerance in the Age of Identity and Empire* (Princeton, N.J.: Princeton University Press, 2006); and Laura Levitt, *Jews and Feminism: The Ambivalent Search for Home* (New York: Routledge, 1997), esp. chaps. 3 and 4.

2. For more on these very different legacies of enlightenment, see the primary sources collected in Paul R. Mendes-Flohr and Jehuda Reinharz, eds., *The Jew in the Modern World: A Documentary History* (New York: Oxford University Press, 1980).

3. Brown, *Regulating Aversion*, 53.

4. On this issue of liberalism's promise and effacement, see Laura Levitt, *Jews and Feminism*, esp. introduction and chaps. 1 and 4.

5. I thank Ayako Sairenji and David Watt for sending me back to particular essays in *Judaism*. These articles include the following: Abraham Menes, "Religious and Secular trends in Jewish Socialism," *Judaism* 1.3 (July 1952): 218–26; Herbert Parzen, "Eastern European Immigrants and Jewish Secularism in America—1882–1915," *Judaism* 3.2 (Spring 1954): 154–64; C. Bezalel Sherman, "Nationalism, Secularism, and Religion in the Jewish Labor Movement," *Judaism* 3.4 (Winter 1954): 354–65; Abraham Menes, "The East Side—Matrix of the Jewish Labor Movement," *Judaism* 3.4 (Winter 1954): 366–80; Samuel Kreiter, "Sh. Niger—Yiddish Humanist," *Judaism* 6.4 (Fall 1957): 334–38; Herbert Parzen, "The Passing of Jewish Secularism in the United States," *Judaism* 8.3 (Summer 1959): 195–205; Saul L. Goodman, "Jewish Secularism in America," *Judaism* 9.4 (Fall 1960): 319–30.

6. See Sara Horowitz, "The Paradox of Jewish Studies in the New Academy," in *Insider/Outsider: American Jews and Multiculturalism*, ed. David Biale, Michael Galchinsky, and Susannah Heschel (Berkeley: University of California Press, 1998), 116–30.

7. Parzen, "The Passing of Jewish Secularism," 196.

8. Paula Hyman, "Enlightenment," in *Contemporary Jewish Religious Thought: Original Essays on Critical Concepts, Movements, and Beliefs*, ed. Arthur Cohen and Paul Mendes-Flohr (New York: Free Press, 1987), 167.

9. See Hyman, "Enlightenment," and Brown, "Regulating Aversion," on this point as well as my own discussion in Levitt, *Jews and Feminism*, esp. chap. 3.

10. See Parzen, "The Passing of Jewish Secularism," 196; and Joseph L. Blau, "What's American About American Jewry?" *Judaism* 7.3 (Summer 1958): 208–18.

11. See the *American Heritage Dictionary*, 4th ed. (Boston: Houghton Mifflin, 2006), s.v. "denominate."

12. Hyman, "Enlightenment," 167.

13. See Robert J. Baird, *Inventing Religion in the Western Imaginary* (Princeton, N.J.: Princeton University Press, forthcoming), and his essay in Jakobsen and Pellegrini's *Secularisms*. See also Pellegrini and Jakobsen's account of the genealogy of religion in their introduction to "World Secularisms at the Millennium," *Social Text*, 17–20, as well as their introduction to *Secularisms*. Other key works include: Leigh Schmidt, *Hearing Things: Religion, Illusion, and the American Enlightenment* (Cambridge, Mass.: Harvard University Press, 2000); Jonathan Z. Smith, "Religion, Religions, Religious," in *Critical Terms for Religious Studies*, ed. Mark Taylor (Chicago: University of Chicago Press, 1998), 269–84; Tomoko Masuzawa, *The Invention of World Religions, or, How European Universalism Was Preserved in the Language of Pluralism and Diversity* (Chicago: University of Chicago Press, 2005). For a haunting historical account of these issues, see the entry for "Religion, or Theology," in the first edition of *Encyclopedia Britannica* (Edinburgh: A. Bell and C. MacFaquhar, 1771). For more on this entry and the relationship between Protestantism and Enlightenment, see David Harrington Watt, "Protestantism," in *The International Encyclopedia of the Social Sciences* (New York: Macmillan, 2007).

14. Mendes-Flohr and Reinharz, *The Jew in the Modern World*.

15. Levitt, *Jews and Feminism*.

16. See Levitt, *Jews and Feminism*, chap. 3.

17. See Tracy Fessenden's "The Convent, the Brothel, and the Protestant Woman's Sphere," *Signs* 25.2 (Winter 2000): 451–78; and Parzen's 1954 essay "Eastern European Immigrants and Jewish Secularism," esp. 155–56.

18. On the feminization of American Judaism, see Karla Goldman, *Beyond the Synagogue Gallery: Finding a Place for Women in American Judaism* (Cambridge, Mass.: Harvard University Press, 2000).

19. See Karla Goldman's careful account of these tensions and conflicts in *Beyond the Synagogue Gallery*, esp. in chaps. 4, 5, and 6.

20. This narrative is usually associated closely with what Stephen Steinberg describes as the myth of the "Jewish Horatio Alger" on the one hand and the romanticization of the shtetl on the other. See Steinberg, *The Ethnic Myth: Race, Ethnicity, and Class in America* (New York: Antheneum, 1981); and Caren Kaplan, "'Beyond the Pale': Rearticulating U.S. Jewish Whiteness," in *Talking Visions: Multicultural Feminism in a Transnational Age*, ed. Ella Shohat (Cambridge, Mass.: MIT Press, 1998): 451–84. On the role of Russia and the shtetl in particular in Jewish imagination, see Steven Zipperstein, *Imagining Russian Jewry: Memory, History, Identity* (Seattle: University of Washington Press, 1999).

21. On the differences between Eastern and Western Jewish efforts as modernization and enlightenment, especially in terms of gender, see Paula Hyman, *Gender and Assimilation in Modern Jewish History: The Roles and Representation of Women* (Seattle: University of Washington Press, 1995).

22. Between 1880 and 1920, more than 2 million Jews from Eastern Europe migrated to the United States. They came from the Russian Empire, Poland, Austria-Hungary, and Romania. See Gerald Sorin, *A Time of Building: The Third Migration, 1880–1920* (Baltimore: Johns Hopkins University Press, 1992); Andrew Heinze, *Adapting to Abundance: Jewish Immigrants, Mass Consumption, and the Search for American Identity* (New York: Columbia University Press, 1990); Irving Howe's classic study *The World of Our Fathers: The Journey of the Eastern European Jews to America and the Life They Found and Made* (New York: Harcourt, Brace, Jovanovich, 1976); Charlotte Baum, Paula Hyman, and Sonya Michel, *The Jewish Woman in America* (New York: Plume, 1975); Sydney Stahl Weinberg, *The World of Our Mothers: The Lives of Jewish Immigrant Women* (New York: Shocken, 1988); Susan A. Glenn, *Daughters of the Shtetl: Life and Labor in the Immigrant Generation* (Ithaca, N.Y.: Cornell University Press, 1990).

23. On this issue of multiple Enlightenments, see Jonathan I. Israel, *Radical Enlightenment: Philosophy and the Making of Modernity, 1650–1750* (Oxford: Oxford University Press, 2001).

24. On these issues, see the primary sources collected in Mendes-Flohr and Reinharz's *The Jew in the Modern World*. See also David Weinberg, *Between Tradition and Modernity: Haim Zhitlowski, Simon Dubnow, Ahad Ha-Am, and the Shaping of Modern Jewish Identity* (New York: Holmes and Meier, 1996).

25. See Parzen, "Eastern European Immigrants and Jewish Secularism."

26. See Benjamin Harshav, *The Meaning of Yiddish* (Berkeley: University of California Press, 1990); Emanuel S. Goldsmith, *Modern Yiddish Culture: The Story of the Yiddish Language Movement* (New York: Fordham University Press, 1997); Naomi Seidman, *A Marriage Made in Heaven: The Sexual Politics of Hebrew and Yiddish* (Berkeley: University of California Press, 1997); Chana Kronfeld, *On the Margins of Modernism: Decentering Literary Dynamics* (Berkeley: University of California Press, 1996); Alan Mintz, *"Banished from Their Father's Table": Loss of Faith and Hebrew Autobiography* (Bloomington: Indiana University Press, 1989). For a powerful critique of the politics of modern Hebrew literature, see Hannan Hever, *Producing the Modern Hebrew Canon: Nation Building and Minority Discourse* (New York: New York University Press, 2002).

27. See Mendes-Flohr and Reinharz, *The Jew in the Modern World*; Lucjan Dobroszycki and Barbara Kirshenblatt-Gimblett, *Image Before My Eyes: A Photographic History of Jewish Life in Poland Before the Holocaust* (1977; New York: Schocken, 1994); Michael Steinlauf, *Bondage to the Dead: Poland and the Memory of the Holocaust* (Syracuse, N.Y.: Syracuse University Press, 1997), esp. chap. 1 on Polish Jewish cultural production; and Carol Balin, *To Reveal Our Hearts: Jewish Women Writers in Tzarist Russia* (Cincinnati: Hebrew Union College Press, 2000).

28. I am grateful to Paul Reitter for his fascinating account of the power of Yiddish theater in German Jewish imagination. Paul Reitter, "Karl Krauss's Yiddish Theater," conference paper, Los Angeles, Association for Jewish Studies, December 2002.

29. Alexander Harkay, *English-Yiddish Dictionary* (New York: Hebrew Publishing Company, 1929). See also the discussion of *Weltlikh* verses, secular, in Goodman, "Jewish Secularism in America."

30. See *Image Before My Eyes* for examples of more liberal enactments of Jewish religious life in cosmopolitan Poland.

31. Mordecai Kaplan, 1917, as quoted by Abraham Karp in his introduction to *The American Synagogue: A Sanctuary Transformed*, ed. Abraham Karp (Cambridge: Cambridge University Press, 1987), 31.

32. For a particularly nostalgic look at this phenomenon, see the highly popular videos produced by WLIW21 Public Television about the creation of "Jewish Americans": *A Laugh, a Tear, a Mitzvah* (New York: WLIW21, 1996), 90 min., and *Another Mitzvah* (New York: WLIW21, 1997), 90 min.

33. In addition to the extensive treatment of the importance of the Yiddish press presented in the various articles from *Judaism*, especially Parzen, "East European Immigrants and Jewish Secularism," see Maxine S. Seller, "Defining Socialist Womanhood: The Women's Page of the Jewish Daily Forward in 1919," *American Jewish History* 76.4 (1987): 416–38; Riv Ellen Prell, *Fighting to Become Americans: Jews, Gender, and the Anxiety of Assimilation* (Boston: Beacon Press, 1999); and Barbara Schreier, *Becoming American Women: Clothing and the Jewish Immigrant Experience, 1880–1920* (Chicago: Chicago Historical Society, 1995).

34. See Prell, *Fighting to Become Americans*, esp. chaps. 2 and 3.

35. On the role of Yiddish theater as well as the Yiddish press and literature in promoting secular Jewish culture in the United States, see Parzen, "East European Immigrants and Jewish Secularism," 161–62.

36. On these issues, again, see Parzen, "East European Immigrants and Jewish Secularism." This is a position close to my own heart. It is the position taken by my own grandparents. See my discussion of my maternal grandmother's citizenship in the introduction to *Jews and Feminism*.

37. Samson Raphael Hirsch, *The Nineteen Letters on Judaism* (New York: Feldheim, 1969). See also the various primary sources collected in *The Jew in the Modern World*, ed. Mendes-Flohr and Reinharz.

38. Haym Soloveitchik, "Rupture and Reconstruction: The Transformation of Contemporary Orthodoxy," *Tradition* 28.4 (Summer 1994): 64–130. I think Ellen Frankel for this reference.

39. On the growth of ultra-orthodoxy at the expense of more modern forms of Jewish orthodoxy, see Samuel G. Freedman's *Jew vs. Jew: The Struggle for the Soul of American Jewry* (New York: Simon & Schuster, 2000); Samuel Heilman, *Defenders of the Faith: Inside Ultra-Orthodox Jewry* (New York: Schocken, 1992); and Heilman and Menachem Friedman, "Religious Fundamentalism and Religious Jews: The Case of the Haredim," in *Fundamentalism Observed*, vol. 1 of the Fundamentalism Project,

ed. Martin Marty and R. Scott Appleby (Chicago: University of Chicago Press, 1991), 197–264. For a more historical account of U.S. orthodoxy, see Jenna Joselit, *New York's Jewish Jews: The Orthodox Community in the Interwar Years* (Bloomington: Indiana University Press, 1990).

40. On postvernacular Yiddish culture, see Jeffery Shandler, *Adventures in Yiddish Land: Postvernacular Language and Culture* (Berkeley: University of California Press, 2006). The demise of Yiddish culture after World War II is connected not only to the Holocaust and the destruction of so much of what was Eastern European Jewish culture; it is also linked to the aging and assimilation of the first generation of Eastern European Yiddish-speaking immigrants who came to the United States at the turn of the century. Another aspect of this move away from Yiddish culture in the United States is connected to the cold war and McCarthyism. Many of the most radical adherents to various forms of Yiddish politics and cultural production were blacklisted during the fifties. For more on this, see Michael Staub, *Torn at the Root: The Crisis of Jewish Liberalism* (New York: Columbia University Press, 2002).

41. For a more developed reading of Klepfisz's essay and her secular Jewishness, see Laura Levitt, "Feminist Spirituality," in *Spirituality and the Secular Quest*, ed. Peter Van Ness (New York: Crossroad, 1996), 305–34.

42. This move echoes the more expanded argument made by Shandler in *Adventures in Yiddishland*.

43. See Klepfisz, especially the final section of her essay devoted to *Di tsukunft*, the future, 159–84. See also Levitt, "Feminist Spirituality"; quote on 161.

44. Robert Gordis, "Towards a Renascence of Judaism," Judaism 1.1 (January 1952): 3–11.

45. Gordis, *Towards a Renascence*, 4.

46. Ibid., 5.

47. An example of this is Nathan Rotenstreich's "Secularism and Religion in Israel," *Judaism* 15.3 (Summer 1966): 259–83. This has become the dominant reading of Jewish secularism. See, for example, Ben Halprin, "Secularism," in *Contemporary Jewish Religious Thought*, 863–66.

48. Parzen, "The Passing of Jewish Secularism," 195.

49. Ibid.

50. Ibid.

51. Ibid.

52. Ibid., 195, 196.

53. Ibid., 199, 197.

54. Ibid., 197.

55. Ibid., 205.

56. Goodman, "Jewish Secularism in America," 320.

57. Ibid., 321.

58. Lehrer, as cited by Goodman, "Jewish Secularism in America," 321. These seem to be Goodman's own translations. As his notes suggest, these passages come from a Yiddish text, Leibush Lehrer's *Yiddishkeit und Andere Problemen*.

59. Goodman, "Jewish Secularism in America," 324.

60. As Goodman explains, this is a distinction Dewey makes in his *Common Faith* (Goodman, "Jewish Secularism in America," 330).

61. Goodman, "Jewish Secularism in America," 330; Dewey, as cited by Goodman, ibid.

62. Ibid.

63. It should also be noted that Goodman continued to write and think about these issues. His later publications include the anthology *The Faith of Secular Jews* (New York: Ktav, 1976).

64. For more on these various forms of communal expression, especially in relation to a younger generation of U.S. Jews, see Steven M. Cohen and Ari Kelman, "The Continuity of Discontinuity: How Young Jews Are Connecting, Creating, and Organizing Their Own Jewish Lives" (New York: The Andrea and Charles Bronfman Philanthropies, 2007); and Steven M. Cohen and Ari Kelman, "Cultural Events and Jewish Identities: Young Jewish Adults in New York" (New York: The National Foundation for Jewish Culture, 2006). Cohen offers an account of their most recent study in "Continuity Beyond Communal Walls," *The Forward*, May 25, 2007. For a broader account of new Jewish cultural expression in the transnational present, see David Shneer and Caryn Aviv, *New Jews: The End of Jewish Diaspora* (New York: New York University Press, 2005).

65. One important venue for this new work, especially in the academy, is the work of the Posen Foundation. The foundation has taken a leading role in promoting new scholarship on the legacy of secular Jewish

forms of expression. They have sponsored new scholarly works, books, and encyclopedia projects, as well as courses and programs of study at numerous colleges and universities in the United States and internationally. For more information about the Posen Foundation go to *http://www.culturaljudaism. org/ccj/grants* (accessed June 29, 2007). Under the auspices of this program, at Temple University we have instituted a new undergraduate certificate program in secular Jewish studies.

66. On this problem of excess as a form of mimicry, where assimilation is always already partial and incomplete, see Laura Levitt, *Jews and Feminism*, introduction and chap. 1, as well as the discussion of Jewish whiteness in Caren Kaplan, "'Beyond the Pale.'"

67. As cited by Goodman, "Jewish Secularism in America," 326.

An Exception to Exceptionalism: A Reflection on Reinhold Niebuhr's Vision of "Prophetic" Christianity and the Problem of Religion and U.S. Foreign Policy

Michael G. Thompson

> Adequate spiritual guidance can only come through a more radical political orientation and more conservative religious convictions than are comprehended in the culture of our era.
> —Reinhold Niebuhr, *Reflections on the End of an Era*, 1934

I s there an inevitable relationship between conservative Protestantism and a foreign policy of "benevolent hegemony"? Does a "more religious" or "more theological" public discourse of foreign affairs simply lead to heightened nationalism and messianism? When President George W. Bush borrowed from the gospel of John to refer to the United States as "light shining in darkness" (his figure cast in front of the Statue of Liberty) he seemed to confirm a pattern that historians have long demonstrated: that Protestant religion is complicit with, and indeed facilitates, a view that the United States' role in the world is as the guardian and bearer of universal values. American exceptionalism (the idea of the United States as a chosen nation with a unique role in world history) has been linked to numerous conflicts, interventions, and wars: from westward expansion in the 1800s, to "making the world safe for Democracy" in 1917, to containment of communism in the 1940s and '50s. One could be forgiven for presuming, therefore, that the relationship between Christianity and foreign affairs was somehow static and inevitable.[1]

I wish to propose a counternarrative: what if there was an exception to exceptionalism? By looking at perhaps the most influential Christian thinker on politics and foreign affairs in the twentieth century—theologian and public intellectual Reinhold Niebuhr (1892–1971)—in one of the most critical periods of the United States' political and military relationship to the world, I hope to tease apart the often-presumed relationship between orthodox ("conservative") Protestant religion and American exceptionalism. I suggest that it was the development of Niebuhr's "prophetic" theology—his very turn toward orthodoxy in religion—that acted as a critical lever over and against the cold war cultural hegemony of American exceptionalism, even while his practical politics coincided with the dominant view.[2] Prophetic, of course, doesn't refer to the act of predicting the future; rather, for Niebuhr, the prophetic was about living in the present, in a concrete historical moment. The prophetic vision was an "answer"—wrought out of an atmosphere of crisis—to the perennially plaguing question of how the church ought to relate to the "public square" in a modern secular democracy. It was a paradox: a desire to escape or transcend modern culture, while at the same time relate to it. In a crude sense it referred to the idea of being "inside" (relevant to) the culture while remaining "outside" (transcending) it: the two were to remain in tension, in a dialectical relationship of both insider *and* outsider. However, the prophetic stance needs to be understood primarily as a theological vision, not just as a biographical paradox. It was theological because it made a statement about God in his relation to the world: that God was both transcendent and related to the world and to human history. It was also theological insofar as it envisioned the church as mimicking God's dialectical transcendent-related relationship to the world. Specifically, the prophetic church would love justice more than it had; it would be involved in the world, but it would resist and criticize every form of pretension and self-glory on the part of its surrounding culture. Importantly, therefore, the church's relationship to the nation as nation would involve resistance to claims of absolute or transcendent status: such claims were idolatry. Niebuhr's original target was, of course, 1930s fascist Europe. Yet this approach toward nation and nationalism was a continuous element of his "prophetic" and "realist" theology, and in the late 1940s and '50s, Niebuhr's sights increasingly turned, instead of on Europe, towards American nationalism and exceptionalism. In a secondary sense, then, we also need "more theology" to understand Niebuhr the theologian. This is to move closer to the historian's goal of treating subjects on their own terms.[3]

Paying attention to theology, however, doesn't dispense with the need for narrative, for exploring change and complexity through time. The emergence of Niebuhr's prophetic stance was never simple or inevitable. In fact, the life and career of Reinhold Niebuhr coincided with a period of enormous oscillation and crisis: from the high hopes of Wilson's crusade for democracy to the plunge into postwar despair; from public outrage at those "merchants of death," the munitions makers, in the 1930s, to the explosion of nuclear weapons in Hiroshima and Nagasaki in 1945; from the League of Nations as "Kingdom of God" to isolationism, and back again; from the Paris Peace Pact to the North Atlantic Treaty Organization; from the formation of the United Nations to calls for unilateral invasion of China. Niebuhr's thinking was formed in response to the enormous crises the Western world faced in this period. As he reflected in 1939, it wasn't so much scholarship as "the pressure of world events" that constituted his theological education.[4] For Niebuhr, as for many "mainline" liberal Protestants, World War I had left a severe case of "moral nausea" and revulsion toward war, and he was one of many committed pacifists of the 1920s. Pacifism was—alongside labor reform and Prohibition—part of the search for a whole "Christian social order." In the 1930s however, Niebuhr's pacifism began to be stretched by his need to account "realistically" for power: first in the quest for economic justice within the United States, where he saw power as necessary (and right) for an industrial revolt; and second, Niebuhr began to see power as necessary to counter international aggressors, such as the Japanese in Manchuria or the Italians in Abyssinia. When Germany invaded Europe in contravention of the ill-fated Munich agreement, Niebuhr bitterly renounced what he saw as the whole of "liberal culture's" inability to account for evil in human history, and indeed in human beings. In Niebuhr's mind, only an orthodox Christian view of human sin could account for the current situation. His new "Christian realism" was accompanied by membership in a raft of organizations advocating U.S. aid to the allies. This meant Niebuhr was explicitly encouraging Christians to accept the possibility, even the desirability, of war with Germany. The enormity of this crisis must not be lost: Niebuhr was turning against many friends and allies in the Christian-pacifist camp, who, like him, were opposed to anything that reeked of "holy war" imperialism. The end of war gave rise again to the question of international order, and Niebuhr called for the United Sates to assume its national "responsibility" as a world power. Power had to be balanced with power; the United States needed to be "tough" with the Russians, whose insecurity and expansionist ideology meant they couldn't be trusted. Social democracies—which for Niebuhr were intrinsic to a Christian and humanist "Western civilization"—had to be protected and cultivated in Europe, and the United States had to take a lead in ensuring this. Thus Niebuhr straddled and wrestled with some of the defining historical fault lines in the country's political relationship to the world: isolationism to globalism, pacifism to realism, and anti-imperialism to internationalist promotion of democracy.[5]

Niebuhr's prolific output has made him to this day a seminal figure in American political philosophy, foreign policy-making, and theology. His hyperactive output took the form of monographic works such as *Moral Man and Immoral Society* (1932), *The Nature and Destiny of Man* (1941, 1943), and *The Irony of American History* (1952), to name just three of his most influential works. It took the form of journalistic editorial work and opinion writing in Christian periodicals such as *Christian Century* and *Christianity and Crisis* (which he helped found and edit), as well as ostensibly "secular" journals such as *Nation, New Republic* and *Atlantic Monthly*. In total, Niebuhr is said to have written 21 books, contributed to another 126, and penned more than 2,600 articles.[6] Much more of Niebuhr's output was expressed in his role of activist-organizer. Niebuhr almost inevitably rose to leadership in every fellowship, league, and organization he joined, and there were many: the Fellowship of Socialist Christians, the Fellowship for a Christian Social Order, the Fellowship of Reconciliation, the League for Independent Political Action, the League for Industrial Democracy, the YMCA, the Federal Council of Churches, and the Socialist Party of New York, just to name *some* of those in the early 1930s. Somehow all of this took place in addition to Niebuhr's being professor of Christian ethics at Union Theological Seminary between 1928 and 1960, where his role varied from lecturing in packed theaters to mentoring students in his and his wife Ursula's New York apartment. And one must not forget that Niebuhr's magnetism was distinctly felt in his oratory and preaching, not only in Union's chapel, or earlier in his parish in Detroit, but also at student and youth gatherings on the preaching circuit all over the East Coast and the Midwest. Some of Niebuhr's influence therefore must be put down to his phenomenal work rate. Yet his influence also had much to do with how he "located" himself, not just as a kind of theologian, but as a public—we might even use the word "secular"—intellectual and leader.

At the height of his career in the 1940s and '50s, Niebuhr could accurately have been labeled a public intellectual. His media presence expanded as he appeared frequently as host or guest on radio shows, was featured in *Life* magazine twice, and even made the cover of *Time* magazine in 1948 as "theologian for a lenten age."[7] His influence as a political thinker, especially on international affairs waxed even greater. Political philosopher and foreign affairs "realist," Hans Morgenthau, labeled Niebuhr the "greatest living political philosopher of America."[8] George Kennan, another "realist" and cold war foreign policy strategist, was famously reported to have called Reinhold Niebuhr "the father of us all" (though this has been disputed).[9] Niebuhr sat with Kennan for a time on his State Department foreign policy think tank. He was invited to join the Council on Foreign Affairs in 1947 and was chosen to represent the U.S. delegation to the UNESCO conference in Paris in 1949. Even still, there was a deeper intangible way in which Niebuhr influenced his culture, one that went beyond his prolific output and high-profile networks. In cold war historian Walter LaFeber's terms, "not since Jonathan Edwards' day in the 1740s had an American theologian so affected his society. . . . he provided a historical basis and rationale for the tone, the outlook, the unsaid, and often unconscious assumptions of this period."[10]

What demands closer attention, however, is Niebuhr's positioning of himself when he was so immersed and accepted in the public square. Even while being "inside," Niebuhr attempted to maintain the perspective of one on the "outside." Just as the self-conscious trajectory of Niebuhr's work was a search for a place in the center, at the same time his explicit mission and hope for the church, and for himself, was the development of a culturally independent, "prophetic" church, whose perspective came not from within modern culture but from beyond its horizons.

In his 1935 *An Interpretation of Christian Ethics* Niebuhr set out to challenge the dependence of American Protestantism "upon the very culture of modernity."[11] Niebuhr's alternative is "prophetic religion." For Niebuhr, the culture of modernity, which he saw as underpinning both Marxism and bourgeois liberalism, consisted in the belief that the ideal could be realized through human effort. It interpreted history as having a "self-contained" meaning. In contrast, argued Niebuhr,

> the significance of the Hebrew-Christian religion lies in the fact that the tension between the ideal and the real which it creates can be maintained at any point no matter what the moral and social achievement, because its ultimate ideal always transcends every historical fact and reality.[12]

Through stressing the transcendent ethic, prophetic religion avoided the conflation of God with a given social and political order. But for Niebuhr prophetic religion also had to avoid the withdrawal and escape from history represented by "mystic" religions. These made "the transcendent irrelevant to the historical process."[13] Prophetic religion, then, consisted in a tension or dialectic of both transcendence and relatedness. Put more simply, the prophetic stance referred to being in the world but not of the world: both "insider" and "outsider." The implications of this theological dialectic are crucial for Niebuhr's commentary on foreign affairs.

For Niebuhr, the insistence on God's transcendence meant the pretensions of any group laying claim to absolute virtue were idolatry. The exceptionalism of a nation cannot, for Niebuhr, in any sense be total or essential. A nation may be capable of relatively more good or more justice, but never total good or total justice. Moreover, a nation or society will almost always act in its own interests, not out of abstract virtue or altruism. According to Niebuhr, such "realism" must inform our moral and political calculus. Furthermore, Niebuhr's insistence on the theology of God's transcendence stands in negation to the interpretation of history that underlies exceptionalism. Exceptionalism and nationalism hold that history has an apparent and observable meaning. Indeed other secular metanarratives, such as Marxism and liberal progressivism, share the same sense of history's "obvious meaning." This may be seen as a kind of historical "immanentism," the idea that God, or some other "transhistorical" principle, acts within—*immanent* to—history in an empirically observable manner (hence Marx's "scientific" view of history). Whether secular or religiously derived, however, immanentism allows for the nation to claim status as the actualization of an ideal, and thus to claim virtue in its actions. This may be found in the assertion of the communist vanguard or the call for a Christianized colony in the Philippines. Indeed at the heart of American "Manifest Destiny" or "Redeemer Nation" culture is a belief in the transcendent working, acting immanently, in history. In the famous words of Julia Ward Howe, God's "truth is marching on." For Niebuhr, however, honoring the transcendence of God meant resisting immanentist claims made by the nation-state.

Yet the theology of "transcendence" was only one pole of the dialectic for Niebuhr. The other pole of "relatedness" also had immediate bearing on his approach to foreign policy. Indeed, the very fact that Niebuhr *approached* foreign policy represented a deep assumption that religion ought to relate to social and political life. This is where many have rightly found Niebuhr to be thoroughly liberal in his presuppositions. Theological ethicist Stanley Hauerwas's important criticism of Niebuhr is that his theological ethics were actually not theological, in that they were not addressed to the church, but were rather designed to provide an "ethos" for the nation-state.[14] He and others have noted that Niebuhr's roots were in the tradition of Schleiermacher and Kant—as well as William James—in that he presumed religion ought to be translated into rational, universally applicable norms that are *useful* for society. Indeed, it was exactly the "relatedness" of Niebuhr's theology that allowed him to talk of "national responsibility" when the United States faced the prospect of war in 1940 or to call for U.S. support for the rebuilding of a democratic Germany in 1946.

As a work of history, this essay is concerned with the nexus where theology became political. For Niebuhr, this was seen most clearly in his journalism and editorializing. In these, the everyday (or every week) events were brought into contact with the shifting contours of his theology: the transcendent and the historical were related. Therefore, relying on these shorter journalistic works as evidence—in dialogue with certain book-length works—we will seek to explore the development of Niebuhr's prophetic stance in the 1930s and its implications for the political contesting of the United States' role in the world through World War II and the early cold war.

The Making of Niebuhr's "Prophetic" Stance

To understand Niebuhr's response to the perceived crisis of the 1930s, it is first necessary to place him in the context of the social gospel worldview of the 1920s—albeit in very general terms. Liberal Protestant Christians of the social gospel movement, influenced by the Enlightenment belief in human goodness, rationality, and progress, stressed a God of immanence and order in relation to historical and social experience. God was alive in history, behind progress: he was relevant, not "other." Biblical revelation was therefore submitted to the rule of modern reason; Jesus was seen as a moral teacher and example, the means to social progress. This resulted in a historical optimism whereby God and history were united in the march of Progress. Walter Rauschenbusch, who arguably embodied the social gospel movement more than any other single figure, expressed a vision that made the progress of society at large contingent upon the confluence of Christianity with social knowledge, "a scientific comprehension of social life."[15] The conclusion of Rauschenbusch's 1907 grand statement *Christianity and the Social Crisis* read:

> Perhaps these nineteen centuries of Christian influence have been a long preliminary stage of growth, and now the flower and fruit are almost here. If at this juncture we can rally sufficient religious faith and moral strength to snap the bonds of evil and turn the present unparalleled economic and intellectual resources of humanity to the harmonious development of a true social life, the generations yet unborn will mark this as the great day of the Lord for which the ages waited.[16]

The social gospel was thus built on a purported harmony between God and human society. Its optimistic view of human nature supported the expectation that God's will would be made manifest in and through human history. The "day of the Lord" would occur with human cooperation. Consequently, during its whole working life, the social gospel movement stressed the "relevance" of Christianity or "religion" to society at large. Just as God was immanent, and involved in human history, so the church's role was to work as a positive agent within modern society. Rather than disjuncture, there was a perceived harmony, a symbiosis between the progress of the world and the work of the church. The role of the church in liberal social gospel thought was to work *within* the given order, promoting love, peace, and goodwill.

Pacifism thus became a sacred plank in the social gospel's hope for the world. Nations were required to learn to love and trust, to create a "universal brotherhood" through sacrificial acts rather than mutual mistrust. This was seen as the natural human order of things.[17] In 1928 we find Niebuhr delivering an address on the eve of leaving Detroit for his new post at Union Seminary in New York. Niebuhr himself is preaching what he later would call the "if only" position with regard to international relations. The idealism of the message is reflected in the title, "Christianizing International Relations." The ideal is imposed on the reality. "Universal brotherhood" is the norm to which the nations ought to strive: "The family relation must ultimately become the basic relation of all men in order to establish the Fatherhood of God and the Brotherhood of Man. You can define the whole of Christianity in these terms."[18] There is no separation between the pragmatic, "the strategy of life," and the essence, "the whole of Christianity." Rather, "nations must be made to see and to submit themselves to the dominion of the Christ Spirit of service and sacrifice."[19]

As the twenties turned into the thirties, Niebuhr's ethical and political liberalism started to strain. His rhetoric began to shift away from the possibility of working within a given order to that of fundamental contradictions between the given order and Christianity. The Great Depression created such a sense of crisis that Niebuhr remarked, "We cannot save our civilization at all except we change its whole basis . . . Nothing less than that will save us."[20] In light of this, Niebuhr and colleagues, including John C. Bennett, Sherwood Eddy, and Kirby Page, founded the Fellowship of Social Christians in the winter of 1930–31. Members had to "recognize the essential conflict between Christianity and the ethics of capitalistic individualism."[21] The symbiosis was beginning to break.

In such an atmosphere, Niebuhr penned one of his most famous books, *Moral Man and Immoral Society*.[22] The title reflects a paradox that constituted one of the main theses of the work. That is, individual morality is distinct from social morality. Patriotic individuals may sacrifice themselves for their country and yet the country may be acting out of egoism and hubris in wronging another nation. Further, members of a dominant class such as the middle class may in themselves hold a certain "private" virtue (honesty, thrift, prudence), yet the very structure of relations on which that class survives may be intrinsically unjust and immoral; and the class may act complacently and selfishly in maintaining the status quo.

A particular section of Niebuhr's work was devoted to "The Morality of Nations." Anticipating Benedict Anderson's "imagined community" thesis, Niebuhr wrote of the power of the nation "to avail itself of the most potent symbols to impress its claims upon the consciousness of the individual. Since it is impossible to become conscious of a large social group without adequate symbolism." The nation in modernity is able to place such a claim on the individual, Niebuhr argued, and "achieves a potency in the modern soul, so unqualified, that the nation is given carte blanche to use the power, compounded of the devotion of individuals, for any purpose it desires."[23] If nations are selfish, they are even more hypocritical. The modern nation feels the need to justify or cloak its interests in moral terms. A nation feels compelled to "claim general and universally valid objectives" for itself. According to Niebuhr, "in the imagination of the simple patriot the nation is not a society but Society." And here is where the underlying structure of this error is laid bare: "Though its values are relative, they appear . . . to be absolute."[24] In this sense, nationalism has a religious potency in its "instinct" for the absolute; thus patriotism and religion become intertwined. Significantly for our purposes, *Moral Man* introduces the binary of absolute and relative, universal and particular, into Niebuhr's political thought. It becomes a fundamental lever with which Niebuhr is able to criticize nationalism and future U.S. foreign policy.

Meanwhile, tensions had been emerging in Niebuhr's pacifism. In articles published in the *World Tomorrow* and *Atlantic Monthly*, Niebuhr had begun to express a "qualified" rather than an "absolute" pacifism.[25] His careful dissection of "necessary" and "unnecessary force" was, however, fraught with ambiguity and imprecision, a problem of which Niebuhr seems to have been aware. In a specially commissioned "intellectual autobiography" published in 1956, Niebuhr remarked of his earlier pacifism, that it became a "dubious compound of the prudential ethics of a commercial civilization and the absolute demands of the Gospel ethics."[26] This "dubious compound" of prudentialism and idealism in Niebuhr's thought would be placed under immense strain, and eventually implode.

Perhaps surprisingly it was domestic politics and economic justice rather than international war and peace that pushed Niebuhr over the edge on pacifism. Niebuhr's decision to leave the pacifist Fellowship of Reconciliation in 1934 had to do with the permissibility of violence in a hypothetical labor uprising. Niebuhr reluctantly agreed that Christian leaders ought to support the proletariat in using force to resist capitalism if necessary.[27] The *Christian Century* published Niebuhr's explanatory letter, "Why I Leave the F.O.R." Here Niebuhr calls himself explicitly a "Christian Marxian." Thus he asserted that there was no neutrality in the class struggle. "Neutrality is morally more dangerous . . . because it works to the advantage of entrenched interests against advancing forces."[28] Rather, if power is the basic reality, then confusion came in attempting to establish an absolute ethic in a relative and contested world. For Niebuhr to accept violence and reject pacifism in the name of economic justice meant that the identification of Christian ethics with political progress was to break.

However, not only did Niebuhr find pacifism an unacceptable option in the pursuit of domestic social justice, but he was also beginning to criticize pacifism's viability as a norm for international relations. As the Japanese invaded Manchuria in 1931, in a rare published argument with his theologian brother Helmut Richard, Niebuhr criticized the West's noninvolvement as rooted in blatant self-interest.[29] As Mussolini stormed into Abyssinia and fascism continued to spread in Europe, Niebuhr argued that pacifism was "against the wall." Writing in the *American Scholar*, Niebuhr expanded on his separation of the two realms of ethics: the one of relative choices and pragmatism, and the other of the absolute ethics of the gospel. "Absolutistic scruples . . . tend to increase the anarchy that they abhor. . . . The political order must be satisfied with relative peace and relative justice."[30]

Yet Niebuhr's biggest critique of pacifism actually became its ties with liberalism. Liberalism, Niebuhr argued—and this became central to his theology—rested on a fundamentally optimistic view of "the goodness of human nature, and interpretation of human history in terms of the idea of progress, and a belief that collective behavior differs only in a certain tardiness in reaching the ideals of the latter."[31] Each of these three themes—human nature, the interpretation of history, and the ethics of collective life —would become explicitly inverted in Niebuhr's burgeoning prophetic orthodoxy. Pacifism was the target of Niebuhr's changing politics; yet his theological sights rested on much bigger prey, the central tenets of modern liberalism itself. Pacifism was indicative of a larger problem for Niebuhr, a theological and cultural illusion: "it is only a Christianity that suffers from modern liberal illusions that has ever believed that the law of love could be made an absolute guide of social morality and politics."[32]

*****

By 1937 Niebuhr was noticeably speaking as one "outside" the social order yet still intimately involved in it. Niebuhr had enjoyed a strong relationship with figures in the English Christian Left and ecumenical movements (alongside colleagues John C. Bennett and Henry Pit van Dusen), and so found himself invited to deliver an address at the World Conference on Church, Community, and State in Oxford in 1937. This precursor to the World Council of Churches was almost entirely Protestant in organization; the Roman Catholic Church had declined an invitation. The German Evangelical Church was prevented from sending delegates for reasons that naturally made church-state questions appear all the more vital. The Oxford Conference was dedicated to the problem of the church's relationship to the whole social order, seen to be in total crisis. In this climate of novel formulation and reconceptualization of the church's task, Niebuhr delivered a stinging, tightly argued address titled "The Christian Church in a Secular Age."

All so-called secular positions, argued Niebuhr, are actually positions premised on a faith, organized by a center of unconditioned belief. "Every estimate of values involves some criterion of values which cannot be arrived at empirically."[33] While he still preferred Marxism to fascism, and perhaps to "bourgeois liberalism," Niebuhr's target was in fact all "political faiths." Importantly, as an indicator of his burgeoning theological orthodoxy, Niebuhr finally invoked the word "sin" rather than "egoism," and quoted from St. Paul's letter to the Romans (the keystone of "classical" Augustinian, Lutheran theology) to define what he meant. All political faiths were guilty of the same sin: self-glorification. Niebuhr here defined what he saw as the quintessence of sin: having rejected God, society made false gods out of some particular element in life: liberals out of Reason; fascists out of a Romantic love of vitality, blood, and force; and Marxists out of a mixture of both. Drawing on the crucial theme developed in *Moral Man*, the sin of pride involves the relative claiming absolute status. "It is by this reason that men make pretentious claims for their partial and relative insights, falsely identifying them with absolute truths."[34] This treatment of the sin of pride linked back to the earlier absolute/relative binary, and would not only form the basis of his famous Gifford Lectures, but would also inform his political journalism of the late 1940s. Thus, the belief in sin both marked his move toward theological orthodoxy and served as the basis for prophetic criticism.

The ramifications of this theological stance for Christians and the nation-state were explored in a little tract published in 1937 by the Student Christian Movement in Britain titled *Do the State and Nation Belong to God or the Devil?* Despite leaning toward theological orthodoxy, Niebuhr laid his case squarely against the historical track record of orthodox Christianity.

> If we sum up this record of orthodox Christianity, both Catholic and Protestant, we are forced to the conclusion that it has consistently failed to maintain the prophetic criticism against both the nation and the state which inheres in a prophetic religion's faith in a God of transcendent majesty, who judges the pretensions of majesty, inevitably made by temporal rulers and particular human communities.[35]

Here we see both the object of prophetic criticism—the pretensions of rulers and human communities—and the means by which they are criticized, "faith in a God of transcendent majesty." States and nations, argued Niebuhr, constantly tended toward a religious self-veneration.

> There is consequently a religious overtone in all political loyalties; that is, conditioned, relative and partial human institutions tend to make unconditioned claims upon the lives of individuals and to secure the acceptance of such claims.[36]

On the one hand, Niebuhr conceded, a qualified reverence toward centers of power is appropriate where the order is tolerably just. But on the other hand, the tendency of power to preclude justice "requires an unrelenting critical attitude toward all government."[37] The prophetic stance according to Niebuhr is not softened by the majesty of human government, but "speaks a word of judgment against every ruler and every nation."[38]

The crisis of the 1930s had seen Niebuhr's view change on three essential matters. Whereas in the earlier liberal social gospel period God was stressed as being immanent to the historical process, involved in human society, in Niebuhr's turn to his "prophetic" orthodoxy of the late 1930s, God was transcendent—a judge. He was "other" from the historical process. This correlated with his changed view of human nature. The early Niebuhr understood human nature, perhaps unconsciously, as being inchoately good, capable of enlightenment through reason that would lead to "self-transcendence" and virtue. As Niebuhr leaned more heavily on Marx, reason was replaced by self-interest as the dominant force in human behavior. As Niebuhr retained his Marxian roots, but brought even Marxism under criticism, the rhetoric of egoism turned into the language of "sin." Sin was universal, even in the proletariat, and even in the most virtuous individuals. The "Nature of Man" was the theme of Niebuhr's

Gifford Lectures in 1939 in Edinburgh, later published as *The Nature and Destiny of Man* in two volumes. In this most famous of his synthetic works, Niebuhr took from the Reformation (Martin Luther) the idea of the totality and originality of sin, and from the Renaissance the idea of man's freedom and ability to reason. Man was free, but corrupted his freedom through sin. This view of human nature radically altered Niebuhr's expectations for history. Rather than progress, judgment and catastrophe were to be expected. Undoubtedly the world political climate in 1939 reinforced this expectation.

The Prophetic Stance in World War II and Cold War America

Niebuhr's rise to public prominence coincided with two of the greatest crises for U.S. foreign policy: the shift from neutrality to interventionism in the years leading up to the attack on Pearl Harbor, and the formation of cold war "containment" doctrine with regard to Russia in the late 1940s. Niebuhr's relationship to both events has been extensively documented, so it is not worth giving too much space to recounting the story when others have done so in depth.[39] Nevertheless, a sketch of these events may be helpfully refracted through two particular disputes involving Niebuhr. We will first examine Niebuhr's disagreement with Charles Clayton Morrison, a leading Christian pacifist over the issue of U.S. neutrality in 1939–41; and secondly we will examine Niebuhr's opposition to Henry Wallace on the nature and alleged threat of communism in 1946.

As war threatened in Europe, the "post-Wilsonian" atmosphere prevalent in 1930s America created a general fear about fighting overseas for abstract ideals. A suspicion of waging "holy war" was particularly prominent among social gospel pacifists. The editor of the leading liberal Protestant periodical, *The Christian Century* (*CCY*), Charles Clayton Morrison expressed this concern, framing it in almost Niebuhrian terms of not identifying the nation's actions with God's will. In *CCY* Morrison condemned President Roosevelt as making an "Invitation to a Holy War." Again, responding to Henry Luce's declaration of an "American Century," Morrison fumed:

> The world is in a mess; now let the omnicompetent Anglo-Saxon step in to straighten it out! . . . [This is] the most ambitious imperialism ever projected . . . which will gradually but inevitably bring to focus against itself the jealousies and hatreds of all the other nations and races on earth.[40]

Surely such a theme would have seemed perfectly congruent with Niebuhr's "prophetic" stance against all national pretensions. Yet Morrison became

Niebuhr's chief journalistic opponent, resulting in Niebuhr and his colleagues starting an alternative journal, *Christianity and Crisis* (*C&C*), in direct opposition to *Century*. Why was this?

Niebuhr's disagreement with Morrison was focused on the issue of pacifism versus intervention. Yet it was the whole approach to foreign politics that was at stake for Niebuhr. The first edition of the new journal *Christianity and Crisis* outlined this problem. As Niebuhr explained in his inaugural article, "The Christian Faith and the World Crisis," the new "little" journal was devoted to "an exposition of our Christian faith in its relation to world events." According to Niebuhr, confusion reigned in American Protestantism both over what Christianity was and how it related to world events. Niebuhr argued that false interpretations of the faith led to "false analyses of our world and our duties in it."[41] Pacifism, Niebuhr argued, was based on the theological error of moral perfectionism. Embedded in liberal culture, it presumed an optimistic and progressive view of human nature. Thus Morrison and others failed to "realize to what degree the sinfulness of all men, even the best, makes justice between competing interests and conflicting wills a perennial necessity of history." A faulty doctrine of sin led to ignorance of the need to balance power with force. Niebuhr had earlier outlined his own purported rejection of *all* liberal convictions in *CCY* in 1939. History, argued Niebuhr, had "proved" liberalism wrong: "I conclude that the whole of contemporary history proves that liberal culture has not seen the problem of mankind in sufficient depth to understand its own history."[42]

Further, Niebuhr accused America of disavowing its "responsibilities" to preserve and defend "the rich inheritance of our civilization." Thus Niebuhr insisted that although Christians ought to "judge not" other nations when they themselves were sinful, and although they ought to resist all "holy wars," *discriminatory choices still had to be made.* The peril of Nazism was clear, argued Niebuhr; it did no good to celebrate one's sensitive conscience by equating the United States with Nazi tyranny. In this first edition of *Christianity and Crisis*, therefore, Niebuhr called for Christians to support Roosevelt's "measures short of war," such as the suggested Lend-Lease Bill, recognizing all the while that these could result in war. For Niebuhr, the threat that Nazism posed to "civilization" was a worse evil than war.

It is not clear exactly what civilization was for Niebuhr; most often it was defined negatively. Of the positive content, it must be noted that it was limited to the West, to a felt "transatlantic community" and to "the liberties and legal standards which are the priceless heritage of ages of Christian and humanistic culture."[43] It did have something to do with democracy. Niebuhr's wartime release, *The Children of Light, and the Children of Darkness* framed democracy as crucial to, indeed partly constitutive of, "Western Civilization."[44] Yet here Niebuhr explicitly distanced himself from a "Wilsonianism" that sought to spread democracy globally while overlooking "organic" factors of culture, community, kin, and tradition.[45]

Just as Niebuhr's dispute with Morrison and *Christian Century* had thrust him into greater controversy and greater leadership, so too did his conflict with Henry Wallace in 1946. Then the issue at stake was not whether churches should support war against Hitler, but how the United States should approach Russia. In late 1946 Niebuhr himself was still undecided on the existence of a Russian threat: "One may assume that patience and lack of provocation may through the years allay Russian fears and mitigate Russian truculence," he wrote in September in *C&C*.[46] Traveling to Germany that September seemed to provide the context for Niebuhr to harden his opinion, however.

Niebuhr went to Germany for the U.S. State Department to investigate the condition of education in the American quarter of occupied Germany. Whatever the value of his State Department reports, the impact of his "endless stream of journalistic junk"—as he labeled it to his wife, Ursula—would be far more significant in shaping the cold war than the original purpose of the trip had reflected.[47] While in Stuttgart, Niebuhr happened to hear the address given by Secretary Byrnes in which he promised that the United States would remain in Germany "as long as required." This cheered Niebuhr immensely. He wrote to Ursula on September 6, 1946, "The high period today was Secretary Byrnes's address. . . . It was the best thing yet done for this sad nation." Against this background, Niebuhr read and heard of Henry Wallace's criticism of Byrnes's proposals.

Speaking in Madison Square Garden just days after Byrnes's "get-tough" speech, Henry Wallace (who was on the cusp of leaving the Democratic Party, in which he had served as Roosevelt's secretary of agriculture) publicly disagreed with Byrnes. He had done so privately with President Truman already. Wallace argued mere U.S. "toughness" would only serve to make Russia act "tougher." Instead, Wallace hoped to set an atmosphere of "friendly peaceful co-operation" in which Americans and Soviets "would gradually become more alike."[48] Niebuhr's view of Russia, however, had undergone a profound change during his short stay in Germany. Writing in *Life* magazine on October 21, 1946, he vehemently opposed Wallace's foreign policy views. Perhaps for the first time, he implied that the Russians were like the Nazis, and Wallace like

Chamberlain at Munich. "The Wallace line of criticism is dangerous because it is based upon illusions similar to those held by the conservatives of another decade in regard to Nazism." Wedged between color ads for pipe tobacco and cleaning agents (a long way from the spartan *Christianity and Crisis*), Niebuhr's six-page article implicitly placed him at the helm of a new liberal foreign policy, in contrast to the "confusion" with which other, "sentimental" liberals approached international affairs.[49]

A true liberal response, argued Niebuhr, would see the reality and couple strategic firmness with positive "healthy" growth. In the *Nation* magazine in September 1946, Niebuhr argued that to "save" civilization in Western Europe—namely Germany—communism had to be repelled with a *positive* social, economic, and political policy as well as military firmness. "If Western Germany remains an economic desert and Western Europe an economic chaos, communism will spread despite the present unpopularity of Communist parties."[50]

Given Niebuhr's call for a creative "two-pronged" foreign policy—firmness with Russia and positive growth in Germany—it is not surprising that he applauded the Truman administration's foreign policy of the next half decade. Truman's pledge of aid to Greece and Turkey in March 1947 was commented on with pride by Niebuhr: pride that his nation, so recently isolationist in temperament, was beginning to shoulder its international responsibilities. "Though it was rather silly to . . . talk of the necessity of preserving 'democratic' governments," he cautioned.[51] The Marshall Plan embodied a proposal for the positive economic aid Niebuhr had long been calling for. In *C&C*, Niebuhr expressed desperate hopes for its passage through Congress. "No decision of war-time was more fateful than those which our nation is now called upon to make."[52]

As outlined in the introduction to this paper, Niebuhr's reputation as a leading political thinker increased greatly in the years following 1946. The late 1940s were the high point of Niebuhr's "public" status. His foreign policy recommendations were congruent with, acting upon and being acted upon, the policy of the Truman administration. What did this congruency mean? Was it congruency or complicity? As we shall see, the coincidence of Niebuhr's practical policy recommendations with the dominant view can't be allowed to hide the vast body of reflection that formed the backdrop to whatever policy or politics he may or may not have agreed with.

*****

Mark Hulsether's "X-hand, Y-hand" characterization of Niebuhr's thought is a helpful way to understand its dialectical nature. In his history of *Christianity and Crisis,* Hulsether suggests that Niebuhr would posit an X-hand with a paradoxically related Y-hand in most of his journalistic criticism. Niebuhr would argue "X but at the same time Y."[53] Hulsether's charge is that in reality, the X-hand (support for the cold war consensus) drowned out any genuine critique in the Y-hand. But this ignores the vital structure of Niebuhr's thought. That is, if the X-hand is a realistic acceptance of policy alternatives available within the limitations of a situation, and the Y-hand is a broader qualification of the relative merit of the policy in the light of the gospel ethic, then the X-hand will be concrete, and the Y-hand will be abstract. If we examine the shape of Niebuhr's own prophetic dialectic—being in, but not of, being related but transcendent—then we will expect to see discriminating choice between a relative good on the one hand, and indiscriminate judgment formed from an absolute good on the other hand. We would expect the X-hand to offer a suggestion for limited concrete action, and the Y-hand to offer at the same time a broader religious "prophetic" critique. Hulsether uses the criterion of social policy for both the X- and Y-hands. It is not surprising, then, that the Y-hand sounds weak when its frequencies are being tested in the wrong bandwidth. Yet I would argue that the Y-hand was a lever against the whole cultural prism of American nationalism and exceptionalism that governed the period. The rhetorical structure of Niebuhr's "X-hand, Y-hand" approach is expressive of the theological structure of the transcendent and related: the two relate despite, or because of, their contradictions.

Niebuhr's prophetic Y-hand was written into a great deal of his journalism in the post–World War II period. It served to relativize many of the "goods" that American nationalism held to be universal. Firstly, while Niebuhr was an American liberal, American liberalism was never a final good for him. While he was a close colleague of Arthur Schlesinger Jr., and belonged to the same centrist school of politics, his whole view of history and humanity differed. Schlesinger noted that Niebuhr's insights contributed to his "faith": but this is not Christian faith. Rather says Schlesinger, Niebuhr spurred on his faith in "freedom," faith in American liberal traditions and "the possibility of re-charging the faith in democracy with some of its old passion and principle."[54] For Niebuhr, such faith was idolatrous: "For whether it is in ourselves, or in mankind, or in civilization, or in America, that we are asked to have faith, the admonition always points to an object of faith which is less than God and which certainly does not deserve unreserved commitment or adoration."[55] In the August 4, 1947, edition of *C&C*, Niebuhr's article "Democracy as a Religion" begins with this observation:

> If one may judge by the various commencement utterances of the past month, Americans have only one religion: devotion to democracy. They extol its virtues, are apprehensive about the perils to which it is exposed, pour maledictions upon its foes, rededicate themselves to its purposes and claim unconditioned validity for its ideals.[56]

As Niebuhr had urged in *The Children of Light*, democracy was probably the best available option for organizing a government, in that freedom and order could be brought to support each other most successfully given human nature (let this be the X-hand).[57] Nevertheless, Niebuhr is no Fukuyama. "[Democracy] is a worthy object of qualified loyalty. But is it a proper object of unqualified loyalty?" Here Niebuhr is drawing on the absolute/relative binary, which shapes his transcendent/related prophetic stance. The equating of the relative good with absolute status always involves pretension and ultimately idolatry. "It tempts us to identify the final meaning of life with a virtue which we possess, and thus to give a false and idolatrous religious note to the conflict between democracy and communism for instance."[58] (Let this be the Y-hand.)

Niebuhr's prophetic Y-hand was drawn increasingly against U.S. self-idolatry as the cold war developed. Niebuhr warned against the hubris of taking a war for democracy into Asia. General MacArthur wished to enter China; Senator Taft now wanted to stand against communism in both continents. Niebuhr stuck with the position that Europe was the strategic center. Writing in *C&C* on Christmas Day 1950, Niebuhr (ironically) rejected all claims of being an "appeaser," and trained his gun on U.S. opinion:

> Our journalistic strategists dismiss our European allies as "appeasers" and plan to stand nobly as the solitary "beacon light of liberty" shining into both continents, presumably with an atomic bomb in our hand, so that those who do not respect us may at least fear us . . . This is a time when the churches should speak, to warn against the folly which comes from pride.[59]

Niebuhr saw a strategic miscalculation premised on a moral miscalculation, that is, on an "idolatrous conception of the perfection of American democracy, and its appeal to other peoples."[60] In a stream of journalism and essays, Niebuhr warned of the dangers of presuming the universal applicability of American values, especially when such calculations ignored the political and cultural complexities of other peoples. Addressing what he saw as the particular weakness of conservative foreign policy-making in the United States, Niebuhr remarked that "the impingement of American power upon Asiatic life without adequate comprehension in America of the vast complexities of Asiatic politics is one of the most frightening aspects of the present international situation."[61] He had warned of much the same in 1946: "the sheer enforcement of ideas and principles which lack the universal validity which we ascribe to them, will render them the more odious."[62]

Yet Niebuhr's prophetic critique went beyond U.S. tendencies, back to "the very culture of modernity." A longtime target of Niebuhr's criticism had been "modern man," who assumed he was master of his own destiny. In April of 1948, Niebuhr penned the following warning in the context of a tremendous sense of foreboding about nuclear war:

> If the Christian faith has any word to speak to the nation in such a dread time as this, it must certainly contain these warnings drawn from the Gospel, reminding us that we face not merely a Russian or communist peril but the threat of a divine judgment. We are drifting toward a possible calamity in which even the most self-righteous assurance of the justice of our cause will give us no easy assurance.[63]

Such a Y-hand stance transcends policy alternatives. The invocation of God the judge didn't serve to bolster the United States' sense of right in the conflict with communism, but rather relativized it against a greater right.

The prophetic critique of "modern man" was pronounced most clearly in what was Niebuhr's most significant book of the period, *The Irony of American History*. Here again, while Niebuhr was strongly anticommunist he called for U.S. self-criticism. The self-criticism was to be based on the recognition that modern liberal culture shared the same assumptions as communism. Communism, according to *Irony*, was actually a close cousin of the same modern liberal optimistic faith in man out of which the United States had grown. That is, humans pretended to be masters of their destiny. "The hope is that man may be delivered from his ambiguous position of being both creature and creator of the historical process and become unequivocally the master of his own destiny."[64] Consequently, both liberalism and communism overestimated human virtue and falsely located the source of evil:

> In the liberal world the evils in human nature were ascribed to social institutions or to ignorance or to some other manageable defect in human nature or environment. Again the communist doctrine is more explicit and therefore more dangerous. It ascribes the origin of evil to the institution of property. The abolition of this institution by Communism therefore prompts the ridiculous claim of innocency for one of the vastest concentrations of power in history.[65]

The prophetic target Niebuhr had set out in 1937 had been "the pretensions of majesty, inevitably made by temporal rulers and particular human communities."[66] Ten and fifteen years later the target remained the same, even while Niebuhr's public status had grown. Rather than being complicit, Niebuhr consciously criticized the whole cultural web of assumptions out of which cold war politics were shaped, even while he shaped those very politics.

Conclusion

This essay, while written from the disciplinary standpoint of history, is concerned with the need for more theology in two ways. First, methodologically, historians need more theology, not less, in order to historically understand religious subjects, especially theologians. Critics of Niebuhr the Cold Warrior have sometimes not been theological enough in method, and have thus missed the ongoing prophetic critique Niebuhr offered of American exceptionalism. Second, Niebuhr demonstrates the possibility that being *more theological*, not less, leads to a transcendence of the prism of American exceptionalism in approaching foreign policy. This may have resonance for the present. Walter Russell Mead rightly noted in *Foreign Affairs* in 2006 that mainline Protestantism has steadily declined in policy-making influence, while in his words, "evangelical power is here to stay."[67] While Mead sidestepped the issue of evangelicals and exceptionalism, I wonder whether there is any reason that Niebuhr's "exception to exceptionalism" could not find synergy with an evangelical worldview that already accepts the premises of prophetic theology: namely belief in a transcendent God and the universality of sin.

Notes

My thanks to Neville Meaney and Stephen Robertson of the Department of History, University of Sydney, and Nikki Thompson for their invaluable criticisms on this essay.

1. "Benevolent hegemony" is used by Francis Fukuyama to refer to the neoconservative framing of American foreign policy in his *After the Neocons: America at the Crossroads* (London: Profile Books, 2006). This treatment of President Bush's 2002 speech to the nation can be found in Richard M. Gamble, *The War for Righteousness* (Wilmington, Del.: ISI Books, 2003), 23. For works exploring the influence of American nationalism and exceptionalism in warfare and foreign policy, see, for example, E. L. Tuveson, *Redeemer Nation* (Chicago: University of Chicago Press, 1968); Anders Stephanson, *Manifest Destiny: American Expansionism and the Empire of Right* (New York: Hill and Wang, 1995); John Fousek, *To Lead the Free World: American Nationalism and the Cultural Roots of The Cold War* (Chapel Hill: University of North Carolina Press, 2000); and Gamble, *War for Righteousness*. For a classic statement relating religion, exceptionalism, and U.S. foreign policy, see John B. Judis, *The Chosen*

Nation: The Influence of Religion on U.S. Foreign Policy, The Carnegie Endowment for International Peace, Policy Brief, March 2005, http://www.carnegieendowment.org/files/PB37.judis.FINAL.pdf (accessed Aug. 31, 2006). The briefing argues "America's difficult moments have come when it has allowed religious conceptions to color its understanding of the real world." Niebuhr does appear as an exception to the rule in the briefing, but the reasons why aren't really explored.

2. Cultural hegemony is here used in the Gramscian sense of an "organic," "ethico-political" moment in history, rather than an ideology imposed by "top-down" coercion. The concept of Christianity as a "critical lever" comes from Allan W. Loy's exploration of Marxism and theology in which he argues that Christianity can be potentially more critical than Marxism, having a transcendent critical lever from "beyond" the culture. Allan W. Loy, "Praxis: Karl Marx's Challenge to Christian Theology," *St. Mark's Review* 113 (March 1983).

3. While Niebuhr humbly, but perhaps fairly, remarked, "I cannot and do not claim to be a theologian," his work in the fields of ethics and apologetics, not to mention his preaching, meant he was in fact *doing* theology, despite not perhaps having the training or professional vocation of a "theologian." Moreover, he was received as a theologian by an American public that didn't discriminate between "practical" and systematic theology. Reinhold Niebuhr, "Intellectual Autobiography," in *Reinhold Niebuhr: His Religious, Social, and Political Thought*, ed. C. W. Kegley and R. W. Bretall, 1–23 (New York: Macmillan, 1961), 1. I am heavily indebted here to Langdon Gilkey's treatment of Niebuhr's "vertical dialectic" in his *On Niebuhr: A Theological Reflection* (Chicago: University of Chicago Press, 2001), 16–18. While Niebuhr's "insider-outsider" vision was helpfully highlighted by Mark Kleinman in *A World of Hope, A World of Fear* (Columbus: Ohio State University Press, 2000), Kleinman relied on psychological explanations at the expense of theological ones (19, 20–21, 51, 54).

4. Reinhold Niebuhr, "Ten Years That Shook My World," *The Christian Century*, April 26, 1939, 546, cited in Larry Rasmussen, *Reinhold Niebuhr: Theologian of Public Life* (Blackburn, U.K.: Collins, 1989), 4.

5. Much of this outline is indebted to Richard W. Fox, *Reinhold Niebuhr: A Biography* (New York: Pantheon Books, 1985). For "moral nausea," see Reinhold Niebuhr, "Pacifism Against the Wall," *The American Scholar*, Spring 1936, in *Love and Justice: Selections from the Shorter Writings of Reinhold Niebuhr*, ed. D. B Robertson (Cleveland: Meridian Books/World Publishing, 1967), 260. For rejection of "liberal culture," see Niebuhr, "Ten Years That Shook My World," 4.

6. Rasmussen, *Reinhold Niebuhr*, ix.

7. Rasmussen, *Reinhold Niebuhr*, 13; Reinhold Niebuhr: "The Fight for Germany," *Life*, October 21, 1946, 65; "For Peace, We Must Risk War," *Life*, September 20, 1948, 38; and "Faith for a Lenten Age" (cover and article), *Time*, March 8, 1948, 71.

8. R. H. Stone, "Niebuhr, Reinhold," *The Reader's Companion to American History*, Houghton Mifflin, http://college.hmco.com/history/readerscomp/rcah/html/ah_065000_neibuhrreinh.htm (accessed September 15, 2004).

9. Fox, *Reinhold Niebuhr*, 238.

10. Walter LaFeber, *America, Russia, and the Cold War, 1945–66* (New York: John Wiley & Sons, 1967), 40–41.

11. Reinhold Niebuhr, *An Interpretation of Christian Ethics* (1935; San Francisco: Harper, 1963), 1.

12. Ibid.

13. Ibid.

14. See Stanley Hauerwas, "On Keeping Theological Ethics Theological" (1983), in *The Hauerwas Reader*, ed. John Berkman and Michael Cartwright (Durham, N.C.: Duke University Press, 2005), 58–62.

15. On Niebuhr's liberal social gospel background, see Sidney Ahlstrom, *A Religious History of the American People* (New Haven, Conn.: Yale University Press, 1972), 786–87; and Arthur Schlesinger Jr., "Reinhold Niebuhr's Role in American Political Thought and Life," in *Reinhold Niebuhr*, ed. Kegley and Bretall, 127–28.

16. Cited in Ahlstrom, *A Religious History*, 785–86.

17. Heather A. Warren, *Theologians of a New World Order: Reinhold Niebuhr and the Christian Realists, 1920–48* (Oxford: Oxford University Press, 1997), 19–34.

18. Reinhold Niebuhr, "Christianizing International Relations," in *Young Reinhold Niebuhr: His Early Writings, 1911–1931*, ed. W. G Chrystal (New York: Pilgrim Press, 1977), 201–2.

19. Ibid., 208.

20. Fox, *Reinhold Niebuhr*, 129.
21. Ibid.
22. Reinhold Niebuhr, *Moral Man and Immoral Society*, partly reprinted as "The Morality of Nations," in *The Puritan Ethic in United States Foreign Policy*, ed. D. L. Larson (Princeton, N.J.: D. Van Nostrand, 1966).
23. Niebuhr, "Morality of Nations," 83.
24. Ibid., 86.
25. Reinhold Niebuhr, " A Critique of Pacifism," *The Atlantic Monthly*, May 1927, in *Love and Justice*, ed. Robertson, 247; Reinhold Niebuhr, "Pacifism and the Use of Force," *The World Tomorrow*, May 1927, in *Love and Justice*, ed. Robertson, 253.
26. Reinhold Niebuhr, "Intellectual Autobiography," in *Reinhold Niebuhr*, ed. Kegley and Bretall, 8.
27. Fox, *Reinhold Niebuhr*, 155–57.
28. Reinhold Niebuhr, "Why I Leave the F.O.R.," *Christian Century*, January 3, 1934, in *Love and Justice*, ed. Robertson, 254.
29. Fox, *Reinhold Niebuhr*, 133.
30. Niebuhr, "Pacifism Against the Wall," 267.
31. Ibid., 261.
32. Niebuhr, "Why I leave the F.O.R.," 258.
33. Reinhold Niebuhr, "The Christian Church in a Secular Age," reprinted in *The Essential Reinhold Niebuhr*, ed. R. McAfee Brown (New Haven, Conn.: Yale University Press, 1986), 80.
34. Ibid.
35. Reinhold Niebuhr, *Do the State and Nation Belong to God or the Devil?* (London: Student Christian Movement Press, 1937), 29–30.
36. Ibid., 9.
37. Ibid., 21–22.
38. Ibid., 42.
39. See Fox, as well as Charles C. Brown, *Niebuhr and His Age: Reinhold Niebuhr's Prophetic Role and Legacy*, new ed. (Harrisburg, Pa.: Trinity Press International, 2002), and Mark Hulsether, *Building a Protestant Left: Christianity and Crisis Magazine, 1941–1993* (Knoxville: University of Tennessee Press, 1998).
40. Cited in Hulsether, *Building a Protestant Left*, 21–22.
41. Reinhold Niebuhr, "The Christian Faith and the World Crisis," *Christianity and Crisis*, February 10, 1941, 4–5.
42. Niebuhr, "Ten Years That Shook My World," 4.
43. Niebuhr, "The Christian Faith and the World Crisis," 6.
44. Reinhold Niebuhr, *The Children of Light, and the Children of Darkness* (New York: Scribner's, 1945).
45. Niebuhr, *The Children of Light*, 163–65.
46. Reinhold Niebuhr, "Editorial Notes," *Christianity and Crisis*, September 16, 1946, 3.
47. Reinhold Niebuhr, letter to Ursula Niebuhr, September 3, 1946, in *Remembering Reinhold Niebuhr: Letters of Reinhold and Ursula M. Niebuhr*, ed. Ursula M. Niebuhr (San Francisco: Harper Collins, 1991), 201.
48. Kleinman, *A World of Hope*, 209.
49. Niebuhr, "The Fight for Germany," 67.
50. Reinhold Niebuhr, "Europe, Russia, and America," *Nation*, September 14, 1946, 289.
51. Reinhold Niebuhr, "European Impressions," *Christianity and Crisis*, May 12, 1947, 2.
52. Reinhold Niebuhr, "The Marshall Plan," *Christianity and Crisis*, October 13, 1947, 2.
53. Hulsether, *Building a Protestant Left*, xxxvi–vii.
54. Arthur Schlesinger Jr., *The Vital Center* (Boston: Houghton Mifflin, 1949), online at http://www.writing.upenn.edu/~afilreis/50s/vital-center.html (accessed August 1, 2004).
55. Reinhold Niebuhr, "Religiosity and the Christian Faith," *Christianity and Crisis*, January 1955, cited at Religion-Online, http://www.religion-online.org/showarticle.asp?title=519 (accessed February 14, 2004).
56. Reinhold Niebuhr, "Democracy as a Religion," *Christianity and Crisis*, August 4, 1947, 1.
57. Niebuhr, *The Children of Light*, xi.

58. Niebuhr, "Democracy as a Religion," 1.
59. Reinhold Niebuhr, "Editorial Notes," *Christianity and Crisis*, December 25, 1950, 170.
60. Reinhold Niebuhr, "Ten Fateful Years," *Christianity and Crisis*, February 5, 1951, 2. See also Niebuhr's "The Idolatry of America," *Christianity and Society*, Spring 1950, in *Love and Justice*, ed. Robertson, 94–97.
61. Reinhold Niebuhr, "American Conservatism and the World Crisis," *Yale Review*, March 1951, 393.
62. Reinhold Niebuhr, "As Others See Us," *Christianity and Crisis*, December 9, 1946, 6.
63. Reinhold Niebuhr, "Amid Encircling Gloom," *Christianity and Crisis*, April 12, 1948, 42.
64. Reinhold Niebuhr, *The Irony of American History* (London: Nisbet, 1952), 57.
65. Ibid., 3.
66. Niebuhr, *Do the State and Nation Belong to God or the Devil?* 29–30.
67. Walter Russell Mead, "God's Country?" *Foreign Affairs*, September–October 2006, online at http://www.foreignaffairs.org/20060901faessay85504/walter-russell-mead/god-s-country.html (accessed June 18, 2007).

Cesar Chavez in American Religious Politics: Mapping the New Global Spiritual Line

Luis D. León

It wasn't that saving my soul was more important than the strike. On the contrary, I said to myself, if I'm going to save my soul, it's going to be through the struggle for social justice.

Cesar E. Chavez[1]

When Cesar Estrada Chavez (1927–1993) founded the United Farm Workers Union (UFW) in 1962, he concomitantly inspired the Chicano political movement and largely occasioned its attendant cultural renaissance. On July 4, 1969, he was featured on the cover of *Time* magazine. The accompanying article dubbed him the "mystical" and "earthy" leader of the Mexican American civil rights movement, and the Chicano Martin Luther King Jr. The symbolism of the date, Independence Day, bespeaks Chavez's psychosocial location: he had become a prophet of U.S. civil religiosity. Today he is unequivocally the most widely remembered Chicano public figure in the United States and globally.[2]

Chavez was broadly recognized for his social justice work during his life, but since his death in 1993, he has been multiply memorialized, awarded the Presidential Medal of Freedom, nominated for the Congressional Gold Medal, celebrated in an official California state holiday, and commemorated in an official U.S. stamp. In 2006, he was counted among the first group of inductees into the California Hall of Fame—the few posthumous awardees included naturalist John Muir, as well as Chavez nemesis Ronald Reagan. Should the movement to establish a national holiday on his birthday prove successful, this honor would be the equivalent of reaching full U.S. sainthood—trumping in significance even the ongoing efforts to canonize him as an official Catholic saint.[3]

At Chavez's funeral, Art Torres, California Democratic Party state chairman, spoke for millions of Latina/os when he declared: "[Cesar Chavez] is our Gandhi, our Martin Luther King."[4] Chavez's political leadership became, even before his death, intimately linked to his larger status in the community as a charismatic leader who, as Richard Rodriguez put it, "wielded spiritual authority."[5]

This essay explores the nature of that "spiritual authority" and argues for its significance in any comprehensive understanding of Chavez and his importance as a leader for Chicanos. In his national ascendancy, ironically, a distinct but amorphous Christian identity became pivotal in his efficacious campaign for the hearts and minds of Americans. As devotee Gary Soto has professed, "In the course of this movement, Cesar became—whether he accepted this status or not—a spiritual leader for all Chicanos."[6] In what follows I argue that he indeed accepted this role, albeit with initial reluctance, and that his religious identity, complex and fluctuating, erudite and theological, was central to establishing what Los Angeles Catholic Archdiocese bishop Roger Mahoney described as his "prophetic" vocation.[7]

Chavez signified in various religions, though he identified broadly as "Christian," and he produced an unmistakably Christian ethics. However, his variegated theology has resulted in a religious identity that is ultimately irretrievable as, I argue, he intended it to be. Still, this essay seeks a clearer understanding of his sacred acts as they intersected his political practices.

Chavez did not separate religion and politics into two discrete personal and public dimensions that informed each other. Rather, he melded these two realms into prophetic narratives and practices, directly responding to and engaging the unlikely place of Christianity in American political discourse. Chavez was a prophetic agent in a broadly spiritual, ecumenical, and political sense. He is best understood as a prophet in the particular sense that Max Weber defined: a leader whose vision is not produced in a vacuum, but instead responds from within, outside, and on the boundaries of his inherited tradition.[8]

Yet biographers (especially those writing in Chavez's wake) neglect his unmistakably prophetic role within American religious and political history, grossly underestimating the level of his intellectual and spiritual engagements. Therefore, as a part of a larger revisionist project, this essay attends first to Chavez's religious identity, paying close attention to his own philosophies, through writings, interviews, and speeches. The secondary literature on Chavez and the UFW regularly presents conflicting dates and other details. Hence, I rely first on interviews and accounts with the Chavez family and on the documents produced by the Cesar E. Chavez Foundation.

I argue that Chavez's radical ecumenicalism positioned him beyond Catholicism, and that a closer scrutiny of this positioning allows a revised and enhanced perspective on the intersection of religions and politics in the United States.

My conclusion expands on the social ethics of Chavez, proposing a critical model to understand the twenty-first century, waxing not "scientifically" but theologically—that is, as advancing an understanding of the transcendent within the limitations of the temporal and the terrestrial.

I have come to neither praise nor condemn Cesar, but to describe his role in American political religiosity, unpacking and expanding his program for social change, which is, as I see it, a model for social justice. This focus obviates the banal academic mandate to render criticism of the subject in order to prove "objectivity," as if perfectly neutral. Of course, human perfection is impossible—in my work on Chavez, and in Chavez's own life—and I simultaneously resist also the impulse to lionize him for certainly he was all too human. Efforts to both canonize Chavez and to condemn him are more interesting for what they reveal about the narrators, and the power of memory and forgetting, than for what they say about the man himself.

A Prophet from the Desert

Chavez was a prophetic agent: a person, a *human*, who advocates for social change by critical discourses and acts based in religious and moral convictions vis-à-vis the status quo. Certainly he was not a perfect human, an "angel" (as he would say), nor a saint, but a charismatic leader—a leader with a powerful magnetic appeal, according to Weber. Chavez's authority was not conferred by virtue of an institutional office such as priest; according to many testimonies—including those printed in the *New York Times* and *Time* magazine—it adhered naturally. "Natural" charismatic endowment is Weber's key criteria for the prophetic designation. Additionally, the prophet speaks on behalf of the poor and the oppressed as if bringing a novel revelation from God, or by stressing existing doctrines that have gone overlooked—each resonating with (re)fresh(ed) narratives of salvation.[9]

Prophets typically emerge from out of crisis events that occasion the need for social criticism and change. Many undergo a life cycle punctuated by times of separation, trial, and return, known as the "hero's tale" or "song."[10] Like Gandhi and Martin Luther King Jr., Chavez's formation replicates in broad patterns classical training for his quasi-religious work. He was born and died in the same county. At the ground base of his struggle was a longing to return to his childhood home, a 160-acre ranch that his father and grandfather built from a parched space of neglected Arizona desert. In 1937, the Bruce Church Corporation engineered a foreclosure of the ranch so the property would be available for acquisition. In addition to the ranch, the Chavez family owned and operated a few small businesses in town that ultimately failed because of the many unpaid accountants they extended to the community, and drought years had cost the ranch a fortune. In spite of the family's relentless efforts to keep their property, the cards were stacked in favor of Bruce Church, who needed the land to straighten out his property line.

Chavez marks the exile from his homeland as fundamental to his own memory: "I bitterly missed the ranch. Maybe that is when the rebellion started. Some had been born into the migrant stream. But we had been born on the land, and I knew a different way of life. We were poor, but we had liberty. The migrant is poor, and he has no freedom."[11] His goal was to reoccupy the primal desert soil, which, in a sense, he achieved. He died in his homeland while in the midst of a court trial against the Bruce Church Corporation; his death was pivotal in gaining the jury's sympathy and favorable decision.[12] His formative childhood experiences of injustice led him down the path to working for social change; through the faith of his family he learned "heroic" and prophetic values.

But young Cesar learned also from stories and books, and the fictions of his life begin with a distortion of this fact. Orthodox narratives of his days start with the misnomer "common man from common origins." That is not exactly correct, for while poor, his family was never "common," "simple," or even "humble," as in uneducated. His grandmother, Dorotea Chavez, or "Mama Tella," was raised in a Mexican convent, where she learned Latin and Spanish. His grandfather, Cesario Chavez, or "Papa Chayo," fought in the agrarian reforms that boiled into the Mexican Revolution, catalyzed by the philosophies of "land" and "liberty." Cesar's mother, Juana Estrada, was a woman of uncommon faith. She was a *curandera*, skilled in the elaborate world of indigenous postcolonial curing. "My mother had a reputation in the valley for her skill in healing," Chavez notes, "a skill she put to constant use, for she couldn't bear to see anyone in pain, and there were no doctors in the valley. She was especially knowledgeable in the use of herbs, choosing some to cool a fever, others to cure colic, and mixing brews for specific illnesses. Her faith in her skill was as strong as her belief in the saints and the Virgin of Guadalupe."[13]

Chavez is careful to position his mother's indigenous faith as equal in importance to her Christian faith. He credits her for his initial adoption of a theology of peace. "When I look back I see her sermons had a tremendous impact on me. I didn't know it was nonviolence then, but after reading Gandhi, St. Francis, and other exponents of nonviolence, I began to clarify that in my mind. Now that I'm older I see she is nonviolent."[14] Cesar's father, Librado Chavez, taught him to abhor the behaviors associated with the macho racist stereotype, and also taught him to fight for social justice. Librado was uncommonly active in the earliest efforts to unionize farm workers.

Cesar left school at age fifteen, upon graduating from the eighth grade in 1942, in order to return to work the fields full time, thereby liberating his mother from the back-breaking work. This was also a rebellious period in his life, and his identity underwent a brief but conspicuous transformation during his "pachuco" or zootsuit period. He began to smoke, drink beer, and dance: the erotic choreography and uninhibited parties of the pachucos and pachucas gave Chicana/o youth a Dionysian idiom for expressing their alienation and rage. The adolescence of prophetic "heroes" is often characterized by rebellion, followed by a continually morphing personal identity.

In 1946 Chavez joined the U.S. Navy and served in the Pacific. "Those were the worst two years of my life: this regimentation, this super authority that somehow somebody has the right to move you around like a piece of equipment. It's worse than being in prison. And there was a lot of discrimination."[15] While in the navy he was exposed to racism and suffering on a global scale, crystallizing his resolve to advance universal justice, beginning at home. This episode marks a phase of total separation from a world in which he was familiar, and immersion into a hostile environment in which he was made to battle and endure an unjust and unrelenting force.

It was during Chavez's military service that an incident occurred at a local theater that would further impress upon him the urgency of working for democratic morality; this has been called his "Rosa Parks" moment. On shore leave, he was not in uniform.

> For a long time, movie theaters throughout the San Joaquin Valley were segregated. It was just accepted by the Mexicans then. In Delano, the quarter-section on the right was reserved for Mexicans, blacks, and Filipinos, while Anglos and Japanese sat elsewhere. . . .
>
> This time something told me I shouldn't accept such discrimination. It wasn't a question of sitting elsewhere because it was more comfortable. It was just a question that I wanted a free choice of where I wanted to be. I decided to challenge the rule, even though I was very frightened. Instead of sitting on the right, I sat down on the left. . . .
>
> It was the first time I had challenged rules so brazenly.[16]

He was forced from the cinema and detained in jail. He was not formally charged, and was released after a police officer threatened and degraded him. In the same way, the Chicano movement was ignited largely by veterans who became intolerant of racial discrimination, for such was inimical to democratic values that military indoctrination held sacred. As his response to segregation in a San Joaquin Valley theater suggests, Chavez's experience in the navy educated him in the religion of the nation-state, especially its transcendent promises of freedom, justice, and equality—until death.

In 1946 Chavez returned to California and married Helen Fabela. The couple settled in San Jose. There he began his role as husband, father of eight children, and a leader in the infamous barrio know as "sal si puedes," or "escape if you can." In 1952 he befriended a missionary priest from the San Francisco diocese, Father Donald McDonnell. McDonnell mentored Chavez in the church's teachings on farmworkers and social justice, involving Chavez in his labor camp ministry and recommending readings for him. Contrary to popular fiction, Chavez continued to educate himself after leaving school, but his apprenticeship with the missionary priest focused and increased his reading.

That same year Chavez met Fred Ross—a man whom Chavez claims "changed" his life. Ross was a forty-two-year-old organizer who worked with the Community Service Organization (CSO) directed by Saul Alinsky. Cesar soon became a disciple of Ross, who secured a position for his young apprentice also as a community organizer. But much of Chavez's first three years in the CSO were spent isolated in an office working through piles of Western and Eastern classics, accompanied by cigarettes, cans of Tab cola, and a giant, dog-eared dictionary. He read voraciously, including works on photography, art, philosophy, politics, economics, and religion. Typical of the biographers, Peter Matthiessen trivializes his intellect, but reports on his reading nonetheless: "He is a realist, not an intellectual, and his realism has been fortified by *extensive acquaintance* with political treatises, from St. Paul to Churchill, and from Jefferson to 'all the dictators': His self-education, in the CSO years, included readings in Goebbels and Machiavelli and Lord Acton."[17] His wife, Helen, once expressed her fear when she and her husband came across a bookstore: "I hope it isn't open. Books and camera stores—he'll be in there all night."[18] Today Chavez's personal library housed at La Paz reflects an impressive bibliographic mind. Indeed, much like Gramsci's organic intellectual, his erudition was occasioned and nurtured by and within a political movement.

Chavez credits Ross as his most influential mentor; he worked at the CSO under the tutelage of both Alinsky and Ross for ten years before leaving to organize farmworkers on his birthday, October 31, 1962. The date marks a rebirth for Chavez. Like Gandhi's return to India from South Africa, and King's return to his home church in Atlanta, Chavez returned to Delano to confront the master beast who had plagued his people for generations. The time had arrived for him to assume the prophetic role for which he had been training all his life.

At its apex, Chavez's prophecy revealed another of America's great sins to itself—the national abomination that was the treatment of the farmworkers, laying bare their mass suffering. He tore down the opaque veil that blinded Americans to the injustice in their own backyard—a condition tantamount to slavery in its offenses to the sacred orthodoxy the citizenry professed. In the course of his work, Chavez learned to transliterate racial and cultural politics into public Christianity: "Everywhere we went, to school, to church, to the movies, there was an attack on our culture and language, an attempt to make us conform to the 'American way,'" Chavez exclaimed. "What a sin!"[19] Chavez's movement, like American political theology more broadly, captures, reassembles, and synthesizes the confessional fragments of traditional dogmas, capitalizing on the ambiguities and overlaps in their lexicons of the sacred and the profane—all the while appealing to the Deity of reason and nature, revealed by the will of the majority.

Indeed, Chavez was all too human, and he knew that romantic notions of him could not be sustained and would inevitably give way to disillusionment and bitter criticism. Movements animated by the charismatic endowment of their founders are inextricably tied to a singularly ineffable quality. Intense personal charisma cannot be sustained and will inevitably suffer decline, or "routinization"; such was true of the UFW.

Rightly or not, aspects of Chavez's life and leadership have been publicly criticized: his imperial leadership style, the demands for utter loyalty, and the direction he took the UFW during the latter years of his life—especially the time he dedicated to fund-raising. Yet, early on Chavez described himself as a "practical" man, and recognized that organizations without money are powerless. As he saw it, there were two essential human ingredients for a successful movement, time and money: "An individual who is willing to give his time is more important than an individual who is willing to give his money. I think money would be number two."[20] In this he took cues from King, but especially Gandhi: "It's amazing how people lose track of basics. Gandhi was one of the best fund-raisers the world has ever seen! (*Laughter.*) But people don't look at it that way! They don't!"[21] Nonetheless, these fund-raising efforts have recently been condemned. Miriam Pawell of the *Los Angeles Times* discloses her bias in this regard. After all, why would a social movement need money in the United States? Pawell speaks for many, rushing her righteous indignation: Chavez, like other racialized public leaders, is not allowed to develop and change. Indeed, his image is most consumable when frozen as a striking farmworker holding picket signs, or as a fasting penitent. By contrast, his progression dispels comfortable notions of an isolated problem easily fixed by national paternal care.[22] Chavez cut an imposing figure as an American prophet on the world stage decrying the ideology of capitalism that privileges the rich.

Chavez never claimed that he would remain forever in the fields, organizing workers, picketing, and fasting. In fact, as early as 1978 he publicly declared that his role was more akin to that of a teacher: "I think my role has changed from one of an organizer to possibly one of a teacher. . . . Mostly I want to teach people to initiate and accept change within the movement because we can't live in the late '70s with the concepts we had in the mid '60s. The things we did in 1965 are no longer necessary, valid, or even important."[23] In 1981, the *Los Angeles Times* ran a story entitled "UFW Transforming Itself from 'Cause' to "Businesslike Union.'" It reported: "Even as a costly modernization program continues, the union stresses its role as a social cause, a near-religion requiring vows of poverty from its top officers, attorneys, doctors, nurses, and even the lowest level of file clerk."[24] By 1983 Chavez told the UFW annual convention that he had formed a "Chicano lobby" to support Democratic candidates.[25] That same year he addressed a lesbian and gay coalition, called Project Just Business, at Circus Disco in West Hollywood.[26] He was, as has been noted, many things to many people, and he continued to evolve throughout his life.

The Myth of Cesar Chavez

Chavez's public memory has emerged as a highly contested political field of self-interest and (un)holy constructs. Some scholars and activists, anxious to claim Chavez as "one of the people," insistently and publicly remember Chavez as a simple, ignorant man with little in the way of self-reflection, religious or otherwise. Luis Valdez and other Chicano political leaders have helped to script this fiction of simplicity and ignorance. "The essence of his [Chavez's] greatness," claims Valdez,

> is his simple humanity. All who had the opportunity to know and work with him in his day-to-day struggle know this to be true: he was not a saint; he was not a miracle worker; he was just a man. That's why his impact on history is so remarkable. This is the common man, inspiring leader and unforgettable brother that lives.[27]

While most memories of Chavez misrepresent his complexity (especially posthumously), cofounder of the UFW Dolores Huerta disagrees: "But in truth, I find him a very complicated person."[28] Similarly, Stan Steiner wrote of him in 1969: "Chavez is an enigma to many. He is a different man to different people."[29]

Even inasmuch as Valdez and others remember Chavez singularly as an ordinary man, they clash over the issue of canonization. Fred Dalton's treatment of Chavez follows the work of Chicano priest and scholar Virgil Elizondo; it reads as a hagiography, professing Catholic identity for "Cesar." In fact, professions of Catholic loyalty are rampant in the print on Chavez, especially in the posthumous literature, which often popularizes the myth, already circulating in his life, declaring Chavez a "devout" Catholic believer. Dalton writes: "While César [sic] respected other religious and moral traditions, actively promoted an ecumenical spirit within the union, and incorporated meditation and yoga into his own spirituality, he was quite open about his commitment to the [Catholic] Church. Chavez *always* identified himself as a member of the *Catholic* faith community."[30]

In reality, such claims of an exclusive commitment never came from Chavez himself. Although he was baptized Catholic, his catechism was informal and he was schooled in a form of Mexican home-based Catholicism. Attitudes and values toward the church in Mexico stem largely from the anticolonial philosophy of the Mexican Revolution, which rejected the hierarchy as a feudal institution yet which privileged Catholic symbols that had been indigenized and therefore possessed the potential to mobilize masses of people for revolution.[31] Cesar's formation as a Catholic was informed by this history: he rarely attended mass as a child, but was prepared for confirmation by his grandmother, and was confirmed without formal church instruction. As an adult, Chavez attended mass, but he was also active in many faith congregations—including Pentecostal. Moreover, his Catholic subjectivity became decreasingly pronounced throughout the duration of his work. When asked about his religious identification in his later life, he responded: "For me, Christianity happens to be *a* natural *source* of *faith*. I have read what Christ said when he was here. He was very clear in what he meant and knew exactly what he was after. He was extremely radical, and he was for social change."[32] He bespeaks a savvy Christian identity with a hearty salute to his Pentecostal and otherwise Protestant followers in his claim to have studied the scriptures. Indeed, his earliest organizing efforts in Delano began in Pentecostal house churches in his neighborhood. He prayed with churchgoers, and there he developed the idea for singing in the union.[33]

Chavez's spiritual practices were diverse not only within Christianity, but beyond; he was fascinated by the study of and engagement in other religions. Around his neck he sported a Jewish mezuzah. "I'm sure Christ wore a mezuzah," he once quipped. "He certainly didn't wear a cross."[34] According to artist and curator of the Cesar Chavez museum in Phoenix, Jim Covurrubias, the labor leader returned periodically to the Arizona desert to fast privately and to consult with an indigenous healer or *curandera*.[35] Cesar's granddaughter, Julie Rodriguez, spokesperson for the Chavez family, explained that her grandfather's spirituality was manifest as a physical commitment: "His spiritual beliefs affected his diet as well; he was a vegetarian and . . . became a macrobiotic. Cesar understood embodying the way of nonviolence as centering himself and understanding himself as one with the universe. He was the optimal example of a lifelong learner. I have never come in touch with someone who was so self-aware."[36] Later in his life, Chavez developed a commitment to the quasi-religious practices of Synanon, imposing the "Game" strategy on his union staff—much to the staff's dismay.[37]

It is, of course, impossible for anyone to judge Chavez's level of faithful commitment to Catholicism, but his strategic intentions are made clear in his writings. In a 1968 academic paper read at a Chicano studies conference, Chavez called upon the church to live out its teachings of social justice.

> The Church is *one* form of the presence of God on Earth, and so naturally it is powerful. It is powerful by definition. It is a powerful moral and spiritual force which cannot be ignored by any movement. Furthermore, it is an organization with tremendous wealth. Since the Church is to be servant to the poor, it is our fault if that wealth is not channeled to help the poor in our world.
>
> In a small way we have been able, in the Delano strike, to work together with the Church in such a way as to bring some of its moral and economic power to bear on those who want to maintain the status quo, keeping farmworkers in virtual enslavement.[38]

Chavez's reasoning here is logical and sound: the church must practice what it preaches, and because it is rich and globally influential, those resources could be wielded for tremendous advantage. However, these same words have been distorted, twisting the narrative into a magical incantation: "A devout Roman Catholic, he described the church as a 'powerful moral and spiritual force' in the world. God controls the earth's events and people, seeing to it that good causes triumph . . . Chavez felt that he could be divinely guaranteed of eventual success if he persisted in presenting his righteous case."[39]

This paternalistic reading completely neglects the historical context for the statement. Three years into the grape strike and boycott, the Catholic Church remained officially "uncommitted," arguing that their endorsement would bias and thus invalidate their role as presumed mediators between the striking farmworkers and the growers—many of whom were Italian Catholics and major contributors to the church. Yet, Protestant denominations had served farmworkers well before the strike and thus became immediate supporters of the UFW. The earliest efforts began in 1928 with the National Council of Churches Migrant Ministry. In 1957, the California Migrant Ministry crystallized and advanced aid to farmworkers, bringing a newly endowed focus and a director whose activities included enlisting the support of mainline Protestant churches.[40] Many churches offered financial support as well as personnel, and the grape boycott was officially endorsed by the California Council of Churches, the National Council of Churches, and the International Council of Churches. One minister reflects: "In the 1960s and '70s virtually every major religious body in the United States and many in Europe and Canada gave attention to U.S. farm workers, took positions on what the workers were doing, and were a significant force in rallying 17 million Americans to participate in the common act of not buying grapes."[41]

Still, the Catholic Church resisted. Chavez formally petitioned the American bishops for their expressed support in 1968, and again in 1969; on both occasions his request was denied. In 1969 the church formed an ad hoc committee to deal with the farmworkers, but it remained officially neutral until the middle of the lettuce boycott in 1973.[42] During this time, however, individual priests and nuns worked for the strikes and boycotts—and to these efforts Chavez has attributed the initial victories of the union.[43] Though the church remained officially neutral, California bishops remained split, some supporting the UFW, others siding with the growers. Catholic groups helped to finance the strikes early on, and individual priests and nuns marched on picket lines in California, defying the church's position. Whereas many commentators represent Chavez's simple, almost naive devotion to the church, clearly his actual engagements with Catholic institutions combined religion and the practical exigencies of political struggle.

But Chavez eventually grew weary of the church's official neutrality. In 1971, Franciscan Mark Day recounted the following exchange.

> I asked Cesar about his feelings toward the church one evening, Day recounted, when he and his wife, Helen, had supper at Guadalupe Church rectory with me and some visiting priests.
>
> "Most farm workers are Chicanos," Cesar said, "and most Chicanos are Catholics. The church is the only institution which our people are closely associated with. When the church

does not respond to us, we get offended, and we are tempted to lash out against it."

"You know," he continued, "there are many changes in the church today. But many of these changes, like the new ritual of the mass, are merely external. What I like to see is a priest get up and speak about things like racism and poverty. But, even when you hear about these things from the pulpit, you get the feeling that they aren't doing anything significant to alleviate these evils. They are just talking about them.

"Here in Delano, the church has been such a stranger to us that our own people tend to put it together with all the powers and institutions that oppose them."[44]

While Dalton and others evince Chavez's commitment to the Catholic Church with this very same passage, the practical union leader meant it as a criticism and careful mechanism for his own religious positionality; it nowhere represents a buttress for his own Catholicism; nor does his 1968 admonition to the church represent a fatalistic, primitive faith (as some have argued).

There was one occasion when Chavez clearly identified himself as specifically and emotionally Catholic—upon meeting Pope Paul VI, on September 25, 1974. Chavez did not request the audience, however; it was initiated by U.S. bishops as part of their new campaign supporting the farmworkers. Chavez had been planning a trip to Europe that fall to urge labor leaders there to enforce the lettuce boycott. The flight was paid for by the National Council of Churches. During the visit, Cesar followed standard procedure and kissed the pope's ring. He then dramatically unfolded a UFW flag and presented it to the Pontiff while photographers shot pictures. Of this meeting Chavez remarked: "I have difficulty expressing its meaning, except that being a Catholic, having a chance to see the Holy Father in person, to have a special audience, is like a small miracle." The Vatican later made a statement supporting the farmworkers, which Chavez said was the most important aspect of the meeting: "And what was really significant was the statement that he made about the farm workers and the Mexican-Americans in the United States."[45]

After the meeting, Chavez responded with an enthusiasm that was at once sentimental and pragmatic: he makes clear his emotional identification with the church and his feelings of awe, but he stops far short of claiming that his is a Catholic movement, or that he himself is solely committed to the church.

Chavez was pragmatic in developing a social ethics looking toward the church, especially liberation theology, but not allowing himself to be beholden to it. Efforts to canonize him as a Catholic evince his success in gaining the church as a base of support. At the same time, there are stakes involved in refusing to concede a specifically or singularly Catholic identity to Chavez. Every indication is that he saw himself as far more ecumenical than is often assumed. By contrast, connecting Chavez solely to the institutional church enables his co-optation in support of sundry church positions and projects that he reviled—especially those involving the church's misogyny, homophobia, and pedophilia.

The Sacrificial Body: Performing Nonviolence

Chavez is best understood as a complex thinker and ecumenical believer, whose political work was deeply influenced by Gandhi, based in the spirituality and philosophy of nonviolent sacrificial struggle for social justice. And nothing exemplifies this commitment so much as his leadership in Delano, the central California town at the heart of the state's agribusiness. For more than a century, police and local sheriff departments had been deployed as militia forces by growers, who successfully thwarted efforts at unionization and workers' rights. Chavez's return to the Central Valley would mark the beginning of change. Intent on forming a union even at great personal cost, he called for a grape boycott in 1965, a battle that was bitterly fought for five years. In 1966 the first union contracts were signed, and the dream of a union was realized. However, negotiating new and lapsed contracts became a series of fierce battles involving endless picket lines and lawsuits.

The fledgling union was dwarfed by labor's Goliath. Agribusiness was California's economic giant: it enjoyed the favor of local and federal politicians. Moreover, the initial victory motivated the Teamsters'/Mafia union to compete for deals: they offered growers "sweetheart" contracts that decreased benefits and pay for labor; the Teamsters had previously ignored Chicano fieldworkers. Mafia goons savagely attacked striking women and children, brutalizing them under the gleeful gaze of police officers, who stood nearby idly, gawking. Inevitably, police arrested the bloodied strikers, even while they had been the victims rather than the perpetrators of a crime.

These events drew media attention, and as a result in 1966, the U.S. Senate Subcommittee in Migratory Labor held hearings in Sacramento. The arrest of strikers was a preemptive measure, pleaded the sheriff. This tortured reasoning occasioned Robert Kennedy's now famous quip: "Can I suggest that in the interim period of time, the luncheon period of time, that the sheriff and the district attorney read the Constitution of the United States?"[46] Kennedy's support of the union came partially as payback for Chavez's organizing efforts throughout the 1950s. During those years, Chavez, UFW's first vice president Dolores Huerta, and activist Fred Ross registered and delivered nearly 300,000 new Latino Democrats in California, making it the most powerful Chicano group in the United States. This campaign coalesced around the "Viva Kennedy" slogan, which is thought to have tipped California's electoral votes for John F. Kennedy in 1960. Working with the Community Service Organization, Chavez learned the potentials and pitfalls of the democratic process; he never trusted it blindly as a panacea.

As the grape strike continued throughout the late 1960s, growers stubbornly refused to sign contracts and continued to attack strikers. Despite Chavez's best efforts, retaliatory violence erupted in the UFW, and some of the growers' properties were burned and goons assaulted. Chavez himself never abandoned his foundational principal, nonviolent sacrificial love: "Love is the most important ingredient in nonviolent work—love the opponent—but we really haven't learned yet how to love the growers," he explained.

> I think we've learned how not to hate them, and maybe love comes in stages. If we're full of hatred, we can't really do our work. Hatred saps all that strength and energy we need to plan. Of course, we can learn how to love the growers more easily after they sign contracts.[47]

Certainly he had many sacred models for this political philosophy of love, including Jesus Christ and Saint Francis of Assisi.

Most biographers assert that Chavez was introduced to Gandhi by Father Donald McDonnell in San Jose in 1948. However, Chavez's own version is more complicated, and also contradictory. In 1975 he claimed that McDonnell introduced him to many books, including Louis Fischer's *Life of Gandhi*; he further stated that his exposure to the Indian guru was limited to newsreels and newspapers. In 1990, however, three years prior to his death, he was quoted as follows:

> I was eleven or twelve years old, and I went to a movie. In those days, in between movies they had newsreels, and in one of the newsreels there was a report on Gandhi. It said that this half-naked man without a gun had conquered the might of the British empire. . . . It really impressed me because I couldn't conceive of how that had happened without guns. Even though I had never heard the name Gandhi before. . . . since then, I have made a life project of reading about Gandhi and his message.[48]

The long versions of the stories are reconcilable in all but one detail, and noteworthy especially inasmuch as Chavez was more inclined to cite Gandhi as his muse later in his life. Still, Gandhi's influence was central to his work from the start. It begins from the following maxim: "Nonviolence also has one big demand—the need to be creative, to develop strategy. Gandhi described it as 'moral jujitsu.' Always hit the opposition off balance, but keep your principles."[49] For Chavez, morality meant consistency in ethics, but moral values could also be deployed for political gain in the public marketplace of ideas.

In this, he also drew from the prophetic tradition of Martin Luther King Jr., whose acumen for narrating public morality revitalized and established fresh grammar for discourses of American civil religion. Chavez and King communicated with each other, spoke on the telephone, and announced their collaboration on King's Poor People's March and Campaign in 1968. After King's assassination, the Reverend Ralph Abernathy and Coretta Scott King were present at many of Chavez's public actions, including his subsequent fasts in 1972 and 1988. Chavez published an homage to King titled "Martin Luther King, Jr.: He Showed Us the Way."[50]

King founded the Southern Christian Leadership Conference (SCLC) in the 1950s with the messianic and prophetic mission to "redeem the soul of America."[51] The ideological power of this motivation illustrates the suasion of an American identity embedded in a Protestantism that continues to be reshaped and retold by its most recent professors. In the tradition of the Black Church, King rendered the meaning of Christian redemption from his own experience. Chavez followed suit.

A conception of social evil is possible within many traditions and appears as a formative trope in the politics of Gandhi, King, and Chavez. All three went beyond the boundaries of their inherited traditions and thrived in the spiritual borderlands: King's pilgrimage to India, Gandhi's multiple self-religious identities, and Chavez's radical Christian ecumenicalism combined with indigenous teachings and practices. They all intersected, however, in their commitment to nonviolent social change, coalescing with the organization of workers.

For Chavez, organizing workers required exposing the injustice in Delano to a national audience. To this end he engineered several key public events to transform the UFW from a Western farmworkers union into a (mostly) Latino/a civil rights movement with international fame. By November of 1968, the New York Times described his work as "a civil rights issue" and "a quasi-religious cause"; these events transformed the strike, into "The Cause," or "La Causa."[52]

The first event was a march from Delano to Sacramento that was modeled after King's "prayer pilgrimage" and Gandhi's Salt March. The march took place during holy week of 1966 and culminated in a massive interfaith ceremony on Easter Sunday. It was called "Pilgrimage, Penitence, and Revolution." Its charter, the "Plan of Delano," was penned by Luis Valdez and Chavez and expressly mimicked Emiliano Zapata's "Plan of Ayala"; it articulated the group's central articles of faith. Each marcher was literally sworn in, verbally declaring allegiance to the plan while resting one hand on it and holding a crucifix in the other. Dolores Huerta performed each initiation. The plan itself was recited each night of the procession, in "spirited" ceremonies. An avowed "Plan of Liberation," its religious professions were multiple:

> The Penance we accept symbolizes the suffering we shall have in order to bring justice to these same towns, to this same valley. . . . The Pilgrimage we make symbolizes the long historical road we have traveled in this valley alone, and the long road we have yet to travel, with much penance, in order to bring about the Revolution we need.[53]

Theirs was a distinctly Mexican American civil religion: drawn from revolutionary traditions yet consonant with the major teachings of the Constitution, principally freedom and liberty, but also justice, equality, and progress. The UFW added to this creed a motherly femininity embodied by the Virgin of Guadalupe, while emphasizing dynamic human sacrifice.[54] Chavez stressed the sacrificial element: "The thing we have going for us is that people are willing to sacrifice themselves. When you have that spirit, then nonviolence is not very difficult to accomplish."[55]

Nonviolent sacrificial struggle was the heart of the movement; it was linked with religious symbols to increase its rhetorical appeal. The marchers claimed to "seek, and have, the support of the church in what we do." However, the "church" is not specifically identified, even while the plan quotes *Rerum Novarum*—the church's key statement on justice for workers. Still, the marchers were careful to qualify their relationship to the symbols and orthodoxy of Catholicism: "At the head of the pilgrimage we carry LA VIRGEN DE GUADALUPE because she is ours, all ours, Patroness of the Mexican people. We also carry the Sacred Cross and the Star of David because we are not sectarians, and because we ask the help and prayers of all religions. . . . GOD SHALL NOT ABANDON US." The plan is rife with God talk, and emerges de facto as its own theological statement. "We seek our basic, God-given rights as human beings. Because we have suffered—and are not afraid to suffer—in order to survive, we are ready to give up everything, even our lives, in our fight for social justice. We shall do it without violence because that is our destiny."[56] The ceremony ending the pilgrimage was celebrated on Easter Sunday, on the steps of the State Capital building. Governor Pat Brown was not counted among the ten thousand; his absence was conspicuous. He spent the holiday at the Palm Springs' home of Frank Sinatra.

Even more than the peregrination, Chavez's fasting impressed the hearts and minds of Americans with the plight of the farmworkers. Chavez embarked upon three public fasts, following Gandhi's example in number and duration. In 1972 he fasted for twenty-five days in Phoenix, for "social justice." In 1988, he fasted in Delano for thirty-six days, protesting the use of pesticides. But it was his first fast in 1968, the "love fast," that transformed his movement from a strike and boycott into a moral crusade and Chavez into its prophet. Again, the symbolism of time, free and accessible, was a central trope in the event: it began on February 14. Like the first fast of Gandhi, Chavez's actions were precipitated by violence erupting within his own movement: Chavez wanted to recommit the movement to its foundational principles. Ignoring the counsel of his advisors, he told his followers he was embarking upon the fast because he loved them.

During this initial starvation period, Chavez cloistered himself in a small "cell" at Forty Acres, which subsequently became a makeshift pilgrimage site. Chavez stressed the distinct yet broadly religious quality of his actions, preaching the favor of God. Each night an ecumenical "religious ceremony" was celebrated, involving rabbis; Catholic priests sporting bright red vestments adorned by a UFW black eagle; Presbyterian, Methodist, and Episcopalian ministers; and Pentecostal preachers.[57] Of these events Jerry Cohen observed:

> I visited the Forty Acres on several occasions during the fast. It was both a fascinating and awesome spectacle to view. By the second week of the fast a sprawling tent city had sprung up around the little service station at the forty acres. Farm workers from all over California came to live in the tents and to share in the event. . . . the deliberate pace, the quiet voices, the huddled figures, the sharing of food and drink—all these gave the impression of serious religious vigil. . . . I'm not religious at all, but I would go to those masses at the Forty Acres every night. No matter what their religious background, anyone interested in farm workers, or with any sense about people, could see that something was going on that was changing a lot of people. The feeling of the workers was obvious. They talked at those meetings about their own experiences, about what the fast meant in terms of what the Union was going to mean to them. That was a really deep feeling, but it wasn't religious in the sense that somebody like me couldn't relate to it.[58]

Like that of the nation-state, the religion of the UFW was open to all who professed even secular beliefs in the sanctity of freedom, liberty, equality, and justice—but a belief in a monotheistic God served best to elevate these principles above the earthly terrain into a cosmic arena. People from all backgrounds experienced spiritual conversions through their devotion to the Chicano guru.[59]

The fast was terminated in dramatic fashion, covered by media from around the globe. Senator Robert F. Kennedy returned for the event, and fed bread directly to the leader who had mortified his flesh to enhance reliance on his spirit. In fact, Chavez claims to have received a fresh revelation from God during his retreat that was read aloud during the mass:

> Our struggle is not easy. Those who oppose our cause are rich and powerful, and they have many allies in high places. We are poor. Our allies are few. But we have something the rich do not own. We have our own bodies and spirits and the justice of our cause as weapons. . . . We must admit that our lives are all that really belong to us. So it is my deepest belief that only by giving our lives do we find life. I am convinced that the truest act of courage, the strongest act of [humanity] is to sacrifice ourselves for others in a totally nonviolent struggle for justice. To be [human] is to suffer for others. God help us to be [human]![60]

On this same occasion, Martin Luther King Jr. sent a telegram to Chavez.

> As brothers in the fight for equality, I extend the hand of fellowship and goodwill and wish continuing success to you and your members. The fight for equality must be fought on many fronts—in the urban slums, in the sweatshops of the factories and fields. Our separate struggles are really one—a struggle for freedom, for dignity, and for humanity. You and your valiant fellow workers have demonstrated your commitment to righting grievous wrongs forced upon exploited people. We are together with you in spirit and in determination that our dreams for a better tomorrow will be realized.[61]

During his famed initial "spiritual fast," Chavez received visitors while he meditated, reposing in a full lotus position. He was asked to explain the fast. In one characteristic response, he pointed to a blank wall. "See that white wall? Well, imagine ten different-colored balls, all jumping up and down. One ball is called religion, another propaganda, another organizing, another law, and so forth. When people look at that wall and see those balls, different people look at different balls; each person keeps his eye on his own ball. For each person the balls mean many different things, but for everyone they can mean something!"[62]

The meaning of the fast, like the movement itself, paralleled the religious dimension of the state in that it was broadly coded, enabling mass appeal. Prior to the fast, Chavez further clarified his motivations in a letter to the to the National Council of Churches: "My fast is informed by my religious faith and by my deep roots in the Church. It is not intended as a pressure on anyone but only as an expression of my own deep feelings and my own need to do penance and to be in prayer." "Penance" is a Catholic rite, but not exclusively. Again, Chavez deploys circumlocution, positioning, and deft border crossing while emphasizing the ritual's distinctly religious aspects. Orthodoxy in this case is belief itself, rather than a discrete faith.

Cesar Chavez and the American Faithful: True Believers without True Belief

As a social movement within a democratic republic, Chavez's campaign was for American hearts and minds. "America is comprised of groups," he once remarked. "So long as the smaller groups do not have the same rights and the same protection as others—I don't care what you call it, Capitalism or Communism—it is not going to work. Somehow, the guys in power have to be reached by counter power, or through change in their hearts and minds."[63] Thus, his appeal was not exclusively to any particular religious group—even while his base was predominantly Christian, and specifically Catholic. He appealed to those religious sentiments around which all like-minded believers congealed, while attaching those amorphous "moods and motivations" to his political cause. He once explained as follows: "See, everybody interprets our work in a different way. Some people interpret us as a union, some people interpret our work as an ethnic issue, some people interpret our work as a peace movement, some people see it as a religious movement. We can appeal to broad sectors because of these different interpretations"[64] Taking my cue from Chavez himself, I interpret his work as a *broadly* religious movement—one not distinctly Catholic.

Inasmuch as his description of his group is antithetical to a traditional church orthodoxy, it recalls President Eisenhower's famous one-liner: "America makes no sense unless it is founded on a deeply held religious faith—and I don't care what that faith is." Comparing King's SCLC to Chavez's UFW, one theorist writes: "Both agencies attempted to convince the larger public that the symbols of their respective movements were in keeping with the values of the nation as they had been inculcated into the metaphors of earlier historical situations and became part of the accepted civil religion by the majority."[65] The prophetic translation and iteration of the American story was central to Chavez's rhetorical appeal.

Chavez's vision began with the organization of farmworkers, but he always intended that union to catalyze a much larger social transformation. "And if this spirit grows within the farm labor movement, one day we can use the force that we have to help correct a lot of things that are wrong in this society. But that is for the future. Before you can run, you have to learn to walk."[66] Learning to walk involved deconstructing the codes that legitimized racism and the mass exploitation and suffering of the many for the benefit of the few; hence, he read, beginning with classical philosophy, economics, politics, and religion. From this he fathomed the moral and ethical foundation of U.S. democracy, and engaged it—a system that is marked by the advances and limitations of the European Enlightenment.

In the eighteenth century Rousseau addressed the ideological limits of a democratic republic voided of its divine right: mass secularization would strip social inequities of the sacred vestments that clothed the status quo in an aura of truth and legitimacy. The naked injustice of economic inequality threatened the peace of society. But rather than proposing broad reform, Rousseau first theorized a "civil religion," whereby sacred authority would become the manufactured domain of what he called the state's "spiritual dimension," through the continuing confluence of history and revelation. Though avowedly secular, the liberal republic could retain its sacred authority in what is perhaps modernity's greatest sleight of hand: a secular state whose sacred authority is reflexive, or self-generating. In the American democratic system, as De Tocqueville proposed, the authority that the masses once attributed to the Mind of God alone could now be found in the Will of the People, writ large and revealed by the democratic process.

Rather than a sui generis religious system, civil religion is perhaps best described as a national collection of myths, symbols, and rituals that express Judeo-Christian teaching along nonspecific religious lines within national narratives of transcendent significance. The symbols themselves are shadow representations of the majority traditions that can be reflected by minority faiths. Hence, Robert Bellah's 1965 liberal reprisal of Rousseau is a corruption of the original aristocratic intention. What the French modernist first described was not a self-supporting institution aligned with the state, but a "religious dimension" of the nation capturing and synthesizing mass religious sentiments supporting it. His "civil religion" would function as a mystifying agent of the state that would enable believers to reassemble and affirm the fragments of primitive beliefs, hopes, and fears shattered by enlightened thought within the certainty of their collective. For Rousseau, this spiritual dimension of the republic could free the rulers from devotion to medieval institutions in favor of populist tropes, all the while reproducing the ultimate stakes of heaven and hell as a psychic technique of social regulation. The religion of the democratic republic could suit modern demand for tangibility, efficacy, and participation.

Political discourse in the United States is a triumph of Rousseau's theories. On June 27, 2005, Supreme Court justice Antonin Scalia spoke for millions of faithful Americans when explaining his vote to allow the Ten Commandments to be displayed on public space: "It is a profound religious message, but it's a profound religious message believed in by the vast majority of the American people. . . . the minority has to be tolerant of the majority's ability to express its belief that government comes from God, which is what this is about."

For such believers, the state's divine legitimacy is implicit, allowing it to (re)produce its own discourses of the holy. Devotion to the state was described by Nietzsche's Zarathustra as the "New Idol." The modern death of God left a void filled by a generalized mysticism that surrounds, shapes, and inflects the democratic process so that it becomes a sacred system. Hence, the principle of majority rule is the process whereby God's will is revealed. Echoing Rousseau, Nietzsche's prophet declared that all nations invent and speak their "own tongues of good and evil." The history of the twentieth century has repeatedly proven the efficacy of this tool as a mechanism of mass political suasion—even while its patent abuses are obvious and repetitive. Bellah and other liberal twentieth-century theorists have promoted the deist rendering of modern national religion as a tongue for good, celebrating a consensus social spirituality and ethics indebted to Enlightened principles of justice and equality. In this way they overlook the great suffering and injustice legitimized by religious nationalism.

The danger of a nation-state dedicated to popular spiritual beliefs manifests in self-interested, myopic forces that concomitantly manipulate love, fear, and hatred into a Christian theocracy. As President Jimmy Carter warns: "Although considered to be desirable by some Americans, this melding of church and state is of deep concern to those who have always relished their separation as one of our moral values."[67] For better or worse, state constructs of the sacred fall short of tight control over effervescent moods and motivations, and therefore new and unorthodox spiritual energies are continually produced. Conversely, antihegemonic religious stories circulate throughout the population within, outside, and in direct opposition to churches and other institutions functioning as regulatory mechanisms.

Religious nationalists have invested in modern normative models of human subjectivity; at times, racial and erotic identities are attached as appendages to grand economic, political, and cultural narratives. Ironically, civil religion is also a democratic field of social relations, and the complicated truths of race, gender, and sexuality rupture the architecture of the state's version, opening new spaces to theorize the nation, beginning with the most primal element in statecraft—the human body and soul. Racism begins from a narration of a "natural" order to the world, delimiting a hierarchy of races crafted through Enlightenment discourses. Gandhi, King, and Chavez confronted these racializing narratives, demonstrating that people of color are equally children of God.

In this way, Chavez's fasts proposed his own corporality as the metonymic national body upon which to imprint a fresh template of virtuous being. His body was broken and suspended in a deathlike state before a resurrection to enliven a praxis of new life and national redemption. His explanation for the fast, "love," strengthens the allegorical tie to the sacrificial Christ—a signification not lost on most observers. Chavez redefined God and the national good for an American community of believers (and make-believers).

Mapping the Spiritual Line for the Twenty-first Century

There is no small irony in the coalescing of religion and politics into the civil rights movements of the second half of the twentieth century—a century ushered in by the "death of God." Religious authority emanating from church pulpits does not flow securely into the hands of government officials, no matter how successful the politician or party. Instead, democratic impulses continually disestablish religious boundaries, thereby establishing the conditions for spiritual dominance to circulate as so many individuals' and groups' will to power. America's most remembered leaders thrived from this reality, King and Chavez foremost. At best, they functioned as theologians of American civil religion who moved the national logos against racial intolerance, toward the promise of universal Christian grace. But the pendulum continues to swing.

On the current coalescence of religion and politics, President Carter warns: "It is the injection of these beliefs into America's government policies that is cause for concern. These believers are convinced that they have a personal responsibility to hasten this coming of the 'rapture' in order to fulfill biblical prophecy. Their agenda calls for a war in the Middle East against Islam . . . At this time of rapture, all Jews will either be converted to Christianity or be burned."[68]

To this warning Sam Harris adds: "Many who claim to be transformed by Christ's love are deeply, even murderously intolerant of criticism. While we may want to ascribe this to human nature, it is clear that such hatred draws considerable support from the Bible. . . . most disturbed of my correspondents always cite chapter and verse."[69] For Harris, religious designations and their attendant oppositional identities are divisive and immoral beyond the faulty logic of other social cleavages: "Religion raises the stakes of human conflict much higher than tribalism, racism, or politics ever can, as it is the only form of in-group/out-group thinking that casts the differences between people in terms of eternal rewards and punishments."[70]

Chavez's work and the current religious state of emergency in the United States lead me to conclude that the problem of the twenty-first century is the problem of the spiritual line, an ideological border delineated by social constructs separating good from evil, saved from damned, straight from gay, Christian from Muslim, Muslim from Jew, and the religious from the secular. This is not to say that race is no longer a problem. Rather, racial hatred is now further complicated, receded, and recast in a drama starring saints and sinners. No government or individual legitimate in the eyes of the world can openly sanction racial hatred. Yet, they all respect religious difference. Chavez's religious politics were thus prescient regarding our current religious crisis. In narrating his own nuanced spiritual identity he mitigated the insistence on fundamentalist belief, rightly attributing to religious identity the randomness of birth: "To me, religion is a most beautiful thing. And over the years, I have come to realize that all religions are beautiful." Here he echoes the famous aphorism of Gandhi: "All religions are true, and all contain error." Hence Chavez advanced multiculturalism before it became an academic industry.

In contrast to religious leaders confident in their ability to judge the difference between sinners and saints, Chavez recognized the continuing fall of the human condition (including, of course, his own) and its need for redemption, a spiritual conversion: "We need a cultural revolution. And we need a cultural revolution among ourselves not only in art but also in the realm of the spirit."[71] Chavez knew that in the United States, democratic change arises from the soul of the majority and that that soul could be touched and informed—transformed—by religious discourse emerging from prophetic agency. Yet religiosity was only one tactic he deployed as a key dimension of his arsenal. The quintessential organic intellectual, he was armed with many discourses, including religious and constitutional, and tactics, including strikes and boycotts. He further recognized that strategies need to change and develop following the vicissitudes of history. In this regard, he cited Gandhi's rendering of "moral jujitsu. Always hit the opposition off balance, but keep your principles."[72]

Notes

1. Cesar Chavez, quoted in Jacques Levy, *Cesar Chavez: Autobiography of La Causa* (New York: Norton, 1975), 276.
2. Throughout I refer to the late leader by his last name, Chavez, unless clarity requires a more familiar reference. This usage directly rejects the more common and, I argue, disrespectful first-name references to him in the literature by authors who never met him. Too often racist and sexist discursive

practices allow women and minorities first-name references within academic grammar; regrettably, this is especially true in the literature on Chavez.

3. On civil religion, see especially Robert Bellah, "Civil Religion in America," *Daedalus* (Winter 1967); and *The Broken Covenant: Civil Religion in Time of Trial*, 2nd ed. (Chicago: University of Chicago Press, 1992).

4. Art Torres, quoted in Richard Griswold del Castillo and Richard A. Garcia, *César Chávez: A Triumph of Spirit* (Norman: University of Oklahoma Press, 1995), 154.

5. Richard Rodriguez, *Days of Obligation: An Argument with My Mexican Father* (New York: Penguin, 1992), 68.

6. Gary Soto, in *The Fight in the Fields: Cesar Chavez and the Farmworkers Movement*, edited by Susan Ferris and Ricardo Sandoval (New York: Harcourt Brace, 1997), xvi.

7. Ibid.

8. Max Weber, "The Prophet," in *The Sociology of Religion*, trans. Ephraim Fischoff (Boston: Beacon, 1963), 46–59.

9. Ibid., 9.

10. See Joseph Campbell, *The Hero with a Thousand Faces* (Princeton, N.J.: Princeton University Press, 1949).

11. Cesar Chavez, quoted in Ronald B. Taylor, *Chavez and the Farm Workers* (Boston: Beacon Press, 1975), 61.

12. See Griswold del Castillo and Garcia, "Conclusion: A Legacy of Struggle," in *Triumph of Spirit*, 172–78.

13. Chavez, quoted in Levy, *Cesar Chavez*, 11.

14. Ibid., 19.

15. Ibid., 84.

16. Ibid., 84–85.

17. Ibid., 280–81.

18. Helen Chavez, quoted in Peter Matthiessen, *Sal Si Puedes (Escape If You Can): Cesar Chavez and the New American Revolution*, 2nd ed. (Berkeley: University of California Press, 2000), 231.

19. Chavez, quoted in Levy, *Cesar Chavez*, 84.

20. Chavez, quoted in "A Conversation with Cesar Chavez," in *Readings on La Raza: The Twentieth Century*, ed. Matt S. Meier and Feliciano Rivera (New York: Hill and Wang, 1974), 251.

21. Chavez, "People Are Willing to Sacrifice Themselves: An Interview with Cesar Chavez" in *Peace Is the Way: Writings on Nonviolence from the Fellowship of Reconciliation*, ed. Walter Wink (Maryknoll, N.Y.: Orbis, 2000), 228.

22. Miriam Pawel, *Los Angeles Times*, January 10–14, 2006. The Cesar E. Chavez Foundation has categorically answered her shrill charges on their Web site at *www.cecf.org.*

23. Cesar Chavez quoted in William P. Colleman, "At 51, Cesar Chavez Emphasizes Teaching," *Los Angeles Times*, March 26, 1978, 3.

24. Harry Bernstein, "UFW Transforming Itself from 'Cause' to 'Businesslike Union,'" *Los Angeles Times*, October 25, 1981, 20.

25. Robert Lindsey, "Cesar Chavez Tries New Directions for United Farm Workers," *Los Angeles Times*, September 19, 1983, 16.

26. Doug Smith, "UFW Leader Addresses 100 at Buffet-Dance," *Los Angeles Times*, March 31, 1983, WS1.

27. Luis Valdez, quoted in Susan Drake, *Fields of Courage: Remembering Cesar Chavez and the People Whose Labor Feeds Us* (Santa Cruz, Calif.: Many Names Press, 1999).

28. Dolores Huerta, quoted in Matthiessen, *Sal Si Puedes*, 176.

29. Stan Steiner, *La Raza: The Mexican Americans* (New York: Harper and Row, 1970), 62.

30. Fred Dalton, *The Moral Vision of Cesar Chavez* (Maryknoll, N.Y.: Orbis, 2003), 46; emphasis added.

31. I have written at length on this issue in my book *La Llorona's Children: Religion, Life, and Death in the United States Mexican Borderlands* (Berkeley: University of California Press, 2004); see especially chap. 2, "Virtual Virgin Nation: Mexico City as Sacred Center of Memory," 59–90.

32. Chavez, quoted in Catherine Ingram, *In the Footsteps of Gandhi: Conversations with Spiritual Social Activists* (Berkeley: Parallax Press, 1990), 27; emphasis added.

33. See Levy, *Cesar Chavez*, 50.

34. Chavez, quoted in Matthiessen, *Sal Si Puedes*, 326.
35. Interview by the author with Jim Covarrubias, Phoenix, Arizona, December 8, 1999.
36. Julie Rodriguez, interview by the author, March 1, 2006.
37. See Pat Hoffman, *Ministry of the Dispossessed: Learning from the Farm Workers Movement* (Los Angeles: Wallace Press, 1987), 113.
38. Cesar Chavez, "The Mexican American and the Church," *El Grito* 4 (Summer 1968): 215–18, 215.
39. Richard J. Jensen and and John C. Hammerbeck, "Introduction," in *The Words of Cesar Chavez*, ed. Richard J. Jensen and John C. Hammerbeck (College Station: Texas A&M University Press, 2002), xxii–xxiii.
40. For a history of the Migrant Ministry, see Sydney D. Smith, *Grapes of Conflict* (Pasadena, Calif.: Hope Publishing House, 1987).
41. Hoffman, *Ministry of the Dispossessed*, 6–7.
42. See Marco G. Prouty, *Cesar Chavez, the Catholic Bishops, and the Farmworkers Struggle for Social Justice* (Tucson: University of Arizona Press, 2006).
43. See especially George G. Higgins with William Boyle, *Organized Labor and the Church: Reflections of a Labor Priest* (New York: Paulist Press, 1993).
44. Mark Day, *Forty Acres: Cesar Chavez and the Farm Workers Movement* (New York: Praeger, 1971), 58.
45. Chavez, quoted in Levy, *Cesar Chavez*, 524–25.
46. Robert Kennedy, quoted in James Terzian and Kathryn Cramer, *Mighty Hard Road: The Story of Cesar Chavez* (New York: Doubleday, 1970), 107.
47. Chavez, quoted in Levy, *Cesar Chavez*, 196.
48. Chavez, quoted in Ingram, *In the Footsteps of Gandhi*, 119.
49. Chavez, quoted in Levy, *Cesar Chavez*, 270.
50. Chavez, "Martin Luther King, Jr.: He Showed Us the Way," *Maryknoll*, April 1978, 52–55.
51. Ibid.
52. Dick Meister, "'La Huelga' Becomes 'La Causa,'" *New York Times*, November 17, 1968.
53. From the "Plan of Delano," by Luis Valdez and Cesar Chavez (n.d., n. p.).
54. See Spencer Bennett, "Civil Religion in a New Context: The Mexican-American Faith of Cesar Chavez," in *Religion and Political Power*, edited by Gustavo Benavides and M. W. Daly (Albany: State University of New York Press, 1989).
55. Chavez, "People Are Willing to Sacrifice Themselves," 227.
56. From the "Plan of Delano"; capitalization in original.
57. Chavez noted the involvement of preachers in Matthiessen, *Sal Si Puedes*, 186.
58. Jerry Cohen, quoted in Levy, *Cesar Chavez*, 283.
59. See especially Hoffman, *Ministry of the Dispossessed*.
60. Chavez, quoted in Levy, *Cesar Chavez*, 286.
61. Martin Luther King Jr., telegram to Cesar Chavez, March 1968, reprinted in full in Levy, *Cesar Chavez*, 246.
62. Chavez, quoted in Matthiessen, *Sal Si Puedes*, 186.
63. Chavez, quoted in Griswold del Castillo and Garcia, *A Triumph of Spirit*, 150.
64. Chavez, quoted in Ingram, *In the Footsteps of Gandhi*, 114.
65. Bennett, "Civil Religion in a New Context," 4.
66. Cesar Chavez, "The Organizer's Tale," in *Chicano: The Evolution of a People*, ed. Renato Rosaldo et al. (Minneapolis: Winston Press, 1973).
67. Jimmy Carter, *Our Endangered Values: America's Moral Crisis* (New York: Simon and Schuster, 2005), 64.
68. Ibid., 114.
69. Sam Harris, *Letter to a Christian Nation* (New York: Knopf, 2006), vii.
70. Ibid., 80.
71. Cesar Chavez, "Introduction," in Day, *Forty Acres*, 12.
72. Chavez quoted in Levy, *Cesar Chavez*, 270.

Ties That Bind and Divisions That Persist: Evangelical Faith and the Political Spectrum

D. Michael Lindsay

A merican evangelicals have exerted significant political influence over the last thirty years. Particular policies and strategies of action have contributed to the alliance between conservative political life and evangelical activism. However, many evangelicals also identify with concerns and priorities of the political Left. Evangelicals in politics reflect a significant degree of cohesion, but there are also significant divisions among evangelicals in government, ones that have political consequences. This essay traces the expressive and institutional components of political activism that have contributed to cohesion between evangelical leaders and conservative politics. It then analyzes similar initiatives among the political Left. I conclude with an assessment of these developments and suggest why the political Right has been more successful. Data for this essay are based on interviews with 360 national, public leaders as well as leaders of evangelical institutions. Informants for this essay include two former presidents of the United States; nearly fifty cabinet secretaries, governmental leaders, and senior White House staffers; more than a hundred presidents, CEOs, or senior executives at large firms, both public and private; a dozen accomplished Hollywood professionals; more than ten leaders from the world of professional athletics, and a handful of leaders from the artistic and philanthropic arenas, among others. This study involves the largest and most comprehensive examination on the role of faith in the lives of public leaders ever conducted.

Evangelicalism and Politics

Tucked off to the side of the Oval Office sits a small, private room, opposite the eastern doors that open onto the Rose Garden. When Jimmy Carter was president, he would often retreat to that private study if there was a matter of national concern. He says, "I would kneel and ask God to give me wisdom and strength and let me adequately entertain the opinion of others [and] not be overly arrogant."[1] When done, he would return to the Oval Office, often to face looming issues, such as the energy crisis or the Soviet invasion of Afghanistan, yet he felt these times of prayer gave him a sense of "equanimity." And in many ways, episodes like these were exactly what evangelicals in this country had longed for: a like-minded president praying from the inner chamber of political power.[2] Within a matter of a few years, though, their support would recede and eventually return with Carter's political opponent riding high on a wave of evangelical approval. How could evangelicals switch allegiances so quickly, and how, in the intervening years, have they come to exert political influence? Several studies have explored the rise of evangelical political influence, largely addressing the topic as a social movement.[3] Such studies present evangelicals as political outsiders seeking to bring about their vision for the United States through grassroots civic engagement or sometimes through militant force.[4] Others have documented the role of evangelicals as a powerful voting bloc, especially within the Republican Party, in recent decades.[5] Yet very little of what we know about evangelical political life has been based on interview data with actual political leaders who are evangelicals. How do we account for the rise of an evangelical political presence in Washington? And what about the number of prominent Democrats who identify with American evangelicalism? I examine issues such as these based on interviews with 360 national leaders, including political elites from every administration between 1976 and 2006.[6] I find evidence of remarkable cohesion among evangelical leaders in government, which has contributed to their political success over the last thirty years. At the same time, evangelicalism has been a movement with significant divisions that have political consequences. The presumed congruency between evangelicalism and the political Right ignores large segments of the evangelical population and several important leaders within the movement. However, political conservatives have successfully tapped into two elements of political life—the expressive and the institutional—that have facilitated an alliance between evangelicals and the political Right. In the process, evangelicalism has established for itself a greater political presence, becoming an even more important figure in American public life.

Rising evangelical influence in politics has been most evident in campaigns for the nation's highest office. The personal spirituality of the presidential hopeful is particularly important to evangelical voters. Indeed, voting in presidential elections entails an *expressive component* that is often overlooked by political commentators.[7] This expressive component relies on communicating to voters through a shared discourse. On the campaign trail, presidential candidates can allude to shared ideals, background experiences, and priorities through public speeches and press interviews. Others noted many years ago that voting, like all cultural phenomena, has a distinctly expressive dimension within a pluralistic democracy.[8] People enact certain cultural rituals as a way of expressing norms and beliefs that they hold dear. Casting a ballot for a particular candidate can become an expressive symbol, a way of affirming individual values in the larger public square. By identifying with the candidate in a fundamental way—as might happen if religious identity is salient for both a candidate and a voter—voting for the candidate can become an implicit vote for oneself. Evangelical voters support evangelical candidates as a means of self-affirmation, a tactic that, when successful on election day, reinforces one's own sense of conviction.[9] This further strengthens the movement and explains why some evangelicals have voted for co-religionists whose economic policies may actually hurt them.[10] Voting in a presidential race may express both political interests and personal affinities that boost one's sense of values and beliefs.

In light of this expressive symbolism, how exactly is a political leader's religious faith communicated to potential supporters? It may be expressed directly, as was the case when Carter casually referred to himself on the campaign trail as "born again."[11] And later, Ronald Reagan likewise linked himself publicly with evangelicals. In a "National Affairs Briefing" sponsored by the Religious Roundtable in Dallas, Reagan acknowledged the nonpartisan nature of the meeting and then delivered his oft-repeated remark, "I know you cannot endorse me, but I endorse you."[12] Such identification with evangelicals was significant in garnering evangelical support, as his landslide reelection campaign in 1984 showed.[13] As others have shown, the changes in voting patterns of evangelicals that began in 1972 and continued in 1980 were complete by 1984 when Reagan brought the evangelicals firmly into the Republican fold.[14]

★★★★★

Republican presidents, and most notably George W. Bush, have excelled at another element of the expressive symbolism associated with presidential politics in ways that elicit evangelicals' support—namely, presidential appointments. Every new president has the opportunity to name hundreds to Senate-confirmed appointments and several thousands to lesser advisory boards and political jobs within the administration. The sheer number of executive appointments means that it can take up to a year before a president has all of these positions filled. When a constituency throws its weight behind a candidate, those voters invariably hope to enjoy the spoils of their victory: the promise of presidential appointments. President Carter shares a basic theological outlook with the younger President Bush, but their administrations looked very different. Practically none of Carter's senior advisors were evangelical, while Bush appointed many to senior positions. Most of Carter's top appointments came from individuals associated with the Trilateral Commission and the Council on Foreign Relations, neither of which had much evangelical representation.[15] Alonzo McDonald, who served President Carter in a role that is equivalent to today's deputy White House chief of staff, acknowledged that he didn't "know of anybody" in the White House except the president and his liaison to the religious community who spoke much about their faith.[16] By contrast, George W. Bush has surrounded himself with more evangelicals than any U.S. president over the last fifty years. Even among those who are not evangelical, there is a general affinity for religious faith; for example, former White House chief of staff Andrew Card is married to a mainline Methodist minister. And while evangelicals still constitute only a minority of senior staff positions, within the president's top level of advisors, I found the following who would either self-identify as evangelical or who could affirm the definition I apply in this study: Claude Allen (assistant to the president), John Ashcroft (attorney general), John Danforth (U.S. representative to the United Nations), John DiIulio (assistant to the president), Donald Evans (secretary of commerce), Michael Gerson (assistant to the president), Glenn Hubbard (chairman of White House Council of Economic Advisors), Karen Hughes (counselor to the president), Stephen Johnson (EPA administrator), Kay James (Office of Personnel Management director), David Leitch (deputy White House counsel), Mel Martinez (secretary of housing and urban development), Harriet Miers (White House counsel), Donald Powell (FDIC chairman), and Condoleezza Rice (national security advisor and secretary of state).[17] Additionally, I found dozens of deputy assistants to the president, special assistants to the president, presidentially nominated ambassadors, along with deputy and assistant secretaries at various federal departments who match the president's style of evangelical faith.[18] And whereas previous administrations had a regular Bible study attended by six to ten White House staffers, today's White House Christian Fellowship is attended by fifteen to a hundred people when it meets every Thursday during the lunch hour. Similar Bible studies can be found throughout this administration, across numerous federal departments and agencies.

Some non-evangelicals, such as speechwriter David Frum, were surprised how evangelical the Bush White House was when they went to work there, while others, like Jay Lefkowitz, an observant Jew who served as Bush's chief domestic policy advisor, have said it was never a problem for them. [19] The sheer number of evangelicals in top positions is a novelty, yet even in that context, the Bush administration can hardly be described as an "evangelical administration." The number of prominent Jews in the administration, for example, demonstrates the diversity of religious outlooks within the Bush White House. [20] David Leitch, who served as deputy White House counsel says, "I think there are a lot of evangelicals in the administration . . . but I certainly don't view it as an evangelical administration . . . it's not a religious organization; it's [the federal] government." [21] Regardless of discourse like this from administration officials, the Bush White House consulted with evangelical leaders more regularly and forged closer relations with the conservative wing of evangelicalism than any administration in recent history.

By contrast, Democratic administrations have not included many evangelical appointees, despite the evangelical faith of the president. As had been the case under President Carter, none of President Clinton's closest advisors shared his evangelical faith, as has been acknowledged by those inside the Clinton White House. [22] And many informants report outright hostility toward people of faith among some Clinton administration officials. Several senior White House officials and cabinet secretaries from the Clinton administration saw a significant divide between secular rationality and evangelical belief. Robert Reich, who served as secretary of labor from 1993 to 1997, wrote about an "underlying battle" between "those who believe in the primacy of the individual and those who believe that human beings owe blind allegiance to a higher authority," between "those who believe that truth is revealed solely through scripture and religious dogma, and those who rely primarily on science, reason and logic." [23] This overall ethos, ranging from general indifference to blatant animosity toward evangelical faith, contributed to an environment in which evangelicals did not feel welcome. [24] In fact, during the last six years of President Clinton's administration, White House staffers disbanded the in-house Bible study that had met continuously at the White House since the Eisenhower administration. [25]

In sum, Republican administrations have more effectively tapped the expressive component of political life in forging close relations with American evangelicals. Through public speech and symbolic expressions such as presidential appointments, political conservatives have created social space in which self-identified evangelicals could rise in political prominence. This cohort of evangelicals has become a distinct, visible segment within the political elite. And because evangelical identity was salient for these individuals—because it was an identity they embraced—it was an identity they carried with them into the professional realm. Evangelicalism, then, became more than a religious category for their lives; it was part of who they were, influencing them both professionally and personally. Beyond this expressive dimension, evangelicals have benefited from organizations and institutional arrangements that have facilitated their ascent in American politics. To that we now turn.

★★★★★

In 1981, a group of conservatives founded the Council for National Policy (CNP), an exclusive organization that included conservative leaders Phyllis Schlafly (Eagle Forum) and Paul Weyrich (Free Congress Foundation). According to the group's Web site, "members are united in their belief in a free enterprise system, a strong national defense, and support for traditional western values."[26] The organization was started as a conservative Christian alternative to the Council on Foreign Relations. Evangelical pastor and writer Tim LaHaye (of *Left Behind* fame) cofounded the group, and evangelical leaders can be found throughout the group today. Members include Pat Robertson (CBN), Donald Wildmon (American Family Association), Tony Perkins (Family Research Council), James Dobson (Focus on the Family), Ted Baehr (Christian Film and Television Commission), Robert Reccord (North American Mission Board), and Sam Moore (Thomas Nelson). CNP holds multiday conferences three times a year at exclusive hotels and resorts, and just before the 2004 Republican Convention, the group met at New York's Plaza Hotel. Meetings often include discussions about taxes and economic issues, marriage policy, and national defense, along with a host of other issues. Then, at the end of the evening, time is set aside for prayer for anyone who wishes to attend. Several Reagan-era officials (such as Edwin Meese and Donald Hodel) have held leadership positions within the group; in fact, Hodel served as the group's president from 2004 to 2006. Because of the group's strict policies regarding outsiders attending CNP meetings, the conservative gathering has eluded media attention.[27] Council meetings are closed to the media and general public, and organizational documents state: "The media should not know when or where or who takes part in our programs, before or after a meeting." Special guests may attend only with advance, unanimous approval of the executive committee, and detailed biographies of speakers, members, new members, guests, and spouses are all provided in briefing packets. All nonmembers wear different-colored name tags so members can spot outsiders easily. The few hundred members pay at least $1,750 annually for CNP involvement, and Gold Circle members pay up to $10,000 per year to the group. Peb Jackson, a seasoned fund-raiser and executive with various evangelical organizations ranging from Focus on the Family to Young Life to Rick Warren's PurposeDriven, has been involved with CNP for many years. Indeed, CNP facilitates ongoing interaction between evangelical leaders and conservative political leaders who are also evangelical in religious outlook. This is important to laying the foundation for elite cohesion.

Groups such as the Council for National Policy provide opportunities for evangelicals to interact in an explicitly nonreligious setting. Political interests and current social issues draw people together, but in the process, discussions about faith arise. I find that groups like CNP and more informal gatherings like the Bible study fellowships that honeycomb Washington today provide the social context through which personal friendships among national leaders are forged. As these groups cross institutional sectors, introducing governmental leaders to business leaders, important social ties develop. While I do not find empirical support for the tight cohesion that some have suggested exists among the nation's elites, I do find evidence of ties that encompass deep loyalty and interconnectedness that surely must be contributing to evangelicalism's ascent on the national stage. But does such cohesion translate into political power?[28]

Since Max Weber, some scholars have equated the concept of power with domination, the probability that a person can carry out his or her own will, despite resistance. [29] Legitimated power, in Weber's formulation, is authority. Steven Lukes, in his original text, *Power: A Radical View*, argued that power involved both observable decision making and informal influences such as persuasion and manipulation.[30] But it also included nonobservable phenomena such as the shaping of preferences. More recently, though, Lukes has published a second edition to the text whereby he repudiates his earlier assertion that equated power with domination.[31]

Building on a more efficacious view of power that regards it as a transaction, I find evidence of a particular form of influence, which I term *convening power.*[32] This involves the ability to bring disparate actors together for dialogue and perhaps joint action, falls within this broader stream that sees persuasion as a form of social power, and includes both the ability to set agendas and to coordinate activity. Harold Kerbo claims that elite power is the power over social networks, yet he fails to explicate exactly how that power operates.[33] I believe convening power clarifies the issue. Among other possibilities, convening power enables leaders to marshal resources, to share information, to deflect criticism, and to set agendas. Elite power is the power to convene; this is accomplished through the structural benefits afforded elites through their positions within various social networks. The power that they wield over these social networks involves the ability to bring people together, to introduce and to recruit others for shared objectives. Within elite circles, persuasion is far more effective than domination. After researching the political influence of evangelicals for several years, I find the ability of political leaders to convene groups to be among their most powerful resource. This has been critical to evangelicalism's alliance with political conservatives, for Republicans have used their convening power to bring together evangelical constituents with other conservative groups. Because they serve as nodes of information and introduction within high-status social networks, elite actors wield a form of social power that exists over and above micro-level interactions such as decision making and agenda setting. This is the power to convene, and leaders in government are structurally well situated to act on their convening power. As one Hollywood executive told me, "when you get a call from the White House, whether it's the man you voted for or not, you take their call."

The centripetal force of inner-circle power has been documented by many, and American evangelicals have come to wield considerable political influence as they have become part of the inner circles of political power, often through presidential appointments.[34] Notwithstanding the influence such individuals must certainly exert in other social arenas, senior advisors to the president can nudge policy initiatives—born in part from their religious convictions. They also can introduce movement leaders to others within the corridors of Washington power.[35] These individuals in the political inner circle, therefore, serve as critical nodes within larger networks of both the evangelical community and governmental leaders. The larger evangelical movement has, no doubt, benefited from the participation of some of their adherents within influential circles. Individuals within elite networks have drawn upon the convening power that accompanies their structural position in overlapping networks of powerful people; that, in turn, has contributed to wider evangelical influence in American political life, especially among political conservatives. Yet it has also been a critical mechanism for evangelical influence on more centrist and liberal social concerns—examples include changing attitudes on the environment and AIDS policy.

Throughout the course of my research, I witnessed multiple examples of convening power flowing from one social arena to another—such as from the political sector to the entertainment world, and vice versa. In essence, the power that resides in the hands of elites is their ability to use the web of relational and structural arrangements in which they are located to influence other parties. Sometimes, the individuals involved see this as a way to act on their religious convictions. Consider this example, describing an interaction that took place between the entertainer Kathie Lee Gifford and New York's Governor George Pataki. Gifford states:

> The one time I got involved in politics was with Governor Pataki. We were having dinner one time in the Hamptons, at a friend's home, and we [a charity for children with AIDS that Gifford supports] were suing the State of New York because they had blinded HIV testing for pregnant women [such that they could not learn the tests' results]. And as a result, babies were coming into the world with the HIV virus and sometimes full-blown AIDS. [If those same babies would have received] a cocktail of AZT and some other [drugs while in utero], it would go from over 40 percent to less than an 8 percent chance that [these women] would have an AIDS baby . . . All they [the State of New York] were doing was tracking pregnant women, testing them, and sending the blinded test results to the CDC to track the disease.
>
> Here's where I say my ministry is, if I have one. If I were off in Africa as a missionary, I wouldn't be sitting in the Hamptons having dinner with George Pataki. . . . I'm his dinner partner, and I've got him for two hours, and I can sit with him and tell him why it's immoral that pregnant women are not told the test results so that they could get a very simple cocktail and, as a result, bring a child into this world that will probably not have the AIDS virus.
>
> He listened to me intently and because I was knowledgeable . . . he said, "We're on the wrong side of this lawsuit. . . . This is wrong and . . . I'm going to do something about it." . . .
>
> Within one month, he mandated that all of HIV testing in New York State be unblinded so that the woman would know the results and . . . could get the in utero protection. That's the first year that the death rates of AIDS went down in New York State.[36]

To summarize, evangelicalism is a salient identity for many within the political elite, and through both expressive and institutional elements, evangelicalism has been aligned with the political Right. Groups like the CNP and strategic, symbolic acts like presidential appointments have solidified relations between the evangelical community and the Republican Party. Even though the theological outlook of Jimmy Carter and George W. Bush are strikingly similar, their administrations differ in terms of evangelical influence. However, it would be a mistake to assume that the cohesion that exists between conservative politicians and evangelical leaders reflects all of American evangelicalism. Republicans have used their convening power to bring conservative politicians and evangelical leaders closer together, but countercurrents can also be found among the political elite. To that issue we next turn.

Movement Divisions with Political Consequences

While remarkable cohesion can be found between conservative politics and American evangelicalism today, similar mechanisms have contributed to alliances between Democratic politicians and segments of the evangelical community. Just as the CNP provided an institutional hub through which Republican politicians and evangelical leaders interacted and formed alliances, so also is there an organizational context for the political Left. Democrats in office have also drawn upon the expressive component of political life to reach out to evangelicals in ways not unlike the strategies of Republicans. And while Democratic administrations have not used their convening power or presidential appointments to the same degree in building alliances with evangelical constituents, my research suggests that many in office today are presently considering such tactics.

*****

Throughout its history, American evangelicalism has been central to protesting movements committed to reform on selective moral issues. In the nineteenth century, the abolitionist movement benefited from evangelical mobilization.[37] And in the twentieth century, religious arguments motivated *both* those who favored and those who opposed the civil rights movement, with evangelical publications such as *Christianity Today* alternating between positions.[38] In this regard, American evangelicalism has been historically more defined by political issues than theological concerns; in essence, theology has birthed and buttressed particular positions. No doubt, this springs from the movement's lineage as part of the larger family of Protestant Christianity. The curious development in recent years has been the alliance of evangelical reform and conservative politics, but this was certainly not the case for previous generations. In the hundred years following the Civil War, the American South and the working class of the North—large segments of the evangelical constituency—consistently cast their ballots for Democratic candidates. Franklin Roosevelt's patrician background and New Deal policies expanded the Democratic reach to include many within the intellectual elite and those "limousine liberals" who favored state-sponsored support for the poor, even as they received no personal benefit from such initiatives. Kennedy's Camelot solidified this marriage between the nation's intellectual elite and the Democratic Party, and during his campaign, John F. Kennedy went to great lengths to assure voters that his religious convictions would not determine his positions on various issues. Kennedy went so far as to tell the Greater Houston Ministerial Association, "I want a chief executive whose public acts are responsible to all and obligated to none . . . whose fulfillment of his presidential office is not limited or conditioned by any religious oath, ritual, or obligation."[39] President Kennedy offered these words with the hope of expunging anti-Catholic bias from the voting booth. The result was the election of the United States' first Catholic president and an additional brick added to the wall separating church and state.

The unintended consequences of Kennedy's assurances drove a deep wedge between the sacred and secular realms, especially within the Democratic Party—a reality that has both pleased and haunted Democrats ever since. Gradually, the social conservatism of many southerners and the working class unraveled from the fabric of the Democratic Party, and with the civil rights legislation of the 1960s, many whites fled the party as quickly as blacks rallied around Democratic candidates. In 1972, the Democrats nominated George McGovern, and with his nomination a dominant force emerged at the Democratic Convention, that of secular progressives. As others have shown, the 1972 convention in Miami gave a group of delegates called the "secularists"—those who seldom or never attend religious services along with those who self-identify as either atheist or religiously agnostic—control of the party.[40] In the years since, these so-called secularists have become increasingly identified with the Democratic Party and its leadership. And data from the American National Election Study shows the increasing divide between secular progressives and religious traditionalists. Whereas about 5 percent of first-time, white delegates to the Republican Convention in 1992 would be classified as "secularist" according to these categories, 60 percent of first-time, white delegates to the Democratic Convention would be thus classified—up from 33 percent in 1972.[41] What began as a divide within Democratic delegates at the 1972 convention became a divide between parties as the secularist progressive camp became increasingly prominent within the Democratic Party and religious traditionalists became more visible within the ranks of Republican leadership.

Despite these developments, though, evangelicals have not altogether abandoned the political Left. In fact, there remains a vibrant constituency of liberal or progressive evangelicals, which has been around for decades.[42] During the administration of George W. Bush, this camp has grown increasingly vocal under the leadership of outspoken evangelicals such as Jim Wallis, Tony Campolo, and Ron Sider. From tax cuts that came at the expense of welfare for the poor to environmental policies which favored big business, liberal evangelicals have chastised parts of President Bush's domestic agenda. And when the president gave the 2005 commencement address at Calvin College, a strong evangelical institution in the heart of conservative western Michigan, one-third of the faculty signed a full-page ad protesting the president's policy on Iraq.[43] Indeed, around the country, leaders expressed frustration with the Bush administration during their interviews with me. One business leader became so bothered with certain Bush policies that he said he wouldn't vote George W. Bush if he were running for "dogcatcher."[44] Others voiced concern that programs such as the faith-based initiatives eroded the wall separating church and state, saying "it takes only one or two generations to lose the religious liberty that we have known as Americans."[45] Bruce Kennedy, former CEO of Alaska Airlines, said, "I never dreamed I'd be anything but a Republican," yet in 2004 he became what he called an "ABB" voter, "anybody-but-Bush."[46] Even stronger opposition can be found among Hollywood evangelicals, where producers, directors, and actors not only refused to support Bush, but actively supported and campaigned for Gore in 2000 and then again for Kerry in 2004.

All of these individuals are part of a larger group of the electorate, dubbed "freestyle evangelicals."[47] These are evangelicals who, for the most part, disapprove of matters such as homosexuality and abortion but also express concern about the environment and fiscal policies that hurt the poor. Among these, some have supported liberal or progressive evangelical activism, such as the grassroots movement Call to Renewal. Established in 1995 by Tony Campolo and Jim Wallis, Call to Renewal is a policy advocacy group aimed at eradicating poverty in the United States through governmental intervention. Policies that Call to Renewal endorses include federal subsidies for affordable housing, wider health-care coverage, and higher minimum wages to ensure what they call "a living family income." A similar group is Sojourners, which is an evangelical ministry that publishes a magazine of the same name.[48] Wallis also founded Sojourners, and in 2006, its activities were subsumed under the Call to Renewal organization. Although Wallis and his work have been present in Washington since 1975, only about 200,000 people are on the group's mailing list currently.[49] Indeed, the presence of "freestyle evangelicals" and these groups that oppose political conservatives bear witness to the "kaleidoscopic diversity" of American evangelicalism that exists today.[50] Fully 70 percent of evangelicals in America do not identify with the Religious Right.[51]

*****

The emergence of this less conservative faction—at least in terms of politics—within American evangelicalism does suggest that it is a mistake to overlook the range of opinions that exist within evangelicalism. While there is general consensus among the leaders I interviewed against homosexuality, there is significant disagreement on the best way to respond. A growing number of moderate evangelicals told me that they favor a warmer relationship with gay and lesbian groups. In the spring of 2006, a group of young evangelicals visited several Christian universities on the Soulforce Equality Ride in an effort to eradicate discrimination against gays and lesbians at evangelical schools. One initiative they sought was to allow gay and lesbian students to come out of the closet without being expelled from their schools, which is the policy on some evangelical campuses. Although Soulforce participants in the project, most of whom self-identified as evangelical and some of whom self-identified as gay or lesbian, were not welcomed at all of the institutions they visited, several universities organized panel discussions in which Soulforce activists participated.[52] Of course, such conversations are largely symbolic, but they do suggest an increasing openness to those involved with the homosexual movement.[53]

Liberalizing attitudes on homosexuality, at least in some quarters, come at the same time as adjustments among evangelicals regarding gender norms. Although research has confirmed that conservative religion is often joined to sexism in one form or another, American evangelicalism has spawned feminist ideals as well.[54] For instance, R. Marie Griffith demonstrated how the largest evangelical women's organization in the world provides a crucible through which evangelical women achieve a surprising degree of power, autonomy, and personal liberation—even when affirming traditional evangelical dogma.[55] By the same token, Sally K. Gallagher discovered the paradoxical reality that an overwhelming majority of evangelical families affirm that husbands should be the head of the home (90 percent) while also saying that marriage should be an equal partnership between husband and wife (87 percent). Moreover, 78 percent affirm both claims. Hence, evangelical attitudes around responses to gender are complex and, at times, contradictory.[56]

Among the women leaders that I interviewed, several spoke about particular challenges they faced. The relations among family, professional life, and evangelical commitment are complicated for many of these women. Even though most of their own families do not exhibit the patriarchal tendencies of wider evangelicalism, elite informants felt torn between family desires and professional ambition. The overall ethos of American evangelicalism has not supported many of these women as they have juggled competing demands.[57] I also found several structural issues that reinforce some elements of a gender bias, even as a few evangelical women have entered the elite. Men-only spiritual retreats, especially among business leaders, exclude evangelical women from the opportunity to interact with professional peers and have, in subtle ways, widened the gap between men and women within the evangelical elite. These modes of exclusion keep women who rise to the top still outside; to borrow Gwen Moore's pithy phrase, "women in formal positions of power remain outsiders on the inside."[58]

Beyond issues of gender and sex, race has provided another touchstone in shaping the political life of contemporary evangelicalism. Whereas most white evangelicals today tend to vote Republican, black Protestants continue to be loyal Democrats. These political divisions have largely emerged out of religious and historical divisions in the U.S. context. The most comprehensive study on race relations within American evangelicalism comes from Michael Emerson and Christian Smith.[59] Drawing on national survey and extensive interview data, they conclude that "white evangelicalism likely does more to perpetuate the racialized society than to reduce it."[60] Factors cited include the tendency of evangelicals to minimize racial concerns and treat racism as an individual-level problem bereft of structural causes as well as the tendency to assign blame to blacks themselves for racial inequality. While they acknowledge that white evangelicals have expressed great interest in recent years toward improving black-white relations, they find that the structural challenges endemic to American capitalism, the housing market, our nation's educational system, and elite networks perpetuate forms of racial inequality that evangelical good intentions have little chance of overcoming. Additionally, evangelical congregations—which are almost entirely homogeneous with regard to race—Emerson and Smith find actually *facilitate* racial inequality. It seems, therefore, that evangelical organizations, at least at the macro level, are not doing much to end racial divisions.

And yet a number of recent works have chronicled the role played by evangelicalism in undoing some of this country's racial inequality.[61] Most of these have detailed activities between blacks and whites at the level of individual interactions, group efforts, and congregational experiments in racial reconciliation. Such efforts must not be overlooked, for micro-level developments among public leaders can play a significant role in producing change within social structures. Nevertheless, Emerson and Smith argue that structural changes are required for religiously shaped race relations to adjust in this country, and I found no evidence of significant macro-level changes taking place.[62] When various leaders discussed racial issues in their interviews, invariably they would allude to personal, cross-racial friendships. Typically, this involved friendships that did not cross party lines: black and white Republicans might know each other and be friends, and the same occurred among Democrats. However, nearly all discussions of race that emerged in these interviews were relegated to individual interactions. Larger structural considerations were not raised, which is surprising since several dozen interviews were conducted in the wake of Hurricane Katrina, when issues about race and poverty were at the forefront of public discussion.

★★★★★

In the 1990s, evangelicals were actively involved on both sides of the Clinton impeachment proceedings. While several conservative evangelicals, including independent counsel Kenneth Starr, were prominent in the investigation and then the impeachment of the president, other evangelical leaders were huddling with him in spiritual solidarity. Bill Hybels, the pastor of the nation's largest megachurch at the time, Willow Creek Community Church in suburban Chicago, was a close friend and pastoral advisor to President Clinton throughout his term in office. Other evangelical leaders such as Tony Campolo and Gordon McDonald advised the president, and in the months following the Lewinski scandal, the three of them met regularly with the president for spiritual counsel.[63] In 2000, while emceeing a session of Willow Creek's Leadership Summit for several thousand evangelical pastors, Hybels interviewed President Clinton about a range of topics. To the ire of some in attendance and many others in the evangelical world, Hybels did not use that opportunity to confront the president on the tension between his self-identification as a Christian and his lying under oath about the relationship with Lewinski. But Robert Seiple, another evangelical leader who served in the Clinton administration, could relate to Hybels's predicament. He first met the president at a prayer meeting in 1993 that Hybels organized.[64] After the meeting, according to Seiple, those in attendance "got the dickens beat out of us by the rest of the evangelical community because we did not raise the issue of sanctity of life and abortion." The reason, Seiple says, is "all of us were taken aback" when the president opened the meeting by asking them to tell him "things that would help [his] spirituality." Seiple continues, "Say what you want about the guy, [but] this is a guy that's reaching out. So that's what we talked about."[65] President Clinton and his wife, Hillary Rodham Clinton, have also had a long relationship with evangelical icon Billy Graham.[66] Several evangelical leaders have advised Democratic leaders, have campaigned for Democratic candidates, and have stood with Democrats such as Bill Clinton when others in their faith community disapproved.

In the years since, tensions between evangelicals and the Democratic leadership have grown, not abated. George W. Bush's outspoken identification with evangelicals has helped maintain the symbolic boundaries between Democrats and Republicans on matters of religious conviction. To complicate matters, many evangelical Democrats have grown increasingly frustrated with their party. Over the course of my research, many Democratic informants expressed disappointment with the party, calling it "fouled up" because of reluctance on the part of party leadership to talk about faith or similar matters "publicly." [67] Tony Campolo, a Democrat and evangelical leader who has been close to Bill and Hillary Clinton for many years, says his party is "ashamed of Jesus," a reality he believes continues to cost them votes.[68] While speaking to thirty-seven of the forty-four Democratic senators at a 2006 meeting organized by Hillary Clinton, Campolo asked the group: "In your speeches . . . do you ever quote Socrates? . . . Jefferson? . . . Aside from the fact that I'm saying he's the Son of God . . . you would have to admit that [Jesus] has to stand among the greatest moral teachers of all time. Why wouldn't you quote the greatest moral teacher of all time?" The senators had no response, and Campolo believes it shows just how "ashamed" the Democratic Party can be on matters of religion.

Beliefnet.com editor Steve Waldman related to me a story of accidentally being copied on an internal e-mail within the campaign of a Democratic contender in 2004. Waldman had invited the various presidential candidates to talk about their spiritual lives in an online column early in the primary season. While staffers for one Democratic candidate debated whether their candidate should participate, part of their e-mail correspondence was sent to Waldman by mistake. The line that stood out to him was from a senior campaign strategist to fellow staffers. In response to Waldman's request, the leader asked his colleagues, "Do we talk about that stuff?"

Recently, though, the Democratic leadership has undertaken several steps to reach out to faith communities. Burns Strider, a self-identified evangelical who grew up as a Southern Baptist in Mississippi, was hired to provide staff leadership for the Democratic Faith Working Group when it was formed in 2004 with the goal of trying to help congressional Democrats connect their faith to the party's agenda. Focused more on the personal connection between faith and policy, as opposed to strategy and communicating with the media, Strider says the Faith Working Group is for members with "authentic faith" from a variety of religious traditions, including the evangelical faith.[69] He has since been hired to head religious outreach for Hillary Clinton's campaign. There is also now a consulting firm for Democrats focused on helping their candidates connect with faith communities.[70] And throughout the Democratic Party, leaders have begun employing a rhetoric that refers to themselves as the party of "religious progressives," echoing the language of evangelical leaders such as Campolo, Sider, and Wallis. However, in their zeal to portray certain policies as born of religious conviction, some observers think these Democrats are "making the same mistakes that the folks on the right made."[71] Namely, they are attaching religious labels to partisan activities in ways that strike some as disingenuous. Consider, for example, the recent assertion by evangelical progressives that tax policies and the federal budget are "moral issues" of equal magnitude to policy issues regarding human sexuality.[72] These are contested claims, for the framing of issues as "moral" entails political activity unto itself.[73] Framing policy issues in ways that express evangelical concerns and priorities—such as environmental "stewardship" and welfare as "care for one's neighbor"—represent an important strategy among Democrats in connecting with evangelical constituents. After all, it was a Democrat—Jimmy Carter—who was the first major candidate to refer to himself as "born again," and Carter spoke in evangelical tones: "I believe God wants me to be the best politician I can be."[74]

Although my research concludes that Republicans have more effectively and consistently drawn upon the expressive component of political life in building alliances with American evangelicals, counterexamples abound. Symbolic acts, such as the president attending church or invoking religious language, can be ways in which Democrats signal evangelical allegiances.[75] During the 1992 campaign and throughout his presidency, Bill Clinton relied upon religious rhetoric to convey several of his domestic priorities. His "New Covenant" platform resonated with religious constituents, employing biblical references to advocate a closer relationship between the federal government and U.S. citizens.[76] Symbolic acts such as church attendance were also prominent in President Clinton's public life. The 1992 campaign highlighted his faithful participation as a choir member at Little Rock's Immanuel Baptist Church. And during his time in the White House, Clinton and his family regularly attended the 11 a.m. service at Foundry United Methodist Church, an occurrence that was often noted in news accounts of the Clinton presidency.[77]

Further, research has shown that President Clinton employed evangelical discourse in public statements more frequently than other recent presidents.[78] For example, he cited Jesus, Jesus Christ, or Christ on average 5.1 times per year during his administration, which is statistically more significant than citations by President George W. Bush, who averaged 4.7 times per year. Moreover, in the reelection year of 1996, President Clinton spoke of Jesus Christ in nine different statements. "No politician in modern times mixed politics and religion with complete impunity to the extent Bill Clinton did," writes Kengor.[79] Indeed, President Clinton demonstrated that appealing to evangelical sensibilities through public speech and action is not the exclusive purview of Republicans.

Also, the political Left has effectively used institutional contexts in which to build alliances with American evangelicalism. Consider Renaissance Weekend. Founded the same year as CNP (1981), Renaissance began as an extended family retreat over Thanksgiving and has grown to include five annual gatherings around the country. Renaissance Weekends seek to build relational bridges "among innovative leaders from diverse fields" and feature an array of panel sessions on a host of subjects ranging from the Asian economy to zoology discoveries.[80] Like CNP, Renaissance Weekends are private, by-invitation-only meetings that include a wide spectrum of leaders from government, business, and disparate other fields. And like CNP, evangelicals can be found throughout the organization. Both groups provide social space wherein like-minded evangelical leaders can network through informal, off-the-record interaction. They also provide forums through which evangelicals can discuss policy issues with actual policy-makers, away from the glare of the media spotlight. And as one Congressional staffer told me, these gatherings "facilitate friendships among unlikely allies . . . people can become friends, not just acquaintances. . . . I can easily call up any person I met in [this context] and ask them for information [regardless of whether they are in the same political party] . . . Friendships formed in these contexts facilitate that."

Although described as "nonpartisan" gatherings, Renaissance Weekends have included a "Who's Who" of the Democratic Party. Two early participants were Bill and Hillary Clinton. In fact, Renaissance Weekend became not only a critical node within the social networks of those who served during President Clinton's administration but also serves as a hub for liberal evangelicalism in this country. Liberal evangelical leaders, whose faith convictions lead them to progressive political positions on matters such as welfare and the environment, frequent Renaissance Weekends.

In essence, Democrats, like Republicans, have drawn upon both expressive and institutional components of political action to form alliances with American evangelicalism. However, relations between the political Left and evangelicalism are not as cohesive as they are between evangelicals and the political Right, which is not surprising given the divergent paths pursued by the two national parties since the 1960s. It remains to be seen if Democrats' more recent strategies, framing particular policy initiatives, and establishing supportive organizational networks like the Democratic Faith Working Group, will decrease the distance between their party and evangelicals.

Conclusion

Over the last thirty years, American evangelicals have established a significant political presence for themselves, and both Democrats and Republicans have capitalized upon expressive and institutional aspects of political life to foster closer relations with evangelical constituents. Presidential rhetoric and symbolic acts such as presidential appointments have been useful strategies of action. Additionally, groups with political overtones—such as CNP and Renaissance Weekend—have provided opportunities for evangelicals and political leaders to interact with one another. Indeed, within American evangelicalism, there appear signs of an emerging *political bivocality*. In 2004, the National Association of Evangelicals (NAE) released a statement called "For the Health of the Nation: An Evangelical Call to Civic Responsibility." The twelve-page document, originally drafted by *Christianity Today* editor David Neff, called on the evangelical community to support governmental initiatives that upheld traditional notions of marriage and opposed what they believe are "social evils," such as gambling, drugs, abortion, and the use of human embryos for stem-cell research. The statement also called for government protections for the poor, the sick, and disabled through fair wages, health care, and education, among other things. The statement points to an emerging bivocality among evangelicals—that is, an appreciation for both liberal and conservative political priorities. One movement leader referred to this development as "a maturing of the evangelical public mind."[81]

If this is the case, why does there remain such noticeable cohesion between evangelicals and the political Right? Simply stated, Republicans have done a better job of drawing upon the expressive and institutional aspects of political action in ways that resonate with evangelical sensibilities. Republican administrations are populated with more evangelicals, and they have been more explicit in framing campaigns and policies with an evangelical tenor. The institutions founded by political conservatives in which they interact with evangelical leaders are sometimes more explicitly faith oriented, and conservatives have devoted considerable resources in recent years to Washington-based think tanks. Institutions such as the Heritage Foundation, the Family Research Council, and the Ethics and Public Policy Center have benefited from the philanthropy of conservative evangelicals. In addition, their patronage of Washington institutes and research centers has furthered conservative evangelicals' public influence as cable news programs rely more on the expertise of those working at Washington think tanks than on scholars at major, liberal universities.[82] In essence, the avenue of conservative evangelicals' patronage has been granted greater media exposure, expanding their public influence over the last three decades.

The close identification for American evangelicalism with conservative Republicanism has taken place to evangelicals' political disadvantage. To the extent that the courtship between evangelicals and political conservatives began in the 1960s and 1970s, the union between the two has been consummated through the presidency of George W. Bush. Murmurs within the movement by liberal progressives suggest the marriage may not last forever, but research by John Green and others show the remarkable ways in which President Bush has connected with all kinds of evangelicals.[83] Indeed, the Christian Right, which used to exist as an independent political structure in the 1970s and 1980s, has now become integrated into the institution of the Republican Party. As Rosin notes, "Evangelicals in public office have finally become so numerous that they've blended in to the permanent Washington backdrop, a new establishment that has absorbed the local habits and mores. . . . In Washington, the evangelicals are the new Episcopalians—established, connected, respectable."[84] As they have become integrated into the Republican establishment, evangelicals have certainly become more sophisticated politically. Gone is the bombast of placard-bearing protests and in its place are Capitol Hill meetings and West Wing strategy sessions. But this dulling of the edges of the evangelical movement comes with a cost; in fact, a growing number of movement leaders fear that evangelicalism has become "marginalized or pigeon-holed" because of its close association with the Republican Party.[85] In the process, they fear, evangelicalism is being co-opted by the party, diminishing the movement's ability to speak independently to leaders across the political spectrum. As one leader in government says, "it's just very easy, when you get involved in political movements, to let them overtake you."[86] So even as evangelicals have gained attention through their political success working with conservative Republicans, they risk eroding the symbolic boundary that has existed between evangelicalism as a religious movement and the field of conservative politics. This boundary was critical to their ascent in the 1970s and 1980s and facilitated their influence in both parties across several administrations. It remains to be seen how realignments that are presently under way in American politics will change evangelical influence in Washington, yet as this essay has shown, evangelicals have become fixtures within the corridors of American political power.

Notes

I especially thank Paul DiMaggio, R. Marie Griffith, Suzanne Keller, Melani McAllister, Martin Ruef, Robert Wuthnow, Viviana Zelizer, and colleagues in the department of sociology at Rice University, as well as board members of *American Quarterly*, for their helpful feedback on material in this article. I am most appreciative of funding for various phases of this project that has been provided by the National Science Foundation, the Andrew W. Mellon Foundation, the Earhart Foundation, the Society for the Scientific Study of Religion, the Religious Research Association, and the Department of Sociology and Center for the Study of Religion at Princeton University. Finally, Daisy Paul and Laura Hoseley provided invaluable research assistance.

1.   Interview with President Jimmy Carter, November 16, 2004, Atlanta, Georgia.

2.   In this essay, I follow the conventional definition of evangelicalism as being a segment of Christianity that (1) holds a particular regard for the Bible, (2) embraces a personal relationship with God through a "conversion" to Jesus Christ, (3) and seeks to lead others on a similar spiritual journey; see Lyman A. Kellstedt et al., "Grasping the Essentials: The Social Embodiment of Religion and Social Behavior," in *Religion and the Culture Wars: Dispatches from the Front*, ed. John C. Green, James L. Guth, Corwin E. Smidt, and Lyman A. Kellstedt (Lanham, Md.: Rowman & Littlefield, 1996), and David Bebbington, *Evangelicalism in Modern Britain: A History from the 1730s to the 1980s* (London: Unwin Hyman, 1989). Informants are classified as evangelical if they describe themselves using this term or if they affirm these fundamental characteristics. I agree with others (Brian Steensland et al., "The Measure of American Religion: Toward Improving the State of the Art," *Social Forces* 79 [2000]: 291–318) who regard black Protestantism as different in kind from white evangelicalism; hence, I focus on whites in this study of evangelicalism in the United States. Among the few informants (5 percent) who are people of color, all are involved in evangelical groups and programs that are dominated by whites.

3.   George Marsden, *Fundamentalism and American Culture*, 2nd ed. (New York: Oxford University Press, 2006); Sara Diamond, *Roads to Dominion: Right-Wing Movements and Political Power in the United States* (New York: Guilford Press, 1995); Michael Lienesch, "Right-Wing Religion: Christian Conservatism as a Political Movement," *Political Science Quarterly* 97 (1982):403–25.

4.   Christian Smith and David Sikkink, "Evangelicals on Education," in *Christian America: What Evangelicals Really Want*, by Christian Smith (Berkeley: University of California Press, 2000); Mark Rozell and Clyde Wilcox, *God at the Grassroots* (Lanham, Md.: Rowman and Littlefield, 1995). For examples that present evangelicals as militants imposing their will, please see Esther Kaplan, *With God on Their Side* (New York: New Press, 2004); Harvey Cox, "The Warring Visions of the Religious Right," *Atlantic Monthly*, November 1995, 59–69; James Davison Hunter, *Culture Wars: The Struggle to Define America* (New York: Basic Books, 1991); Flo Conway and Jim Siegelman, *Holy Terror: The Fundamentalist War on America's Freedoms in Religion, Politics, and Our Private Lives* (New York: Dell, 1984).

5.   John C. Green, "Religion Gap Swings New Ways," *Religion in the News* 7.3 (Winter 2005); Mark Regenerus, David Sikkink, and Christian Smith, "Who Votes with the Christian Right? Contextual and Group Patterns of Electoral Influence," *Social Force* 46 (1999): 1347–72; Duane Oldfield, *The Right and the Righteous: The Christian Right Confronts the Republican Party* (Lanham, Md.: Rowman

and Littlefield, 1996); Lyman A. Kellstedt et al., "Religious Voting Blocs in the 1992 Election: The Year of the Evangelical?" *Sociology of Religion* 55.3 (1994): 307–26.

6. Informants for this study were selected using a two-stage method of sample selection. First, I identified the nation's largest organizations within one religious tradition—American evangelicalism in this case. Using a variety of personal and professional relationships, I interviewed 157 leaders of evangelically oriented institutions. Most of these informants serve or have served as president or chief executive of at least one evangelical organization or initiative. At the end of these interviews, I asked informants to identify national, public leaders for whom their Christian faith was an important aspect of their life. Since these institutional leaders were associated with evangelically oriented organizations, most of those recommended were individuals who would either identify as "evangelical" or were very familiar with American evangelicalism through contact with at least one program or institution. Almost all of these institutional leaders volunteered to help me secure contact details and/or request an interview with the individuals they recommended. Because of these personal connections, many public leaders who would not normally grant a university researcher an hour-long interview agreed to participate in the study at the recommendation of our mutual contact. This technique, which I call the "leapfrog" method for informant selection, granted me unusual access to leaders in government, business, and culture (N = 203) without the usual impediments of secretarial gatekeepers or organizational barriers. Indeed, this methodological innovation, coupled with the traditional "snowball" method for informant selection, created an unusually large number of high-ranking, willing informants. As with other projects involving elite informants, I also employed the snowball method for selecting informants (John Schmalzbauer, *People of Faith: Religious Conviction in American Journalism and Higher Education* [Ithaca, N.Y.: Cornell University Press, 2003]; Charles Kadushin, "Friendship Among the French Financial Elite," *American Sociological Review* 60 [1995]: 202–21). According to this method, societal leader informants are asked at the end of each interview to identify other, similarly stationed leaders who share their religious commitments; this method is both appropriate and useful for the present study. The leapfrog method, however, represents a methodological innovation by engaging nonparticipants who are well qualified (through both information and network advantages) to help identify potential informants while minimizing the bias of limited interpersonal networks and shared personal identities that typically encumber the snowball method by itself. Of course, the leapfrog method relies upon interpersonal networks as well, but the breadth of these networks is much wider. In this particular study, for instance, informants were selected from 138 more organizational networks than would have been the case if I had relied solely on the snowball method. Also, because the leapfrog method begins with organizations as the unit of analysis, instead of individuals, informants are more likely to represent diverse social locations (geographically, institutionally, and demographically) than is often the case in studies that employ only the snowball method. In subsequent work, I plan to discuss more fully the leapfrog method and its possibilities for other types of studies.

7. For this line of thinking, I am indebted to Robert Wuthnow for pointing me to the relevant literature.

8. Richard A. Peterson, "Revitalizing the Culture Concept," *Annual Review of Sociology* 5 (1979): 137–66; Morris P. Fiorina, "The Voting Decision: Instrumental and Expressive Aspects," *The Journal of Politics* 38.2 (1976): 390–413.

9. That, in my estimation, is why so many evangelicals voted for George W. Bush. According to the Pew Research Center, Bush received 72 percent of the votes from evangelicals in 2000; in 2004, he received 78 percent of their votes. Evangelicals voted for this president as a way of validating their own faith perspective and as a way of legitimating their opinion.

10. In fact, Greeley and Hout (*The Truth about Conservative Christians* [Chicago: University of Chicago Press, 2006]) find that income affects voting patterns in presidential elections for all denominations, but it affects the votes of conservative Protestants almost 50 percent more than it does others' votes. And the impact of family income on voting increased more than the differences among religion did from 1970 to 2000. Despite these economic differences, still more than half of poor conservative Protestants voted Republican in the 1992, 1996, and 2000 elections; evangelicals continue to cast their votes more according to candidates' positions on moral issues than on economic issues.

11. The phrase "born again" refers to a conversation recorded in the New Testament book of John between Jesus and Nicodemus, a spiritual seeker. In the evangelical vernacular, it refers to a decision made by an individual to follow Jesus Christ. That decision, which often entails some experiential or emotional

component, becomes a defining moment in the life of the adherent; from that point, he considers himself to be Christian. Often, evangelicals will use the expression "asking Jesus into my heart" for this born-again experience. Such terminology underscores the movement's devotional piety and high regard for individual agency.

12. Led by evangelist James Robison, the lineup of speakers clearly leaned right on the political spectrum. It came as no surprise, then, when President Carter and Independent candidate John Anderson declined an invitation to address the group.

13. William C. Martin, *With God on Our Side: The Rise of the Religious Right in America* (New York: Broadway Books, 1996).

14. Kellstedt et al., "Religious Voting Blocs"; Jerome L. Himmelstein, *To the Right: The Transformation of American Conservatism* (Berkeley: University of California Press, 1990).

15. Established in 1973, the Trilateral Commission is a private organization that began at the encouragement of David Rockefeller, Henry Kissinger, and Zbingniew Brzezinksi. The approximately three hundred members include private citizens and world leaders from Japan, North America, and Europe.

16. Interview with Alonzo McDonald, July 8, 2004, Birmingham, Michigan.

17. Titles refer to the highest position held by the individual during the years of George W. Bush's presidency; some of these individuals have changed positions over time, and others are no longer in government. It should be noted that an important faction of the Bush's administration, including Vice President Dick Cheney, Deputy White House Chief of Staff Karl Rove, and Secretary of Defense Donald Rumsfeld, have little religious kinship with the president's evangelical faith.

18. The White House staff includes about 130 commissioned officers. The top tier, assistant to the president, includes 15 top advisors to the president on matters such as domestic policy and national security. The second tier, deputy assistant to the president, and the third tier, special assistant to the president, comprise the remaining 115 top jobs within the White House. Assistants to the president serve at the rank of a four-star general, deputy assistants at the rank of a three-star general, and special assistants at the rank of a two-star general. During interviews with various public officials, I often asked them about colleagues who shared their faith commitments. From their responses, I was able to identify several dozen administration officials who share President Bush's faith.

19. After leaving the White House, Frum wrote a book titled *The Right Man: The Surprise Presidency of George W. Bush* (New York: Random House, 2003), in which he opens with the description that this was a "White House where attendance at Bible study was, if not compulsory, not quite uncompulsory, either," a fact he says "was disconcerting to a non-Christian like me" (3–4). For Jay Lefkowitz's perspective see Alan Cooperman, "Openly Religious, to a Point," *Washington Post*, September 15, 2004.

20. Officials of the Jewish faith in the Bush White House include the following: Elliott Abrams (deputy national security adviser), Joshua Bolten (chief of staff), Michael Chertoff (secretary of homeland security), Ari Fleischer (White House press secretary), Blake Gottesman (personal aide to the president), I. Lewis Libby (chief of staff to the vice president), Ken Melman (White House political director), and Paul Wolfowitz (deputy secretary of defense).

21. Interview with David Leitch, December 6, 2004, Washington, D.C.

22. William A. Galston, *Public Matters: Politics, Policy, and Religion in the 21st Century* (Lanham, Md.: Rowman & Littlefield, 2005).

23. Robert Reich, "The Last Word," *American Prospect*, July 2004, 40.

24. The Clinton administration also did not have a close relationship with the only other Democrat—and fellow evangelical—to occupy the White House in recent memory. President Carter reports he received the worst treatment since leaving office from the Clinton administration, while the elder Bush administration treated him the best; Ralph Z. Hallow, "Carter Condemns Abortion Culture," *Washington Times*, November 4, 2005.

25. According to a knowledgeable source, "it wasn't that Clinton said, 'I hate this stuff, let's get rid of it.' But among the people that President Clinton hired, it was a badge of dishonor to be a part of that. [So Christians after the first two years] didn't have an official Bible study, but they met informally and infrequently in people's offices."

26. See *www.policycounsel.org* for more information.

27. For the only major news story on CNP, see David D. Kirkpatrick, "Club of the Most Powerful Gathers in Strictest Privacy," *New York Times*, August 28, 2004.

28. On elite cohesion, see C. Wright Mills, *The Power Elite* (New York: Oxford University Press, 1956).

29. Max Weber, *Max Weber: Essays in Sociology*, edited by Hans H. Gerth and C. Wright Mills (1946; London: Routledge, 1991).
30. Steven Lukes, *Power: A Radical View* (New York: Palgrave, 1974).
31. Steven Lukes, *Power: A Radical View*, 2nd ed. (1974; New York: Palgrave, 2005).
32. With regards to the idea of power as a transaction, see Talcott Parsons, "On the Concept of Political Power," *Proceedings of the American Philosophical Society* 107 (1963): 232–62.
33. Harold R. Kerbo, "Upper Class Power," in *Power in Modern Societies*, ed. Marvin E. Olsen and Martin N. Marger, 223–37 (Boulder, Colo.: Westview, 1993).
34. For more on inner circle power, see Dan Clawson and Alan Neustadtl, "Interlock, PACS and Corporate Conservatism," *American Journal of Sociology* 94 (1989): 779–93; Michael Useem, *The Inner Circle: Large Corporations and the Rise of Business Political Activity in the U.S. and the U.K.* (New York: Oxford University Press, 1984).
35. "Movement leaders" refers to those individuals who served in a leadership position within the evangelical movement, typically heading a prominent evangelical organization. Following Keller (*Beyond the Ruling Class: Strategic Elites in Modern Society* [New York: Random House, 1963]), I differentiate between leaders over a segment of society (such as evangelicalism) and public leaders who occupy positions of societal influence. Billy Graham, as head of the Billy Graham Evangelistic Association and a prominent evangelist, is a movement leader whose authority arose from his position within a segment of American life (namely, the evangelical movement). President Jimmy Carter, an evangelical like Graham, held a position of societal influence that did not depend upon the evangelical movement for the basis of his authority.
36. Interview with Kathie Lee Gifford, May 23, 2005, New York. It also helps that Gifford is a celebrity and therefore more likely to be able to have dinner with Pataki. However, she, like other leaders I interviewed, downplayed the benefits of their location within the structure of social networks that come with celebrity status.
37. Kevin Belmonte, *Hero for Humanity: A Biography of William Wilberforce* (Colorado Springs, Colo.: NavPress, 2002); Victor B. Howard, *The Evangelical War Against Slavery and Caste: The Life and Times of John G. Fee* (Selinsgrove, Pa.: Susquehanna University Press, 1996); John R. McKivigan, *The War Against Proslavery Religion: Abolitionism and the Northern Churches, 1830–1865* (Ithaca, N.Y.: Cornell University Press, 1984); Bertram Wyatt-Brown, *Lewis Tappan and the Evangelical War Against Slavery* (Cleveland: Case Western University Press, 1969).
38. For a study of how religious arguments motivated both those in favor of and opposed to the civil rights movement see Michael O. Emerson and Christian Smith, *Divided by Faith: Evangelical Religion and the Problem of Race in America* (New York: Oxford University Press, 2000).
39. Remarks by Senator John F. Kennedy, June 12, 1960, Greater Houston Ministerial Association, Houston, Texas. Transcript and audio available online at the John F. Kennedy Presidential Library and Museum Web site, www.jfklibrary.org.
40. Louis Bolce and Gerald De Maio, "Our Secularist Democratic Party," *The Public Interest* (Fall 2002); Geoffrey Layman, *The Great Divide: Religious and Cultural Conflict in American Party Politics* (New York : Columbia University Press, 2001).
41. The number of "secularist" Republicans in 1992 is similar to those for the 1972 Republican Convention.
42. In this context, "liberal evangelicals" and "progressive evangelicals" are synonyms, but they are employed by different camps, conservatives and liberals, respectively. See Leo P. Ribuffo, "Liberals and That Old-Time Religion," *Nation*, November 29, 1980, 570–73.
43. The ad appearing in the *Grand Rapids Press* on May 21, 2005, said in part: "We, the undersigned, respect your office, and we join the college in welcoming you to our campus. Like you, we recognize the importance of religious commitment in American political life. We seek open and honest dialogue about the Christian faith and how it is best expressed in the political sphere. While recognizing God as sovereign over individuals and institutions alike, we understand that no single political position should be identified with God's will, and we are conscious that this applies to our own views as well as those of others. At the same time we see conflicts between our understanding of what Christians are called to do and many of the policies of your administration." Some faculty and students also wore stickers to commencement that declared "God Is Not a Democrat or a Republican."
44. Interview with Timothy Collins, September 20, 2004, New York.

45. Interview with Herbert Reynolds, March 26, 2004, Waco, Texas; response via e-mail.
46. Interview with Bruce Kennedy, September 8, 2004, Seattle, Washington.
47. The term arose from various items John Green, a political scientist at the University of Akron, and Steve Waldman, editor of *www.beliefnet.com*, have published on beliefnet.com's Web page.
48. The publication was originally titled *The Post American: Voice of the People's Christian Coalition*, a title it held from 1971 until 1975.
49. By comparison, the conservative group Focus on the Family has a mailing list of more than 2 million.
50. Ayelish McGarvey, "Reaching to the Choir," *American Prospect*, April 2004.
51. Christian Smith, *Christian America: What Evangelicals Really Want* (Berkeley: University of California Press, 2000), 208.
52. Jamie Dean, "Forgiving Their Trespass," *World*, April 1, 2006, online at http://www.worldmag.com/articles/11673 (accessed April 2006).
53. D. Michael Lindsay, *Faith in the Halls of Power: How Evangelicals Joined the American Elite* (New York: Oxford University Press, 2007). Evangelical leader Tony Campolo, a sociologist and frequent speaker, told me that "even Jim Dobson [who has been quite vocal about his opposition to homosexuality] knows that people cannot change their orientation. . . . Anyone with a PhD from a secular university [who] examines the data knows that you cannot change that" (interview with Tony Campolo, March 3, 2006, Cherry Hill, New Jersey). Campolo advocates that Christians who have a homosexual orientation practice celibacy. The president of a prominent evangelical seminary shared with me the story of a student at his seminary who came to talk about her lesbian identity and his subsequent handling of the issue. Episodes like these, while isolated, emerged throughout my research. It is interesting to note the strong opposition voiced by some evangelical leaders to the gay actor Chad Allen's portrayal of Nate and Steve Saint in *The End of the Spear* (2006), yet the lack of opposition to gay actor Ian Charleson's portrayal of Eric Liddell in *Chariots of Fire* (1981). This paradox is not lost on movement leaders. As Marvin Olasky, editor of the evangelical *World* magazine states, "because God has placed us in a modern Babylon rather than ancient Israel, I'm not troubled by the presence of gay actors in movies with theistic themes. . . . Few people urged Christians to boycott . . . films [like *Chariots of Fire*] that wonderfully communicated truths about Christian conscience and divine providence" (Marvin Olasky, "Tighter Lips? Raining on Spear's Parade," *World*, February 18, 2006, online at http://www.worldmag.com/articles/1151 [accessed February 2006]).
54. Regarding conservative religion and sexism, see Charles W. Peek, George D. Lowe, and L. Susan Williams, "Gender and God's Word: Another Look at Religious Fundamentalism and Sexism," *Social Forces* 69.4 (1991): 1205–21.
55. R. Marie Griffith, *God's Daughters: Evangelical Women and the Power of Submission* (Berkeley: University of California Press, 1997).
56. Sally K. Gallagher, *Evangelical Identity and Gendered Family Life* (New Brunswick, N.J.: Rutgers University Press, 2003).
57. When speaking off the record, several women mentioned that their churches offer little support for female executives.
58. Gwen Moore, "Women in Elite Positions: Insiders or Outsiders?" *Sociological Forum* 3.4 (1988): 566–85.
59. Emerson and Smith, "Divided by Faith."
60. Ibid., 170.
61. Brad Christerson, Michael O. Emerson, and Korie L. Edwards, *Against All Odds: The Struggle for Racial Integration in Religious Organizations* (New York: New York University Press, 2005); George Yancey, *Beyond Black and White: Reflections on Racial Reconciliation* (Grand Rapids, Mich.: Baker Books, 1996); John Perkins, and Thomas Tarrants III, *He's My Brother: Former Racial Foes Offer Strategy for Reconciliation* (Grand Rapids, Mich.: Chosen Books, 1994); Raleigh Washington and Glen Kehrein, *Breaking Down Walls: A Model for Reconciliation in an Age of Racial Strife* (Chicago: Moody Press, 1993).
62. Emerson and Smith, "Divided by Faith."
63. Pastor of Grace Chapel in Massachusetts, McDonald admitted to an adulterous affair in 1987. In addition, the Reverend Philip Wogaman, pastor of Foundry United Methodist Church in Washington, where the Clintons attended, was part of the group that provided spiritual counsel for the president.

64. According to Seiple, the group included a variety of evangelical leaders, such as Fuller Theological Seminary president Richard Mouw and *Christianity Today* columnist and popular writer Philip Yancey.

65. Interview with Robert Seiple, November 2, 2004, Philadelphia, Pennsylvania.

66. At his final public event, held in New York City in 2005, Graham came the closest to endorsing a candidate for president since he seated Richard Nixon in the VIP section at his 1968 crusade in Pittsburgh. Graham declared, "I told President Clinton that when he left office, he should be an evangelist because he has all the right gifts for it, and he should leave his wife to run the country" (comment to Greater New York Crusade, June 25, 2005, New York).

67. The "fouled up" comment came from an interview with Rudy de Leon, January 13, 2005, Washington, D.C. The reluctance to talk about faith "publicly" among Democrats came from an interview with Tony Hall, February 4, 2005, Washington, D.C.

68. Interview with Tony Campolo, March 3, 2006, Cherry Hill, New Jersey.

69. Interview with Burns Strider, February 17, 2006, Washington, D.C. I am not sure how "authentic" is defined by Strider, but the context in which he mentioned the term suggests the group is for members who are interested in the relation between religion and politics out of both spiritual and political concern.

70. The group is Common Good Strategies, founded by Eric Sapp and Mara Vanderslice in Washington, D.C.

71. Interview with Robert Seiple, November 2, 2004, Philadelphia, Pennsylvania.

72. See *www.sojo.net* for the best explication of this argument.

73. George Lakoff, *Moral Politics: How Liberals and Conservatives Think*, 2nd ed. (Chicago: University of Chicago Press, 2002).

74. Transcript from "Jimmy Carter" documentary in the *American Experience* series, Public Broadcasting System. See *http://www.pbs.org/wgbh/amex/carter/filmmore/fd.html* (accessed June 12, 2007) for complete transcript.

75. Some have claimed (McGarvey, "Reaching to the Choir"; Amy Sullivan, "Why W. Doesn't Go to Church: Empty Pew," *National Review Online*, October 11, 2004) that George W. Bush attends church significantly less than President Clinton did while in Washington. A careful review of the president's weekly schedule, as released by the White House Press Office, for several administrations reveals that the weekly digest of the president's schedule rarely contains references to church attendance, aside from religious holiday services (such as Easter services attended in a military chapel) or highly unusual event (as in the first White House church service conducted in 1969 at the start of the Nixon administration). Therefore, I find little support, according to the weekly compilation of presidential documents, that President Clinton attended church more often than President George W. Bush does. However, informants have said that, while at Camp David, President Bush uses the chapel more frequently than President Clinton did during his trips to the presidential retreat. By the same token, informed observers say President Bush attends church relatively infrequently while staying at his ranch in Crawford, Texas.

76. This was particularly effective with swing voting blocs such as Roman Catholics in 1992.

77. Amy Goldstein, "Part Of, but Apart From, It All," *Washington Post*, January 20, 1997; Terence Hunt, "Inaugural II Marks Renewal of Democracy," Associated Press news release, January 20, 1997.

78. Paul Kengor, "Talking about God: Clinton vs. Bush," posted on *www.newsmax.com*, September 4, 2004.

79. Kengor cites explicitly partisan statements by President Clinton such as identifying New York's Democratic governor Mario Cuomo as a "prophet" and instructing worshippers to vote. At Shiloh Baptist Church in October of 2000, President Clinton said, "I am pleading with you . . . I have done everything I know to do . . . [But] you have to show . . . make sure nobody takes a pass on November 7th." In addition to speaking at black churches, President Clinton spoke between 1993 and 2000 at twenty-one churches from a variety of religious traditions, including evangelical congregations such as the Willow Creek Community Church.

80. Every attendee, including children, must participate in the program in some way.

81. Interview with Richard Mouw, president of Fuller Theological Seminary, May 27, 2003, Pasadena, California.

82. David Croteau and William Hoynes, *By Invitation Only: How the Media Limit Political Debate* (Monroe, Maine: Common Courage, 1994).

83. Green's research shows that Bush captured a "decisive advantage in a very tight election" (Green, "Religion Gap Swings New Ways") by capturing the votes in 2004 of all kinds of churchgoers, including those who attend only on a monthly basis, a group that is closely divided between Republicans and Democrats.

84. Hanna Rosin, "Right with God: Evangelical Conservatives Find a Spiritual Home on the Hill," *Washington Post*, March 6, 2005.

85. The "marginalized or pigeon-holed" comment came from an interview with Pat MacMillan, November 16, 2004, Atlanta, Georgia.

86. Interview with Pete Wehner, August 4, 2004, Washington, D.C.

"Signaling Through the Flames": Hell House Performance and Structures of Religious Feeling

Ann Pellegrini

"Is Halloween the New Christmas?" This was the question posed by ABC News in a much-circulated online article from October 2006.[1] The article went on to trumpet Halloween as "now the second-biggest decorating holiday of the year—right behind Christmas." Halloween is indeed a multibillion-dollar business. A September 2006 report issued by the National Retail Federation estimated that American consumers would spend $4.96 billion on Halloween in 2006, up from $3.29 billion the previous year. From a strictly financial perspective, though, Christmas need not look over its shoulder for ghosts and goblins any time soon: the average consumer spends $791.10 on Christmas-related purchases, but only $59.06 for Halloween.[2]

But dollars and cents do not tell the whole story. ABC's rhetorical question—"Is Halloween the New Christmas?"—actually opens on to substantive issues regarding religious affect and the politics of feeling in the contemporary United States. Conservative U.S. Protestants have long worried that Halloween's associations with paganism and the occult leave young people susceptible to Satan's seductions. From this perspective, the worry is less that Halloween is the new Christmas than that it provides a route whereby the meaning of Christmas—*Christ*—will be denied altogether. These concerns have led some conservative Protestant churches, by which I mean evangelical, fundamentalist, and Pentecostal denominations, to offer alternative events to trick-or-treating, such as harvest celebrations and hayrides.[3] Others are taking it right to Satan and using Halloween as a platform for creative evangelizing—or "HalloWitnessing," in the words of self-proclaimed "anti-occult expert and Baptist demon exorcism specialist" Dr. Troy Franklin.[4] Even Christian Coalition founder Pat Robertson is seizing the day. Where once he inveighed against Halloween on *The 700 Club*—in one notorious 1982 segment he called for Halloween to be closed down and equated dressing up as a witch to "acting out Satanic rituals and participating in it [Satanism]"—today the Web site for his Christian Broadcasting Network offers concerned parents resources for turning Halloween into an evangelical opportunity.[5] (Suggestions include offering trick-or-treaters religious pamphlets along with their candy.)

Robertson's equation of Halloween with Satanic rituals continues to circulate in the eternal present of the World Wide Web and was quoted as recently as 2004 in a Knight-Ridder article on evangelical concerns about Halloween.[6] The recycling of this quotation, as if it represents Robertson's current approach to Halloween ("I think we ought to close Halloween down"), misses out on the ongoing negotiation many evangelical conservatives are making with secular popular culture in the service of missionizing to young people. These efforts attempt to utilize the vernaculars of youth culture and secular amusements.

One of the most innovative such responses to Halloween and its lurking dangers is the phenomenon of Hell Houses. Hell Houses are evangelical riffs on the haunted houses that dot the landscape of secular culture each Halloween. Some of these haunted houses are seasonal attractions mounted by for-profit amusement parks; others are low-tech fund-raisers run by local community groups. Where haunted houses promise to scare the bejeezus out of you, Hell Houses aim to scare you to Jesus. In a typical Hell House, demon tour guides take the audience though a series of bloody staged tableaux depicting sinners whose bad behavior—homosexuality, abortion, suicide, and, above all, rejection of Christ's saving grace—leads them straight to hell.

This essay discusses Hell Houses' use of theater as a medium of evangelization. I focus my analysis on the Hell House staged by the New Destiny Christian Center in the Denver suburb of Thornton, Colorado, in October 2006. I attended two performances over the course of their ten-day run, and also had an extended interview with Keenan Roberts, the senior pastor of New Destiny Christian Center. I will supplement this discussion with reference to the 2001 documentary *Hell House* and by comparing these performances to a Hell House staged by a "secular" theater group in Brooklyn, New York, in October 2006. My examination is in service of a larger set of questions about how religious feelings are lived, experienced, and communicated. Ultimately, I suggest that to understand how these performances do their evangelical work, cultural critics need to move beyond simply analyzing—and lambasting—the overt content or theology of Hell Houses (what Hell Houses *say*) and focus instead on the affectively rich worlds Hell House performances generate for their participants (what Hell Houses *do*). Such a methodological approach does not bracket political judgments or ethical critique, but lays the ground for them.

*****

Hell Houses first crossed the radar of secular popular culture with George Ratliff's 2001 documentary *Hell House*, a film festival favorite that was also featured on a memorable May 2002 episode of National Public Radio's *This American Life*, "Devil on My Shoulder." The documentary focused on the annual Hell House staged by Trinity Church of the Assemblies of God, in Cedar Hill, Texas. Each year, between 11,000 and 15,000 people flock to this suburb of Dallas to attend Trinity Church's Hell House. Although Ratliff and others have credited Trinity Church with inventing Hell Houses in 1990, in fact the phenomenon can be traced back to at least 1972, when Reverend Jerry Falwell first staged a "Scaremare" at his Thomas Road Baptist Church (TRBC), in Lynchburg, Virginia. Scaremare continues today, now mounted by the youth ministry at Falwell's Liberty University. The Scaremare Web site (*www.Scaremare.com*) describes the annual event as a "balance between a fun house and a house of death." Certainly, Scaremare, Hell Houses, and Judgment Houses (which date to the mid-1980s) all depend upon an audience's familiarity with the horror genre and with the haunted attractions at secular amusement parks.

This is a familiarity shared by the makers of Scaremare and its offshoots as well, who use their knowledge of secular popular culture as a way to connect with the unsaved. Indeed, in *The Book of Jerry Falwell*, anthropologist Susan Friend Harding quotes a TRBC youth minister as saying that Walt Disney World's Haunted Mansion was the immediate inspiration for Scaremare. With Harding, then, we could say that Christian haunted houses are "willfully hybrid" experiences, which combine secular culture and Christianity to extend a Christian message.[7]

Such hybridity has a long history. Notably, the eighteenth-century revivalist George Whitefield—who studied acting in his youth—used the conventions of the theater to win souls to Christ, drawing rapt audiences by the thousands in London and the United States. Whitefield's self-dramatizing sermons—tears rolling down his cheeks, passions on full display—were all the more striking in light of his forceful repudiation of the stage and his embrace of an explicitly antitheatrical theology. Harry S. Stout suggests there is something of mimetic rivalry in Whitefield's postconversion relation to his first passion, theater. Henceforth, Whitefield would do battle with theater as if it were a "*competing church*," but he would do so using his rival's tools.[8] Sometimes you have to traffic with the Devil to do the Lord's work. Engagement with popular culture provided an idiom and affective style that could transcend simple denominational divisions within Protestantism and compete for takers within an increasingly commercialized public square. Stylistically, Whitefield thus anticipated and set the pattern for later trends in American evangelical performance, from the illustrated sermons of Aimee Semple McPherson to the masculine tears of Ted Haggard and Jim Bakker as they testified to their own sinfulness.[9]

Hell Houses are an evangelical phenomenon, but they are hardly representative of evangelical Protestantism as a whole, which is theologically and politically diverse. And yet, I would argue, the religious sensibilities and styles of life that Hell Houses speak to and help to realize are shared across the wider evangelical world. It is these shared religious feelings I am exploring here.

The most prominent exponents of Hell Houses have been Assemblies of God churches, a Pentecostal group that dates to the Holiness movement of the late nineteenth century and to the Azusa Street revival of 1906. Today, the Assemblies of God is the largest Pentecostal denomination in the United States—and, indeed, in the world—with more than fifty million adherents globally. Despite the theological gulf between the dedicated Calvinism of a George Whitefield, for whom conversion was once for all, and the Arminian orientation of the Assemblies of God, who stress free will, progressive sanctification, and (because humans have free will) the possibility of religious "backsliding," what joins them is a striking emphasis on the culture and cultivation of feeling. The appeal is to the heart, not the head. Assemblies, not unlike Whitefield, are willing—in the words of the Assemblies' own mission statement—to use "every effective means to spiritually develop believers in [their] churches and to prepare continuing generations for service."[10] (It is probably no accident that McPherson—a pioneer in the blending of showbiz and salvation—was an Assemblies of God minister early in her preaching career.) This twinned commitment—evangelism and discipleship—is epitomized in the outreach work of Hell Houses.

No one has done more to spread Hell Houses across the United States than New Destiny's senior pastor, Keenan Roberts. He has also made canny use of the mass media, thereby helping to extend the Hell House message beyond the cultural margins. Pastor Keenan, as his congregants call him, has been mounting Hell Houses in the Denver area since 1995, first at the Abundant Life Christian Center in Arvada, and currently at New Destiny. Both are, like Trinity Church in Cedar Hill, Assemblies of God churches.

Pastor Keenan is a charismatic man, whose easy laugh and gift of story belie an intensity of purpose. He went to college on a basketball scholarship, and, at 6' 5", he is a towering physical presence. He must have made quite an impression as a demon guide, a role he played every Hell House season until 2006, when he decided to take a year off from acting in the production. He himself describes his demon guide performance as "the best," and, somehow, I have no reason to doubt him.[11] He "had a great time doing it," he says. "Being big was fun."

Pastor Keenan had not even heard of Hell Houses until the early 1990s, when a fellow youth pastor told him about the basic concept. He was, he says, "immediately gripped" by their potential as an evangelizing tool. He went on to stage his first Hell House in 1993, at a church in Roswell, New Mexico. Pastor Keenan may have been late to the scene of Hell Houses, but he has capitalized on their potential as instruments of outreach and amplification. In 1996 he began selling "Hell House Outreach Kits" (the 2006 edition cost $299), and says they have sold approximately eight hundred kits in the past ten years to churches across the United States and even to a few in Europe (figure 1). Hell House Outreach brilliantly joins marketing with missionizing.

Hell Houses try to tap into their audience's desire for a bounded, "safe" experience of being afraid. Audiences want to gasp and gape in company—and leave without a mark. They want the heart-pounding, stomach-churning catharsis of horror-as-entertainment: at the end of the ride or the film or the performance, you get to return to the world unscathed. The object of fear (a vampire, say) is revealed as unreal, or a terrifying experience (such as a roller coaster ride) is shown to be ephemeral, survivable. By contrast, Hell Houses are playing for keeps. They draw upon even as they move to recode experiences of "safety" and "fear," "reality" and "unreality," in the service of a fundamental spiritual transformation. They want their audiences to see the gruesome realities that await them if they do not live wisely: not just death in its pain and brutality (and, as Charles D'Ambrosio points out, Hell House can only imagine the most gruesome endings), but everlasting damnation.[12] The roller coaster eventually stops, but hell is for all eternity. What's more, within the worlds laid bare by Hell House performances the devil is neither allegory nor projection of the unconscious; he is real and he is coming for you. The relentlessness of this vision is tempered, however, by the promise of a safety more thoroughgoing than any this-worldly happy ending: the saving grace of Jesus Christ.

The primary targets of Hell Houses are teenagers, and this targeting is among the reasons Hell Houses have become so controversial. Detractors accuse them of preaching hate to an especially vulnerable population. In the run-up to the 2006 Halloween season, for example, the National Gay and Lesbian Task

NEW DESTINY CHRISTIAN CENTER
SOARING AT A GODLY ALTITUDE

Welcome   About Us   Ministries   Calendar   Contact Us

Introduction

How-To Kit

Individual Scenes

Hell House FX CDs

Ordering

Hell House Resources

Contained within this section of our site are numerous resources that will assist any church or ministry in the presentation of the Hell House Outreach. These items have been carefully developed over the course of many years and have been utilized with great success in outreaches that have impacted multiplied thousands in person in metro Denver and millions more across the country and around the world. Most of these resources have been uniquely created for the Hell House Outreach and are highly specialized and unavailable from any other source.

Each resource is listed with a brief description, as well as the price. (The price does not include shipping and handling. Shipping and handling charges will be added to your order based on current United States Postal Service mail rates.)

Note: the Hell House Outreach Kit contains different materials and accessories than the ones listed in the Resource Directory area of the site. If a particular church or ministry has not yet purchased the kit, it is the initial resource needed to begin building an outreach for your community. Read thoroughly about the How-To Kit.

Also, the ministry of the Hell House Outreach has now gone entirely paperless both for your convenience as well as ours. All Hell House materials are now digital and sent on disc. This includes all video resource on DVD and all audio resource on compact disc. All textual documents are created in the standard Windows program, Microsoft Word and sent on CD.

We trust you find the following materials helpful in your efforts to reach your community and build the Kingdom of God through dramatic and theatrical means!

Force (NGLTF) released a report accusing Hell Houses and their purveyors of spreading a message of bigotry and homophobia. The Hell House message "literally demonizes [Lesbian, Gay, Bisexual, Transgender] LGBT youth, fueling the harassment and violence many experience on a daily basis." The reports' authors, Sarah Kennedy and Jason Cianciotto, also criticize Hell Houses for perpetuating the "false notion that youth cannot be both LGBT and Christian."[13] Hell Houses have come under criticism from Christian groups as well, such as the Colorado Council of Churches, for engaging in fear-based theology that distorts the Christian message.

Figure 1.
"Hell House Resources," © The Hell House Outreach, Thornton, Colorado,_www.godestiny.org/hell_house/HH_resources.cfm, 2005–2007.

But the literally thousands of men, women, and teenagers across the country who take part in Hell House ministries each year do not think of themselves as spreading hate or intolerance; nor do they see themselves as *unreasonably* manipulating people's fears. In any case, asks Pastor Keenan, "who decided that fear is not an effective teacher?" His rhetorical question here echoes the words of Tim Ferguson, Trinity Church's youth pastor and Hell House coordinator, early in the documentary film: "A part of salvation is being afraid of going to hell." As these exchanges suggest, a Hell House is supposed to scare you, but for a much higher purpose than the secular entertainments it so knowingly mimes. Certainly Pastor Keenan rejects accusations that he is trafficking in hate: "Just because someone doesn't agree with the message, doesn't mean it's a hateful message. . . . We also believe that communicating to people what the Bible says doesn't make this judgmental. We believe the Book to be the all-sufficient source for life direction." The discordance between these ways of understanding the Hell House experience—hate/love, distortion/truth—is as much about affect as it is about ideology or theology. This is salvation as "structure of feeling."

The term "structure of feeling" comes from Raymond Williams, of course.[14] In *Marxism and Literature*, Williams proposes this language as a way to describe "pre-emergent" phenomena, experiences that are "active and pressing but not yet fully articulated."[15] He chose the word "feeling" to "emphasize a distinction from more formal concepts of 'world-view' or 'ideology'."[16] He does not abandon these concepts and concerns so much as push us to take seriously how "formal or systematic beliefs" are embedded in, and arise out of, concrete relations and experiences:

> We are talking about characteristic elements of impulse, restraint, and tone; specifically affective elements of consciousness and relationships: not feeling against thought, but thought

as felt and feeling as thought: practical consciousness of a present kind, in a living and interrelating continuity. We are then defining these elements as a "structure": as a set, with specific internal relations, at once interlocking and in tension. Yet we are also defining a social experience which is still *in process*, often indeed not yet recognized as social but taken to be private, idiosyncratic, and even isolating, but which in analysis (though rarely otherwise) has its emergent, connecting, and dominant characteristics, indeed its hierarchies.[17]

Although Hell House Outreach represents itself as presenting objective realities and Bible-based truth, at the end of the day, the ability to win over converts or spark spiritual rededication does not rise and fall on fact checking or biblical hermeneutics. It is a matter rather of affective congruences. Hell House performances witness to their audiences. The process of conviction may engage preexisting beliefs—such as the notion that homosexuality is wrong, abortion is evil, or Satan is real—but for conviction to take hold something more is required. The participant is invested (or reinvested) in a deeper structure of religious feeling that can tie together disparate, even contradictory, experiences, bodily sensations, feelings, and thoughts.

Perhaps one of the reasons accusations against Hell House—as fomenting bigotry or distorting the Christian message—gain so little traction with Hell House participants is that opponents are arguing "facts." But, you cannot fight feelings with facts.[18] For its adherents, a Hell House sutures gaps, soothes contradictions, and produces resonance amid discord.[19] (As I will make clear below, Hell House's reliance on theatricality means that gaps may reemerge elsewhere.) Pastor Keenan has welcomed the controversies generated by Hell House's depiction of hell-bound homosexuals and blood-covered "abortion girl." He considers such controversies an "incredible blessing." The media storm has been a means of "amplifying the message" well beyond what the church could achieve on its own. And the message is about to get an even bigger staging ground: a fictional treatment of Hell House is in development with producers Adam Shulman and Julie Silverman-Yorn, of Firm Films. Scott Derrickson, a self-identified evangelical and director of the 2005 film *The Exorcism of Emily Rose*, has been tapped to helm the project. The feature film will focus on the controversies that engulf a town when a Christian group stages a Hell House.[20]

This does not mean that Pastor Keenan is insensible to every criticism. During the course of my ninety-minute interview with him, he twice drew an explicit contrast between his own message and ministry and that of Reverend Fred Phelps. Phelps leads the Westboro Baptist Church, in Topeka, Kansas, and he gained widespread notoriety for organizing protests at the funeral of murdered gay college student Matthew Shepard, in 1998. Phelps and his small band of followers (almost all of them family members) held up placards with slogans such as "God Hates Fags" and "Matt in Hell." Phelps and his church continue to court controversy. For example, Westboro Baptist runs an incendiary Web site, Godhatesfags.com.[21] More recently, Phelps has led protests at the funerals of U.S. military personnel killed in Iraq, whose deaths he has interpreted as divine punishment for America's acceptance of homosexuality. "Thank God for Dead Soldiers," read one of the placards. (Phelps's actions have led several state legislatures to pass bills forbidding political protests from being held within five hundred feet of funerals or memorial services.)

Where Phelps is the measure of hateful extremism, it is not hard to come off as reasonable and compassionate. Pastor Keenan described Phelps as a "raving lunatic . . . Everything he says is so opposite of the Bible, in my opinion." In stark contrast, Pastor Keenan asserted, "I care about people in all walks of life and people that are dealing with all kinds of things in their life. I care about people whatever their particular issues might be. I can tell you, I don't hate people. I don't believe that it [Hell House's condemnation of homosexuality] is a hateful message." Pastor Keenan himself analogizes the work of his Hell House to the responsibilities of good parenting: "God's word is very explicit about where to play and where not to play. That doesn't make him or us judgmental for communicating, 'Play here or don't play there.' And good parents are the same way." Pastor Keenan is extremely sensitive to accusations of fomenting hatred and draws what is to him a clear distinction between being hateful and being painfully, even aggressively, honest.

Instead of seeing Pastor Keenan's denials as hypocritical or deluded, I want to take him at his word. Certainly, it is tempting to subsume the rhetorics of Hell House and Pastor Keenan fully under hate. But resisting this temptation can actually give us insight into the way Hell House's structures of religious feeling meet up with—find resonances with—the larger feeling culture not just of evangelicals but of the U.S. public square more broadly. How far is Pastor Keenan, really, from the attitude of "love the sinner, hate the sin" that animates so much public, *secular* discussion and debate over homosexuality? As Janet R. Jakobsen and I have argued elsewhere, "love the sinner, hate the sin" allows people to espouse punitive judgments and promote discriminatory policies against their neighbors and fellow citizens, all the while experiencing themselves as "tolerant" and "open-minded."[22] Indeed, professions of tolerance mixed with stern moral judgment are a routine feature of political life in the United States. Even the Southern Poverty Law Center, the group probably most responsible for bringing hate groups such as the Ku Klux Klan to justice, urges us to "teach tolerance" in order to battle hatred. But what does tolerance really offer—and to whom?

When President George W. Bush came out in favor of a federal constitutional amendment to ban gay marriage, a move that would create a permanent constitutional underclass, he nonetheless concluded his remarks with a call for "kindness and goodwill and decency."[23] Again, this is not a matter of personal hypocrisy or political opportunism per se. This is about larger structures of American political life in which invidious social distinctions are maintained in part by the way they hook into dominant feelings. Feelings of tolerance actually support hierarchy and social domination. Although tolerance is usually promoted as a response to violence and social division, in practice tolerance works to affirm existing social hierarchies by establishing an us-them relationship between a dominant center and those on the margins. To put the matter more starkly, tolerance might feel good—and like good faith—to those who mouth its words; but being tolerated might not always feel all that different from being hated.

I am thus deeply sympathetic to NGLTF's concerns about the effect Hell Houses may have on GLBT and questioning youth. For such youth, witnessing a Hell House depiction of ghouls delighting over a gay man's death from AIDS may well feel like a profound and profoundly alienating blow to the self. Nonetheless, are Hell House's effects on "Christian youth who may be struggling with their sexual orientation or gender identity" as one-way or unidirectional as the NGLTF report worries?[24] For one thing, NGLTF may underestimate the resilience of many queer youth. For another, the uptake of a message is not fully determined by the sender's intentions. Misfires happen all the time, especially when it comes to sexual representations. Can we rule out the possibility that for some young people—GLBT, questioning, or otherwise—just getting a glimpse of same-sex eroticism is a perverse pleasure, revealing possibilities they were not otherwise supposed to contemplate? In other words, what if the very medium Hell House uses to reach its audience, theater, queers the pitch of the message?

*****

One of the things that most interests me about Hell House is its faith in the power of theater to reach in and transform its audience. Pastor Keenan and his ministry understand that propelling the Word forward today requires engaging with this-worldly forms, including contemporary media and technology. Starting with the 2006 version of the outreach kit, all the components are on disc, including a how-to guide to production, a DVD of a Hell House performance, and a compact disc soundtrack containing sound effects and music to amp up the scariness of specific scenes—"from the voice of Suicide to Lucifer's bone-chilling introduction to Hell House to a myriad of others you absolutely cannot find anywhere else," the Web site promises.[25]

Pastor Keenan's script is included in every kit as a rewritable document, allowing individual churches to adapt it to their particular needs. His Hell House features seven scenes. The first five scenes of the basic kit depict what Pastor Keenan calls "social-sin issues," addressing homosexuality, abortion, suicide, drunk driving, and Satanism. Pastor Keenan writes a new script every year for production by his own church group, always reserving two of the five "social-sin" scenes to cover homosexuality and abortion. He says he will continue prioritizing these two topics until God instructs him otherwise. This leaves three scenes whose topical focus can vary from year to year, as new issues present themselves. (For example, the 2006 production featured a brand-new scene on the evils of methamphetamine use. It ended—badly of course—with a fiery car crash, which had some overlap with the drunk-driving narrative of the standard script.)

Churches do not have to buy a new kit every year. Instead, to supplement a kit they have already purchased, they can buy updated and new scenes as stand-alone CDs. The Web site currently advertises sixteen individual scenes for purchase, complete with sound effects and any needed background music. Scene one in the standard script depicts "the funeral of a young homosexual male who believed the born gay lie and died of AIDS." But, for an additional $45, you can get the "Gay Wedding Scene Package":

> This energetic scene will give you another powerful weapon in your arsenal against the homosexual stronghold and the born-gay deception. The demon tour guide conducts the ceremony that actually involves a young married couple. (The wife dons masculine make-up for the necessary male look.) The tour guide pronounces them "husband and husband". Then the scene utilizes a time warp to move several years into the future with one of the partners dying of AIDS as demon imps swarm into a hospital room. This package comes with the originally produced rock-n-roll wedding march CD, the air of evil background music CD and the death drum track also on compact disc.[26]

In the 2006 production, this scene opened the play, underscoring the way homosexuality and same-sex marriage in particular have come to function as *the* defining issue for many Christian conservatives. (A still of New Destiny's gay wedding scene is visible in the center of figure 1.) But there is such a thing as theater that succeeds too well. The "born-gay deception" is a trap set by Satan to ease the path to sin. Pastor Keenan's insistence that the gay male couple be played by a married heterosexual one can be seen as an attempt to minimize risk to both audience and actors. Interestingly, similar precautions are not taken with respect to other, nonsexual scenes; that is, no special warnings are given about making sure to cast only males or only women over child-bearing age in the role of "abortion girl."

Importantly, this is not just about so-called gay sex. One of the extra for-purchase packages in the Hell House kit depicts the "out-of-control sexual appetite" of contemporary youth. Pastor Keenan always casts a young married couple in the role of the teenagers who are about to have sex, the girl giving up "the pearl of her virginity" to the more experienced boyfriend. The stage directions, such as they are, say that the scene will be played in a "tasteful yet sizzling fashion."[27]

Sexual scenes are thus understood to be especially volatile for both actors—and audience. This is a point brought home forcefully in the documentary as well. During an August script meeting, Tim Ferguson invites the Hell House youth leaders to suggest "new twists" on old themes for Trinity Church's 2001 production. One young woman proposes that they include a gay bar scene, with "two girls hitting on one another." Ferguson immediately nixes the idea: "I don't want to do that. The way we do it, it's almost bad enough just being at the hospital bed there for that moment." He is referring to the way they have handled the issue of homosexuality in previous years' productions. Equating homosexuality with AIDS, they typically depicted a gay man dying of AIDS who refuses to accept Jesus into his life, despite the pleas of a female friend at his deathbed. He is spirited off to hell by a demon at the moment of his death. (This is the scene they ended up performing in the 2001 production, too.)

It remains unclear to me just what is "bad enough" about this scene. That an audience member might sympathize with the young gay man's bodily suffering, and thus lose sight of the eternal suffering that awaits? When the young woman persists with her proposal to do a gay bar scene, Ferguson elaborates his objection in another way: "The same reason we don't do a boyfriend-girlfriend scene in Hell House is because you're just together so much over this period of time that I just don't want to go there." Clearly, the concern here is that the intense intimacy of rehearsal will lead to other kinds of intimacies, in which life too much imitates art. In the documentary Ferguson will refer to his desire to use Hell House to "infect" and "infiltrate the culture." He is able to voice anxieties about the effect sexual scenes will have on the young actors, but stops short of recognizing the broader dangers of dallying with forms. And yet, mimesis cannot be so easily contained, no matter what Ferguson, Pastor Keenan, and the Hell House outreach kit may specify. "Tasteful yet sizzling." Can Hell Houses really have it both ways?

This worrisome porousness exists on the side of audiences, too, who bring to Hell Houses their own sets of expectations and vulnerabilities. The Hell House performances I attended in Thornton were small affairs; fewer than 150 people attended each night—total—with a large share of this made up of bussed-in youth groups, who were apparently there because they had to be. This wildly contradicted my own expectations. I was expecting the sort of crowds that show up in Cedar Hill each year. The scale of the Cedar Hill audience, at least as depicted in the documentary, generates surprising juxtapositions between, for example, the earnestness of the drunk-driving death scene and the rowdy anticipation of some obviously intoxicated youths waiting to take their tour of hell. At another moment we learn in a voiceover that after a previous year's production, a warlock contacted the Hell House ministry to tell them that their occult scene was not accurate. The warlock's desire for mimesis, to be given back whole, is a different mimetic desire than the ones Hell Houses' makers seek to activate, but the differences underscore, once again, the volatility of live performance.

The complex, unpredictable interactions among performer, performed, and audience—who must complete the performance—are among the reasons theater's emotional reach cannot be so easily micromanaged. The audience member who knows she is seeing a married couple just playing at being gay men but "really" kissing may find herself alongside another spectator who sees two men exchanging vows and a kiss and then witnesses one stretched in grief over his dying lover's body, a final embrace as his beloved passes from life. The emotional power of this scene exceeds, or potentially exceeds, theological straitjacketing. "Bad enough," indeed.

The final two stops on the Hell House tour are always hell and heaven, in that order. Although the script for these two scenes may vary from year to year, the basic plot points remain the same. In the production I saw, the actor portraying Lucifer spoke through a voice box, which distorted his voice and lent it a menacing quality. The scene as a whole was theatrically accomplished and well thought out. The audience was squeezed together in a claustrophobic basement hell. Condemned souls, young and old, threw themselves piteously against a chain-link fence, screaming for help, while black-garbed imps, their faces completely covered, offered hissing punctuation to Lucifer's speech. The imps were the youngest members of the cast, and their smallness of size made them especially effective as they slithered among the crowd.

In a kind of Hell House 101, a gloating Lucifer neatly summarized the previous five scenes, underscoring the bad choices that were made in each: from the gay men who chose homosexuality but hid behind the excuse that God made them gay, to the young teen suicide whose worldly success could not hide the emptiness of his spiritual life. The sensory overload of this scene was interrupted by a blaze of bright light and a chorus of white-garbed winged angels, who brought Satan's speech to an end and escorted us into our final destination, heaven. Here, a beatific blond Jesus preached the Good News before leading the now-seated audience in a prayer of salvation. The two nights I saw Hell House, there was a low hum from the crowd. Some murmured along; others sat in silence.

In comparison to the pyrotechnics of hell, heaven was a let-down. On one level this is purely an aesthetic problem: sin makes for much more interesting spectacle and narrative than goodness. "Sin" is lush, sensual, readily theatrical. By comparison, "goodness" is generic, saccharine, and bland. Preachiness may be good for the soul, but it is not very fun. This is the open secret of Hell House. For Pastor Keenan and his congregation, though, "God's word does not return void." I may have sat silent and unmoved during the salvation prayer, but I was still listening, still being witnessed to.

The salvation prayer was followed by a brief address by one of New Destiny's associate pastors, who encouraged all of us to fill out an outreach response card. The card, along with information about the church, a clipboard, and pen, had been placed under every chair in "heaven." It had four boxes to check off:

- For the first time I have prayed the prayer of salvation and asked Jesus Christ into my life tonight.
- I rededicated my life to Jesus Christ tonight.
- I am looking for a church/youth group to be involved in.
- Please remember my prayer request on back of this card.

The two evenings I saw New Destiny's Hell House, people dutifully filled out the cards, though no one stayed behind for further prayer or conversation, as we were all invited to do. Everything about the associate pastor's final pitch was warmly and lightly done, in contrast to the hard sell of the preceding tour. As Pastor Keenan avers, Hell House is "very go-right-at-you. But that's the Hell House personality of what we do for a few nights a year . . . [and] that allows us to reach a lot of people in a different way."

The Hell House experience is not just in-your-face missionizing. It is an aggressive theater of transformation. Spreading the Word depends on theater as a kind of contagion passed from performer to audience. We are back to Ferguson's metaphor of "infection." However, this promise—that theater can be catching—is also the reason it has historically been at the center of so much moral hand wringing and outright condemnation. From Plato's tirade against mimesis in *The Republic*, to Tertullian's likening of theater to idolatry in *De Spectaculis* (*Of Spectacles*), to Puritan polemics linking theater to sexual depravity in Phillip Stubbes's 1583 treatise *The Anatomie of Abuses*, philosophers and theologians have worried over theater's capacity to "infect" audiences with the "wrong" sorts of ideas and practices.[28] The worry is not simply that seeing is believing, but that believing might beget doing.

This antitheatrical prejudice is not just yesterday's news, of course. It followed the Puritans to the "New World," and it continues to percolate in debates over "obscenity," public funding of the arts, and age-appropriate media content, just for starters. Nevertheless, as George Whitefield's own career testifies, these suspicions concerning theater's moral dangers have often gone hand in hand with a desire to harness its power for projects of political and/or spiritual renewal—for conversion, even. This too has a long history, from ancient Greek festivals of Dionysus, to the passion plays of medieval Catholicism, to the Ta'ziyeh dramas of Shiite Islam.

As a form, theater has no one political claim. Although political theater generally invokes images of the political Left—think of the work of Bertolt Brecht or of Clifford Odets and the Group Theatre—theatrical transformation does not point one way only. It has become a commonplace for scholars of theater and live performance to refer, in nearly reverential terms, to the worldmaking capacity of performance, its ability to conjure into view new horizons of the possible and to consolidate and reconsolidate oppositional publics or lifeworlds. I share this faith in performance's power to transform its audience into something more . . . into a public, perhaps? Or, even, a revolution? So do the hundreds, if not thousands, of evangelical communities that stage Hell Houses across the United States each year. Could Pastor Keenan and his flock be the face of theater's last true believers? Perhaps Hell House represents the new avant-garde.

Documentary filmmaker and performance studies scholar Debra Levine has elaborated this point, astutely placing Hell Houses within the tradition of Antonin Artaud's "theatre of cruelty."[29] In *The Theater and Its Double* (1938), Artaud called for a theater that, "overturning all our preconceptions, inspires us with the fiery magnetism of its images and acts upon us like a spiritual therapeutics whose touch can never be forgotten."[30] Artaud's theater of cruelty privileges feeling over plot and moves to break down artificial walls between spectator and spectacle by bombarding the audience from all sides with new sensations. This is theater as affective immersion and communal event, and its "therapeutics" are not gentle pats on the back. Conjuring a new theater adequate to its time, Artaud concludes the preface to *The Theater and Its Double* by linking theater to sacrifice and purification: "And if there is still one hellish, truly accursed thing in our time, it is our artistic dallying with forms, instead of being like victims burnt at the stake, signaling through the flames."[31]

These are heady metaphors. But so too is Pastor Keenan's likening of attacks on Hell House to the Crucifixion: "The same will be true of this [criticisms of Hell House] as what was true of Jesus. That is, they tried to crucify him, and we all know how that worked out. People can try to crucify this [Hell House], and you can't kill it because it is about the Good News message." Pastor Keenan offered this comparison specifically in response to a 2004 parody version of Hell House that was performed in Hollywood and featured such celebrities as Sarah Silverman and Bill Maher, who played Satan—and not very well, Pastor Keenan hastens to add. Maher did not seem to know his lines, a sin against professionalism at the very least.

The experience with Hollywood Hell House made Pastor Keenan doubly suspicious when Les Frères Corbusier, an experimental theater company based in New York City, contacted him about staging Hell House in the Big Apple. They did not want to do a parody or a hatchet job. They wanted to do a "straight up" version of Hell House,[32] giving New York City audiences a glimpse into a social world that is otherwise completely foreign to them. (This is hardly an accurate picture of the religious diversity of New York City and the greater metropolitan area, of course, which is home, for instance, to the largest concentration of Pentecostals in the country.) Eventually, the company's executive director, Aaron Lemon-Strauss, convinced Pastor Keenan that the company's motives were sincere.

Les Frères went on to stage their Hell House in St. Ann's Warehouse, in October 2006, in Brooklyn's DUMBO neighborhood. DUMBO, an acronym for "Down Under the Manhattan Bridge Overpass," is an area of reclaimed warehouses, art galleries, hip watering holes and eateries, and increasing rents. St. Ann's is known for its cutting-edge theater and performance events, and its typical audience member probably goes to more art openings than prayer services.

Certainly, the prospect of a "secular" Hell House was media catnip, landing coverage by *Newsweek* as well as articles and reviews in the *New York Times*, the *Denver Post*, the Associated Press, and even *Variety*. Uniformly, the media made much of the fact that the production was a "faithful" and "sincere" presentation of a "real" Hell House. For example, in his October 2006 review of the production, chief *New York Times* theater critic Ben Brantley described it as an "irony-free facsimile" of the real thing and said the company managed to present "its visions of the fiery agonies that await non-believers with nary a wink or a roll of the eyes."[33]

Maybe so, but the sincerity of Les Frères's approach to Hell House may have been its undoing. To my eyes, the performance felt less sincere than "sincere." The quote marks here are not irony alerts. The cast was top notch, professional, filled with talent, and so on. The special effects were well considered, deliberately low-tech and sophisticated at the same time, as in the blood-spurting abortion scene (figure 2), or when Steve, whose marriage to another man we had witnessed just one scene before (figure 3), lies dying of AIDS and is dispatched to hell through a trapdoor in his hospital gurney (figure 4). Nonetheless, the performances came across as a kind of self-referential pointing at what they were not: "Look at me, I am not ironic" as well as "Look at me, I am not a Christian or, at least, not one of *those* Christians." To put the matter in theatrical terms, you could say that Les Frères was coolly Brechtian when it needed to be engaged and Aristotelian, let alone bloody red and Artaudian.

The program notes begin with a disclaimer "FROM LES FRERES AND ARTS AT ST. ANN'S: This authentic depiction of a Hell House is meant to educate and inform about a particular religious movement, not to endorse any specific ideology." Les Frères served up its *Hell House* as a kind of sociological artifact, not a living thing, and the company's anthropological approach proved theatrically limiting. This limitation is related to the company's assertion that it was offering an "authentic depiction of a Hell House." The language here is confusing. Les Frères's claim is smaller than it first appears. They are not putting on a Hell House, but a representation, a "depiction," of one. This sets them at remove—a safe distance, perhaps—from the "real" thing, where the "real" means "religion." The modifier "authentic" is puzzling in this context. What, exactly, is an "authentic depiction"? Is this their way of distinguishing good copies (good because sincere) from bad ones (think: *Hollywood Hell House*)? Staking out claims to authenticity even as they proclaimed their difference, Les Frères members wanted to have their evangelical cake, *without* having to eat it, too.

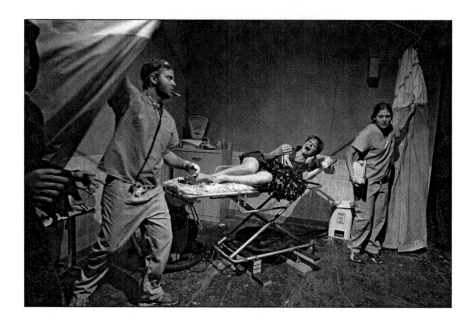

Figure 2.
"Abortion," scene from *Hell House.* Photograph by Joan Marcus, © Les Freres Corbusier, 2006.

It is interesting to speculate how Les Frères's Hell House would have changed if the company had done outreach to evangelical churches, in a kind of reverse missionizing. How would Les Frères's Hell House have appeared—felt—to them? But this would have required recognizing that the religious landscape of New York City already includes many people whose worldview evangelical Hell Houses *do* accurately capture. It would also have meant confronting some significant overlap between the truth-and-consequences theology of Hell House and the worldviews of many urban "hipsters." Les Frères's hipster audience surely included many people who profess pastoral notions of good, spiritually redeeming sex versus bad, corrupting sex or who ascribe to a watered-down version of karmic retribution. For whom, exactly, is a Hell House an otherworldly experience?

There were certainly numerous departures between the evangelical (the "authentic"?) Hell House put on by New Destiny and Les Frères's. Where Pastor Keenan's model recommends seven scenes, each with the dramatic arc of a "one-act play," Les Frères had nine rooms. Pastor Keenan's version suggests using two demon guides per tour; Les Frères's demons worked solo. For the gay wedding scene, Les Frères cast two men in the role of the gay grooms,

Figure 3.
"Gay Wedding," scene from *Hell House*. Photograph by Joan Marcus, © Les Freres Corbusier, 2006.

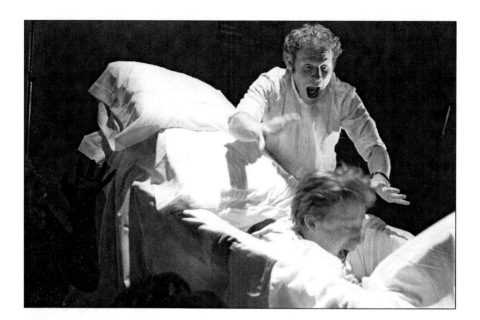

Figure 4.
"Clinic–Steve to Hell," scene from *Hell House*. Photograph by Joan Marcus, © Les Freres Corbusier, 2006.

stopping just short of having the two men kiss. As the grooms' lips were about to touch, one man interposed his hand between their two mouths. Les Frères also freely adapted Pastor Keenan's script. The version they performed combined elements from his script, scenes from the 2001 documentary, and additions by the company itself. The most notable addition was scene 6, which was set at a hipster cafe, or "Café Hell," as the demon guide dubbed it. Three twenty-somethings—two men, one woman—excitedly discuss *The Onion*, Jon Stewart, and the possibility of putting on a show that will make fun of "religious people." At this, a pack of lesser demons drags the trio of ironists away, as the demon guide growls his review: "Do you know what's really hot right now? Sincerity. Painful Sincerity."

Pastor Keenan attended the opening weekend of Les Frères's production. His own verdict on it was not that that it lacked sincerity, but that it needed more "intensity." The intensity of an evangelical Hell House derives in part from the cast and crew's belief that there are cosmic stakes involved in their performance. Ultimately, then, the numerous structural and textual differences between Les Frères's Hell House and Pastor Keenan's pale beside the question of affective sensibility.

Hell House is theater, but it is also something more than theater. As Pastor Keenan observes, "it's not just a play, it's not just a theatre thing, it is something that has tremendous spiritual significance for people's lives." This "not just"—this "excess," let's call it—returns us to the structure of religious feeling. On its Web site, the New Destiny Center claims "outreaches average a 33% salvation and rededication decision rate!"[34] Trinity Church Cedar Hill claims a more "modest," but still significant conversion and recommitment rate of 20 percent. These statistics can be argued over: exactly what is being counted, and how? What does seem unmistakable, though, is the circuit of feeling that passes among the participants in New Destiny's Hell House or Trinity Church's, all of whom, young and old, cast and crew, are embedded in a larger community of meaning making and, as they see it, higher purpose. Conversion is never a finished process, and Hell House is as much about reconfirming the individual participants in their faith commitments as it is about spreading the Good News to others.

As theater, Hell House exceeds religious understanding or sectarian attempts to control its overflow of feeling and meaning making. Pastor Keenan is right: "Being big is fun." So is getting to be other than who you are if only for a night, or maybe more. In "Devil on my Shoulder," the 2002 segment of *This American Life* that focused on *Hell House*, director Ratliff reminds us—if we needed any reminding—that the plum roles in Hell House are the sinners; "nearly everyone wants to play [one]." He continues:

> Not one person auditioned to play Jesus or an angel role. Maybe it's just more fun to be evil on stage than good. Maybe playing a church-going, God-fearing Christian is just not that interesting if you are a church-going, God-fearing Christian. The organizers usually have to go out and recruit some hapless kids to play the good Christian roles.[35]

In the documentary, the filmmaker asks a group of performers what the best scene in Hell House is. One young girl unhesitatingly replies: "Rave scene's the best, because you get to dance." There is vocal assent from her peers.

The pleasures of putting on the theatrical mask are the pleasures of transgressing the everyday, being who you are not, and opening yourself—sometimes dangerously—to the leakiness between roles on stage and off. More than theater, more than religion: Hell House defies neat boundaries between audience and performer, secular culture and religious event. At its best, and sometimes even at its worst, theater can make you susceptible. To what, and whether that is a good thing, depends on who's doing the accounting.

If we measure the success of Hell House in terms of how many people are saved for the first time, then Hell House seems a failure—even Trinity's 20 percent statistic is inflated by the high numbers of spectators who "rededicate." But, there are some queer convergences here. In a jointly written essay "Preaching to the Converted," performance studies scholar David Román and performance artist Tim Miller defend the value of performing for one's "own." Conversion, they argue, "demands a continual testing of identity," not identity once for all, and this "implies vulnerability."[36] Writing from a distinctly queer perspective, Román and Miller argue for community-based performance as an urgent and even life-saving experience of self and communal (re)constitution in the face of an often hostile world. If queer theater is "preaching to the converted," as its critics sometimes sneer, this is precisely what Román and Miller want to valorize.

Evangelical Christians see themselves as marginal and in need of buffering, too, and Hell House offers one way to reconfirm belief in the face of what they feel to be a secular hegemony. Of course, it is important to distinguish here between a feeling of marginalization and the accuracy of such a feeling.[37] This feeling of marginalization remains active and galvanizing despite the undeniable impact conservative Christianity has had on electoral politics and policy-making in the United States over the past two decades. And this is what makes Hell House seem so politically scary to many of its progressive critics, both religious and secular: Hell House speaks for much larger political and cultural currents, and represents a politics of division.

This division even extends to Hell House's fear factor. For evangelical proponents, Hell House uses fear in the service of a higher good. For critics, such as NGLTF or the Colorado Council of Churches, Hell House cruelly manipulates social stereotypes and phobias against vulnerable populations. For a secular critic like the writer Charles D'Ambrosio, Hell House's problem is that it is not scary enough; it fails because it lacks the "anguish and torment . . . you expect a good haunted house to have."[38] For myself, I was not "scared" by the Hell House performances I saw, though I could not be in greater disagreement with the cultural politics or theology of Hell House and its makers. Still, I remain impressed by their can-do theatrical spirit and the palpable sense of fun they seemed to be having. This was a fun that most squarely did not include me. At least not in any simple way. As a queer scholar of performance (not to mention, an atheist) I find my own pleasures—and challenges—in thinking seriously about Hell House, what it does, what it fails to accomplish.

By attending to "meanings and values as they are actively lived and felt,"[39] to return to Raymond Williams's language, progressive scholars might better understand not just Hell House's appeal to its participants, but also the role emotions play in the constitution of conservative cultural politics. As Linda

Kintz argues, "academics and others who feel justifiably threatened by traditionalist conservatism are often unable to understand its appeal because we are not used to understanding beliefs that are not expressed according to our own scholarly expectations. By dismissing arguments that are not articulated in the terms with which we are familiar, we overlook the very places where politics comes to matter most: at the deepest levels of the unconscious, in our bodies, through faith, and in relation to the emotions."[40] This essay represents a modest attempt to listen for these other articulations.

Notes

I thank Julia Bryan-Wilson, Marie Griffith, Janet Jakobsen (as ever!), Heather Lukes, Molly McGarry, and Angela Zito for helping me to think through and clarify the issues taken up in this essay. Some material in it was initially developed for *The Revealer*, an online daily review of religion and the press. I am so thankful to Jeff Sharlet for his sterling feedback on that version. Keenan Roberts and Jeff Beste were generous with their time during my visit to the New Destiny Christian Center in October 2006; I appreciate their hospitality and their permission to reproduce a page from the Hell House Outreach Web site. Aaron Lemon-Strauss graciously provided images from Les Frères Corbusier's *Hell House*; Julia Steinmetz and Nikki DeBlosi offered valuable technological and research assistance from afar and on short notice; Linda Schlossberg did heroic battle with the *Chicago Manual of Style*; and David Eng "skyped" stellar support as I completed the last round of revisions. Finally, special thanks are due my fellow traveler, Debra Levine; conversations with her have sharpened my own thinking about Hell Houses immeasurably.

1. "Is Halloween the New Christmas?" ABC News, October 31, 2006, *www.abcnews.go.com/GMA/Business/story?id=2617781&page=1* (accessed December 11, 2006).
2. Quoted in Chris Serres, "GHOUL DAYS; You Want Scary? There's a New Holiday Shopping Season," *Minnesota Star Tribune*, October 25, 2006, 1D.
3. It is not just conservative Protestants who have expressed religious concerns with Halloween. But conservative Protestants are distinguished by having developed an infrastructure to offer alternative Halloween events.
4. Troy Franklin, "Objective: Halloween Reclamation," *www.objectiveministries.org/antioccult/halloween.html* (accessed December 13, 2006).
5. See *www.cbn.com/special/halloween/* (accessed March 18, 2007).
6. Robertson made his initial assertion on an October 29, 1982, segment of *The 700 Club*. For a recent citation, see Dahleen Glanton, "Halloween Bedevils Some U.S. Churches," Knight-Ridder Newspapers, October 29, 2004, National section. Archived at *http://media.www.pittnews.com/media/storage/paper879/news/2004/10/29/NationalNews/Halloween.Bedevils.Some.U.s.Churches-1788600.shtml* (accessed March 18, 2007).
7. For a discussion of Scaremare, see Susan Friend Harding, *The Book of Jerry Falwell: Fundamentalist Language and Politics* (Princeton, N.J.: Princeton University Press, 2000), 3–4.
8. Harry S. Stout, *The Divine Dramatist: George Whitefield and the Rise of Modern Evangelicalism* (Grand Rapids, Mich.: William B. Eerdmans, 1991), 23; emphasis in original.
9. Ibid., xviii, xxiii.
10. From the Assemblies of God Web site, *www.ag.org/top/about/mission_vision.cfm* (accessed March 18, 2007).
11. Keenan Roberts, interview by Debra Levine and the author, digital recording, Thornton, Colorado, October 29, 2006. Unless otherwise indicated, all quotations of Roberts are from this interview.
12. For more on the aesthetics of horror and the gruesome imagination of Hell Houses, see Charles D'Ambrosio, "Hell House," in *Orphans* (Astoria, Ore.: Clear Cut Press, 2004), 124–39. Brian Jackson

notes the almost "pornographic fixation on the eternal suffering of others," and places Hell Houses in the tradition of Jonathan Edwards's hellfire rhetoric and "scare-for-salvation." Although I think this approach is useful, as will become clear, I connect Hell Houses to the self-conscious theatricality of Edwards's contemporary George Whitefield. See Jackson, "Jonathan Edwards Goes to Hell (House): Fear Appeals in American Evangelism," *Rhetoric Review* 26.1 (2007): 42–59.

13. Sarah Kennedy and Jason Cianciotto, *Homophobia at "Hell House": Literally Demonizing Lesbian, Gay, Bisexual, and Transgender Youth* (Washington, D.C.: National Gay and Lesbian Task Force Policy Institute, 2006), 8, *www.thetaskforce.org/reslibrary/list.cfm?pubTypeID=2* (accessed December 13, 2006).

14. Raymond Williams, *Marxism and Literature* (Oxford: Oxford University Press, 1977), 128–35. In another place, I explore the cross-hatchings of religious and sexual identities as structures of feelings. See Ann Pellegrini, "Testimonial Sexuality; or, Queer Structures of Religious Feeling: Notes Towards an Investigation," *Journal of Dramatic Theory and Criticism* (Fall 2005): 93–102.

15. Williams, 126.

16. Ibid., 132.

17. Ibid.; emphasis in original

18. On this dilemma, see Lauren Berlant, "The Subject of True Feeling: Pain, Privacy, and Politics," in *Left Legalism/Left Critique*, ed. Wendy Brown and Janet Halley (Durham, N.C.: Duke University Press, 2002), 105–33.

19. I borrow the term "resonance" from Linda Kintz's important discussion of the emotional texture of right-wing Christian politics. See Kintz, *Between Jesus and the Market: The Emotions That Matter in Right-Wing America* (Durham, N.C.: Duke University Press, 1998), esp. 6–7.

20. In a 2005 interview with *Christianity Today*, to promote *The Exorcism of Emily Rose*, Derrickson made an impassioned argument for horror as a Christian genre; he could as easily have been talking about Hell House. Calling horror the genre of "non-denial," he said that horror "tackles issues of good and evil more than any other genre, it distinguishes and articulates the essence of good and evil better than any other genre, and my feeling is that a lot of Christians are wary of this genre simply because it's unpleasant. The genre is not about making you feel good, it is about making you face your fears. And in my experience, that's something a lot of Christians don't want to do." He went on to call upon evangelicals to reclaim the gothic from Catholic and secular aesthetics. Scott Derickson, "Horror: The Perfect Christian Genre," interview by Peter Chattaway, *Christianity Today*, August 30, 2005, *www. christianitytoday.com/movies/interviews/scottderrickson.html* (accessed December 11, 2006).

21. For a provocative discussion of Phelps and this Web site, see Michael Cobb, *God Hates Fags: The Rhetorics of Religious Violence* (New York: New York University Press, 2006).

22. Janet R. Jakobsen and Ann Pellegrini, *Love the Sin: Sexual Regulation and the Limits of Religious Tolerance* (Boston: Beacon Press, 2004). The argument of this paragraph and the one that follows was developed jointly with Jakobsen and largely reproduces the language of our co-writing.

23. Bush made these comments in the course of a February 2004 press conference. His call for "civil" dialogue was extensively reported. See, for example, "Bush calls for ban on same-sex marriages," available at: *www.cnn.com/2004/ALLPOLITICS/02/24/elec04.prez.bush.marriage/* (accessed March 19, 2007).

24. Kennedy and Ciancotto, 3.

25. See *www.godestiny.org/hell_house/HH_kitInclude.cfm* (accessed December 13, 2006).

26. From *www.godestiny.org/hell_house/HH_resources_scenes.cfm?p_id=6* (accessed December 13, 2006).

27. All the quoted sections in this paragraph come from "Hell House Resources—Sex Scene Package," www.godestiny.org/hell_house/HH_resources_scenes.cfm?p_id=14 (accessed April 23, 2007).

28. For a now-classic discussion of the history and persistence of antimimeticism, see Jonas Barish, *The Anti-theatrical Prejudice* (Berkeley: University of California Press, 1981).

29. Debra Levine, "Conceiving a Community Theatre of Cruelty," paper presented at "Manhattan Hell House: A Roundtable," the Center for Religion and Media, New York University, October 14, 2005.

30. Antonin Artaud, *The Theater and Its Double* (New York: Grove Press, 1958), 84–85.

31. Ibid., 13.

32. Aaron Lemon-Strauss, quoted in "Visions of Hell," by Matthew Philips and Lisa Miller, *Newsweek*, November 6, 2006, 52.

33. Ben Brantley, "A Guided Tour of Hell, With an Appearance by Satan," *New York Times*, October 14, 2006, B7.

34. See *www.godestiny.org/hell_house/HH_kitResults.cfm* (accessed December 13, 2006).
35. "Devil on My Shoulder," *This American Life*, host Ira Glass, Chicago Public Radio, May 24, 2002, archived at www.thislife.org/Radio_Episode.aspx?sched=925 (accessed June 6, 2007).
36. David Román and Tim Miller, "Preaching to the Converted," *The Queerest Art: Essays on Lesbian and Gay Theater*, ed. Alisa Solomon and Framji Minwalla (New York: New York University Press, 2002), 212.
37. On this point, see Jakobsen and Pellegrini, *Love the Sin*, 118–19.
38. D'Ambrosio, "Hell House," 126.
39. Williams, *Marxism and Literature*, 132.
40. Kintz, *Between Jesus and the Market*, 5.

Critical Faith:
Japanese Americans and the Birth of a New Civil Religion

Jane Naomi Iwamura

America, Manzanar National Monument, California, April 2007. Photograph by Tim May, © *http://www. pbase.com/mityam* Tim May.

On a bright day in April, not far from Independence, California, several charter buses can be seen rambling down some old dirt roads in what appears to be the middle of nowhere. Although the scenery is spectacular—the dusty Owens Valley framed by snow-peaked mountains and a broad blue sky—one can not locate the attraction. What are these people coming to see?

The dirt roads, as well as the abandoned concrete foundations that punctuate the acres of desert scrub, are part of the Manzanar National Historic Site. While many do come here as tourists, today's arrivals converge on the location with a different purpose in mind; they are on a pilgrimage.

The Manzanar Annual Pilgrimage is now in its thirty-eighth year. In 1969, 150 young Japanese Americans journeyed to the site that once served as an internment camp in which their parents and grandparents were detained. "The bitter cold and biting wind gave us our first lesson on how life must have been for the internees. Our humility was reinforced when we learned that what we had brashly called our 'first' pilgrimage was, for two Issei ministers, their 25th—Rev. Sentoku Maeda and Rev. Soichi Wakahiro are gone—but their spirits live on."[1] After this initial pilgrimage in 1969, hundreds more began to make the trip each year. And eventually, a dedicated committee of volunteers would come to organize the annual event. The pilgrimage now takes place over several days and includes speakers, spoken word performances, contemporary bands, and Taiko drumming. The crux of the program is the Saturday afternoon ceremony, which begins with the raising of the ten banners (representing each of the ten internment camps) and a roll call commemorating the former internees. At this moment, the crowd gathers in front of the cemetery monument—a "soul consoling" tower or memorial to the dead erected by the evacuees during their internment—for a service of remembrance.[2] Christian and Buddhist ministers, Catholic and Shinto priests preside and offer chants and prayers. The service is brought to a close as each participant places a flower on the monument—an offering in memory of those who died and suffered within the barbed wire that once enclosed the site.[3] The offering also engenders a hope that such an injustice will never happen again and a commitment to make sure that it never will.

The pilgrimage is at once festival, political forum, and religious ceremony. In considering the relationship between Japanese Americans and religion, it would be easy to focus only on the interfaith service. However, the entire event has spiritual import. As Joanne Doi writes, such a pilgrimage for Japanese Americans represents a "sacred journey" that relives and recollects a "sacred story of suffering and spirit":

> [It is] an attempt to regain our center as human persons and community by reconnecting to our history and each other on the periphery, on the margins. It is not escape but a return to the center of our history, the pivotal events that have marked us as Japanese Americans. In a paradoxical way, the center of our history located on the margins recreates and revitalizes as the truth of who we are shifts into place.[4]

The Manzanar pilgrimage and similar events and institutions committed to the preservation of memory reveal a dimension of Japanese American life that is rich and vital, but seldom recognized by American studies and religious studies scholars alike. What has emerged from the collective experience of war and internment is a faith that is tied to no particular religious tradition, but that takes racial-ethnic identity as its starting point. Japanese Americans have developed no less than their own brand of civil religion.

Critical Faith

As historian Roger Daniels notes: "The wartime exile and incarceration is the transcendent event of Japanese American history."[5] The Nikkei community suffered its most harrowing blow during the Second World War, as those of Japanese ancestry came under suspicion, and West Coast Japanese Americans were rounded up and interned.[6] This event more than any other has become the defining moment in Japanese American history—the one that both informs and haunts Japanese American identity, collective and individual, to this day. Daniel's characterization highlights the overwhelming significance that wartime experience holds for Japanese Americans. But how exactly did this event shape Japanese American historical consciousness and in what ways is the event "exceptional," that is, beyond the realm of the everyday and formative of a larger sense of the group's mission and identity? How does it continue to inform Japanese American political and cultural pathways and take on an almost religious significance?

The history and travails of Japanese Americans have been well documented in numerous historical accounts, literary works, oral histories, and video documentaries.[7] These works also include historical and sociological analyses of the role of religious institutions in Japanese American life. Many of these studies cite the significance of these institutions for the Nikkei population, especially the Buddhist Churches of America (BCA), an organization that has served a "key role in [Japanese American] survival and adaptation."[8] Scholarship that touches upon the intersection of religion and civic life often points out the ways in which ethnic-specific institutions fostered an ethical outlook in concert with American ideals or the cooperative merger of religious and American civic institutions (e.g., the Boy Scouts of America as a temple-sponsored organization).[9] In a more critical vein, Gary Okihiro discusses the way in which Buddhism and other folk religious practices functioned as a means of resistance during the internment period.[10] And more recently, Duncan Williams analyzes the government's treatment of Buddhist ministers during the Second World War in order to draw parallels between the plight of World War II Buddhists and post-9/11 Muslims—parallels that were immediately recognized by the Japanese American political and religious leaders after the fall of the Twin Towers.[11] Here, the consideration of religious identity and its intersection with race offers insight as Americans struggle to deal with the non-Christian, nonwhite other in their midst.

While these studies highlight the role that religion plays in Nikkei civic engagement, they reveal only part of the civil religious story. To offer a more illuminating picture of Japanese Americans, religion, and public life, one is compelled to background conventional definitions of religion and religious affiliation (Buddhist, Protestant Christian, Catholic, etc.), which characterize a great deal of the studies on Japanese American religions, in favor of a new lens. This lens should accommodate a sense of the religious that is more reflective of a Japanese American sensibility. David Y. Hirano states that "the difference between the American view of religion and the Japanese view is that the Japanese did not compartmentalize religion. Religion was a part of and inseparable from life."[12] For immigrant Japanese Americans and, one may argue, their descendants, the boundaries between religion, politics, and culture are porous. In addition, one also needs to consider the elements of Japanese American religious experience that have been most defining for the community itself, for example, interdependence, reciprocity, care, and compassion.[13] These values find their expression outside the bounds of religious institutions and affiliations, and strongly link the individual's identity to a wider sense of the collective.

Such a sensibility is perhaps best illustrated through a concrete example: A third-generation Japanese American (Sansei) recounts how, during his time as a seminary student, he had the opportunity to meet Jitsuo Morikawa—a respected Baptist pastor and theologian in the Japanese American community.[14] He asked Morikawa what he should do after he completed his seminary degree. Instead of steering the young Sansei toward a career as a minister or pastoral care worker, Morikawa counseled that he should think about serving Asian American youth, *not* in a religious capacity but as an Asian American student services administrator who would help instill in these youth pride in their ethnic heritage and offer them a sense of belonging. The young seminary student did just that and now sees his work as a realization of his ministerial training and an extension of his religious background. Such stories as this are not uncommon and demonstrate an interwoven sense of religion (spiritual healing and development), politics (an awareness of discrimination and prejudice), and culture (kinship and acceptance) that is not confined to the walls of the church.

This understanding of religion is not one that is wholly unfamiliar to most in the United States. Perhaps the concept that best embodies this intermingling of the religious, cultural, and political is the one of *American civil religion*. This term achieved its greatest prominence, especially in academic circles, through the writings of sociologist Robert Bellah.[15] "Civil religion," according to Bellah is "that religious dimension found . . . in the life of every people, through which it interprets its historical experience in the light of transcendent reality."[16] For many in the United States, this "transcendent reality" is shaped by both the Christian tradition and Roman republicanism, which in turn lends meaning and justification to the principles of "democracy," "freedom," and "equality" before the law. Americans affirm their faith in these principles and to the nation through a shared set of "beliefs, symbols, and rituals" (e.g., the Bill of Rights, the Lincoln Memorial, the inauguration of the president). Civil religious institutions are historical creations, yet they need no justification. For instance, the Constitution "does not call upon any source of sacredness higher than itself and its makers."[17] Ultimately, civil religion has an integrative function and binds the individual citizen psychically and spiritually to her fellow Americans and to the nation-state.[18]

It is both tempting and treacherous to think of American civil religion in relation to Japanese Americans. Tempting, because Japanese Americans are often upheld as a political "model minority." Despite the unwarranted suspicion and mistreatment Japanese Americans suffered at the hands of the government and their fellow compatriots during World War II, they have "proven" their loyalty and worth as U.S. citizens. They have fought meritoriously in battle and become dedicated public servants. As actor George Takei remarks: "We are part of the fabric of America, from U.S. senators to your schoolteacher to your local banker."[19] In 1941 Japanese American Citizen League leader Mike Masaoka stood in front of the U.S. Senate and declared: "I am proud that I am an American of Japanese ancestry. I believe in this nation's institutions, ideals, and traditions; I glory in her heritage; I boast of her history; I trust in her future."[20] Masaoka penned this "Japanese American Creed" as a declaration of his community's allegiance to the country—an obvious proclamation of American civil religious faith.

It is treacherous to relate Japanese Americans to U.S. civil religion because not all Japanese Americans share Masaoka's fervent belief and unabashed patriotism. There were those who questioned, if not actively resisted, the government's decision to intern 112,000 Japanese Americans, and this legacy of dissent has an active voice in the Japanese American community today.[21]

While Bellah's American civil religion framework is able to accommodate this dissent, it does not necessarily draw our attention to the ways in which the Japanese American community has negotiated internal controversy, nor does it speak to the unique manner in which Japanese American civil religion is expressed. Japanese Americans did not adopt the larger American civil religious discourse part and parcel; to do so would be to retain a naive understanding and credulous embrace of the same institutions that were used to justify their internment. Rather, what emerges out of internment's legacy and an extended history of racial-ethnic oppression is something that one may call a *critical faith*. This critical faith does not abandon civil religious principles (equality before the law, due process, and so on), but finds it necessary to reinterpret these ideals in relation to the Japanese American experience and to make known that experience.

"Times of trial" radically redefine, if not create, civil religious expression. During these moments of crisis, the "deepest questions of national meaning" are raised that often require the formation of new myths, symbols, and rituals to support a transformed sense of a people's self-identity. The "time of trial" for Japanese Americans came in the form of internment—mass incarceration at the hands of the U.S. government. Japanese American historical conscious-ness is not something that was a spontaneous and sudden result of internment. Collectively, Japanese Americans did not seek reparations immediately after the war, nor did they readily acknowledge governmental injustice or even their own psychic trauma. Historical consciousness developed over time, as the com-munity could articulate the abuses suffered and negotiate their own reflective response. One can see this development through a historical examination of the Nikkei debates over internment and the shift from a rhetoric of "loyalty" to one of "justice." From their efforts to properly memorialize the event to the hard-fought battle for redress, Japanese Americans began to realize their critical faith. And the arduous process of recollection and reclamation began to give shape to a new brand of civil religion—one in which it became the community's duty to recount the injustice and to make sure that it did not happen again.

Japanese American civil religion has taken on unique forms and is supported by its own set of sacred texts, sites, and rituals. Perhaps most foundational are two government documents that serve as historical bookends for the intern-ment experience: Executive Order 9066 and the Civil Liberties Act of 1988. On February 19, 1942, President Roosevelt formally approved E. O. 9066, which allowed for the forced removal and detention of Japanese Americans without trial or hearings. Nearly fifty years and eight presidents later, Ronald Reagan would sign into law the Civil Liberties Act of 1988. Although Roosevelt's executive order was officially rescinded in 1976, the Civil Liberties Act would carry the full acknowledgment of the nation's wrongdoing by awarding a $20,000 reparations payment to each surviving internee, along with an official apology from the president made on behalf of the American people. Central to the apology was the acknowledgment that the government's actions "were rooted deeply in race prejudice, wartime hysteria, and a lack of political leadership" and that this moment in American history should not be forgotten or erased. The act, toward this end, also established a public education fund "to finance efforts to inform the public about the internment so as to prevent the recurrence of any similar event." In 2000, Reagan's words—"Here we admit a wrong . . . "—were prominently carved into the stone facade of the National Japanese American Memorial to Patriotism in Washington, D.C., as a permanent reminder of the nation's guilt.

Although the Civil Liberties Act brought a great deal of closure for Japanese American internees, former servicemen, and their descendants, it did not end the ordeal of the concentration camps and racial prejudice. The legacy of internment remains ever present for many Nikkei. Japanese American Nisei still deal with the psychological trauma and lingering feelings of guilt and shame over the event.[22] Their progeny also suffer the effects of the violation, as Sansei, Yonsei, and Gosei "continue to search for a sense of cultural identity and historical integrity."[23] Common to many descendants is an intense recognition of the suffering and sacrifice of the Issei and Nisei, and the need to pay homage to their Japanese American ancestors. The collective memory of internment also compels Japanese Americans to forge sympathetic connections with other communities of color and new immigrant groups who are at risk of suffering the same racist mistreatment and propels an intense mission to safeguard against governmental injustice.

Executive Order 9066 and the Civil Liberties Act could certainly be read as significant historical markers in the development of a national or American civil religious sensibility, the former as a document that represents a shameful moment in America's past, and the latter as an acknowledgment of injustice, if not an act of contrition. However, incorporating these documents and events into the larger American civil religious frame easily erases the agency of Japanese Americans and the civil religious movement that developed to finally bring about the U.S. government's recognition of its misdeeds. It sweeps aside subcultural forms of opposition and resistance that can never be fully assimilated and stand as an "offense" to U.S. national life.

In the following sections, I discuss some of the texts, sites, and rituals that have come to form the basis of a Japanese American civil religion and then go on to analyze the patterns of religious practice and commitment that underwrite this civil religious engagement. My analysis here of the Commission on Wartime Relocation and Internment of Civilians (CWRIC) hearings, the Japanese American National Museum, and the pilgrimage to Manzanar describes the emergence of these events/institutions and highlights their status as significant expressions of a critical faith.[24] An in-depth understanding of Japanese American civil religion provides an example of political *and* religious resistance that has import for other marginalized groups who have formulated similar traditions and for those currently under siege who are engaged in developing their own critical response.

New Testament(s)

> For the forced incarceration during the war, which did so much to thwart my relationships with others, I am bitter. For the fear instilled in me at the hands of my own government, I am bitter. For the unnecessary feelings of shame inflicted on my father and my family for unfounded and never explained reasons, I am bitter.
> —former internee's testimony at the CWRIC hearings[25]

The initial response to mass incarceration of many Japanese Americans could be encapsulated in the phrase "shikata ga nai," or, "it cannot be helped now." The philosophy behind the term should not be mistaken as mere fatalism, but rather implies in its utterance the need to move on with life in the face of circumstances that one cannot adequately explain and does not have the power to change. As an ethnic group who had very little recourse at the time, Japanese Americans were served well by this principle. It allowed Nikkei internees to "concentrate on survival, rather than on the things they'd lost."[26]

In hindsight, the phrase is associated with an attitude of passivity, and this passivity is then read as an essentialized part of the Japanese character. Such an interpretation, however, does not take into account the contextual use of the phrase. The intentional logic behind *shikata ga nai* is that one should not concentrate on the things one cannot change. As such, it bespeaks a spiritual philosophy that allows one to focus on the things one can do something about. The principle is also provisionally applied. As circumstances allow for greater action, *shikata ga nai* does not relieve one of responsibility. Its ultimate aim is not to debilitate, but rather to revitalize in the face of adversities that seem beyond one's control.

As Japanese American regained themselves in the postwar years, a sense of what they believed could and should be changed grew. Nikkei, especially the Sansei generation, who participated in the civil rights and ethnic consciousness movements of the 1960s, actually served as a catalyst for this growing awareness.[27] Through a framework of racial justice, Japanese Americans were able to fully recognize that internment was wrong; they were also able to situate the event within the broader context of the nation's racist history in which blacks, Latinos, and Native Americans were also victims.[28] Ethnic pride, which these movements also encouraged, provided the impetus for cultural recovery and expression. Japanese Americans no longer needed to authenticate their identity vis-à-vis Japan or the United States, but found it imperative to define themselves in relation to their own unique history.

For the Nisei, the process of regeneration and healing was complex. Silence was how this generation and their parents first responded to the event. However, plagued by the ghosts of the war and internment, they could not simply move on as if the past never happened; "I can never forget," as the Japanese American soldiers of the 100th Infantry Battalion and 442nd Regimental Combat Team proclaim.[29] Bolstered by the Sansei example, many Nisei started to come to terms with the trauma that they and the Issei had suffered. They began to realize the import of their experiences and the need to make their stories heard so that their children would know of their suffering. These stories also were meant to serve as a reminder so that "never again shall any group be denied liberty and the rights of citizenship."[30] "I can never forget," transformed into the injunction: "Never forget," and an era of silence eventually evolved into an era of speech.[31]

Hence, the interests of the various generations and groups of Japanese Americans did not coalesce naturally but entailed an extended process of negotiation and awareness. The Civil Liberties Act of 1988 was actually a result of the coalitional efforts of three distinct political groups within the Japanese American community: the Japanese American Citizens League (JACL), the National Coalition for Redress/Reparations (NCRR), and the National Council for Japanese American Redress (NCJAR), as well as Japanese American politicians and everyday citizens.[32] While these organizations and their members were bitterly divided on certain issues (especially when it came to the issue of draft resisters and "no-no boys"—those who refused to take the government's loyalty oath during wartime), they did agree that the U.S. government had committed a grave injustice against the Nikkei community, and that this betrayal needed to be fully acknowledged to the satisfaction of the community.

They also agreed that the story of Japanese Americans was one that needed to be recorded and told for the sake of all in the United States.

The institutionalization of memory therefore becomes significant in the larger mission of education and healing for Japanese Americans. The ways in which memory is reenacted and repurposed lend Japanese American civil religion its distinctive character. One of these ways was made most evident in 1981 at the congressional hearings held by the CWRIC. The commission was established to determine whether the incarceration of Japanese Americans during World War II constituted a military necessity. It also sought to assess the impact of internment on the Japanese American community. More than 750 Japanese Americans in six cities offered emotional, often heart-wrenching testimony to the committee. For these individuals, their families, and the community at large, the hearings proved a cathartic experience: "Nisei testified and spoke of the humiliating and degrading treatment experienced by these American citizens simply because of their race."[33] These testimonies not only chronicled severe financial, cultural, and personal loss, but also gave expression to years of anger, frustration, and rage.

The CWRIC issued its formal report in 1983 and found that "military necessity" was not at the heart of government's decision to incarcerate West Coast Japanese Americans, but rather "race prejudice, war hysteria, and a failure in [U.S.] political leadership."[34] In its report, the commission recommended redress for Japanese Americans, including a reparations payment to each evacuee. While the Civil Liberties Act of 1988 and the presidential apology that accompanied it stand as landmark documents, it is the individual testimonies of the 750-plus internees that are equally if not more significant. In the fullest sense of the word, these accounts form a "testament": tangible proof, a statement of belief, a legacy and covenant. They bear witness to the injustice suffered and introduce into congressional record the good faith and sacrifice of a marginalized people. Furthermore, these testimonies serve as cautionary tales of the type of oppression that racial and religious minorities can experience not only at the hands of fellow citizens, but the U.S. government as well. As humble, yet passionate reminders, they also reveal that such abuse does not end with the traumatic event or with its disclosure, but reverberates through the group for generations.

By all accounts, the CWRIC hearings were a turning point in the struggle for redress. They galvanized the Japanese American community and lent the cause a broad-based support. As Nisei publicly shared their testimonies and heard those of others, they realized that they each had an important story to tell. Common in theme, but individually distinct in detail, these stories spiritually bind Japanese Americans together and are referenced again and again in historical documents, lesson plans, and by the internees and their families themselves.

Re-Siting Memory

In the heart of the Little Tokyo district in downtown Los Angeles, one can cross over to the north end of First Street onto a large plaza. To one's left, one will glimpse a beautifully ornate yet understated doorway that was once the entrance to the Nishi Hongwanji Buddhist temple. Looking to the right, one is struck by a more imposing structure—a contemporary pavilion of glass, steel, and brick. In feel and design, there is a stark contrast between the two buildings. However, both structures are meant to form an integrated unit as part of the Japanese American National Museum.

Viewed together, the two Los Angeles buildings provide a historical metaphor for Nikkei identity. The temple, which initially housed the museum's exhibition space, was built by Japanese immigrants in 1925. Designed by Edgar Cline, it is an eclectic mix of Japanese temple architecture and the Egyptian revival style that was popular in the United States in the 1920s. As is the case with many immigrant churches, the building served a number of functions: worship space, social hall, movie theater, and rental office space. Japanese Americans during the war used the temple to store their belongings as they were led off to internment.

In 1969, the Nishi Hongwanji congregation would construct a new temple just down the street—grand in proportion and Japanese in design. As JANM curator Karin Higa remarks: "[The new temple] seems to reflect the sixties and seventies longing for authenticity and ethnic identity."[35] After the old temple was abandoned, it fell into disrepair and was eventually taken over by the city. It sat, ready for demolition, until it received a new lease on life in 1986 as the proposed site of the new museum and was carefully restored and retrofitted.

The pavilion, in relation to its ancestral relative, reflects a postmodern sensibility. The building's materials and design were chosen to "express the Japanese reverence for materials and craftsmanship, [while] at the same time creating forms that are bold and contemporary and reflect in an abstract way the rich urban context."[36] Both in the reflection of the curved glass wall and in its complementary building materials, the pavilion intentionally mirrors and enters into a dialogue with the older temple (fig. 1). By considering the

Figure 1.
The Japanese American National Museum. Photograph by author.

architecture of both buildings, one can sense an increasing comfort and conscious embrace of the Japanese American past. However, this new ethos does not romanticize that past and attempt to re-create it in every detail, but rather pursues a conversation with what has gone before.

The Japanese American National Museum (JANM) began in 1982 as a joint effort between Little Tokyo businessman and former internee Bruce Kaji, and Japanese American war veterans Young Oak Kim and Y. B. Mamiya. The museum received nonprofit status in 1985, and over the course of the next seven years, Kaji, Kim, and Mamiya, as well as a dedicated corps of volunteers would raise the more than $10 million needed to renovate the old Buddhist temple.[37] Although the museum was without a building throughout the 1980s, it hired a full-time curator/researcher, who embarked on developing its collections, including an extensive photo and moving image archive. It also designed and sponsored its first installations and exhibited these "beyond its metaphorical walls" in Honolulu, New York, and Los Angeles.

The Japanese American National Museum opened its real doors in 1992. The museum then set its sights on the construction of a new pavilion that would house its growing collections and staff; six years and $45 million later, JANM realized that goal as well. The 85,000-square-foot pavilion features a national resource center, life history studio, education centers, and stone and water garden, as well as exhibition and museum staff space. The expansive central hall allows for large-scale special events and lectures. While corporations and governmental agencies provided the bulk of the funding for both building projects, the museum also received amazing widespread assistance from Japanese Americans. In addition to financial support, Japanese Americans across the country generously donated many of the artifacts and photos that now make up the museum's collection.[38]

JANM is set apart from other ethnic museums around the country,[39] not only in terms of its size and resources, but also in terms of its aim: "The mission of the Japanese American National Museum is to promote understanding and appreciation of America's ethnic and cultural diversity by preserving, interpreting, and sharing the experiences of Japanese Americans."[40] While the institution's raison d'être derives from the quest to document the Japanese American experience and preserve historical memory, this memory is harnessed for a larger goal: "to promote understanding and appreciation of America's ethnic and cultural diversity."

This mission is at once general and specific. It is general in the sense that it reaches for universal significance: it pushes Japanese American identity beyond itself. At the same time, it sees Japanese American experience as offering relevant lessons and insights for others in the United States. This universalization however is not abstract. The museum's definition of "American-ness" clearly highlights the ideal of cultural diversity, tackling issues of difference as its primary concern. Here, cultural memory is consciously deployed as a safeguard "against the prejudice that threatens liberty and equality in a democratic society."[41]

JANM's mission is reflected in its exhibits and programming. While much of the gallery space is dedicated to chronicling the Japanese American experience through historical exhibits, the museum also has sponsored shows dedicated to Flo Oy Wong's work on Angel Island and Asian American immigration, contemporary art by Los Angeles artists, and the community history of the multiethnic Boyle Heights area. The museum also sponsors discussion forums, craft classes, artist talks, walking tours, and a wide variety of performances.

Finally, the museum's Life History Program seeks to document the histories of individual Japanese Americans through oral and videotaped interviews, as well as written texts. This is arguably JANM's most significant program, since it perfectly engenders the goals of the museum:

> Oral history is particularly important for the Japanese American community. As a community of color, our history is often marginalized from the mainstream record. Oral history provides a way for marginalized communities to record and interpret the meaning of historical events from their own perspective. No longer is history told about them, but rather history is told by them.[42]

As the program description suggests, oral history constitutes a privileged method and important community practice. Similar oral history projects by other Nikkei organizations and educational institutions across the country abound.[43] Like the personal testimonies offered by former internees at the CWRIC hearings, these accounts uphold the uniqueness of individual lives and offer a multidimensional, multiperspective view of social forces and events that have shaped the Japanese American collective psyche. History becomes something that is not authoritatively dictated and officially sanctioned, but rather mutually informed and more wholly realized; every person has an important story to tell.[44]

In essence, JANM has come to embody the spiritual ethos of the community. The museum becomes a sacred storehouse of cultural memory and spiritually links current generations of Japanese Americans with their immigrant ancestors. By visiting the museum, second, third, fourth, and subsequent generations of Japanese Americans in a sense pay homage to their forebears. In relation to American public life, JANM also concretizes a sense of mission as it compels museum visitors to confront issues of racial oppression, historical injustice, ethnic identity, and cultural survival.[45] Through its various exhibits, programs, and indeed, the very physical presence of the museum itself, JANM enacts a critical faith—a faith in its ability to "transform lives and strengthen community," as well as "create a more just America and ultimately, a better world."[46]

Rituals of Remembrance

Words, images, and sounds all serve as important avenues of memory. However, as S. Brent Plate comments: "Memory is not an activity of the mind only, but of the body and of the minds and bodies of others . . . [R]emembering is a dynamic, interactive process."[47] Rituals play an important role in the preservation of memory as they involve the active bodily participation of all those who are present. Japanese American civil religion similarly involves rituals that bring a community together to remember the past for the sake of the present. These modern-day rituals, such as the annual pilgrimage to Manzanar that opens this article (and the Tule Lake Pilgrimage, which began in 1974), initially brought together Japanese Americans, mainly Sansei, who often lived in the shadow of their parents' and grandparents' silence, and helped them begin to recover a shattered past. As Joanne Doi explains: "These [events] were attempts to search out the truth of the history bound up in the silence of the Nisei and the classroom. The magnitude of the silence of the Nisei helped form the voice of the Sansei; the Nisei's absence of outward emotional response mobilized the Sansei to begin to speak out."[48] In a significant sense, the annual pilgrimages and Days of Remembrance prepared the way for more intense struggles (the fight for redress) and extended projects (the Japanese American National Museum). [49]

Even though many of the ambitious goals of the Japanese American community have been realized, the pilgrimages continue to fulfill an important function. Nisei join their children and grandchildren on these journeys, and the rituals have become intergenerational affairs.[50] As such, they provide the opportunity to share long-suppressed stories and feelings with one another. The pilgrimages also draw non-Japanese Americans from a variety of racial-ethnic backgrounds. At the Manzanar pilgrimage ceremony, Latino schoolchildren can be seen lining the rows in front of the cemetery monument. They, along with Arab Americans, African Americans, Jewish and Anglo Americans, as well as other Asian Americans, listen to the prayers and chanting of the various priests and place flowers on the monument.

As many note, the flower offering is one of the most powerful parts of the service (fig. 2). Through the act of the offering, individuals forge their own relation to the past and contemplate the larger forces that led them to this place and time. They enter into a sacred economy in which the ancestors are enlivened and past, present, and future meld into one. At the very least, they are caught up in the communal nature of the moment. At the end of the ceremony, participants are invited to dance the *Tanko Bushi* (coal miner's dance). This traditional dance, associated with Obon odori festivals observed at Buddhist temples throughout the United States, is performed to honor the dead—most notably to recognize their true unselfish nature and celebrate their release. Those who join in the dance may not fully understand the religious dimensions of the ritual, but they realize their movements in bittersweet and now hopeful remembrance. Through sound, motion, and rhythm, participants become bonded with their Japanese American ancestors and to one other. For the people who share in the annual pilgrimages, psychic connections are highly specific, as each participant is drawn into the history of internment and is led to consider the consequences of injustice and betrayal, as well as recognize

perseverance and reaffirm hope. On multiple levels and in multiple ways, the pilgrimage ritual encourages a spiritual reconciliation and healing that other ethnic institutions—secular and religious—do not usually provide.

Equally significant, the pilgrimages nurture a strong political awareness among its participants. In 2003, for instance, the Manzanar Committee chose "A Call to Action: End Racial Profiling, Speak Out for Peace" as the pilgrimage's official theme. In the 9/11 aftermath, Japanese Americans readily view the government's detention of Arab, Muslim, and Sikh citizens as eerily similar to their own experience. Japanese American organizations were some of the first to protest the unfair treatment of these marginalized groups. As such, there have been new alliances forged among various communities, and many Japanese Americans are discovering that their historical experience is more relevant than ever before.[51]

Figure 2.
Manzanar Pilgrimage 2003.
Photograph by author.

Unlike the government's response in 1942, President Bush in 2001 would make a forthright appeal to the American people to treat Americans of Arab, Muslim, and Sikh descent with "respect and dignity" soon after the fall of the Twin Towers. While Bush's plea drew from the rhetoric of liberal multiculturalism, statements issued by Japanese American organizations politicized the situation by drawing attention not only to the government's racist history, but also to "the link between domestic and foreign policies, or U.S. state racism at home and U.S.-led wars abroad."[52] The stance of these organizations remained critically watchful; the necessity to act propelled by their own unique historical calling: "We should step up and speak out. . . . Maybe [Muslim Americans] can't make any statements against the war because they are feeling so targeted just like we did."[53]

Religious Patterns of Commitment

The year 2004 marked an important event for the Manzanar Committee, the Japanese American community, and those who joined the pilgrimage annually: the U.S. Park Services officially opened the Manzanar Interpretive Center at the Manzanar National Historic Site.[54] The Interpretive Center, much like the Japanese American National Museum, features interactive exhibits chronicling the wartime internment of Japanese Americans, as well as the rich history of the area, educational programs, and its own oral history project. In addition, the on-site "museum" includes a reconstructed guard shack and mess hall. In the

Figure 3.
Memorial service for Japanese American servicemen killed in action. Gila River Relocation Center, Arizona. Photographer unknown, War Relocation Authority.

back of the center is a screen that lists the names of the ten thousand who were interned at the camp. The (re)construction of the camp and its educational arm, the Interpretive Center, appears to bring Japanese American history back into the American civil religious fold. As Sue Embrey, the longtime Manzanar Committee chair seems to concede: "The Interpretive Center is important because it needs to show to the world that America is strong as it makes amends for the wrongs it has committed, and that we will always remember Manzanar because of that."[55] A year later, however, the committee reaffirmed the critical function of the Manzanar Pilgrimage. Embrey proclaimed, "We need to make sure history doesn't repeat itself. Muslim and Arab Americans are being held at Guantanamo Bay without charge or trial. It reminds us of the Issei who were also held without charge for many years during WWII."[56]

In 2005, history would also come full circle as the Japanese American National Museum's sister institution, the National Center for the Preservation of Democracy, would make its home in the old Nishi Hongwanji Buddhist temple. With its aim to "promote the principles of democracy, diversity, and civic involvement,"[57] the National Center appears in lockstep with an American civil religious agenda. But a closer look reveals the center's particular standpoint—one that is informed by its Japanese American historical roots. Its premier exhibition, "Fighting for Democracy"—available both in virtual and physical form—takes the visitor through a series of exercises or scenes that juxtapose and connect the lives of Mexican Americans, African Americans,

Filipino Americans, Chinese Americans, and other ethnic minorities in the United States during the Second World War.[58] While great care is given to highlighting the diversity of wartime perspectives, it is the Japanese American experience that anchors the exhibition and demonstrates the center's emphasis on the "fragility" of individual rights and freedoms.

In an important sense, Japanese American Civil Religion remains in constant dialogue with its American counterpart—sharing much of its language and principles. But the texts, sites, and rituals that inform its stance remain historically unique. They are also influenced by religious and cultural traditions and ways of engaging the world that differ from the religious patterns of Christianity and Roman Republicanism that undergird American civil religion.[59] Attention to these traditions and spiritual sensibilities are key to fully understanding the distinctiveness of Japanese American civil religious formation and the spirit that sustains its vision.

Models for understanding the contours of a racial-ethnic group's civil religious engagement do exist. For instance, Jonathan Woocher in his book *Sacred Survival* delineates the process for American Jews.[60] He outlines a number of Jewish American secular organizations in which ethnicity and religion merge to create a sphere of moral commitment and concern.[61] Japanese Americans, likewise, draw from a traumatic history to create their own civic sphere. The Nikkei example also presents a unique and interesting perspective. Because of the religious diversity of the community, Japanese American civil religious expressions is usually not tied to one particular religious tradition; Japanese Americans had to negotiate, if not transcend, their particular religious affiliations. For the Issei and Nisei generations, such affiliations created cleavages within the community and even contentious rifts within families to the point that some Buddhists and Christians did not speak to each other. The mere fact that Japanese American Buddhists, Protestant Christians, Shintoists, Catholics, and others were interned not only gave rise to a common experience to which these different groups would eventually refer, but also compelled them to find language and rituals that bridged their respective worldviews and sectarian concerns. This is not to say that particular religious traditions were abandoned for a more secular mode of engagement, but rather Japanese Americans found concepts that were faithful to those traditions and drew from a broadly conceived Japanese American spiritual culture. The language Japanese Americans use to express their commitments therefore may not stand out as religious. At the same time, it is subtly underwritten by a transcendent sense of identity and mission forged in the historical trials of internment and war, as well as informed by a particular spiritual culture.

Gary Okihiro, in his essay "Religion and Resistance in America's Concentration Camps," begins to investigate the sources that would foster a Japanese American civil religious outlook. In his investigation of "ethnic religion" in the camps (a term he uses interchangeably with "ethnic culture"), he isolates two "fundamental features of Japanese religious belief": (1) filial piety and ancestor worship; and (2) closeness of man, gods, and nature.[62] The first dimension is especially relevant to an understanding of Japanese American civil religion. As Okihiro states:

> Filial piety, ancestor worship, and family and ethnic collectivity were cultural values which were emphasized in the home and stressed in the Buddhist churches and Japanese language schools. Those internal values were reinforced by external forces such as anti-Japanese agitation, barriers to Nisei assimilation and restrictive employment opportunities, and the concentration camps themselves which were pointed reminders to the Nisei that they were not considered to be "true Americans."[63]

Furthermore, this view of everyday relations and the collective was buttressed by a sense of heritage and peoplehood that was not necessarily tied to either the Japanese or the U.S. nation-state. The invocation of *Yamato damashii* ("Japanese spirit"), while seen by Wartime Relocation Authority officials as an expression of pro-Japan sentiment, was often rather invoked by Nikkei to summon the "customary virtues of perseverance, loyalty, forbearance, and sacrifice for the common good."[64]

Viewing Japanese American spiritual culture in this integrated fashion allows one to identify the distinctive framework upon which a Nikkei critical faith is built. The language of "paying respect" is often invoked during pilgrimages to internment sites, as are notions of "remembrance." These spiritually infused concepts and practices are linked to the ways Japanese Americans honor the dead across religious and sectarian lines. Homage to ancestors is most formally realized in Japanese American Buddhist traditions, in which loved ones who have passed away are memorialized through ritual activities that take place in the home, the temple, and the cemetery. (These traditions are also informally practiced by Nikkei Christians.) A person's death is marked not only by a funeral, but also by a series of memorial services, both privately held by the family (fig. 3) and publicly recognized by the *sangha*, or congregation. While the details and sentiment surrounding these services vary according to Buddhist denomination, such rituals have genealogical links to *senzo kuyô*, or Japanese ancestral memorial rites, which are observed on a regular basis and reinforce a sense of the ongoing interconnectedness between the living and the dead.[65] Within this spiritual economy, the dead do occupy a distinct realm—but one that is in constant engagement with the living and is experienced more as part of the "seamless social continuum," rather than as a radical departure.[66] Memory, therefore, is something that must be continually cared for and ritually maintained.[67]

The Manzanar Pilgrimage and Days of Remembrance can be viewed as *kuyô*, in which participants remember their Japanese Americans forebears and the event that so disrupted their lives. But perhaps more to the point, these events memorialize the *social death* of Japanese Americans—their racial exclusion in the United States—and ritually reaffirm this historical moment and social fact. Participation in these annual gatherings therefore is an obligation that redeploys memory in the service of the living (including future generations) and can be distinguished from similar American civil religious rituals of memorialization, such as the Gettysburg Address. In this "Lincolnian 'New Testament' among the civil scriptures," the Civil War is reinterpreted within the rubric of Christian sacrifice and viewed as an event that demands "a new birth of freedom."[68] In contrast, Japanese American civil religion views death—both individual and social—not simply as a sacrifice in this Christian sense of unimaginable act and necessary rebirth, but rather as an extension of life that tempers the living.[69] The dead—which here includes a sense of what used to be (Japanese American life before internment) and what they had hoped to become (fully accepted American subjects)—are ever present, but only remain so through continual acts of attention and care.[70]

Senzo kuyô also sheds light on the centrality of oral testimony and oral history for Japanese Americans. Within the religious cosmos of Japanese and, arguably, Japanese Americans, individuals do not exist as autonomous beings, but rather as part of a network or web of human relations. As Dorinne Kondo notes, within the Japanese worldview, there is a "fundamental connectedness of human beings to each other."[71]

One of the wellsprings of such an understanding can be traced to the Buddhist tradition, including metaphors of "Indra's net," or still closer to home, "The Golden Chain"—a verse that many Japanese American children learn as part of their Pure Land Buddhist upbringing:[72]

I am a link in Lord Buddha's golden chain of love that stretches around the world. I must keep my link bright and strong. I will try to be kind and gentle to every living thing, and protect all who are weaker than myself. I will try to think pure and beautiful thoughts, to say pure and beautiful words, and to do pure and beautiful deeds, knowing that on what I do now depends my happiness and misery.

May every link in Lord Buddha's golden chain of love become bright and strong and may we all attain perfect peace.

In Amida Buddha's "golden chain," each link is important and one realizes not only that one's existence is dependent on others, but that one's life and actions are also integral parts of the chain. In this everyday religious saying and its broader religious context, the significance of each person is recognized and each one makes an important contribution to the whole. This sense of interdependence permeates not only relations among the living, but also between the living and the dead. Such a framework lends each person's life, his individual perspective, an integrity and importance all its own.

While the "group orientation" of Japanese and Japanese American subjects is often emphasized in scholarly and popular accounts, a sense of the group—whether family, workplace, or nation—is inextricably tied to the value and worth of each individual. Again, through participation in memorial services, Japanese American religious subjects perform and embody this worldview as they both remember those loved ones who have passed away *and* reaffirm their ancestors (and ultimately themselves) as part of a larger network. The centrality of oral history—the need to capture individual voices and stories—emerges from this spiritual ethos. As previously mentioned, no one person's story takes precedence, but rather each provides a unique reflection of the collective experience (as each jewel in Indra's Net reflects the whole of Buddha nature). And without these individual pieces, the collective no longer exists or does so in an impoverished manner. As each person's life contributes to the chain of being, each person's testimony about internment and its legacy becomes a necessary component in the Japanese American civil religious framework.

The testimonies that make up the CWRIC hearings and other oral historical accounts therefore provide not only the epistemological foundation for Japanese American historical consciousness and its vision of justice ("coming to know"), but also the ontological foundation of its meaning and mission ("coming to be"). In a similar vein, the Japanese American National Museum as a repository of memory emerges as a key site and expression of this particular ethic that simultaneously recognizes the integrity of individual experience and the way in which this experience is interwoven into the larger fabric of communal meaning.[73] The museum on many levels can be likened to a Japanese home altar in its structure and function—formal and resolute in its overall focus, yet improvisationally defined by its Japanese American historical actors, supporting members, and multicultural viewing public. Indeed, the interactive experience JANM encourages through its exhibitions, programs, and collection processes serve to weave Japanese American individual lives into the larger frame (in the same way the Buddhist practitioner brings his or her own history to a home altar through *ihai* (mortuary tablets), photographs, and personal reflection). History becomes enshrined in the museum—but in a way that does not simply commemorate, but also enlivens.[74]

The spiritual economy that that I have described is not meant to essentialize the Japanese American character. The religious and political diversity of Japanese Americans must be recognized and one should note that a good degree of conflict and difference has always characterized Japanese American life throughout its 150-year history.[75] As David Chidester and Edward Linenthal emphasize: "Sacred space is inevitably contested space, a site of negotiated contests over the legitimate ownership of sacred symbols" and meanings.[76] Younger generations of Nikkei will undoubtedly bring their particular outlook and experiences to the continuing endeavors and concerns of the "community" and forge their own connections to the past.[77] Still, when consensus does emerge, as, for example, with the Nikkei movement for the passage of the Civil Liberties Act or Japanese American participation on annual pilgrimages, it is important to articulate the patterns of civil religious engagement and the spiritual worldviews—not so readily apparent—that lend ongoing meaning to Japanese American struggles for justice and expand the dominant civil religious perspective.

To Remember Is to Act

> Without being imprisoned in Gila Relocation Camp,
> How would I have become aware of the Buddha's compassion?
> Kakichi[78]

Robert Bellah concludes *The Broken Covenant*—his most extended work on American civil religion—with a call for a "new communalism of intention," one that (as a first step) reaffirms the "outward or external covenant and that includes civil religion in its most classical forms."[79] This external covenant is most prominently expressed in the principles and ideals set forth in the Declaration of Independence, the Constitution, and the Fourteenth Amendment, which Bellah feels have "never been fully implemented." Such commitments, while necessary, tell us little about how the realization of this external covenant is achieved. In post-9/11 America—marked by religious and racial difference—such a call for unity seems moot. Similarly, appeals to tolerance and toleration—seen as "inseparable from [the] principle in freedom and equality" and a civil religious "right, duty, and virtue"—also provide little direction.[80] These conceptions of American civil religion in their abstract appeal are ultimately inadequate for addressing the mounting injustices—from racial profiling to unlawful detainment—taking place in our midst.

Instead of simply turning to old traditions and myths or rushing headlong into new ones in pursuit of a common civic culture, it would behoove us to reinvestigate the ways in which the United States is home to many civil religions. Such a task is not based simply on a greater recognition of non–Judeo Christian religious traditions or solely on the need for retrieval—the intentional recall of lifeways and worldviews "of all the repressed cultures that 'Americanization' tried to obliterate."[81] Marginalized communities have long since taken up the work of retrieval and engaged in the process of articulating their own civil religious visions—visions that draw upon, yet exceed institutionalized forms of religious practice. If repression occurs, it is primarily for the dominant culture, who fails to recognize the ways in which these groups have developed their own sets of rituals, symbols, and beliefs born from historical experience and spiritual necessity and marked by their own integrity and resourcefulness.

For Japanese Americans, internment constituted a time of trial—the transcendent event—that would come to define its identity and mission. Times of trial are often specific to a group and subculturally defined. "A shared experience, no matter how unjust the circumstances, creates an intimate and kindred universe for those who share it," in Karen Ishizuka's apt words.[82] For racial minorities and other marginalized groups, these times of trial are often instigated by U.S. institutions and quickened when the promise of American civil religion is not fulfilled. In response to such crisis, marginalized groups are compelled to develop their own civil religious faith—related to but distinct from U.S. national expressions. Japanese Americans offer an especially paradigmatic case, but one is able to discern similar civil religious movements among Mexican Americans (the Chicano/a vision of Aztlán or the embrace of Cesar Chavez as a civil religious figure), African Americans (forms of Black Nationalism and Pan-Africanism), and Native Americans and indigenous peoples (struggles for land rights and nationhood).[83] Ethnic Muslims and Asian Sikhs in the shadow of 9/11 have also drawn from the example of their historical predecessors; these groups currently under siege are beginning to develop their own distinctive civil religious consciousness that is true to their voice and their vision.

At crucial moments, American civil religion and minority civil religions can converge (as is the case with Martin Luther King Jr. and the civil rights movement, frequently referenced in national address, or the designation of Manzanar as a National Historic Site). But because of the persistent inequities they can never wholly unite. Minority civil religious expression, such as the critical faith of Japanese Americans, therefore becomes crucial in the sustenance of a particular group *and* for the nation as a whole. It is not simply a transcendent sense of its own origins and calling that keeps American civil religion accountable (as Bellah contends), but competing civil religious institutions and forms wrought through the suffering of the nation's oppressed that calls out and ultimately humbles.[84]

Racial prejudice has had a harrowing effect on Japanese Americans. The documents, sites, and rituals of Japanese American civil religion help Japanese Americans emerge from their painful history and make good of that past. As the above sketch reveals, the institutionalization of memory becomes the occasion for education, political action, and healing. While one hopes that intolerance and discrimination are a thing of the past, Japanese Americans are well aware that there is no guarantee that this is or ever will be the case. This vigilant attitude is indeed at the heart of Japanese Americans' critical faith.[85] *Shikata ga nai.* There is nothing I can do to change the past. *Shikata ga nai.* But there is something I can and must do now.

Notes

This project was developed as part of the Social Science Research Council Working Group on Religion, Immigration, and Civic Life; Paul Spickard, Lori Pierce, Sharon Suh, David Yoo, Richard Alba, Albert Raboteau, Josh Dewind, and the other working group members served as valuable conversation partners. Early versions of the paper were presented at "The Most Segregated Hour: Race and Religion in the American West" (Claremont 2004), at the 2006 American Studies Association Annual Meeting, and to the USC Center for Religion and Civil Culture Working Group on Religion and Immigration. Those who were instrumental in the development of this piece include Rudy Busto, Derek Chang, Macarena Gómez-Barris, Pierrette Hondagneu-Sotelo, Janet Hoskins, Clara Irazábal, David Kyuman Kim, James Kyung-Jin Lee, Luís León, Stephanie Nawyn, Roberto Lint Sagarena, and Janelle Wong. Joanne Doi and Hillary Jenks generously shared their work on Japanese American pilgrimage and grassroots history, respectively; and R. Marie Griffith and Melani McAlister, the editors of this special issue of *American Quarterly*, provided helpful suggestions and patient support. To all these individuals and organizations, I am most grateful.

1. Manzanar Committee, "Manzanar History," Manzanar Committee Online, http://www.manzanar-committee.org/manzhistory.html (accessed June 22, 2007).
2. The tower was constructed in 1943. Financed by family contributions, the cemetery monument's construction was supervised by Ryozo Kado, a landscaper and stonemason for the Los Angeles Catholic diocese. Its design is interesting to consider; the obelisk was an especially popular form of grave marker during the Egyptian revival period. In cemetery art, the revival reached its peak in the 1840s and 1850s, but its general influence can be found in turn-of-the-century architecture (such as the Nishi Hongwanji temple that would later house the Japanese American Museum). It is difficult to know what influenced Kado's artistic vision. Perhaps he was aesthetically inclined to the design because of its ancient, non-Christian roots. The obelisk is also reminiscent of the *kasasotouba* style of grave marker found in Japan. See cover photo caption, *SAA Archaeological Record* 4.5 (2004): 1.

3. At the thirty-eighth annual pilgrimage, the service also included a recitation of the opening chapter of the Qur'an led by the Council on American-Islamic Relations executive director, Hussam Ayloush.

4. Joanne Doi, "Tule Lake Pilgrimage: Dissonant Memories, Sacred Journey," in *Revealing the Sacred in Asian and Pacific America*, ed. Jane Naomi Iwamura and Paul Spickard (New York: Routledge, 2003), 280.

5. Roger Daniels, "Incarceration of the Japanese Americans: A Sixty-Year Perspective," *History Teacher* 35.3 (2002): 303.

6. The term *Nikkei* is generally used to refer to Japanese emigrants and their descendants, especially to those Japanese who migrated to North America and Latin American during the Meiji period. In this essay, I use the term interchangeably with "Japanese American," since Japanese Americans often refer to themselves as such. The designation also recognizes a growing awareness among Japanese Americans of their connections with Japanese in Latin America and Cuba.

7. The majority of Japanese Americans who now reside in the United States are not foreign born. Rather, they trace their descent from the largest influx of Japanese immigrants who arrived on U.S. soil at the turn of the century. In search of economic opportunity, these immigrants were met by unfriendly labor conditions and anti-Asian prejudice. Despite these hardships, Japanese American communities thrived as the immigrant generation put down roots, reared their children, and established ethnic-specific networks and institutions, including Buddhist temples and Christian churches.

8. Tetsuden Kashima, *Buddhism in America: The Social Organization of an Ethnic Religious Institution* (Westport, Conn.: Greenwood Press, 1977). See also, David Yoo, *Growing Up Nisei* (Bloomington: University of Indiana Press, 2000).

9. See Lori Anne Pierce, "Constructing American Buddhisms: Discourses of Race and Religion in Territorial Hawai'i" (PhD diss., University of Hawai'i, 2000); See Kashima, *Buddhism in America*, 1977.

10. Gary Y. Okihiro, "Religion and Resistance in America's Concentration Camps," *Phylon* 45.3 (1984): 220–33.

11. Duncan Ryûken Williams, "From Pearl Harbor to 9/11: Lessons from the Internment of Japanese American Buddhists," in *A Nation of Religions: The Politics of Pluralism in Multireligious America*, ed. Stephen Prothero (Chapel Hill: University of North Carolina Press, 2006), 63–78.

12. "Religious Values Among Japanese Americans and Their Relationship to Counseling," (D.M. diss., School of Theology at Claremont, 1974), 2.

13. Peter Yuichi Clark, "Compassion among Aging Nisei Japanese Americans," in *Revealing the Sacred*, ed. Iwamura and Spickard, 43–65.

14. This conversation took place in the 1980s. To read more about Morikawa's legacy, see Hazel Morikawa, *Footprints: One Man's Pilgrimage—a Biography of Jitsuo Morikawa* (Berkeley: Jennings Associates, 1990); and *Jitsuo Morikawa: A Prophet for the 21st Century*, ed. Paul M. Nagano and William L. Malcomson (Richmond, Calif.: Council for Pacific Asian Theology [CPAT], 2000).

15. Bellah first wrote about American civil religion in "Civil Religion in America," *Daedalus* 96.1 (1967): 1–21. The version cited in this article appears in *The Robert Bellah Reader*, ed. Robert Bellah and Steven Tipton (Durham, N.C.: Duke University Press, 2006), 225–245.

16. Robert N. Bellah, *The Broken Covenant: American Civil Religion in Time of Trial*, 2nd ed. (Chicago: University of Chicago Press, 1975), 3.

17. Ibid., 4.

18. Writings on American civil religion since Bellah's 1967 essay on the subject are extensive and cannot be fully reviewed here. Robert Wuthnow ("Divided We Fall: America's Two Civil Religions," *The Christian Century*, April 20, 1998:395–99) and Catherine Albanese ("Civil Religion: Millennial Politics and History," in *American Religions and Religion*, 2nd ed. [Belmont, Calif.: Belmont Publishing, 1992], 432–62) provide useful overviews. For more recent interpretations of Bellah's framework, see Michael Angrosino, "Civil Religion Redux," *Anthropological Quarterly* 75.2 (2002): 239–67; and Grace Y. Kao and Jerome E. Copulsky, "The Pledge of Allegiance and the Meanings and Limits of Civil Religion," *Journal of the American Academy of Religion* 75.1 (2007): 121–49.

19. Carolyn O'Neill, "L.A. museum shares Japanese-American struggles, triumphs," CNN.com, http://www.cnn.com/2000/TRAVEL/DESTINATIONS/06/30/japanese.museum/ (accessed June 22, 2007).

20. This amended version of Masaoka's statement is inscribed on the National Japanese American Memorial to Patriotism in Washington, D.C. The inclusion of the inscription has been the center of great controversy. As Lawrence Hashima notes: "Unmediated, Masaoka's words upon the Japanese American

Memorial may easily be interpreted to equate acquiescence and capitulation as the benchmarks for true patriotism. Alongside the names of those who gave their lives in battle, such an association creates dangerous possibilities in what is expected of citizens, particularly those who are ethnic, racial, or religious minorities" ("Public Memories, Community Discord: The Battle over the 'Japanese American Creed'" American Studies Association, http://epsilon3.georgetown.edu/~coventrm/asa2001/panel11/hashima.html (accessed June 22, 2007).

21. The histories of the Japanese American men who resisted the draft are cataloged in both visual and written form: Eric L. Muller, *Free to Die for Their Country: The Story of the Japanese American Draft Resisters in World War II* (Chicago: University of Chicago Press, 2001); and *Conscience and the Constitution*, VHS, directed by Frank Abe (Hohokus, N.J.: Transit Media, 2000). Journalist and filmmaker Frank Abe maintains a Web site dedicated to the resisters and on which he features commentary and news regarding Japanese Americans and civil liberties issues, including the recent controversy surround Lt. Ehren Watada; see Resisters.com, http://www.resisters.com/index_conscience.htm (accessed June 22, 2007).

22. Japanese Americans often define themselves generationally: Issei (immigrant or "first generation"); Nisei ("second generation," i.e., the first generation born in the United States); Sansei ("third generation"); Yonsei ("fourth generation"), and Gosei ("fifth generation"). This terminology is used throughout the essay.

23. National Asian American Telecommunications Association (NAATA), "Postwar and Impact Today," Exploring the Japanese American Internment through the Internet and Film, http://www.jainternment.org/postwar/ongoing.html (accessed June 22, 2007). Formal efforts by postwar generations of Nikkei to come to terms with the lasting effects of internment and exile include the Sansei Legacy Project, which sponsored the public forum "Legacies of the Camp: Strategies for Healing" in 1998. See the Project's home page, http://www.momomedia.com/CLPEF/sansei/home.htm (accessed June 22, 2007).

24. Other monuments dedicated to the Japanese American wartime experience that can be considered civil religious expressions include the National Japanese American Monument to Patriotism in Washington, D.C., and the Go For Broke Monument in Los Angeles. They do not seem to garner as much multigenerational Nikkei participation and support, however, and their foundations have been primarily maintained by older volunteers. The National Japanese American Monument has especially aroused conflict within the Nikkei community. (See note 20.)

25. Quoted in Teresa Watanabe, "Deja Vu," *Los Angeles Times Magazine*, June 8, 2003, 16+.

26. John Tateishi, quoted in Stephen Magagnini, "A Nation's Apology: Formal Gesture Erases a Half Century of Shame," *Sacramento Bee*, October 8, 2001. See also Karen L. Ishizuka, *Lost and Found: Reclaiming the Japanese American Incarceration* (Urbana: University of Illinois Press, 2006), 125–26.

27. For an extended study of the distinction and interplay between Nisei and Sansei political styles, see Jere Takahashi, *Nisei/Sansei: Shifting Japanese American Identities and Politics* (Philadelphia: Temple University Press, 1997).

28. It is important to note that Japanese American Christian ministers were actively involved in the Asian American movement and Nikkei Christian organizations provided significant spaces that fostered ethnic consciousness and liberal protest. See Chrissy Lau's "Christianity and the Asian American Movement: Clash or Coalition?" and Helen Kim, "*Niseis* of the Faith: Theologizing Liberation in the Asian American Movement," papers presented at the 2006 Asian Pacific Americans and Religion Research Initiative (APARRI) Conference, Berkeley, August 3–5, 2006.

29. Thelma Chang, *I Can Never Forget: Men of the 100th/442nd* (Honolulu: Sigi Productions, 1991).

30. These words prominently appear on the Go For Broke Monument in Little Tokyo, Los Angeles. They are attributed to Ben Tamashiro, who served as part of the 100th Infantry Battalion. "Ben Hiroshi Tamashiro," *Honolulu Advertiser & Star-Bulletin* obituaries, January 1–December 31, 2004," Joseph F. Smith Library, Brigham Young University, Hawai'i, http://w2.byuh.edu/library/Obituaries/2004/T.htm (accessed June 22, 2007).

31. *Speech* and *silence* in relation to the Japanese American experience are complicated terms. While silence regarding the abuse and mistreatment one suffers can have debilitating effects, it can be used strategically as well. For a multivalent understanding of silence and the politics of speech, see King-Kok Cheung, *Articulate Silences: Hisaye Yamamoto, Maxine Hong Kingston, and Joy Kogawa* (Ithaca, N.Y.: Cornell University Press, 1993); and Traise Yamamoto, *Masking Selves, Making Subjects: Japanese American Women, Identity, and the Body* (Berkeley: University of California Press, 1999). Both Cheung and

Yamamoto investigate the trope of silence as it emerges in Japanese American literary production. For a discussion of silence as it is experienced by visitors to the Japanese National Museum, see Ishizuka, *Lost and Found,* 187–90.

32. A good number of studies recount the history and social dynamics of the redress movement. These include William Hohri, *Repairing America: An Account of the Movement for Japanese-American Redress* (Pullman: Washington State University, 1988); Roger Daniels et al., eds., *Japanese Americans: From Relocation to Redress* (Seattle: University of Washington Press, 1992); Leslie Hatamiya, *Righting a Wrong: Japanese Americans and the Passage of the Civil Liberties Act of 1988* (Stanford, Calif.: Stanford University Press, 1993); Yasuko I. Takezawa, *Breaking the Silence: Redress and Japanese American Ethnicity* (Ithaca, N.Y.: Cornell University Press, 1995); Mitchell T. Maki, Harry H. L. Kitano, and S. Megan Berthold, *Achieving the Impossible Dream: How Japanese Americans Obtained Redress* (Urbana: University of Illinois Press, 1999); and Ricardo René Laremont, "Jewish and Japanese American Reparations: Political Lessons for the Africana Community," *Journal of Asian American Studies* 4.3 (2001): 235–50. For an account of the redress movement at a more local/regional level, see: Robert Sadamu Shimabukuro, *Born in Seattle: The Campaign for Japanese American Redress* (Seattle: University of Washington Press, 2001).

33. James Okutsu, quoted in Paul Spickard, *Japanese Americans: The Formation and Transformations of an Ethnic Group* (New York: Twayne, 1996), 155.

34. United States Commission on Wartime Relocation and Internment of Civilians (USCWRIC) et al., *Personal Justice Denied: Report of the Commission on Wartime Relocation and Internment of Civilians* (Seattle: University of Washington Press, 1997).

35. Quoted in Susan Moffat, "Museum to Link Japanese, U.S. Cultures Architecture," *Los Angeles Times,* February 16, 1993, 1.

36. Japanese American National Museum (JANM), "Architectural Fact Sheet—Japanese American Nation Museum Phase II Pavilion," Japanese American National Museum, http://www.janm.org/about/press/p_facts.html (accessed June 22, 2007).

37. The Phase I Campaign actually generated $12.8 million—$2.6 million over the initial goal.

38. For an extended profile of community giving and discussion of the museum's history and development, see Akemi Kikumura-Yano, Lane Ryo Hirabayashi, and James A. Hirabayashi, eds., *Common Ground: The Japanese American National Museum and the Cultures of Collaboration* (Boulder: University of Colorado Press, 2005).

39. Joseph Berger, in "Ethnic Museums Abounding" (*New York Times,* July 4, 2003, E2, 27), outlines institutional efforts similar to JANM's.

40. Japanese American National Museum (JANM), "Mission of the Japanese American National Museum," Japanese American National Museum, http://www.janm.org/general/mission.html/ (accessed August 31, 2002). Leilani Nishime compares the museum's exhibit *Fighting for Tomorrow: Japanese Americans in America's Wars* to a comparable one staged at the Smithsonian National Museum of American History in Washington, D.C. (A More Perfect Union: Japanese Americans and the Constitution). Nishime notes that while the JANM exhibit "tells the same basic story of loss and redemption as the Smithsonian, it still makes room for ambiguity and for a critique of the dominant narrative" (51). See "Communities on Display: Museums and the Creation of the (Asian) American Citizen," *Amerasia Journal* 30.3 (2004/2005): 41–60.

41. Ibid. Nishime speaks of the ways in which the Japanese American patron becomes the "centering norm" and critically shifts the museum exhibit's perspective and function (55).

42. Japanese American National Museum (JANM), "The Museum's Life History Program," http://www.janm.org/lifehist/lhp.php/ (accessed June 22, 2007).

43. For an overview of these efforts, see Arthur A. Hansen, "Oral History and the Japanese American evacuation," *Journal of American History* 82.2 (1995): 625–39.

44. In addition to collecting oral histories as part of the museum's collection, the Life History Program also conducts educational workshops so that members of the community can conduct their own interviews. The program has been so successful that it is now training representatives from other communities of color around Los Angeles to recover, record, and preserve their own lost histories.

45. Some scholars may argue that this is an idealized portrait of JANM and its mission. For instance, Lon Kurashige notes the way in which the museum was unable to resist "outside ethnic descriptions and prescriptions" and the enticement of Japanese corporate interest. "Caught between corporations and

community, the JANM supported a version of history that played down the fractured community politics of the war era" (212). See *Japanese American Celebration and Conflict: A History of Ethnic Identity and Festival in Los Angeles, 1934–1990* (Berkeley: University of California Press, 2002). Takashi Fujitana also speaks about the "model minority" dimensions of JANM exhibitions that highlight Japanese Americans' loyalty and worth as citizens ("National Narratives and Minority Politics: The Japanese American National Museum's War Stories," *Museum Anthropology* 21.1 [1997]: 99–112). Such critical (and necessary) perspectives are rare, however. More prevalent are accounts that point to JANM's groundbreaking work and celebrate its mission and method. See Kikumura et al., *Common Ground*; Ishizuka, *Lost and Found*; and David Yoo, "Captivating Memories: Museology, Concentration Camps, and Japanese American History," *American Quarterly* 48.4 (1996): 680–99. These accounts bear witness to the museum's significance for contemporary Japanese and Asian Americans.

46. JANM, "Mission."

47. S. Brent Plate, ed., *Religion, Art, and Visual Culture* (New York: Palgrave, 2002), 196.

48. Doi, "Tule Lake Pilgrimage," 277. For a more extended version of Doi's insightful analysis of the history and spiritual import of Japanese American pilgrimage to internment sites, see "Bridge to Compassion: Theological Pilgrimage to Tule Lake and Manzanar" (PhD diss., Graduate Theological Union, 2007).

49. The Day of Remembrance takes place every February 19—the day that President Franklin D. Roosevelt signed Executive Order 9066. The first Day of Remembrance took place in 1978 at the Puyallup Fairgrounds in Seattle and is now commemorated by Japanese American civic groups throughout the country. On February 12, 2007, the U.S. House of Representatives passed H.R. 112 and officially designated February 19 as the National Day of Remembrance for the Japanese American Internment.

50. While the fight for redress and subsequent battles successfully brought about the passage of the Civil Liberties Act of 1988 and compensation for those within "denied categories" under the legislation, Japanese America organizations remain active in the struggle for Nikkei civil rights. For instance, Nikkei for Civil Rights and Redress (NCRR) members are engaged in efforts to secure redress for Japanese Latin Americans, who were forcibly removed from their homes in Latin America by the United States and detained at a camp in Crystal City, Texas. See Nikkei for Civil Rights and Redress, "Campaign for Justice: Redress for Japanese Latin Americans!" at http://www.ncrr-la.org/campaign.html (accessed June 22, 2007).

51. For an especially moving effort that utilizes new media to explore the parallels between December 7, 1941, and September 11, 2001, see Rob Mikuriya, "Face to Face: Stories from the Aftermath of Infamy," ITV.org, http://www.itvs.org/facetoface/intro.html (accessed June 22, 2007).

52. Nadine C. Naber, "So Our History Doesn't Become Your Future: The Local and Global Politics of Coalition Building Post September 11th," *Journal for Asian American Studies* 5 (2002): 226–27.

53. Lisa Nakamura, quoted in Naber, "So Our History Doesn't Become," 227.

54. Manzanar was designated a National Historic Site by the federal government in 1992. As such, it has become a "site of national remembrance for all Americans," and the construction of the Interpretive Center further enhances its significance. Robert T. Hayashi recounts the legislative process that brought about the designation and discusses the competing groups and stories that had come to define the place. His essay suggests the ways in which the master narrative of war and internment and narrow definitions of the Nikkei community ("loyal victim," "fearless fighter") that the National Historic Site promotes do not "allow for the voices of all participants to be heard." "Memories are too easily lost in the process of memorializing" (71). "Transfigured Patterns: Contesting Memories at the Manzanar National Historic Site," *Public Historian* 25.4 (2003): 51–71. See also Elena Tajima Creef, *Imaging Japanese America: The Visual Construction of Citizenship, Nation, and the Body* (New York: New York University Press, 2004), 139–41. While the Manzanar Committee works cooperatively with the National Park Service (NPS) to organize the annual pilgrimage, the committee (in its fervent political commitments) and pilgrimage (as a public forum and living expression of memory) serve as a critical counterpoint to the NPS focus.

55. Sue Kunitomi Embrey, "Speech at the National Park Service Opening of the Manzanar Interpretive Center, 4/24/04," Manzanar Committee Online, http://www.manzanarcommittee.org/pilgrimages/manz2004/Speech-embrey.html (accessed June 22, 2007).

56. Sue Kunitomi Embrey, "Press Release, 4/19/05," Manzanar Committee Online, http://www.manzanarcommittee.org/pilgrimages/manz2005/PR-41905.html (accessed June 22, 2007).

57. "Vision and Mission," National Center for the Preservation of Democracy, http://www.ncdemocracy.org/node/1126 (accessed June 22, 2007).

58. "Fighting for Democracy Exhibition," National Center for the Preservation of Democracy, http://www.ncdemocracy.org/node/1097 (accessed June 22, 2007).

59. Bellah describes these defining patterns and the archetypes of "Israel and Rome" in the first chapter of *Broken Covenant* (1–35).

60. Jonathan S. Woocher, *Sacred Survival: The Civil Religion of American Jews* (Bloomington: Indiana University Press, 1986).

61. A significant example of civil religious dialogue between Jewish Americans and Japanese Americans took place on March 9, 1998, in which the two groups discussed the use of the term "concentration camps." The issue ignited nationwide discussion and debate. For an account of the interaction, see Ishizuka, *Lost and Found*, 154–72.

62. Okihiro, *Religion and Resistance*, 225.

63. Ibid., 227.

64. Ibid., 228.

65. The Jodo Shin tradition—which the majority of Japanese American Buddhists are part—does not formally recognize *senzo kuyô*, since the deceased family member automatically gains entrance into the Pure Land through Amida's saving grace and no longer relies on the family's efforts to attain Enlightenment. Such *kuyô* are deemed unnecessary. Still the primacy of an individual's relationship to the deceased endures and is reinforced through parallel rituals that actively engage memory. Also, Jodo Shin practitioners are oftentimes less strict in their motivation and observance and incorporate religious rituals that are *kuyô*-inflected.

66. Michael Pye, "Religion: Shape and Shadow," *Numen* 41 (1994): 61.

67. For an insightful discussion of (Protestant) Westerners' misunderstandings of Buddhist rituals and attitudes toward the dead, see Dickson Kazuo Yagi, "Protestant Perspectives on Ancestor Worship in Japanese Buddhism: The Funeral and the Buddhist Altar," *Buddhist-Christian Studies* 15 (1995): 43–59.

68. Bellah, "Civil Religion in America," 235–36.

69. This is not to downplay the rhetoric of sacrifice that Japanese Americans often adopt in retelling their wartime stories. But here one needs to be careful and consider the ways in which such language is culturally and religiously shaped.

70. The yearly observance of the pilgrimages and Days of Remembrance are also reinforced by conventions of Japanese American religious practice. Buddhist memorials for the dead, or *Hoji*, are held according to a strict timetable—seventh day after death, forty-ninth day, and each year on the anniversary of the loved one's passing. Important anniversaries are also recognized. While only the most devout Japanese American Buddhist may observe these *Hoji*, many do attend annual services, or *Shotsuki Hoyo*, sponsored by their local temples or offer donations (*orei*) to the church in their family member's name. Jodo Shin Buddhist practitioners also participate in more corporate forms of remembrance, such as the yearly *Eitaikyo* service (to honor deceased members who have supported the temple) and *Urabon-e* (general remembrance of the dead).

71. Dorinne K. Kondo, *Crafting Selves: Power, Gender, and Discourses of Identity in a Japanese Workplace* (Chicago: University of Chicago Press, 1990), 9.

72. The Pure Land tradition, from which Shin Buddhism emerged, traces its roots to India and China, and Shinran Shonin (1173–1262) is taken as Jodo Shin's official founder. This sect departs from other strands of Buddhism in that salvation no longer depends on one's merit or individual efforts but is achieved through the invocation of the Buddha's name ("Namu Amida Butsu"). Amida Buddha, the Buddha of Unhindered Light, provides the focus of a Jodo Shin practitioner's faith and devotion. Japanese American children, who attend Dharma school, learn to recite "The Golden Chain" by heart at an early age. The verse formally appears in the *Shin Buddhist Service Book* (Buddhist Churches of America, 1994).

73. It is interesting to note the ways in which the museum's fund-raising campaigns are informed by a Japanese religious sensibility. As Audrey Lee-Sung writes, "in considering support for the institution, many individual made gifts in memory or in honor of their first-generation parents or grandparents. Understanding this, the National Museum made it possible for families to pool their gifts and collectively honor a significant family member. . . . These 'family gifts' enabled more individuals to participate

in the campaign, many of whom may not otherwise have done so, and provided a meaningful way to contribute and recognize family members in the process ("Community Building Through Fundraising," in Kikumura-Yano et al., *On Common Ground*, 67). This practice of remembering family members through financial donation is common among Japanese American Buddhist practitioners. The relevance of *kuyô* can also be extended to the museum's cultural artifacts and reconstructed sites (internment barracks), since *kuyô* can also be performed for inanimate objects. As Hillary Jenks notes, speaking more broadly about the production of Japanese American grassroots history, memories can be activated by "preserved buildings, oral histories, and historical society publications," as well as by cultural artifacts. Such preservation is of ultimate concern to many Japanese American organizations. See "Memories of 'Lil' Tokio', Japanese American History and Community in Southern California," paper presented at the 2006 Organization of American Historians Meeting, Washington, D.C., April 19–22, 2006.

74. For a discussion of the religious economy of the Buddhist home altar in Japanese American contexts, see Jane Naomi Iwamura, "Altared States: Exploring the Legacy of Japanese American Butsudan Practice," *Pacific World: Journal of the Institute of Buddhist Studies* 3.5 (2003): 275–91. Civil religious expressions do not simply replace more conventional forms of religious belief and practice, even though the increasing secularization among Japanese Americans would suggest such a shift. The distinction between the two is perhaps best highlighted in the "Heart Mountain mystery rocks," displayed at JANM. Shinjiro Kanazawa came forward to clear up the mystery and reveal the significance of the rocks: after the death of a child, parents would inscribe stones with passages from Buddhist sutras. As part of Kanazawa's missive, he requested that the museum "at least repose the souls of babies that the pebbles were gathered for, before you exhibit them" (Ishizuka, *Lost and Found*, 180–81).

75. Japanese Americans remain politically and culturally divided on a number of contemporary issues. Perhaps most prominent is the controversy surrounding Lt. Ehren Watada, who refused to deploy to Iraq and thereby challenged the constitutionality of U.S. involvement in that war. Watada's act of resistance as a U.S. military personnel presents interesting contradictions to Nikkei, who once were themselves defined (and often defined themselves) as loyal/disloyal, veteran/resister. The controversy has stirred up old feelings, if not frank discussion, among Japanese Americans. JANM also is embroiled in controversy. Locally, the museum is involved in debates over land use in its immediate vicinity (First Street North). The city of Los Angeles has plans to develop an "art park" in the area that will feature museums and other cultural attractions. Community organizations, such as the Little Tokyo Service Center (LTSC) and the Nikkei for Civil Rights and Redress (NCRR), have long advocated for the construction of a recreation center on site that will serve the needs of the local multiracial community. JANM aligns itself with the city's proposal, which has put it at odds with these progressive Nikkei groups.

76. "Introduction," *American Sacred Space*, ed. David Chidester and Edward T. Linenthal (Bloomington: Indiana University Press, 1995), 15.

77. See *Pilgrimage*, digital video, directed by Tadashi H. Nakamura (Los Angeles: Center for Ethno Communications, UCLA Asian American Studies Center, 2006).

78. Quoted in Gibun Kimura, *Why Pursue the Buddha* (Los Angeles: Nembutsu Press, 1976), 151.

79. Bellah, *Broken Covenant*, 151. While Bellah has honed his views over time, his commitment to a common civil religious culture remains. In his plea to return to the "deepest core of our tradition" (329), he often elides the recognition of cultural difference with "religious individualism." See Bellah, "Civil Religion in America," 319–32.

80. "God Bless America: Reflections on Civil Religion After September 11, 2/06/02," Pew Forum on Religion and Public Life, http://pewforum.org/events/index.php?EventID=R22 (accessed June 22, 2007).

81. Bellah, *Broken Covenant*, 107.

82. Ishizuka, *Lost and Found*, 124.

83. For a discussion of Cesar Chavez as a Latino civil religious figure, see Luís D. León, "Cesar Chavez and Mexican American Civil Religion," in *Latino Religions and Civic Activism in the United States*, ed. Gastón Espinosa, Virgilio Elizondo, and Jesse Miranda (New York: Oxford University Press, 2005), 53–64; and León's article in this issue. Articulations of an African American civil religion can be found in the following treatments: Randall K. Burkett, *Garveyism as a Religious Movement: The Institutionalization of a Black Civil Religion* (Metuchen, N.J.: Scarecrow Press, 1978); David Howard Pitney, *The African American Jeremiad: Appeals for Justice in America* (Philadelphia: Temple University

Press, 2005); and David Howard-Pitney, "'To Form a More Perfect Union: African Americans and American Civil Religion," in *New Day Begun: African American Churches and Civic Culture in Post–Civil Rights America*, ed. R. Drew Smith (Durham, N.C.: Duke University Press, 2003). For contests over indigenous sacred space in relation to U.S. civil religious discourse, see Chidester and Linenthal's description in *American Sacred Space*, 1–5.

84. Bellah would perhaps classify the critical faith of Japanese Americans that I have articulated here as a form of communalist pluralism in which "each community is seen as having its own idea of its own common good, radically different from the idea of other communities" and that "sees society as resting on uneasy treaty relations between communities so autonomous as virtually to be subnations" (Bellah and Tipton, "Citizenship, Diversity, and the Search for the Common Good," in *The Robert Bellah Reader*, 305). I would disagree. There is a common experience that brings the civil religious expressions of minorities in concert with one another and that experience is race. It is important, however, to recognize that each of these expressions is shaped by the group's particular struggles, as well as the unique spiritual resources or "traditions of interpretation" the group deploys to endure the oppression. It is only when we recognize the integrity of these movements, investigate their underpinnings, and take seriously their concerns that we will move beyond rhetorics of "diversity" and "pluralism" and American civil religion's external covenant will be more internally realized.

85. The Japanese American fight for redress has inspired new struggles in other communities of color (Native Americans, Latinos, and African Americans). Ricardo René Laremont argues that "if African reparations are to succeed, similar solidarity will be needed among African communities in Africa and in the African diaspora" (248). As I have tried to argue here, such solidarity is not built upon political strategy alone, but on the foundations of a critical faith that is intimately informed by community-defined practices of memory, healing, and action. See Ricardo René Laremont, "Jewish and Japanese American Reparations: Political Lessons for the Africana Community," *Journal of Asian American Studies* 4 (2001): 235–50.

Back to the Future:
Religion, Politics, and the Media

Diane Winston

If religion and politics make strange bedfellows, what to do with religion, politics, and the news media—the ménage a trois of the moment? Since 2000, many American journalists have had a "come to Jesus" experience, spurred by the rise of politicized religion and religious politics. Manichean worldviews, eschatological narratives, and larger-than-life leaders have long been the media's stock-in-trade, and now "militant Islam" and the "Religious Right" supply the color, conflict, and catchy quotes that make for journalistic catnip. In domestic coverage, the trend is evident in the recent (and extensive) coverage of religion's incursion into the secular political arena. Detailing debates over evolution, abortion, stem cell research, and the definition of marriage, reporters conjure a bitterly divided nation—this despite the fact that many sociologists and pollsters say most in the United States, rather than occupying opposing camps, fall within the "muddled middle."[1]

The news media's current fascination with the interaction between religion and politics is the latest two-step in a long-standing dance. When New England's earliest colonists began cataloguing and circulating news of important events, they framed their stories with a religious perspective: divine providence played a decisive role in covering and interpreting everyday occurrences. Media historian David Paul Nord, probing the place where "printing, printed news and the newspaper first flowered in America," found that "the characteristics of American news—its subject matter and its method of reporting—are deeply rooted in the religious culture of seventeenth century New England."[2] Religious studies scholar Tracy Fessenden pushes the nexus of writing and religion further, surveying three centuries of American literature to show how a specific Protestant identity (Fessenden draws on Catherine Albanese's notion of "public Protestantism") became the default mode for religion in U.S. public life.[3] Fessenden writes, "New England Protestantism elicited assent to its own claims to historical and national primacy by framing the progress of both history and the nation in Protestant terms."[4] As a result, the subsequent construction of "secularism," "pluralism," and "church/state separation" implicitly manifested the binding and buttressing of a North Atlantic Protestant perspective on U.S. democracy, religion, power, and privilege.[5]

This perspective, which Fessenden calls a "strand of post-Calvinist Protestantism whose popularization renders it so pervasive as to become invisible to many observers," became the dominant (if invisible) frame for twentieth-century knowledge workers, including the media.[6] Its particular admixture of religion and politics, that is, secular American democracy, grew so distant from its Christian origins that a political movement of conservative religious leaders coalesced to challenge it. The mainstream media initially dismissed Jerry Falwell's Moral Majority as redneck religion, but public response to Richard John Neuhaus's *The Naked Public Square: Religion and Democracy in America*, published in 1984, demonstrated a pent-up appetite for the inclusion of faith-based ideas and values in public life. Neuhaus's call itself was somewhat disingenuous because religion and religious values were part of public life. Moreover, they had been part of the news mix for 150 tears, ever since James Gordon Bennett, penny press pioneer and publisher of the *New York Herald*, realized religion made good copy.[7] The real issue was not whether to cover religion but whose religion was covered, how it was described, and where the story was played in the newspaper.[8] According to Sarah Forbes Orwig, the amount of religion coverage remained constant between 1893 and 1998, but the type of coverage shifted. "Substantive" coverage—reporting on the substance of faith and initially done through daily devotionals, sermon reviews, and explications of why and what people believe—evolved into conflict stories about theology and politics. "Functional" coverage, entwining religion with politics to illustrate faith's role in society, gradually changed from hard news stories to human-interest pieces on social activism.[9]

In 1984, religious conservatives gleaned little substantive or functional coverage. Their belief that Christianity should have explicit bearing on public life and governance was at odds with the notion of secular American democracy. But in the two decades since, Neuhaus and his confederates have gained significant ground in framing public understanding of religion's role in American life and, as a result, in altering the dominant news narrative.[10] Reporters, whose perspective had obscured the resurgence and strengthening vitality of conservative religion, eventually adopted the new frame as their own, as much due to skillful manipulation as world events. Since September 11, an increased interest in self-conscious religious identity has advantaged conservative Christianity while moderate and progressive strands have been marginalized, if not ignored.[11] Thus, despite the current catch phrase that journalists are "getting" religion, many remain clueless.[12] Why and how this is says as much about the confluence of religion, politics and media in the United States as it does about the state of contemporary news media.

The Promised Land

Ever since the Pilgrims' landing at Plymouth Rock, the religious tropes of the "Promised Land" and the "Beloved Community" have molded understandings of national destiny in the United States. Before the Puritans disembarked from the *Arabella*, John Winthrop wove themes of a divinely ordained domain and a celestially oriented citizenry in a homily to inspire his fellow travelers. But while Winthrop enshrined and entwined religion and politics in the colony's creation story, subsequent generations lacked his passionate vision. An ascetic city on high could not compete with the good life down below. The secular narrative, celebrating self and material success, trumped the Puritan story—at least initially. I say initially because even though the mission failed, the message persisted as successive generations made numerous efforts to create a "beloved community" or to reach a "promised land." In the early-to-mid-nineteenth century, Moravians, Shakers, and Latter-day Saints as well as members of the Oneida, Amana, New Harmony, and Brook Farm communes sought the former, determined to restore a reconciling and redemptive society through their commitment to communal life. Antebellum evangelicals, more intent on the latter, wedded religious fervor to social change in campaigns for abolition, female suffrage, and labor reform. These postmillenial Christians, in search of the promised land, believed their efforts would ring in a thousand-year reign of peace, piety, and prosperity. Neither stream held sway for long. Changing human nature proved no more successful in small groups than in sweeping social movements. Communes faltered when leaders died; campaigns fizzled after initial victories were won. Ultimately, the nineteenth century's grand reli-giopolitical schemes, badly battered in the Civil War, were felled by modernist attacks and buried by public indifference.

Nevertheless, in the century between the Civil War and civil rights, these two dominant motifs endured, however tangential to the national agenda. Press coverage, fluctuating between "kooks and spooks" and martyrs and saints, focused less on movements than on their leaders: swamis and yogis, faith healers and holy rollers, Jewish reformers and Catholic crusaders, Daddy Grace and Father Coughlin, Sister Aimee and Dorothy Day. Each represented an epiphe-nomena addressed sequentially and in isolation. A few ensemble pieces proved the exception—the Ku Klux Klan, the Scopes Trial, the Nation of Islam. But these were less about the constituted power of belief than religion gone bad. Between the 1940s and the early 1960s, several "great men" commanded attention. Reinhold Niebuhr and Paul Tillich embodied the national conscience. Mahatma Gandhi and David Ben Gurion proved conviction could transform powerless communities into the sovereigns of promised lands. But it wasn't until the mid-twentieth century when the Rev. Martin Luther King Jr., leading the faith-based movement for social change he came to symbolize, truly captured public imagination by uniting both themes in a call of singular power. King, who understood the "beloved community" as an intentional commitment to "reconciliation and redemption," focused media attention with a familiar story--the journey to the promised land. When television cameras captured Bull Connor—a latter-day pharaoh armed with dogs, whips, and hoses—terrorizing an oppressed people, the images seared the Exodus narrative on the national psyche. The civil rights movement attracted unprecedented print and broadcast coverage partly through the luck of timing. Mass media made possible almost instantaneous coast-to-coast communication. Newspapers reached a national audience by the turn of the century, and radio followed suit in the 1920s. By the mid-1950s, at least half of the population owned television sets. King's biographers disagree on just how media savvy the young minister was, but the combination of his rhetorical skills, the movement's use of nonviolence and its telegenic protests drew national print and broadcast coverage to bus boycotts, sit-ins, school desegregations, and marches.[13]

Ironically, the historical moment at which King's crusade caught fire was the apotheosis of the secular revolution. By midcentury, the United States' postwar credo reflected its now dominant faith in science and belief in technology. At a juncture when the marketing slogan "better living through chemistry" summed up American confidence in science and technology, journalists, like most other professionals, regarded science and secularism as the twin engines of American progress.[14] The ascendancy of these new cultural touchstones further marginalized traditional religion. The shift came quickly. Less than a decade after President Eisenhower inserted God in the Pledge of Allegiance (1954) and onto the nation's currency (1955), the Supreme Court ejected prayer (1962) and Bible reading (1963) from the nation's public schools, deeming the First Amendment's establishment clause more critical than its safeguard of free expression.

A far different perspective had dominated the nineteenth century. Even though religious swindles, scandals, and scalawags were fair game for the penny press, respect and reverence for traditional religion was widely represented in news columns and opinion pages, and Episcopal and Presbyterian clergy were frequently quoted as civic spokespeople.[15] When defining the limits of acceptable thought or discourse, editors deferred to these authoritative sources. Yet, by the century's closing decades, as legal and scientific authorities gained increasing status in a society grown progressively more professionalized and secularized, educators, editors, and publishers eager to professionalize journalism "actively sought to minimize and ultimately undermine traditional religion."[16] By downplaying the importance of faith and promoting science, advocates for the profession of journalism demonstrated that their field was "best suited to succeed religion in the modern world."[17] The mantle passed to journalism to interpret and explain the twentieth century.

Editors, cognizant of their responsibility to interpret the world for readers, encouraged reporters to write colorful, lively pieces. (This boosted newspapers' sales, too.) In the mid-1920s, Charles Merz, who later became an editor of the *New York Times*, instructed his staff to treat conflict as a key element in reporting and writing.[18] He noted presciently, given the column inches subsequently allotted to clergy sex scandals, "if theology and religion envy sex and crime and sigh for front-page space, all that theology and religion need to do is produce a good personal encounter."[19] These two trends—the declension of religion's prestige in the larger culture and the rise of the conflict narrative as a media trope—dramatically converged in the coverage of the 1925 Scopes trial. Following H. L. Mencken's vivid stories of the "Tennessee buffoonery," the newspapers of the day painted William Jennings Bryan and his supporters as troglodytes opposed to science, reason, and common sense.[20] The actual arguments and outcome—and the larger context for the debate—were rarely noted.[21]

This model—true believers as fools, men of science as heroes—defined mainstream coverage for the next fifty-plus years. The polarization had epistemological as well as practical utility: it validated the scientific model of the world and provided colorful prose. It also fit the default mode of public Protestantism. As Fessenden writes: "To consider the career of secularism within American culture is therefore also necessarily to consider the consolidation of a Protestant ideology that has grown more entrenched and controlling even as its manifestations have become less visibly religious."[22] As religion's role in culture and society disappeared from mainstream news, the faithful read their own outlets to track the intersection of religion and current events. Protestants could choose from *Christianity and Crisis*'s progressive perspective, the more mainstream *Christian Century*, or the evangelically oriented *Christianity Today*. Catholics had *Commonweal* and *America*; Jews perused *Commentary* or *Jewish Currents*.

Throughout the first five decades of the twentieth century, religious people protested against war, injustice, and discrimination, but most of their activities were below the radar and if covered by journalists treated as singular phenomena. Then in 1955, the Montgomery bus boycott propelled Martin Luther King Jr. to the symbolic center of the civil rights movement. King combined southern authenticity with northern sophistication, theater with storytelling, and church politics with realpolitick. Fluent in the cadences and imagery of both the Hebrew Scriptures and the New Testament, he was equally conversant with Reinhold Niebuhr's school of Christian realism and Mahatma Gandhi's concept of *satyagraha* (resistance through mass civil disobedience).

Gathering the various streams of religious liberalism that had flowed since the nineteenth century, King provided public expression of the United States' culturally subsumed moral center. His leadership channeled these disparate tributaries into a mighty river of progressive evangelicals, mainline Protestants, Roman Catholics, Unitarians, Jews, and much of the African American church. Though this accomplishment was treated as ancillary to his work for racial and economic equality, King reinvigorated religious liberalism as a theological and practical project.[23] Gaining the attention of the news media was key, but that attention could break as well as make a movement. Several writers have explored the fate of religious liberalism in the mid-1960s, and the demise of this once mighty coalition.[24] The reasons were many: clashing egos, the atomizing impact of modern society, and, to a great degree, needs outstripping popular support—there were too many fronts to sustain. Negative press coverage exacerbated the problems. When King turned to the issues of poverty, labor unrest, and the Vietnam War, he was criticized by fellow civil rights workers, savaged by politicians, and excoriated in the media. Religious progressives who had made common cause with King splintered into antiwar organizing, feminism, black nationalism, La Raza, and gay liberation to name just some of the movement's offshoots. The Six-Day War sidetracked Jews, and the assassination of Robert F. Kennedy cast white liberals adrift. King's assassination proved too much for an interracial coalition grown increasingly frayed, and when he was shot, his dream died, too. Religious liberalism grew increasingly diffuse, and each emerging trend or interest group became grist for the media mill, which co-opted, lampooned, or marginalized its message.[25]

In the wake of King's accomplishments and the vacuum left by the loss of his leadership (and in reaction to it, too), another religiously inspired mass movement arose. The Rev. Jerry Falwell said that the civil rights campaign inspired the founding of the Moral Majority, an interreligious conservative coalition, which surged to national attention in the 1980s. When King began organizing, Falwell, like many white U.S. evangelicals, criticized the civil rights movement's deployment of church folks in politics. But King's successes, in tandem with Supreme Court decisions banning prayer and Bible reading in public schools and legalizing abortion, changed Falwell's opinion. The Lynchburg, Virginia, minister became convinced that religious conservatives needed to follow the liberals' example: organize, protest, and work for change. From the outset, Falwell and his followers received support from Republican political operatives such as Richard Viguerie and Paul Weyrich.[26] The new movement grew rapidly. Falwell did not need to articulate the biblical tropes of Exodus and *koinonia* because they were implicit in his message: as with King, the beloved community was headed to the promised land. (*Koinonia*, from the New Testament Book of Acts, describes the initial gathering of Jesus' followers after his death, and encompasses their arrangements for mutual support. It has come to represent an ideal form of Christian fellowship, such as the beloved community.) But this time, the community itself and the land to which it journeyed had more in common with John Winthrop's vision of a Christian commonwealth than with the Kingdom of God envisioned by the slain civil rights leader. Tellingly, both visions depended on religion's influence in politics. But where King sought social change, Falwell wanted cultural transformation.

The Promised Land Community (Right)

Although the religious antiwar movement persevered after King's assassination, there was no viable faith-based, mass movement when the Moral Majority took shape in the late 1970s. The new organization was newsworthy because it defied expectation: southern religious conservatives had not been a national political force for a long time. But the debate over abortion and concomitant appeal for "traditional family values," calling on women to be homemakers and mothers rather than careerists, provided the new movement with a defining cause, a fund-raising strategy, and an opening salvo in what would become the "culture war." (The ideological conflict was formally christened with the publication of James. D. Hunter's 1991 *Culture War: The Struggle to Define America.*) Although the increasingly strident debate over abortion provided ongoing headline fodder, much of the media missed an equally important religion and politics story unfolding at the same time.

In the late 1970s, a small group of Southern Baptist leaders announced their plan to take over their denomination, the Southern Baptist Convention (SBC). With 13 million members then—closer to 16 million now—the SBC was and remains the largest Protestant denomination in the nation. Conservative leaders were open about their intention: they wanted to end what they saw as a liberal drift in seminaries, Sunday schools, and mission boards. By drawing a theological redline within the denomination, they also hoped to spur members' support for conservative social and political views.[27] The late 1970s had been a good time for Southern Baptists. One of their own, Jimmy Carter, was in the White House. In 1976, when Carter won the presidency, news outlets dubbed it "the year of the evangelical." Millions of Americans now knew what "born again" meant. The press was reassuring. According to NBC news anchor John Chancellor: "We've checked this out. Being born again is not a bizarre, mountaintop experience. It's something common to millions of Americans—particularly if you're Baptist."[28]

Something else common to many conservative Baptists and born agains was dissatisfaction with what seemed like political success. By their lights, President Carter was a huge disappointment. He was far too liberal in domestic policy and way too soft on foreign affairs. The tipping point was the revolution in Iran. When Islamic revolutionaries toppled the Shah and took fifty-four U.S. citizens hostage, Carter, eschewing the use of force, was powerless to free his countrymen. To Southern Baptist conservatives, it was all of a piece. If liberalism were not stopped, it would drain their denomination's vitality just as it had sapped the nation's strength. Through a stealth strategy of electing supporters to advisory boards that had previously rubber-stamped administrative decisions, the conservatives infiltrated key denominational bureaucracies. By the mid-1980s Sunday school materials were more sectarian, missionary boards more evangelical, and seminaries more insistent on doctrinal purity. Denominational leaders proclaimed that God did not hear the prayers of the Jews, women could not be ordained, and abortion was a national sin. Southern print and broadcast media covered the takeover. Some even reported that moderate Southern Baptists warned it was a dry run for what would soon occur in the Republican Party. But when the national media parachuted in—usually to cover the annual convention and the election of the denominational president—all they saw were blustering buffoons—pompadoured men and polyester-clad women vying for control of what elites considered a backwater faith.

The issues in play for Southern Baptists—traditional family values, America's divine destiny, and faith as the nation's organizing principle—were central, fifteen years later, in the 2000 race for president of the United States. The same issue that split the Southern Baptist Convention—traditional versus cosmopolitan values or, in more practical terms, the authority of the Bible versus the *New York Times*—became the core of the Republican's election strategy. George W. Bush anchored his campaign in the language of personal piety: Jesus Christ, his "favorite philosopher," had changed his life.[29] Throughout the campaign and for several years after, members of the press, unwilling or unable to query Bush's religious rhetoric, simply repeated what they heard. The "echoing press" amplified and legitimized what communications scholar David Domke calls Bush's "political fundamentalism."[30] Even when Bush wove religious themes into political discourse to a degree unprecedented in presidential history, reporters just jotted it down.

Why did most of the mainstream media miss the takeover of the Southern Baptist Convention and only intermittently cover the rise of the Religious Right during the 1980s and 1990s? How did reporters fail to see the transformation of the Republican Party into a haven for conservative religious ideologues? And what made it possible for the Religious Right's ideological frame to shape news coverage of religion and politics? The simple answer is that many journalists could not comprehend what unfolded before their eyes. Ideological blinders and narrative conventions prevented them from perceiving that religious conservatives were organizationally shrewd, media savvy political operators. Even when repeating the Right's religious formulas during the 2000 presidential debates or President Bush's post-9/11 speeches, reporters never doubted their own objectivity. Few questioned whether, much less how, they had become part of the story.

That story had shifted since the 1980s. At the same time that some conservative Christian leaders founded the Moral Majority and others began the takeover of the Southern Baptist Convention, still others launched a strategy to defund and delegitimate mainline Protestant moderates and progressives. This plan proceeded on two tracks—internally, fomenting dissension over the role of gender and sexuality in mainline denominations, and externally, using the secular press to air allegations against religious moderates. Although these campaigns have been documented by historians and reported in the alternative and online media, the mainstream press rarely mentions its own role in the Right's purposeful campaign to marginalize religious moderates and progressives as an active force for social change.[31]

The campaign was instigated by the Institute for Religion and Democracy (IRD), a think tank organized under the aegis of Coalition for a Democratic

Majority (CDM), conservative Democrats (most of whom subsequently became Republicans) alarmed over the party's post-1968 liberal drift. IRD began in 1980 and, by 1985, was funded by right-wing foundations including Bradley, Scaife, and Olin. Reminiscing about IRD's start-up in a commemorative issue of its house journal *First Things*, its editors recalled their initial concerns about "the ambiguous witness of the churches on the cause of human freedom." In the waning days of the cold war, IRD leaders had worried that "numerous Christian leaders and some churches associated with the National Council of Churches (NCC) advocated a 'moral symmetry' between the Soviet Union and the United States."[32] Begun in 1950 to promote Christian unity, the mostly Protestant and transdenominational National Council of Churches then represented some 45 million American Christians, and counted mainline Protestant denominations, the historic black Protestant denominations, and Eastern Orthodox churches among its members. IRD's concern with the mainline's activities led to stories in *Reader's Digest* and on *60 Minutes* that claimed NCC leaders supported and funded Marxist guerrillas, liberation theology, and other communist fronts in Third World nations. Richard Neuhaus, a founding member of IRD and later editor-in-chief of *First Things*, was the architect of both media exposés. In fact, the *60 Minutes* piece opens with Neuhaus contesting the NCC's claim to be the primary defender of American Christian values.

In 1987, four years after the *Reader's Digest* and *60 Minutes* pieces appeared, Richard H. Gentry, then a professor of communications at Trinity University in San Antonio, delivered a paper on these events, "The National Council of Churches' Alleged Leftist Bias: To What Degree Did Two Major Media Set the Agenda for Debate on the Issue?"[33] at the Annual Meeting of the Association for Education in Journalism and Mass Communication. Surveying a wide range of print media two years before and two years after the attacks on the NCC, Gentry sought to determine the extent to which *Reader's Digest*, then the most widely read magazine in the United States, and *60 Minutes*, the most widely watched television news program, had set the baseline for the debate over the NCC's political leanings.

Gentry determined that the two attacks on the NCC resulted in a flood of critical coverage in both religious periodicals and general circulation media. Still, his survey indicated that no firm conclusions could be drawn about the media's role in setting the national agenda in this instance. His findings did suggest that using mass media to dramatize an issue might lead to negative side effects. Missing from his analysis, however, was an investigation into the meaning of IRD's role in the *60 Minutes* and *Reader's Digest* pieces and how the group's shrewd use of mass media hobbled the NCC and mainline denominations.

Today, almost twenty-five years since the first stories appeared, the IRD and several like-minded peer organizations continue to accuse the NCC and other mainline Protestant groups of a leftist bias.[34] Each time a news outlet runs a story on a current charge, it contextualizes the debate within the *60 Minutes/Reader's Digest* reportage, allowing the old allegations to echo on. The conservative media strategy is successful because it keeps alive the image of mainline Protestantism as a seedbed for left-wing ideologues. Stories hinge on the mainline's intentionality (e.g., is this another example of a leftist bias?) rather than its activities. Consequently, mainline Protestants' social and political initiatives, often from the get-go, are discredited among the general public and tainted within their own ranks.

In recent years, the IRD also has actively promoted denominational schism, by cultivating fifth-column forces within the United Methodist Church, the Presbyterian Church, USA, and the Episcopal Church.[35] Diane Knippers, who headed the IRD from 1983 until her death in 2005, was the "chief architect" of an attempt to overturn the governing structures of the mainline denominations "to diminish and discredit the religious left's influence."[36] With single-minded purpose, the IRD has succeeded in making the theological and ecclesiastical debate over sexual orientation—the ordination of gays and lesbians, same sex marriage, and acceptance of GLBT people as church members in good standing—into a wedge issue among Methodists, Presbyterians, and Episcopalians.

Through its support for opponents of "sexual deviance" within those denominations, the IRD has bolstered its own internal networking as well as the siphoning of denominational funds to conservative alternatives. These tactics stymied efforts of Protestant denominations to focus on social problems and political issues from economic justice to the environment. Moreover, they have kept the mainstream media focused on the conflict over homosexuality. As Gentry's study suggests: it's not the mainstream media but rather the religious conservatives who have established the terms of the debate. But the mainstream media has, by adopting the Religious Right's framing of the debate over religion, assisted its rise to power.

Even as the Religious Right impeded both the creation and the coverage of a progressive religious movement, its organizational media strategy fostered the development and promotion of its own social and political agenda. Spokesmen stayed on message, providing strong sound bites and mobilizing faithful constituencies. In media terms, they framed, explicated, and illustrated their stories. A recent study underscores their success: between January 2005 and June 2006, a survey of ten general interest/consumer magazines and six daily newspapers identified 369 pieces that mentioned the Religious Right and only 58 that mentioned the Religious Left, religious liberals, or religious progressives.[37] What explains the dramatic shift in media coverage of Christian conservatives? Several converging factors fueled this change. Augmenting the Religious Right's media skills was the political Right's linkage of patriotic and religious rhetoric. After the terrorist attacks of September 11, 2001, the Bush government yoked American politics to the conservative Christian project, and the press reiterated this message without question or comment for nearly five years.[38] Why did it take the mainstream media so long to interrogate the president's religious rhetoric and the significance of religion in public life?[39] In part, the "echoing press" reflects the post-9/11 political climate. But it also underscores the news media's ignorance of both the actual role and the rhetorical importance of religion in many Americans' lives. Last, but hardly least, industry corporatization, the increasing number of media conglomerates beholden to the bottom line, blunted journalistic muckraking. Publishers are wary of offending audiences and advertisers, especially over highly volatile religious issues.

The Promised Land (Left)

Throughout much of the twentieth century, mainline Protestantism enjoyed power disproportionate to its numbers insofar as its creeds and commitments remained largely contiguous with public Protestantism. Moreover, the status of its membership, often the local and national business, political and cultural elite, as well as the wealth of its coffers, reflected in real estate holdings and pension funds, lent it the moral authority to support moderate social change. Indeed, from the early days of the social gospel through the civil rights movement, a self-conscious sector of the Protestant mainline saw itself as the nation's social conscience. This is not to say that the majority of mainline Protestants supported a progressive agenda; rather, a significant portion of the religious leadership did, and their efforts were usually well publicized.

That publicity, however, did not reflect the mainline's understanding of how journalists worked. Unlike evangelicals whose zeal to proselytize made them early adopters of new technologies, mainline Protestants were slow to embrace media innovations. In the early days of television, many in the mainline dismissed the new medium as a waste of time. Others, citing social scientific research commissioned by their own organizations, deemed it an ineffective way to sway viewers' opinions. (In other words, they believed that it could not be used for evangelism.) Both arguments overlooked the salient point that religious people could not afford to ignore television's increasing influence in American society.[40] Religious moderates and progressives were at a double disadvantage: they had little inclination and even less skill at using the mainstream media to advance their cause. Their adversaries, on the other hand, proved preternaturally savvy about both.

The mainline's disinclination to make use of the mainstream media was compounded by several factors. As noted, these Protestants operated in a larger media environment that was indifferent, if not hostile, to religion. Moreover, after the successful deployment of the Religious Right's media strategy, starting in the 1980s, the mainline denominations lost control of the news narrative and were trapped by the stories being told about them. The dominant post-Scopes caricature—religious conservatives as buffoons—was replaced by the depiction of religious liberals as bleeding hearts or commie shills. Adding to the portrait of liberal ineptitude and irrelevancy was coverage of the "graying" mainline, its attendant membership losses, and its financial woes. Even when mainline Protestants took action—objecting to budget cuts for the poor, campaigning to secure debt forgiveness for developing nations, or seeking corporate responsibility—their activities were virtually unnoticed by the press.[41] According to United Church of Christ figures for the past nine years, conservative Christian leaders have appeared more than forty times on the Sunday morning talk show circuit while Methodists, Lutherans, Presbyterians, Disciples, American Baptists, and African Methodist Episcopalians have never been represented.[42]

The mainline contributed to its own media as well as social, cultural, and political marginalization by ignoring groups who could become allies. The founders of the Religious Right saw the strategic wisdom of building coalitions to extend their base. Before the Moral Majority appeared, theological differences divided evangelicals from Pentecostals, and fundamentalists from both. Catholics were beyond the pale, as were Jews and Mormons. But Falwell and his associates welcomed all who shared their social and political agenda. From the outset, morality rather than theology was the glue that bound the group together.

Mainline Protestants, on the other hand, allowed their old partnerships to unravel. Many Jews separated from former allies over the issue of Israel; specifically, they could not reconcile some mainliners' support for the Palestinian cause. Roman Catholics became alienated from Protestants on the issues of abortion and "traditional family values." Rather than make common cause on matters they agreed upon, every stripe of Protestant, Catholic, and Jew started its own environmental, peace and justice, or human rights caucus. Leigh Eric Schmidt, a historian of American religion, reviewed some of these missed opportunities at a 2005 meeting with journalists.[43] Drawing upon his own examination of the historical connection between liberalism, spiritual seeking, and progressive politics, Schmidt addressed the contemporary relevance of these movements with reporters seeking to understand the role of religion in U.S. society. He identified a cluster of characteristics—cosmopolitanism, the pursuit of justice, creativity, and self-cultivation—that define "seekers," an umbrella term for all those committed to spiritual experience and ethical action. Why, Schmidt wondered, are these seekers left out of media narratives or, when they do appear, depicted as nutty New Agers or style-setting but shallow "metrospirituals"?

In Schmidt's view, today's seekers are the spiritual progeny of nineteenth-century evangelicals who fought for abolition, temperance, and women's rights. Their antecedents also included Quakers, Unitarians, and Transcendentalists, all believers that spiritual depth would lead to social activism. Today those who share this twofold concern are also found among Jews, Muslims, Buddhists, Hindus, and the unaffiliated. Citing the Higher Education Research Institute study that UCLA is conducting on more than 112,000 college students, Schmidt said that 48 percent of those surveyed were categorized as seeking, doubting, questing, or conflicted but nevertheless engaged with spiritual questions and looking for ways to improve the world.[44] Schmidt noted that these students wanted to "integrate their spirituality with a social ethics of caring and interfaith ecumenicalism," suggesting that the current growth of seekers, particularly among college students, indicates a significant cultural shift.[45]

Schmidt predicted that change is coming; recent polls suggest it may have already begun. John Green, a senior fellow with the Pew Forum on Religion and Public Life, has said that according to survey data there were as many moderate/progressive values voters in the 2004 election as there were conservatives.[46] Moreover, in the years since that election, issues ranging from global warming to the spread of HIV/AIDS in Africa to human rights abuses in American prisons have galvanized seekers and religious moderates even as they have drawn evangelical and Catholic support as well. The mainstream media has covered some of these developments, especially when they feature evangelicals' taking unexpected stances. A slew of stories have described evangelical pastor

Rick (*The Purpose Driven Life*) Warren's work to assist HIV/AIDS sufferers in Africa. Likewise the press took notice when Richard Cizik, as vice president of governmental affairs for the National Association of Evangelicals, advocated "creation care" and "going green" as religious priorities.[47] But the nitty-gritty, day-to-day work of reforming the criminal justice system, health care, education, housing, and myriad other social ills goes unnoticed as groups ranging from the Progressive Jewish Alliance to the Interfaith Alliance to Clergy and Laity United for Economic Justice persevere in a media vacuum.

Part of the reason that the progressives' work is so rarely reported is that it flies in the face of the media's definition of news. News occurs when someone famous does something unexpected and (in the best of all possible worlds) generates conflict. Much of the religious progressives' activity occurs below the radar: unknown men and women work on small canvasses over extended periods. Their labors are not unexpected since progressive people are assumed to care about economic justice, human rights, better housing, and safe neighborhoods. Work for these aims is unsung, ongoing, and incremental. The efforts don't seem newsworthy, and most of the leaders don't know how to provide compelling sound bites. Moreover, now that the mainstream media has reframed its religion narrative around the culture wars and the marginalization of the mainline, it's difficult to change the plot.

Progressive religion, likewise, resists the American metanarrative: God's people in God's land doing God's business, that is, getting rich. In *The Protestant Ethic and the Spirit of Capitalism*, Max Weber explored the religious grounding of individualism and the quest for material success. Still, Weber could not have anticipated how these Calvinist strands would be rewoven by twentieth-century Pentecostals who believe earthly rewards offer but a foretaste of a heavenly pay-out.[48] Even Christians who don't subscribe to the prosperity gospel do not necessarily equate piety with poverty or salvation with austerity. Shopping has been sacralized. According to recent statistics, the Christian music industry amassed $650 million in 2005, and religious book sales, including red-hot Christian fiction, accounted for 11 percent of book publishing revenue, or $1.9 billion, in 2004.[49] The very vitality of the Christian market—everything from religious T-shirts to faith-based films—makes the progressives' urge to clothe the naked and feed the hungry seem naive by comparison. The Left's vision for the promised land—one in which greed and materialism are considered sins—is antithetical to the current cultural moment.

This is why, as Schmidt observed to reporters, many people, trends, and stories are left out of the news mix. Seekers are trivialized, campus spirituality is minimized, and local faith-based organizing is ignored. Trend stories that buck the narrative are rarely reported. For example, newspaper and television audiences are unlikely to know about the recent moves to develop an American Islam. This initiative catalyzes the creation, study, and development of an indigenous Muslim tradition, which draws on U.S. culture—rather than Saudi, Pakistani, or Egyptian—for contextualizing religious laws and customs.[50] The result could have a profound affect on U.S. culture and society as well as international relations. Equally significant, since September 11, many young Muslims have become religiously observant and, at the same time, deeply committed to participating in U.S. society. As these young adults assume careers in politics, journalism, and entertainment, their influence will change the ways non-Muslims see, experience, and think about Islam.[51]

Among evangelicals, a network of young pastors and academics are cultivating alternatives to the megachurch. Members of the emerging church movement, "emergents" for short, define themselves as "missional" (responding to the needs to the world instead of just the church), "relational" (putting people first), and "traditional" (practicing authentic, orthodox Christianity). They favor the term *self-sustainability*, applying it to the way they live, their idea of church, and their relationship to the U.S. economy. Although their efforts have been reported, the coverage suggests the movement is marginal to the conservative religious trajectory.[52] Most emergents organize communities in urban neighborhoods where their presence can make a difference. They do not believe in setting up social ministries; rather, they encourage members to find appropriate ways to make a difference in their neighbors' lives. Although most emergents come out of the evangelical tradition, there are similar movements within mainline Protestant and Roman Catholic churches as well as Jewish synagogues.[53] Emergents eschew political labels, but they look, act, and sound like progressives who take their faith seriously. Their Web sites link to antiwar, human rights, and social justice activities. Critical of consumerism and materialism, they attempt to, in the Bible's words (Micah 6:8), "act justly and walk humbly."

If this sounds familiar, it should. Christians have sought to restore a Jesus-centered society for two thousand years. It's a return to the notion of *koinonia*, the foundation for the beloved community, and in its seamless web of belief and behavior, religion becomes political and politics become religious. But emergents are not usually counted among the Religious Left. They're not linked on most "mainline" Web sites or invited to discussions on the future of religious progressivism. Yet they are part of the larger community that Schmidt suggests exemplifies the fusion of spirituality and ethical action that defines religious liberalism.

Emergents and American Muslims are just two examples of religious groups that are missing from mainstream media coverage. Unlike mainline Protestants, they have not been targeted by the Religious Right (they're not powerful enough to matter), and their stories don't fit the current narrative. They are likely to remain invisible unless someone or something compelling enough forces the news media to pay attention. Even then, it may take repeated instances (the press has been discovering evangelicals for the past thirty years) to shift from the Religious Right's narrative frame to an alternate one. The media's structural antagonism to religion makes such change difficult. In 1993, Hillary Clinton's efforts to inject a religious dimension into the political calculus with her call for a "politics of meaning," raised attacks from the Left as well as the Right.[54] The mainstream media reported her speech as if it were a boldly cynical grab for the moral high ground. (Jimmy Carter's 1979 "crisis of spirit" speech—asking the American public to turn the oil shortage and the American hostage crisis into an opportunity for reflection and redemption—was similarly dismissed.) Jeremiads addressing finitude, limits, and sin—in other words, religious critiques that question American triumphalism and national destiny—have as little appeal for the public as they do for the news media.

Then again, change happens. Just as the Scopes story gradually gave way to the saga of the culture wars, the narrative will inevitably shift again. In the two years following the 2004 election, more stories were written about religious progressives than in the two years before, and if the trend continues, the numbers will rise in the run up to the 2008 presidential race. Just as telling is the media response to public declarations of progressive faith. Barak Obama's June 2006 speech at the Call to Renewal conference elicited a (mostly) positive reaction from the *National Review* as well as the *Washington Post*.[55] The talk didn't make the *New York Times*, but that is a sanctum sanctorum of secularism.[56]

Obama told the crowd of religious progressives that their secular colleagues needed to stop disdaining people of faith if they wanted to have an impact. "Some of the problem here is rhetorical," the Illinois senator said. "If we scrub language of all religious content, we forfeit the imagery and terminology through which millions of Americans understand both their personal morality and social justice."

The news media has been doing exactly that for almost a century. Its unwitting participation in public Protestantism long obscured a clear view of religion in society. Still blind to their own biases, journalists cleave to narratives that reinforce the status quo. Current tropes of culture war may have decentered public Protestantism, but the Religious Right's narrative marginalizes individuals, groups, and ideas that challenge its lock on the prevailing religiopolitical framework. Intriguingly, the current moment, leading up to the 2008 presidential election, offers a tantalizing view of what might be. Several declared candidates, including Sam Brownback, Hilary Clinton, John Edwards, Barak Obama, and Mitt Romney—have thoughtful stances on the relationship between religion and politics. But the temptation of catchy headlines and slick sound bites threatens to bury complexity in glib controversy: we're left with Mitt's "Mormon problem," Brownback's "fundamentalism," and Obama's dues to a "radical" preacher.[57] In each case, the reality is much more interesting.

Almost four hundred years ago, the Puritans looked at the world around them for evidence of God's plan. Then, they reported the divine doings they observed in essays, sermons, almanacs, and, eventually, newspapers. The teleological cast of these reports put religion at the center of their world, the lens through which they judged an event's importance. In the intervening centuries, the explicit power of religion to define the news receded. The centrality of divine providence gave way to secularism, and the vision for a city on a hill became a validation of secular democracy. Yet a religious perspective, public Protestantism, still underlay critical decisions of what was newsworthy and how it should be interpreted. That perspective helped shape how reporters covered not only the Scopes trial and the takeover of the Southern Baptist Convention but many seminal social, cultural, legal, and political issues, ideas, and events of the twentieth century. Up through the 1980s and the impact of the Religious Right on the journalistic narrative, public Protestantism, an unmarked category, influenced broad and deep understandings of religion in public life while, at the same time, constructing, through the news media, a "secular" political sphere. It took the Religious Right's incursion to show this secular sphere was not a neutral one and to force an alternative narrative into the media. That narrative, privileging culture wars and clashing civilizations—has led the news in a new direction and, in the process, forced a reinterpretation of formerly given categories such as secular and religious, public and private. Future interventions of Muslims and emergents, Obamas and Romneys may yield yet another iteration of religion and politics, but the fundamental dynamic: the entwining intimacy of God, man, and a damned good story will remain fundamental to the American destiny—and its chroniclers.

Notes

1. "The Muddled Middle" was the title of Jonathan Reeder's *Slate* review of Alan Wolfe's *One Nation After All: What Americans Really Think About God, Country, Family, Racism, Welfare, Immigration, Homosexuality, Work, the Right, the Left and Each Other* (*Slate*, March 11, 1998).
2. David Paul Nord, *Communities of Journalism: A History of American Newspapers and Their Readers* (Urbana: University of Illinois Press, 2001), 34, 31.
3. For a discussion of "public Protestantism," see Catherine L. Albanese, *America: Religion and Religions*, 3rd ed. (Belmont, Calif.: Wadsworth, 1998), 396–429.
4. Traci Fessenden, *Culture and Redemption: Religion, the Secular, and American Literature* (Princeton, N.J.: Princeton University Press, 2006), 19.
5. For an example of how this process is enacted through politics, the courts, and public opinion, see Sarah Gordon, *The Mormon Question: Polygamy and Constitutional Conflict in Nineteenth-Century America* (Chapel Hill: University of North Carolina Press, 2001).
6. Fessenden, *Culture and Redemption*, 249.
7. Stewart Hoover, *Religion in the News: Faith and Journalism in American Public Discourse* (Thousand Oaks, Calif.: Sage Publications, 1998), 19–20; Sarah Forbes Orwig, *Substantive and Functional Representations of Religion in Four American Newspapers, 1893–1998* (PhD diss., Boston University, 1999), 11–14.
8. Orwig, *Substantive and Functional Representations*, 234–35.
9. Ibid., 234.
10. A report titled "Left Behind: The Skewed Representation of Religion in Major News Media" on the Media Matters for America Web site, May 2007, found that the mainstream media cites conservative religious leaders almost three times more frequently than their progressive counterparts. See *http://mediamatters.org/leftbehind/?f=h_top* (accessed June 22, 2007).
11. For more on this, see Sean McCloud, *Making the American Religious Fringe: Exotics, Subversives, and Journalists, 1955–1993* (Chapel Hill: University of North Carolina Press, 2004).
12. For daily critiques of religion coverage in the mainstream media, see *http://www.getreligion.org/* and *http://therevealer.org/* (accessed June 22, 2007).
13. Taylor Branch, e-mail message to Nick Street, September 15, 2006.
14. Richard Flory, "Promoting a Secular Standard: Secularization and Modern Journalism, 1870–1930," in *The Secular Revolution: Power, Interests, and Conflict in the Secularization of American Life*, ed. Christian Smith (Berkeley: University of California Press, 2003), 397. The actual slogan alluded to, trademarked by DuPont, was "Better Things for Better Living . . . Through Chemistry."
15. Ibid., 400–402.
16. Ibid., 397.
17. Ibid.
18. Ibid., 412.
19. Ibid.
20. See http://www.positiveatheism.org/hist/menck01.htm (accessed June 22, 2007).
21. For an in-depth perspective on the case, the trial, and the principals, see Edward J. Larson, *Summer for the Gods: The Scopes Trial and America's Continuing Debate over Science and Religion* (New York: Basic Books, 1997); also http://www.law.umkc.edu/faculty/projects/ftrials/scopes/scopes.htm (accessed June 22, 2007).
22. Fessenden, *Culture and Redemption*, 5.
23. Recent works on religious liberalism include Gary Dorrien's masterful trilogy *The Making of American Liberal Theology: Imagining Progressive Religion, 1805–1900* (Louisville, Ky.: Westminster–John Knox Press, 2001), *The Making of American Liberal Theology: Idealism, Realism, and Modernity, 1900–1950* (2003), and *The Making of American Liberal Theology: Crisis, Irony, and Postmodernity, 1950–2005* (2006). See also David L. Chappell, *A Stone of Hope: Prophetic Religion and the Death of Jim Crow* (Chapel Hill: University of North Carolina Press, 2004); Charles Marsh, *The Beloved Community: How Faith Shapes Social Justice, from the Civil Rights Movement to Today* (New York: Basic Books, 2004); and Leigh Schmidt's *Restless Souls: The Making of American Spirituality* (San Francisco: HarperSanFrancisco, 2005).
24. Recent analyses of historical clashes between the National Council of Churches and the Institute for Religion and Democracy include Bill Berkowitz, "Institute on Religion and Democracy Slams Left-

Leaning National Council of Churches," posted on Media Transparency, January 19, 2007, *http://www.mediatransparency.org/story.php?storyID=174*; Jason Byassee, "Hardball Tactics: The Mainline and the IRD," *Christian Century*, May 16, 2006; and Mark Tooley, "Methodist Renewal: A Response," *Sightings*, Martin Marty Center, August 7, 2003.

25. See, for example, Tom Wolfe, *Radical Chic and Mau-Mauing the Flak Catchers* (1970; repr., New York: Bantam, 1999); and Norman Podhoretz, *Making It* (New York: HarperCollins, 1980).

26. See Paul Weyrich's letter to conservatives on February 16, 2000, in which he outlines the history of the "Moral Majority" and the left-wing U.S. movement he calls "Cultural Marxism" (*http://www.nationalcenter.org/Weyrich299.html* [accessed June 22, 2007]), and Sara Diamond's account of the innovative ways that conservative religious and political groups used the media: *Spiritual Warfare: The Politics of the Christian Right* (Cambridge, Mass.: South End Press, 1989).

27. For more on the conflict within the Southern Baptist Convention, see Walter Shurden, *Going for the Jugular: A Documentary History of the SBC Holy War* (Macon, Ga.: Mercer University Press, 1996); Arthur Farnsley, *Southern Baptist Politics: Authority and Power in the Restructuring of an American Denomination* (University Park: Pennsylvania State University Press, 1994); and Nancy Ammerman, *Baptist Battles: Social Change and Religious Conflict in the Southern Baptist Convention* (New Brunswick, N.J.: Rutgers University Press, 1990).

28. William Martin, *With God on Our Side: The Rise of the Religious Right in America* (New York: Broadway Books, 1996), 150.

29. Bush named Jesus Christ as his favorite philosopher during a debate among Republican presidential candidates in Des Moines, Iowa, on December 13, 1999.

30. David Domke, *God Willing? Political Fundamentalism in the White House, the "War on Terror," and the Echoing Press* (London: Pluto Press, 2004).

31. In an interview with Larry King on December 2, 2002, *60 Minutes* producer Don Hewitt said he regretted the NCC segment. "We once took off on the National Council of Churches as being left wing and radical and a lot of nonsense," Hewitt told King. "And the next morning I got a congratulatory phone call from every redneck bishop in America and I thought, 'Oh my God, we must have done something wrong last night,' and I think we probably did."

32. "Documentation: Christianity and Democracy," by the First Political Task Force of the Church, *First Things*, October 1996, *http://www.firstthings.com/article.php3?id_article=3929&var_recherche=Documentation%3A+Christianity+and+Democracy* (accessed February 19, 2007).

33. Found at *http://eric.ed.gov/ERICWebPortal/Home.portal?_nfpb=true&_pageLabel=RecordDetails&ERICExtSearch_SearchValue_0=ED284233&ERICExtSearch_SearchType_0=eric_accno&objectId=0900000b801170b1* (accessed February 19, 2007).

34. I receive regular e-mail updates from IRD detailing NCC activities.

35. See Frederick Clarkson, "The Battle for Mainline Churches," *The Public Eye*, Spring 2006; and John H. Thomas, "The IRS, the IRD, and Red State/Blue State Religion," a speech that Thomas, general minister and president of the United Church of Christ, gave at Gettysburg College on March 6, 2006, *http://news.ucc.org/index.php?option=com_content&task=view&id=483&Itemid=56* (accessed February 19, 2007).

36. See *http://dir.salon.com/story/news/feature/2004/01/06/ahmanson/index.html* (accessed June 22, 2007).

37. Research for Diane Winston by USC Annenberg graduate student Haley Poland.

38. Questioning began with Ron Suskind's article "Faith, Certainty, and the Presidency of George W. Bush," in *New York Times Magazine*, October 17, 2004.

39. In an effort to make up for lost time, the *New York Times* assigned reporter David D. Kirkpatrick to the "conservative" beat beginning in January 2004.

40. See Michele Rosenthal, *American Protestants and TV in the 1950s: Responses to a New Medium* (New York: Palgrave, 2007).

41. See Robert Wuthnow and John Evans, *The Quiet Hand of God: Faith-Based Activism and the Public Role of Mainline Protestantism* (Berkeley: University of California Press, 2002); Robert Edgar, *Middle Church: Reclaiming the Moral Values of the Faithful Majority from the Religious Right* (New York: Simon and Schuster, 2006).

42. See *http://www.ucc.org/ucnews/jul06/mainline.htm* (accessed February 19, 2007). See too the May 2007 Media Matters for America report.

43. See *http://www.eppc.org/publications/pubID.2527/pub_detail.asp* (accessed June 22, 2007).

44. "Spirituality in Higher Education: A National Study of College Students' Search for Meaning and Purpose," Alexander W. Astin and Helen S. Astin, co-principal investigators, and Jennifer A. Lindholm, project director. See online at http://www.gsels.ucla.edu/heri/cirpoverview.php (accessed June 22, 2007).

45. Ibid.

46. See Green's comments in Jane Lampman, "Religion and Public Life: Americans Yearn for a Middle Way," *Christian Science Monitor*, August 30, 2006, *http://www.csmonitor.com/2006/0830/p15s02-lire. html* (accessed June 22, 2007).

47. In March 2007, Cizik was chastened by his right flank for paying too much attention to global warming and not enough to sexual immorality; see *http://www.nytimes.com/2007/03/03/us/03evangelical. html?_r=1&oref=slogin* (accessed June 22, 2007).

48. See Milmon F. Harrison, *Righteous Riches: The Word of Faith Movement in Contemporary African American Religion* (New York: Oxford University Press, 2005); Shayne Lee, *T.D. Jakes: America's New Preacher* (New York: New York University Press, 2005). See, too, Michael Luo, "Preaching a Gospel of Wealth in a Glittery Market," *New York Times*, January 16, 2005, sec. 1.

49. See the Recording Industry Association of America's 2005 Consumer Profile at http://www.riaa.com and "Crossing Over Lines between the Christian and Trade Markets Continue to Blur with Growth on All Fronts," *Publishing Trends*, May 2005.

50. There are not many academic or journalistic sources. See Sherman Jackson, *Islam and the Blackamerican: Looking Toward the Third Resurrection* (New York: Oxford University Press, 2005). The Zaytuna Institute (*http://www.zaytuna.org/*) seeks to provide educational resources for American Muslims and the development of an American Islam. In 2005, the Western Knight Center for Specialized Journalism held a conference on Islam in America, and several panels addressed this issue: *http://www.wkconline. org/index.php/seminar_showcase/islam_2005* (accessed June 22, 2007).

51. Very little has been published by academics or journalists on this topic. One unpublished paper, "Muslim Communities in the U.S.," written by Nadia Roumani for the Four Freedoms Fund, explores indigenous and immigrant Muslim communities, national Muslim organizations, stated priorities, and strategies for meeting community needs. As a follow-up, Roumani convened an "American Muslim Young Adult Community Leaders Retreat" at the Pocantico Conference Center in New York in July 2006 with activists working on Muslim civic and political engagement. Roumani highlights several organizations active in this sector including the Muslim Public Affairs Council (MPAC, *www.mpac. org*); Inner-City Muslim Action Network (IMAN, *http://www.imancentral.org/*); Abraham's Vision (*http://www.abrahamsvision.org/*); and Muslim Advocates (*http://www.muslimadvocates.org/more. php?id=8_0_2_0_M* [accessed June 22, 2007]).

52. Eddie Gibbs and Ryan Bolger, *Emergent Churches: Creating Christian Communities in Postmodern Cultures* (Grand Rapids, Mich.: Baker Academic Publishing, 2005); see also *http://www.emergentvillage. org/* and *http://www.theooze.com/main.cfm* (accessed June 22, 2007).

53. See, on Jews, *http://www.jewishjournal.com/home/preview.php?id=15322 http://www.synagogue3000.org/ emergentweb/jewishemergent.html* and, on mainline Protestants, *http://dixonkinser.blogspot.com/2007/02/ emergent-mainlines-report.html* (accessed June 22, 2007).

54. See, for example, Michael Kelly, "Saint Hillary," *New York Times Magazine*, May 23, 1993; and Nina Martin, "Who Is She?" *Mother Jones*, November–December 1993.

55. See Peter Wood, "Obama's Prayer: Wooing Evangelicals," *National Review*, July 6, 2006; and E. J. Dionne, "Obama's Eloquent Faith," *Washington Post*, June 30, 2006.

56. See Robert Pettit, "Religion Through the Times: An Examination of the Secularization Thesis through Content Analysis of the *New York Times*, 1855–1975" (PhD diss., Columbia University, 1986).

57. For examples: *http://www.washingtonmonthly.com/features/2005/0509.sullivan1.html*, *http://www. foxnews.com/story/0,2933,256078,00.html*, and *http://www.rollingstone.com/politics/story/9178374/ gods_senator/print* (accessed June 22, 2007).

Testimonial Politics: The Christian Right's Faith-Based Approach to Marriage and Imprisonment

Tanya Erzen

In January 2005, Joaquin Phoenix, who played Johnny Cash in the film *Walk the Line*, visited Folsom State Prison to perform a version of "Folsom Prison Blues," the song Cash recorded live during his famous visit in 1968. The actor had been invited by the evangelical Prison Fellowship Ministries (PFM), whose chaplain wanted to inspire inmates with Cash's "story of redemption." Redemption through Jesus Christ is the message of PFM and its affiliate Prison Fellowship International, which runs evangelical-based programs for prisoners in the United States and nine other countries. "If we're ever going to see the crime rate go down, we have to do more than simply lock criminals up. We must transform their hearts through faith in Jesus Christ," writes Chuck Colson, the founder of PFM.[1] As Jorge Valdes, an inmate and self-described former "drug kingpin" testifies, "prison will not change any human being. Rehab centers will not change any human being. Tortures will not change any human being—only an intimate relationship with Jesus Christ."[2]

A few months earlier, Exodus International, the umbrella organization for the ex-gay movement, had launched an advertising campaign in several media markets. They featured Alan Chambers, Exodus's president, clasping his wife, Leslie, in his arms.[3] The title above Alan and Leslie reads, "I Questioned Homosexuality. By finding my way out of a gay identity, I found the love of my life in the process. Gay marriage would only have blinded me to such an incredible joy." His testimony follows: "My name is Alan Chambers, and I lived for nine years with a homosexual orientation. Today I'm married to Leslie, and we're beginning a family with our first child this year." The advertisement was designed to promote the message that legalizing gay marriage will prevent gay men and women from realizing that they can transform themselves into born-again heterosexuals.

Such testimonies, with their narratives of sin, redemption and personal transformation, are central to the way some organizations of the Christian Right view both marriage and imprisonment. Christian Right organizations such as PFM, Exodus, and Focus on the Family mobilize evangelical testimonies of conversion to produce political stances and affiliations. I define the Christian Right as a broad coalition of politically active conservative Christians who hold a view of America based on theological ideas that the government should be based on biblical values and morality.[4] These Christian Right organizations employ testimonial politics to argue against same-sex marriage and for a mode of prisoner rehabilitation based on transformation as a born-again Christian. The premise is that belief in Jesus will transform a person: from homosexual to married ex-gay Christian, prisoner to upstanding Christian citizen. From this perspective, a new life as an evangelical Christian ultimately supersedes previous identities.

The nature of the evangelical born-again narrative is crucial to how conservative Christian organizations conceive of their role in politics. Testimonial politics rely on redemption narratives in which evangelical Christians become born-again as new persons. They equate their born-again experience with their belief in the death and resurrection of Jesus, and thereby place themselves within a sacred and cosmic order in which they hear and internalize God's voice. Individual testimonies serve as evidence that God speaks to and transforms people, and this concept bolsters conservative Christian ideas about the role of Christianity in politics. The testimonies provide a way for Christian organizations to claim that, when it comes to marriage and prison, a higher Christian law supersedes that of the state.

Testimonial politics emphasize how the experience of becoming a born-again Christian transforms individuals, eliminating the need for social programs focused on structural economic issues. Christian programs of rehabilitation in the prison and anti-same-sex marriage campaigns appeal to constituents because they emphasize that transformation is individual. The campaigners against gay rights and same-sex marriage and for evangelical prison programs emphasize the individual and even grassroots nature of their activism. However, testimonial politics enable issues to appear to be about individual transformation, even if they are highly coordinated national political campaigns in which Christian Right organizations dictate policy stances and provide political resources.

Personal narratives of individual transformation are central to testimonial politics, and they work in conjunction with a neoliberal vision in which social services are privatized rather than funded by the federal government. The rationale behind the federal office of faith-based initiatives created by President Bush is that faith-based organizations can provide services more efficiently than government organizations can. Testimonial politics support the faith-based policies of economic privatization that place the onus for solving social problems on the individual and on the power of God to transform lives. The testimonies of individuals provide an explanation or cause for both homosexuality, in the case of the ex-gay movement, and for criminality, in the case of evangelical prison programs. In this view, the answer to imprisonment, homosexuality, drug addiction, and poverty is conversion to evangelical Christianity.

Testifying to Transformation

At a church service in an airy, immaculate chapel at a correctional facility for women, approximately a hundred inmates sit in gleaming cedar pews. A band plays on the stage as the pastor introduces Deborah, a prisoner who now volunteers for Prison Fellowship Ministries. Deborah testifies that she is thirty-one, with four children, and she is two years into an eighteen-year sentence at an Alabama prison for theft. She had blasted her way through alcohol, drugs, and prostitution to support her $1,000-a-day crack addiction. "If you keep this up, it's going to catch up with you," a drug counselor had warned her. Deborah recalls,

> I was dead. My body was walking around, but inside I was dead. I heard music from the other side of the room: a group of Prison Fellowship volunteers and inmates singing an old gospel song, "Victory in Jesus." *I heard an old, old story, how a Savior came from glory! How He gave His life on Calvary to save a wretch like me* . . . That song just filled and warmed my body, and I went to join the singers. My hands went up in the air, tears starting coming out of my eyes, and I asked God to please help me. I was like the Prodigal Son down in that pig slime. And then the son "came to himself." I was like that: I came to myself and said, "I'm going to my Father."[5]

Later, with one of the Prison Fellowship volunteers, she prayed to commit her life to Christ.

At another church service in a rented community center in California, a man faces a nondenominational Christian congregation. Mitch, a stooped man in his late forties, talks about the years he lived a double life, participating in his church while having secret affairs with men. He relates how his church forced him to resign as a youth pastor when they discovered he was a homosexual.

> This is the part where I came to the place and I said God, either you let me go or you change my life, but I can't live in the middle anymore. I can't struggle with Christianity and how I believe the Bible teaches that homosexuality is wrong and still struggle with the feelings and the emotions and the attractions. Then I remember one night, I was walking to the adult

bookstore to cruise. I really didn't want to, but I felt like I had no power over myself.

I began to shake my fists. I was crying in the middle of the night in downtown Richmond. I started screaming, "God I hate you, I hate you, get out of my life. I don't want you anymore. You're sadistic. You don't care. You won't set me free. You won't let me act out. You just want me to suffer, and I'm not going to do this anymore." And that was right before the doors opened up for me to come here.

A week later, Mitch jumped in his car and drove out to California to attend a residential ex-gay program for men. Now he tells the congregation that he still fights the temptation to look at pornography, but he is transformed.

After Deborah and Mitch's testimonies, the congregations rise to their feet and applaud vigorously. Both pastors ask the people in the audience to gather around the speakers and pray for them. The church members pour down the aisles to lay their hands on Deborah and Mitch, kneeling and standing around them. Deborah and Mitch are witnesses to the persuasive power of a born-again conversion that engenders new identities from the shells of their sexual and criminal ones. Their testimonies are narratives of self-transformation that connect the testifier's life to a sacred reality, and they impart to listeners the experience of being filled with the word of God. The testimonies have an explicit proselytizing purpose to bring their message of redemption through Jesus to others.

Although Deborah and Mitch speak of their own personal circumstances, both of their narratives are part of a wider evangelical template.[6] Evangelicalism in the United States describes a vast, varied, and interactive aggregation of many different groups, such as Pentecostals, Charismatics, Vineyard Fellowships, Assemblies of God, and Churches of the Nazarene. Religious practitioners within evangelicalism believe that people must have an intimate relationship with Jesus and that only an individual desire to follow him will suffice for salvation. In the simple meaning of the word itself, "evangelical" is about good news, and many modern evangelicals understand their mandate as spreading this good news and winning souls for Jesus by testifying to their own life-changing experiences. Within evangelicalism, some churches and denominations understand the Bible as infallible, true, and literal, in contrast to the liberal Protestant view that considers the Bible a product of human history and context. Theologically, evangelicalism refers to a belief system that includes the necessity for personal salvation through becoming born again or saved, faith in the inerrancy of the Bible, and belief that Jesus Christ is the Son of God and a person with whom one can have an intimate relationship. The idea of grace is central to how Mitch and Deborah conceive of their transformations. In their worldview, God's grace extends to all people regardless of their sins as long as they ask for forgiveness. As they are reborn, the guilt of sin disappears, and an inward process of renewal takes place as the individual leads a Christian life.

Deborah and Mitch's narratives of redemption attest to their engagement with this wider evangelical belief system, especially in the manner in which they invoke a sacred reality and connect their individual lives with the presence and voice of God. Susan Harding describes this process as a "supernaturalizing mode of interpretation" in which disbelief becomes false and the supernatural becomes reality.[7] The supernatural manifests itself through testimony or hearing God's voice, and the individual begins to understand his or her previous identity as a fiction that has been overcome in the service of a new identity in Jesus. Just as Mitch calls out to God that he won't set him free, Deborah testifies, "*I heard an old, old story, how a Savior came from glory! How He gave His life on Calvary to save a wretch like me.*" They are born again religiously, and this transforms a person into an ex-gay or noncriminal. They have taken on a pure identity in which they can access their previous lives while attesting to their new ones through a relationship with God. Both Mitch and Deborah speak to and identify with God or Jesus in their testimonies. They attest to a transformation that begins when they internalize the spirit and words of God. Deborah tells the listeners, "That song just filled and warmed my body, and I went to join the singers. My hands went up in the air, tears starting coming out of my eyes, and I asked God to please help me. I was like the Prodigal Son." The impetus behind the evangelical testimony is that listeners will hear and absorb the saved speaker's language and sacred view of the world as part of their own conversion.

Confession of past indiscretions is central to the testifier's contention that she has become a new person through a born-again conversion. Mitch confesses that "I was walking to the adult bookstore to cruise," before he cried out to God. The idea that no matter how many illicit sex acts or crimes you have committed, there is still the possibility of forgiveness if you publicly confess is specific to evangelical concepts of grace and transformation. As the testimonies demonstrate, nothing is too private or painful to share, and those with the most unsettling tales become the most sought-after speakers.

Conversion is a process of acquiring a specific religious language or dialect that is recognizable to other Christians. Through participation in evangelical groups, a person internalizes the structure of a testimony, and in the telling the confessions become retrospective narratives that are shaped by the evangelical culture around them. The testimonies reinterpret individuals' past lives in the language of sin and salvation and in the light of their new evangelical Christian identity. Robyn R. Warhol and Helena Michie write that Alcoholics Anonymous has a similar master narrative for recovery groups that "functions mnemonically to provide the speaker with a structure for shaping the individual story's details."[8]

The testimonial narratives of Mitch and Deborah are autobiographical, but they are also capacious enough to allow many people to hear the story of their lives in the accounts. They testify publicly about the most private and harrowing aspects of their lives. They begin with a traumatic story about past lives of addiction to pornography and prostitution. In each of them, Mitch and Deborah reached a crisis point, and during that moment they found themselves either calling out to God or hearing God for the first time. Each testimony results in the discovery of the relationship with God, and finishes with participation in an ex-gay ministry or the Christian prison program along the path to conversion.

The testimonies of transformation are part of the proselytizing mandate of contemporary evangelicalism. Harding writes, "What distinguishes fundamental Baptists from others is the degree to which they have formalized rhetorical techniques for converting others."[9] The dramatic testimonies of Mitch and Deborah are meant to be a cathartic, public enactment that provides evidence of the power of Jesus in transforming lives. In the proselytizing culture of evangelicalism, Mitch and Deborah have located themselves in a sacred reality, and they believe that they speak the words of God. Bella Brodski writes that testimony needs an audience to fulfill itself.[10] By giving witness to their transformed selves, Deborah and Mitch try to convince others that their only option is to disavow their previous lives of sin.

The testimonial narrative marks people's entrance into an evangelical community and signifies their new identities. However, in the focus on individual transformation, the testimonies place the blame on a person's choices rather than on the aspects of society that make it difficult to live as a gay man or woman, or on the drug sentencing laws that put Deborah in prison for eighteen years. By making Jesus the only one who can transform a person, testimonials also remove some agency from the individual, negating his potential power to alter the structures around him. Instead, individuals can allow themselves to be transformed only by God.

The Political Uses of Testimony

The testimonies of Mitch and Deborah are not just compelling evidence for listeners, but they contain a hybrid religious and political rhetoric formulated to change more than individuals. They are part of a strategic political mode of organizing around gay rights, marriage, and faith-based government funding for Christian Right organizations such as Focus on the Family, Prison Fellowship Ministry (PFM), and the ex-gay movement. These groups are invested in more than saving souls. They are involved in cultural and moral reform aimed at transforming the state. They highlight individual testimonies as a way to remold the criminal justice system, prisons, and laws governing marriage and sexuality into a biblical Christian worldview. Focus on the Family and PFM mobilize testimonies as part of the argument that their political initiatives are sacred and directed by the laws of God.

The Christian ex-gay movement is a global network of religious ministries that attempt to change and convert gay men and lesbians to nonhomosexual Christians through psychological, self-help, therapeutic, and biblical approaches. Exodus International counters same-sex marriage initiatives with the evidence of people who testify about their conversions from homosexuality to heterosexuality. The ex-gay movement understands homosexuality as a choice, a developmental disorder, and an addiction that can be overcome only by fostering a personal relationship with God.[11] The theological premise of the movement is that sexuality and religion are not only incompatible but contrary to the word of God.[12] While the ex-gay movement cites some studies to prove that men and women do change, they rely mainly on ex-gay narratives of sexual conversion.

Ex-gay testimonies create a new form of self-revelation and identity formation centered on coming *out* of homosexuality. In the Exodus office, an entire wall is filled with different shelves for every type of testimony: homosexuality, lesbianism, masturbation, pornography, and transgender identities; there is material for parents and teenagers. Every month, the newsletter has a testimony or story on the front cover. Most of these stories feature a ministry leader who has been out of the lifestyle for several years. Barbara Swallow, a former lesbian, gives a testimony called "All Things Made New." The subheading reads: "After being molested, I decided it wasn't safe being a girl. So I began to construct a new Barbara who wasn't female at all."[13]

Rather than simply using testimonies as proof that change in a person's sexuality can occur, Exodus also actively participates in political debates over same-sex marriage policy. Since Alan Chambers became president of Exodus in 2001 and moved the headquarters to Orlando, Florida, Exodus now explicitly attempts to influence public policy through its speaking engagements, media appearances, advertising, and members' own testimonies, and the organization cultivates relationships with prominent Christian conservatives such as James Dobson of Focus on the Family and members of the Bush administration. Testimonies of ex-gay men and women now serve as the basis of the marriage initiatives at the state level. In June 2006, Chambers was invited by officials in Washington to meet President Bush and testify during the Senate debates over a federal marriage amendment.

Exodus designed the advertising campaign featuring Chambers to oppose same-sex marriage. In the first ad, Alan Chambers writes, "I grew up with the secret shame of being sexually molested by an older man," and this generated his homosexual feelings at age ten. "I never imagined my marriage partner could *ever be a woman*. I just assumed that if I ever 'got married,' it would be with a man."[14] The Chambers ad reads,

> Like so many of the gay men I came to know, I was starved for genuine male love and affirmation. But after years of searching, I realized that acceptance in the gay community always wore the same tired nametag called "sex," and every sexual encounter with a man only emptied more of me than it filled.
>
> And so the questions began.
>
> In all honesty, my search for answers was difficult. . . . Changing old responses and patterns, then finding security on the deepest level, takes time. *But, it was totally worth the journey!*
>
> Here's the truth. *If I had a gay marriage option ten years ago, I'd never have dealt with the root issues of my homosexual behavior.* I'd probably be in and out of half a dozen "marital" relationships. And I'd never know the complete peace I now have about my past. Leslie is not my diploma for "healing," nor is she a prop that shows how I've abandoned a sexual identity. She is my perfect complement and completes me in ways no male relationships can ever do . . . physically or emotionally.
>
> I'm living proof that change *is* possible.[15]

Chambers testifies that legalizing gay marriage will prevent gay men and women from realizing "the root issues of their homosexual behavior," and that it will deter them from becoming what God intends—that they are truly heterosexual. The Exodus advertisement also implies that Chambers's homosexuality is a result of developmental and societal influences, citing sexual abuse and his lack of male affirmation as causes of his "homosexual orientation."

However, his testimony is not only designed to convert others or simply support the ex-gay movement. The claim "I'm living proof that change is possible" also solidifies the rationale for anti-gay marriage policies. The ex-gay movement has effectively convinced many conservative Christians that homosexuality is a choice or a developmental condition. It has also enabled opponents of gay marriage to persuade others that gay identity is a false life-style and identification, and that gay people do not merit rights or protections like that of the right to marry. This conceptual shift is crucial to the anti–gay marriage movement, whose members are careful to claim that they are not advocating bigotry or discrimination. Christian Right leaders can argue that gay identity is nonexistent by showcasing people like Alan Chambers. How can they deprive someone of a right, they counter, when the very identity that right is protecting is something they believe does not exist? The battle against gay marriage is not about discrimination or rights because gay people can choose to change their sexuality.

The anti-same-sex marriage movement utilizes ex-gay testimonies to impose its view of Christian morality on the state and legislation. Evangelical prison programs like PFM also focus on individual transformation as the basis for a new model of rehabilitation. The InnerChange Freedom Initiative (IFI) is the twenty-four-hour Christian immersion program sponsored by Prison Fellowship Ministry. PFM has contracted with state corrections departments to administer entire wings of men's medium security prisons in Texas, Missouri, Minnesota, Iowa, and Kansas, and they are finalizing plans for a women's program in Arkansas in 2006. The program begins eighteen to twenty-four months before an inmate is released. To be eligible to join InnerChange, inmates must be at least two years away from parole and must proclaim their status as born-again Christians. They spend the day working at a job and attend classes to develop their life skills and spiritual maturity. The classes focus on time management, anger control, family relations, and job preparedness. There are also classes dedicated to biblical doctrine and scripture memorization. Evenings are filled with more Christian teaching and discipleship seminars. During Phase Two of the program, inmates must perform community service, and they are encouraged to apologize and make restitution to their victims. Six months into the program, each inmate is matched with a Christian church volunteer who mentors him during his remaining time in prison. After the inmate's release, the volunteer continues to mentor him for six to twelve months, during which time the former prisoner must hold a job and be an active church member.

Participants in the program must accept Jesus as their personal savior by publicly stating a version of the sinner's prayer that they acknowledge they are sinners, and that Jesus paid the penalty for their sins. The program explains that when you accept Jesus Christ as your savior, "you became a new person inside—your spirit is now alive in Christ!" The InnerChange program is based on the idea that sin is the root cause of imprisonment, and teaches that inmates should "learn how God can heal them permanently, if they turn from their sinful past, are willing to see the world through God's eyes, and surrender themselves to God's will."[16]

> We are invited to experience new life in Christ—to be rescued out of our darkness and into His light—but we cannot earn our salvation. The Bible makes this clear: "For it is by grace you have been saved, through faith—and this not from yourselves, it is the gift of God—not by works, so that no one can boast" (Ephesians 2:8–9). There is only one way to receive this gift: "Believe in the Lord Jesus Christ, and you shall be saved." (Acts 16:31)[17]

The program is clear that InnerChange is a transformation model, not a therapeutic community. "IFI seeks a radical transformation from the inside out that is only possible through the miraculous power of God's love. This type of transformation cannot happen through human relationships alone."[18] According to Chuck Colson, the founder of PFM, the transformation that InnerChange promises "happens through an instantaneous miracle." The miracle is becoming born again and accepting Jesus Christ as one's personal savior. Rehabilitation occurs through redemption from Jesus, and prisoner testimonies are the proof that the program is effective. One example is the testimony of Jorge Valdes, self-identified as "one of the biggest drug lords in the world," who delivered 150 kilograms of cocaine a month to California, laundered the money, and took in hundreds of thousands of dollars.

> I began buying big houses, fancy cars, and clothes. I learned all about the business. My dreams were all coming true. One night during a separation with my third wife, as I slept with two other women, my two-year-old daughter Krystle knocked on the locked bedroom door, crying. Struck with shame, I ordered the women out and scalded myself in the shower attempting to wash the feelings away. I found my daughter whimpering, asleep on the hard floor. How could I be so evil?

Once in prison for his drug business, Jorge writes,

> Seeing the truth of Christianity lived out right in front of me and feeling the terrible consequences of my former life bearing down, I fell to my knees in desperation and asked Jesus into my life—this time with all my heart. I felt refreshed. Strangest of all, I felt clean! As though all the dirt of my life had suddenly been power-washed away.[19]

The rationale behind InnerChange is that the experience of imprisonment can be mediated only through born-again Christian conversion in which individuals allow their lives to be directed by God or by asking Jesus into their lives. However, these testimonies are not solely about conversion; like Alan Chambers, Jorge Valdes, through his testimony, also supports the political stance of PFM, which advocates a Christ-centered approach to rehabilitation and crime. Testimonies are mobilized to reform not only the soul of the prisoner or gay man but to instate a form of religious citizenship and laws about marriage, gay rights, and prisoners that accord with a conservative Christian worldview.

The Battle against Secularism

The ex-gay movement, Focus on the Family, PFM, and other conservative Christian organizations understand themselves as waging a battle against secularism. In their book *Love the Sin*, Janet Jakobsen and Ann Pellegrini compellingly argue that U.S. secularism is in fact a form of what they term "stealth Protestantism."[20] They write that the unstated religious assumptions of secularism in the United States are Protestant, and that Christianity shapes legislation, policy, and jurisprudence, especially regarding sex. Christian conservatives such as James Dobson and Chuck Colson argue precisely the opposite in order to build support for their political and policy stances. They often use the language of victimization to describe the situation of a conservative Christian religious worldview in the United States. Focus on the Family and PFM rely on testimonial politics to claim that Christian morality is embattled but should ultimately override secular laws and policies.

Their campaigns against same-sex marriage and for the right to promote evangelical programs in state prisons illustrate their mandate to convert not just individuals but the state as well. Focus on the Family attempts to reshape laws based on conservative Christian views of gender, family, and sexuality. While PFM also seeks to re-create the state prison as a religious institution dictated by Christian values, the key distinction is that PFM receives state and federal funds to do so. For Colson and Dobson, religious freedom is actually the freedom to be a conservative Christian with theological, political, and cultural worldviews similar to those of Focus on the Family and Prison Fellowship Ministry. Dobson has made similar arguments about same-sex marriage. He argues that laws granting the right to marriage to nonheterosexual couples violate Christian beliefs and values, and that it is his duty to promote Christian values in public policy and politics.

In the case of Focus on the Family, how the organization understands homosexuality is paramount to its policy arguments about gay marriage. Led by Dobson since 1977, Focus on the Family is a conservative Christian conglomerate with daily radio broadcasts; more than sixteen publications geared toward youth, parents, teachers, physicians, and church leaders; overseas missionary organizations; and other media ventures. Dobson sends a monthly letter to his mailing list in which he outlines his thoughts on current political controversies, and he has been crucial in furthering the agenda of the anti-gay marriage movement because of the financial and media resources of his organization.[21] His book *Marriage Under Fire: Why We Must Win This Battle* lays out eleven reasons not to support same-sex marriage and is widely quoted by other anti-marriage organizations.[22]

Dobson refers his millions of readers and listeners who have questions about their sexuality to Exodus. Through his sponsorship of Love Won Out conferences, which feature ex-gay speakers, Dobson has increased visibility for the ex-gay movement and presented these speakers to a Christian audience that would otherwise have never addressed the issue of homosexuality. In his other publications, such as *Citizen Magazine*, a monthly publication about issues affecting the family, Dobson's rhetoric is more explicitly anti-gay and it includes legislative updates and suggestions for action. In one issue he writes: "Homosexuality has become the cause du jour of those who seek to undermine the family. Though homosexuals comprise only 2–3 percent of the population, they exert incredible influence over the political arena. Abetted by a pro-homosexual news and entertainment media, the radical gay activists' assault on morality has reached a fever pitch."[23] He then informs readers that homosexuals have achieved "a form of gay marriage in Vermont and are pushing for recognition of same-sex unions in the other 49 states."[24] He urges them to write their representatives and get involved on the state level. In the past, his newsletters also endorsed anti-gay ballot initiatives, such as Amendment 2 in Colorado.[25]

Dobson is part of a larger network of Christian Right leaders of which Chuck Colson is also a part. Both men have been members of the Council for National Policy, a secretive organization of evangelical leaders and conservative politicians founded by Tim LaHaye who meet regularly to network and discuss national policy. Members have included Oliver North, Bob Jones, Pat Robertson, Tom DeLay, and Jerry Falwell, and other prominent officials such as Clarence Thomas, John Ashcroft, and President Bush have addressed the group. The council recently met in Florida to discuss which presidential candidate for the 2008 elections would most likely represent a conservative Christian platform.[26] Chuck Colson is no stranger to national politics. Before he founded PFM and Prison Fellowship International (PFI) in 1976, he was a former Nixon aide, who served seven months in prison for obstruction of justice as part of his Watergate crimes.[27] Upon his release he wrote a book, *Born Again*, and refashioned himself as an advocate for the redemptive power of evangelical Christianity on criminals. As governor of Texas, Bush supported and promoted the PFM pilot programs in a Texas prison. Colson has published multiple books and writes regular columns for *Christianity Today*, and his daily radio column "Breakpoint" is broadcast on a thousand religious radio stations across the country. In his columns, he frequently expresses disdain for the concept of the separation of church and state, gay rights, abortion, evolution, and stem-cell research. As a testament to his influence, Colson received the Templeton Prize in 1993, a million-dollar cash reward given annually to people who have done significant work to advance conservative Christianity. Colson has written that gay marriage will lead to further imprisonment of young men because they do not learn moral values.

> Now, some don't like the moral or philosophical arguments for a marriage amendment. Others dislike dealing with a contentious social issue at all or simply do not like amending the Constitution. My response to these people is, "Do you want to continue to see our prisons fill with kids who have been raised like feral children in the wilderness? Do we want to risk further damage to the integrity of the family?"[28]

Despite Colson's affiliation with the Christian Right on issues such as gay marriage and abortion, his political views on crime and imprisonment sometimes resist easy classification as conservative. He opposes mandatory minimum sentencing laws that send people to prison for first-time drug offenses and is an advocate of better work-release and after-care programs for prisoners. Colson promotes rehabilitation, restorative justice, and the improvement of living conditions in prisons as long as the rehabilitation entails a conversion to evangelical Christianity.

Both Focus on the Family and PFM deploy testimonial politics to argue for a vision of the law and citizenship based on conservative evangelical morality. In the mid-1990s, several graduates of ex-gay ministry programs obtained positions as policy specialists in the gender and sexuality division of Focus on the Family. They modified Dobson's strident anti-gay rhetoric and instituted the Love Won Out conferences in churches throughout the United States. The conferences feature ex-gay speakers as a bid to encourage churches to minister to homosexuals and refer gay congregants to ex-gay ministries. Dobson now regularly cites ex-gay testimonies as proof of sexual change and directs callers and clients of Focus on the Family to Exodus. The alliance between Focus on the Family and Exodus has marked an important political shift for the way conservative Christian organizations address the issue of homosexuality. Rather than claiming gay rights are about demanding "special rights" and "the right to perversion," Focus on the Family and other Christian Right organizations now employ a testimonial approach to gay politics.[29]

Using this approach, "marriage recovery" initiatives such as Mayday for Marriage deliberately bill themselves as a pro-marriage movement rather than one that is anti-gay, a "distress call for the destruction of traditional marriage."[30] Mayday formed to "preserve the definition of marriage as the union between a man and a woman." "Because of God's love through Jesus Christ in our lives, we love every man, woman and child, regardless of race, gender and even sexual orientation," the mission statement reads.[31] The organization appropriates the language of coming out to proclaim that many Christians have "publicly come out of the closet and taken a stand for marriage." In the same way, the ex-gay movement sponsors "National Coming out of Homosexuality" events in which ex-gays testify to leaving their homosexuality behind.

The testimonies of ex-gay speakers such as Chambers enable Christian marriage campaigns to lobby state legislatures that gay marriage is not legitimate because "change is possible." Thirty-eight states have passed "Defense of Marriage Acts" (DOMAs), and a dozen states are considering constitutional amendments to protect marriage. Exodus was directly involved with the organization Florida 4 Marriage and the Florida Coalition to Protect Marriage, which attempted to gather enough signatures to put an amendment of the Florida state constitution on the ballot that defines marriage as only a relationship between one man and one woman. Although they were short of the 611,000 needed to place the initiative on the November ballot, the petitions remain valid for several years, and the organization intends to renew its efforts in time for the November 2008 election.[32] During 2005, members of Exodus collaborated in press conferences in nine cities across Florida. "Our organization represents hundreds of thousands of people, like myself, who felt trapped by homosexuality and found an escape through Jesus Christ," said Randy Thomas, membership director for Exodus.[33]

The testimonial approach to the politics of marriage also enables anti-gay marriage organizations to evade the charge that they seek to undermine the rights of gay men and lesbians by denying gay identity. Glenn T. Stanton, a policy analyst and writer for Focus on the Family who specializes in the marriage issue carefully notes that "no U.S. court has ever recognized, nor has any scientific study ever established, that homosexuality is rooted in nature and therefore is the same as heterosexuality. Scientists understand that homosexuality is rooted in a collection of biological, psychological and social factors. We cannot treat them as the same thing."[34] His argument rests on the testimonies of men and women who claim to have changed their sexualities. For Stanton, the Christian marriage movement is not about rights or discrimination, because homosexuality is not an immutable status like race. He argues, "Being black or white, Hispanic or Asian is not like being homosexual. Again, no academic institution in the world nor any U.S. court has ever established that homosexuality is unchangeable, as are race, nationality or gender."[35] The distinction between race as immutable and sexuality as a choice garnered support for marriage amendments at the state level in 2004, and Dobson sponsored a conference for African American pastors in May to discuss the ways in which marriage is not a civil rights issue.[36]

Testimonies, including Colson's own personal testimony, have been central to the evidence that PFM presents to verify the success of InnerChange prison programs and refute criticisms that they violate the separation of church and state. Recently, the contention that InnerChange is proselytizing to a captive population led to a lawsuit sponsored by Americans United for the Separation of Church and State. The lawsuit argued that the program promotes evangelical Christianity at state expense. In June 2006, U.S. District Judge Robert W. Pratt ordered the InnerChange Freedom Initiative to shut down and reimburse the state of Iowa the $1.5 million it had received to fund the program in the Newton Correctional Facility. The ruling by Judge Pratt reads:

> For all practical purposes, the state has literally established an Evangelical Christian congregation within the walls of one its penal institutions, giving the leaders of that congregation, i.e., InnerChange employees, authority to control the spiritual, emotional, and physical lives of hundreds of Iowa inmates. There are no adequate safeguards present, nor could there be, to ensure that state funds are not being directly spent to indoctrinate Iowa inmates.[37]

In response, Charles Colson and PFM president Mark Early have launched a campaign to discredit the ruling, solicit funding, and appeal the decision.

Just as PFM uses prisoner testimonies as proof that InnerChange is effective, when the program lost the lawsuit, Colson and Mark Early mobilized prisoner narratives to assert that the lack of a program would harm prisoners and increase recidivism. Some of these testimonies include that of Jeff, a former prison inmate and current PFM volunteer.

In July of 1986 Jeff entered the Federal Correctional Institution at Danbury in Connecticut where he would be completing his federal sentence. Jeff halfheartedly attended a Bible study while at Danbury. But at that session, he was given a small Gideon Bible. He took it back to his dorm and, by the light of a full midnight moon, read 1 Corinthians 13. Jeff recalls, "It was like BANG! A thunderbolt hit me. I was changed. I knew right then who my Lord and Savior was. I knew who Jesus was, and I knew that this little book that I held was the Truth!"[38]

Another testimony that Colson and Early cite to buttress their claims that Judge Pratt's ruling harms prisoners is that of prisoner Gregg Hanson. "Until he came under the influence of IFI, he was part of a breeding ground for criminals, a grad school where you learned how to be a better crook. This place now has become the opposite of that. Why would a judge—why would anybody—want to put a stop to that?" In 2003, Colson joined Tom DeLay in issuing a joint press release celebrating InnerChange after the University of Pennsylvania's Center for Research on Religion and Urban Civil Society released a study showing that InnerChange graduates were rearrested and reimprisoned at much lower rates than a control group.[39] However, this study was discredited by a public policy professor who questioned the methodology and argued that the recidivism rates for prisoners in the InnerChange programs are equal and possibly higher than other prisons.[40] Colson and Early also argue that revoking the federal funds they received for the InnerChange program is an instance of discrimination and a violation of their religious freedom. Mark Early, the president of PFM writes:

> Prison Fellowship wants to see a level playing field for people of faith. People of faith should not be excluded from providing services in the public square to those who have volunteered to receive them. We want prisoners to be able to take part in a program—yes, even a Christ-centered one—that will help them change their lives for the better if they desire to do so.[41]

However, neither Charles Colson nor James Dobson envision a level playing field for all faiths. In a recent *Breakpoint* column called "Allah Blues," Chuck Colson warned about the dangers of radical Islam in America's prisons, asserting that prisons are "breeding grounds for future terrorists." Colson argued that "no religious sect should be allowed to preach a doctrine that promotes violence, especially in prison." His solution: "The surest antidote to the poison of hatred and revenge spread by some radical Islamists is Christ's message of love, forgiveness, and peace."[42] Colson has made it clear that he would not support state-funding for an Islamic immersion program in America's prisons.

Since 2004, Florida has converted two medium security prisons for men and women into "faith and character" institutions designed to rehabilitate prisoners through access to religious services. Lawtey and Hillsborough Correctional Facilities are state prisons that rely on volunteers to provide religious services and programming to their populations.[43] While they strive to serve inmates of all religious backgrounds, the overall programming is directed through a local Christian nondenominational church that donated the chapel and runs the main education and faith programs. The group is acutely aware of the legal troubles plaguing PFM and is therefore careful to reiterate that its funding is not state-based. Aside from these programs, most state and federal prisons have long-standing chaplaincy programs that provide counseling, materials, and services to Muslim, Buddhist, Jewish, Christian, and Native American prisoners. However, PFM is the only organization in the United States that receives state funding for a program in which conversion to evangelical Christianity is mandatory and that specifically excludes other religious groups. There is no equivalent religious immersion program for a non-Christian tradition. Therefore, the outcome of the Iowa court case presents a challenge to the concept of faith-based initiatives, calling into question whether taxpayers' money should fund religious organizations with a proselytizing mission.

The Brave New World of Privatization

The issue of state funding is central to the controversy around PFM. Colson argues that the state has failed to adequately address the question of imprisonment and that state funding for his evangelical program will provide another model of rehabilitation. This argument claims that state funds are best used to transform individuals into born-again Christians. Politics based on testimony provide compelling anecdotal evidence to listeners, but they also support the current Bush administration's focus on economic privatization and the decrease in funding for federal social programs such as welfare, social security, education, and job training. Testimonial politics enable organizations to claim that religion itself is the cure for socioeconomic problems and that transformation is an individual process rather than a social or structural one.

In 2001, President Bush signed an executive order creating the White House Office of Faith-Based and Community Initiatives (FBCI). The rationale behind the faith-based policies was to ensure that religious organizations were equal competitors for government funding. The Bush administration claimed the federal government had discriminated against faith-based organizations in the past. Since 2001, faith-based organizations have received $1.1 billion in federal and state funding with the mandate to focus their efforts on at-risk youth, ex-offenders and prisoners, homeless men and women, substance abusers, and welfare-to-work families. The FBCI chose the Prison Fellowship Ministries as one of four national partners for a $22.5 million workplace reentry program for ex-offenders.[44] Former PFM officials also lead Dare Mighty Things, which received a $2.2 million grant by the Department of Health and Human Services and now serves as a clearinghouse for faith-based and community groups applying for federal money.[45]

By joining an InnerChange program, inmates can transfer from more dangerous parts of the prison system. They have access to privileges such as keys to their own cells, private bathrooms, big-screen televisions, and family visits. Completing the InnerChange program usually means that inmates have an easier time with the parole board, and graduates are guaranteed a space in work-release programs as well as help finding a job and housing. InnerChange offers substance-abuse treatment and free computer training. PFM has received an influx of government money while most prisons have eliminated education, addiction, and job-training programs. One man who is not in InnerChange, noted that "the Christians do lots of stuff the state used to do, like vocational programs, but now they're only for believers."[46] The program represents the cutting edge of the faith-based initiatives, which seek to have religious groups take over social services once provided by state and federal agencies and, in so doing, fulfill two goals: bringing more people to Christ and shrinking government. As Colson elaborated in a radio interview, "What's at stake is not just a prison program, but how we deal with social problems in our country. Do we do it through grassroots organizations or big government? We know what works."

Funding for the conservative Christian opposition to same-sex marriage does not come from the state but through Christian Right organizations like Focus on the Family that raise money through membership fees, donations, royalties, and subscriptions.[47] However, Focus's campaign against same-sex marriage aligns it with arguments against social spending and for privatization. In his book *Marriage Under Fire*, Dobson argues that legalizing gay marriage will open up the economic benefits of marriage to everyone. In one passage he cautions that the "brave new world" of same-sex marriage would bankrupt government and businesses. "Could your business afford health-care benefits for 5 or 9 people in a group marriage? In fact . . . what would keep two heterosexual single moms—or even six of them—from 'marrying' simply so they can receive family health, tax and social security benefits together? The increased cost to business and government would be crippling."[48] He also writes,

> The health care system will stagger and perhaps collapse. This could be the straw that breaks the back of the insurance industry in Western nations, as millions of new dependents become eligible for coverage. Every HIV-positive patient needs only to find a partner to receive the same coverage as offered to an employee. . . . It may not be profitable for companies to stay in business.

The implication is that nonheterosexual families are a parasitical drain on social services and examples of big-government spending gone awry.

Ex-gay spokesperson Randy Thomas uses his testimony to support Dobson's arguments. "The (health-care costs) of homosexual males and homosexual females, when it comes to sexually transmitted diseases and other issues, run a lot higher in those communities." According to him, "to mandate spousal health coverage for those communities is to mandate higher bills for us all."[49] The implication is that American families will be unable to afford health insurance because the price of premiums will skyrocket due to the "lifestyles" of gay and lesbian married couples. Tony Perkins, head of the Family Research Council, which works closely with Focus on the Family, writes that "we only have so (many) resources and if we're going to say "It's OK to live in a risky lifestyle, we're going to take care of you,' somebody, somewhere is not going to get the health care coverage that they need."[50] These arguments about the imagined financial stress on health care provision become one way of endorsing a view that alternative marital arrangements are economically detrimental. "Society benefits from the well-being of marriage; nearly every dollar spent by our government on social welfare is in reaction to a marriage breaking down or failing to form," writes Glen Stanton.[51]

Awakening the Grass Roots

PFM, the ex-gay movement, and Focus on the Family have created significant grassroots networks of state and local affiliates, ministries, and prison programs. Prison Fellowship has a presence in the majority of prisons in the United States, in addition to an international presence in eighty-eight countries. PFM boasts that more than 150,000 prisoners participate in its Bible studies and seminars each year, while its newspaper is the most widely distributed prison newspaper in the United States. For Focus on the Family, the goal of the Love Won Out conferences is to establish referral networks between the churches and ex-gay ministries, and to help churches create their own ex-gay support groups. With local churches as the infrastructure for activism, the conservative Christian marriage movement has nurtured political participation from church pastors and their congregations. Dobson believes that marriage is the issue that will awaken the grass roots. He writes, "Evil has a way of overreaching, and that appears to have happened regarding the blatant and lawless assault on marriage and biblical morality. In a strange way, the threats we are facing today could be the vehicle for a revitalized church. It is an exciting thing to watch."[52]

Dobson and Colson utilize testimonies to promote the idea that their organizations are grassroots in nature, but the policy ideas and concepts about marriage, sexuality, imprisonment, and faith-based services stem directly from national conservative Christian organizations. Colson claims the program is concerned only with the transformation of prisoners, but his connections to prominent Christian Right leaders and officials in the Bush administration provide his organization with resources that filter down to the local level. Mayday for Marriage and Florida 4 Marriage characterize themselves as citizen driven, reflecting the beliefs of ordinary people, but their policy stances are generated by national Christian Right organizations and Dobson's books and articles. The national coordination by Focus on the Family binds the grass roots to the national conservative Christian movement.

John Stemberger is the chairman of Florida 4 Marriage and the president of the Florida Family Policy Council (FFPC), a state affiliate of Focus on the Family. The Florida Family Policy Council is a local node in the wider network of conservative Christian organizations. The Florida Family Policy Council seeks to educate and inform Florida citizens about public policy issues "that would impact marriage, children and families. . . . through public policy education, issue research and grassroots advocacy." The FFPC's policy reports and materials about marriage and families are culled directly from the policy specialists at Focus on the Family. These documents are in turn vital training materials for marriage activists. As a result, there is a uniformity of conservative Christian arguments against same-sex marriage from the national to the local level.

Conservative Christian political campaigns against same-sex marriage and for evangelical prison programs both mobilize around the issue of religious freedom and the claim that they are initiated at the state and local level. Using testimonies enables them to evade the charge that these are national campaigns aimed at imposing conservative Christian morality on the state.

The version of faith that Dobson and Colson espouse fuses a corporate vision of social provision with evangelical ideals of personal transformation.

This model of testimonial politics exempts the government from social welfare spending, placing the onus on individuals to remold themselves into particular kinds of Christian citizens. In the case of PFM, the state foots the bill for an evangelical prison program designed to transform individuals into Christians as a form of rehabilitation. Colson argues that these programs will save the state money in the long term because they will reduce recidivism and the cost of long-term sentences. For Focus on the Family, the idea behind the anti-same-sex marriage movement is that limiting the economic benefits of marriage to heterosexuals will also keep the state from having to support multiple household arrangement that could lead to bankruptcy. PFM and Focus on the Family have made effective political uses of testimony to challenge the values of the state and to convince constituents that individual transformation, not government programs, is the most effective way to address marriage, sexuality, and imprisonment.

Testimony as a political strategy is risky because proclaiming a born-again identity can backfire. In November 2006, Ted Haggard, pastor of the 14,000-member New Life Church, president of the National Association of Evangelicals, and close advisor to the Bush administration became the subject of a major scandal when a Colorado man reported that Haggard had paid him for sex and drugs. After initial denials and in the face of mounting evidence, Haggard resigned. In a letter read aloud at New Life, Haggard confessed to being a "deceiver and liar" who had waged a lifelong struggle with "repulsive" homosexual urges. James Dobson immediately announced that he and a team of two pastors would be overseeing Haggard's "therapeutic restoration" based on the principles of the ex-gay movement. Both Haggard and Dobson had campaigned widely against gay rights. Most recently, they had been involved in an anti-gay marriage initiative in Colorado. Three months after Haggard's letter and resignation, the press reported that Haggard was "cured" of homosexuality and "no longer gay."

Haggard has yet to testify, but his narrative could become a powerful tool in the testimonial politics of the Christian Right. As a disgraced public figure who may emerge transformed and purified, Haggard stands as yet another example for conservative Christians of how giving one's life to Jesus supersedes all other modes of transformation. Whether Dobson or Colson's conservative Christian version of testimonial politics and morality will continue to predominate within American evangelicalism is debatable, especially with the death of Jerry Falwell in May 2007. Increasingly, highly influential evangelical leaders such as Rick Warren of Saddleback Church and Joel Hunter of Northland Church, with thousands of evangelicals in their megachurches, have shifted the emphasis of evangelical politics. They proclaim torture, war, global health, and climate change as central moral issues for Christians. These divisions have splintered the conservative evangelical coalition that has been dominant during the Bush administration. The change of direction may also damage the effectiveness of conservative Christian testimonial politics in which the specter of crime and same-sex marriage hold sway.

Notes

Many thanks to Melani McAlister and R. Marie Griffith for their insightful comments on this essay.

1. Charles Colson, "The God Pod: Moral Reform at Jester II," *Breakpoint Commentary #71021*, October 21, 1997.
2. Jeff Peck, "Getting Away Clean: The Life and Times of a Transformed Cocaine Kingpin," *Prison Fellowship Ministries, Jubilee Extra*, June 1991, 1.
3. A copy of this advertisement and Alan Chambers's testimony are available on the Exodus International Web site at *http://www.exodus.to/pdf/AlanLeslieAd.pdf* (accessed June 13, 2007).
4. For historical perspectives on the emergence of the Christian Right, see Clyde Wilcox, *God's Warriors: The Christian Right in Twentieth-Century America* (Baltimore: Johns Hopkins University Press, 1992); Mark Shibley, *Resurgent Evangelicalism in the United States: Mapping Cultural Change since 1970* (Columbia: University of South Carolina Press, 1996); and Matthew Moen, *The Transformation of the Christian Right* (Tuscaloosa: University of Alabama Press, 1992). Other work in sociology and political science that examines the Christian Right as a social movement and political mobilization includes Sara Diamond, *Roads to Dominion: Right-Wing Movements and Political Power in the United States* (New York: *Guilford Press*, 1995); Robert C. Liebman, *The New Christian Right: Mobilization and Legitimation*; Steve Bruce, *The Rise and Fall of the New Christian Right* (Oxford: Clarendon, 1988); Jerome Himmelstein, *To the Right: The Transformation of American Conservatism* (Berkeley: University of California Press, 1990). Work that explicitly connects the Christian Right to American evangelicalism includes Jose Casanova, "Evangelical Protestantism: From Civil Religion to Fundamentalist Sect to New Christian Right," in *Public Religions in the Modern World* (Chicago: University of Chicago Press, 1994), 135–66; and Michael Lienesch, *Redeeming America: Piety and Politics in the New Christian Right* (Chapel Hill: University of North Carolina, 1993).
5. Becky Beane, "The Road Home: The Father's Love—and the Helping Hands of PF Volunteers—Puts Ex-prisoner on the Right Path," *Prison Fellowship Ministries, Jubilee Extra*, 1998, 1.
6. On the history of evangelicalism, see Nathan Hatch, *The Democratization of American Religion* (New Haven, Conn.: Yale University Press, 1989); Christine Heyrman, *Southern Cross: The Beginnings of the Bible Belt* (New York: Alfred A. Knopf, 1997); Laurence Moore, *Religious Outsiders and the Making of America* (New York: Oxford University Press, 1986); Whitney Cross, *The Burned-over District: The Social and Intellectual History of Enthusiastic Religion in Western New York, 1800–1850.* (Ithaca, N.Y.: Cornell University Press, 1950); Jose Casanova, "Evangelical Protestantism"; Randy Balmer, *Blessed Assurance: A History of Evangelicalism in America* (Boston: Beacon Press, 1999); Mark Noll, *The Rise of Evangelicalism: The Age of Edwards, Whitefield and the Wesleys* (Downers Grove, Ill.: InterVarsity Press, 2004); Ferenc Szasz Morton, *The Divided Mind of Protestant America, 1880–1930* (Tuscaloosa: University of Alabama Press, 1982); Ernest R. Sandeen, *The Roots of Fundamentalism: British and American Millenarianism 1800–1930* (Chicago: University of Chicago Press, 1970); Betty DeBerg, *Ungodly Women: Gender and the First Wave of American Fundamentalism* (Minneapolis: University of Minnesota Press, 1990); and Margaret Bendroth, *Fundamentalism and Gender: 1875 to the Present* (New Haven, Conn.: Yale University Press, 1996). For analyses of contemporary evangelicalism and

the emergence of nondenominational conservative Christian congregations, see Christian Smith, *American Evangelicalism: Embattled or Thriving* (Chicago: University of Chicago Press, 1998); Don Miller, *Reinventing American Protestantism: Christianity in the New Millennium* (Berkeley: University of California Press, 1997); Christian Smith, *Christian America? What Evangelicals Really Want* (Berkeley: University of California Press, 2002); Heather Hendershot, *Shaking the World for Jesus: Media and Conservative Evangelical Culture* (Chicago: University of Chicago Press, 2004); and Nancy Ammerman, *Bible Believers: Fundamentalists in the Modern World* (New Brunswick, N.J.: Rutgers University Press, 1987). Other recent ethnographies, such as Brenda Brasher's *Godly Women: Fundamentalism and Female Power* (New Brunswick, N.J.: Rutgers University Press, 1998), and R. Marie Griffith's *God's Daughters: Evangelical Women and the Power of Submission* (Berkeley: University of California Press, 1997), analyze gender and power within specific groups that define themselves as fundamentalist and/or evangelical. It is important to note that while the categories of evangelicalism and fundamentalism tend to be used widely, many people who might fit into these religious belief systems would describe themselves simply as Christians. Some will define themselves as fundamentalist when their other options are to call themselves mainline, liberal, or other.

7. Susan Harding, *The Book of Jerry Falwell: Fundamentalist Language and Politics* (Princeton, N.J.: Princeton University Press, 2001), 37.

8. Robyn R. Warhol and Helena Michie, "Twelve-Step Teleology: Narratives of Recovery/Recovery as Narrative," in *Getting a Life: Everyday Uses of Autobiography*, ed. Sidonie Smith and Julia Watson (Ann Arbor: University of Michigan Press, 2002), 329.

9. Harding, *The Book of Jerry Falwell*, 37.

10. Bella Brodski, "Testimony," in *The Encyclopedia of Life Writing*, ed. Margaretta Jolly (London: Fitzroy-Dearborn, 2001).

11. For a more detailed analysis of the ex-gay movement, see Tanya Erzen, *Straight to Jesus: Sexual and Christian Conversions in the Ex-Gay Movement* (Berkeley: University of California Press, 2006).

12. In *Christianity, Social Tolerance, and Homosexuality: Gay People in Western Europe from the Beginning of the Christian Era to the Fourteenth Century* (Chicago: University of Chicago Press, 1980), John Boswell discusses the biblical arguments that conservative Christians use to condemn homosexuality. See also Kathy Rudy, *Sex and the Church: Gender, Homosexuality, and the Transformation of Christian Ethics* (Boston: Beacon Press, 1997). For recent ethnographic work that addresses the conflict between sexual identities and religious beliefs within contemporary Christianity, see Dawne Moon, *God, Sex, and Politics: Homosexuality and Everyday Theologies* (Chicago: University of Chicago Press, 2004), and Melissa Wilcox, *Coming Out in Christianity: Religion, Identity, and Community* (Bloomington: Indiana University Press, 2003). Mel White's memoir, *Stranger at the Gate: To Be Gay and Christian in America* (New York: Penguin Books, 1995), details his struggle with his sexuality and identity as a Christian.

13. Barbara Swallow, *Exodus International Newsletter*, July 2000. Swallow published a book-length testimony of her personal story titled, *Free Indeed: One Woman's Victory Over Lesbianism* (Seattle: Exodus International North America, 2000).

14. See http://www.exodus.to/marriage.shtml (accessed June 15, 2007).

15. Ibid.

16. IFI Freedom Initiative, Program Details, *http://www.ifiprison.org/generic.asp?ID=971* (accessed August 22, 2006).

17. Prison Fellowship Ministries mission statement, *http://www.prisonfellowship.org/* (accessed August 5, 2006).

18. Ibid.

19. The two quotes are from Peck, "Getting Away Clean."

20. Janet Jakobsen and Ann Pellegrini, *Love the Sin: Sexual Regulation and the Limits of Tolerance* (New York: New York University Press, 2003).

21. Before Focus, Dr. Dobson was best known as an advocate of traditional discipline. His book *Dare to Discipline* advocated corporal punishment for children. In 1991, Focus relocated to an eighty-three-acre campus in Colorado Springs as a nonprofit organization. Previously connected to the Family Research Council (FRC), headed by Gary Bauer, Focus and FRC separated officially in 1992 so that FRC could pursue lobbying activities and not risk the tax-exempt status of the wider organization. In this way, Dobson has been able to pursue political change in Washington while running the culture industry of Focus.

22. James Dobson, *Marriage Under Fire: Why We Must Win This Battle* (Sisters, Ore.: Multnomah Publishers, 2004).
23. James Dobson, "Family News from Dr. James Dobson," *Focus on the Family Newsletter*, June 1998.
24. Ibid.
25. Amendment 2 was a 1992 Colorado ballot initiative that sought to amend the Colorado constitution in order to legally forbid the state, its municipalities, school districts, or agencies from guaranteeing nondiscrimination to those with "homosexual, lesbian, or bisexual orientation." The amendment passed in November 1992, but was subsequently overturned by the U.S. Supreme Court.
26. David Kirkpatrick, "Christian Right Labors to Find '08 Candidate," *New York Times*, February 25, 2007.
27. "Watergate Revisited: The Key Players," *Washington Post*, June 2005 http://www.washingtonpost.com/wp-srv/onpolitics/watergate/charles.html (accessed August 31, 2006).
28. Charles Colson, "Without Anti-Gay Marriage Amendment, 'Feral Children' Flood Prisons," *Right Wing Watch: A Regular Look at the Worst from the Right Brought to You by PFAW Foundation*, June 6, 2006, http://www.pfaw.org/pfaw/general/default.aspx?oid=19453 (accessed August 5, 2006).
29. According to Focus, Dobson's syndicated radio broadcast is heard on more than 3,000 radio facilities in North America and in nine languages on approximately 2,300 facilities in more than ninety-eight countries. By the mid-1990s, Focus had an annual budget of over $100 million. See Sara Diamond, *Not by Politics Alone: The Enduring Influence of the Christian Right* (New York: Guilford Press, 1998), 30–36. For a comprehensive recent examination of the centrality of Dobson and Focus on the Family to American politics, see Dan Gilgoff, *The Jesus Machine: How James Dobson, Focus on the Family, and Evangelical America Are Winning the Culture War* (New York: St. Martin's Press, 2007). For more information, see the Focus on the Family Web site at www.family.org.
30. See http://www.maydayformarriage.com/initiative.aspx (accessed June 15, 2007).
31. Ibid.
32. Florida 4 Marriage press release, February 1, 2006, at http://florida4marriage.org/ (accessed May 28, 2006).
33. Exodus International Press Release, "Ex-Gay Organization Joins Hundreds of Clergy, Business & Political Leaders in Endorsing the Florida Marriage Protection Amendment," January 6, 2006, http://www.exodus.to/news_2006_0106PR.shtml (accessed June 23, 2006).
34. Glenn Stanton, "Is Marriage in Jeopardy?" *CitizenLink: Focus on Social Issues, Focus on the Family*, August 27, 2003, http://www.family.org/cforum/pdfs/fosi/marriage/is_marriage_in_jeopardy.pdf (accessed March 18, 2006).
35. Ibid.
36. On May 30, 2006, and for three consecutive days, Focus on the Family sponsored a three-part broadcast Web and radio conference with African American pastors to discuss the issue of gay marriage. The program was titled "Marriage and the African-American Church." During the radio show, Dobson stated: "As you all very well know marriage is under vicious attack, now I think from the forces of hell itself." http://www.family.org/fmedia/broadcast/a0040243.cfm (accessed May 30, 2006).
37. Rob Boston, "Victory in Iowa," Americans United for the Separation of Church and State, http://www.au.org/site/News2?page=NewsArticle&id=8313&abbr=cs_ (accessed August 23, 2006).
38. Ron Humphrey, "Man on the Run: A Former Fugitive Now Helps Others Find Their Way," *Prison Fellowship Ministries, Jubilee Extra*, http://www.prisonfellowship.org/articleslist.asp?ID=21 (accessed August 15, 2006).
39. The study can be found at www.prisonfellowship.org/media/ifi/Docs/crrucs_innerchange.pdf (accessed July 18, 2006).
40. Mark A. R. Kleinman, "Faith Based Fudging," *Slate Magazine*, August 5, 2003, http://www.slate.com/id/2086617 (accessed August 28, 2006).
41. Mark Early, "InnerChange Freedom Initiative and the Ruling," http://www.pfm.org/generic.asp?1D=2416 (accessed January 2007).
42. Chuck Colson, "The Wrong Kind of Prison Fellowship," *Breakpoint Commentary*, October 18, 2005.
43. For information on the evolution of the faith and character model, see http://www.dc.state.fl.us/facilities/region2/255.html. I am currently working on a book about the Florida faith and character prisons titled *Disciplining Bodies and Souls: Creating Sacred Identities in the Faith-Based Prison*.

44. Esther Kaplan, "Follow the Money," *The Nation*, November 1, 2004, 1.
45. Ibid.
46. Samantha Shapiro, "Jails for Jesus," *Mother Jones*, November/December 2003.
47. For a breakdown of Focus on the Family's expenses and revenue, see *http://charityreports.give.org/Public/Report.aspx?CharityID=941* (accessed June 15, 2007).
48. Dobson, *Marriage Under Fire*, 23.
49. Quoted in Keith Peters, "Same-Sex 'Marriage' to Drive Up Health-Care Costs" *Family News in Focus: Family News in Policy and Culture*, Focus on the Family publication, April 16, 2004, 2.
50. Ibid.
51. Stanton, "Is Marriage in Jeopardy?"
52. Dobson, *Marriage Under Fire*, 23.

"It Will Change the World If Everybody Reads This Book": New Thought Religion in Oprah's Book Club

Trysh Travis

> You can't create a popular political movement in such social formations without getting into the religious question, because it is the arena in which this community has come to a certain kind of consciousness. This consciousness may be limited; it may not have successfully helped them to remake their history. But they have been "languaged" by the discourse of popular religion.
>
> —Stuart Hall, "On Postmodernism and Articulation"

Oprah Winfrey announced the formation of her eponymous book club in the fall of 1996 with the statement that she "wanted to get the country reading again."[1] Inadvertently, perhaps, she invoked an idealized past in which a highly literate citizenry enjoyed the pleasures of the imagination while simultaneously creating a robust and vibrant public sphere. That invocation has set the tone for much of the scholarship that has followed in the book club's wake—scholarship that has been almost exclusively laudatory, and that has praised the club as a triumph of what we might call the cultural politics of progressive multiculturalism.[2] That politics retains the ideals of the classical public sphere, but undoes its traditional elitism to include—indeed, to privilege—the voices of those who have been historically excluded from and silenced by its discursive modes: women, children, racial and ethnic minorities, the differently abled, the sexually transgressive, and "others" of all stripes. Seen through this lens, Oprah's Book Club turns what Brian Street has called "ideological literacy" into a form of empowerment that—in this articulation, anyway—serves the cause of cultural democracy by challenging existing hierarchies and giving voice to issues that are salient to the historically disempowered but still deemed out of bounds in traditional politics.[3]

In this essay I argue that observers of the club have managed to achieve this interpretation by repressing two essential dimensions of Winfrey's enterprise. The first is the hypercapitalist nature of her undertaking. By "hypercapitalist" I mean, following Baudrillard, a cultural logic that aims both to commodify all areas of life and all interpersonal transactions and to efface the intentionality of those processes and thus render them "natural."[4] Winfrey, the CEO and sole owner of Harpo Entertainment, Inc., a multimillion-dollar global media corporation, operates from within a hypercapitalist frame of reference. Obviously, she operates from within other frames of reference as well, but the political economy underpinning her endeavors cannot simply be bracketed out of the analysis. As Peter Golding and Graham Murdock have argued, "the different ways of financing and organizing cultural production have traceable consequences for the range of discourses and representations in the public domain," and the commercial dimension of Oprah's Book Club, as we shall see, is fundamental, not incidental, to its workings.[5]

The second dimension repressed in most accounts of the book club is its religiosity. By "religiosity" I mean, following Paul Tillich, an orientation toward "ultimate concerns" that, while connected to the workings of the material, day-to-day world, also transcends it.[6] Scholars writing about Winfrey frequently note her religiosity, typically folding it into discussions of her working-class, African American roots. African American religious tradition has played a key role in Winfrey's life—she was brought up a Baptist and attended all-day Sunday school, and she credits the techniques she mastered in the Baptist Training Union for much of her performance style. "Whenever she is feeling down," one biographer explains, "Oprah reaches for her Bible and cues up Aretha Franklin's 'Amazing Grace' on the stereo." But Winfrey has also distanced herself from what she calls "the very narrow view" of religious faith that she grew up with, one in which the image of "God [as] a man with a long white beard and a black book checking off the things you can do" was intended to "[keep] you under control."[7] Instead she has embraced—and used her media outlets to showcase—a hybrid faith, one whose roots, perhaps, lie in the black church, but whose distinctive and quite visible flowers most closely resemble the New Thought religions that developed during the late nineteenth and early twentieth centuries.[8] As critics writing from within a variety of traditional denominations have been quick to point out, New Thought principles—mysticism, universalism, idealism, and the belief in the power of thought to alter material reality—feature prominently across the various iterations of Harpo Entertainment.[9] More important, Winfrey explicitly credits her phenomenal success to her faith in those principles, and invites her legions of fans to join her in the rewards of that faith: "I believe in the God force that lives inside all of us," she explains, "and once you tap into that, you can do anything."[10] More so even than the economic dimension of her undertakings, the presence of this faith must be acknowledged and taken seriously if we hope to gain a real understanding of Winfrey's apparently limitless appeal and of her book club's popularity in its historical moment.

As an attempt at that understanding, then, this essay examines the presence of New Thought ideals within Oprah's Book Club. I look first at the beliefs and practices of New Thought religions, which, despite (or perhaps because of) their enormous popularity at the turn of the nineteenth century and resurgent presence since the 1960s, have largely been written out of twentieth century cultural and intellectual history.[11] A complete reckoning with the enormously complicated and varied body of New Thought theology is beyond the scope of this short article; instead, I offer an overview of New Thought's distinctive idealism sufficient to illuminate the larger tradition that Oprah Winfrey's public persona and media products—including the book club—extend.

Second, to make more specific my claims about the hypercapitalist nature of Winfrey's enterprise, I explore the way that New Thought ideas figured into what marketing experts call "Brand Oprah," the commoditized version of Winfrey's personality and worldview. In 1994, Winfrey made a pronounced and quite conscious turn toward the spiritual—just at the time that she also began to pursue a new and more affluent audience through nonbroadcast media. Whatever else it may have been for Winfrey, New Thought religiosity was a successful strategy for "brand enhancement," distinguishing her from her competitors and unifying her rapidly diversifying collection of media properties. The spiritually enhanced message of Brand Oprah was disseminated through a variety of programming innovations; the most successful of them was the book club.

Turning to talk about the club itself, the third part of this essay explores the ways in which it functioned as a tutorial in New Thought idealism. Following Winfrey's lead, guests on the book club episodes of *The Oprah Winfrey Show* learned to treat the book as an enchanted object, the product of forces greater than the author him- or herself. Relying on New Thought's assumption that the power of the mind can overcome socially constructed reality, the club framed reading as an imaginative exercise capable of transforming the world. As Winfrey's champions repeatedly point out, book club discussions routinely touched on some of the most highly charged political issues in the United States today—poverty, violence against women, and persistent racism, to name just a few. The conversations that resulted, as Kimberly Chabot Davis has argued, may have been "stepping stones for individuals to move towards more public-oriented" and recognizably "political" engagement.[12] But in response to those issues, the club promoted heightened consciousness and flows of affect, interventions in a realm that, while linked to the social, also transcends and supersedes it.

By way of conclusion, I speculate briefly about the politics of such transcendence. Millions of Americans are, to use Stuart Hall's term, "languaged"—given a sense of their identity and purpose—by popular religious and spiritual discourses retailed to them through consumer outlets such as Harpo Entertainment—entities only tangentially related to church-based religions. As John Frow has noted, few members of the professoriate find themselves "languaged" in this way, and as a result, academic attempts to develop adequate schemas or vocabularies through which to analyze such discourses remain relatively underdeveloped.[13] But the baby-boom generation, as Wade Clark Roof has argued, is dominated by such unchurched "seekers"—a 2005 poll found that 79 percent of people in the United States identify themselves as "spiritual," whereas only 64 percent claimed to be "religious."[14] Thus, glossing over the workings of this faith—in the lives of millions of individual believers as well as within the culture at large—compromises our ability to make meaningful political engagements with and/or interventions in the world outside the academy. Oprah Winfrey means it literally when she says "it will change the world if everybody reads this book."[15] When widely held, such beliefs have powerful consequences for more traditional politics—liberal or radical. As a result, left-leaning academics (and I include myself in that category) need to reckon seriously with them.

Historicizing "Thought-as-Power"

Despite the fact that Sydney Ahlstrom described New Thought in 1972 as "a major force in American religion," it remains relatively obscure to most scholars of twentieth-century U.S. popular culture not trained in religious history.[16] To date, the treatment of New Thought most likely to be read by cultural and intellectual historians and by literary and cultural studies scholars remains T. J. Jackson Lears's 1981 *No Place of Grace*, which lumps the various strains of New Thought together under the sobriquet of "mind cure" and treats them as a subset of a wide-ranging antimodern "popular occultism."[17] In Lears's telling, the mind cure mystics of the late nineteenth and early twentieth centuries shilled an "overtly . . . therapeutic" (176) version of the *mysterium tremendum*, one premised on "platitudinous vagueness" (173) and "flatulent pieties" (58). Other scholars have shared Lears's views but not his knack for the cutting phrase; the rhetorical flair of *No Place of Grace*, combined with its intellectual heft, helped to entomb New Thought within American studies' conceptual graveyard.

That internment is unfortunate, because Ahlstrom's assessment of New Thought's importance—not only to those who identify as followers of a particular sect, but also to the broader U.S. culture—is correct. In his otherwise unsympathetic gloss on New Thought ideas, Richard Huber grudgingly admits they were widely held: in the early twentieth century, nearly four hundred centers and churches disseminated New Thought ideas to around a million adherents across the country. By the Second World War, "leaders of the movement were estimating that from fifteen to twenty million people in America were being influenced by New Thought teachings."[18] Beryl Satter—whose insightful *Each Mind a Kingdom* offers a necessary corrective to Lears's dismissal of New Thought—notes that its influence has only grown since then, thanks to a variety of out-of-church regimes based on some of its key principles. Norman Vincent Peale's *The Power of Positive Thinking*, the teachings of 12-step groups like Alcoholics Anonymous, "self-actualization" corporations such as EST, Lifespring, and Silva Mind Control—all of these, Satter argues, are elaborations of New Thought's central message, which she identifies as "thought-as-power."[19]

It may be easier, however, to acknowledge New Thought's importance than to say with precision what it entails. Originating alongside Transcendentalism in antebellum New England, New Thought was informed by first-century Christian mysticism and Eastern religious traditions as well as new theories of (among other things) electricity, neurology, and nutrition. Its theology is idealist, syncretic, hybrid—and frustratingly inconsistent. For example, Satter, focusing on one stream of doctrine, explains that for believers "the mental or spiritual world was the true reality," and the "material world of daily life, the world of 'matter,' was merely a secondary creation of the mind."[20] The range of New Thought beliefs, however, was such that Marie Griffith, looking at a slightly different constellation of believers, can accurately claim that "the *body* was the real source of might, site of potential transformation, and basis for revealing the inner truth about the human self."[21] The common assumption these variations share looks something like this: although the human body is "matter," human essence is the work of God and therefore humanity itself is divine. Religious practice is a means to free up that divinity, either by reaffirming the transience and irrelevance of "matter," or by disciplining it through various mental and physical regimes.

This idealism explains what was "new" in New Thought: unlike traditional creedal religions that "dwelt on sin [and] emphasized . . . darkness and misery . . . distress and suffering," its proponents argued that humanity "is by divine purpose, by birth, and [by] true human inheritance, free. [Man] must come forth and 'claim his freedom,' the true freedom of his inner or spiritual nature. He should take his clue from the ideal, not from the actualities of his natural existence."[22] Believers develop the ability to transcend "the actualities of . . . natural existence" through visualization, affirmation, and prayer (sometimes accompanied by diet and exercise schemes). Together these practices slough off the dross of "matter" and correctly align the faithful with the divinely ordained order of things, bringing health and harmony, peace and abundance into their lives.

The "thought-as-power" dynamic that forms the taproot of New Thought originated and manifests itself most sharply in the belief in mental healing. New Thought's founder, Maine clockmaker Phineas Parkhurst Quimby (1802–1866), advocated what he called "Christ Science"—basically the idea that illness results from false or erroneous beliefs. The healer's role (following Christ's example) is to help purge the sufferer of those beliefs, with the result that the chimera of illness drops away.[23] Quimby's insights into the power of mind over matter were complemented by the "mental medicine" theories of his disciple Warren Felt Evans (1817–1889). To help strengthen belief, Evans advocated the cultivation of "the divine within"—the spark of the Godhead that dwells in each human and connects her to God—through guided meditation and ritualized affirmations. He deliberately deployed these incantatory, antirational practices to counter skepticism and argument, which he saw as the dominant discourses of worldly society and the source of much of the mental anguish that manifested itself as bodily sickness.[24] Proper nurturance of the divine within required mental discipline but also mental relaxation; it was both a labor of faith and a result of faith. Living these paradoxical conditions would result in a victory over corporeal infirmity.

The elaboration of Quimby and Evans's theories into "religions"—institutions with explicit theologies and doctrines, canons of scripture and standards for worship, structures for ordination and knowledge transmission—was undertaken by a host of middle-class white women late in the nineteenth century.[25] Many became believers in New Thought after lives of chronic illness, and they carried Quimby's "Christ Science" to others so afflicted through a host of small and flexible denominations—Divine Science, Religious Science, Science of Being, the Homes of Truth, and the Unity Church, to name just a few. After a series of false starts and partial alliances, a variety of these sects came together in 1916 to form the International New Thought Alliance (INTA). The group's 1919 "Declaration of Principles" distills the ideas of various thinkers into one coherent statement, which deserves to be quoted at length.

We affirm the freedom of each soul as to choice and as to belief. . . . The essence of New Thought is Truth, and each individual must be loyal to the Truth he sees. The windows of his soul must be kept open at each moment for the higher light, and his mind must be always hospitable to each new inspiration.

> We affirm the good. This is supreme, universal and everlasting. Man is made in the image of the good, and evil and pain are the tests and correctives that appear when his thought does not reflect the full glory of this image. . . .
> We affirm health, which is man's divine inheritance. . . .
> We affirm the divine supply . . . Within us are unused resources of energy and power. He who lives with his whole being, and thus expresses fullness shall reap fullness in return. . . .
> We affirm the teaching of Christ that the Kingdom of Heaven is within us, that we are one with the Father. . . .
> We affirm these things, not as a profession, but practice . . . not in words alone, but in the innermost thoughts of the heart expressed in living the life.[26]

This multidimensional creed inserts New Thought religions firmly into the long tradition of dissenting denominations and sects—Pietist Christians, Quakers, Swedenborgians, Sufis, Bahá'ís—who reject doctrine and theology in favor of "higher light . . . inspiration" and who believe that "evil and pain" are mere shadows that will fade once the "unused resources of energy and power" associated with divinity and available to all believers are brought to bear upon them.

New Thought has remained something of an unwanted stepchild to these august creeds, however, thanks to its association with middle-class white women and its enmeshment within consumer capitalism. As Satter demonstrates, many early New Thought leaders identified with the postbellum woman movement, and advocated for temperance, suffrage, and public health reform. In doing so, they exposed themselves to masculine ridicule—in their own day as well as in subsequent generations: Lears's condemnation of "mind-cure mystics" can be read as a centennial edition of Henry James's screed against the "somnabulists . . . trance-speakers [and] lady-editors of newspapers advocating new religions" in 1885's *The Bostonians.*[27]

The stigma attached to New Thought only increased when, around the turn of the century, most "tracts shifted their focus from the attainment of health through denial of desire to the attainment of prosperity through the expression of desire."[28] By the 1930s, "thought-as-power" seemed to be synonymous with nothing so much as profane capitalist accumulation, as evidenced by the popularity of books like Napoleon Hill's 1937 best seller *Think and Grow Rich*. As Leigh Schmidt has pointed out in his nuanced re-reading of the ministry of Ralph Waldo Trine, for many New Thought mystics "capitalist materialism [could seem] as misbegotten as scientific materialism" and devotion could take an ascetic, rather than acquisitive form.[29] The heterogeneity of New Thought religiosity, however, has proved less interesting to most scholars than the suspicious affinity between the logic of "the divine supply" and the political economy of consumer capitalism. The perception of New Thought theories, practices, and institutions as pathologically bourgeois and feminized has helped to assure their marginalization within the academy. But the very aspects of New Thought that have caused scholars focused on the contestatory dimensions of U.S. popular culture to overlook it, however, have also made it easy for brokers of popular women's culture—such as Oprah Winfrey—to appropriate.

Enhancing and Extending "Brand Oprah"

As Jane Shattuc has observed, critics attempting to analyze Oprah Winfrey face unique challenges. Her success has been built on her "girlfriend to the world" persona, a performance of "trust, human-to-human connectedness, and realness" buttressed by a relentless public relations machine.[30] What marketing experts call "Brand Oprah" anchors a multimillion-dollar business, and as a result, Shattuc argues, "all we know and see of [Winfrey] is subject to corporate decision making. . . . There [is] no authentic Winfrey; there [is] the image of Winfrey's authenticity."[31] Fans, journalists, and a significant portion of the scholarly community have found that image a very convincing one. This is nowhere more evident than in writing about Oprah's Book Club, which has typically treated it as the spontaneous outgrowth of Winfrey's well-known love of reading.

The epistemological conundrum that Shattuc identifies not withstanding, Winfrey's enthusiasm for books seems genuine. But we need nevertheless to acknowledge that the club was a strategic and commercial endeavor, part of a larger marketing campaign that Harpo Entertainment undertook during the mid-1990s. The goal of that campaign was both "brand enhancement"—the addition of perceived value to the brand—and "brand extension"—the creation of new products retailed under it.[32] These were intended to help Harpo evolve from a television production company that was (save for the phenomenal success of *The Oprah Winfrey Show* itself) relatively undistinguished into what then-CEO Jeff Jacobs called "an intellectual property company" that "'multi-purpos[es] our content' for various outlets" and thereby delivers an older, more affluent audience to its advertisers.[33] New Thought religiosity provided the enhancement for Brand Oprah; the book club was one of several strategies for its extension.

Winfrey has never shied away from religious talk. During the early part of her career she spoke routinely to interviewers about her churchgoing life, favorite Bible passages, habits of prayer and meditation, and abiding personal faith. "There's only one way I've been able to survive being raped, molested, whipped, rejected . . . being fat and unpopular," she told *McCall's* in 1987. "As corny as it sounds, my faith in God got me through."[34] Her allegiance to traditional Christianity coexisted easily alongside an interest in more esoteric spiritualism: Barbara Grizutti Harrison ranted at length against what she called Winfrey's "New Age" pretensions in the *New York Times Magazine* in 1989. From the time her show went national in 1986 until the early 1990s, eclectic spirituality was part of its heterogeneous programming, rubbing shoulders with relationship and beauty advice, self-help and home-making tips, interviews with celebrities and trauma victims, and, occasionally, explorations of social issues. The promiscuous mixing of topics; animated conversations among audience members, host, and invited guests; and Winfrey's own exuberant performance style created a show that many scholars celebrated for its willingness to disrupt the polite conventions of broadcast television.[35]

Winfrey began to refine this boisterous mode, however, in the wake of what critics have called "the talk show wars" of the early 1990s.[36] When she debuted in 1986, Winfrey's only competitors were Phil Donahue and Sally Jesse Raphael. She quickly bested them in the ratings and held her own against newcomers Geraldo Rivera and Morton Downey Jr. in 1987 and '88. In the early 1990s, however, a blizzard of new talk shows appeared, whose young hosts, sensational topics, and production designs aimed to create maximum conflict and disruption among the guests and the studio audience. By the spring of 1993, Winfrey faced competition from twenty nationally syndicated programs, each regularly treating topics like "When Your Best Friend Is Sleeping with Your Father," "Get Bigger Breasts Or Else," and "Women Who Marry Their Rapists." Determined to maintain her ratings hegemony, Winfrey went with the flow, hosting programs such as "I Had My Father's Baby," "Disgruntled Employees Who Kill," and "Husbands Who Work with Brazen Hussies Are Lured into

Illicit Relationships; Wives Vent Frustration."[37] But while she continued to lead the field both in market penetration and in ratings, her overall share of the audience dropped an unprecedented 7 percent between 1993 and '94.[38]

In response, Winfrey announced a dramatic departure from what she called "the trash pack."[39] In a series of high-profile interviews (*TV Guide, People, Entertainment Weekly*) and on her season opener, she acknowledged that "I've been guilty of doing trash TV and not even thinking it was trash. I don't want to do it anymore."[40] Contrasting herself to the scandal mongers on other networks, Winfrey declared that

> the time has come for this genre of talk show to move from dysfunctional whining and complaining and blaming. I have had enough of people's dysfunction. . . . We're all aware that we do have some problems and we need to work on them. What are you willing to do about it? . . . That's what our shows are going to be about.[41]

By self-consciously rejecting "dysfunction" in favor of "awareness" and the "need to work," Winfrey set herself apart from her low-brow competitors; she also laid the foundation for the new brand message that she would develop over the next several years.

Though Winfrey never identified them as such, New Thought principles—the invocation of the divine within, the importance on attuning the mind to a divine plan, the INTA belief that those "who express fullness shall reap fullness in return"—formed the heart of that message. In a *Ladies Home Journal* interview, she credited her new approach to her show to feeling "connected to the bigger picture of what God is." In 1993, she explained, she had "asked [God] for freedom. . . . And this year I asked for clarity." As a result, she had "become more clear about my purpose in television and this show."[42] That purpose was to promote a spiritual message that would counter negative forces at work in the personal lives of individual viewers as well as in the world at large. The competition might pander to its audiences with programming that showcased negativity, but Winfrey would offer something different. "I feel that my show is a ministry," she explained in another interview, and she aimed to use it—along with the other media outlets that she was developing—for the greater good.[43]

Thus in 1994 Winfrey shifted both program content and production design in order to focus her audience's attention on positive and uplifting topics. Participation by rowdy audience members and dysfunctional guests declined and the show took on a more staid look, with Winfrey interviewing guests (increasingly celebrities or "experts") about their accomplishments, hopes, and dreams.[44] Among these were several authors who preach a "thought-as-power" gospel, including James Redfield, Thomas Moore, Larry Dossey, and Steven Covey. A particularly noteworthy presence during this season, media studies scholar Janice Peck has argued, was Marianne Williamson, revered teacher on the New Thought best seller *A Course in Miracles* and spiritual leader of Detroit's Church of Today, an outpost of Unity Church. Peck describes how, during her guest spot, Williamson told an

> unhappy welfare mother that her problem lay in thinking that depression and being on welfare were "more powerful than God." Rather than thinking, "I'm the victim," Williamson told the [woman] she should think "I have within me the power to break through these constrictions."

The episode concluded with a "Prayer for America," and with Winfrey's encomium to prayer as "a secret weapon [that] can help with every single problem before you."[45] That message was reinforced in episodes throughout the season, which bore titles such as "Thank You Day," "Dreams Really Do Come True," and "Would You Know a Miracle If You Saw One?"[46]

The enhanced Brand Oprah proved successful: Winfrey won daytime Emmy Awards in 1994 and '95, and in '96 received broadcasting's highest honor, the George Foster Peabody Individual Achievement Award. Bolstered by this recognition, she continued to develop her spiritual message. The 1997 season began with the announcement of Winfrey's philanthropic "Angel Network," and the 1998 season created a whole regimen of "Change Your Life TV," reflecting Winfrey's desire to be "'more dedicated than ever to . . . television that [is] a light in people's lives.'"[47] To help bring that "light," Change Your Life TV devoted regular episodes to a group of motivational and inspirational experts, including "Dr. Phil" McGraw, John Gray, Iyanla Vanzant, and Suze Orman.[48] Their insights, combined with a five-minute daily segment titled "Remembering Your Spirit," would aid viewers with "going inside, removing yourself from the chaos, confusion, and the noise of the world and finding a way to bring peace to yourself."[49]

Such spiritual injunctions are not exclusive to New Thought denominations. The discourse of "looking for something deeper" and "finding a way to bring peace to yourself" can be described as part of the "deep yearning for the sacred" that Robert Wuthnow has argued "characterizes much of the American public."[50] It is also possible to argue that Winfrey and her guests are merely the *Restless Souls* whose spiritual exploration, meditation, and questioning is part of the post-nineteenth-century liberalization of Protestantism that Leigh

Schmidt explores in his book of that title. But for those who would plumb the political implications of Winfrey's show, it seems important to reckon with her assertion that "changing your life [is] about really changing the way you think, the way you see your life, the way you see your family, your children, your relationships."[51] By asserting the primacy of idealism—of "the way you think" and "the way you see" as the principle ways you "chang[e] your life"—Winfrey allied herself quite specifically with New Thought principles, which relegate material conditions and worldly power to a distant second place.

The spiritual concerns that began to shape *The Oprah Winfrey Show* in 1994 not only enhanced Brand Oprah, but also served to unify the proliferating extensions of the brand. Winfrey created an interactive Web site in partnership with AOL in 1995; in the fall of '98 she launched the independent Oprah.com site, promoting it as a way for viewers to "expand their relationships" with and to use the "information and resources provided by Oprah and the 'Change Your Life TV' experts."[52] The "Change Your Life" slogan that unified the electronic media shifted to accommodate *O: The Oprah Magazine* when it appeared in 2001. The new tagline—"Live Your Best Life: Your mission is true happiness. Your purpose is your destiny"—linked the print and electronic manifestations of Harpo with a series of "personal growth summits" Winfrey hosted around the country.[53] All platforms shared underwriters and content—in the form of meditations, affirmations, and inspirational narratives and images—intended to fulfill that "mission" and "purpose" as well as to distinguish Winfrey's properties from what she called her competitors' "mental poison."[54]

It was within this trajectory of brand enhancement and brand extension that Oprah's Book Club first appeared. The idea originated with an assistant producer, and Winfrey, fearing a ratings decline into "horrible numbers," had to be convinced to pursue it.[55] But when she announced the club as part of the season premiere in September 1996, the response was immediate, enormous, and overwhelmingly favorable. The latter quality made the press attention particularly welcome. Cynical critics had reviled Change Your Life TV from its inception, remarking acidly, "You don't [change] your life by watching TV—you [change] your life by turning off the TV and going back to school," and crowing that the show was "losing about a million viewers each time a 'Change Your Life' segment was aired."[56] But critics could not admire the book club enough; by the end of the year, editorials praising Winfrey for promoting reading and cultural uplift had appeared in almost every major newspaper. Her plan to sell club selections in Starbucks and donate the proceeds to literacy education was similarly hailed as an example of bold civic leadership. The iconography of the book, apparently, was strong enough to neutralize—in critics' minds—the spiritualized discourse of Change Your Life TV. It is ironic, therefore, that the discourse continued to percolate, even to boil, within the book club itself.

Reading to Change the World

Between the fall of 1996 and the spring of 2002, Oprah's Book Club worked something like this: approximately every six weeks, Winfrey announced on-air the selection of a new title—usually, though not exclusively, a work of recent fiction—and solicited readers' letters in response to the book.[57] A select few letter writers then joined Winfrey and the author to discuss it, often over a meal. Taped highlights from this conversation, interspersed with Winfrey interviewing the author, a montage of the author's thoughts on his/her creative process, studio audience members comments, and so on, constituted the on-air book club; readers could also discuss the book on a dedicated bulletin board at the Oprah.com Web site. Although it began as one segment within the larger program, the book club quickly expanded to fill the whole hour-long *Oprah Winfrey Show*. Occasional features such as trips to the locales where the books unfolded were added for variety's sake, but the core of the club remained unchanged over its history: taped excerpts of Winfrey, her guests, and the author discussing plot, characters, themes, and other elements they liked and disliked about the book. At the center of these discussions was a consideration, often tearful, of how the incidents or characters in the books resonated with the readers' own lives.

Though no empirical research has yet documented precisely how many of Winfrey's viewers read along with the club, retail and library records suggest that the number was in the millions. Generalizing with any precision about those reading experiences is difficult; as any number of book historians have demonstrated, individual readers derive wildly varying meanings from the texts they encounter. Furthermore, contemporary Western reading is, for the most part, a private experience, and one encumbered by powerful notions of "good" and "bad" that are instilled in readers by the educational system and the popular press alike.[58] Individual idiosyncrasies and cultural norms alike shape the readers' encounter with the meanings that authors (not to mention genre, language, and the mechanisms of book marketing) encode in a text. As Janice Peck and Kimberly Chabot Davis have noted, the discussion among readers on the Oprah.com bulletin boards is varied and often unruly, with different readers and reading strategies competing for hermeneutical hegemony. Thus, speculating about what reading along with Oprah's Book Club meant to the mass of her fan base is risky.[59]

Less diffuse, however, is the reading Winfrey encouraged and showcased on-air, an interpretive mode focused on empathetic identification and the cultivation of "openness"—a state of affective transcendence that derived from and reinforced the New Thought ideals articulated across the Harpo properties. The basic assumptions of this hermeneutic are well known: a bare-bones version of it can be seen in the reading for psychological validation ("I liked this character; I could relate to her") that forms the baseline in most college classrooms, and it resembles in many ways what Wayne Booth has called "ethical criticism," a reading mode in which "one serves one's 'self' in part by *taking in* the new selves offered in stories."[60] What distinguishes the club is the way it took this practice to a higher level. Following Winfrey's example, guests used the emotional connection inherent in identifying with a literary character as the first in a multistage imaginative process that would make the social and political hierarchies that marked their lives dissolve into meaninglessness and be replaced by harmonious flows of love and kindness. Like original New Thought teachings, and like the larger project of "Change Your Life TV," this literary version of "thought-as-power" did pose a critique—sometimes tacit, sometimes explicit—of the rational, differentiated modern world, and named its structures of domination and difference as the source of individuals' pain. But the club's reading mode also ratified the foundational idealism and mysticism of New Thought, and its focus on a higher spiritual realm meant that it did not enjoin action in the world against such structures.

The club's otherworldly orientation was established early on by its depiction of books themselves as mystical objects. The first episode of Oprah's Book Club, in which Jacquelyn Mitchard described the origins of *The Deep End of the Ocean* in "a dream I had three years ago," laid down this template. "I woke my husband up about 5:00 that morning to tell him about this wonderful story," Mitchard explained, but "he got cancer and he only lived a few months." After his death, "everyone who loved me kept telling me . . . 'think about security . . . Don't think about dreams anymore,'" but she persevered with the novel as a way of honoring her dead husband's spirit. Juxtaposing the realist advice she received with her "dreamy" book project, Mitchard affirmed the importance of New Thought's idealist worldview; the believer's sense that an intricate connectivity structures the world was manifest in the fact that Mitchard "finished the book exactly two years to the day after Dan died."[61]

Throughout the course of the book club, this sense of authorship as a mystical practice and of the book as an enchanted object framed the readings of specific texts. Winfrey's questions to authors established the terms of the discussion—"Did the characters, like, visit you, like little people in your house, or little people in your head?"—and few authors challenged it.[62] Typically, authors explained their work with statements such as "the story was so large in me that there were times I felt like I couldn't keep up with it"; "I start writing a book and somehow [the characters] emerge from—from someplace"; "it was like a flower . . . I had never imagined it, but I thought it was beautiful," and so on.[63] Toni Morrison, frequently invoked as an exemplary guest in the club, is more accurately viewed as an exceptional one: each time she appeared on the show, Morrison would draw attention to the writer's craft, with comments such as "I love to hear it when [people] say . . . 'I had to read every word.' And I always wanted to say, 'Yeah—and I had to write every word.'"[64] While approvingly noted by Winfrey and the guests, Morrison's commitment to the labor of writing did not carry over to other episodes.[65] More often, books were treated as the products of efflorescent forces that periodically surged into the workaday world through the portal formed by the author and her word processor.

The club's enchanted books invited a similarly nonrational reading. Toni Morrison was again an exception that proved this rule, urging frustrated readers of *Paradise* "to have an intellectual response to the issues being debated here" and promising that it "may be easier than you think." In every Morrison episode, Winfrey and her guests praised the author's intellection, noting her rich, allusive language and puzzle-like plots, which required careful note taking and multiple readings. But as Timothy Aubry has argued, the club's chief goal was not the cultivation of such an "intellectual response," even with a heady author like Morrison.[66] In direct contrast to the author's suggestion, Winfrey exhorted readers of *Paradise*, "don't read this book just with your head!"[67] A too-cerebral analysis, she suggested, could in fact detract from what made the reading experience truly valuable.

For Winfrey, that value lay in a sense of interpersonal connectedness, which had the capacity to change not only personal life, but also the broader social world. Her own belief in reading's transformative power, she explained in an interview, resulted from "growing up [with] a sense of loneliness." Thus Francie Nolan, the protagonist of Betty Smith's *A Tree Grows in Brooklyn*, had become a best friend to the solitary teenage Winfrey: "There was a tree outside my apartment, and I used to imagine it was the same tree. I felt like my life was like hers."[68] The importance of this fictive community only increased as she grew older. Like Smith's novel, Maya Angelou's *I Know Why the Caged Bird Sings* helped Winfrey break down a feeling of alienation brought on by childhood sexual abuse. The emotional connectedness engendered by reading created a community that Winfrey felt compensated her for the affective sparseness of her childhood, which she attributed to growing up as a "little Negro child . . . unloved and so isolated."[69] Tapping into an imagined community available through books had been, for Winfrey, a key to unlocking spiritual isolation; accordingly, identification with the protagonist was the starting point for book club reading. She actively solicited that identification, urging would-be guests to explain in their letters to her "how the book touched you" or "how you were affected by it." Similar questions guided the on-air discussions as well, with Winfrey asking guests, "Did you see yourself?" or, "[Is] this story like your own in any way?"[70]

Identification was not an end in itself, however. Rather, it was the first step toward a richer connection of the self to the world, a mode of engagement that Winfrey referred to as "openness." Regularly discussed during book club episodes, openness was a cognitive and emotional state that reflected the New Thought investment in the transformation of "the dualism of . . . soul and body" into "an indivisible and inseparable unity."[71] As she discussed books, Winfrey modeled a clear three-stage process of "opening" in which empathy melted the perceived barriers separating readers from one another and merged them into an enchanted community.

One of the club's first episodes, devoted to Ursula Hegi's *Stones from the River*, exemplifies the journey Winfrey hoped readers would make: into the narrow confines of individuated selfhood, through a critical engagement with society, and finally into a transcendent space of affective union, a state characterized by the dissolve of "difference." Hegi's novel tells the story of Trudi Montag, a dwarf who works in a library and hides Jews from the Nazis in wartime Germany. When a guest named Kathleen noted that Hegi's novel "opened [my] eyes to the differentness of being a dwarf," Winfrey concurred, remarking, "it's expanded me. . . . I think I'm pretty open-minded . . . but it opened me up in a way."[72]

The pursuit of openness had an undeniably solipsistic dimension. Midway through the Hegi discussion, Winfrey compared Trudi Montag's attempts to stretch her diminutive body to her own childhood identification with Shirley Temple, revealing that "I remember, like, putting a clothespin on my nose with two cotton balls trying to get my nose . . . to point up." [73] Taken in context, however, this turn to personal experience is not merely narcissistic. Within the club's interpretive community, readers are initially drawn deeper into their individuated selves by equating their own experience with that of others. But that rudimentary point-to-point comparison then reverses itself: readers "open" out into the larger world when they recognize the ways in which both sets of experiences are similarly structured by divisive social hierarchies. Winfrey's Shirley Temple reverie ended with her reflection that "you can't change who you are . . . that's how I identified . . . that's what slavery did to black people, is to teach us self-hatred for the way we looked."[74] By naming the social institutions and mores that create and enforce hierarchy (anti-Semitism, slavery, "lookisms" of all kinds), readers served to speed it on its way to dissolution. At the close of the *Stones from the River* episode Winfrey noted that once she "open[ed] . . . up to a new way of thinking" she recognized that "[even] if you are a dwarf, then . . . there is no difference between yourself and myself . . . there is no difference, you know."[75] This dissolve of the gap between the self and its others was the goal of Winfrey's pedagogy of openness.

The second stage of the process of "opening"—the moment where reading prompts a recognition that social hierarchies affect all members of the human community—bears some scrutiny. The *Stones from the River* episode is fairly typical in the way it notes issues of social inequality; it is unusual in the kind of action it countenances. A guest whose Jewish parents had lived in Germany during the Second World War recounted that "when the Nazis marched into [her father's] office . . . and told him Jews cannot be attorneys anymore . . . most of the secretaries went along with it, and yet, one stood up and she said, 'Why? Why are you doing this?' . . . They still did it, but at least she said, 'It's not all right.'"[76] In this instance, the act of opening yourself to others, of extending your subjectivity to include them, became the grounds for social action in the form of refusing to cede power to an oppressive political regime. Winfrey and the guests agreed that after reading *Stones* it would be hard to just "do that phony little laugh thing" or to "seeth[e] inside [because] you don't like" the injustices that you see in the world.[77] Having "opened" themselves to Trudi Montag, they would take her resistance to the Nazis as a model for future action.

The formulation of such concrete plans to resist unjust or immoral behavior in the world, however, was infrequent in the club. Typically, Winfrey and her guests simply moved past the hierarchical divisions of society that their reading had brought to light and into the utopian space of "no difference." The final book club episode of the 1996–97 season, devoted to Maya Angelou's memoir, *The Heart of a Woman*, demonstrates this dynamic. The episode's unstructured discussion—it was staged as a dinner and pajama party at Angelou's home—touched on a variety of social ills, including sexualized violence (one guest, like Angelou herself in *I Know Why the Caged Bird Sings*, had been a victim of childhood sexual abuse) and urban crime (*Heart of a Woman* treated Angelou's response to her son's involvement with a gang). As Winfrey and her guests celebrated Angelou's response to both issues, the author explained that "I had to tell the truth [because] to tell the truth liberates."[78]

This sentiment allies its adherents with the radical tradition of "speaking truth to power," but Angelou's elaboration on truth telling pushed the discussion away from further consideration of the material conditions that produce urban gangs and the sexual politics that suborns incest. To tell the truth, she explained, "reminds human beings, all of us, that [we] are more alike than we are unalike. . . . Nothing human can be alien to me."[79] Winfrey elaborated on this insight, asking, "Don't you believe . . . that the heart of every woman—and man, too, for that matter . . . really is the same? That's what I try to tell people."[80] That transcendent human sameness, all agreed, was obscured in the world today by the stringency of what Angelou called "these lean and mean and terrifying days." That structure of terror, Winfrey argued, was maintained in part by the fact that "there's a whole generation of people, particularly in our culture, who never learned to say, 'I love you.'" Urging guests to break that pattern, Angelou reminded them that "in order to change, you have to . . . say, 'It stops here. The cruelty stops here. The silences stop here. From me on, there will be kindness. From my mouth on, there will be tenderness. From my throat, there will be softness.'" The changed hearts for which Angelou advocated represented the ultimate realm of meaning for club members; Winfrey consecrated it as such when she followed Angelou's speech with her customary toast of "here's to books." "Opened" by their identification with Angelou's insights, she and her guests had connected to a spiritual truth that transcended their lived reality, which all agreed was a world of "cruelty . . . silences . . . and hard words."[81]

Not every episode of the book club elaborated the idealist tenets of Change Your Life TV as eloquently as the Maya Angelou episode, but most provided something similar. Even Toni Morrison, who resisted incorporation into the discourse of the enchanted book, could not avoid being swept up in this dynamic. Early in the episode dealing with *The Bluest Eye*, Morrison talked explicitly about the "racism" that dominated the period in which she wrote the novel (1965–69) and excoriated the "hierarchy of race" that structured protagonist Pecola Breedlove's life.[82] As with Angelou, however, no sooner was the issue of racism introduced than it was redefined as a lack of love. By the end of the broadcast, Pecola was recast as suffering "the ravages of an unloved life," and guests were enjoined to bring more love into the world as a way to right social wrongs.[83] Glossing her own representation of the consequences of racism, poverty, and patriarchy, Morrison observed that "the most important thing is . . . do your eyes light up when your child walks into the room?"[84] Reading's greatest value in this context was its ability to inspire that transcendent love, leading Winfrey to triumphantly predict that "it will change the world if everybody read[s] this book."[85] Encouraging this sympathetic expansion of the individual spirit, and directing its flow into a larger and unbounded community of the heart was the purpose of Oprah's Book Club.

The reading experiences of the millions of individuals who read along with Winfrey's selections remain largely unknown to scholars. The reading experience showcased on the televised book club, however, is available to us and, when viewed in the context of Brand Oprah's New Thought–inflected message, seems of a piece with it. That alignment was no coincidence. As Ted Striphas has observed, the fans "invited to participate on air were considered by the show's producers to be ideal readers," interpreters who could be relied upon to produce readings that would resonate with Winfrey's larger themes.[86] Kathleen Rooney, one of the few academic critics to attend a taping, has noted that producers seeded the studio audience with "ringers" to ensure that the Q&A portions of the show would stay on-message.[87] When contrarian readings did bubble up in discussion, Winfrey dismissed them quickly. To one guest's remark that he "d[id] not have compassion" for a protagonist in Andre Dubus's *House of Sand and Fog*, Winfrey snapped, "Would you give us a break here, George?" In the episode devoted to Barbara Kingsolver's *The Poisonwood Bible*, an African American audience member claimed that she "really dislike[d]" one of the Anglo-American main characters "because she got everything that I want. She got my African husband and my homeland," to which Winfrey replied testily, "OK. It's just—it's just a book."[88] Perhaps more than anything else, the fact that these outliers could not be recuperated into the enchanted community demonstrates the ways in which the book club functioned as part of the enhanced message of Brand Oprah, a message crafted to invite readers to believe that by exercising "thought-as-power" they would ultimately create a world of "no difference."

Beyond "Cultural Democracy"

In September 2001, Winfrey chose Jonathan Franzen's *The Corrections* as the club's forty-second selection, and Franzen stunned the literary world by expressing not joy but trepidation. Damning Winfrey with remarkably faint praise—"I like her for liking my book"—he first worried that her endorsement might "put off" potential readers, particularly men, who associated the club with what he called "schmaltzy, one-dimensional" fiction, and then fretted that, as "an independent writer," he didn't want her "corporate logo on my book."[89] A media frenzy erupted, and Franzen's subsequent fumbling attempts to retract his remarks or apologize only dug him in deeper with Winfrey's defenders. Journalists pilloried him as a "pinch-nosed and ivory-towered" elitist "living in [a] solipsistic dream world."[90] Academic critics quickly followed suit, disregarding Franzen's admittedly pallid gesture toward a critique of the corporate culture industry (Winfrey's "corporate logo on my book") in order to focus on his "virtually indefensible" suggestion that the "readers drawn by [*The Oprah Winfrey Show*] were in some way unintelligent, and therefore undesirable."[91] Speaking for many in the academy, Cecilia Konchar Farr observed that "like most high cultural critics," Franzen "was blind to changes in reading habits led by the middle or lower classes, by people of color or women." Such outmoded mandarins would soon be vanquished, she predicted, because "Oprah is shaping and advocating cultural democracy . . . advanc[ing] on Old World privilege and elitism with her guerilla force of women readers behind her. Refusing her own authority and highlighting everyday women's voices . . . this TV talk show host is changing the way America reads."[92] For many left-leaning academics, the Oprah-Franzen contretemps offered a unique opportunity to glimpse the hegemon in action, articulating the discourse and inhabiting the subject position against which—both professionally and personally—they defined themselves.

Let me be clear: Oprah's Book Club did validate and empower readers, and for anyone who cares about either the tangible or intangible benefits of literacy, that can only be a good thing. For many women (and some men), club reading offered the opportunity to continue an education that had been cut short by other obligations, or to carve out a space of imaginative freedom from the demands of daily working and domestic life, or to deepen an appreciation for contemporary fiction. Similarly, Winfrey's foregrounding of African American experience within the club—in her talk about her own life, in the books she selected, in the comments she elicited from guests—broadened public perceptions of history and literature in important ways, as John Young has demonstrated. And, as Kimberly Chabot Davis has argued, readers' responses to club selections "could be seen as an incipient form of political action"—provided that they occur "in a larger chain of events, alongside other moments of critical thinking and encounters with alternative viewpoints that might shift an individual's perspective."[93] As my readings above suggest, however, Winfrey's perceived "advoca[cy] of cultural democracy" may not have been the most important cultural work performed by her book club.

What I have attempted to demonstrate here is the way that the book club's pedagogy of reading elevated the sensations of love and wonder to the center of its participants' conceptual worlds and validated readers based on their ability to experience those sensations. Its New Thought–derived worldview explicitly celebrated the spirit for its ability to transcend the market—while simultaneously deploying the spirit, through the discourse of Brand Oprah, to serve the market's ends. The ideal readers who appeared on the *Oprah Winfrey Show* modeled for the viewing audience the importance of rising above the clutter and chaos of a material existence defined by "don't think about dreams anymore" and "cruelty . . . silences . . . and hard words."[94] Rather than remain trapped by those harsh realities, the club urged, readers should commit themselves to the higher realm of the spirit. The mental act of making that commitment would, somehow, redound upon the real world. Accounts of the club's importance that rush to tout its populist cultural democracy without considering its invocation of a commercialized and faith-based politics risk missing the opportunity truly to understand what Stuart Hall calls the "certain kind of consciousness" through which millions of Winfrey's fans are "languaged."

Although there are important exceptions, as noted in this essay, it seems difficult to deny that the majority of secular progressive academics have been content for some time to overlook the growth of popular, unchurched spiritual and religious practices, particularly among the white, native-born middle class. Without a shred of irony, we have preferred instead to invest in our own version of "thought-as-power": if we visualize class-conscious resistance in popular cultural forms, practices, and communities, then it will materialize in the political world. The academic Left needs to maintain its vision of the utopian, but we can no longer afford to ignore the social structures and cultural forms that offer competing visions of utopia—especially when they are offered to, and eagerly accepted by, audiences far larger than those we touch through our writing and our teaching.

Scholars working to explain or to intervene in popular culture and politics need to determine how the affective energy called up by the kind of faith I have described here manifests itself in the lives and the communities—and perhaps in the voting habits—of those who are "languaged" by it. We would also do well to ask whether the institutions and networks necessary to transform flows of good feeling into what Ann Ferguson calls "revolutionary love" can precipitate out of a discourse that has its roots in such a counterrevolutionary marketplace.[95] What kind of labor would be required to call them forth? And, building on that, how should those who remain skeptical of the assertion that "it will change the world if everyone reads this book" attempt to work in concert with those who do believe it? If we want genuinely to understand the cultural politics of the world outside the academy, we need to recognize the terms through which the inhabitants of that world—who are often the staff members at our institutions, our students, neighbors, and family members—articulate hope, desire, and fear. The terms of that articulation are often mystical ones, and a clearer vision of them may afford us the opportunity to see and to affect the ways that many Americans outside the academic Left imagine and desire "the political."

Notes

I owe a debt of gratitude to the following, without whose assistance this essay would never have seen the light of day: Rita Barnard, James English, Janice Peck, and Richard Fox; my writing group, Julie Kim, Leah Rosenberg, Jodi Schorb, and Ed White; and, as always, Mark Fenster.

1. *The Oprah Winfrey Show*, September 17, 1996, 15. All citations to the Oprah Winfrey Show are to pages within the transcripts, which are available from Burrelle's Information Services, Box 7, Livingston, N.J. 07039. This essay treats only the club's original incarnation, which extended from fall 1996 through the spring of 2002. I do not discuss the "classic literature" club of 2003–2005, whose aims and production values differed substantially from the original, or the revived contemporary authors club that began in fall 2005; it has not convened often enough for meaningful generalizations to be made about it.

2. See, for example, Cecilia Konchar Farr, *Reading Oprah: How Oprah's Book Club Changed the Way America Reads* (Albany: State University of New York Press, 2004) and Kathleen Rooney, *Reading with Oprah: The Book Club That Changed America* (Fayetteville: University of Arkansas Press, 2005). Elizabeth McHenry's *Forgotten Readers: Recovering the Lost History of African American Literary Societies* (Durham, N.C.: Duke University Press, 2002) and Elizabeth Long's *Book Clubs: Women and the Uses of Reading in Everyday Life* (Chicago: University of Chicago Press, 2003) make similar arguments in chapters devoted to the club. See also Ted Striphas, "A Dialectic with the Everyday: Communication and Cultural Politics on Oprah Winfrey's Book Club," *Critical Studies in Mass Communication* 20.3 (September 2003): 295–316, and, taking slightly different tacks, Timothy Aubry's "Beware the Furrow of the Middlebrow: Searching for Paradise in "The Oprah Winfrey Show," *Modern Fiction Studies* 52.2 (Summer 2006): 350–73; John Young's "Toni Morrison, Oprah Winfrey, and Postmodern Popular Audiences," *African American Review* 35.2 (Summer 2001): 181–204; and Eva Illouz's treatment of the club in passing in *Oprah Winfrey and the Glamour of Misery* (New York: Columbia University Press, 2003). Important exceptions to this interpretive mode are Janice Peck's "The Oprah Effect: Texts, Readers, and the Dialectics of Signification," *Communications Review* 5 (2002): 159–67, and Kimberly

Chabot Davis's "Oprah's Book Club and the Politics of Cross-Racial Empathy," *International Journal of Cultural Studies* 7.4 (December 2004): 399–419.

3. Brian Street, *Literacy in Theory and Practice* (New York: Oxford University Press, 1984).

4. In "The Precession of the Simulacra," Baudrillard argues that "the form of advertising has imposed itself and developed at the expense of all the other languages as an increasingly neutral, equivalent rhetoric, without affects"; Sheila Faria Glaser, trans., *Simulacra and Simulation* (Ann Arbor: University of Michigan Press, 1994), 88. Jeremy Rifkin develops this idea and denominates it "hypercapitalist" in *The Age of Access* (New York: Tarcher/Putnam, 2000), 10.

5. Peter Golding and Graham Murdock, "Culture, Communications, and Political Economy," in *Mass Media and Society*, ed. James Curran and Michael Gurevitch (London: Arnold, 1996), 15.

6. Paul Tillich, *The Dynamics of Faith* (New York: Harper, 1958).

7. George Mair, *Oprah Winfrey: The Real Story* (New York: Birch Lane, 2002), 344; Barbara Grizutti Harrison, "The Importance of Being Oprah," *New York Times Magazine*, June 11, 1989, 48+.

8. Critics frequently scorn Winfrey as "New Age," but New Age occultism, which includes past life regression, shamanism, crystals, and so on, is distinct from New Thought and appears less frequently in Winfrey's spiritual discourse.

9. Noted in Kathryn Lofton, "Practicing Oprah; or, the Prescriptive Compulsion of Spiritual Capitalism," *Journal of Popular Culture* 39.4 (August 2006): 599–621.

10. Winfrey quoted in Janet Lowe, ed., *Oprah Winfrey Speaks* (New York: John Wiley and Sons, 1998), 122.

11. Important exceptions to this trend, in addition to the works discussed in the text, are William Leach's *Land of Desire* (New York: Pantheon, 1993), and, more recently, Susan Gillman, *Blood Talk: American Race Melodrama and the Culture of the Occult* (Chicago: University of Chicago Press, 2003).

12. Davis, "Cross-Racial Empathy," 414.

13. "Is Elvis a God? Cult, Culture, Questions of Method," *International Journal of Cultural Studies* 1.2 (August 1998): 199–212. For further discussion of this issue, see Jon Butler, "Jack-in-the-Box Faith: The Religion Problem in Modern American History," *The Journal of American History* (March 2004), http://www.historycooperative.org/cgi-bin/justtop.cgi?act=justtop&url=http://www.historycooperative.org/journals/jah/90.4/butler.html (accessed May 23, 2007).

14. Wade Clark Roof, *A Generation of Seekers: The Spiritual Journeys of the Baby Boom Generation* (San Francisco: HarperSanFrancisco, 1993); Jerry Adler, "In Search of the Spiritual," *Newsweek*, August 29–Sept. 5, 2005, http://www.msnbc.msn.com/id/9024914/site/newsweek/ (accessed March 3, 2007).

15. *The Oprah Winfrey Show*, May 26, 2000, 17.

16. Sydney Ahlstrom, *A Religious History of the American People* (New Haven, Conn.: Yale University Press, 1972), 1019.

17. T. J. Jackson Lears, *No Place of Grace* (New York: Pantheon, 1981), 173.

18. Richard Huber, *The American Idea of Success* (New York: McGraw-Hill, 1971), 125.

19. Beryl Satter, *Each Mind a Kingdom* (Berkeley: University of California Press, 1999), 6–7.

20. Ibid., 3.

21. Marie Griffith, *Born Again Bodies: Flesh and Spirit in American Christianity* (Berkeley: University of California Press), 108; emphasis in original.

22. Horatio Dresser, *A History of the New Thought Movement* (New York: Thomas Crowell, 1919), 160.

23. Excluded from this discussion is Quimby's most famous patient and student, Mary Baker Eddy (1821–1910). Although she was the first mental healer to elaborate her beliefs into a religion, Eddy did not consider her First Church of Christ, Scientist to be part of "New Thought" and was hostile to those who practiced and worshiped under that name. Tensions between Christian Science and New Thought are explored in Satter, *Each Mind a Kingdom*, 57–79, and in Charles Braden, *Spirits in Rebellion* (Dallas: Southern Methodist University Press, 1987), 14–21.

24. Braden, *Spirits*, 122.

25. While Satter's book focuses on a "New Thought network [that] appears to have been entirely white," she also notes that "discussions of . . . New Thought were common in African American race uplift manuals" of the late nineteenth century (16); both Satter and Griffiths demonstrate the salience of New Thought ideas to the African American followers of Father Divine. Their suggestive discussions point to the need to articulate and historicize the relationship between New Thought and the evolving philosophy of black "womanism," an intellectual genealogy within which Oprah Winfrey can be usefully situated.

26. Braden, *Spirits*, 196.
27. Henry James, *The Bostonians* (New York: Library of America, 1991), 77.
28. Satter, *Each Mind a Kingdom*, 14.
29. Leigh Schmidt, *Restless Souls: The Making of American Spirituality* (San Francisco: HarperSanFrancisco, 2005), 155.
30. Jane Shattuc, *The Talking Cure:* TV Talk Shows and Women (New York: Routledge, 1977, 56–57; Lowe, *Winfrey Speaks*, 37, 34.
31. See Steve Rebello, "Brand Oprah: Connecting with 20 Million 'Customers' a Day," *Success* 45.5 (1998): 64.
32. On branding theory, see Douglas Holt, *How Brands Become Icons* (Cambridge, Mass.: Harvard Business School Press, 2004).
33. Jeff Jacobs is quoted in Patricia Sellers, "The Business of Being Oprah," *Fortune*, April 1, 2002, 50+.
34. Quoted in Bill Adler, ed., *The Uncommon Wisdom of Oprah Winfrey: A Portrait in Her Own Words* (New York: Carol Publishing, 2000), 120.
35. Preeminent examples of this reading of talk show discourse can be found in Shattuc, as well as in Josh Gamson, *Freaks Talk Back: Tabloid Talk Shows and Sexual Non-Conformity* (Chicago: University of Chicago Press, 1998).
36. Shattuc, *Talking Cure*, 137–69.
37. Competitors' toxic titles cited in Vicki Abt and Mel Seesholtz, "The Shameless World of Phil, Sally, and Oprah: TV Talk Shows and the Deconstructing of Society," *Journal of Popular Culture* 28 (Summer 1994): 181, and Shattuc, *Talking Cure*, 145, 146. Winfrey's toxic programs aired on March 18, May 27, and August 20, 1993.
38. Mair, *Real Story*, 340.
39. Quoted in Lowe, *Oprah Speaks*, 150.
40. Quoted in Dana Kennedy, "Oprah Act Two," *Entertainment Weekly*, September 9, 1994.
41. Quoted in Adler, *Uncommon Wisdom*, 76.
42. Quoted in Lowe, *Oprah Speaks*, 128.
43. Ibid., 126.
44. Shattuc, *Talking Cure*, 154–55.
45. Winfrey quoted in *The Age of Oprah: The Making of a Cultural Icon for the Neoliberal Era* (Boulder, Colo.: Paradigm, forthcoming 2008), n.p.
46. Positive show air dates: September 19 and December 28, 1994, and January 16, 1995.
47. Quoted in Kathleen Lowney, *Baring Our Souls: TV Talk Shows and the Religion of Recovery,* (New York: Aldine de Gruyter, 1999), 90–91.
48. "'Change Your Life'—Log On with Oprah," *Business Wire*, October 19, 1998, *http://www.findarticles.com/p/articles/mi_m0EIN/is_1998_Oct_19/ai_53093122* (accessed November 11, 2006).
49. Quoted in Wendy Parkins, "Oprah Winfrey's Change Your Life TV and the Spiritual Everyday," *Continuum: Journal of Media and Cultural Studies* 15.2 (July 2001): 149.
50. Robert Wuthnow, *Sharing the Journey: Support Groups and America's Quest for Community* (New York: Free Press, 1994).
51. Quoted in Parkins, "Spiritual Everyday," 145.
52. See "'Change Your Life'—Log On with Oprah."
53. See *http://www.oprah.com/spiritself/ss_landing.jhtml* (accessed May 3, 2001). The site text has changed since this access date, and no longer includes the statements about mission and purpose.
54. Quoted in Lowney, *Baring Our Souls*, 91.
55. D. T. Max, "The Oprah Effect," *New York Times Magazine*, December 26, 1999.
56. Quoted in Lowney, *Baring Our Souls*, 140–41.
57. The club selected two memoirs: Maya Angelou's 1981 *The Heart of a Woman* (June 18, 1997) and Malika Oufkir's 1999 *Stolen Lives: Twenty Years in a Desert Jail* (June 20, 2001). Three short children's books by Bill Cosby, *The Meanest Thing to Say*, *The Treasure Hunt*, and *The Best Way to Play* (all 1997) were featured on December 8, 1997. The definition of "recent" was flexible, as one spokesperson noted: "The only real criteria we have is that the author has to be alive, so that he or she can appear on the program" (quoted in Rooney, *Reading with Oprah*, 109).

58. For discussion of the way educational and cultural norms put pressure on the private reading act, see Janice Radway, *A Feeling for Books: The Book of the Month Club, Literary Taste, and Middle-Class Desire* (Chapel Hill: University of North Carolina Press).

59. Davis, "Cross-Racial Empathy," 408–9; Peck, "Oprah Effect," 159–67.

60. Wayne Booth, *The Company We Keep* (Chicago: University of Chicago Press, 1988): 138; emphasis in original.

61. Jacquelyn Mitchard, October 18, 1996, 17.

62. Winfrey, June 23, 2000, 11.

63. Melinda Haynes, June 15, 1999, 16; Isabel Allende, March 28, 2000, 11; Ann-Marie MacDonald, April 5, 2002, 12.

64. Toni Morrison, November 18, 1996, 13.

65. Peck notes that Barbara Kingsolver (August 23, 2000) also attempted to assert the conscious labor and practice that led to *The Poisonwood Bible*, only to have Winfrey "corral" the discussion. Peck, "Oprah Effect," 169.

66. Aubry, "Furrow of the Middlebrow."

67. Winfrey, March 6, 1998, 11, 6.

68. Marilyn Johnson and Dana Fineman, "Oprah Winfrey: A Life in Books," *Life*, September 1997, 46–48, 53, 54, 56, 60.

69. Lynette Clementson, "Oprah on Oprah," *Newsweek*, January 8, 2001, 38–44.

70. Questions asked on programs airing May 9, 1997, 18; May 26, 2000, 20; April 9, 1998, 12; and May 9, 1997, 15.

71. Braden, *Spirits in Rebellion*, 108. Substantive images and talk of openness occur, for instance, in episodes devoted to Christina Schwartz's *Drowning Ruth*, Isabel Allende's *Daughter of Fortune*, Malika Oufkir's *Stolen Lives: Twenty Years in a Desert Jail*, Janet Fitch's *White Oleander*, Ann-Marie McDonald's *Fall on Your Knees*, and Toni Morrison's *Paradise*.

72. "Kathleen" and Winfrey, April 8, 1997, 9.

73. Ibid., 15.

74. Ibid.

75. Ibid., 13

76. Ibid., 10

77. Ibid., 11.

78. Angelou, June 18, 1997, 4.

79. Ibid., 4–5

80. Ibid., 5.

81. Ibid., 9.

82. Morrison, May 26, 2000, 2, 8.

83. Ibid., 16.

84. Ibid., 9.

85. Ibid., 18.

86. Striphas, "A Dialectic," 300.

87. Rooney, *Reading With Oprah*, 104.

88. Guests on programs airing January 24, 2001, 18, and August 23, 2000, 2.

89. David Kirkpatrick, "Winfrey Rescinds Offer," *New York Times*, October 24, 2001, C4; "Oprah's Stamp," *Portland Oregonian*, October 12, 2001, oregonlive.com (accessed October 29, 2001).

90. Jeff Giles, "Errors and 'Corrections,'" *Newsweek*, November 5, 2001, 69; Verlyn Klinkenborg, "The Not-Yet-Ready-for-Prime-Time-Novelist," *New York Times*, October 30, 2001, A16.

91. Rooney, *Reading with Oprah*, 44.

92. Farr, *Reading Oprah*, 97, 107–8.

93. Davis, "Cross-Racial Empathy," 413, 412.

94. From the programs airing October 18, 1996, 17, and June 18, 1997, 9.

95. Ann Ferguson, "Feminist Communities and Moral Revolution," in *Feminism and Community*, ed. Penny A. Weiss and Marilyn Friedman (Philadelphia: Temple University Press, 1995), 367–97.

Contributors

Evelyn Alsultany

Evelyn Alsultany is an assistant professor in the Program in American Culture at the University of Michigan. Her recent publications include "The Primetime Plight of Arab-Muslim-Americans After 9/11: Configurations of Race and Nation in TV Dramas," in *Arab American Identities Before and After September 11th* (2007) and "From Ambiguity to Abjection: Iraqi-Americans Negotiating Race in the United States," in *The Arab Diaspora: Voices of an Anguished Scream* (2006). She is the co-editor (with Nadine Naber and Rabab Abdulhadi) of a special issue of the *MIT Electronic Journal of Middle East Studies* on Arab and Arab American Feminist Perspectives (Spring 2005). She is currently working on a co-edited book project (with Ella Shohat) on the cultural politics of the Middle East in the Americas. She is also working on her book manuscript, tentatively entitled, *The Changing Profile of Race in the United States: Representing Arab and Muslim Americans in the U.S. Mainstream Media Post-9/11.*

Edward E. Curtis IV

Edward E. Curtis IV is Millennium Scholar of the Liberal Arts and Associate Professor of Religious Studies and American Studies at Indiana University-Purdue University Indianapolis (IUPUI). He is the author of *Black Muslim Religion in the Nation of Islam, 1960–1975* (UNC Press, 2006) and editor of the *Columbia Sourcebook of Muslims in the United States* (Columbia University Press, 2008). Curtis is currently at work on a new synthesis of Muslim history in the United States (under contract with Oxford University Press).

Jodi Eichler-Levine

Jodi Eichler-Levine is Assistant Professor of Religious Studies at the University of Wisconsin, Oshkosh, where she teaches courses in Jewish Studies and Women's Studies. She recently completed her Ph.D. in Religion at Columbia University. Her current project is on the uses of the past and the telling of violence in religious children's literature; her research and teaching interests also include American Jewish life; religion and popular culture; the overlapping constructions of race, ethnicity, gender, and religion; and biblical afterlives in contemporary America.

Tanya Erzen

Tanya Erzen is an assistant professor in the Department of Comparative Studies at Ohio State University, where she teaches courses in religious studies and American studies. She is the author of *Straight to Jesus: Sexual and Christian Conversions in the Ex-Gay Movement* (2006), which received the Ruth Benedict Prize and co-editor of *Zero Tolerance: Quality of Life and the New Police Brutality in New York City* (2001). Erzen is currently working on a book about faith-based prisons entitled *Bodies and Souls: Evangelicalism and the Faith-based Politics of Imprisonment.*

R. Marie Griffith

R. Marie Griffith is a professor in the Department of Religion and a faculty member in the American Studies and Gender Studies interdepartmental programs at Princeton University. Her research and teaching focus on gender, embodiment, and sexuality in twentieth-century U.S. religion. Her books include *God's Daughters: Evangelical Women and the Power of Submission* (1997); *Born Again Bodies: Flesh and Spirit in American Christianity* (2004); *Women and Religion in the African Diaspora*, co-edited with Barbara Savage (2006); and *American Religions: A Documentary History* (2008). She is now writing a book that analyzes America's long religious and political battles over the linked issues of sex education, abortion, birth control, pornography, homosexuality, marriage, and abstinence.

Clarence E. Hardy III

Clarence Hardy is an assistant professor in the Religion Department at Dartmouth College. He teaches courses in American religious culture and contemporary Christian thought with a special focus on twentieth century black religious culture in the United States. He is the author of *James Baldwin's God: Sex, Hope and Crisis in Black Holiness Culture* and has written pieces for the *Journal of Religion and Christianity & Crisis*. He is currently at work on a book titled, *We Grappled for the Mysteries: Black God-Talk in Modern America.* It will span the 1920s through the Civil Rights period and consider how black descriptions of the divine have evolved in the modern period.

Rosemary R. Hicks

Rosemary R. Hicks is a doctoral candidate in the Columbia University Religion Department focusing on Islam in the United States and intellectual histories of pluralism. With a grant from the American Association of University Women, she is writing an ethno-history investigating how Muslims in New York engage in inter-religious endeavors while identifying as religious and political moderates. She is interested in how various groups have responded to increased religious and ethnic diversity by forming alliances around particular issues and/or appealing to neo-liberalism in the midst of disagreements over secularism, multiculturalism, and issues of gender and sexuality. She has organized two graduate student conferences examining theoretical and methodological issues in religious studies and has published in *Comparative Islamic Studies* (2007) and the *Journal of Feminist Studies in Religion* (2004). She has lectured in women's studies and American religious history courses, taught "Islam in the United States," and spent the summer of 2007 in Lebanon finishing her fourth year of Arabic study.

Jane Naomi Iwamura

Jane Naomi Iwamura is an assistant professor of Religion and American Studies & Ethnicity at the University of Southern California. She has published articles on Asian American religions and religious experience, as well as on the representation of Asian religions in American popular culture in *Semeia, Pacific World, Amerasia Journal,* the *Journal of Asian American Studies,* and in the volume *Religion and Popular Culture in America.* She is coeditor (with Paul Spickard) of *Revealing the Sacred in Asian and Pacific America* (2003) and is currently working on a book tentatively titled, *The Oriental Monk Comes West: Asian Religions and the American Popular Imagination, 1950–1975.*

Prema Kurien

Prema Kurien is Associate Professor of Sociology at Syracuse University. Her research focuses on the relationship between religion, ethnicity, and international migration. She is the author of two books, *Kaleidoscopic Ethnicity: International Migration and the Reconstruction of Community Identities in India,* (2002) which was co-winner of the book award from the Asia and Asian American section of the American Sociological Association, and *A Place at the Multicultural Table: The Development of an American Hinduism* (2007). In 2007 she was a fellow at the Woodrow Wilson International Center and conducted research on Indian American political activism. She is also completing a study focusing on transnationalism and the generational transmission of religion among a group of Indian American Christians. In addition to the two books, she has published over twenty articles in journals and edited books.

Luis D. León

Luis León is assistant professor of American religions in the department of religious studies at the University of Denver. He is the author of *La Llorona's Children: Religion, Life, and Death in the United States–Mexico Borderlands* (California, 2004). He is co-editor with Gary Laderman of *Religion and American Cultures: An Encyclopedia of Traditions, Diversity, and Popular Expressions* (ABC-CLIO, 2003). His research and teaching areas include American religions and cultures, Latin@ borderlands, method and theory, and gender and sexuality. He is currently completing a book on the intersections of religion and politics in the life and work of Cesar Chavez.

Laura Levitt

Laura Levitt is the author of the forthcoming *American Jewish Loss after the Holocaust* (NYU Press, 2007) and *Jews and Feminism: The Ambivalent Search for Home* (1997). She is co-editor with Miriam Peskowitz of *Judaism since Gender* (1997); and with Shelley Hornstein and Laurence Silberstein an editor of *Impossible Images: Contemporary Art after the Holocaust* (2003). She edited "Changing Focus: Family Photography and American Jewish Identity," *The Scholar & Feminist Online*, 1.3(Winter 2003) *www.barnard.edu/sfonline*. She is the director of the Jewish Studies Program at Temple University where she teaches in the Religion Department and in the Women's Studies program.

D. Michael Lindsay

D. Michael Lindsay is assistant professor of sociology at Rice University where he is also the Faculty Associate of Leadership Rice and Assistant Director of the Center on Race, Religion, and Urban Life. Lindsay is currently undertaking a multi-year study on leadership and American culture entitled the PLATINUM Project, which examines Public Leaders in America Today and the Inquiry into their Networks, Upbringing, and Motivations. Results from the project's first phase are explored in his most recent work, *Faith in the Halls of Power: How Evangelicals Joined the American Elite* (Oxford, 2007).

Melani McAlister

Melani McAlister is Associate Professor of American Studies and International Affairs at George Washington University. She is the author of *Epic Encounters: Culture, Media, and U.S. Interests in the Middle East since 1945* (University of California Press, rev. ed. 2005, orig. 2001), as well as academic articles in, among others, *American Quarterly*, the *Journal of American History*, as well as commentary in *The New York Times*, the *Washington Post*, and the *Nation*. She is currently working on a study of Christian evangelicals, popular culture, and foreign relations, tentatively titled: *Our God in the World: The Global Visions of American Evangelicals*. In fall 2007, McAlister will be a fellow at Princeton's Davis Center for Historical Studies.

Brian McCammack

Brian McCammack holds a Master's degree in American Studies at Purdue University and is currently a doctoral student in the History of American Civilization program at Harvard University. His research examines issues of space and place in the nineteenth and twentieth centuries and has been focused more narrowly on intersections of contemporary environmental thought and religion.

John T. McGreevy

John T. McGreevy is Professor of History at the University of Notre Dame. He is the author of *Catholicism and American Freedom: A History* (Norton, 2003).

Ann Pellegrini

Ann Pellegrini is Associate Professor of Performance Studies and Religious Studies at New York University. She is the author of *Performance Anxieties: Staging Psychoanalysis, Staging Race* (1997); co-author, with Janet R. Jakobsen, of *Love the Sin: Sexual Regulation and the Limits of Religious Tolerance* (2003); and co-editor of two volumes, *Queer Theory and the Jewish Question* (2003) and *Secularisms* (forthcoming in spring 2008).

Barbara Dianne Savage

Barbara Dianne Savage is Geraldine R. Segal Professor of American Social Thought and a Professor of history at the University of Pennsylvania. She is the author of *Broadcasting Freedom: Radio, War, and the Politics of Race, 1938–1948* (University of North Carolina Press, 1999) and co-editor (with R. Marie Griffith) of *Women and Religion in the African Diaspora* (Johns Hopkins University Press, 2006). She is completing a book on the politics of African American religion to be published by Harvard University Press in 2008. Special thanks to Joellen El Bashir of the Moorland Spingarn Research Center, Howard University for her assistance with the Mays Papers Collection.

Kevin M. Schultz

Kevin M. Schultz is assistant professor of history and Catholic studies at the University of Illinois, Chicago. His research concerns the intellectual, social, and religious history of twentieth century America, and he has published essays in the *Journal of American History, Labor History*, and various edited volumes. His book, *Making Pluralism: Catholics and Jews in Postwar America*, is forthcoming from Oxford University Press. He received his PhD from University of California, Berkeley in 2005 and completed much of the research for this essay while a post-doctoral fellow at the Institute for Advanced Studies in Culture at the University of Virginia

Michael G. Thompson

Michael G. Thompson is a PhD Candidate in the History Department of the University of Sydney, Australia, where he works and teaches in the field of U.S. history. His research focuses on Anglo-American Christianity, war, peace, and world crisis from the 1920s to the 1940s, with a particular interest in Reinhold Niebuhr. He has also written and lectured for the Centre for Apologetic Scholarship and Education (CASE), at New College, University of New South Wales, on Christianity, war, and politics.

Trysh Travis

Trysh Travis is an Assistant Professor of Women's Studies at the University of Florida, specializing in the gendered history of twentieth-century books and reading. Her work has appeared in *American Literary History* and *The Journal of Modern Literature*, as well as *The Chronicle of Higher Education* and *Bitch: Feminist Responses to Popular Culture*. This essay draws on material from her forthcoming book "The Language of the Heart: Reading, Writing, and 12-Step Recovery."

Diane Winston

Diane Winston holds the Knight Chair in Media and Religion at the Annenberg School for Communication at the University of Southern California. She is author of *Red-Hot and Righteous: The Urban Religion of the Salvation Army* and is currently examining representations of religion, spirituality and ethics in post 9/11 television dramas. Winston is also writing a book on how the mainstream news media's coverage of religion skews American political discourse.

Neil J. Young

Neil J. Young is a doctoral candidate in U.S. History at Columbia University. He is currently writing his dissertation, "We Gather Together: Catholics, Mormons, Southern Baptists and the Question of Interfaith Politics, 1972–1984."

Index

Printed in the United States
111470LV00001B/1-54/P